Southeast
Guide to

2nd Edition
Saltwater

Fishing ^and Boating

Edited by Vin T. Sparano

International Marine
Camden, Maine

About Our Experts

Herb Allen, a regional and field editor for *Florida Sportsman*, was outdoors editor at the *Tampa Tribune* for 19 years. A freelance writer and photographer with more than 500 credits in magazines such as *Field & Stream*, *Outdoor Life*, and *Gulf Coast Fisherman*, Allen has won a number of journalism and conservation awards, including "Florida's Best Outdoors Columnist" for nine consecutive years and the National Wildlife Federation's President's Award. He is a member of the International Fishing Hall of Fame.

 Eric B. Burnley has been fishing the coastal waters from Cape Cod to Cape Hatteras for more than 40 years and has been a full-time outdoor writer for the past 20 years. A native of Delaware, he currently lives in and guides out of Virginia Beach. Burnley has been involved in fisheries management issues on the local, state, and federal levels and has served on advisory boards for striped bass, summer flounder, black sea bass, and weakfish. He has contributed articles to all national outdoor publications and is author of *Surf Fishing the Atlantic Coast*. In 1990, Burnley was awarded Conservationist of the Year by the Virginia Beach Anglers Club.

Dean Travis Clarke is executive editor of *Sport Fishing* magazine, a regular contributor to most saltwater publications, and a specialist in marine electronics.

Gary Diamond, a freelance writer for more than 20 years, contributes frequent columns to the *Washington Post* and such magazines as *The Fisherman* and *Game & Fish*. He has been instrumental in developing interest in striped bass restoration projects on the East Coast.

Jan Fogt is a contributing editor to *Sportfishing*, *Boating*, and *Marlin* magazines whose work also appears regularly in *Salt Water Sportsman* and *Power and Motoryacht*.

Jerry Gibbs is fishing editor of *Outdoor Life* and a member of the Fishing Hall of Fame.

Barry Gibson has been a charter captain in Boothbay Harbor, Maine, for the past 24 years, specializing in species ranging from bass and blues to sharks and giant tuna. A strong proponent of responsible fisheries management, he has been an advisor to the International Commission for the Conservation of Atlantic Tunas (ICCAT) and is currently completing a third term on the New England Fishery Management Council, of which he served as chairman in 1992. He is also active in numerous conservation and professional organizations. A world-record holder for bigeye tuna on fly, Gibson has fished extensively in North and South America.

Ed Jaworowski is a saltwater expert who writes regularly for *American Angler*, and *Fly Fishing Salt Water*, among other magazines.

Lefty Kreh, an active outdoor writer and photographer for more than 40 years, has written for almost every major outdoor magazine in this country and abroad. He is the retired outdoor editor of the *Baltimore Sun* and appears on the mastheads of six outdoor magazines. Lefty has also starred in a number of fly fishing videos and television shows, and is the author of several books, including *Salt Water Fly Fishing, Salt Water Fly Patterns,* and the *L.L. Bean Guide to Outdoor Photography.* He has fished in all 50 states and in all Canadian provinces, as well as in Central and South America, Europe, Iceland, Australia, New Guinea, and New Zealand.

Buddy LaPointe, president of Florida's Marathon Guides Association, is a full-time backcountry fishing guide working out of the Grassy Key Marina area.

Joe Malat, an instructor at saltwater fishing schools, writes regularly for *Salt Water Sportsman*, *The Outer Banks Sportfishing Report,* and *The Fisherman* magazines.

Bob McNally, a full-time outdoor writer and professional photographer in Jacksonville, Florida, published his first article in a national publication at the age of 18. He's since written more than 2,000 features for every major outdoor magazine in the country.

Doug Olander, a marine biologist, is editor-in-chief of *Sportfishing* magazine and a contributing editor to *Marlin* magazine.

George Poveromo, field and boating editor for *Salt Water Sportsman*, is a nationally recognized sport fishing expert, writer, and photographer. The author of hundreds of articles, he has fished extensively along the U.S. coast, as well as in Europe, Australia, Bermuda, Mexico, the Bahamas, Africa, and numerous Caribbean, Central American, and South American destinations. In 1983, *Motor Boating & Sailing* magazine voted him one of the top eight U.S. anglers. Poveromo lives in South Florida.

John N. Raguso, an expert at taking a small boat offshore, is a regular contributor to *Sport Fishing, Boating, Trailer Boating, NY Outdoors, Fishing World,* and *Power and Motoryacht.*

Tom Richardson contributes many articles and photographs to *Salt Water Sportsman*, as well as writing its "New Gear" and "Traveling Fisherman" columns. He has fished the Caribbean and Central America,

as well as many spots around the U.S., but his home waters are in Buzzards Bay, Massachusetts. Recently, Richardson was awarded first place in the Salt Water Magazine Category of the Outdoor Writers Association of America writing contest.

Al Ristori has written thousands of newspaper and magazine articles and is the author of three books, including *North American Salt Water Fishing* and *Fishing for Bluefish.* Over his 29-year career as an outdoor writer, Ristori has fished all over the world and has held world records for bluefin tuna and mako shark. He is the past president of Save Our Stripers, has served on the Mid-Atlantic Fishery Management Council, and is currently on the Northeast Director's Recreational Advisory Committee of the National Marine Fisheries Service. He was honored as Mako Marine Outdoor Writer of the Year in 1984 and won the Saltwater Writing Award in the 1989 Outdoor Writers Association of America contest.

Jim Sharpe, host of the television show "Fish'n In the Florida Keys," is a columnist and contributing editor to *Sportfishing* magazine.

Mark Sosin is an award-winning writer, photographer, and television producer. During his 30-year writing career, he has authored 24 books on the outdoors and contributed more than 3,000 articles to major magazines. He is producer and host of "Mark Sosin's Saltwater Journal," a director of The Billfish Foundation, and a trustee of the University of Florida's Whitney Laboratory. He is also a past president of the Outdoor Writers Association of America and the recipient of its Excellence in Craft Award, as well as its prestigious Ham Brown Award. Sosin is a member of many journalists' organizations and has been voted into both the International Fishing Hall of Fame and the Freshwater Fishing Hall of Fame.

To Betty,

Who shares my love of the sea, but
who has also learned to tolerate a husband
who chases fish and dreams.

Published by International Marine®, with Vin T. Sparano
Communications, Inc.

10 9 8 7 6 5 4 3 2 1

Copyright © 1996 Vin T. Sparano

Library of Congress Cataloging-in-Publication Data
Southeast guide to saltwater fishing and boating / edited by
Vin T. Sparano.
    p.   cm.
   Includes index.
   ISBN 0-07-059892-4 (alk. paper)
   1. Saltwater fishing—South Atlantic States—Guide-
books. 2. Boats and boating—South Atlantic States—
Guidebooks. 3. Saltwater fishing—South Atlantic States.
4. Boats and boating—South Atlantic States.
I. Sparano, Vin T.
SH464.S64S68   1996
799.1'66148—dc20   95–50259
                                     CIP

International Marine/ Ragged Mountain Press

A Division of The McGraw-Hill Companies

Questions regarding the content of this book should be
addressed to:
    International Marine
    P.O. Box 220
    Camden, ME 04843

Questions regarding the ordering of this book should be
addressed to:
    The McGraw-Hill Companies
    Customer Service Department
    P.O. Box 547
    Blacklick, OH 43004
    Retail customers: 1-800-822-8158
    Bookstores: 1-800-722-4726

The Southeast Guide to Saltwater Fishing and Boating is
printed on acid-free paper.

Printed by Malloy Lithographing
Design by Faith Hague
Production and page layout by Janet Robbins
Edited by Jonathan Eaton, Tom McCarthy

Contents

Chapter 4
FLORIDA'S GULF COAST 157

Chapter 5
COMMONLY CAUGHT SPECIES, INCLUDING AN ANGLER'S GUIDE TO SHARKS 183

Part 2
FISHING AND BOATING TECHNIQUES AND GEAR 208

Chapter 6
TACKLE 210

Chapter 7
LINES, LEADERS, AND HOOKS 222

Foreword

There's a sense of urgency about the time we spend in the outdoors today. Forecasters who sang of the great increase in leisure hours we were to have are silent now. New demands that zoom in from unexpected places make priceless each hour we can spend near the sea. To avoid wasting one moment of a fishing or boating trip, to live it safely, to be there when things are right normally demands extensive research of many sources on your part—another big time investment. No more. In your hands is the key to making that next adventure anywhere along our coast from Virginia to Florida, as well as the Gulf, a brilliant success. It would take more free time than you have all year just trying to collect the amount of material Vin Sparano has distilled and organized in this guide.

That the premiere edition of the *Guide* was a resounding success is obvious, or there would not be this second, even better work. Just glance at the table of contents, then thumb quickly through the index of this volume. The fare of fascinating information is like an endless banquet for which you need exercise no restraint. Pick a place you want to fish or cruise or simply poke about. You'll learn how to access the spot by boat or afoot, what the services are, how the fishing's likely to be and for what. Want to spend just some of the time afloat? You'll learn how and where to find a charter or party boat or a small rental skiff to meet your needs.

If you want to do some further research on your own, you'll find the names and whereabouts of important state agencies to whom you can turn for more information. The latest in both boat and fishing tackle and their maintenance are here, too. Having trouble with your line kinking? Want to match tackle to the fish you're after, learn to catch bait better, or care for those fish you decide to keep? It's all here. So are helpful sections on boating electronics, mooring and anchoring safely, and making knots for every occasion.

And then there is this. Some of the coast's most knowledgeable saltwater anglers and boaters have supplied a selection of stories about their home waters—waters so familiar these experts could find their way as easily around them as around their homes when the lights go out. Read carefully, for their information can supply the core around which to build your own adventures—trips for a particular species or for exploring areas off the usual beat of most visitors to an area.

For Vin Sparano, the sea has been that complex, lifelong mix of passion, learning ground, and source of renewal that she has for so many who love her. This is evident in the completeness of the *Guide*, which is certain to increase both the joy and the confidence of sportsmen and women exploring our ever changing and always irresistible coast.

JERRY GIBBS,
Fishing Editor, *Outdoor Life*

You are holding the second edition of the *Southeast Guide to Saltwater Fishing & Boating*. I firmly believed that the first edition of this coastal guide was the most comprehensive book of its kind along the East Coast. Many fishermen must have agreed with me, because that first edition was a bestseller. It wasn't unbeatable, however, which I've proved with this second edition that is even better.

My mission with these guides, however, has not changed. The purpose of the *Southeast Guide* is to provide any inshore, offshore, or beach fisherman with the most comprehensive data available today, including advice from nationally known and local fishing experts. The new, updated edition of the *Southeast Guide to Saltwater Fishing & Boating* is once again a total package that will tell you when, where, and how to fish inshore and offshore for every saltwater gamefish.

How can I determine if I have done a thorough job? That's easy. With the completed manuscript in hand, I start fishing in Virginia and follow the coast south. If I arrive at a state or region for which I can't find enough detailed information to plan a successful fishing trip, I know I have failed. But that hasn't happened yet! I have gathered huge amounts of fishing data and hot-spot locations for every coastal state. Much of the information included here is from local experts and fishing guides. I have also relied on state fish and game departments and private sources to compile complete listings of launch ramps, marinas, charter and party boats, beach access points, bait and tackle shops and other resources that traveling fishermen will find useful.

This book's usefulness, is not limited to traveling fishermen. Regardless of how many years you've fished the salt water in your state, I am certain you can still find much to learn about your local waters. For example, while researching my home state of New Jersey, I discovered hot spots and techniques I'd never tried.

Books of this scope are never the work of one person. I want to thank Jon Eaton and Tom McCarthy at International Marine for their support, patience, and skill in handling a huge amount of data that would have driven many editors to a career change. Finally, I want to offer my sincere gratitude to all the federal and state marine fisheries divisions and local experts for their generous assistance.

This guide is for you . . . the coastal fisherman. If you like it, I want to know. More importantly, if you don't like it, or want more specific data, write to me and I'll try to fix it in the next edition. I can always be reached through International Marine in Camden, Maine.

Good luck and good fishing.

VIN T. SPARANO, Fairfield and Barnegat Light, New Jersey, November 1995

Preface

Vin Sparano, right, and a sailfish he caught on the fly.

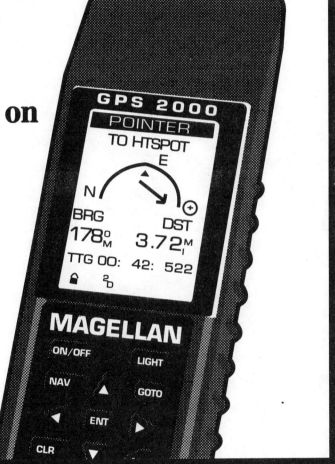

Part One

Fishing the Southeast, A Regional Guide

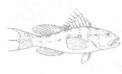

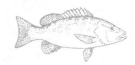

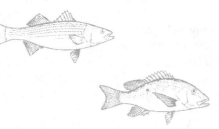

False Cape, Virginia, to Altamaha Sound, Georgia

The section of coast lying between False Cape, Virginia, and Altamaha Sound, Georgia, is characterized by sandy barrier islands, tidal waterways, and saltmarshes, all of which vary as we proceed southward. From just north of False Cape to about Cape Lookout, North Carolina, a series of long, narrow, low barriers, called the Outer Banks, parallels the coastline and separates the sea from a 2,500-square-mile system of large interconnecting sounds. Only five inlets provide passage from the sea into this vast enclosure. These sounds of North Carolina appear to be the most important nursery grounds for coastal migratory fishes along the entire Atlantic seaboard. From Cape Lookout to about Winyah Bay, South Carolina, these sandy barriers continue to skirt most of the coast. They are shorter than those in the Outer Banks and the sounds behind are, at most, only a mile or two wide. They are connected with the sea by two dozen or so inlets. From Winyah Bay to Altamaha Sound, Georgia, the barriers become a series of rather large, irregularly shaped islands, called sea islands. Between these and the mainland lies one of the largest coastal salt-marsh areas in the world, through which cuts a system of anastomosing waterways.

The line of the outer coast along a large stretch of this section is carved into three long, crescent-shaped embayments, demarcated by four prominent points of land—Cape Hatteras, Cape Lookout, and Cape Fear in North Carolina and Cape Romain in South Carolina. How these embayments with their capes were formed is not precisely understood, though it appears that prevailing ocean currents were, and still are, of primary importance in creating them. Along here the principal current, the Gulf Stream, flows northward along the edge of the continental shelf, at speeds of 1 to 4 knots. As great volumes of water break away from the nearshore margin of the stream, they become mixed with continental-shelf water and evidently form a series of three counterclockwise eddies, each of which cuts into one of the embayments.

The nearly flat, sandy expanse of land, called the coastal plain, begins at the fall line some 150 miles inland and continues out from shore to about the 600-foot contour. The submerged part of the coastal plain forms the gently sloping plateau of the continental shelf. The width of the shelf, which is about 55 miles off False Cape, Virginia, diminishes to less than 20 miles off Cape Hatteras, North Carolina. South of there the shelf broadens continuously until it reaches 75 miles off Georgia.

The sea floor over the continental shelf varies from smooth, almost featureless expanses of sand, to shoals and dome-shaped sand ridges, to outcroppings and ledges of rock and stone and coral heads. Scattered throughout are the wrecks of over 500 vessels with their cargoes. Between Cape Hatteras and Cape Look-

Cobia are tough fighting trophies for inshore anglers all along the Southeast coast. Cobia also rank high as a table fish, especially when finger-size pieces are floured and deep-fried. (BILL CORK)

out some 50 or so of these wrecks, especially the largest ones, were sunk during World War II by German U-boats that struck at coastal shipping as well as the convoys gathering for the crossing to Europe and Africa. It is no wonder that this stretch of water became known for a while as Torpedo Junction after a popular song of the war years, Tuxedo Junction. Of all the vessels that have been recorded as sunk along this section by one cause or another, most have been either buried by the shifting sand or eaten away by boring organisms and rust.

TIDES

Along the open sea coast of this section, as elsewhere along the east coast, high and low tides occur twice daily. Here, however, there is more geographic variation in the tidal range than anywhere else south of Cape Cod, Massachusetts. Between False Cape and Cape Hatteras where the shoreline is nearly straight, the tidal range is between 3 and 3½ feet. Between Cape Hatteras and Cape Canaveral, Florida, the shoreline is deeply concave. In the middle of this concavity, about off Savannah, Georgia, the sea floor slopes much more gradually than at either end. The combination of the shoreline's shape and the bathymetric configuration produce a funnel effect, causing tides to be highest in the center and lowest at the ends. Thus, at Tybee Light off Savannah and at Sapelo Island, Georgia, the tidal range is 7 feet. Northward from about Savannah it progressively decreases to 5½ feet at Charleston, South Carolina, to 4 feet at Cape Fear, North Carolina. From Savannah southward, the range progressively decreases to 6 feet at Fernandina Beach, Florida, to 5 feet at St. Augustine, Florida, to 3½ feet at Cape Canaveral.

Tidal ranges within the bays and sounds vary according to location. In Back Bay and Currituck Sound in northern North Carolina there are no detectable tides, and in the large Albemarle–Pamlico Sound complex the tidal range is often less than one-half foot. Here, winds are the principal force controlling the level of the water. From about Bogue Sound in central North Carolina, where the tides range only about 2½ feet, they gradually increase to 5 feet in the estuaries near Charleston and to 8 feet in those near Savannah. Some coastal rivers have complicated tidal patterns, especially those south of Charleston. At the mouths of these rivers the tidal range is that of the open sea, but as one proceeds upstream it increases as much as 3 feet more. This can happen within a mile or as far as a dozen miles upstream; beyond that, it decreases.

SEASONS AND WEATHER

Along this stretch of coast summers are warm and long, and winters mild and short. From about mid-April in the northernmost area and mid-March in the southernmost, to early November, the weather is warm, the humidity high, and the winds usually gentle. The prevailing southerly or southwesterly winds bring warm, moist air from the Gulf of Mexico, and the weather usually remains uniform for weeks at a time. The calmest winds and highest temperatures, occasionally reaching over 100°F, occur during July and August. Even though skies are clear much of the time during summer, there are periods of frequent showers or thunderstorms. Gale force winds sometimes accompany thunderstorms, and when they do they can cause serious trouble to small boatmen in unprotected waters.

Anytime between May and November severe tropical cyclonic storms, called hurricanes, occasionally strike this section of coast. It is from August to October, however, that they are most common and intense. The very high tides and exceptionally large waves raised by these storms batter the coast, eroding great sections of the beach and often causing considerable damage to shore installations as well as to boats and their dockage. As a hurricane approaches, the strong easterly winds push huge volumes of water along ocean beaches, through the inlets, into the sounds, and against the mainland shore. After the eye, i.e., the calm section in the hurricane's center, passes, the winds shift around to a westerly direction. Now the seawater plus the runoff from the torrential rains are pushed back to the barrier islands. The resulting high water washing over low places along these islands often forms new inlets, most of which remain open only a short time before being filled with sand.

Fall is a short transitional period in which the temperature diminishes, and the warm, gentle southerlies gradually become more variable, then shift to northerly and become progressively stronger. Winter is marked by

3

brief stormy periods followed by crisp, clear days. The combination of a few warm days followed by a sudden drop in temperature at night sometimes causes fog. This, however, usually burns off by the afternoon. Only occasionally do severe winter storms with sleet, snow, and freezing temperatures affect this area. When they do, the accompanying winds often reach gale force. Usually these blow out of the south and west, then swing around to the north and east. Confronted with this situation, ship captains have sought refuge on the north and lee sides of the capes only to have the winds shift suddenly, thus exposing them to face the full fury of a northeaster. In olden days sailing ships, beating upwind into the teeth of such a gale in close water, often foundered, broached, and then sank or were driven ashore before-the-wind. This accounts for over two-thirds of the more than 350 vessels wrecked along the beaches of the Carolinas being located on the north and east sides of the capes.

Spring, like fall, is a short transitional period. The frequency of storms decreases, winds prevail from the southwest, temperatures rise, and the weather becomes more uniform as it gradually merges into the summer regime.

FISH MOVEMENT AND MIGRATION

It is generally accepted that of all environmental properties combining to influence the movements of sea fishes, the dominating one is temperature. In this section the water temperature over most of the continental shelf is governed chiefly by the weather, while along the edge of the shelf it is governed by the Gulf Stream flowing from warmer latitudes.

Of all the species of fishes occurring along shore and in the estuaries during the year, about a third tolerate the seasonal range in water temperature between 35° and 90°F and so remain permanent residents. These species, of which the most abundant are silversides and anchovies, may move short distances into deeper water to avoid extreme winter cold or summer heat; but none of them seem to go very far.

Of the fishes living farther out in moderate depths, nearly all, including sea basses, porgies, snappers, groupers, and grunts, are permanent residents living at the bottom in a band of water that varies only between 60° and 68°F. This band extends the year-round from south of the Florida Keys at least to Cape Hatteras. Its northern end in winter marks the limit beyond which the hardier of the warm-water reef-dwelling fishes are not permanent residents. Although in summer this band extends as far as Ocean City, Maryland, the great majority of these fishes do not move with it, for they are closely associated with coral reefs, and these end at about Cape Hatteras. True, we do find a few reef fishes in northern waters every summer, but usually these are either the very young ones that have been carried there by the Gulf Stream or very large and old ones that tend to roam.

Nearly a quarter of the species occurring in this section remain within the sounds and bays only through their first year or two of life. Then, as they become older, almost all move off into deeper ocean water for the coldest months and return to the protected waters in the spring. This becomes the migratory pattern for the rest of their lives. Among these are the sea trouts, the drums, the kingfishes, spot, croaker, and the flukes. Beginning in late fall some of them, notably spot, croaker, and the flukes, move offshore, where they spawn during winter. Almost immediately after hatching the young move inshore, through the inlets, and into the upper reaches of the sounds and bays. Meanwhile the adults remain offshore, not to return until spring.

Most of the species occurring in this section are seasonal migrants generally arriving in spring and remaining until fall. Their arrivals, sojourns, and departures coincide with the occurrence of a band of surface water ranging from 72° to 84°F that extends seasonally from south of the Florida Keys to North Carolina. These warm-water migrants travel either alongshore (pompano, tarpon, Spanish mackerel) or in deeper water farther offshore (king mackerel, sailfish, barracuda, black-fin tuna, Atlantic bonito, skipjack tuna, white and blue marlins). As the water gradually cools in the fall, both groups of these fishes make their return migrations.

Other species that are abundant in this section only during the warm months include little tunny, wahoo,

Spanish mackerel make for great, easy-to-do family fishing trips. (BOB MCNALLY)

Head or party boats are good solutions for vacationers. Tackle and bait are always available, and mates are friendly and helpful to beginners. (ERIC BURNLEY)

great amberjack, and dolphin. These remain offshore through the winter in a band of surface water that ranges from about 60°F on the landward side to 72°F on the seaward side and extends during that season from Florida to Cape Hatteras. At the same time we find several temperate-water fishes along a part of the coast where this band washes the shore, i.e., between Cape Hatteras and Cape Lookout. Notable among these are bluefish, most of which have spent the summer from Cape Hatteras to Cape Cod. On their southward migration in the fall a few bluefish may overwinter off North Carolina but most of them continue south, some going as far as Florida. They return in the spring, staying in this section a few weeks or so before moving toward their northern summering grounds.

A few boreal fishes migrating from northern areas arrive off Cape Hatteras in early winter when the water over this part of the continental shelf becomes cold enough; and they stay there until it warms in the spring. This cape marks the southernmost limit of bottom-dwelling, cold-water fishes, because a band of water 50° to 55°F that extends along the bottom southward from the Gulf of Maine reaches this far. These temperatures are within the tolerance range of several common North Atlantic groundfishes, including cod, pollock, haddock, and squirrel hake. The course of this cold-water band as well as its extent varies seasonally, approaching the Virginia and northern North Carolina shore in winter and moving toward the edge of the shelf in late spring, there to remain until the following winter.

HISTORY

In olden times, various coastal Indian tribes depended largely upon fish and shellfish that abounded in the waterways and along the shores. They shot fish with arrows, speared them with sharpened stalks of cane, and, at times when fish gathered in shallow water, captured them in nets made of fibers of wild hemp and wild flax. As for anadromous fishes that run upstream to spawn, such as river herrings, shad, and striped bass, the Indians sometimes poisoned them with solutions extracted from the bark and roots of certain trees, but more often trapped them in long stone weirs at the ends of which were baskets woven of cane or grapevine. They also took oysters and clams from brackish water, using their meats for food and making their shells into implements and jewelry. Some tribes even ground oyster shells into a powder and used it for whitewashing their mud-and-grass plastered houses.

The first Europeans to come here, Spaniards, took little notice of how the Indians lived, for they came seeking instant wealth. Originally they sought a shorter passage to Asia and its treasures, but their discovery of silver and gold, among the Caribbean Islands where they had settled, captured their attention. Later, as Europeans of other countries came to this section, they established settlements north of what is now Florida and took to raising crops for which the land was well suited; chiefly tobacco in Virginia and the northern part of North Carolina and rice and indigo in southern North Carolina, South Carolina, and Georgia.

Except in settlements along the water where fresh fish and shellfish were lavishly abundant and could be taken almost at will, the fisheries during early times were initially neglected. In those days, New Englanders had a monopoly on the trade in salt cod and mackerel, which they bartered in the southern colonies for tobacco, rice, and other agricultural commodities. The only important fishery in this section was around Charleston, South Carolina, which, by the middle of the 1700s, ranked among the five largest cities in the colonies. Fishermen would sail small boats, called smacks, as far as 30 miles up and down the coast from Charleston and 10 to 20 miles offshore. Black sea bass, porgies, grunts, sheepshead, snappers, and other fishes were handlined, placed in large livewells built into the smack, and brought into the harbor to be sold alive.

Several medical doctors in the Charleston area, who like others in their profession were often good naturalists, made a hobby of collecting fishes. They often sent these specimens to the famous scientist, Carolus Linnaeus, in Sweden, to be technically described and named. Consequently, they were included in his great work, *Systema Naturae*, a catalog of all plants, animals, and minerals known to exist. The system established in this work has become the basis of modern zoological and botanical classification. Many of the scientific names Linnaeus gave to South Atlantic fishes are in use today.

The worldwide importance of whaling during the time this section was settled influenced people living near the coast to be on the lookout for whales. Anyone lucky enough to find one washed ashore would try out the blubber for its oil and extract from the roof of the

Anglers will have their hands full when they hook into these broadbacked amberjacks. You can catch them by trolling, bottom fishing, and jigging inshore waters.
(ERIC BURNLEY)

whale's mouth the horny plates, called whalebone. The refined oil was used for making candles, as fuel for lamps, and as a lubricant; the whalebone, when suitably prepared, was used for making whips, umbrellas, and stays for dresses and corsets. Not until the early 1700s, however, when a few New England whalers made Cape Lookout their base, was there a full-time fishery for whales. Their initial success stimulated the local people to engage in whaling from shore in small boats, a practice which continued for over 150 years, although with varied success.

Meanwhile, farmers and plantation owners living along the lower parts of rivers would let their chores go for a few weeks in the spring while they caught and salted enough fish to last the year. These were chiefly species that migrated upstream to spawn in the freshwater reaches. Even though it was easy to catch more than the farmers and plantation owners could use, it was not until the mid-1700s that a large enough market developed to make peddling these fish profitable. Expansion of this market encouraged people to take up fishing as a full-time occupation. In turn, this stimulated improvement of fishing gear. The shore haul seine, which in early days proved to be the most efficient piece of equipment for capturing fish, was continually lengthened,

sometimes reaching over a mile and a half long, and requiring teams of oxen to pull it ashore. A single sweep by one of these seines took fish from a 1,200-acre area. During the late 1700s and the early 1800s, fishing for anadromous species became important in the Chowan, Roanoke, Tar, Neuse, and Cape Fear Rivers in North Carolina; the Waccamaw, Pee Dee, Santee, and Edisto Rivers in South Carolina; and the Savannah, Ogeechee, Altamaha, and Satilla Rivers in Georgia.

It was not until the 1870s, however, that the importance of fishing along the southeast coast began to be fully realized. The connection of most towns by either steamships or railways at last furnished a reliable means of shipping fish to the distant markets of Baltimore, Philadelphia, and New York City. The introduction of the pound net into this area in the early 1870s stimulated the development of extensive fisheries in many of the sounds and bays. At the same time, the introduction and rapid growth of the iced-fish trade here made it possible to keep fish fresh and, thus, to offer a more desirable, higher priced seafood than salted fish. The salt-fish trade that had concentrated on mullet, spot, sea trouts, bluefish, and Spanish mackerel rapidly gave way to a fresh-fish trade with expanded distant markets. Improved transportation and larger markets stimulated tonging and dredging of oysters. Even the shrimps and blue crabs, which fouled fishermen's nets and had always seemed a nuisance to be destroyed, began to be appreciated. Even so, who could have foreseen in the 1880s that these two shellfishes were destined to rank among the highest priced of our seafoods?

Judging from brief references in early accounts, the gentlemen landowners along this section of the coast took to angling very early in the 1700s, partly for sport, partly for subsistence, and partly for food for their slaves. Red drum seems to have been the favorite then and remained so for a long time. Sheepshead, another popular catch, aroused the first serious concern about diminishing abundance. The cause of the depletion seemed to be quite evident. The most convenient good fishing spots for sheepshead had been around the trunks of trees that had fallen into the water from where they grew near the edge of the shore. It was about these submerged trunks that sheepshead had gathered to feed. During the early 1800s, however, planters had deforested the land to increase their acreage for cotton. Consequently, there were no longer any trees along the shores to provide suitable habitat for these fish. This is one of the earliest symptoms in the United States of man's growing dilemma between conflicting needs. People solved the problem of creating suitable habitat by sinking weighted log pens in areas where there had formerly been good fishing. These log pens, probably the first artificial reefs in America, provided a substrate for a great variety of encrusting animals and seaweeds, about which small, free-living invertebrate animals dwell. This community attracted the sheepshead, as well as other fishes, and the "reefs" are said to have been quite successful. For some unexplained reason, however, the practice was discontinued sometime during the late 1800s.

By 1880 shore communities were becoming resorts, attracting people from the interior who visited the coast not only for business but for recreation, and that included fishing. The Outer Banks, Beaufort and Southport, North Carolina; Charleston and Beaufort, South Carolina; and Savannah, Georgia, as well as other towns, attracted anglers seeking red drum, sheepshead, black drum, sea trouts, and bluefish. The popularity of the coastal resorts continued to attract anglers through the 1800s and into the 1900s.

In the mid-1900s, an unprecedented number of people migrated from the interior to the coast and many became permanent residents. The accompanying growth of seashore resorts stimulated the reclamation of saltmarshes for housing and industrial requirements. Other human activities, including channeling of the shallow waterways for the increasing number of boats, have been generally deleterious to marine life. For example, ditching to control mosquitoes damaged about half of the over one million acres of saltmarshes along this section of coast, and dredging and filling for real estate projects destroyed some 20,000 acres of saltmarshes.

The estuaries, too, i.e., the sounds, bays, and river mouths, have been seriously affected. Since estuaries are essential to the survival and well-being of many of our fishes, the progressive deterioration and loss of estuarine areas contribute significantly to a decline in fish species abundance. Our most ubiquitous inshore species, silversides, anchovies, and killifishes, spend their lives entirely within estuaries. Other important species, including spotted and gray sea trouts, red and black drums, and silver perch, depend on estuaries even though they spend only a small portion of their lives at sea. Spot, croaker, northern and southern flukes, sheepshead, pinfish, tarpon, and ladyfish seasonally return from the sea to the estuaries year after year throughout their lives. Striped bass, which along here live mostly in the brackish reaches of estuaries, move up rivers to spawn. After remaining there for several weeks to several months, they return to the estuaries. Menhadens, important as bait species as well as for commercial use, spend much of their time in estuaries during the first year or so of their lives. Adult alewives and blueback herring, shad, and Atlantic sturgeon must pass through estuaries on their way upstream to spawn, and the juveniles as well as the adults that survive spawning must pass through estuaries on their way to the sea. Some young of bluefish, black sea bass, spadefish, and porgies find estuaries beneficial to some degree for their survival. Estuaries are the habitat not

The increasing number of boats and facilities for them have had an adverse impact on the saltmarshes necessary for fish production. (BOB MCNALLY)

only of oysters, hard clams, and bay scallops but of other kinds of shellfishes including shrimps and blue crabs.

Ironically, the tragic damage to estuarine areas from man's various activities could have been avoided with proper land use planning. It is not too late to save what remains, but any hope of doing so depends upon effective action now!

Anglers in Virginia, South Carolina, and Georgia need a license to fish in salt or brackish water, and there are state and federal regulations on many saltwater fish in all states. Some states have minimum size limits as well as daily catch limits for large striped bass and red drum. Also, there may be minimum size limits for a few other species. Most states have regulations governing the type of gear, method of capture, and catch limits for oysters, clams, and shrimps taken by recreational fishermen for home consumption. Some may set seasons and require a permit to oyster or shrimp. All of the states have minimum size limits for both the hard and soft stages of blue crabs, and prohibit keeping egg-bearing females. It's important to note that fishing regulations are perishable, often changing from year to year. A prudent angler will check for the latest rules before dropping a hook.

To obtain copies of current fishing and shellfishing regulations, contact the following offices:

- Virginia—Marine Resources Commission, P. O. Box 756, 2600 Washington Avenue, Newport News, 23607-0756
- North Carolina—District Offices of the Department of Marine Fisheries, Morehead City, (800) 682-2632
- South Carolina—Wildlife and Marine Resources Department, Marine Resources Division, P.O. Box 12559, 217 Fort Johnson Road, Charleston, 29412
- Georgia—Department of Natural Resources, Coastal Resources Division, 1 Conservation Way, Brunswick, 31523-8600, (912) 264-7218

FALSE CAPE TO DIAMOND SHOALS

LAND CONFIGURATION AND WATER DEPTH

The dominant feature of this section and the one following is the chain of long, narrow barrier sandbars that skirts the coast for about 150 miles between False Cape and Cape Lookout. These are the Outer Banks. They average less than half a mile wide and, except in a few places where steep, wind-blown hills or ridges of sand rise 50 to 150 feet, they are usually less than 10- to 15-feet high. Smooth, sandy beaches devoid of vegetation, average about 100 yards wide and extend along the ocean side of the Outer Banks. Rising from the beaches are grassy dunes and behind the dunes, low, gently downward-sloping ground, covered by grasses and shrubs, extends to the intertidal zone of the sounds.

To the west of the Outer Banks, a large, complex system of interconnecting bays and tidal lagoons, locally called sounds, extends nearly the entire length of North Carolina.

FISH AND FISHING

The coast from False Cape, Virginia, down to Duck, North Carolina, provides good surf fishing action from April to November and is not as heavily fished as the beaches to the south. Currituck Sound, which lies behind this strip of beach, has excellent fishing for large-mouth bass in the summer and striped bass during the spring and fall. Access to the Sound is provided at Grandy, Poplar Branch, and Coinjock off of State Route 158. Beach access is a bit difficult unless you have a four-wheel-drive vehicle.

The bottom formations along this stretch of beach

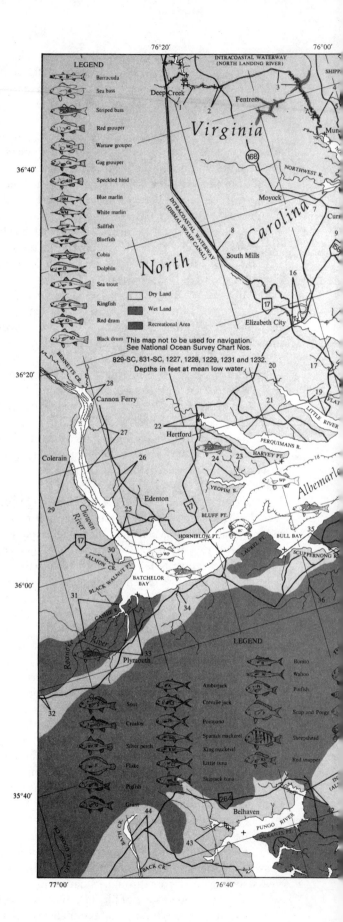

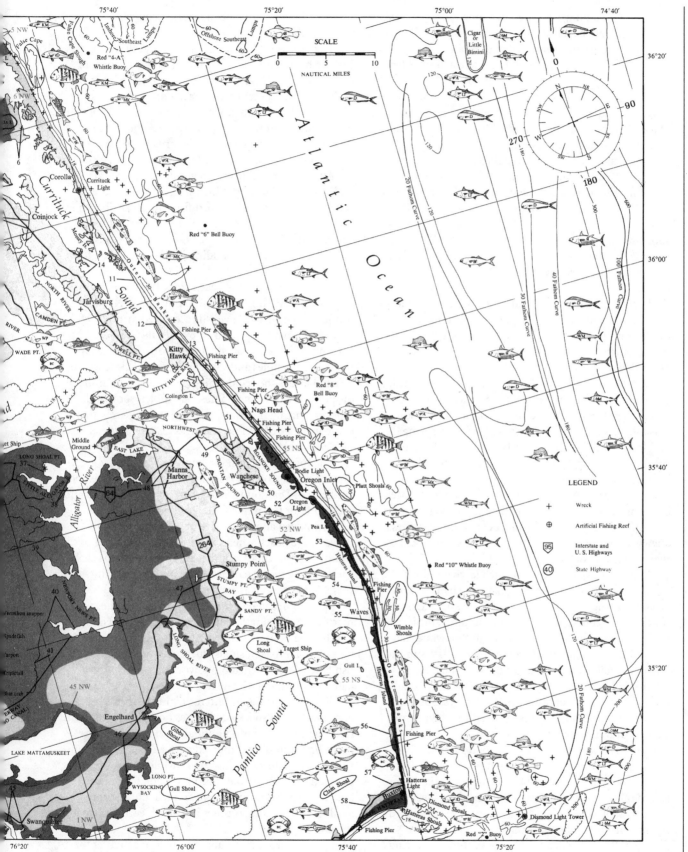

SCALE

0   5   10

NAUTICAL MILES

LEGEND

+	Wreck
⊕	Artificial Fishing Reef
95	Interstate and U. S. Highways
40	State Highway

are always changing, and you must look for new holes and sloughs after each storm. The successful surf angler will work these depressions with cut mullet, bloodworms, leadhead jigs, or MirrOlures to catch speckled trout, blues, spot, sea mullet, and croaker.

A large pier used to monitor wave action and other scientific studies is the biggest fish attracter around Duck. You must fish the area from a boat. The closest inlet lies 20 miles to the south, but big king mackerel and cobia are taken here during the late summer and early fall. Farther south, you may choose from a number of fishing piers spaced along the beach between Kill Devil Hills and Nags Head. Most of the fish caught from these structures are small bottom species such as spot, croaker, sea mullet, and gray trout, but during the late summer big cobia, tarpon, king mackerel, and the occasional shark are taken on live bait fished from the end of the piers.

Surf fishing is very popular here. There are numerous access points with public parking all along the oceanfront. Driving on the beach requires a special permit from each municipality and is restricted to fall and winter.

Surf fishing from south Nags Head to Oregon Inlet is controlled by the National Park Service, which, to date, has not required a permit or enforced a season closure. Speckled trout are taken here in the spring and fall with pompano a possibility during the late summer. Surf fishing here is difficult without a beach buggy.

Oregon Inlet provides the only opening to the ocean between Rudee Inlet to the north and Hatteras Inlet to the south. This is one of the most dangerous passages anywhere in the world and should not be attempted by inexperienced boaters.

During the winter you can catch large numbers of small yellowfin tuna by trolling ballyhoo baits or artificial lures along the edge of the Gulf Stream. As the waters warm during the spring and summer, fishing improves for dolphin, wahoo, blue marlin, white marlin, and sailfish. King mackerel show up in late summer and in the fall, with live bunker the bait of choice.

Inside Oregon Inlet, the waters of Pamlico Sound offer a wide variety of fishing opportunities. Speckled trout attract the most attention. They are caught from shallow draft boats or by anglers wading the flats close to shore. The old ferry dock at the bottom of the Bonner Bridge is a favorite stepping-off point for anglers who fish Green Channel. Puppy drum are taken in the sound on the same grubs and plugs used on speckled trout, as well as on live and dead baits. Live bait fished on the bottom in the deeper channels will produce flounder. Blues and Spanish mackerel show up during the summer and are taken on small spoons trolled just below the surface. On occasion these fish will chase bait across the top of the water and you can catch them on

poppers, bucktails, or metal lures and on white streamer flies.

The Oregon Inlet Fishing Center and Pirate's Cove Marina have a large fleet of charter boats for inshore and offshore fishing. In addition, there is a boat ramp at the Fishing Center that will accommodate anything you can put on a trailer. You can rent boats suitable for fishing in the sound from Hatteras Jack located in Rodanthe. He also offers a guide service for those who may not be familiar with the local waters.

All of Pea Island from Oregon Inlet to Rodanthe is closed to surf fishing vehicles, but there are several walk-on areas available to surf fishermen. The beach is severely eroded here so the walk from the road to the surf is quite short. One of the best fishing spots is across from the maintenance buildings halfway between the inlet and Rodanthe.

You can drive on the beach from Rodanthe all the way down to Buxton. The surf along this stretch has produced the all-tackle world record red drum, a 94-pound, 2-ounce trophy taken by the late Dave Deuel, and continues to produce other big drum, especially in the fall. Deep holes and sloughs are found close to the beach. Besides the red drum, they hold good numbers of speckled trout, small blues, sea mullet, spot, and croaker. During the summer, Spanish mackerel often come in range of surf-casters who toss small metal lures on light tackle.

The town of Buxton is adjacent to one of the greatest surf fishing locations in the world. The point is the land end of Diamond Shoal where the Gulf Stream and the Labrador Current collide. In the spring and fall, big red drum feed along the edge of the shoal and will move to the beach when the wind blows hard out of the south. A good run of summer flounder develops each spring along the beach just south of the point; thin strips of cut fresh fish are the top bait.

Spanish mackerel are caught throughout the summer from the point. Small metal lures are used and the best fishing occurs during early morning or late afternoon. Spot, croaker, small blues, sea mullet, and blowfish take bottom-fished bloodworms, squid, and cut bait from spring until late fall.

The jetties at Cape Hatteras Lighthouse hold excellent numbers of speckled trout, as does the beach to the north and south of this national landmark. Most are taken on leadhead jigs dressed with rubber tails. Plugs such as MirrOlures are also used, while cut fresh mullet is effective when the water is dirty. Look for the best action on specks in the spring and fall, but they are available during the summer if you fish early or late in the day.

Speckled trout and puppy drum are the target for anglers who wade the shallow waters of the sound. This, too, is an early or late day fishery as big fish do not stay in shallow water when the sun is high. Boaters who work the sound may find big tarpon late in the summer and a few channel bass in the spring but speckled trout and puppy drum provide most of the action.

DIAMOND SHOALS TO NEW RIVER

LAND CONFIGURATION AND WATER DEPTH

The long, narrow barrier sandbars that make up the Outer Banks continue along this stretch of coast. Instead of running nearly due south as they have for 90 miles, however, they abruptly turn southwesterly at Cape Hatteras. From there to Cape Lookout they form a sweeping 60-mile-long arc in the coastline. This arc, consisting of the southern end of Hatteras Island and all of Ocracoke Island, Portsmouth Island, and Core Banks, forms the inside edge of the coastal concavity known as Raleigh Bay. Barden Inlet, the shallow opening between Core Banks and Shackleford Banks, roughly marks the end of the Outer Banks.

The complex system of sounds described in the previous map section continues here. Pamlico Sound extends southward from Roanoke Island some 60 miles before dividing into three main arms: Pamlico River, Neuse River, and Core Sound. Pamlico River is not a river but a 35-mile-long extension of Pamlico Sound averaging about 18 feet deep. The principal tributary, Tar River, enters the arm of the sound at the town of Washington. Similarly, Neuse River up to the town of New Bern is also a 35-mile-long extension of the sound. The principal tributaries, Neuse and Trent Rivers, enter near the town of New Bern. Core Sound is a narrow saltwater bay 25 miles long. It is shallow, rarely exceeding 10 feet deep, and averaging only about 4 feet. Bogue Sound is merely a westerly extension of Core Sound some 30 miles long by 3 miles wide. South of Bogue Banks the coast continues and, for the most part, is skirted by a series of short barrier islands that separate the sea from narrow, interconnecting shallow sounds.

The sea floor off this section of coast consists mostly of sand, and slopes downward at widely varying rates. Off Cape Hatteras, a series of submerged, shifting sandy shoals, called Diamond Shoals, extends nearly 10 miles seaward. Owing to the shallowness of these shoals, many of which are less than 15 feet under the surface, waves break far out to sea beyond sight of land. This area is very dangerous to navigators, what with the shallowness of the shoals, the often strong, erratic currents that sweep over them, and the difficulty in making proper allowance for the nearby Gulf Stream. Beyond Diamond Shoals the sea floor slopes

Dolphin are frequently taken close to shore during the late summer months along the Southeast coast.
(BILL CORK)

downward at a rate of 60 feet a mile for 10 miles to a depth of 600 feet—the edge of the continental shelf. At Cape Lookout, another series of sandy shoals similar to those at Cape Hatteras, extends nearly 10 miles seaward. The distance from the end of Cape Lookout Shoals to the edge of the shelf is about 25 miles, and here the slope is only about 25 feet a mile. The sea floor around Cape Lookout, while mostly comprised of sand, has numerous rock outcrops, especially between Cape Lookout Shoals and the shelf edge. Even tropical reef-building corals occur along the edge of the shelf.

The Gulf Stream passes about 15 miles from Cape Hatteras. This is closer than anywhere else along the coast after it leaves Florida at West Palm Beach.

FISH AND FISHING

The waters south of Cape Hatteras feel the warmth of the Gulf Stream, especially between Diamond Shoals and Cape Lookout Shoals. This warm water produces excellent fishing close to the beach for such species as sailfish, marlin, yellowfin tuna, barracuda, amberjack, king mackerel, dolphin, and wahoo. Hatteras Inlet, between Hatteras and Ocracoke Islands, provides a reasonably safe outlet to the ocean, and you can be in the Gulf Stream after a short 12-mile run. The run to the 100-fathom line is considerably longer out of Beaufort Inlet, but the Stream moves very close to shore

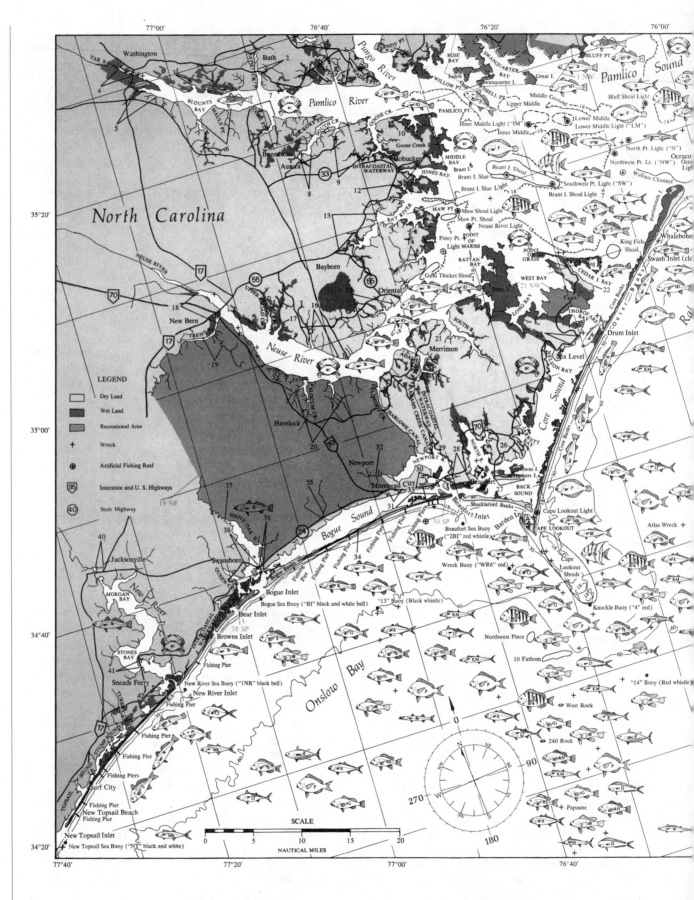

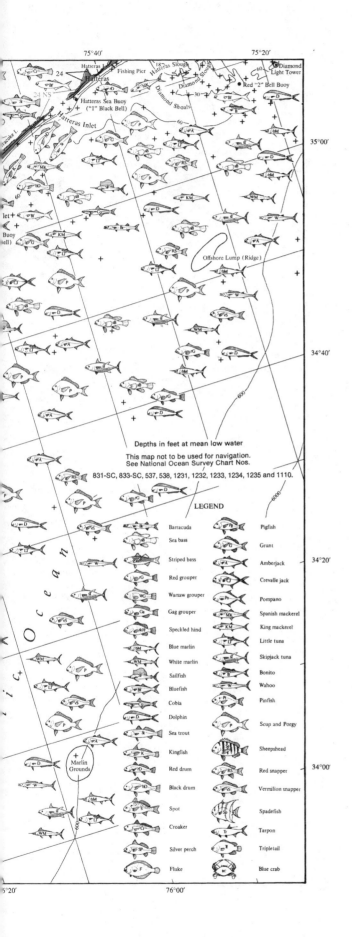

during the summer, bringing sailfish, dolphin, and king mackerel within a few miles of shore.

Big red drum remain the trophy fish for surf casters. They show up during the spring and fall. The south side of the point is the channel bass hot spot, but competition for a piece of open beach is intense, especially when the wind blows hard out of the south. The drum may be less concentrated along the beach south of the point, but at least you will not feel as if you are fishing in Times Square at midnight on New Year's Eve.

That chunk of mullet you toss in the surf for drum may also attract a big bluefish, but these creatures have been hard to come by for the past few years. Drop down to smaller baits and hooks for a mixed bag of bottom fish including flounder, spot, croaker, gray trout, and sea mullet. The north side of the Frisco Pier attracts fair numbers of speckled trout, with MirrOlures or rubber-tail grubs being the most productive lures.

Ocracoke Island is accessible only by water, but ferries run a regular schedule across Hatteras Inlet. Surf fishing here is good for flounder, puppy drum, sea mullet, spot, and croaker. The best action is usually found on the north or south ends, but the entire beach can be productive.

Speckled trout, puppy drum, and flounder provide good action in the sounds behind Hatteras and Ocracoke Islands. The Dredge Island inside Hatteras Inlet and Wallace Channel at Ocracoke Inlet are two good locations for light tackle fishing.

The barrier islands from Ocracoke down to Atlantic Beach are difficult to reach but well worth the effort. Portsmouth Island is served by a private ferry that can carry four-wheel-drive vehicles. There is primitive camping, as well as a few cottages, available on the island. Those who fish here find big channel bass, puppy drum, flounder, spot, and croaker all along this natural beach.

Tarpon have become a popular target for anglers fishing the Pamlico Sound. Oriental is a favored jumping-off spot. Late summer is the prime time, with bottom fished mullet a favorite bait.

The beach at Cape Lookout is very popular with boaters, who can leave their craft safely moored on the sound side and walk over to fish the surf. The sound behind Cape Lookout and Shackleford Banks holds speckled trout, flounder, cobia, and gray trout.

The jetties at Beaufort Inlet have become a hot spot for speckled trout, while boats running out of here find big king mackerel over rocks, wrecks and artificial reefs within five miles of the beach. The offshore fleet concentrates its efforts around the Big Rock just inshore of the 100-fathom line.

There are several large head boats sailing from Morehead City and Atlantic Beach that can carry you to an exciting fishing adventure for a reasonable price. The boats run 12-, 18-, and 22-hour trips that produce grouper, snapper, triggerfish, grunts, amberjack, tuna, cobia, and king mackerel. Most of this action occurs over live bottom 25 to 40 miles offshore, but the longer trips allow fishing the Gulf Stream for top water as well as bottom action.

Bogue Sound is very shallow, but the grass beds can produce speckled trout and puppy drum. Flounder are found in the deeper channels, but boat traffic can be a problem during the summer.

Several piers provide fishing access all along the beach from Beaufort to Bogue Inlet. Most of their patrons are happy catching bottom fish such as spot, croaker, sea mullet, and gray trout, but a hardy crew of live bait fishermen work the end of the piers for king mackerel, cobia, and tarpon. They do not see a lot of action, but when they do connect, it is usually with a trophy-size fish.

Surf fishing is very popular here, yielding good bottom fish action all year. Speckled trout may stage a good run in the fall when MirrOlures and grubs seem to produce better than live bait.

Red drum can be taken from Bear Beach between Bogue and Bear Inlets, but access is by private boat only. Spring and fall are the best times for drum, with the usual variety of bottom fish available during the rest of the season.

The Camp Lejeune Marine Corps Base controls the remainder of the coast from Bear Inlet down to New River. There is a large area of restricted water extending several miles out to sea and boaters should avoid this location at all times.

NEW RIVER TO OCEAN FOREST

LAND CONFIGURATION AND WATER DEPTH

Most of the outer coast from New River, North Carolina, to Ocean Forest, South Carolina, consists of a series of low, sandy barrier islands separated from each other by narrow inlets. The waterway between the barrier islands and the mainland varies in width from a few hundred feet to a mile or so and is bordered by saltmarshes. Along most of its length, the waterway is divided by saltmarsh islands into a network of branching channels. This estuarine passage, with its narrow waterways and its numerous islands, is in sharp contrast to the broad expanses of the Albemarle–Pamlico Sound complex just north of here.

The most prominent feature of this section is the sandy headland of Cape Fear. This has been formed over many thousands of years, much of it by sediments being washed continuously from the interior down the

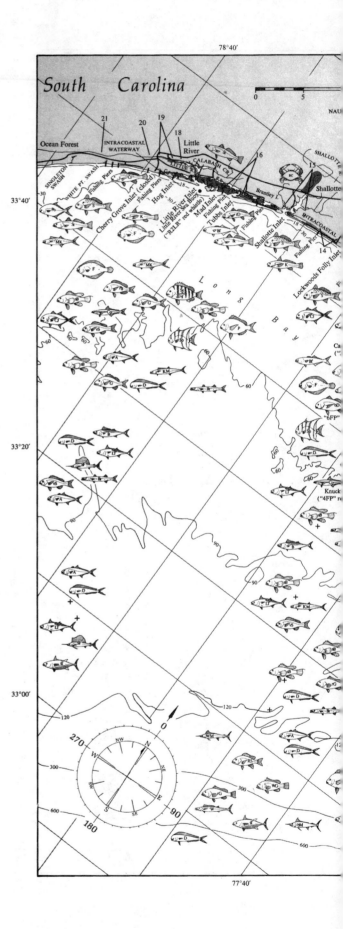

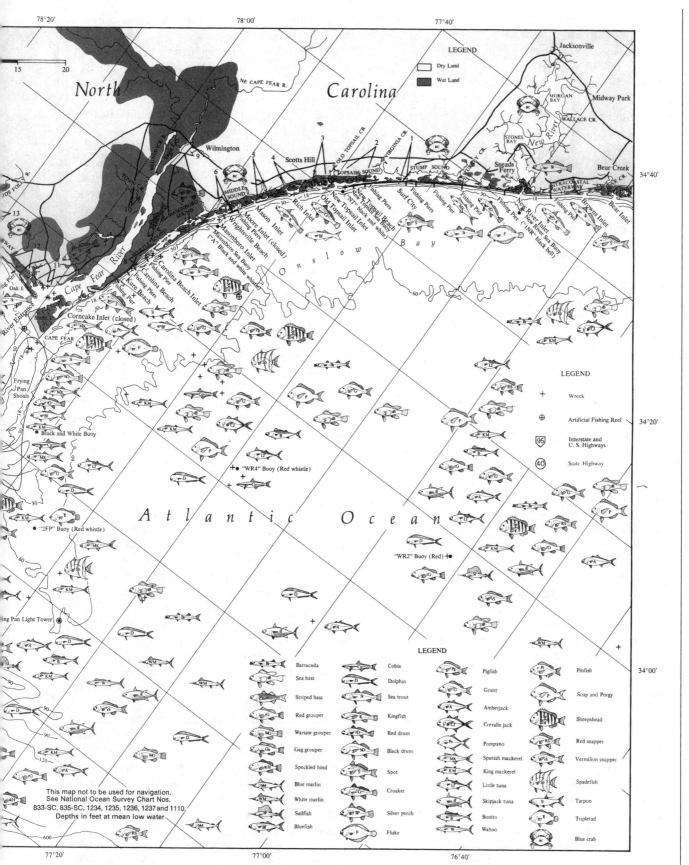

LEGEND

Dry Land

Wet Land

North

Carolina

Jacksonville

Midway Park

MORGAN BAY

WALLACE CR.

STONES BAY

New River

Sneads Ferry

Bear Creek

Wilmington

Scotts Hill

OLD TOPSAIL CR.

VIRGINIA CR.

TURKEY CR.

INTRACOASTAL WATERWAY

TOPSAIL SOUND

STUMP SOUND

MIDDLE SOUND

MASONBORO SOUND

Onslow

Bay

New Topsail Beach
New Topsail Beach
"NT" black and white
Surf City

Fishing Piers

Fishing Pier

Fishing Pier

New River Inlet
New River Sea Buoy
("1NR" black bell)

Browns Inlet

Bear Inlet

Mason Inlet
Rich Inlet
Old Topsail Inlet

Moore Inlet (closed)

Wrightsville Beach
Masonboro Inlet
Masonboro Sea Buoy
("A" Black and white whistle)

Carolina Beach
Carolina Beach Inlet
Carolina Beach
Kure Beach

Fishing Piers

Cape Fear River

Oak Is.

Smith I.

River Entrance

CAPE FEAR

Corncake Inlet (closed)

Frying Pan Shoals

Black and White Buoy

"2FP" Buoy (Red whistle)

"WR4" Buoy (Red whistle)

"WR2" Buoy (Red)

Atlantic Ocean

Frying Pan Light Tower

LEGEND

Wreck	+	
Artificial Fishing Reef	⊕	
Interstate and U. S. Highways	95	
State Highway	40	

LEGEND

Barracuda	Cobia	Pigfish
Sea bass	Dolphin	Grunt
Striped bass	Sea trout	Amberjack
Red grouper	Kingfish	Crevalle jack
Warsaw grouper	Red drum	Pompano
Gag grouper	Black drum	Spanish mackerel
Speckled hind	Spot	King mackerel
Blue marlin	Croaker	Little tuna
White marlin	Silver perch	Skipjack tuna
Sailfish	Silver perch	Bonito
Bluefish	Fluke	Wahoo

Pinfish	
Scup and Porgy	
Sheepshead	
Red snapper	
Vermilion snapper	
Spadefish	
Tarpon	
Tripletail	
Blue crab	

This map not to be used for navigation.
See National Ocean Survey Chart Nos.
833-SC, 835-SC, 1234, 1235, 1236, 1237 and 1110.
Depths in feet at mean low water

Cape Fear River and deposited at the river's mouth. The silt in the sediments is particularly noticeable during windy periods for being lighter in weight than the sand; it is easily agitated by the waves and, being darker, it imparts a milky brown color to the water. The vast sedimentary deposits are partly visible at the surface at Cape Fear, which protrudes 15 miles seaward of the general trend of the coastline. But beyond Cape Fear, another 30 miles of deposits lie hidden under the surface of the sea. This submerged area, Frying Pan Shoals, prompted early explorers and mariners to call its landfall the "Cape of Feare" due to its treacherousness. Cape Fear and Frying Pan Shoals separate two large coastal concavities, Onslow Bay to the north and Long Bay to the south.

Beyond Frying Pan Shoals, the sea increases in depth from 60 feet to 600 feet in 20 miles, a declivity of about 30 feet a mile. Off both Onslow and Long Bays, however, the bottom slopes much more gradually, though with some variation. Within a mile of the beach the sea bottom drops about 30 feet; 10 to 15 miles beyond that, 2½ feet a mile; and 40 to 50 miles beyond that, 14 feet a mile.

Actually, the slope of the bottom here is very gentle, and most of the shelf in this section would look like a vast plain of sand if one could gaze over its surface. It does, however, have patches of shell fragments mixed with the sand, and areas where limestone and sandstone outcrops project above the bottom. Many of these outcroppings are encrusted with corals as well as seaweeds, sponges, and sea fans. Because of the abundance of these sessile invertebrates and the fishes that gather there, fishermen call these areas "live bottom." Inshore of about the 100-foot contour, the live-bottom areas are frequented by black sea bass, scup, spot, and gray sea trout; offshore of this contour, by snappers, groupers, and the various porgies other than scup. Along the 250-foot contour is a series of living tropical coral reefs bathed by the Gulf Stream during most of the year. This is the most northerly occurrence of such reefs along the east coast of the United States.

HISTORY

Early settlers fished mostly for species found close-at-hand to coastal villages, principally anadromous types such as shad, river herring, sturgeon, and striped bass. In the spring and early summer, as large numbers of these fishes collected in the brackish and fresh waterways on their way upstream to spawn, they were trapped in fishermen's nets. With no refrigeration, the great bulk of the catch was salted to preserve it for later use or plowed into the fields as fertilizer. Only a small part of the catch was used immediately.

Later, the supply of river-caught fishes could not meet the year-round demands of increasing popula-

tions living in coastal settlements. Consequently, fishermen turned to the seashore to supply their needs. There, striped mullet became the object of an important ocean fishery in this section, as it still is. Mullet are particularly available here during fall and early winter owing to their habit of collecting in large schools close to shore where they are easily caught in seines fished from beaches.

As the number of people living near the coast continued to increase, so did the demand for fresh fish. The expanded market led fishermen to seek other species during the slack time between the spring and fall runs. One which they found ideally suited to their needs was black sea bass, locally called blackfish. These were plentiful throughout the year just a short distance from the shore. They shipped well; their sweet, flaky flesh stayed firm; and most important, they sold well in the market. Beginning in the mid-1800s as the fishery developed, sea bass were sought during the summer when the seines were laid up. Each morning, if the weather proved suitable, fishermen would sail out to the rocky grounds 1 to 15 miles offshore, fish all day with handlines, and return to port about dusk. It was not until the early 1900s that sea bass along this stretch of coast were fished during winter as well as summer. In the winter fishery, three or four men would ship together on a small naphtha-powered boat and handline off Bear Inlet, Wrightsville Beach, and Southport, North Carolina, on grounds which they called "blackfish rocks."

FISH AND FISHING

Surf fishing from New River Inlet to Cape Fear can produce channel bass, flounder, speckled trout, pompano, spot, croaker, and sea mullet. Access is reasonably good down to New Topsail Inlet. You will need a shallow draft boat to reach the barrier islands south of that point.

The sounds and marshes between the barrier islands and the mainland hold speckled trout, gray trout, and flounder, but much of the area is uncharted and can prove difficult to navigate. Those who stray from the Intracoastal Waterway or marked channels to the inlets may find good fishing or may find themselves hard aground on a sandbar or mud flat.

King mackerel rule the inshore fishery and attract thousands of anglers to big-time tournaments. Live menhaden are the most popular bait, followed by frozen cigar minnows, large plugs, and spoons. Most private and charter boats are equipped with large livewells to accommodate the bunker, and they have developed a system of slow trolling that presents the bait in a very life-like manner.

In addition to king mackerel, inshore waters harbor good numbers of Spanish mackerel plus a few big tarpon and cobia. The top location for all of these fish is over a wreck, rock, or artificial reef, as the bottom is relatively flat. Bottom fishing is good over this same structure for sea bass, snappers, amberjack, and the occasional grouper. Drifting the inlets or along the beachfront can produce flounder, croaker, spot, trout, and a few small bluefish.

Wrightsville Beach boasts a large charter fleet as well as access for private trailer boats. Masonboro Inlet opens to some of the best king mackerel fishing along the coast. Locals, as well as visiting anglers, target these fish from early summer until late fall. When warm blue water from the Gulf Stream moves inshore you can find sailfish and dolphin over the rocks, wrecks, and reefs that normally hold king mackerel. Many sails are hooked and lost each year on the small treble hook rigs employed for big kings. Those who target sailfish with lures or bait rigs using more appropriate hooks have a much better success rate.

The Cape Fear River dumps out into the ocean between Oak Island and Bald Head, creating one of the best fishing locations along the North Carolina coast. The nutrient-rich waters of the river create a feeding zone which interacts with the ocean waters, attracting cobia, tarpon, king mackerel, and other gamefish. Once again, slow trolling with live bait is the most popular technique, but those who target tarpon and cobia may have better success fishing the same bait with larger hooks on the bottom or slow drifted in a chum slick.

Moving south from the Cape Fear River, you will find a series of barrier islands with easy access for the shore angler as well as the boater. Numerous launch ramps are available, and many small marinas provide long- or short-term accommodations. There is public access to the surf all along this section of the coast, but parking can be a problem. The best bet for surf fishing here is to rent one of the many oceanfront homes and fish the beach from your back yard.

Surf fishing may provide a relaxing way to pass the time but for more consistent action try one of the many piers found on the barrier islands. You can catch a wide variety of fish including spot, croaker, sea mullet, trout, sheepshead, and pompano by simply baiting a hook with fresh shrimp, cut mullet, or sand fleas and dropping it over the side.

The end of the pier is usually reserved for big-game fishing, most of which is done with live bait. Quite often, those anglers use a trolling rig with a heavy-duty surf rod to cast a sinker out as far as possible. Then, they use this line to carry a live bait attached to much lighter tackle. A release clip on the trolling line allows the fish to take the bait without any encumbrance from the sinker or other terminal gear. The action may not be fast and furious, but these piers have produced some real monsters over the years. Pier jockeys have taken amberjack weighing over 100 pounds, king mackerel up to 60 pounds, cobia over 50 pounds, and at least one shark that weighed in at well over 1,000 pounds.

Most of the piers provide a tackle shop, a restaurant or snack bar, and a nearby motel or campground for overnight or long-term accommodations. Many anglers who spend their vacation time at their favorite pier will end up with more fish for less money than is possible from any other fishing platform.

OCEAN FOREST TO ALTAMAHA SOUND

LAND CONFIGURATION AND WATER DEPTH

From the northern boundary of this map section southward to Murrells Inlet, the coast consists of a nearly straight sandy beach of the mainland. There are no long, narrow barrier islands sheltering shallow bays and sounds; no saltmarshes, like those characterizing most of the Middle Atlantic and Southeastern coastal states. From Murrells Inlet to the Winyah Bay Entrance, however, the coast becomes a succession of sandy spits and barrier islands. These are rather ill-defined, for only a thin belt of saltmarshes with meandering tidal creeks extends between them and the mainland. From about the Winyah Bay Entrance southward to Florida, the coast becomes more incised, and the barrier islands, locally called sea islands, become broader. These large islands range up to nearly 15 miles long by as much as 5 miles wide. Between them and the mainland, a great expanse of saltmarsh stretches farther than one can see. Passages between the sea islands range from one-tenth of a mile to several miles wide. The depths of these passages, 15 to 70 feet or more, are astonishing, not only in comparison with their width but also with the depth of the sea bordering the coast. While the average depth of the passages is 35 feet, you need to sail more than 5

The sounds and marshes between the barrier islands provide consistent fishing for flounder, a summertime favorite. (ERIC BURNLEY)

miles out from shore along this section before again getting into water that deep.

Just outside the mouths of the passages the sea floor is composed chiefly of bars and tidal deltas. Most of these shoal areas are 2 miles or so long, but some of them extend out as far as 6 miles. About 15 to 20 miles beyond the shoals the sea floor slopes down to 60 feet, the offshore limit of this section. Although there are scattered stony outcroppings, ridges, and ledges, as well as coral heads, shipwrecks, and artificial reefs throughout this inner edge of the continental shelf, the bottom is mainly sand or sandy-silt.

One of the most remarkable features along the United States Atlantic coast is the extensive and highly dynamic estuarine system. The part extending from Winyah Bay, South Carolina, to about Jacksonville, Florida, covers over 2,000 square miles. Stretching inland from the barrier islands, in places as much as 25 miles, the system consists of broad saltmarshes cut by a myriad of tidal waterways meandering in arborescent patterns. These, variously called ditches, creeks, and channelways, depending on their depth, vary in width from less than a foot to over a mile. Separating the saltmarshes at intervals of about 20 miles are sounds and bays that receive the discharge of coastal rivers.

The estuarine system in this area is exceedingly fertile and productive, as elsewhere along the Atlantic coast. Nutrients released by microbial decomposition of plant and animal material within the system, as well as nutrients carried there by freshwater streams, become caught in the cycle of the teeming estuarine life, from plants to minute animals and shellfish to fishes to bacteria to bottom sediments. The action of tides in the estuary is biologically crucial, for it moves nutrients back and forth, thereby slowing their escape from the system and giving the microscopic plants and other minute organisms time enough to incorporate them into living matter. Thus, the vastness of the estuarine system, the volume of the nutrients, and the slow back and forth movement of the water combine to make this area exceedingly rich.

Until recently, the saltmarshes bordering the tidal waterways were believed to be useful only as dumping grounds for wastes or to fill for real estate. Now they are known to be among the most fertile parts of the world, producing more plant material than the richest farmland. Even more significant than their high productivity is the fact that only about half of what grows in the saltmarshes is used by organisms living there. The rest is eventually washed into the brackish water. This dead plant material becomes decomposed by bacteria and transformed into organic detritus. The detritus, together with the large phytoplankton populations, feed shellfish and the myriad tiny grazing animals, which in turn feed larger organisms, including fishes.

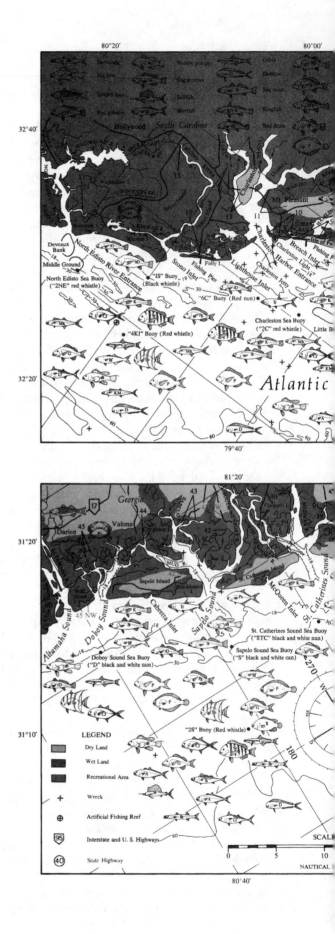

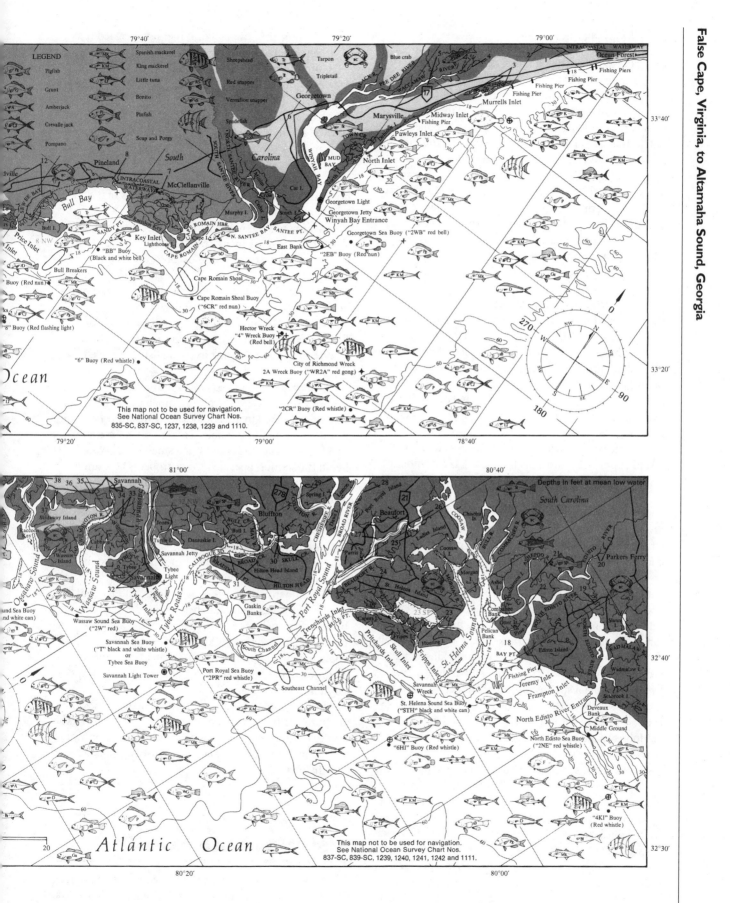

LEGEND

Pigfish

Grunt

Amberjack

Crevalle jack

Pompano

Spanish mackerel

King mackerel

Little tuna

Bonito

Pinfish

Scup and Porgy

Sheepshead

Red snapper

Vermilion snapper

Spadefish

Tarpon

Tripletail

Blue crab

This map not to be used for navigation.
See National Ocean Survey Chart Nos.
835-SC, 837-SC, 1237, 1238, 1239 and 1110.

Georgetown

Marysville

Midway Inlet
Fishing Pier

Pawleys Inlet

North Inlet

Murrells Inlet

Ocean Forest

Fishing Piers

Fishing Pier

Fishing Pier

Fishing Pier

INTRACOASTAL WATERWAY

PEE DEE RIVER

WACCAMAW RIVER

South Carolina

Pineland

McClellanville

INTRACOASTAL WATERWAY

Bull Bay

Key Inlet

Lighthouse

Cape Romain

Murphy I.

Cat I.

South I.

WINYAH BAY

MUD BAY

TOWN CR.

NORTH SANTEE RIVER

SOUTH SANTEE RIVER

N. SANTEE BAY

SANTEE PT.

Georgetown Light

Georgetown Jetty

Winyah Bay Entrance

Georgetown Sea Buoy ("2WB" red bell)

East Bank

"2EB" Buoy (Red nun)

Cape Romain Shoal

Cape Romain Shoal Buoy ("6CR" red nun)

Hector Wreck
"4" Wreck Buoy (Red bell)

City of Richmond Wreck
2A Wreck Buoy ("WR2A" red gong)

"2CR" Buoy (Red whistle)

Price Inlet

Bull I.

SANDY PT.

"BB" Buoy (Black and white bell)

Bull Breakers

Buoy (Red nun)

"8" Buoy (Red flashing light)

"6" Buoy (Red whistle)

Ocean

Atlantic Ocean

This map not to be used for navigation.
See National Ocean Survey Chart Nos.
837-SC, 839-SC, 1239, 1240, 1241, 1242 and 1111.

Savannah

Skidaway Island

Raccoon Key

Ossabaw Sound

Wassaw Sound

Wassaw Island

Tybee Island

Tybee Light

Tybee Inlet

Wassaw Sound Sea Buoy ("2W" red)

Savannah Sea Buoy ("T" black and white whistle) or Tybee Sea Buoy

Savannah Light Tower

Wassaw Sound Sea Buoy
nd white can)

und Sea Buoy

Bluffton

Beaufort

Chisholm Is.

South Carolina

Parkers Ferry

WILMINGTON R.

SKIDAWAY R.

HILTON HEAD

WALL R.

Jones

Turtle

Cabbage

Daufuskie I.

Hilton Head Island

Savannah Jetty

Savannah

CALIBOGUE SD.

Tybee Roads

South Channel

Gaskin Banks

Port Royal Sea Buoy ("2PR" red whistle)

Southeast Channel

COLLETON RIVER

BROAD RIVER

CHECHESSEE R.

SKULL CR.

Bull I.

Spring I.

Parris I.

Port Royal Sound

Trenchards Inlet

BULL PT.

Capers I.

Pritchards Inlet

Skull Inlet

Fripps Inlet

BROAD CR.

BEAUFORT RIVER

COOSAW R.

St. Helena I.

Morgan I.

COMBAHEE R.

Coosaw I.

Ashe

Otter I.

Combahee Bank

Pelican Bank

BAY PT.

Hunting I.

Fripps I.

St. Helena Sound

Savannah Wreck

St. Helena Sound Sea Buoy ("STH" black and white can)

"6HI" Buoy (Red whistle)

Fishing Pier

Jeremy Inlet

Frampton Inlet

North Edisto River Entrance

Deveaux Bank

Middle Ground

North Edisto Sea Buoy ("2NE" red whistle)

"4KI" Buoy (Red whistle)

WADMALAW

Wadmalaw I.

Edisto Island

SOUTH EDISTO RIVER

NORTH EDISTO RIVER

EDISTO RIVER

Slann

Seabrook I.

Depths in feet at mean low water

FISH AND FISHING

While the saltmarsh along this coast provides a nursery area for much of the marine life in the surrounding ocean and bays, the lack of solid ground makes fishing from shore impossible. The development along the barrier islands has cut off quite a bit of beach access to the general public, but several fishing piers remain open and they are the best method for reaching the water without a boat.

Myrtle Beach has become a premier vacation spot for golfers, but it still offers reasonably good access for fishermen from the piers and from the charter boat fleet out of Murrells Inlet. Pier fishermen can expect to catch spot, croaker, sheepshead, sea mullet, and trout while bottom fishing with sand fleas, bloodworms, and fresh shrimp. Live bait action from the end of the piers produces king mackerel, cobia, and tarpon.

The charter boat fleet will fish the inshore and offshore waters for a wide variety of species. King mackerel always top the list, but you can also expect to find Spanish mackerel, cobia, amberjack, and barracuda on the inshore grounds. Bluewater trips produce sailfish, marlin, yellowfin tuna, wahoo, and dolphin. Bottom fishing can be good over live bottom, wrecks, and reefs; sea bass, grouper, triggerfish, and snappers are taken on a regular basis.

Private boat owners will find dockage and launch ramps in this area. Murrells Inlet also has a number of restaurants and motels that cater to the traveling angler.

Surf fishing is somewhat restricted due to private development along the shoreline and the long, gradual drop-off that does not provide much fish-holding structure. The inlets and jetties can be good for flounder and speckled trout, especially during the winter.

Moving down to Charleston Harbor you will find fairly good surf fishing from Folly Beach, Sullivans Island and Isle of Palms. Big red drum are taken out of Breach Inlet, and pompano are found all along the beach. Live sand fleas dug from the surf make the best pompano bait.

Boaters sailing out of Charleston find king mackerel, Spanish mackerel, cobia, and amberjack by trolling live bait or metal spoons. Bottom fish include sea bass, grouper, snapper, and triggerfish. Dolphin and sailfish provide most of the offshore action.

Johns Island on the North Edisto River has a marina that will give boaters access to the open ocean as well as inshore locations such as Botany Bay and Frampton and Jeremy Inlets. Look for speckled trout, tarpon, drum, croaker, and spot from the waters close to shore. King mackerel, cobia, and amberjack rule the inshore waters, while sailfish and dolphin are taken further off the beach.

Flounder fishing is good out of Fripp Inlet. You may also expect to catch sea mullet, croaker, and spot. A state park on Hunting Island allows anglers good access but shore fishing is not very productive due to the relatively flat beach. Fripp Island to the south does have fair

beach fishing around the Skull Inlet for speckled trout, flounder, and red drum.

Hilton Head Island has become a major vacation spot offering some of the most luxurious accommodations along the coast. It is also a good jumping-off spot for offshore fishermen who find sailfish, dolphin, tuna, and wahoo in or near the Gulf Stream. The beach is long and shallow but the inlets do produce a chance for shorebound fishermen to catch trout, flounder, or croaker. Small boat anglers can expect to find a mix of bottom fish in the channels and tidal creeks that divide the marshland.

Savannah is the next major fishing center down the coast. In spite of its many commercial activities, there are plenty of fish to be found on both the inshore and offshore grounds. Some of the best action occurs along the saltmarshes that line the coast and hold good numbers of speckled trout and flounder.

Many public boat ramps service this section of the Georgia coast, providing access for any fishing boat that will fit on a trailer. These ramps are listed at the end of this section.

A myriad of rivers and creeks drain the marshes into sounds from Wassaw down to Altamaha. The shoreline is usually covered in grass and fishing from the bank can be difficult if not impossible. There is some access for surf fishing along the ocean but a small boat is your best bet in the sounds. Speckled trout probably account for most of this fishing activity. They are taken on plugs, grubs, and live bait. A shrimp suspended under a cork and cast over submerged grass beds can be extremely effective. Live mullet or shrimp worked around creek mouths, jetties or over oyster bars is a good way to take flounder. These fish are found not only in the sounds but along the oceanfront.

A number of artificial reefs, wrecks, and live bottom attract king mackerel, spadefish, cobia, amberjack, and bottom fish such as sea bass, grouper, and snapper. Live bait is the first choice for king mackerel, amberjack, and cobia but all will hit plugs and spoons. Small bits of clam work on spadefish while cut fresh bait is always good for bottom fishing.

Sailfish and dolphin will move close to the beach in the summer but marlin and tuna stay well offshore. The run to deep water may be as much as 70 miles or more and should only be attempted in well-equipped, seaworthy boats.

FISHING REGULATIONS

What follows are abstracts of fishing regulations for Virginia, North Carolina, South Carolina, and Georgia. This information should be used for general purposes only. Regulations are constantly revised, and in some areas, local and federal restrictions apply as well. Because regulations change frequently, and because the regulations themselves are far more detailed than presented here, all anglers should contact the state agencies listed at the beginning and end of this chapter.

VIRGINIA

Virginia requires a license to fish the Chesapeake Bay and its tributaries. This does not include the seaside of the Eastern Shore or Virginia Beach. Any angler between 16 and 65, including anyone fishing on a licensed charter boat, head boat, fishing pier, rental boat, or private boat must obtain a license, unless the owner of the boat or pier has a blanket license.

All the following restrictions are subject to change. For the latest information, call the Virginia Marine Resources Commission (VMRC) in Newport News at (804) 247-2200. The VMRC monitors VHF Channel 17. The "hotline" number to report violations is (800) 541-4646.

Regulations for black drum, cobia, gray trout (weakfish), red drum, summer flounder, and speckled trout have been under review; check for the latest limits and restrictions.

Minimum Size and Other Restrictions

Amberjack (Rudder Jack, Rudder Fish): 32"; All fishermen are limited to 2 per person per day.

Black Drum (Drum, Drumfish): 16"; Any person buying, or catching and selling, black drum is required to obtain a Commercial Harvest Permit from the VMRC. Limit of one per day.

Bluefish: None; Hook and line fishermen are limited to 10 per person per day.

Cobia (Bonita): 37"; All fishermen are limited to 2 per person per day.

Gray Trout (Weakfish): 12"; Limit of 4 per day

King Mackerel: 14"; Hook and line fishermen are limited to 5 per person per day.

Red Drum (Redfish, Channel Bass): 18"–27"; No more than 5 per day, 1 of which may exceed 27".

Shad (American Shad): It is illegal to catch American shad in Virginia tidal waters, except during the announced open season. Contact one of the VMRC offices for more information.

Sharks (All species, excluding dogfish): None; Hook and line fishermen are limited to 1 per person per day.

Spanish Mackerel: 14"; Hook and line fishermen are limited to 10 per person per day.

Speckled Trout (Spotted Sea Trout): 14"; Limit of 10 per day.

Striped Bass (Rockfish, Rock, Striper): It is illegal to catch or take striped bass in Virginia tidal waters, except during the announced open season. Contact one of the VMRC offices for more information.

Sturgeon: It is illegal to catch or possess any sturgeon in Virginia. Short-nosed sturgeon is an endangered species and is protected by federal law.

Summer Flounder (Fluke): 14"; Limit of 8 per day.

Tournaments

The Virginia Saltwater Fishing Tournament, inaugurated in 1958, awards wall plaques to all anglers catching fish meeting established minimum weights. There are no entry fees or registration requirements. Fish must be caught with a rod and reel in a sportsmanlike manner and weighed at one of the almost 100 designated weigh stations. Awards programs are also sponsored for the "catch-and-release" of certain species of fish and for the Junior Angler Awards (for children under 16). For more information, contact the Virginia Saltwater Fishing Tournament, 968 Oriole Drive South, Suite 102, Virginia Beach, VA 23451, (804) 491-5160.

NORTH CAROLINA

Minimum Size and Other Restrictions

In North Carolina, no one may possess aboard a vessel or while engaged in fishing any fish subject to limits without head and tail attached. It is unlawful to possess sturgeon, Nassau grouper, and jewfish in this state.

Conservation measures for some species often cause regulatory changes. Check with the local Department of Marine Fisheries office (phone numbers are listed at the end of the chapter) for the most recent regulations.

Black and Gag Grouper: 20" TL; Bag limit of 5 of per day per species

Black Sea Bass (South of Cape Hatteras): 8" TL

Blue Marlin: 86" FL; Bag limit of 1 per day

Bluefish: 12" TL; Bag limit of 20 per day

Cobia: 33" FL; Bag limit of 2 per day

Dolphin: None; Bag limit of 10 per day

Flounder: 13" TL; Bag limit of 6 per day

Gray Trout: 14" TL; Bag limit of 14 per day

Great Amberjack: 28" FL; Bag limit of 3 per day

King Mackerel: 20" FL; Bag limit of 5 per day

Red Drum: 18" TL; Bag limit of 5 per day

Red Snapper: 20" TL; Bag limit of 2 per day

Sailfish: 57" FL; Bag limit of 1 per day

Shark (except dogfish shark): None; No Finning

Spanish Mackerel: 12"; Bag limit of 10 per day

Spotted Sea Trout: 12" TL; Bag limit of 10 per day

Striped Bass: Check with local Dept. of Marine Fisheries office as to seasons, areas, size, and bag limits.

Vermillion Snapper: 10″ TL; Bag limit of 10 per day

White Marlin: 62″ FL; Bag limit of 1 per day

TL = Total length, measured from tip of nose to tip of tail

FL = Fork length, measured from tip of lower jaw to middle of fork in tail

Tournaments
(All telephone area codes are 919.)

May
- Annual Red Drum Classic, Manteo (473-3906)
- Ocracoke Surf Fishing Tournament, Ocracoke (928-4351)
- Memorial Day Blue Water Fishing Tournament, Crystal Coast area

June
- Outer Banks Celebrity Tournament, Manteo (473-3906)
- Hatteras Marlin Fishing Club Invitational Tournament, Hatteras (986-2454)
- Annual Blue Water Open Billfish Tournament, Hatteras (986-2166)
- Big Rock Blue Marlin Tournament, Morehead City

July
- Annual Youth Fishing Tournament, Outer Banks (441-7251)
- Cap'n Fannie's Billfish Tournament, Crystal Coast area
- East Coast Got-Em-On-Live-Bait King Mackerel Classic, Pleasure Island
- Morehead City Rotary King Mackerel Tourney

August
- Annual Alice Kelly Memorial "Lady Angler" Billfish Tournament, Manteo (473-3906)
- Annual Pirates Cove Billfish Tournament, Manteo (473-3906)
- Annual Ducks Unlimited Billfish Release Tournament, Manteo (473-3906)
- Ladies' King Mackerel Tourney, Crystal Coast area
- Capt. Stacey King Mack Masters Tourney, Crystal Coast area

September
- Annual Pirates Cove White Marlin Release Tournament, Manteo (473-3906)
- Annual Oregon Inlet Billfish Release Tournament, Nags Head (441-6301)
- Annual King Mackerel and Bluefish Tournament, Manteo (473-3906)

- Atlantic Beach King Mackerel Tournament, Atlantic Beach

October
- Nags Head Surf Fishing Club Invitational Tournament, Nags Head (441-7251)
- Carolina Beach Surf Fishing Tournament, Carolina Beach
- Cape Hatteras Anglers Club Invitational Surf Fishing Tournament, Buxton (995-4253)

SOUTH CAROLINA

A license for saltwater fishing for personal consumption is not required. All anglers fishing from boats with rods and reels are required to purchase a Recreational Fisheries Stamp for $5.50 annually. Exempt are those under 16 years of age or over 65 (who hold a valid South Carolina Gratis Over 65 Hunting and Fishing License), certain persons who are disabled, and anglers fishing from licensed charter fishing vessels.

Licensing and other regulations are highly subject to change, so contact the appropriate state agencies listed at the end of this chapter for current regulations, restrictions, and exemptions.

Minimum Size and Other Restrictions
Atlantic Sturgeon: Legal size limits and open seasons (if any) are set by the Marine Resources Division. All sturgeon caught outside of these limits must be released immediately into the waters where caught.

Black Sea Bass: 8″ TL

Blue Marlin: 86″ FL; Bag limit of 1 per day

Channel Bass (Red Drum): 14″ TL; Bag limit of 20 per person per day; no more than 1 exceeding 32″ TL

Cobia: 33″ FL; Bag limit of 2 per person per day

Flounder: 12″ TL; Bag limit of 20 per person per day

King Mackerel: 12″ FL; Bag limit of 3 per person per day

Nassau Grouper: 12″ TL

Red Grouper: 12″ FL

Red Snapper: 12″ TL

Sailfish: 57″ FL; Bag limit of 1 per day

Shad (American, Hickory): None; Lawful to catch only with regular state fishing license

Shortnose Sturgeon: Unlawful to catch at any time

Spanish Mackerel: 12″ FL; Bag limit of 10 per person per day

Spotted Sea Trout: 12″ TL; Bag limit of 20 per person per day

Striped Bass: None; Bag limit of 10 per person per

day (5 per person per day in Wando River and Cooper River seaward to Highway Bridge 17)

Tarpon: None; Bag limit of 1 per person per day

White Marlin: 62″ FL; Bag limit of 1 per day

Yellowtail Snapper: 12″ TL

TL = Total length

FL = Fork length, measured from the tip of the lower jaw to fork of tail

GEORGIA

All species under state or federal regulations must be landed with head and tail intact. Additionally, it is illegal to sell gamefish in Georgia, including striped bass, except for provisions made by law.

With the following exceptions, saltwater sportfishing in Georgia requires no license, creel limits, time limits or other restrictions common to inland, freshwater fishing.

For general information concerning saltwater sportfishing in Georgia, as well as updated information on all regulatory changes, contact the Coastal Resources Division, Department of Natural Resources, 1 Conservation Way, Brunswick, GA 31523-8600; (912) 264-7218.

Minimum Size and Other Restrictions

Amberjack: 28″ FL; Creel limit 3; March 16–Dec. 31

Black Sea Bass: 8″ TL; no limit; All year (f)

Bluefish: 12″ FL; Creel limit 15; March 16–Nov. 30

Blue Marlin: 86″ FL; Creel limit 1; All year (f)

Cobia: 33″ FL; Creel limit 2; March 16–Nov. 30

Dolphin: 18″ FL; Creel limit 15; All year

Gag Grouper: 20″ TL; Creel limit 10; All year

King Mackerel: 15″ FL; Creel limit 5; All year

Red Drum: 14″ TL; Creel limit 5; All year (None greater than 27″)

Red Snapper: 20″ TL; Creel limit 2; All year (f)

Sailfish*: 57″ FL; Creel limit 1; All year (f)

Sheepshead: 8″ FL; Creel limit 25; All year

Spanish Mackerel: 12″ FL; Creel limit 10; March 16–Nov. 30 (f)

Spotted Sea trout: 12″ TL; Creel limit 25; All year

Sturgeon, Atlantic: 75″ FL; Feb. 15–April 15

Tarpon*: 40″ FL; Creel limit 1; March 16–Nov. 30

White Marlin*: 62″ FL; Creel limit 1; All year (f)

An asterisk (*) denotes gamefish or no sale status.

FL denotes fork length and TL denotes total length. For billfishes, length is from the tip of lower jaw to the fork of tail.

(f) = Same as federal regulations

Gigging

Only flounder may be taken with a gig in the saltwaters of Georgia.

Striped Bass

Fishermen who take striped bass in the Ogeechee, Altamaha, Satilla and St. Marys River systems, including the saltwaters, are restricted to a creel and/or possession limit of two striped bass which must be 22 inches or longer in length. Fifteen of any one species, or a combination of white bass and/or hybrid striped-white bass, may be possessed. The Savannah River downstream of Clarks Hill Reservoir, including the saltwater portion, is **closed** to striped bass fishing.

Artificial Reefs

Georgia has eight established artificial reefs located from 7 to 23 nautical miles offshore. These areas are designated **Special Management Zones** by the federal government. Within these zones, only hand-held hook-and-line gear and spearfishing gear (including power heads) may be used. Fish traps, bottom longlines, gill nets and trawls are prohibited. Jewfish may not be taken by any type of gear.

The state is in the process of establishing several new nearshore artificial reefs to increase fishing opportunities for the expanding recreational fishery. Artificial reef brochures and other recreational fishing information can be obtained by writing or calling the Coastal Resources Division, Georgia Department of Natural Resources.

Red snapper is a popular species with reef and wreck fishermen everywhere. (BOB MCNALLY)

King of the Capes

by Eric Burnley

There are few spectacles in saltwater fishing as awe-inspiring as seeing a 30-pound-plus king mackerel leap out of the water and pounce on a hapless menhaden. This is especially exciting if the menhaden happens to be attached to your fishing line. Fortunately for those of us who fish along the Virginia–North Carolina coast, this is not a rare occurrence, especially in the later part of the season when king mackerel follow bait fish on their southern migration.

The Virginia capes and the Outer Banks of North Carolina have accounted for numerous shipwrecks, and each one of these structures is a potential fuel stop for the hungry mackerel. Not every wreck holds kings every day, but armed with a loran full of good numbers and a livewell full of bait, you should be able to locate some action during the course of your fishing trip.

Before setting out on your quest for a big king mackerel, you will need some special equipment, especially if you plan to use live bait. The first priority is a container that will keep three or four dozen menhaden alive for six or eight hours. The livewell must be round and the water must circulate constantly or the bait will not survive. If you ever have the opportunity to watch a school of pogies, you will see them moving in a big, slow circle. They will try to do the same thing when confined to your livewell. Many newer boats include a suitable livewell as standard equipment, but those of us with older models must improvise. Several companies produce after-market livewells. You should be able to find a model to fit your boat and your fishing requirements.

Once you have the livewell, your next problem will be filling it with menhaden. Unfortunately, no one sells live bait in Virginia Beach or Oregon Inlet, so

The numerous shipwrecks off the Virginia capes and North Carolina's Outer Banks are potential fuel stops for the hungry mackerel.
(JOHN PHILLIPS)

you must catch your own bait before you can catch a king mackerel. Most recreational fishermen use a cast net on the inshore waters or in the sounds, while some charter boat operators will employ a gill net set for menhaden. Before using either device, check with the local authorities; it may save you a citation for using unlicensed gear.

Live-bait fishing for kings requires a terminal rig that will not pass IGFA muster but is the only practical method for hooking these silver lightning bolts. A king hits a bait at top speed, cuts out the part he wants, and leaves the remainder. If you use a single hook rig, the remainder will contain that hook. In order to solve this problem, a rig using two or three small treble hooks on a light wire leader is employed. The small hooks and light leader are required to conceal the armament from the sharp-eyed kings.

In most hook-ups you will snag the mackerel anywhere from just ahead of

the dorsal fin, to his cheek, to his chin. In rare instances the hook will be firmly embedded in his mouth, but even then care must be taken to keep light pressure on the fish or those little trebles will straighten and pull out.

A soft tip rod is used as a shock absorber to further decrease pressure on the hook. Most experienced anglers will set a light drag and use their educated fingers to apply pressure to the line when they feel it is safe to move the fish.

Live bait may be slow-trolled or played out behind a drifting boat. Many boats will not troll slowly enough for this style of fishing without taking the motor in and out of gear. On the other hand, drift fishing puts one at the mercy of wind and current. A compromise is to use the motor to correct your drift direction in what might be called a power drift. This method works well around small structure such as wrecks, while slow trolling allows you to cover more ground when you work along shoals or over open bottom. In all cases it is a good idea to tow a chum bag close astern.

Live-bait fishing may be the most popular method for taking king mackerel, but it certainly is not the only method. Trolling with a wide variety of lures and baits or jigging metal lures on light tackle may also produce good numbers of kings. A ballyhoo and Sea Witch combination is the ham and eggs of fishing in Virginia and North Carolina. Rig the Sea Witch on 40- to 60-pound single-strand wire to prevent bite-offs by the sharp-toothed mackerel. The 3½ Huntington Drone, the Hopkins Hammered Spoon, and the Tony Accetta, size 14 to 16, also produce good numbers of kings. These may be rigged on 60-pound monofilament leader, since king mackerel attack from the rear and seldom come in contact with the line.

Big swimming plugs from Rapala, Cisco Kid, Rebel, Storm, Halco, Manns, and Magna Strike work exceptionally well on king mackerel. As a general rule you will catch more fish when you pull plugs and spoons, but many anglers believe you catch bigger fish on live bait. Captain Robbie Robinson at the L.B. Huntington Company disputes this notion; he has pictures of king mackerel in excess of 50 pounds taken on Drone Spoons.

Downriggers and planners may improve the efficiency of your plugs, spoons and bait rigs. Kings feed at different levels so it pays to fish from the surface down to 15 or 20 feet. Dropping a jig over a wreck also allows you to fish the entire water column.

Jigging is an exciting way to catch kings because you are holding the rod and can actually feel the strike. We use light tackle with 10- to 20-pound line on a revolving spool reel. It is very important to control the jig on the drop because this is when the fish are most likely to hit. I tie my jig directly to the running line, as the fish seem to be leader shy. A short shot of wire or heavy monofilament would save a few lures from bite-offs, but would also result in fewer hook-ups. Stingsilvers and Hopkins are the most popular lures for this style of fishing, but Crippled Herring and J & J Tin jigs have proven effective.

King mackerel movement is controlled by bait concentrations and water temperatures. The fall weather has been quite mild for the past few years, keeping water temperatures reasonably warm along the Virginia Coast. However, once the water drops below 70°F the kings will move south and east, ending up in the vicinity of Diamond Shoals where many of them will spend the winter.

Federal management plans supported by state regulations have increased the population level of king mackerel, which should provide good fishing well into the future. King mackerel are great sport and excellent table fare, but we should kill only those we plan to use ourselves. ■

Boat Ramps

Virginia

Owls Creek: One mile south of Rudee Inlet off of General Booth Boulevard.

North Carolina

Oregon Inlet: Located adjacent to the Oregon Inlet Fishing Center off of NC Route 12.

Charter Services

Virginia

Virginia Beach Fishing Center: (804) 422-5700
Fisherman's Wharf: (804) 425-1388

North Carolina

Oregon Inlet Fishing Center: (919) 441-6301
Pirate's Cove: (919) 473-3906

Virginia Is for Cobia

by Jan Fogt

More than any gamefish I know, cobia are ubiquitous. You find them off the coasts of Texas, Florida, the Carolinas, Australia, Kenya, and Argentina, around reefs, wrecks, and channel markers. They seem to have a different name in every port: lemonfish, ling, cabio, crab-eater. And while the all-tackle world record of 135 pounds, 9 ounces was caught in Western Australia, every year off Virginia they catch 100-pound cobia. Fishermen here don't talk much about it because they don't want a bunch of outsiders horning in on their cobia, so don't tell anyone where you read this.

Before you start stampeding for Virgina, let me tell you a few things about cobia.

They aren't pretty like party-colored dolphin and the silver bullet (wahoo). They are, in fact, the color of day old coffee, with a creamy white underbelly. But being a crab-loving gamefish, cobia taste great, and thanks to a body image more like a torpedo, they fight hard.

Cobia are not boat shy. As Florida fishermen will attest, they'll readily hit a streamer or plastic squid, but up on the Chesapeake, where fishermen tend to make a habit of catching big ones, cobia seem to favor something a little tastier than plastic and feathers—like "peeler crabs" and squirmin' eels.

Cobia on the East Coast are migratory fish, roaming coastal regions from the gulf coast of Texas to the Delmarva Peninsula. Delmarva is their northernmost range but neither Maryland nor Delaware seem to produce the numbers or size of fish that frequent Virginia's waters.

Virginia may be a great place for lovers, but it's also a perfect hangout for cobia. Bordered by the Atlantic Ocean to the east, the Chesapeake Bay to the west, and by the Potomac, Rappahannock, James, York and Rapidan Rivers, which empty into the bay at Virginia, the area is a regular fish factory for crabs, mackerel, menhaden, and eels.

This doesn't take into account the

25

proximity of the continental shelf, the Gulf Stream 62 miles offshore, or the impact of the plankton-rich Labrador Current and its offshoot Virginia Littoral Drift that converge and mix with the Gulf Stream.

Food isn't the only drawing card. As any cobia specialist will attest, structure is almost as important to cobia as food, and Virginia seems to have more than its share.

Maritime Virginia is a land of bridges, tunnels, and buoys. Without even counting the 126 ships that make up the U.S. Navy's Atlantic Fleet, the seaport City of Norfolk is one of the east coast's busiest harbors. Add to this list light towers, weather buoys strung almost 25 miles offshore, artificial reefs and wrecks, and tunnel bridges—modern marvels with more than 2,500 concrete pilings. All these factors, along with a plenitude of more than 100 channel markers leading into the Chesapeake, combine to make this a cobia addict's paradise.

"But I'm not really a cobia fisherman," protests Capt. Tommy English. Fishing a drizzly gray-lady day off Virgina Beach, the captain of the Rudee Inlet-based charter boat *Anxious*, who is more accustomed to hunting marlin and tuna, was doing an admirable job maneuvering around Virginia's famous buoy line, juggling brisk winds and current to keep us within casting distance of the marker and a safe distance from the chain. Standing shoulder to shoulder across the transom, we were casting 20-pound spinners loaded with squirming eels. Wrapping around themselves in a knot, the lively baits were welcome fare to finicky cobia, which, this late in the season, often grow wary of more common offerings such as live spots, menhaden, and mullet. With few boats around, the cobia were climbing on top of each other. And though there were no 100- or even 80-pounders caught, we fought 15- to 30-pounders until the bait ran out.

Unlike English, Claude Bain and Herb Gordon do spend a lot of time hunting cobia during their seasonal

A crab-loving gamefish, cobia taste great, and thanks to a torpedo-like body, they fight hard. (JAN FOGT)

appearances from May through October. Bain, executive director of the Marine Resource Commission's Virginia Saltwater Fishing Tournament, spends a great deal of time researching saltwater fishing opportunities of interest to angling tourists such as myself. Gordon is an independent insurance agent. As their banter suggested, all three are old friends. "I can't believe you haven't tried using live eels for cobia before this," Gordon said to English. "I don't want to mess with any more slimy stuff than I can help," said English. "That goes for salesmen, too."

The problem with eels, explained Bain, is their protective coating or slime. "It dries like concrete or Superglue. Even with soap and water, the stuff doesn't come off."

"Yuck," said English.

Nevertheless, the American eel is one of the most effective and underutilized baits, not just for cobia, but for white and blue marlin and tuna, says Bain. Part of the problem with eels is getting them. Spawned offshore in the Sargasso Sea, fingerling eels migrate thousands of miles back to coastal areas along the Atlantic and Gulf of Mexico to mature in brackish and freshwater systems. While their range

is large, it's only in the Mid-Atlantic states that they are harvested. You can catch them yourself using baited pots and even crab traps set out in the rivers but, because of the time and effort involved, most people just buy them live for $2 each at tackle shops, explains Bain.

Live eels, such as those we used to catch cobia as English suggested, require special handling. They can be kept alive in aerated livewells or buckets, but you have to make sure the overflow pipe in the well is screened. Otherwise you might find your $24 investment in bait is gone, warns Connie Barber of Bubba's Marina. Located on Lynnhaven Inlet, Bubba's is a popular gathering place for cobia specialists such as Bain and Gordon. "They'll squirm out of livewells through the overflow pipe," he explains. Most people keep them alive by storing them on ice in a cooler, (placed between layers of newspaper or seaweed so their skin and gills stay moist). Ice lowers the body temperature, making them easier to handle and hook.

Live eels are easily rigged by hooking behind the head with the hook facing forward, under the gill plates, through the lower jaw and head in front of the eyes, through both eyes, or in the tail under the dorsal fin. Both Barber and Bain prefer hooking them through the tail, which not only makes them swim better, but limits tangling when fishing with more than one bait. For trolling around the Chesapeake Bay Bridge-Tunnel, they hook them through the mouth and out the bottom lip so the barb points down, like a ballyhoo rig. "Eels have a knack of coiling up and unhooking themselves when hooked with the barb pointed in the other direction," Barber said. And to minimize the slime, (caused by contact with air), Barber handles the eels with gloved hands, taking them off the ice and plunging them right over the side in the water to rig them.

Live eels are Cobia candy, says Gordon as he hooks his third cobia in less than 10 minutes. It's true that cobia love eels, but eating isn't always hooking, as I found out. There's a trick to it all right, agrees Gordon. The trick is you have to let them eat, and eat, and eat. '"Til you can't stand it anymore," adds Bain. "You'd think a fish with a mouth and head that big would have no problem gulping down a 12- to 16-inch eel in short order, but for some reason it takes 15, 20, even 30 seconds to swallow one."

Cobia fishing has only been popular off Virginia since about the early 60s, says Bain, which is when some of the biggest fish were caught. Virginia Saltwater Fishing Tournament statistics, which have been kept for almost 40 years, suggest this was also one of the best cobia runs ever recorded along the Mid-Atlantic. From the tournament's inception, the minimum weight for a tournament citation cobia has been 45 pounds. In 1963, the state issued 326 citations for cobia; in 1964, it gave out 224 citations. In the last couple of years, citation awards have averaged 125 to 200 a year. While cobia seem to be constant in these waters, fishing did slack off for about 20 years between 1970 and 1988. Bain speculates that weather, seasonal population swings, and overfishing were to blame. "This being the northern fringe of their range, presumably there are times when the cobia just don't get up this far because of poor spawning years or decreased abundance," he explains. "But I think we've also seen evidence, in recent years at least, how things can improve because of good management. Since the federal plan limiting catches (three or more miles offshore) to two per person of 33 inches or more went into effect in 1982, we've definitely seen the cobia population rebound, especially the small ones. We're catching a lot of 2- to 5-pound fish along with the 40- to 60-pounders that seem to predominate."

Cobia are a primary target fish along the Gulf Coast and in the Florida Keys, but in Virginia they remain pretty much a bycatch for the charter and party boat industry. "Most of those who fish hard for them are trailer boaters like myself and Herb, who are targeting them at the Bridge-Tunnel early in the season, and offshore along the buoys later on in the summer and fall. Very few work people fish for them in March and April when the cobia are up on the Bay side of the Eastern Shore (barrier islands such Cape Charles, Cedar Island, Metompkin, Parramore) and at the C-1 Buoy, Latimer Shoal, Cabbage Patch, Kiptopeke, which are all good early season fishing locations as well," says Bain. The fish will be in the bay on the west shore from mid-June through August at Bluefish Rock, and at the mouth of the Back River, York Spit, and York Spit Channel. They'll also be located around buoys marking the entrance of the Chesapeake Bay.

By mid-season the fish are at the "V" and "4A" buoys, Chesapeake Light Tower, and Santore wreck, and are staked out along the 17.6-mile-long Chesapeake Bay Bridge-Tunnel, which links the mainland to the Eastern Shore. Crossing the bay at depths of 25 to 70 feet, the Bridge-Tunnel forms one of the largest artificial reefs in the world, says Bain.

Trestle and tunnel fishing differs from buoy fishing. The Bridge-Tunnel is a productive cobia hangout from mid-July through mid-September, especially between the second island and the high-level bridge when fished with live spot, menhaden, croakers, and even small bluefish trolled uptide of the span, so the current washes baits towards the pilings. This can be an extremely effective technique early in the season, adds Bain, when the fish haven't been hit as hard. Artificials also work. A Hopkins 550 and Pet #19 spoons and even plastic eel-imitating jigs catch cobia as well, but the one foolproof bait—providing you can get it—is live peeler crabs.

Peeler crabs are crabs which are hours away from shedding their hard shells in anticipation of a new shell. Because most crabs molt between spring and early July, "you only have a limited window of opportunity," to use them for bait, says Connie Barber. Hooked using 7- to 8/0 long shank hooks, you want to flip the shell and fish the crab with the hook threaded through the middle part of the meat, so the crab swims easily, or hooked through the back foot, so it swims deep. Medium to small crabs are best, "but sometimes you have to take what you can get," adds Barber, "so I'll cut them in half. Live is best, but fresh is almost as good."

Fishing the Bridge-Tunnel, when anchoring or drifting around the structure, Bain likes to use what he calls a "fish finder" rig. Approaching the structure, he'll rig a crab or half a menhaden on a 9/0 hook with a 2- to 4-ounce sinker (depending on the current) just above a length of 100-pound leader. Fished live, baits are used on the bottom with a float and at mid-depth using short shank 6/0 to 8/0 hooks. A lot of fishermen will also use chum to enhance the appeal of their baits. Ground menhaden or even a dollop of bunker or menhaden oil can attract fish.

The buoy hop begins in August, when the fish move to the marker buoys in the Baltimore Channel, then offshore. At this time of year the fish are both bigger and harder to catch after weeks of being tempted with live spots and menhaden. "A lot of times you'll see cobia swimming around the buoys but they won't bite." More or less sitting targets at this time of year, they've been shown pretty much everything there is so it takes something special like a live eel to make them bite, says Bain. At other times, it's like fishing in a barrel, he adds.

Generally, however, when you see them on the surface they're feeding more aggressively. Cobia aren't spooky, but at the same time you don't want to motor up to the markers full bore, says Bain, because if you approach cautiously, they'll often swim to the boat. The reason they are on the surface, he said, is current. When current is slack, they come to the surface to feed, which is an ideal situation for live-baiting with croakers, bluefish, or eels, or even casting artificials like a plastic eel or black plastic worm. But most of the time, conditions don't seem to favor buoy fishing. The wind and current will be running, or there will be a crowd of boats around the marker, which forces you to compensate, Bain says. Understanding tidal current can be a big help. A lot of times you can actually outrun the tide and stay ahead of the change,

just by knowing which way to move up and down the buoy line. "You always want to stay on the slack side of the current, so you can fish your baits with no weight. And because you're not using lead, you want to hook the bait—usually in the tail or behind the dorsal—so it swims down rather than horizontally. Occasionally," he admits, "I'll resort to a 1- to 2-ounce egg sinker above the leader, but I don't like

to." Early morning and late afternoon—when fishing competition is at a minimum—seems to be prime time on buoy lines as long the current is right, adds Bain, but don't try to cover all bases by using multiple hook rigs and a trace of wire (for stray king mackerel) if you really want to catch cobia, he warns. "Dumb as they might seem, a big cobia can and will smell a rat." ■

Specks and Spot-Tails

by Joe Malat

It's pitch black, and dead calm. Still a half hour until first light. I can barely see, silhouetted against the lights of the Nags Head Fishing Pier, a handful of anglers. They are scattered along a short stretch of beach, each one casting artificial lures into the calm surf.

Time passes, my mind is wandering. I'm casting and retrieving on autopilot, and the only sound is the periodic slap of the small waves breaking on the beach at my feet.

Suddenly, to my left, I hear the high-pitched staccato sound a spinning reel makes as a good fish runs out line in strong, short spurts. I strain my eyes to pierce the semidarkness, but I can't see many details. The thick body and blunt nose of the fish tells me it's a puppy drum, as the angler drags his prize high and dry on the sand.

I hear someone else down the beach with a fish on, and I start to get edgy, impatient. My autopilot has disengaged, and I'm working the lure, feeling my lead-head jig bump the sand and the Wiffle tail swim against the current as I move it through the surf.

Three more casts, no fish. What's the deal?

My lure flutters to the bottom, the line suddenly comes tight and pulls away. I'm hooked up. It's give and take as seconds pass. He's so close I could

Nell Malat with a puppy drum caught in the Outer Banks surf.
(JOE MALAT)

reach out and touch him with my rod tip, and suddenly the fish comes half way out of the water and shakes his head. Soon I drag a beautiful speckled trout, glistening in the pre-dawn moonlight, up onto the sand at my feet.

My hands start to shake. They always do when I catch the first one—not knowing if this is the first of many, or the only trout I'll catch that day.

But I really don't care. The first one is the best.

A grizzled, salty surfcaster once told a very impressionable teenager that speckled trout were a gentleman's fish. We both stood ankle-deep in the suds. "A good speckled trout angler has skill, finesse, and a fair amount of

luck," he half muttered, half boasted as he brought a trout to the beach on almost every cast. Meanwhile I couldn't buy a strike.

I dearly love speckled trout. Catching them is fun, but I just enjoy fishing for them. Catching them is not a matter of mustering all of your strength to cast 8 ounces of lead and a big gob of bait a hundred yards. Light tackle, small rods and reels, and an effective, sometimes delicate, presentation of the lure is key. I suppose that's what the old man meant by the term "gentleman's fish."

These splendid fish are available in varying numbers from the North Carolina surf almost nine months a year. A few specks are caught from the Outer Banks' beaches in the spring. Small fish, rarely weighing more than a pound, may cooperate sporadically during the summer. But the fall is the time to pursue speckled trout from the beach.

I fish for them on the beaches north of Oregon Inlet, between Nags Head and Kitty Hawk. The peak of the season along those beaches is late September through October. The trout may linger for a while longer if the big blues don't arrive early. (The specks vacate the premises to keep from being eaten by the foraging bluefish.) Specks can be found in the Hatteras surf well into December, if the weather cooperates.

Speckled trout will eat almost any kind of fresh bait, but most veteran trout anglers prefer to fool them with artificial lures. Six- to seven-foot spinning rods, mated to light saltwater reels filled with good quality 8- or 10-pound-test monofilament line, will cover any situation. The light line is necessary to cast the small lures, but heavy enough to handle the biggest trout, provided the operator has a delicate touch with the reel's drag.

MirrOlures are molded from hard plastic to resemble small baitfish, and are a traditional favorite. A trout's preferred lure color may change from day to day, but proven hues are red and white, green, and occasionally a flashy hot pink color. A couple years ago, when this bright color started to consistently take fish, I was skeptical, but its track record has been proven. The key to catching speckled trout on a MirrOlure is an effective retrieve. That usually means slow, with an occasional twitch of the rod tip to make the lure jump. Canny veterans will often work a MirrOlure with the rod tip pointed down toward the water, to better feel the swimming action of the lure through the rod.

MirrOlures may be traditional favorites, but lead-head jigs and soft-plastic tails are equally popular with both fish and fishermen. Head weights vary from ¼ to ½ ounce, and the lures are occasionally rigged in tandem. The most effective tail color or style is a source of constant debate among speckled trout aficionados. Brand names such as Mr. Wiffle, Tout, Mr. Twister, and Gotcha, are standards. These tails come in every color of the rainbow, literally, but every year a predictable range of the spectrum takes most of the trout. Regulars prefer lime or dark green, white, red and white, green firetail, or maybe a white firetail. The firetails are tipped with bright red at the curly end of the lure. Tail lengths may vary from 2 to 6 inches, with a compromise between the two extremes seen most frequently.

Roney Leitner holds a speckled trout that hit his MirrOlure in the surf at Nags Head. (JOE MALAT)

Again, method and technique is everything with these lures. The most often seen retrieve is a steady cranking motion, punctuated with an erratic jig or jerk of the rod tip to make the lure hop and dance through the water column. There are times, however, when a slow, steady retrieve is the only way to fool the fish. It pays to experiment and to watch the guy next to you if he's catching fish and you are merely beating the water to a froth. I can speak from experience on that one.

A while back, on an early fall morning, the trout made a good showing in the surf at daybreak, just south of Jennette's Fishing Pier in Nags Head. To my chagrin, I was only an unwilling spectator for much of the bite. An angler only 5 yards to my left was putting me to shame and was hooked up almost constantly, while I was going fishless.

Not that I'm competitive or anything, but it was killing me. After he caught six fish, and I was still blanked, I stopped fishing and started watching. His "retrieve" was a very s-l-o-w crank of the reel handle as soon as the lure settled to the bottom. I mimicked him and immediately started to share in the bonanza. When the sun was full in the

sky and the trout moved off the beach to deeper water, he had two fish for every one of mine, but at least I didn't get skunked.

Puppy drum are juvenile red drum, easily recognized by one or more dark spots at the base of the tail and a beautiful copper-like hue over the entire body. These distinctive, identifying marks have earned them the nickname of "spot-tails," a name that is more common in Florida and Georgia. They are frequently mixed with the speckled trout, and can be caught in the same locations. The puppies will go for the identical lures and colors that attract the trout, and the seasonal availability of both species also overlaps.

Recently, sensible fisheries management practices for red drum, such as bag and size limits, have positively affected this species. The results are encouraging for anglers: strong numbers of red drum in the 2- to 5-pound class.

As with most surf-caught species of fish, location is everything. Trout and drum, like most fish, come into the surf to feed. They like to search for food in the deeper pockets of water that pepper the Outer Banks coastline. They travel these holes and sloughs, pronounced "slews," that are formed between the outer sandbars and the beach. Often these sloughs are narrow, not more than 30 yards wide, but they may be several feet deep.

The best way to locate a "fishy-looking" slough is to go to the beach at low tide. Look for places where the beach is steep, and the waves break on the outer sandbar, flatten out, and break again on the beach. A featureless, gradually sloping beach, with no significant contours, will be viewed by the observer as a series of short, choppy waves, breaking all the way to the beach. The contours of any beach are always changing, but along the Outer Banks, productive, fish-holding sloughs are frequently formed to the north of many of the fishing piers.

Specks and puppy drum may bite at any stage of the tide. I prefer the end of the falling tide and the first couple hours of the incoming tide. Slack tide, with no moving water, is generally not productive. Water clarity is also a major player in the formula for success. Clear water is necessary for the fish to see a lure, and a rough surf with heavy, breaking waves will make casting difficult if not impossible. The ideal conditions for the fish are also the best for the angler; calm to moderate surf with light winds and clear water.

However, if the surf is calm enough to fish, most dedicated trout fishers will be on the beach just before first light, no matter what the stage of tide. There are many days when the only action occurs during a brief period when the day is just getting underway. A strong second choice would be the period immediately before and after sunset, especially if the trout made an appearance earlier in the day.

Specks and spot-tails are perhaps the elite of the inshore fish along North Carolina's Outer Banks. To fool them with small artificial lures and light tackle in the surf is to meet them on an equal footing at the edge of the sea, and share in an experience that is truly unique. The experience is addictive; once you catch them, you have to go back and try again.

I think those who know these fish, and have caught them, will hear what I'm saying and nod slowly in agreement. If you don't know them yet, how can you resist? ■

FISHING ACCESS

VIRGINIA

The waters along the Virginia coast—120 miles of ocean shoreline, 300 miles of bayfront land, and over 1,300 miles of shoreline on the saltwater reaches of four tidal rivers—provide a huge spawning and nursery area for many species of fish. The Chesapeake Bay is the largest and most productive estuarine complex in the country. The cool, plankton-rich Labrador Current and its offshoot, the Virginia Littoral Drift, rub shoulders with the warm waters of the Gulf Stream off the Virginia coast, bringing a mix of species from the mid-Atlantic and south Atlantic. In fact, Virginia is the southernmost range of abundance for several temperate-water species of fish and the northernmost range of abundance for several subtropical species. The large Eastern Shore peninsula is flanked by a chain of uninhabited and unspoiled barrier islands protecting rich marshes, bays, and sounds.

The construction of the Chesapeake Bay Bridge-Tunnel across the mouth of the Chesapeake Bay created a 17-mile-long fish haven, which many locals refer to as one of the world's largest artificial reefs. In addition, the Virginia Marine Resources Commission (VMRC) maintains an active artificial reef program, and there is good access to all fishing areas through ramps, marinas, piers, charter boats, and guides.

The following access information includes piers and ramps located north of False Cape, and is included for the angler who may wish to try his luck in the Norfolk–Virginia Beach area. For more information on angling in northern Virginia, pick up a copy of *The Northeast Guide to Saltwater Fishing and Boating,* Second Edition (International Marine, 1996).

Fishing Piers
(All telephone area codes are 804.)
Norfolk–Virginia Beach
Chesapeake Bay Bridge-Tunnel
• Sea Gull Fishing Pier (464-4641)
Norfolk
• Harrison's Boat House & Fishing Pier (587-9630)
• Wolloughby Bay Fishing Pier (588-2663)
Virginia Beach
• Lynnhaven Inlet Fishing Pier (481-7071)
• Sandbridge Fishing Pier (426-7200)
• Virginia Beach Fishing Pier (428-2333)
Lower Peninsula
Hampton
• Buckroe Beach Fishing Pier (851-9146)
• Grandview Fishing Pier (851-2811)
Newport News
• James River Fishing Pier, James River Bridge (247-0364)

Launch Ramps
Virginia Beach
Owls Creek

NORTH CAROLINA

North Carolina offers a variety of forms of saltwater fishing. The Outer Banks consist of mile after mile of beautiful beaches and prime surf fishing. Albemarle

Blue marlin are the big prize of blue-water trollers. (BOB MCNALLY)

and Pamlico Sounds are home base for numerous head and charter boats. The Gulf Stream comes as close as 12 miles offshore—the closest to land north of Florida—bringing with it tuna, dolphin, and trophy fish such as blue and white marlin and sailfish. The area off the Outer Banks is one of two areas in the world offering the best chance of landing blue marlin weighing 1,000 pounds or more.

For all practical purposes, recreational fishing runs from April through November in North Carolina. Even in winter, however, king mackerel and bottom fish can be found around the hundreds of shipwrecks and many artificial reefs in mild weather, and speckled trout and red drum can be caught inshore in any month.

Fishing Piers
(All telephone area codes are 919.)

Atlantic Beach
- Oceanna Fishing Pier (726-0863)
- Sportsman's Pier (726-3176)
- Triple "S" Fishing Pier (726-4170)

Carolina Beach
- Carolina Beach Fishing Pier (458-5518)
- Center Fishing Pier (458-5739)

Elizabeth City
- Avon Fishing Pier

Emerald Isle
- Bogue Inlet Fishing Pier (354-2919)
- Emerald Isle Fishing Pier (354-3274)

Hatteras
- Cape Hatteras Fishing Pier

Holden Beach
- Holden Beach Fishing Pier

Holly Ridge
- The Scotch Bonnet Pier

Kill Devil Hills
- Avalon Fishing Pier (441-7494)

Kitty Hawk
- Kitty Hawk Fishing Pier

Kure Beach
- Kure Beach Fishing Pier (458-5524)

Long Beach
- Long Beach Ocean Crest Motel & Pier
- Oceancrest Pier
- Yaupon Beach Fishing Pier

Morehead City
- Indian Beach Fishing Pier (247-3411)

Nags Head
- Jennette's Fishing Pier
- Nags Head Fishing Pier (441-5141)
- Outer Banks Fishing Pier

Pine Knoll Shores
- Iron Steamer Resort Pier (247-4213)

Rodanthe
- Hatteras Island Resort

Shallotte
- Ocean Isle Fishing Pier

Sneads Ferry
- Salty's Pier

Sunset Beach
- Sunset Beach Fishing Pier

Surf City
- Barnacle Bill's Fishing Pier
- Surf City Ocean Pier

Topsail Beach
- The Jolly Roger Fishing Pier

Wilmington
- Ocean City Fishing Pier

Wrightsville Beach
- Johnnie Mercer Fishing Pier
- Oceanic Restaurant & Grill

Marinas
(All telephone area codes are 919.)

Marsh Harbor Marina, Box 4100 Calabash, NC 28459, 579-3500

Pelican Pointe Marina, 2000 Sommerset Rd., S.W., Ocean Isle Beach, NC 28469, 579-6440

The Plaza at Ocean Isle Beach LOC, 19 Causeway Dr., Box 5280, Ocean Isle Beach, NC 28469, 579-6019

Tripp's Fishing Center, 4133 Dawght Rd., Shallotte, NC 28459, 754-6985

Hughs Marina, 1800 Village Point Rd., Shallotte, NC 28459, 754- 6233

Intracoastal Marina, 2504 Sunrise Street S.W., Supply, NC 28462, 842-9333

Captain Pete's Seafood, 101 S. Shore Dr., Holden Beach, NC 28462, 842-6675

Holden Beach Marina, 3238 Pompano St., Supply, NC 28462, 842-5447

Oak Beach Inn & Marina, Box 10578, 57th Place W., Long Beach, NC 28461, 278-9977

Southport Marina Inc., W. West Street, Southport NC 28461, 457-5261

City of Southport Dock, Yacht Basin Drive, Southport, NC 28461, 457-7900

Bald Head Island Marina, Box 3069, Bald Head Island, NC 28461, 547-7380

Carolina Beach Municipal Docks, Canal Dr., Carolina Beach, NC 28428, 458-2985

Carolina Beach State Park Marina, Box 475, Carolina Beach, NC 28428, 458-7770

Snow's Cut Landing Marina, 100 Spencer Farlow Dr., Carolina Beach, NC 28428, 458-7400

Oceana Marina, 401 Virginia Ave., Carolina Beach, NC 28428, 458-5053

Inlet Watch Yacht Club, 801 Paoli Ct., Wilmington, NC 28409, 392-7106

Carolina Inlet Marina, 801 Paoli Ct., Suite 101, Wilmington, NC 28409, 392-0580

Wilmington Marine Center, 3410 River Rd., Wilmington, NC 28412, 395-5055

Masonboro Boatyard Marina, 609 Trails End Rd., Wilmington, NC 28409, 791-1893

Bradley Creek Boataminium, 6338 Oleander Dr., Box 4867, Wilmington, NC 28409, 350-0029

Boathouse Marina Inc., 6334 Oleander Dr., Wilmington, NC 28409, 350-0023

Dockside Marina, 1306 Airlie Rd., Wilmington, NC 28409, 256-4796

Caroyacht Corp., 2002 Eastwood Rd., Wilmington, NC 28409, 256-9901

Airlie Marina, 1402 Airlie Rd., Wilmington, NC 28409, 256-4796

Bridge Tender Marina, Box 1037, Wrightsville Beach, NC 28480, 256-6550

Wrightsville Marina, Box 1215, Wrightsville Beach, NC 28480, 256-6666

Sea Path Yacht Club Inc., Box 135, 330 Causeway Dr., Wrightsville Beach, NC 28480, 256-3747

Atlantic Marine Sales & Service, 130 Short St., Wrightsville Beach, NC 28480, 256-9911

Carolina Yacht Yard, 2107 Middlesound Rd., Wilmington, NC 28405, 686-0004

Oak Winds Marina, 2127 Middle Sound Loop Rd., Wilmington, NC 28405, 686-7319

Johnson's Marine Service Inc., 2029 Turner Nursery Rd., Wilmington, NC 28405, 686-7565

Canady's Marina, 26244 Mason's Landing Rd., Wilmington, NC 28405, 686-9116

Mason's Marina, 7421 Mt. Pleasant Dr., Wilmington, NC 28405, 686-7661

Pearsall's On The River, 478 Blossoms Ferry Rd., Castle Hayne, NC 28429, 675-3094

Scott's Hill Marina, 2570 Scott's Hill Loop Rd., Wilmington, NC 28405, 686-0896

Harbor Village Marina, 101 Harbor Marina Dr., Hempstead, NC 28443, 270-4017

Bushes Repair Center, Box 3330, Hwy. 50, Topsail Beach, NC 28445, 328-3141

Topsail/Beaufort Marina, 904 S. Anderson Blvd., Topsail Beach, NC 28445, 328-5681

Swan Point Marina, 123 Page St., Box 10, Sneads Ferry, NC 28460, 327-1081

New River Marina, Box 307, Sneads Ferry, NC 28460, 327-9691

Sneads Ferry Marina, Hwy. 172, Sneads Ferry, NC 28460, 327-1621

Old Ferry Marina, 150 Old Ferry Rd., Hwy. 172, Sneads Ferry, NC 28460, 327-2258

Gottschalk Marina, Julian C. Smith Dr., MCB Camp Lejeune, NC 28542, 451-8307

Tideline Marine, 52 Kerr St., Jacksonville, NC 28540, 455-2979

Ivey Marina, 110 South Marine Blvd., Jacksonville, NC 28540, 346-6663

Casper Marine Service, Box 728, 301 Water St., Swansboro, NC 28584, 326-4462

Dudley's Marina, Box 1128, Hwy. 24, Swansboro, NC 28584, 393-2204

The Flying Bridge/Swansboro Yacht Basin, Box 26, Hwy. 24, Swansboro, NC 28584, 393-2416

Island Harbor Marina, End Of Old Ferry Rd., Box 4370, Emerald Isle, NC 28594, 354-3106

Osprey Oaks Marina, Rt. 1, Box 141, Newport, NC 28570, 393-2492

Spooner's Creek Yacht Harbor, Rt. 2, Morehead City, NC 28557, 726-2060

Coral Bay Marina, Hwy. 70 W., Box 1287, Morehead City, NC 28557, 247-4231

Harbor Master, 4408 Central Dr., Box 1048, Morehead City, NC 28557, 726-2541

70 West Marina, 4401 Arendell St., Box 826, Morehead City, NC 28557, 726-5171

Crow's Nest Marina, 409 Morehead Ave., Box 267, Atlantic Beach, NC 28512, 726-4048

Sea Water Marina, Atlantic Beach Causeway, Atlantic Beach, NC 28512, 726-1637

Causeway Marina, 300 Morehead Ave., Box 2366, Atlantic Beach, NC 28512, 726-6977

Bailey's Marina, 116 Morehead Ave., Box 638, Atlantic Beach, NC 28512, 247-4148

Fort Macon Marina, 422 E. Fort Macon Rd., Box 370, Atlantic Beach, NC 28512, 726-2055

Anchorage Marina, 517 E. Fort Macon Rd., Box 7, Atlantic Beach, NC 28512, 726-4423

Triple S Marina Village, 1511 E. Fort Macon Rd., Box 1010, Atlantic Beach, NC 28512, 247-4833

Morehead City Yacht Basin, 208 Arendell St., Morehead City, NC 28557, 726-6862

Dockside Marina, 301 Arendell St., Box 3398, Morehead City, NC 28557, 247-4890

Morehead Sports Marina, Rt.4, Box 17, Beaufort, NC 28516, 726-5676

Radio Island Marina, Inlet Dr., Box 570, Beaufort, NC 28516, 726-3773

Beaufort Marine Discount, 421 Front St., Beaufort, NC 28516, 728-4077

Beaufort Inn, 101 Ann St., Beaufort, NC 28516, 728-2600

Airport Marina, Corner Beaufort St. & Turner St., Beaufort, NC 28516, 728-4725

Town Creek Marina, Rt. 4, Box 25, Beaufort, NC 28516, 728-6111

Beaufort City Docks, 500 Front St., Beaufort, NC 28516, 728-2503

Fisherman's Inn Marina, S.R. 1395, Box 218, Harkers Island, NC 28531, 728-5780

Harker's Island Fishing Center, S.R. 1335, Box 400, Harkers Island, NC 28531, 728-3907

Barbour's Harbor Marina, Island Rd., Box 72, Harkers Island, NC 28531, 728-6181

Calico Jack's Marina, Star Rt., Box 308, Harkers Island, NC 28531, 728-3575

East Bay Boat Works Inc., 11 Fullard St., Box 230, Harkers Island, NC 28531, 728-2004

Bock Marine, Hwy. 101, Core Creek, Rt. 1, Box 633, Beaufort, NC 28516, 728-6855

Sea Gate Marina, 7 Sea Gate Blvd., Newport, NC 28570, 728-4126

Matthews Point Marina, Rt.1, Box 176, Havelock, NC 28532, 444-1805

Cedar Creek Campground & Marina, Inc., 111 Canal Dr., Sealevel, NC 28577, 225-9571

Drum Inlet Seafood, Hwy. 70 East, P.O. Box 186, Atlantic, NC 28511, 225-4581

Sheraton Motel & Marina, 1 Bicentennial Park, New Bern, NC 28560, 638-3585

Ramada Marina, 101 Howell Road, New Bern, NC 28562, 636-8888

Duck Creek Marina, P.O. Box 40, Bridgeton, NC 28519, 637-2045

Northwest Creek Marina, 104 Marina Dr., New Bern, NC 28560, 1-800-443-9129, 638-4133

Minnesott Beach Yacht Basin, P.O. Box 128, Arapahoe, NC 28510, 249-1424

Oriental Marina, P.O. Box 8, Oriental, NC 28571, 249-1818

Deaton Yacht Service, 200 Neuse Dr., Oriental, NC 28571, 249-1180

Whittaker Creek Yacht Harbor, P.O. Box 357, Oriental, NC 28571, 249-0666

Sea Harbor Marina, P.O. Box 442, Harbor Way St., Oriental, NC 28571, 249-0808

Hobucken Marina, Hwy. 304, Hobucken, NC 28537, 745-7182

Whichard's Beach Marina, P.O. Box 746, Washington, NC 27889, 946-4275

Twin Lakes Campground and Yacht Basin, 1618 Whichard's Beach Rd., Rt. 2, Box 605, Chocowinity, NC 27817, 946-5700

Park Boat Company, 214 Hwy. 17 South, Washington, NC 27889, 946-3248

Carolina Wind Yachting Center Inc., 411 West Main St., Washington, NC 27889, 946-4653

Eastern Carolina Yacht Service/Broad Creek
Marina, 300 McCotters Marina Rd., Washington,
NC 27889, 975-2046

McCotters Marina, Rt. 7, Box 221 G, Washington,
NC 27889, 975-2174

Quarter Deck, P.O. Box 119, Bath, NC 27808,
923-2361

Cee Bee Marina, Rt. 2, Pungo Creek, Bellhaven, NC
27810, 964-4375

River Forrest Marina, 600 East Main St., Bellhaven,
NC 27810, 943-2151

Marlin C. Robb & Son Boatyard & Marina, 316 East
Front St., Bellhaven, NC 27810, 943-2110

Dowry Creek Marina, S.R. 1710, P.O. Box 341, Bellhaven, NC 27810, 943-2728, 943-2728

Vanhorn's Bayside Marina & Campground, Rt. 1,
Box 69, Scranton, NC 27875, 921-6621

Rose Bay Marina, Hwy. 246, Rt. 1, Box 205, E.
Scranton, NC 27875, 926-1041

Fisherman's Wharf Marina, Oyster Creek Rd., Swan
Quarter, NC 27885, 926-4271

Oyster Creek, Rt. 1, Box 56, Swan Quarter, NC
27885, 926-4131

Clarks Marina, Landing Rd., Swan Quarter, NC
27885, 926-3801

Big Trout Marina, Box 246, Englehard, NC 27824,
925-6651

Park Service Docks, Box 340, Ocracoke, NC 27960,
928-5111

O'Neal's Dockside, Rt. 12, Box 282, Ocracoke, NC
27960, 928-1111

Teach's Lair Marina, Box 520, Hatteras, NC 27943,
986-2460

Hatteras Harbor Marina, Box 537, Hatteras, NC
27943, 986-2166

Oden's Dock, Box 477, Hatteras, NC 27943, 986-2555

Village Marina, Box 503, Hatteras, NC 27943,
986-2522

Willis Boat Landing, Box 215, Hatteras, NC 27943,
986-2208

Scott Boatyard & Marine Repair, Box 312, Buxton,
NC 27920, 995-4331

Oregon Inlet Fishing Center, Box 2089, Manteo, NC
27954, 441-6301

Mill Landing Marina, Box 483, Nags Head, NC
27957, 473-3908

Gwaltney Boats, Box 1803, Manteo, NC 27954,
473-3338

Pirates Cove Marina, Box 1997, Manteo, NC 27954,
473-3906

Salty Dawg Marina, Box 489, Manteo, NC 27954,
473-3405

Manteo Waterfront Marina, Box 545, Manteo, NC
27954, 473-3320

Manns Harbor Marina, Box 76, Manns Harbor, NC
27953, 473-5150

Alligator River Marina, U.S. 64, Columbia, NC
27925, 796-0333

Sawyers Marina, Box 166, Columbia, NC 27925,
796-6381

Edenton Marina, 607 W. Queen St., Box 700, Edenton, NC 27932, 482-7421

Elizabeth City Shipyard & Marina, 722 Riverside
Ave., Elizabeth City, NC 27909, 355-0171

City Marina, Hwy. 158E, Camden Cswy., Elizabeth
City, NC 27909, 338-2886

Mariner's Wharf, Box 426, Elizabeth City, NC
27907, 335-4365

Riverside Boatworks, 722 Riverside Ave., Elizabeth
City, NC 27907, 335-2118

The Pelican, 43 Camden Cswy., Elizabeth City, NC
27909, 335-5108

Paradise Marina & Grocery, Box 1, Camden Pt.
Shores, NC 27974, 336-3646

Harrison's Marina, Box 69, Coinjock, NC 27923,
453-2631

Midway Marina, Box 87, Coinjock, NC 27923,
453-3625

Carl Davis Coinjock Marina, Rt. 1, Box 8, Coinjock,
NC 27923, 453-3271

Launch Ramps
Alligator River

East Lake Ferry (Dare County)—From the junction
of US 64 and 264 near Manns Harbor, take US 64
west 10.9 miles to SR 1153. Turn right onto SR
1153 and travel 0.2 miles to the area. The access
road is located on the left at the end of SR 1153.

Frying Pan (Tyrrell County)—From the junction of
US 64 and NC 94 in Columbia, take NC 94 south
6.8 miles to SR 1307. Turn left onto SR 1307 and
travel 5.5 miles to the area.

Gum Neck Landing (Tyrrell County)—From the
junction of US 64 and NC 94 in Columbia, take
NC 94 south 13.1 miles to SR 1321. Turn left onto
SR 1321 and travel 2.8 miles to SR 1320. Turn left
onto SR 1320 and travel 1.6 miles to SR 1316.
Turn right onto SR 1316 and travel 0.6 miles. The
access road to the area is located on the left at the
end of SR 1316.

Bogue Sound

Morehead City (Carteret County)—From the junction of US 70 and NC 24, travel US 70 east 1.5
miles. The area is located on the right side of the
highway.

Beaufort (Carteret County)—From Beaufort, travel US 70 east to SR 1310 (Lennoxville Rd.). Go 1.5 miles, turn right onto SR 1312. The area is 100 yards on the left.

Cape Fear River

Federal Point/Ft. Fisher (New Hanover County)—From Wilmington, travel south on US 421 to the end of the road near Ft. Fisher.

Chowan River

Eldenhouse Bridge (Chowan County)—The area is located adjacent to US 17 at the north end of the Chowan River Bridge.

Currituck Sound

Popular Branch (Currituck County)—At Coinjock, take US 158 east 4.9 miles to NC 3. Turn left and go 2.2 miles to the end of the road.

Dawson Creek

Dawson Creek (Pamlico County)—At the junction of US 17 and NC 55, take NC 55 east to Oriental. Cross the bridge onto SR 1308, go 3 miles, take SR 1302, go 1 mile and turn right onto a gravel road. The area is 0.3 mile on the left.

Intracoastal Waterway

Cedar Point (Carteret County)—Take NC 24 west from the junction of NC 58 and NC 24. Go 2.3 miles to the area.

Coinjock (Currituck County)—From Coinjock, take US 158 east 0.3 mile to SR 1405. Turn left and go 0.4 mile to SR 1141. Bear right on SR 1141 and go 0.2 miles to SR 1142. Turn right and go 1.2 miles. The area is on left at Canal Bridge.

Holden Beach (Brunswick County)—Take NC 130 to Holden Beach. Turn left and travel 0.2 mile. Turn left and the area is on the left, under NC 130 bridge.

Oak Island (Brunswick County)—From Southport, take NC 211 west to NC 133. Turn left and go 1.7 miles south to SR 1101. Turn left. The area is 0.5 mile on the left.

Snow's Cut (New Hanover County)—From Wilmington, take US 421 south. Cross over waterway bridge onto SR 1577, go 0.5 mile to SR 1532 (Spencer Farrow Rd.), and then go 0.5 mile to the area.

Sunset Harbor (Brunswick County)—From Supply, at the junction of US 17 and NC 211, go 7 miles southeast on NC 211 to SR 1112. Turn right. The area is 0.5 mile on the left.

Turkey Creek (Onslow County)—From the junction of NC 50 and US 17, take US 17 north 4 miles to Folkstone. Turn northeast onto SR 1518 (Old Folkstone Rd.). Go 1.5 miles to ST 1529,

then 1.9 miles to ST 1530. Turn east and go 0.9 miles to the area.

West Onslow Beach (Onslow County)—Take NC 210 east from the intersection of US 17 and NC 210. Go 10 miles to Highrise Bridge. The area is on the northeast side of the bridge on the left.

Wrightsville Beach (New Hanover County)—From the junction of NC 132, exit to US 74 east. Go 5 miles, cross the ICW bridge, and exit to the right. Go under the bridge and proceed to the area.

Kitty Hawk Bay

Avalon Beach (Dare County)—From the east end of the Wright Memorial Bridge on US 158, travel east 6 miles to Avalon Dr. Turn right, and go 0.6 mile to Bay Dr. Turn left and go 0.1 mile to Dock Street. The area is on the left.

Neuse River

Bridgeton (Craven County)—From Bridgeton, take US 17 north for 2 miles to SR 1431 (Wildlife Rd.) and turn left. The area is at the end of the road.

New River

Jacksonville (Onslow County)—Located on US 17 adjacent to the New River Bridge, down by the USO Building.

Pamlico River

Smith's Creek (Beaufort County)—From Bridgeton, at the junction of US 17 and NC 55, take NC 55 east 14 miles to Bayboro. Take NC 304 north 5.9 miles. Turn onto NC 307 east, go 7.6 miles to NC 33. Turn west and travel 2.9 miles. The area is located west of Hobucken.

Pamlico Sound

Engelhard (Hyde County)—From the junction of US 264 and NC 94 near Lake Mattamuskeet, take US 264 east 14.7 miles to SR 1315. The access road is on the right side of US 264.

Stumpy Point (Dare County)—Take US 264 from the junction US 64 and US 264 near Manns Harbor. Travel west 12.4 miles to SR 1100. Turn left and go 2.5 miles to the area.

Pasquotank River

Elizabeth City (Pasquotank County)—From the junction US 17 and US 158 in Elizabeth City, take US 17 north 1.3 miles to Knobb's Creek Dr. Turn right and travel .8 miles to the Sewage Treatment Plant Road. Turn left and go 0.2 mile to the area.

Salters Creek

Salters Creek (Carteret County)—From Beaufort, take US 70 east to near Sealevel. Cross Highrise Bridge and take the road to the left. The area is at the end of the road.

Smith's Creek

Oriental (Pamlico County)—From US 17 and NC

55, take NC 55 east 24 miles to Oriental. Take SR 1306 (North St.) one block to SR 1367. Turn left; the area is located at the end of the road.

Four-Wheel-Drive Beach Access Information
(All telephone area codes are 919.)

Kure Beach
Kure Beach Town Hall—458-8216

Carolina beach
Carolina Beach Police Dept.—458-8208

Topsail Beach
Topsail Beach Town Hall—328-4851

Surf City
Surf City Police Dept.—328-7711

Emerald Isle to Pine Shores
Emerald Isle Police Dept.—354-2024

Atlantic Beach
Atlantic Beach Police Dept.—726-2523

Cape Lookout
Cape Lookout National Seashore Office—240-1409

Ocracoke to Nags Head
Cape Hatteras National Seashore Office—473-2111

Nags Head
Nags Head Town Hall—441-5508

Kill Devil Hills
Kill Devil Hills Police Dept.—441-7491

Corrola
Currituck Sheriff's Dept.—232-2216

Pier fishing—quiet, relaxing, and time well spent.
(HERB ALLEN)

Artificial Reefs
The information on North Carolina's artificial reefs is listed in the following order: reef number, reef name (depth), buoy loran C, latitude/longitude, compass heading and distance.

AR130: (58 ft.); 26979.1/40726.0; 36°00'18"N, 75°32'00"W; 003° magnetic—12.3 miles from Oregon Inlet sea buoy.

AR140: (57 ft.); 26975.0/40690.0; 35°56'45"N, 75°32'00"W; 001° magnetic—8.9 miles from Oregon Inlet sea buoy.

AR145: LCU-1468 (65 ft.); 26941.4/40685.7; 35°54'01"N, 75°23'48"W; 049° magnetic—8.1 miles from Oregon Inlet sea buoy.

AR160: Oregon Inlet (77 ft.); 26940.7/40574.1; 35°44'40"N, 75°27'20"W; 150° magnetic—4 miles from Oregon Inlet sea buoy.

AR191: Black Walnut Point (18 ft.); 36°00'00"N, 76°40'00"W; 140° magnetic from marker 2 at entrance to Edenton Channel, 1 mile due north of Black Walnut Point.

AR220: (54 ft.); 26951.0/40182.0; 35°08'11"N, 75°40'33"W; 111° magnetic—4.9 miles from Hatteras Inlet sea buoy.

AR225: (69 ft.); 26945.0/40175.0; 35°06'48"N, 75°39'18"W; 120° magnetic—6.2 miles from Hatteras Inlet sea buoy.

AR230: Mr. J.C. (72 ft.); 26957.0/40155.0; 35°06'19"N, 75°43'22"W; 148° magnetic—3.7 miles from Hatteras Inlet sea buoy.

AR250: (83 ft.); 26987.3/40024.0; 34°57'00"N, 75°55'00"W; 156° magnetic—5.1 miles from Ocracoke Inlet sea buoy.

AR255: (84 ft.); 26995.9/39998.0; 34°55'30"N, 75°58'00"W; 184° magnetic—6.1 miles from Ocracoke Inlet sea buoy.

AR275: Drum Inlet (55 ft.); 27052.0/39870.2; 34°50'13"N, 76°16'12"W; 140° magnetic—2.0 miles from north side of Drum Inlet. *Warning: Drum Inlet is not a maintained inlet. Please use local knowledge and exercise caution when using this inlet.

AR285: George Summerlin (65 ft.); 27062.2/ 39682.7; 34°33'51"N, 76°25'32"W; 120° magnetic—14.3 miles from Beaufort Inlet sea buoy.

AR291: Bayview (Pamlico River) (20 ft.); 35°25'55"N, 76°45'42"W; 100 ft. offshore Town of Bayview, near mouth of Bath Creek.

AR292: Quilley Point (Pungo River); 35°28'15"N, 76°34'15"W; 135° magnetic—southeast of ICWW Channel, 1.2 miles southeast of Marker No. 7.

AR296: Hatteras Island Business Association (14 ft.); 26950.0/40280.0; 35°17'20"N, 75°37'30"W;

150° magnetic—1 mile north of Frisco Channel Marker No. 6.

AR298: Ocracoke (15 ft.); 27019.5/40132.7; 35°10′42″N, 75°59′59″W; 035° magnetic—1.5 miles from Big Foot Slough channel entrance.

AR300: Hardees (90 ft.); 27039.3/39574.8; 34°19′00″N, 76°24′30″W; 153° magnetic—24.0 miles from Beaufort Inlet sea buoy.

AR302: Yancey (149-165 ft.); no buoy; 34°10′20″N, 76°14′60″W; 143° magnetic—35.4 nautical miles from Beaufort Inlet sea buoy.

AR305: Carteret County Sportfishing Association (104 ft.); 27080.9/39489.9; 34°16′30″N, 76°38′30″W; 184° magnetic—22.5 miles from Beaufort Inlet sea buoy.

AR315: Atlantic Beach (49 ft.); 27127.9/39661.2; 34°40′00″N, 76°45′00″W; 300° magnetic—3.9 miles from Beaufort Inlet sea buoy.

AR320: Clifton Moss (50 ft.); 27138.6/39637.3; 34°39′00″N, 76°49′00″W; 282° magnetic—6.4 miles from Beaufort Inlet sea buoy.

AR330: Howard Chapin (60 ft.); 27139.7/39569.5; 34°33′55″N, 76°58′35″W; 247° magnetic—10 miles from Beaufort Inlet sea buoy.

AR340: J. Paul Tyndall (58 ft.); 27162.4/39545.3; 34°34′38″N, 76°58′35″W; 118° magnetic—7.2 miles from Bogue Inlet sea buoy.

AR342: Bogue Inlet (49 ft.); 27177.0/39549.8; 34°36′42″N, 77°02′18″W; 107° magnetic—3.9 miles from Bogue Inlet sea buoy.

AR345: Swansboro Rotary Club (60 ft.); 27160.2/39524.8; 34°32′15″N, 76°58′30″W; 133° magnetic—8.4 miles from Bogue Inlet sea buoy.

AR350: New River (31 ft.); 27225.7/39403.7; 34°29′48″N, 77°21′24″W; 210° magnetic—1.25 miles from BW buoy New River Inlet.

AR355: (60 ft.); 27210.0/39324.4; 34°21′18″N, 77°19′54″W; 185° magnetic—9.7 miles from New River Inlet sea buoy.

AR360: Topsail (44 ft.); 27256.9/39252.5; 34°20′42″N, 77°36′12″W; 85° magnetic—2.5 miles from BW "NT" buoy New Topsail Inlet.

AR364: (54 ft.); 27233.1/39224.5; 34°15′40″N, 77°30′24″W; 126° magnetic—8.7 miles from New Topsail Inlet sea buoy.

AR364: Billy Murrell (44 ft.); 27267.4/39160.6; 34°14′48″N, 77°42′54″W; 050° magnetic—6.2 miles from Masonboro Inlet sea buoy.

AR366: (66 ft.); 27214.6/39225.0; 34°13′00″N, 77°25′06″W; 127° magnetic—13.9 miles from New Topsail Inlet sea buoy.

AR368: (66 ft.); 27211.7/39125.0; 34°09′30″N, 77°25′48″W; 140° magnetic—15.5 miles from New Topsail Inlet sea buoy.

AR370: Mears Harris, Jr. (52 ft.); 27267.8/39106.3; 100° magnetic—3.5 miles from Masonboro Inlet sea buoy.

AR372: (48 ft.); 27261.4/39068.9; 34°06′00″N, 77°45′00″W; 154° magnetic—5 miles from Masonboro Inlet sea buoy.

AR376: (60 ft.); 27243.1/39077.2; 34°03′00″N, 77°38′00″W; 142° magnetic—9.9 miles from Masonboro Inlet sea buoy.

AR378: Carolina Beach (40 ft.); 9960—27275.5/57509.2; 34°02′00″N, 77°52′00″W; 7980—45336.0/58990.4; 208° magnetic—8.9 miles from Masonboro Inlet sea buoy.

AR382: Dredge Wreck (58 ft.); 27241.5/39047.0; 160° magnetic—13 miles from Masonboro Inlet sea buoy.

AR386: Lennon/Hyde (78 ft.); 27218.3/39082.2; 33°57′00″N, 77°33′00″W; 143° magnetic—17.8 miles from Masonboro Inlet sea buoy.

AR391: Brices Creek; Old rock pit.

AR392: New Bern (15 ft.); 27211.2/29858.9; 140° magnetic—2.6 miles from Union Point Park, Neuse River.

AR396: Oriental (15 ft.); 35°01′50″N, 76°39′30″W; 900 yards southeast of Whitehurst Point near Oriental.

AR420: Yaupon Beach (30 ft.); 7980—45347.9/59184.8; 33°51′15″N, 78°06′30″W; 315° magnetic—3.0 miles from Cape Fear River sea buoy.

AR425: Yaupon Beach (30 ft.); 7980—45354.7/59169.6; 33°53′06″N, 78°07′24″W; 336° magnetic—4.4 miles from Cape Fear River sea buoy.

AR440: Brunswick County Fishing Club (42 ft.); 7980—45365.8/59246.6; 33°50′00″N, 78°13′00″W; 169° magnetic—4.5 miles from Lockwood Folly Inlet sea buoy.

AR445: (53 ft.); 7980—45352.0/59289.0; 33°45′00″N, 78°14′00″W; 185° magnetic—9.3 miles from Lockwood Folly Inlet sea buoy.

AR455: (46 ft.); 7980—45373.0/59306.0; 33°18′00″N, 78°18′00″W; 156° magnetic—7 miles from Shallotte Inlet sea buoy.

AR460: (38 ft.); 7980—45398.0/59323.0; 33°50′00″N, 78°22′00″W; 183° magnetic—3 miles from Shallotte Inlet sea buoy. (Project completed by Long Bay Artificial Reef Association.)

Boating Information
Department of Environmental Health and Natural Resources District Offices

Elizabeth City, (800) 338-7805 or (919) 264-3911

Washington, (800) 248-4536 or (919) 395-3900

Wilmington, (800) 248-4536 or (919) 395-3900

North Carolina Boating Regulation Information

Boat Registration Section, 512 N. Salisbury Street, Raleigh, NC 27604-1188, (919) 662-4373

Vessels for Hire/Captains Licenses Regional Examination Center

Coast Guard Marine Safety Office, 192 Trade Street, Charleston, SC 29401-1899

Boating Safety Course Information

(800) 336-BOAT

Ship to Shore Call

Southern Coast: Contact Wilmington Marine Operator on Channel 26

Northern Coast: Contact Morehead City Marine Operator on Channel 26

Shore to Ship Call

(919) 726-1070

Camp Lejeune Marine Corps Base

For information on traveling the Atlantic Intracoastal Waterway through Camp Lejeune Marine Corps Base, contact the Onslow Beach swing bridge for waterway opening information.

Coast Guard

For search and rescue, contact the nearest Coast Guard Station or Coast Guard Group Fort Macon at (919) 247-4540 or (919) 247-4545. All initial radio calls to the Coast Guard for emergency assistance should be made on channel 16/156.8 mhz.

Coast Guard Stations

(All telephone area codes are 919.)

Oak Island, (919) 278-5592

Wrightsville Beach, (919) 256-3469

Swansboro, (919) 354-2719

Fort Macon, (919) 247-4546

Ocracoke, (919) 928-3711

Hobucken, (919) 745-3131

Cape Hatteras, (919) 995-6411

Hatteras Island, (919) 986-2175

Oregon Inlet, (919) 987-2311

Coinjock, (919) 453-3411

To Report the Following

Illegal Activity: (919) 247-4540 or (919) 247 4544

Oil Pollution Incident: (919) 247-4544 or (800) 424-8802

Boating Accident or Loss of Life: Contact nearest Coast Guard station

SOUTH CAROLINA

Fishing Piers

South Carolina fishing piers are located mainly along the Grand Strand area, which extends from the North Carolina state line southward to Georgetown, South Carolina. These ocean piers range from 670 to 1,045 feet in length. These structures provide easy access to fishing for thousands of anglers each year and one of the most leisurely and inexpensive forms of angling enjoyment. Spot, croaker, whiting (kingfish), pompano, silver perch (yellowtail), and bluefish are the primary species harvested, although everything from sea trout and flounder to king mackerel, tarpon, and cobia may be caught from these platforms.

Most fishing piers are open from April through November though a few remain open year-round. Operating hours are generally from 6 or 7:00 A.M. to 10 or 11:00 P.M; however, during the summer many piers remain open all night. These piers are lighted and a wide selection of baits such as dead shrimp, bloodworms, mullet, and earthworms are available at each pier, along with a complete line of fishing tackle. All of the piers offer rod and reel outfits for rent and have snack bars or restaurants.

Pier anglers generally use a small- to medium-size rod and reel with a double hook bottom rig with dead shrimp for bait. This method is effective on such species as whiting, spot, croaker, and pompano. Live shrimp or mud minnows are preferred for such species as weakfish (summer trout), speckled trout, and flounder. Larger rods and reels with 50- to 80-pound-test line are usually employed when fishing for king mackerel, cobia, or tarpon. Small live fish such as bluefish, mullet, or menhaden from 4 to 10 inches long are often floated near the surface as bait. Each pier usually has regulations governing the latter form of fishing. One should inquire about these regulations before fishing.

Grand Strand piers are noted for fall spot fishing. This delicious pan fish migrates in large schools southward past the piers during October and November, and hundreds of anglers turn out to fish for them. Many anglers fill coolers, buckets, and barrels with these fish in just a couple of hours during these runs.

South Carolina's fishing piers include:

Paradise Pier (Fee)
Hunting Island State Park
Port Royal Boardwalk
Broad River Pier
Haigh Landing

Coastal Marinas and Facilities

Marinas on the South Carolina coast offer a wide variety of services and accommodations to the recreational angler. These may range from bait and tackle stores to machine shops capable of rebuilding diesel parts. If the trip you plan to the coast requires extensive services, such as a boat slip for a week or more, it would be wise to secure facilities well in advance because demand is heavy during the warm season.

The visiting angler should also take caution when mooring to fixed docks to ensure that his boat doesn't get caught in a rising tide. Tides may fluctuate more than 9 feet on this coast, and even large cabin cruisers have capsized and sunk when they got caught under a dock during a flood tide. Most marinas now use floating docks which reduce this risk significantly.

If you trailer your boat to the coast, make sure you can launch and load your boat with a minimum of your trailer submerged. Saltwater is highly corrosive and can ruin your axles, bearings and even your car if you don't take immediate steps to rinse off saltwater after exposure.

Marinas and launch ramps are often congested, and you should avoid littering and polluting them.

Fish should be cleaned at sea or at home rather than throwing their remains overboard in a marina. Many local marinas have cleaning stations and receptacles for your refuse. These facilities are usually free, so take advantage of the hospitality offered and use them.

Marinas are oases for the boatman, as he can replenish his supplies and find safe moorings there. Marina operators are also one of the best sources of information about current fishing conditions. Therefore, the slight additional cost of purchasing some of your supplies at a coastal marina is usually more than offset by the current fishing information that comes with your purchases.

The following marinas have launch ramps, rentals, or both. Launch ramps are designated (LR); rental, (R).

Bella Marina, P.O. Box 1100, N. Myrtle Beach (LR)

Palmetto Shores Marina, P.O. Box 3063, N. Myrtle Beach, Intracoastal Waterway (LR)

Bucksport Marina, P.O. Box 38, Bucksport, Intracoastal Waterway (LR)

Inlet Port Marina, Murrells Inlet (LR)

Wacca Wache Marina, Murrells Inlet, Intracoastal Waterway (LR), (R)

Georgetown Landing Marina, Georgetown, Pee Dee River (LR)

Gulf Auto Marina, Front Street, Georgetown, Sampit River (LR)

Exxon Marina, St. James St., Georgetown, Sampit River (LR)

Belle Isle Marina, Georgetown, Winyah Bay (LR)

Leland Marina, Water Street, McClellanville, Jeremy Creek (LR)

Wild Dunes Yacht Harbor, Isle of Palms, Intracoastal Waterway, (LR), (R)

Creekside Yacht Harbor, Isle of Palms, Hamlin Creek (LR)

Castaway Texaco Marina, 101 Palm Blvd., Isle of Palms, Intracoastal Waterway (LR) (R)

Shem Creek Marina, 526 Mill St., Mt. Pleasant, Shem Creek (LR)

Toler's Cove, P.O. Box 492, Charleston, Intracoastal Waterway (LR)

Ashley Marina, Lockwood Blvd., Charleston, Ashley River (LR)

Charleston City Marina, Lockwood Blvd., Charleston, Ashley River (LR)

Stono Marina, 2409 Maybank Hwy., Johns Island, Stono River (LR)

Bohicket Marina Village, 1880 Andell Bluff, Johns Island, Bohicket Creek (LR)

Mariners Cay Marina, Folly Road, James Island, Folly River (R)

Botany Bay Marina & Boat, Rockville Yard, Botany Bay (LR)

Edisto Marina, Edisto Beach, (803) 869-3504

Downtown Marina of Beaufort, 1010 Bay St., Beaufort, Beaufort River, (803) 524-4422 (LR)

Fripp Island Marina, Fripp Island, (803) 838-5661

Port Royal Landing, (803) 525-6664

Marsh Harbor Marina, Lady's Island, (803) 524-4797

Beaufort Marina, Lady's Island, Factory Creek, (803) 524-3949 (LR)

Skull Creek Marina, Skull Creek, Hilton Head, (803) 681-4234 (R)

Outdoor Resorts Marina, Hilton Head, Intracoastal Waterway, (803) 681-3241 (LR)

Broad Creek Marina, Hilton Head, Broad Creek, (803) 681-7335 (LR)

Shelter Cove Marina, Hilton Head, Broad Creek, (803) 758-3910 (R)

Palmetto Bay Marina, 164 Palmetto Bay, Hilton Head, Broad Creek, (803) 758-3910 (R)

Harbor Town Yacht Basin, Lighthouse Road, Hilton Head, Calibogue Sound, (803) 671-2704 (R)

South Beach Marina, Hilton Head, Calibogue Sound, (803) 671-6640 (LR), (R)

Dataw Island Marina, (803) 838-8262

Launch Ramps

Public and privately operated launch ramps are present throughout the coastal counties of South Carolina. These facilities provide ready access to all marine waters of the state. Public landings usually consist of the bare essentials: a concrete or gravel ramp and a parking lot which may be graveled. Privately owned landings typically provide much better facilities which normally include docks, bait and tackle shops, fueling docks and, in many cases, a freshwater washdown area. The added facilities are usually worth the $1 to $4 launching fee.

Prior to using a ramp for the first time it is a good idea to inquire about its condition. Many ramps have sharp drop-offs which can damage a trailer or prevent the retrieval of a boat. The water may recede from some ramps on ebb tide so that a boat returning from the water cannot reach the ramp. Ramps built of oyster shell or riprap are inadequate to handle large boats and one should use them with caution. These problems are more commonly associated with the public ramps than with privately operated facilities.

When launching or loading your boat, park in a way that takes as little room as possible and always remove your trailer from the ramp as soon as you are able. It is inconsiderate to others to tie up a ramp while organizing your boat. This can be done in the parking lot or in the water. Never leave your boat unattended for any length of time. You may return to find your boat floating out in the creek with an incoming tide or stranded on land with the water receding. Safe and courteous boating is no accident: you make it happen.

The following launch ramps are available along the South Carolina coast:

Edisto Marina

Johnson Creek Fishing Landing

Capers Creek

Brainards, Intracoastal Waterway

Exxon, Intracoastal Waterway

Highway 9, Intracoastal Waterway

Wortham's Ferry, Waccamaw River

Davis Landing, Waccamaw River

Star Bluff Landing, Waccamaw River

Red Bluff Landing, Waccamaw River

Lee's Landing, Waccamaw River

Hardee's Ferry, Waccamaw River

Pitch Landing, Waccamaw River

Cox's Ferry, Waccamaw River

Jackson Bluff, Waccamaw River

Peach Tree Landing, Waccamaw River

Socastee, Intracoastal Waterway

Hague Marina, Intracoastal Waterway

Bucksport Marina, Intracoastal Waterway

Yanhannah Ferry, Great Pee Dee River

Waccamaw, Waccamaw River

Inlet Port Marina, Murrells Inlet

Pawleys Island, Midway Inlet

Hagley Plantation, Waccamaw River

Shrine Club, Black River

Dunbar Landing, Black River

Meeting Street, Sampit River

New Meeting Street, Sampit River

Moultrie Landing, Sampit River

Belle Isle Marina, Winyah River

South Island Ferry, Winyah River

Collins Landing, Santee Bay

Pole Yard, Santee Bay

Robert E. Ashley, Jeremy Creek

Buck Hall, Intracoastal Waterway

Moore's Landing, Intracoastal Waterway

Claude W. Blanchard, Wando River

Detco Landing, Wando River

Isle of Palms Marina, Intracoastal Waterway

Tolers Cove Marina, Intracoastal Waterway

Creekside Marina, Hamlin Creek

Shem Creek Landing, Shem Creek

J. Mitchell Graham, Cooper River

Ralph M. Hendricks, Cooper River

Wando Woods, Ashley River

Church Creek Landing, Church Creek

North Bridge, Ashley River

Floyd Flemming, Wappoo Creek

R.E. Seabrook, Wappoo Creek

Municipal Yacht Basin, Ashley River

Sol Legare Landing, Stono River

J.F. Seignious, Folly River

Limehouse, Stono River

Bulow Landing, Rantowles Creek

Cherry Point, Bohicket Creek

Penny Creek, Penny Creek

Wiltown Bluff, Edisto River

Dawhoo Bridge, Dawhoo River

San Russ Landing, Russell Creek

Steamboat Landing, Steamboat Creek

Fontaines, Big Bay Creek

Flowers Seafood Co., Big Bay Creek

Brick Yard, Ashepoo River

Bennetts Point, Ashepoo River

Wiggins Boat Landing, Old Chehaw River

Fields Point Landing, Combahee River

Bush Island, Harbor River

Johnson Creek Fishing Landing, Johnson Creek

Russ Point, Fripp Inlet

Fripp Island Marina, Old House Creek

Sams Point, Lucy Creek

Jenkins Creek Landing, Jenkins Creek
Corner Lake, Coosawhatchie River
Dawson's Landing, Coosawhatchie River
Tutens Landing, Boyds Creek
Salvesburg Landing, Boyds Creek
Grays Hill, Whale Branch
Bolen Hall, Euhaw Creek
Edgar C. Glenn Landing, Chechessee
Broad River, Broad River
Pigeon Point Road, Beaufort River
Beaufort City Marina, Beaufort River
Public Landing, Beaufort River
Battery Creek Landing, Battery Creek
Beaufort River, Beaufort River
U.S. Naval Hospital, Beaufort River
Capers Creek, Capers Creek
Station Creek, Station Creek
Trask Landing, Colleton River
C.C. Hague Landing, Mackay Creek
Buckingham, Mackay Creek
Broad Creek, Broad Creek
Bluffton County Landing, May River
All Joy Landing, May River
South Beach Marina, Beach Hole Creek

Artificial Reefs

An artificial reef is an underwater area in which man has placed materials intended to attract and hold large numbers of various fish in order to enhance either commercial or recreational fishing efforts. The reasons for the success of artificial reefs are varied and not completely understood, but it is known that the materials placed in the water for this purpose often provide a source of food, habitat, and physical orientation for many different fish. The success of reefs in transforming virtually barren expanses of ocean bottom into productive fishing grounds is well-documented.

The majority of the ocean floor in nearshore waters off South Carolina (as well as off most of the East Coast and Gulf Coast states) is flat, featureless sand bottom. This type of bottom is generally associated with meager fish populations. Only in limited areas where natural rock outcroppings, ancient coral reefs, or ledges occur is productivity high enough to warrant fishing efforts. The only additional areas which maintain large enough fish populations to be of interest to recreational anglers not wanting to go too far offshore are near materials which man has placed in the ocean either unintentionally or intentionally. This includes everything from shipwrecks and oil drilling platforms to well-placed artificial reefs.

Almost any imaginable stable, solid material

placed in the ocean will, in a short time, become a point of attachment for a wide variety of organisms such as algae, barnacles, corals, and sponges. Other species such as crabs, shrimp, mussels, and clams will soon take up residence on and around these materials. In a matter of weeks to months the originally barren foreign debris begins its transition into a highly productive biological community. A variety of fish very quickly begin to populate the reef and the surrounding waters, becoming the top level of the food chain in this new community.

The practice of constructing artificial reefs to enhance fisheries has been in use for almost two hundred years, with credit being given to the Japanese for initial discovery of their usefulness. The first recorded artificial reefs in the United States were built in South Carolina around 1830.

Local fishermen were becoming frustrated over declining catches of sheepshead, which fed on the barnacle-encrusted branches of dead trees that had fallen into the waters adjacent to shore. The clearing of land for agricultural purposes near the shoreline had depleted the supply of fallen trees. Fishermen decided to create new habitat for the barnacles in hopes of luring the fish back to areas where they were once plentiful. They constructed large, square enclosures out of oak and pine logs and sunk them at selected locations by ballasting them down with stones. The logs soon became covered with barnacles and the sheepshead indeed returned to these areas to feed.

Artificial reef construction has changed a great deal in practice while remaining basically the same in principle. Our understanding of how reefs work and what makes the best type of reef for specific purposes has advanced greatly. The technology of reef design and construction has also developed significantly, especially in countries such as Japan where multi-million dollar reef programs are in operation.

In the United States, the construction and utilization of artificial reefs has expanded greatly in recent years. Since artificial reefs in the U.S. are primarily designed for use by sportfishermen, this growth can be attributed chiefly to a vast increase in the number of people participating in recreational fishing, in both fresh and saltwater. With more and more people competing for a limited number of good fishing locations, especially in the marine environment, the addition of artificial reefs to once unproductive waters has helped take pressure off of existing natural areas and better distribute the total fishing effort over a much wider range.

Despite their early historical success with artificial reefs, it was not until the early 1960s that South Carolinians again became interested in reef construction. Realizing the tremendous success of artificial reefs in Florida and Japan, among others, local organizations of sportfishermen began to take on the task of artificial

Anglers can catch puppy drum from sounds as well as the surf. Drum can reach weights up to 100 pounds and 20- to 40-pounders are not uncommon.
(ERIC BURNLEY)

reef construction. In 1967, the State of South Carolina began appropriating a special fund to assist these groups in the construction of offshore reefs. By 1973, six had been established.

In 1973, a state-maintained Artificial Reef Program was established by the South Carolina Wildlife and Marine Resources Department's Marine Resources Division. Over the past 22 years, this program has overseen the construction of 10 additional artificial reefs, bringing the state's current inventory to 16. These reefs are distributed along the coast from Little River Inlet to Hilton Head Island. Easy boat access to a reef is now available from almost anywhere on the coast. Each of the reefs is marked by at least one yellow artificial reef buoy.

South Carolina's artificial reefs have been constructed from a wide range of materials. Everything from discarded automobile tires, junked car bodies, and concrete pipe to old barges, boats, and ships has been used at one time or another. Recent examination of the reefs has revealed that some of these materials attract more sea life than others. By learning from years of experience, the state hopes to construct future reefs

that will maximize benefits to the fish inhabiting them as well as to the various human users of the reefs.

In addition to maintaining a series of successful benthic (bottom type) artificial reefs along the coast, the Marine Resources Division has pioneered development of a type of artificial reef which is suspended off the bottom. This grouping of mid-water fish attractors is known as a trolling alley because of the type of fish that are attracted to it and the way the reef is designed for fishing. Large numbers of open-water fish such as mackerel, jacks, barracuda, and cobia are found around these structures. They are fished by trolling past the structures, which are placed in rows up to a mile long. Buoys mark each end of the trolling alley on three such reefs at present. It is hoped that with continuing success, this type of reef design can be expanded to most of the existing artificial reefs in the system.

Through continued expansion and improvement of existing reefs and carefully planned additions of new benthic reefs and trolling alleys, South Carolina's Artificial Reef Program will be able to continue to provide enhanced areas for sportfishing in coastal waters. If properly designed, constructed, and utilized, these areas will provide years of successful service to the many recreational fishermen who depend on them for a good day of fishing.

Little River Reef

This reef was built as a cooperative reef by the North Carolina Division of Marine Fisheries and the South Carolina Department of Wildlife and Marine Resources. Construction began in July, 1975. Over 25,000 auto and truck tires have been placed on the reef in large bales. Yellow nun buoys with masts and radar reflectors mark the northeast and southwest corners of the 1500' × 3000' reef.

Since most of the reef consists of low profile material, with depths ranging from 30 to 35 feet, a depth recorder may not indicate a great deal of vertical relief. Fishing in the area between the two buoys should yield good results. The best fishing has been for sea bass, flounder, and mackerel.

The reef is located on a heading of 125°M, 2.7 miles from the end of the South Jetty at Little River Inlet, Lat. 33°49.2'N, Long. 78°30.0'W or Loran C 45424.0/59402.6. This reef can be plotted on NOAA Chart 11535.

Paradise Reef

The second oldest artificial reef currently in the system, construction was begun at this site in March 1968. The 1500' x 3000' reef contains a variety of materials including three Navy landing craft, three barges, one life boat, five cement mixer drums, half of a boat hull, cement pipe, and over 60,000 automobile tires. Two nun buoys and two smaller can buoys mark the four corners of the reef, with most of the material lying around the edges between the buoys. The larger structures should be easy to locate with the use of a depth recorder. Water depth is 30 to 35 feet over the reef.

This has been one of the state's more popular reefs over the years, providing good catches of sea bass, flounder, sea trout, and some Spanish and king mackerel. Amberjack, cobia, and barracuda have also been caught on occasion.

The reef is located 105°M, 3.2 miles from the end of the South Murrells Inlet Jetty, Lat. 33°31.0'N, Long. 78°58.0'W and Loran C 45465.0/59762.1 and can be plotted on NOAA Chart 11535.

Ten Mile Reef

Expanded in 1982 to include a one-mile-long trolling alley, this one-square-mile reef boasts some of the best king mackerel fishing in any area along the coast. The reef was begun in August 1973, and the original materials on the reef consisted of a 200-foot ship, a 60-foot landing craft, a 40-foot dredge tender, eight large steel camels, and over 14,000 auto and truck tires. One hundred twenty mid-water fish attractors were added when the trolling alley was put in, and 100 additional fish attractors were placed on the reef in May, 1984.

A yellow nun buoy and can buoy are found at the northwest corner of the reef. Most of the bottom materials are found between and around these two buoys, offering good bottom fishing in this area. The trolling alley consists of two parallel rows of mid-water fish attracters running from the northwest corner nun buoy to the southwest corner nun buoy one mile away. The water over the reef is 35 to 45 feet deep.

The reef is located on a heading of 130°M, 9.5 miles from the South Jetty at Murrells Inlet. The northwest corner of the reef is at Lat. 33°26.2'N, Long. 78°52.6'W or Loran C 45427.0/59741.1. The southeast corner is at Lat. 33°25.2'N, Long. 78°51.4'W or Loran C 45418.0/59736.7. The reef is accurately depicted on NOAA Chart 11535 dated May 1984.

Pawleys Island Reef

Also begun in August 1973, this 1500' x 1500' reef offers much the same conditions as are found on Paradise Reef to the north. The materials at this reef consist of four landing craft hulls, half of a boat hull, and 25,000 auto tires in bales. One yellow nun buoy marks the center of the reef and one yellow can buoy is placed 600 feet north of this. Most of the material lies between these two buoys. Water depth is 25 to 35 feet.

The reef is located at Lat. 33°26.0'N, Long. 79°00.7'W or Loran C 45456.9/59814.9 and is on heading 177°M, 5.5 miles from the Murrells Inlet Jetty. It can be plotted on NOAA Chart 11535.

Georgetown Reef

Although a permit for construction on this 3000' × 3000' reef was not issued until 1980, the area itself was already a popular location for local fishermen. The permitted area is centered around the remains of a ship which sank around 1916 off of the mouth of Winyah Bay. Since 1980, additional materials have been sunk

adjacent to this wreck. A 95-foot barge and 11 large steel scaffolds were added earlier. Two additional 100-foot barges were sunk in June 1984.

A yellow nun buoy and smaller can buoy mark the reef. The two newest barges are located about 100 yards north of the nun buoy. The average water depth at the reef is 35 to 40 feet. Since all of the materials placed on this reef are high profile steel structures, individual items are easy to locate with even the simplest of depth recorders.

The reef is located on a heading of 074°M, 7.6 miles from the last South Jetty mound as you exit Winyah Bay. It can be plotted at Lat. 33°14.3'N, Long. 79°00.0'W or Loran C 45411.3/59882.8 on NOAA Chart 11535.

Gray Bay Inshore Reef

This reef, constructed in 1982, was the second of two inshore artificial reefs constructed by the South Carolina Wildlife and Marine Resources Department. Located in an estuarine environment, it is much more accessible to a wider variety of anglers including those with the smallest of boats. The 2000-foot-long reef can be located by running up Long Creek off the Intracoastal Waterway behind the Isle of Palms. Water depths at low water range from 5 to 10 feet.

The reef is marked by a series of range markers and buoys which indicate the orientation of the groups of structures on the bottom. A variety of materials were used on the reef, including PVC pipe, steel pallets, concrete pipe, and baled auto tires. Mooring buoys have also been placed in strategic locations over the reef to allow boats to stay in good positions without using their own anchors. Fishing for such species as sea trout, red drum, and sheepshead should be much improved as the reef begins to age.

NOAA Chart 11518 shows the location of the reef between Goat Island and Eagle Island, about three-quarters of a mile north of the Isle of Palms. Boaters should use caution in navigating the narrow and often shallow areas in getting to the reef.

Capers Reef

Often referred to as "R-8" due to its close proximity to the red Coast Guard buoy "8", this reef was originally begun by the efforts of interested anglers and divers in the Charleston area in May 1968. Since that time a wide variety of materials has been added to the 1500' × 1500' area. Five landing craft, several steel and wooden hulled boats, a school bus body, a tank truck body, a steel caisson, 100 steel milk crates, an amphibious vessel, and 30,000 auto and truck tires are scattered around the reef. Most recently, in January 1984, a 97-foot steel hulled fishing trawler was sunk approximately 200 feet north of the Coast Guard buoy, which is on the southeast corner of the reef.

A yellow nun buoy marks the approximate center of the reef, and most of the other materials are located around this buoy. The reef bears 090°M, 12.1 miles from the offshore end of the Charleston Jetties. Good fishing is found on the reef especially in the late spring and early summer when bluefish, amberjack, mackerel, and cobia are abundant. Sea bass, porgies and an occasional grouper are also taken when bottom fishing.

The reef can be plotted on NOAA Chart 11521 at Lat. 32°44.5′N, 79°34.4′W or Loran C 45438.2/60370.4. Water depth ranges from 35 to 45 feet.

Kiawah Reef

The Kiawah Artificial Reef originated as an experimental reef in July 1967. Built by the U.S. Fish and Wildlife Service and the Bears Bluff Laboratory, it is the oldest known artificial reef in South Carolina still in existence. The reef originally consisted of 70 scrapped automobile bodies, barged out and sunk in 45 feet of water, 7.5 miles off Kiawah Island. In 1971, the South Carolina Wildlife and Marine Resources Department assumed responsibility for the reef and began expanding the area to improve its suitability for recreational angling.

At present the 1500′ × 3000′ area contains three tugboats, two mine sweepers, two landing craft, one drydock, several small boats, a 200-foot barge, four 50-foot pontoons, and over 30,000 auto tires. Recently an 800-yard-long mid-water trolling alley was added to improve the success of fishing for pelagic species such as mackerel, barracuda, and amberjack. The reef is marked by a single yellow nun buoy with mast and radar reflector. The new trolling alley runs from this buoy to a point 800 yards due north. Water depth over the area ranges from 30 to 45 feet. Excellent fishing opportunities are available for a wide variety of popular pelagic sportfishes as well as grouper, sea bass, porgy, and sheepshead.

The reef is located at Lat. 32°29.0′N, Long. 080°00.3′W or Loran C 45493.1/60693.6, bearing 201°M, 7.0 miles from the mouth of Strong Inlet or 115°M, 6.5 miles from the buoy "2NE" off of the mouth of the North Edisto River. This reef may be plotted on NOAA Chart 11521.

South Edisto Inshore Reef

Located in the South Edisto River, this 1500′ × 3000′ artificial reef became the first state-maintained inshore artificial reef in October 1980. As is the case with the Gray Bay Inshore Reef, it was designed to allow access to South Carolina's artificial reefs from smaller boats not capable of transits far from shore. The reef is laid out in four 100-yard-long bands of material running perpendicular to the shoreline about 200 yards offshore. Each band can be located by using a set of range markers on the shore.

The structures on this reef consist of PVC pipe units, steel pallets, concrete culvert pipe, and anchored auto tires. A series of mooring buoys are also in place to allow for easy access to the materials without anchoring.

The reef can be located on NOAA Chart 11517,

approximately 1.7 miles upstream from the mouth of St. Pierre Creek on the northern bank of the South Edisto River. Water depths over the reef range from 15 to 30 feet. The structures are located near naturally productive waters for sea trout. Fishing in this area should also be good for red drum, black drum, flounder, sheepshead, croaker, spot, and bluefish.

Edisto Offshore Reef

Originated as a mid-water trolling alley in the spring of 1980, this one-mile-square artificial reef is the farthest offshore of any in the South Carolina system. Over the years the mid-water fish aggregation devices (FADs) have been successful in attracting large numbers of king and Spanish mackerel, barracuda, amberjack, and dolphins to the area. Even an occasional sailfish is taken on the reef when water temperatures are suitable. The one-mile-long trolling alley is laid out between two yellow nun buoys. New FADs were placed on the reef in the spring of 1984.

To enhance fishing for bottom fish as well as pelagics, a ship was sunk near the northernmost buoy and a tugboat was recently placed near the buoy at the southern end. Large numbers of black sea bass, gag grouper, and porgies have been seen by divers in and around these vessels. The water over this reef is from 50 to 72 feet deep.

Edisto Reef can be plotted on NOAA Chart 11480 at Lat. 32°14.1′N, Long. 79°50.5′W or Loran C 45382.0/60689.6. The reef bears 158°M, 23.5 miles from Stono Inlet. Because of its distance offshore, only those with the proper navigational equipment and training should venture out to this reef.

Fripp Island Reef

This 1500′ × 3000′ reef was originated by Beaufort-Jasper Outdoorama, Inc., in 1968. In 1975 the reef was transferred to the South Carolina Wildlife and Marine Resources Department's Artificial Reef Program. The reef is composed of low profile materials such as concrete culvert pipe, scrap steel, and over 50,000 automobile tires. Bottom fishing for black sea bass, porgy, and flounder is good in this area, and best accomplished by drifting over the widely scattered materials. During the spring and fall, large sea trout inhabit the reef and are caught by drifting live minnows or shrimp across the bottom.

The reef is marked by one large yellow nun buoy and one smaller can buoy. The majority of the materials on the bottom lie to the northwest of these buoys. Water depth ranges from 30 to 38 feet.

Fripp Island Reef can be plotted on NOAA Chart 11513 at Lat. 32°15.5′N, Long. 80°22.5′W or Loran C 45546.0/60969.0. It is most easily reached from Hunting or Fripp Islands bearing 140°M, 5.8 miles from Fripp Inlet. Navigation in the waters in this inlet can be tricky, so seek the advice of local sources prior to exploring this area.

Some of South Carolina's artificial reefs are suspended off the bottom and attract such species as this big cobia as well as mackerel, barracuda, and jacks. (JOHN PHILLIPS)

Hunting Island Reef

Lying only 2.5 miles southeast of the Fripp Island Reef, this reef was also initiated by Beaufort-Jasper Out-doorama, Inc., and transferred to the state in 1975. It is also referred to as "6HI" due to its close proximity to the red Coast Guard buoy given that designation. Bearing 143°M, at 8.5 miles from Fripp Inlet, Hunting or Fripp Islands are the most ready points of access.

The materials on the reef include three barges, a dredge tender, two landing craft, eight barge sections, a cabin cruiser hull, and approximately 30,000 single and baled auto tires. Two yellow nun buoys mark the reef, with most of the material lying between the buoys. This reef can be plotted on NOAA Chart 11513. The center of the reef is at Lat. 32°13.0'N, Long. 80°20.3'W or Loran C 45525.1/60964.5.

Both bottom fishing and trolling over the reef have proven to be very successful. Mackerel, barracuda, amberjack, sea bass, and porgy are common on the reef. Drifting is often the best method of bottom fishing.

FishAmerica Reef

Constructed in June 1984, this is the newest of South Carolina's artificial reefs. The reef was built in only 9 feet of water 2.5 miles east of Hilton Head Island and consists entirely of heavy pieces of concrete culvert pipe. The Hilton Head Fishing Club and the South Carolina Wildlife and Marine Resources Department worked together in planning and constructing the reef. FishAmerica Foundation of Tulsa, Oklahoma, provided the primary financial support.

The reef is located at Lat. 32°07.9'N, Long. 80°41.7'W or Loran C 45616.7/61186.2, and can be plotted on NOAA Chart 11513. Over 400 tons of pipe were placed on the reef in four parallel rows lying between the four yellow can buoys that mark the corners of the reef. Material comes up to within 5 feet of the surface at low water, so only shallow draft vessels should attempt to navigate over the reef. Access to the area is about equal distance from the mouths of both Calibogue Sound and Port Royal Sound.

Although it will take several years for the reef to develop to its full potential, results should soon become apparent by improved fishing in this area. This spot should be ideal for such species as mackerels, bluefish, and sea trout.

Betsy Ross Reef

Sunk with the aid of U.S. Marine Corps explosive experts in December 1978, this 440-foot-long liberty ship is the largest single piece of material on any of South Carolina's artificial reefs. The South Carolina Wildlife and Marine Resources Department obtained the ship with the aid of the Lt. Governor's office, from the Liberty Ship Reserve Fleet anchored in the James River near Norfolk, Virginia. The *Betsy Ross*, formerly named the *Cor Caroli*, saw combat service during World War II and was awarded a battle star for her participation in the invasion of Bougonville in 1944.

The vessel now lies in 85 feet of water, 18 miles off of Hilton Head Island, at Lat. 32°03.2'N, Long. 80°25.0'W or Loran C 45504.3/61062.8. It can be plotted on NOAA Chart 11513. Masted yellow nun buoys lie at the bow and stern of the ship so it is very easy to locate.

Due to the depth of the water and the size of the ship fishing on and around this structure is very good. Both trolling and bottom fishing enthusiasts will be well pleased by a visit to this reef.

Hilton Head Reef

Begun in 1977 as a cooperative venture between the Georgia Department of Natural Resources and the South Carolina Wildlife and Marine Resources Department, this 1800' × 1800' reef in 50 feet of water has proven itself as a popular location for all types of fishing. A combination of artificial structures and nearby live bottom areas yields a thriving population of black sea bass, porgy, grouper, sheepshead, amberjack, barracuda, mackerel, and cobia.

Three yellow nun buoys mark the reef, 11.5 miles off of Hilton Head Island. The buoy at the northwest corner marks an area where over 25,000 auto tires were

45

placed. The buoy due south of this one marks a 200-foot barge added to the reef in 1982, and the southeast corner buoy is near two smaller barges sunk in 1977. A 45-foot ex-Navy dive boat was also added to the northeast corner of the reef in 1982.

The reef can be plotted on NOAA Chart 11513 at Lat. 31°59.7'N, Long. 80°35.7'W, 6.0 miles from the last set of buoys in Port Royal Sound Channel, or 093°M, 9.5 miles from buoy "6" in the Tybee Roads Channel.

This reef, as well as the *Betsy Ross* Reef, is very popular for both fishermen and scuba divers. During summer months it is not uncommon to find many boats using each reef. Please be considerate of those arriving before and after you while sharing this resource.

Offshore Fishing Wrecks

General Sherman Wreck

Sunk in rough weather in January 1874, off of Cherry Grove, the remains of the cargo vessel *General Sherman* were finally located and identified by divers in 1979. Formerly having served as a Confederate blockade runner under the name *Prince Royal*, the 150-foot steel-hulled vessel was originally put into service in 1861. After being captured by Union forces, she was renamed the *General Sherman* and put into service as a blockade ship until the end of the war.

The *Sherman* now lies in 45 to 55 feet of water on a heading of 183°M, 7.0 miles from the mouth of the Little River Inlet Jetties. The wreck can be plotted on NOAA Chart 11535 at Lat. 33°43.7'N, Long. 73°32.3'W or Loran C 45413.3/59455.6. In May 1984 the South Carolina Wildlife and Marine Resources Department placed a large yellow nun buoy about 50 feet to the east of the largest portion of the wreckage. This buoy will allow anglers in the area to more easily locate this popular fishing spot.

Most of the *Sherman* has been reduced to a broad area of low profile steel plates and beams. Several portions of the vessel do still rise 10 to 12 feet off the bottom, offering a good solid mark on any type of depth recorder. Originally known as the "Cherry Grove Wreck," this area has yielded good catches of mackerel, amberjack, barracuda, black sea bass, porgy, and grouper over the years. During winter months, good-sized tautog have also been seen on the wreck. Scuba diving here is also very popular.

City of Richmond Wreck

Located at Lat. 33°01.8'N, Long. 78°55.5'W and marked by a red Coast Guard buoy "WR2A," this 250-foot steel-hulled ferryboat can be most easily reached from the entrance of Winyah Bay. The wreck bears 136°M, 14.3 miles from the mound on the seaward end of the jetty at the Winyah Bay entrance, and is shown on NOAA Chart 11531.

The remains of the vessel lie in 50 feet of water, with some parts of the wreckage coming up to a depth of 19 feet. Bottom fishing is excellent for grouper, porgy, and black sea bass. Amberjack, barracuda, mackerel, cobia, and bluefish are also caught over the area. The wreck is also a popular spot for local divers due to the abundance of marine life and generally good visibility for this region.

Hector Wreck

Over the years the remains of this steel-hulled freighter have been broken up, scattered, and partially buried by the relentless pounding of the sea. The remains of the *Hector* lie in 30 feet of water at 176°M, 11.6 miles from the seaward most mound at the Winyah Bay Jetty. Parts of the coral- and sponge-encrusted wreckage come to within 18 feet of the surface. The wreck is located at Lat. 33°00.5'N, Long. 79°06.1'W or Loran C 45379.6/60026.8.

A red Coast Guard buoy ("WR 4") lies about 500 yards due east of the wreckage. The high profile of the many large pieces of material makes the spot easy to locate with any type of depth recorder. The wreck is marked on NOAA Chart 11531.

The area is well populated with large black sea bass, sheepshead, and porgies, making bottom fishing very popular. Trolling over the wreckage can also be profitable, especially in the spring when large bluefish are common.

Fripp Island Drydock Wreck

The Fripp Island Drydock is located at Lat. 32°17.1'N, Long. 80°24.9'W or about 3 miles on a heading of 150°M from Fripp Inlet. The 120 × 80 × 20-foot structure sank while being towed from Jacksonville, Florida, to Charleston. It was accidentally discovered by a local trawler and eventually buoyed by the South Carolina Wildlife and Marine Resources Department in July 1979. The single yellow can buoy aids the trawlers in avoiding the structure and allows anglers to take advantage of the excellent fishing offered.

Divers and anglers have been pleased by the large number of sea bass, sheepshead, and bluefish around the wreck. Numerous red drum, trout, barracuda, cobia, and triggerfish have also been landed at this popular fishing spot. The wreck itself is easy to find due to its close proximity to the buoy and the vertical relief it offers from the otherwise flat bottom in 32-foot-deep water. The drydock rises to within 10 to 12 feet of the surface and can be found on NOAA Chart 11513.

General Gordon Wreck

The remains of the 250-foot steel-hulled sailing vessel, *General Gordon*, are a popular spot for local fishermen in the area of Port Royal Sound. Just 2.0 miles due east of buoy "14" in the Port Royal Sound Channel, it is easily accessible even for smaller boats. The depth of the water is about 6 feet over the wreck, with the bottom around the area being 18 feet deep. The wreck can be plotted on NOAA Chart 11513 at Lat. 32°10.1'N, Long. 80°33.2'W.

A large yellow nun buoy was placed near the wreck to make locating it easier for anglers. The Loran C coordinates for the wreck are 45580.6/61097.1. The buoy is in 18 feet of water about 200 feet north of the wreck itself. Although the wreck is small, it is heavily fished by those interested in bottom fishing or trolling.

Gaskin Banks Wreck

Located about 3.4 miles east-southeast of Hilton Head Island, this scattered accumulation of material is not really a wreck as such. It consists of many steel railroad rails, which are believed to have been the lost cargo from a barge which transited the area a number of years ago. Most of the rails lie in 6 to 10 feet of water at Lat. 32°05.8'N, Long. 80°42.1'W or Loran C 45609.8/61200.9.

The area is frequently marked by plastic jugs or small buoys left by anglers from the Hilton Head area. Larger boats should use extreme caution especially at low tide. Anglers have been very successful in this area, so the wreck is heavily fished. The location may be plotted on NOAA Chart 11513.

GEORGIA

Fishing Piers

The following list of piers includes only those from the South Carolina border to Altamaha Sound (Chatham, Bryan, Liberty, and McIntosh counties). For a list of piers to the south of the Sound, see page 105.

Chatham County

Chimney Creek Marina
I-95 at Exit 16. (GA204). East on GA 204 for 14.4 mi. to US 80. East on US 80 for 14.6 mi., turn right and immediately left onto D.A.V. Rd. Drive 0.3 mi. Parking area on left.

Frank Downing Fishing Piers
I-95 at Exit 16 (GA 204). East on GA 204 for 10.4 mi., right on Montgomery Crossroads. Drive 1.2 mi. to Waters Ave. Turn right on Waters Ave. and drive 3.3 mi. to Moon River Bridge.

Lazaretto Creek Fishing Pier
I-95 at Exit 16 (GA 204). East on GA 204 for 14.4 mi. to US 80. East on US 80 13.3 mi. At Lazaretto boat ramp turn right and follow road to dock.

Salt Creek Park
I-95 at Exit 16 (GA 204). East on GA 204 for 1.8 mi. to US 17. North on US 17 for 4.2 mi. Parking area on left.

Tybee Island Pier
I-95 at Exit 6 (GA 204). East on GA 204 for 14.4 mi. to US 80. East on US 80 for 17.5 mi. to Chatham Ave., Tybee Island. Turn right and drive 0.1 mi. to pier.

Bryan County

Tivoli River Fishing Piers
I-95 at Exit 15 (GA 144). East on GA 144 for 10.1 mi., right at forestry tower, Belfast Rd. Drive 0.7 mi. to fishing piers.

Liberty County

Riceboro Creek Fishing Piers
I-95 at Exit 12 (US 17). North on US 17 for 5 mi. to Riceboro city limits. Drive 1.8 miles to bridge at Riceboro Creek. Docks on both sides of bridge.

McIntosh County

Blue N' Hall Fishing Dock
I-95 at Exit 10 (GA 251). South on GA 251 for 1.2 mi. to US 17. South on US 17 for 0.9 mi. to GA 99 on left. North on GA 99 for 4.4 mi. to Blue N' Hall Park sign. Turn right, follow dead end road to docks.

Champney River Catwalk
I-95 at Exit 10 (GA 251). South on GA 251 for 1.2 mi. to US 17. South on US 17 for 3.3 mi. to Champney River Bridge. Turn left into parking area at south end of bridge.

Harris Neck Fishing Piers
I-95 at Exit 12 (US 17). South on US 17 for 1.0 mi. to GA 131. Left on GA 131, drive 6.2 mi. to bridge at Harris Neck National Park entrance.

The Southeast coast offers hundreds of miles of beach suitable for productive surfcasting.(BOB MCNALLY PHOTO)

Bank or Surf Fishing

The following list includes only those banks and beaches from the South Carolina border to Altamaha Sound (Chatham, Bryan, Liberty, and McIntosh counties). For shore access areas to the south of the Sound, see page 106.

Chatham County

Tybee Island North End Beach
   I-95 at Exit 16 (GA 204). East on GA 204 for 14.4 mi. to US 80. East on US 80 for 15.6 mi. Left at Tybee Museum sign on left. Drive 0.8 mi., turn left into parking area behind Fort Screven.

Tybee Island Pier
   I-95 at Exit 16 (GA 204). East on GA 204 for 14.4 mi. to US 80. East on US 80 for 17.5 mi. to Chatham Ave., Tybee Island. Turn right and drive 0.1 mi.

Tybee Island South End Beach
   I-95 at Exit 16 (GA 204). East on GA 204 for 14.4 mi. to US 80. East on US 80 for 17.3 mi. to Tybee Island Parking Lot 3. Left to beach parking areas. Jetties are south of parking lots.

Liberty County

Liberty County Recreational Park
   I-95 at Exit 13 (GA 38). West on GA 38 for 1.5 mi. to Isle of Wight Road. Turn right, drive 1.9 mi. Parking area on right before Jones Creek Bridge.

Coastal Marinas

(All telephone area codes are 912.)

   The following list of marinas includes only those from the South Carolina border to Altamaha Sound (Chatham, Bryan, Liberty, and McIntosh counties). For a list of marinas to the south of the Sound, see page 106.

Chatham County

Ambos Marina, 354-4133
Bona Bella Marina, 355-9601
Bull River Marina, 897-7300
Chimney Creek Fish Camp, 786-9857
Coffee Bluff Marina, 925-9030
Delegal Creek Marina, 598-0023
Fountain Marina, 354-2283
Hogan's Marina, 897-3474
Isle of Hope Marina, 354-8187
Landings Harbor, 598-1901
Sail Harbor Marina, 897-2896
Savannah Bend Marina, 897-3625
Palmer Johnson Savannah Inc., 352-4956
Tidewater Boat Works, 352-1335

Tuten's Fish Camp, 355-8747
Tybee Island Marina, 786-7508
Young's Marina, 897-2608

Bryan County

Fort McAllister Marina, 727-2632
Kilkenny Marina, 727-2215

Liberty County

Half Moon Marina, 884-5819
Yellow Bluff Fish Camp, 884-5448

McIntosh County

Belle Bluff Marina, 832-5323
Dallas Bluff Marina, 832-5116
Fisherman's Lodge, 832-4671
McIntosh Rod and Gun Club, 437-4677
Pine Harbor Marina, 832-5999
Shellman Bluff Motel and Marina, 832-5426
Shellman Fish Camp, 832-4331

Launch Ramps

The following list of ramps includes only those from the South Carolina border to Altamaha Sound (Bryan, Liberty, and McIntosh counties). For a list of ramps to the south of the Sound, see page 106.

Bryan County

Demeries Creek Boat Ramp—GA Highway 144, Richmond Hill

Fort McAllister Historic Park—Rt. 2, Box 394-A, Richmond Hill, (912) 727-2339 (Savage Island, campers only)

Ogeechee Fish Camp—GA Highway 144, east of Richmond Hill

Liberty County

Liberty County Recreational Park—Isle of Wight, (912) 876-5359

Sunbury Boat Ramp—off GA Highway 38, Sunbury

McIntosh County

Blue-N-Hall Boat Ramp—off GA 99, Ridgeville

Champing River Park Boat Ramp—US 17 south of Darien

Harris Neck Creek Boat Ramp

Driving Directions For Non-Boating Anglers

F.W. Spencer Park
   I-95 at exit 16 (GA 204). East on GA 204 for 14.4 mi. to US 80 for 5.8 mi. Left on Islands Expressway, drive 1.5 mi. Spencer Park on right.

Blythe Island Regional Park
   I-95 at exit 6 (US 17). South on US 17 for 0.6 miles to GA 303. North on GA 303 for 3.6 mi. to park sign. Turn right into park, drive 1.4 mi. to pier.

St. Simons Island Pier
  I-95 at exit 6 (US 17). North on US 17 for
  9.1 mi. to Torras Causeway. East on Causeway
  for 4.0 mi. Bear right on King's Way. Drive
  5.7 mi. to Mallory St. Turn right, drive .2 mi.
  to pier.

Mackay River Fishing Pier
  I-95 at exit 6 (US 17). North on US 17 for 9.1 mi.
  to Torras Causeway. East on Causeway 2.3 mi. to
  Mackay River Bridge. Parking area on right.

Little River Catwalk
  I-95 at exit 6 (US 17). North on US 17 for 9.1 mi.
  to Torras Causeway. East on Causeway for 2.3
  mi. to Little River Bridge. Parking area on right.

Back River Fishing Piers
  I-95 at exit 6 (US 17). North on US 17 for 9.1 mi.
  to Torras Causeway. East on Causeway 1.5 mi. to
  Back River Bridge. Parking area on left.

Gould's Inlet
  I-95 at exit 6 (US 17). North on US 17 for 9.1 mi.
  to Torras Causeway. East on Causeway for 6.3 mi.
  Causeway becomes Demere Rd. Left at East Beach
  Causeway, drive 0.3 mi. Bear left on Bruce Dr. at
  Coast Guard station. Road dead ends at inlet
  parking area.

Jekyll Island Pier
  I-95 at exit 6 (US 17). North on US 17 for 5 mi.
  Right on Jekyll Causeway (GA 50), 6.3 mi. Left
  on Beachview Dr., 4.3 mi., right on Clam Creek
  Rd. Pier and parking area at end of road.

St. Andrew Picnic Area
  I-95 at exit 6 (US 17). North on US 17 for
  5 mi. Right on Jekyll Causeway (GA 50),
  6.1 mi. to Riverview Dr., Jekyll Island. Turn
  right, drive 2.3 mi. Right at radio tower into
  parking area.

Satilla River Waterview Park
  I-95 at exit 4 (GA Spur 25). West on GA Spur 25
  for 2.5 mi. to US 17. North on US 17 for 0.7 mi.
  Fishing dock entrance on right at park sign.

Harriet's Bluff Boat Ramp
  I-95 at exit 3 (Harriet's Bluff Rd.). East for 5 mi.,
  right at Harriet's Bluff sign. Drive 0.4 mi., turn
  right on Crooked River Dr. for 0.3 mi. Parking
  area on left.

Crooked River State Park
  I-95 at exit 2 (GA 40). East on GA 40 for 3.6 mi.
  to King's Bay Rd. North for 2.1 mi. to GA Spur
  40. Left on GA Spur 40 for 4.2 mi. to end of road
  beyond park entrance.

St. Mary's Boat Ramp
  I-95 at exit 2 (GA 40). East on GA 40 for 8.8 mi.
  to waterfront. Right at waterfront pavilion, drive
  0.1 mi. Parking area on left.

St. Mary's Waterfront Pavilion
  I-95 at exit 2 (GA 40). East on GA 40 for 8.8 mi.
  GA 40 dead ends at fishing dock.

Artificial Reefs

Most anglers know fish aren't caught everywhere; they're usually taken at specific "drops" or "holes." Fish congregate at places where the bottom offers shelter and food.

Placing natural or manmade materials in otherwise unproductive areas creates new "drops," or artificial reefs. For fishermen this means more fish and better fishing.

Using wooden vessels, car bodies, refrigerators, and other scrap, Georgians began artificial reef construction in the 1930s. Faced with a typically flat and featureless ocean floor, sportfishing clubs sought to create offshore fisheries similar to those found over scattered wrecks and at Gray's Reef, one of the few natural reef areas, or live bottoms, found within 40 miles of the coast.

The success of these early artificial reefs was short-lived, as most deteriorated or were lost. With increased state and federal funding, the Georgia Department of Natural Resources initiated an artificial reef construction and research program in 1972. Since then, eight reefs have been built 7 to 23 miles offshore. Today, almost 173,000 scrap tires, 21,000 tons of concrete, a WWII wreck, 40 fiberglass boat molds, and 19 surplus vessels make up Georgia's artificial reef system. Groups such as the Savannah and the Golden Isles sportfishing clubs have also been active in offshore reef development.

Within days of reef replacement, fish arrive to take advantage of the new haven. Soon the sunken materials become encrusted with barnacles, algae, anemones, and other small animals that make up the typical reef community. In time, the transformation is complete. Like oases in the desert, the reefs present a stark contrast to the surrounding ocean floor, a home for a variety of fish species, and sportfishing action to challenge any offshore angler.

Recreational fishing on Georgia's artificial reefs occurs year-round, but is most concentrated from mid-spring through late fall. During these warmer months, bluefish, cobia, and little tunny show up earliest, followed by amberjack, king and Spanish mackerel, sharks, barracuda, crevalle jack, and an occasional dolphin, sailfish, or tuna. Popular bottom fish include black sea bass, red and vermilion snapper, grouper, sheepshead, spadefish, triggerfish, and others. Weakfish and large red drum also are caught on the reefs during winter and spring.

Fishing techniques used off Georgia are similar to those used elsewhere, but coastal marina operators and local fishermen often can provide tips. For gamefish such as mackerel, offshore anglers usually troll or live-line. For bottom fish, anglers may resort to a two-hook bottom rig with squid or cut bait.

Whatever is biting, anglers and divers should stay

abreast of federal and state regulations associated with many offshore species. The South Atlantic Fishery Management Council has declared the offshore artificial reefs "Special Management Zones," a designation prohibiting fish trapping and the landing of jewfish.

Georgia's offshore resources are not inexhaustible. Ethics long accepted for freshwater fishing are also applicable in marine waters. The Georgia Department of Natural Resources encourages releases of excess or undersized fish, billfish, and non-desirable species, as well as participation in national tagging projects and conservation programs that help Georgia maintain its productive offshore fisheries.

Yellow nun buoys with 4- to 6-foot towers and radar reflectors are maintained by the Department of Natural Resources at offshore reefs to warn large ships of possible obstructions and help smaller vessels locate and use the reefs. Placed away from submerged material to avoid entanglement, the buoys also help fishermen and divers locate the various structures at each reef and provide important backup should electronics fail. The buoys and their towers are not constructed to withstand the stress produced by vessels tying to them. Without the radar reflector atop the mast, large ships and boats alike may not be able to detect the buoy at all. The U.S. Coast Guard strictly protects these buoys. Boaters tying to the buoys are subject to imprisonment and fines, half of which may be awarded to persons reporting the violation.

When fishing offshore, boaters are far from cover or help should an emergency situation occur. While many of the rules for safe boating are common sense, certain precautions are especially important if you're venturing out to the artificial reefs. Take advantage of the information and safety courses offered through the Georgia Department of Natural Resources, the U.S. Coast Guard, and other agencies. Consult with local marina operators and fishermen, and monitor the weather conditions. Always play it safe—don't take chances.

In recent years, interest in scuba diving off Georgia's coast has increased, especially during warmer months. Visibilities can vary daily, depending on tides, seas, water depth, and distance offshore. Currents can also be very strong. Georgia's artificial reefs are constructed to provide food and shelter for fish. Wrecks and other reef material may become unstable and collapse. Entanglement and entrapment are dangers unavoidably associated with reef materials. It is up to divers to evaluate each situation for safety in light of their own training and abilities.

Reef A

Located seven nautical miles east of Little Cumberland Island, bottom material at this site consists of 1,700 tire units and concrete wharf rubble from the Kings Bay Naval Submarine Base. While tire units are scattered throughout, major concentrations are located approximately 250 yards northeast of the buoy. Con-

crete rubble is found 400 yards to the east and south, with vertical relief up to 10 feet.

Reef C (WR2)

Located 13.5 nautical miles east of Cumberland Island, this site was formerly buoyed by the U.S. Coast Guard to mark a freighter sunk during World War II. Repeatedly salvaged, the wreckage now bears little resemblance to a ship and consists primarily of large, encrusted boiler sections. Placed in the early 1970s, scattered tire units with heavy marine growth are found approximately 600 yards southeast of the buoy, but have settled and are difficult to find. More easily marked are the 12- to 15-foot stacks of concrete wharf rubble, 400 yards to the north, south, and east-southeast of the buoy.

Reef F

Two 55-foot LCMs, 6,000 tire units, and 40 fiberglass boat molds placed by the Golden Isles Sport Fishing Club make up Reef F, nine miles off Jekyll Island. The vessels are 670 and 1,300 yards east of the buoy, with the boat molds in an east-west line 675 yards north of the LCMs. Both exhibit up to 12 feet of relief. Most tire units are 75 to 400 yards north and northeast of the buoy.

Gray's Reef National Marine Sanctuary

Also known as the Sapelo Live Bottom (SLB), Gray's Reef was designated a National Marine Sanctuary in 1980 by President Jimmy Carter. Located 17.5 nautical miles east of Sapelo Island, Gray's Reef constitutes the largest and most accessible nearshore live bottom off Georgia. Ranging from low-relief hardpan to rocky ledges up to 8 feet, live bottom occurs sporadically throughout the 17-square-mile area. Major ledge areas are located southwest, west, and east of the buoy. Certain activities are prohibited in the Sanctuary, including trapping and collecting.

Reef G

The largest of Georgia's artificial reefs, Reef G is located 23 nautical miles east of Little Cumberland Island. The reef consists of 3,000 tire units located 100 to 250 yards to the north, northeast, south, and west of the buoy, as well as several wrecks, including the 441-foot liberty ship, *E.S. Nettleton*; a 33-foot utility boat; and the 100- and 108-foot tugboats, *Tampa* and *Recife*. Often conspicuously marked by schools of baitfish, the *Nettleton* and *Recife* are well away from the buoy to take advantage of deeper waters and to ensure permitted depth clearances are maintained. Vertical profiles at Reef G range from 5 feet over the tires to almost 40 feet over the liberty ship.

Reef J

Located 17.4 miles east of St. Catherine's Island, four vessels have been placed at Reef J including the 180-foot buoy tender *Sagebrush*, the 55-foot ferry *Janet*, the 105-foot tugboat *Elmira*, and the 444-foot *A.B. Daniels*, the second of two liberty ships obtained for the state's reef program. Sunk in 1975, the *Daniels* is in two pieces as a result of Hurricane David in 1979, which moved the ship's stern almost 200 yards south of the main wreck. Other materials include 1,000 tire units scattered between the buoy and the *Daniels*. Relief ranges from 5 feet over the tires to 30 feet over the vessels. Small ledges and scattered pieces of live bottom are found to the south and east of the buoy.

Reef KC

Nine nautical miles southeast of Tybee Island, this artificial reef is largely composed of tires, with 5,700 units scattered throughout the area. Major concentrations are found 75 to 400 yards southeast, southwest, west and northwest of the buoy. One vessel, the 95-foot LCU *Motherlode*, lies south of the buoy. Relief exhibited by the tires and vessel ranges from 3 to 7 feet.

Reef L

Located 23 nautical miles east of Ossabaw Island, Reef L was started in 1977 and has become one of the state's largest offshore reefs. It is composed of two 90-foot barges; a 150-foot dredge, the *Henry Bacon*; and the 55- and 100-foot tugboats *Delta Diamond* and *Senasqua*. Almost 2,000 tire units also are scattered between the two steel barges. Concrete culvert placed by the Savannah Sport Fishing Club also can be found scattered southeast of the buoy. Exhibiting 4 to 5 feet of relief, both the tire units and culverts may, at times, be difficult to locate. The wrecks, with 10- to 30-foot profiles, are easily detected on depth finders.

Reef T (Hilton Head Reef)

Representing a joint construction effort by Georgia and South Carolina, Reef T is located 11.7 nautical miles east of Tybee Island. South Carolina presently maintains three primary markers to help anglers locate three wrecks and a mid-water trolling alley deployed between the northern and southern buoys. Concentrated to the north and south of the northernmost wreck, 1,000 tire units can also be found, exhibiting 4 to 5 feet of relief. Vessel profiles range from 5 to 10 feet. Scattered, low-relief live bottom is present on and near the reef.

To avoid conflicts, courtesy, communication, and compromise are the rules. Do not start diving where others are fishing, and do not start fishing where others are diving. Consult with trolling fishermen and inform them of your intentions and schedules. Once initial dives are completed, move away and spend surface intervals off reef structures.

FISHING BY SEASON IN NORTH CAROLINA

OFFSHORE FISHING

At one time it was believed that fishing in North Carolina's offshore waters began in late April and ended with the first cold weather of October, but that belief was founded more on the fact that it was the fishermen, not the fish, who were more likely to be absent in the cold winter months. Many species, the reef fish for example, remain along the coast year-round. Catches of up to 50 dolphin have been taken off Hatteras in December, and the crews of the Diamond Shoal light tower found these colorful fish present all year. The run of bigeye tuna begins in mid- to late-winter. The fall run of king mackerel extends well into November, and some are caught year-round off of Cape Fear.

Nevertheless, comfort and weather considered, most offshore trips occur between the first of May and the end of October. In that period, with some extensions at either end in the case of certain species, you can expect to land an astonishing variety of great gamefish. Here are some prospects:

Amberjack

Known for its strong, deep-running fight, these fish will test the angler and his tackle. Once hooked, they are constantly battling to escape. Most amberjack are landed by recreational fishermen using live or cut baits or by trolling with spoons and other deep-running artificial lures. Amberjack are most prevalent in May or June. These predators forage over reefs and wrecks in small groups.

Dolphin

You can catch this colorful species trolling with lures in offshore waters. Most anglers seem to prefer using brightly colored man-o-wars, feathers, skirts, and other lead-headed lures rigged with 6/0 to 9/0 hooks baited with squid or mullet strips. Some of the preferred lures are green and yellow feathers, red artificial squid, and purple jelly bellies. For those using standard rods and reels, 30- to 80-pound-test line is recommended. For optimum results, baits are trolled at 4 to 6 knots adjacent to weed lines.

Some of the more adventurous anglers may fish with saltwater fly rods and streamer flies. Dolphin are attracted to floating objects and weed lines. Light-tackle fishermen often drift near weed lines, casting artificial lures for dolphins. The season extends from late April or May through November. June yields the best large fish catches; July through September offer the best opportunities for small fish.

Blue Marlin

Sportfishermen are able to catch this species by trolling artificial and natural baits. Using an artificial, hookless teaser in the wake can lure these marlin to the surface. Heavy rods and reels with 50- to 150-pound monofilament line should be used to fish for blue marlin. Suggested baits are artificial lures, squid, mackerel, mullet, and ballyhoo. Several "granders" (1,000 pounds or more) have been taken off North Carolina. The primary season for blue marlin extends from late May through September.

Sailfish

Recommended baits are artificial lures, squid, and fish, including mullet, spanish mackerel, and ballyhoo. One way to spot a sailfish is to look for fish that are "tailing," that is, swimming with the upper part of the tail fin and dorsal fin above the water. Sailfish are caught from May through October, but peak catches occur from July through September.

White Marlin

Many fishermen prefer light tackle: 20- to 30-pound-test monofilament line, 2/0 to 6/0 reels, and fiberglass rods. Live bait can be whole squid or fish, or strip bait trolled at the surface. Some of the favorite artificial baits are plastic squids, lures with feathers or nylon tails, and spoons. White marlin are caught all year off North Carolina's coast.

Bluefin Tuna

The best catches occur from April through July. These fish can be caught by trolling and float fishing as the bluefin often prey on bait found near the ocean's surface. With the aid of high spotter towers, anglers sometimes troll two lines, each with a single large squid or mullet on a 12/0 to 14/0 hook. One of the favorite rigs is the daisy chain, with six or seven fish (usually mackerel) strung onto a wire leader. The last fish is impaled or sewn on the largest hook.

Yellowfin Tuna

Yellowfin also feed at the ocean's surface on fish and invertebrates. When hooked, yellowfin fight hard and often dive. They are found near floating objects, so many anglers troll near logs, seaweed, and other debris. Sportfishermen also catch this tuna by trolling brightly colored lures at high speed at the surface. This species is the most important tuna taken in North Carolina, and it is caught year-round.

Wahoo

This species often concentrates over high-relief rock or coral bottom and wrecks. The best season for wahoo is from mid-April through October. The best ways to catch these fish are by trolling at high speeds or live-lining from boats.

REEF FISHING

Black Sea Bass

A fine fare in the pan and fun to catch by the one's, two's, or three's, black sea bass are a favorite. Ranging in size from ½ to 8 pounds, the bass can be enjoyed by youngsters fishing on the soundside dock and by small-boat or head boat fishermen fishing the near-shore artificial reefs and ledges. A multihook bottom rig baited with squid, mullet, shrimp, or hotdogs will hook up with the naturally aggressive black sea bass. This aggressiveness makes the bass a ready biter of jigs and grubs. Fished year-round, the best catches occur in June and July.

Grouper

Its strong fight and great taste make grouper one of the most preferred reef fish for the angler year-round. The two most common species of grouper taken in North Carolina are the gag and the scamp. The appetite of groupers makes them quick hitters on baits like cigar minnows, whole squid, and octopus. Depths of 50 to 270 feet over low- or high-relief ledges are best, but the artificial reefs will produce groupers as well. Other species of groupers taken in North Carolina are the speckled, red, and rock hinds, and snowy grouper.

Snapper

The two primary species of snapper caught throughout the year off North Carolina are the vermilion and red snappers. Other species of snapper which may be caught are the silk, blackfin, mutton, dog, and cubera snapper. Vermilion snappers are caught using squid or cut bait on a multihook bottom rig. The other species will also take squid or cut bait; however, the larger ones are usually taken on cigar minnows or Spanish sardines in July and August. April and May offer the best opportunities for catching small fish. Fishing is most successful at night over wrecks and reef structure.

Porgies

The red porgy, which is often referred to as "pink snapper" or "silver snapper," is the most common reef species of porgy taken off North Carolina's coast year-round. While large fish range from 4 to 12 pounds, the average is from 1 to 3 pounds. Their natural prey are crabs and starfish, but the red porgy can be taken by hook and line using squid or cut fish for bait. Other species of porgies taken on offshore reefs are the knobbed, jolthead, whitebone, and the spottail pinfish. The prime season is between March and November.

INSHORE, INLET, AND SOUND FISHING

The ocean waters up to around 10 miles off the coast, the inlets, and the 2,000 square miles of inland sounds provide a wide range of saltwater fishing. The variety of fishing is reflected in the fact that it is conducted aboard everything from large Gulf Stream cruisers to small flat-bottomed skiffs.

The big boats fish these protected waters when weather conditions make it unwise to venture offshore, when they have no offshore charters and, most importantly, when certain species of fish like Spanish and king mackerel, bluefish, stripped bass, and red drum are running in inshore waters. There is also a small fleet of charter vessels which cater to inshore parties rather than to offshore anglers.

Protected waters are found in the vicinity of all of North Carolina's sportfishing centers. These areas offer great opportunities for casting, trolling, and bottom fishing from small craft. Skiffs and outboard motors are available on a rental basis in many areas, and there are launching ramps for private boats.

Persons who cannot handle a casting or spinning rod, but are too active to be satisfied with bottom fishing, can find fun gigging for flounder at night, raking up a mess of cherrystone clams on a tidal flat, or hunting the scuttling, succulent blue crab with a net and pail or handlines baited with chicken necks.

The best time for inlet, inshore and sound fishing varies for each species. There is good fishing for some species all year. Here are some of the prospects:

Red Drum
Sometimes known as channel bass, this is the second largest member of the drum family, occasionally reaching a length of 60 inches and weighing more than 90 pounds. Fishing is best in the spring and fall months. These fish are often seen in head-down position, browsing and rooting on the bottom for food. Surf fishing and sight casting are the preferred methods of capture by anglers. Some of the suggested baits are streamer flies, Hopkins lures, cut bait, lead jigs, and medium-sized floating plugs.

Bluefish
When bluefish are feeding they are likely to strike at anything in the water, including swimmers. Cut bait, Hopkins lures, and spoons are used to catch this species from piers, jetties, bridges, boats, and the surf. Surf fishing is most popular, especially in the fall and early winter for large fish. Some of the typical gear includes a heavy surf rod, 10- to 20-pound-test monofilament line, two 6/0 hooks baited with cut fish and a sliding 5-ounce pyramid sinker. A wire leader measuring 9 to 18 inches is important as bluefish will bite through dacron and monofilament line.

Spanish Mackerel
Spanish are a North Carolina favorite. Spawning extends from April through September, so the prime season runs from late April or May through November. The best catches occur in August and September. You can use almost any small, shiny metal lure to catch them. Spanish migrate close to shore so they can be caught from small craft as well as larger boats, piers, bridges, and jetties. Spanish mackerel have become very abundant in recent years, recovering from overfishing in the early and mid-1980s.

King Mackerel
King mackerel are most plentiful from May through October. Anglers can troll, cast, and float fish for kings. The larger fish are caught by slow trolling with multiple small hooks and live menhaden throughout the summer and fall. When the weather is right kings can be taken throughout the winter off much of North Carolina's coast. They move closest to shore (sometimes into the sounds) in late summer and fall. King mackerel are the primary species targetted by saltwater tournament fishermen, with contests almost every weekend from May to November. The largest fish taken in the tournament are often in the 40- to 60-pound range.

Cobia
These fish are rugged fighters when hooked and are considered to be the best eating fish by some anglers. Some anglers cast or troll, but most prefer to bottom fish using cut or live bait. These fish prefer channels or deep holes in bays and sounds, as well as waters around stationary or floating objects such as buoys, pilings, and artificial reefs. Inshore buoys and beacons are often bypassed by fishermen; however, they are excellent places to catch cobia. May through mid-October is the prime season, with the choicest catches from mid-June to August.

Tarpon
Tarpon are powerful and active swimmers, famous for their leaps when hooked. When they strike there is no doubt what fish has taken the bait. Anglers prefer two basic methods: casting artificial lures from an anchored or drifting boat, and float-fishing with live bait. The major fishing areas are the "tarpon hole" on Cape Fear Shoals and several ocean piers from Bogue Banks southward. July is the best month for catching Tarpon, but the season runs from April to October or early November.

Black Sea Bass
This species is a popular catch among deep-sea anglers. It inhabits wrecks, rocks, coral, and shell bottom offshore, rock jetties near inlets, and the area around piers and pilings in some of the sounds. It is most abundant and larger in the offshore waters. Black sea bass are caught all year, but the best fishing is from April to July. Most are caught in the ocean in depths of 45 to 120 feet by bottom fishing from drifting or anchored boats. Baits used include crabs, squid, clams, worms, shrimp, and cut fish. Many fishermen regard black sea bass as one of the best eating fish.

Spotted Sea Trout
These fish are found in the shallow waters of estuaries and the Intracoastal Waterway during spring and fall

and along the ocean beaches during the winter. The season for these fish is all year, but the best fishing is from September through April. Average weights vary from 1 to 5 pounds. Preferred fishing methods are bottom fishing, jigging, and casting from shore, but trolling also works. Suggested baits include live and dead shrimp, as well as live minnows. The most productive lures are stingray grubs and MirrOlures. This species is very sensitive to water temperature, and major kills occur during severe winters.

Striped Bass

This species is known as rock or rockfish in North Carolina. Methods of fishing vary depending on water conditions and according to local tradition and regulations. Trolling, casting, jigging, and bottom fishing are some of the preferred methods for catching striped bass. The species has been overfished and sportfishing is permitted only from late fall into early spring. Stripers are found in the larger coastal rivers, with the heaviest concentration in the Albemarle Sound–Roanoke River area. Large striped bass from northern spawning areas overwinter off the Outer Banks from Cape Hatteras northward, but are not often caught by anglers.

Weakfish

North Carolina waters produce both the weakfish and spotted sea trout—major attractions for sportsmen. Weakfish up to 14 pounds have been taken, but the average is much smaller. Weakfish are taken in the surf, inlets, sounds, and coastal rivers much of the year, but most are taken directly after a spell of cold weather in the fall and winter.

Along with these top sporting fish, the enormous inland sounds produce a great variety of bottom fish including croaker, spot, pigfish (hogfish), sheepshead, and black drum.

SURF FISHING

Along the entire coast from Calabash to Currituck, the best surf fishing is usually near the inlets. The five best inlets are Drum Inlet, Ocracoke Inlet, Hatteras Inlet, Oregon Inlet, and Beaufort Inlet. The intersection of northerly and southerly flowing currents at Cape Hatteras, makes it the premier surf fishing area in North Carolina, and one of the very best sportfishing locales on the Atlantic Coast.

There are many species to keep fishermen busy. Bluefish and spotted sea trout are taken in the surf, particularly on the rising tide of brisk fall mornings. Big red drum are landed during the spring and fall, especially at Oregon Inlet, Ocracoke Inlet, Cape Hatteras, and along the Hatteras Island beach.

Pompano

Most pompano are in the 1- to 2- pound class, and are taken in the surf during September and October with small spoons, small shrimp, or sand fleas on small hooks. Pompano is an excellent gamefish and is also caught from bridges, jetties, and piers. Many are also caught by fishing on the bottom with natural baits, although some are caught by casting and trolling artificial lures. Pompano is one of the best eating of all the saltwater fishes.

Flounder

Flounder are common in the surf, especially in the fall and early winter. Throughout the sounds and coastal rivers, flounder are taken by rod and reel, as well as by stalking them at night in shallow water with a gig, using a lantern or special underwater lights to find them. These flat, fine-flavored fish may be caught on artificial lures, spoons, and Sea Hawks skipped along a sandy bottom, but the standard rig is a short wire leader, a short shanked hook, and a live minnow fished in jerks along the bottom. Flounder are present year-round. Three different species are taken in North Carolina, with southern flounder dominating in lower salinity areas and summer flounder and Gulf flounder most common near the inlets and along the ocean beaches. The three species are difficult to tell apart.

PIER FISHING

Pier fishing is, in a sense, an extension of surf fishing. All of the surf fish mentioned are taken from piers as well. Because these piers may reach out 1,000 feet or more from the beach, they generally provide more consistent sport for bluefish, Spanish mackerel, spot, and other species which are not tied by their feeding habits to surf sloughs. Pier pilings provide habitat to wary species such as the sheepshead. Sea mullet (called kingfish by scientists), another favorite, provide particularly fine sport for pier fishermen during balmy spring nights.

FISHING BY SEASON IN SOUTH CAROLINA

OFFSHORE FISHING

Spring and fall offer the best in offshore fishing. Spadefish, mackerel, and cobia congregate at artificial reefs and a variety of bottom fish frequent the natural reefs farther offshore. Trolling yields killifish, tuna, dolphin, and wahoo.

Many of the bluewater fish that occur 50 miles offshore in the early spring may move to within 15 miles

Lucky anglers can sometimes pick up good-size groupers from the offshore reefs. It takes stout tackle to keep these big fish from breaking lines in bottom structure.
(JOHN PHILLIPS)

of the coast in summer. Everything from sea bass on the reefs to blue marlin in the Gulf Stream is biting. Summer also offers the angler the best weather of the year, sometimes with four or five consecutive days of flat, calm conditions. However, the steamy days of July and August send many of the fish that normally inhabit the surface to deeper water during the hot part of the day and feeding activity occurs mostly in the early morning and late afternoon and evening.

Although the weather in winter might not be as predictable, many offshore species of gamefish linger in local waters or pass through on their southern migrations and can be caught early in the season. Cold, stiff northeasterly winds are the norm for the winter season, but anglers who take advantage of the one to three days of calm weather between winter storms often enjoy excellent offshore fishing.

INSHORE FISHING

To most anglers, spring in South Carolina signals the beginning of a new fishing year. As days lengthen and coastal waters grow warm, fish that have avoided the cold of winter by moving offshore or to the south return to inshore waters to feed.

Inshore fishing slows somewhat in summer. However, more different fish are available to inshore anglers than at any other season; among them, spotted sea trout, red and black drum, whiting, king and Spanish mackerel, bluefish, tarpon, sheepshead, jack crevalle, and several species of shark. As a general rule, inshore fishing is better during the summer at dusk and dawn.

As with offshore fishing, the fall months offer some of the year's best fishing in South Carolina's inshore coastal waters. The most abundant inshore fish in fall are spotted sea trout, red drum, southern flounder, sheepshead, and spot.

Fishing is much slower during the winter months in the cooler, inshore coastal waters. Fish that do overwinter in these areas feed and move around less.

Amberjack
Amberjack inhabit South Carolina's offshore waters throughout the year, moving into shallow areas from April through December. Like king mackerel, they are a top-of-the-food-chain predator in live bottom areas and natural and man-made reefs. Amberjack average 20 to 40 pounds in these waters, but can exceed 90 pounds.

Atlantic Spadefish
Spadefish inhabit the coastal waters of South Carolina from April to November in close association with natural and artificial reefs and shipwrecks. Usually ranging from 3 to 8 pounds, these fish browse on organisms growing and living on reef structures. On calm days in spring, schools of spadefish cruise the surface with their long dorsal fins sticking out of the water.

Barracuda
Barracuda provide some of the most action-packed fishing on artificial reefs and coastal shipwrecks during the summer, although they are notoriously picky about feeding at this time of the year. During the fall, barracuda can be abundant at artificial reefs in more than 40 feet of water and over live bottom areas that support concentrations of bottom fish. Barracuda in this area range between 8 and 40 pounds in weight.

Billfish (White Marlin, Blue Marlin, Sailfish)
May and June are the peak months for bluewater trolling for billfish. They can be found as early as the first of March after a mild winter, but the season usually begins the first of April. Billfish are more scattered during the summer months since water temperatures no longer restrict them to the Gulf Stream. The most productive fishing areas are in 300 to 1,200 feet of water.

Sailfish reach peak abundance in the summer. July and August offer anglers their best opportunities to catch a sail off South Carolina. During this time, numerous small sails will be hooked within 10 miles of the beach, but these fish are usually well below the 57-inch fork length minimum set by law. Weedlines, current rips, and natural reefs are the best areas to find these prime gamefish.

Most blue marlin caught in local waters during the summer are in the 125- to 200- pound range, which is below the 86-inch fork length minimum.

Blue and white marlin and sailfish can all be caught off the coast of South Carolina during the fall. Marlin usually inhabit waters in excess of 200 feet in depth, while sailfish frequently occur in less than 50 feet of water.

Because billfish stocks have been depleted and because these large fish are not particularly good food fish, every effort should be made to tag and release them.

Black Drum

Black drum are bottom-feeding cousins of the red drum. They feed on crabs, shrimp, clams, and mussels and do not consume fish. The best places to find them are around rocks, pilings, and bridge piers. Smaller black drum are delicious, but larger fish (over 15 pounds) have a coarse flesh. Anglers who catch larger fish they do not plan to eat should tag and release them.

Black Sea Bass (Blackfish)

Black sea bass ranging from $\frac{1}{2}$ to 5 pounds are abundant on artificial reefs and natural live bottom areas in 50 to 90 feet of water along the entire coast. These bottom areas and rocky outcroppings are the so-called "blackfish banks."

Winter is one of the best times to catch blackfish on artificial reefs. Decreased fishing allows their populations to build. When fishing for black sea bass at artificial reefs, it is necessary to anchor boats directly over the reefs, since these fish will not stray from the protection of the reef material. By early spring, sea bass have built their populations on the shallower reefs and live bottom areas to their highest levels, offering the small-boat offshore angler the best fishing of the year on these nearshore reefs. During the heat of summer, blackfish slow their feeding during the middle part of the day and they scatter, meaning they can be found in more areas but in much smaller schools.

Bluefish

Large bluefish of 8 to 20 pounds regularly winter off the South Carolina coast. From January through early May, these voracious gamefish inhabit natural reefs in 70 to 200 feet of water. These bluefish are thought to be the same population enjoyed by surf fishermen along North Carolina's Outer Banks. In April and May, large bluefish on their way north can be caught by small-boat anglers near the mouths of estuaries and around jetties, where currents are relatively strong. An excellent place to encounter large bluefish in the spring is at the tip of the south jetty at the mouth of Charleston Harbor during ebb tides, especially when they occur at dusk and dawn.

Cobia

Cobia in the 20- to 60-pound range arrive at artificial reefs in late April or early May and somewhat later in shipping channels along the coast. These adults stay in nearshore waters and bays for three to four months prior to spawning. During the remainder of the year, they associate with the deep-water snapper–grouper community.

Dolphin, Wahoo, Yellowfin Tuna

Summer offers anglers the best opportunity to catch these gamefish close to shore. Good concentrations of wahoo and dolphin occur as close to shore as the 90-foot contour, although areas from 180-feet to 600-feet deep will hold the best concentrations of these species. Yellowfin tuna prefer to stay in somewhat deeper waters—from 300 to more than 600 feet. As summer progresses, the size of both dolphin and wahoo gradually declines. At summer's start, 10- to 20-pound dolphin and 35- to 50-pound wahoo are the norm, but average weight drops to 8 pounds for dolphin and 20 pounds for wahoo by summer's end. Conversely, yellowfin tuna increase in size throughout the year, averaging 45 pounds by late summer.

By fall, dolphin, wahoo, and yellowfin tuna are most abundant in 200 to 1,200 feet of water about 30 to 70 miles offshore. Wahoo tend to be loners, but dolphin and tuna often travel in schools, providing lots of action once the fish are located.

Bluewater trolling for these fish can begin as early as the first of March following mild winters, but normally begins the first of April and peaks in May and June.

Flounder

Flounder are abundant in estuaries during the summer months. Good areas to catch flounder are in the Grand Strand around inlets and in inlets north of Charleston, such as Dewees Inlet, Capers Inlet, and Prices Inlet. The best flounder fishing in the fall is near Dewees, Capers, and Stono inlets and in inlets near lower Charleston Harbor. Winter finds flounder in offshore waters, where they spawn from December to March. When inshore waters warm in the spring, in late April or May, flounder reappear there.

Jack Crevalle

When inshore waters warm in the summer, a southern visitor enters the estuaries of South Carolina to terrorize menhaden and other small bait fish. These are the "jacks." They do not make spectacular long runs like large king mackerel or perform graceful jumps like tarpon, but jacks are one of the toughest fishes encountered in inshore waters. At night or at dusk or dawn, jacks lurk around rips during ebb tide. During the daytime, schools of jacks frequently can be spotted milling on the surface. Jacks are not good food fish and should be tagged and released.

King Mackerel

Fall usually provides the year's best king mackerel fishing. Kings occur virtually everywhere from just outside bays and sounds out to 180 feet of water, with the most productive fishing in about 50 feet of water. During mild winters, king mackerel fishing remains productive, with the best fishing in 70 to 180 feet of water in areas where natural reefs occur and bottom fish congregate. Kings move into shallow coastal waters around the mouths of bays near the end of April and peak in this area in mid- to late May. King fishing during the summer has its ups and downs. The larger female fish normally occur in nearshore waters just outside the bays and sounds, while the smaller males are more abundant in 60 to 120 feet of water. It is usual for the mackerel to sound to avoid the heat of the day during the summer.

Red Drum

In spring, red drum inside estuaries range up to about 10 pounds, but this is the time of year when trophy red drum, some exceeding 30 pounds, reappear in the surf. Best fishing is on the incoming tide; experienced anglers will often check the beach at low tide to scan for the deeper holes. Where the beach profile is steep, waves break close to shore and carry away more sand, and red drum move into these deeper cuts to feed.

During July, small juvenile red drum leave the shallow creeks to form schools in the main estuaries. They are very easy to catch at this time, but most are smaller than the legal minimum size. In late summer, anglers are frequently successful in catching fish of 20 to 30 pounds around jetties and at the mouths of bays and sounds. By fall, large trophy red drum of 15 pounds or more occur along the front beaches and near inlets.

Large trophy red drum are generally unavailable to anglers during the winter months, however smaller fish are present inside South Carolina's estuaries during colder weather. Fish that were spawned two Septembers ago are anywhere from 14 to 18 inches in length and 1 to 2 pounds in weight. Red drum that were spawned three Septembers ago are also in inshore waters and can be caught by the patient angler who doesn't mind the cold. These fish are from 4 to 8 pounds in weight. The time to fish for red drum is just after low tide, when the water begins to flood but before the tide reaches the marsh grass. Early afternoon on warmer sunny days is probably the best time to fish. As the tide floods, red drum move into increasingly shallow water until they swim onto the surface of the flooded marsh, where they remain until the tide starts to fall.

Sheepshead

Sheepshead can be caught around docks, jetties, pilings, and bridge piers, where they feed on barnacles and mussels scraped from the structures. One of the best places to catch sheepshead in the fall is at the jetties of Charleston Harbor.

Snapper and Grouper

These large bottom fish inhabit natural reefs in 70 to 300 feet of water. Winter offers an excellent opportunity to catch them where they abound on rock outcroppings and live bottom areas. Gray triggerfish, red and whitebone porgies, blueline tile fish, hogfish, and grunts commonly are caught along with snappers and groupers. These fish tend to occur in fewer but larger congregations during the winter, making them more difficult to locate. Once they are found, however, the fishing is often fast and furious.

Spanish Mackerel

Spanish mackerel occur in local waters from late April until November, with the best action usually found in May and June. Some Spanish mackerel will enter the bays and sounds, but most inhabit nearshore waters from 2 to 15 miles out. On calm days, schools of top-feeding Spanish can be spotted from long distances by watching for flocks of terns diving on schools of bait fish. Best schooling activity normally occurs prior to 10:00 A.M. and after 5:00 P.M.

Spot

This species is one of the most widely sought-after fishes by small-boat anglers and pier fishermen along the Grand Strand in the fall. During this time, spots are migrating south along the coast from North Carolina to spawn. Good places to catch spot are off the piers along the Grand Strand and in areas along the Intracoastal Waterway, especially at the intersection of Inlet Creek north of Charleston.

Spotted Sea Trout

When inshore water temperatures exceed 60°F in the spring, spotted sea trout that overwintered inside estuaries become much more active. Trout begin spawning in late April and early May, and, since spawning requires a great deal of energy, spring trout go on a feeding binge. In late March and early April, good catches of trout can be made in the upper parts of the estuaries. Some anglers call spotted sea trout "tide-runners," because when tidal currents are moving, fish start feeding. When there is no tidal current and the water is still, feeding is reduced. When the tidal currents are running, spotted sea trout prefer areas with structure, such as oyster beds, rocks, and pilings.

During the hot summer months, trout fishing is erratic, as the fish do not form the large schools typical of cooler periods of the year. As water temperatures begin to decline in late September and after the first good northeaster, spotted sea trout begin to move back into the rivers from the lower parts of the estuaries and along the coast. In the Charleston Harbor area, good incoming tide spots are the points at Hobcaw and Foster Creeks in the Wando River; good outgoing tide spots are near the drydock in Beresford Creek and the point at Guerin Creek in the Wando. The point at Orange Grove Creek in the Ashley River is good on either an incoming or outgoing tide.

During the colder months of the year, spotted sea trout tend to stay inside the estuaries at least until March or early April. They can be found in many of the tributaries of the main rivers.

Whiting

During the summer, whiting can be caught in the surf around the groins and in the sloughs and cuts along open beaches. Whiting feed on small worms, crabs, and shrimp. Generally weighing less than a pound, whiting do not fight as hard as many of the other inshore fishes. They make up for it by being excellent table fare.

FISHING BY SEASON IN GEORGIA

Amberjack

Congregate around structures, wrecks, and artificial reefs.

April–December nearshore. Year-round offshore.

Atlantic Spadefish

Form large schools around offshore structures. Often seen finning at the surface while feeding or spawning.

May–November, nearshore. Year-round offshore.

Barracuda

May–October

Black Drum

Oyster beds, pilings, submerged structures. Common in summer in sounds and along outer beaches of barrier islands.

April–October.

Black Sea Bass

Offshore, bottom fish. Year-round.

Bluefish

"Big Blues" abundant on offshore reefs and Navy towers. Small "snapper" and medium "chopper" blues appear at jetties and outer bars. April–December.

Cobia

Occur singly or in schools. Congregate over wrecks. April–November nearshore. Year-round well offshore.

Croaker

Sandy bottoms in deep water. Don't stray far from the estuaries. March–April, August–November.

Dolphin

Open ocean, warm water. Gather under floating debris and weed lines. June–September nearshore. Year-round well offshore.

Flounder

Hard mud/shell or sand bottoms. May–December.

Gray Triggerfish

Can be found nearshore where barnacles and similar animals grow. May–November nearshore. Year-round offshore.

Groupers

May–December nearshore. Year-round offshore.

Jack Crevalle

May–October

King Mackerel

Large "smoker" kings can be caught within sight of land when waters warm up to the high 60s. Schools of smaller "snake" kings are more common when water temperatures are in the 70s. Distinct spring/fall migrations, but taken throughout warmer months at artificial reefs, live bottoms, Navy towers, and any feature that holds baitfish. April–December nearshore. Year-round well offshore.

Kingfish

Southern, northern, and gulf kingfish prefer higher salinities found along the outer beaches of the barrier islands. Prefer sandy bottom, often swimming in so close that they are temporarily stranded by receding waves. April–June.

Little Tunny, Bonito

Schools in nearshore waters in early spring. April–November nearshore. Year-round offshore.

Red Drum

Oyster beds in creeks, rivers. Adults most abundant in or just beyond surf zone along outer beaches of barrier islands. May–December.

Red Porgy, Pink Porgy, Silver Snapper
Move to deeper waters with age. April–December nearshore. Year-round well offshore.

Red Snapper
Caught on or near reefs. Young fish found close to shore, while adults favor deeper and cooler waters. May–November nearshore. Year-round offshore.

Sailfish
Seen within sight of land. Often spotted at the surface June–September.

Sharks
Most sharks prefer warmer water and migrate yearly. March–November nearshore (except spiny dogfish in winter). Year-round offshore for Atlantic sharpnose and nurse.

Sheepshead
Barnacle-encrusted pilings of artificial reefs, wrecks, and other structures. Also found nearshore in spring. Year-round.

Spanish Mackerel
Smaller fish form large schools off the outer bars and jetties in spring. April–November.

Spot
Hard clay or mud bottoms in deep water. March–June.

Spotted Sea Trout
Oyster beds in creeks, rivers bordered by marsh grass. Preferred habitat along edges of marsh. October–December.

Summer Trout (Weakfish)
Sandy bottom in deep water. March–September.

Vermilion Snapper
Large schools of small fish common over low-relief live bottom; adults found in deeper waters. June–November nearshore. Year-round well offshore.

Wahoo
Most common offshore, but are caught at the Navy towers and Snapper Banks in summer. May–September nearshore. Year-round well offshore.

Whiting
Sandy/dead shell bottoms in deep water. April–June.

Wahoo is only one of many species that prowl the offshore waters of South Carolina. Anglers can also catch king mackerel, dolphin, tuna, blue marlin, white marlin, and sailfish. (JOHN PHILLIPS)

FISHING RECORDS

VIRGINIA

Amberjack: 118 lb.; Chesapeake Light Tower; 1986
Bluefish: 25 lb., 4 oz.; Bluefish Rock; 1986
Cobia: 103 lb., 8 oz.; Mobjack Bay; 1980
Cod, Atlantic: 35 lb.; Off Wachapreague; 1969
Dolphin: 71 lb., 8 oz.; Off Virginia Beach; 1991
Drum
   Black: 111 lb.; Cape Charles; 1973
   Red: 85 lb., 4 oz.; Wreck Island; 1981
False Albacore: 25 lb., 4 oz.; Off Virginia Capes; 1964
Flounder: 17 lb., 8 oz.; Baltimore Channel; 1971
Mackerel (King): 51 lb., 3 oz.; Off Virginia Beach; 1991
Marlin
   Blue: 1,093 lb., 12 oz.; Norfolk Canyon; 1978
   White: 131 lb., 10 oz.; Off Virginia Beach; 1978
Porgy: 5 lb., 5 oz.; Off Chincoteague; 1978
Sailfish: 68 lb., 8 oz.; Off Virginia Beach; 1977

Seabass (Tie): 9 lb., 8 oz.; Off Virginia Beach; 1990

Seabass (Tie): 9 lb., 8 oz.; Off Virginia Beach; 1987

Shark

Blacktip: 76 lb., 10 oz.; Off Virginia Beach; 1988

Blue: 266 lb.; The Cigar; 1987

Bull: 256 lb.; V-Buoy; 1982

Dusky: 673 lb.; S.E. Lumps; 1982

Hammerhead (Great): 430 lb.; S.E. Lumps; 1984

Hammerhead (Scalloped): 245 lb.; The Cigar; 1977

Hammerhead (Smooth): 272 lb.; Off Virginia Beach; 1988

Lemon: 312 lb., 12 oz.; Sandbridge; 1976

Mako: 728 lb.; Chesapeake Light Tower; 1983

Sandbar: 213 lb.; Triangle Wrecks; 1986

Sand Tiger: 339 lb.; Cape Charles; 1983

Spinner: 129 lb., 8 oz.; Off Chincoteague; 1991

Thresher: 115 lb., 4 oz.; Off Virginia Beach; 1980

Tiger: 1,099 lb., 12 oz.; S.E. Lumps; 1981

White: 131 lb.; S.E. Lumps; 1981

Sheepshead: 19 lb.; Chesapeake Bay Bridge-Tunnel; 1979

Spadefish: 13 lb.; The Cell (Chesapeake Bay); 1988

Striped Bass: 61 lb.; Mattaponi River; 1981

Swordfish: 381 lb., 8 oz.; Norfolk Canyon; 1978

Tarpon: 130 lb.; Off Oyster; 1975

Tautog: 24 lb.; Off Wachapeague; 1987

Tuna

Bigeye: 274 lb., 8 oz.; Norfolk Canyon; 1988

Bluefin: 204 lb.; Off Virginia Beach; 1977

Yellowfin: 203 lb., 12 oz.; Norfolk Canyon; 1981

Wahoo: 109 lb.; Off Virginia Beach; 1994

NORTH CAROLINA

Albacore (false): 26 lb., 8 oz.; Off Wrightsville Beach; 1991

Albacore (true): 57 lb.; Off Oregon Inlet; 1971

Amberjack: 125 lb.; Off Cape Lookout; 1973

Barracuda: 67 lb., 7 oz.; Cape Lookout; 1985

Bass

Black Sea: 8 lb., 12 oz.; Off Oregon Inlet; 1979

Striped: 60 lb.; Hatteras Island Surf; 1972

Bluefish*: 31 lb., 12 oz.; Off Cape Hattaras; 1972

Cobia: 103 lb.; Emerald Isle Pier; 1988

Dolphin: 77 lb.; Off Cape Hatteras; 1973

Drum

Black: 87 lb.; Cape Lookout; 1990

Red*: 94 lb., 2 oz.; Hatteras Island Surf; l984

Flounder: 20 lb., 8 oz.; Carolina Beach; 1980

Grouper

Strawberry: 28 lb., 8 oz.; Off Topsail Beach; 1972

Warsaw: 245 lb.; Off Wrightsville Beach; 1967

Grunt, White: 4 lb., 8 oz.; Off Cape Lookout; 1969

Hogfish: 2 lb., 4 oz.; Atlantic Ocean; 1991

Jack, Crevalle: 47 lb.; Off Cape Hatteras; 1989

Mackerel

King: 79 lb.; Off Cape Lookout; 1985

Spanish*: 13 lb.; Ocracoke Inlet; 1987

Marlin

Blue: 1,142 lb.; Off Oregon Inlet; 1974

White: 118 lb., 8 oz.; Off Oregon Inlet; 1976

Perch, White: 1 lb., 13 oz.; Pembroke Creek; 1986

Pompano

African: 27 lb., 8 oz.; Off Holden Beach; 1991

Florida: 7 lb., 13 oz.; New River Inlet; 1981

Sailfish: 100 lb.; Off Ocean Isle; 1987

Shark

Blue: 478 lb.; Crystal Fishing Pier; 1961

Dusky: 610 lb.; Nags Head Pier; 1963

Hammerhead: 710 lb.; Nags Head Pier; 1960

Lemon: 421 lb., 8 oz.; Kure Beach Pier; 1978

Mako: 768 lb.; Off Oregon Inlet; 1983

Scalloped: 234 lb.; South of Cape Point; 1990

Thresher: 145 lb.; Off Cape Lookout; 1980

Tiger: 1,150 lb.; Yaupon Beach Pier; 1966

Sheepshead: 18 lb., 7 oz.; Off Carolina Beach; 1982

Snapper, Red: 40 lb.; Off Cape Lookout; 1970

Spadefish

Atlantic: 8 lb., 2 oz.; Pamlico Sound; 1978

Longbill: 98 lb.; Off Cape Hatteras; 1978

Swordfish: 441 lb.; Off Wrightsville Beach; 1979

Tarpon: 164 lb.; Indian Beach Pier; 1978

Tautog: 16 lb., 2 oz.; Off Oregon Inlet; 1991

Tuna

Bigeye: 300 lb.; Off Oregon Inlet; 1989

Blackfin: 32 lb.; Off Wrightsville Beach; 1972

Bluefin: 732 lb., 8 oz.; Off Cape Hatteras; 1979

Skipjack: 22 lb., 3 oz.; Off Wrightsville Beach; 1968

Yellowfin: 237 lb.; Off Cape Lookout; 1979

Tunny, Little: 26 lb., 4 oz.; Off Wrightsville Beach; 1990

Wahoo: 127 lb.; Oregon Inlet; 1973

*World all-tackle record

SOUTH CAROLINA

Albacore: 37 lb., 4 oz.; Charleston; 1976

Amberjack: 98 lb., 8 oz.; Fripp Island; 1981

Barracuda, Great: 65 lb.; Georgetown; 1948

Bass, Black Sea: 7 lb., 12 oz.; Charleston; 1975

Bass, Striped: 44 lb., 8 oz.; Beaufort; 1983

Bluefish: 21 lb.; Charleston; 1975

Bonito, Atlantic: 6 lb., 3 oz.; Little River; 1973

Cobia: 83 lb., 3 oz.; Broad River; 1976

Croaker: 4 lb., 9 oz.; Charleston; 1979

Dolphin: 69 lb., 10 oz.; Mt. Pleasant; 1988

Drum

 Black: 89 lb.; Port Royal; 1978

 Red (Channel Bass): 75 lb.; Murrells Inlet; 1965

Flounder, Southern: 17 lb., 6 oz.; South Santee; 1974

Flounder, Summer: 3 lb., 8 oz.; Murrells Inlet; 1982

Grouper

 Gag: 46 lb., 7 oz.; Murrells Inlet; 1986

 Red: 30 lb., 2 oz.; Charleston; 1976

 Scamp: 23 lb., 10 oz.; Charleston; 1972

 Snowy: 30 lb.; Murrells Inlet; 1981

 Speckled Hind: 45 lb.; Little River; 1973

 Warsaw: 310 lb.; Murrells Inlet; 1976

Grunt: 18 lb., 8 oz.; Murrells Inlet; 1971

Hogfish: 20 lb., 8 oz.; Murrells Inlet; 1988

Houndfish: 9 lb., 4 oz.; Murrells Inlet; 1974

Jack, Crevalle (tie): 37 lb., 2 oz.; Charleston Harbor; 1979

Kingfish (Whiting) (tie): 2 lb., 10 oz.; Pawleys Island; 1968

Ladyfish: 4 lb., 8 oz.; Bulls Island; 1968

Mackerel

 King: 62 lb.; Charleston; 1976

 Spanish: 11 lb.; Myrtle Beach; 1983

Marlin

 Blue: 640 lb.; Charleston; 1975

 White: 108 lb.; Charleston; 1981

Pompano, Florida: 8 lb., 12 oz.; Charleston; 1975

Porgy: 18 lb., 4 oz.; Charleston; 1984

Porgy, Red: 10 lb., 8 oz.; Murrells Inlet; 1985

Runner, Rainbow: 14 lb., 14 oz.; Georgetown; 1985

Sailfish: 75 lb.; Georgetown; 1968

Sea Trout, Spotted: 11 lb., 13 oz.; Murrells Inlet; 1976

Shark

 Bigeye Thresher: 406 lb.; Edisto Island; 1978

 Blacktip (tie): 133 lb.; Port Royal; 1968

 Bull: 477 lb., 12 oz.; Stono Inlet; 1985

 Dusky: 466 lb., 12 oz.; Charleston; 1981

 Hammerhead: 588 lb., 3 oz.; Charleston; 1989

 Lemon: 332 lb.; Charleston; 1983

 Sandbar: 199 lb., 4 oz.; Charleston; 1984

 Sand Tiger: 304 lb., 8 oz.; Charleston; 1984

 Shortfin Mako: 302 lb., 12 oz.; Georgetown; 1978

 Silky: 248 lb.; Charleston; 1981

 Spinner: 105 lb.; Charleston; 1985

 Tiger: 1,780 lb.; Cherry Grove; 1964

Sheepshead: 15 lb., 4 oz.; Charleston; 1969

Snapper

 Red: 37 lb., 8 oz.; Little River; 1964

 Vermilion: 6 lb., 10 oz.; Charleston; 1975

Spadefish

 Atlantic: 9 lb., 11 oz.; Fripp Island; 1989

 Longbill: 53 lb.; Mt. Pleasant; 1986

Spot (tie): 1 lb., 1 oz.; Charleston; 1967

Swordfish: 500 lb.; Georgetown; 1978

Tarpon: 154 lb., 10 oz.; Hilton Head; 1987

Tilefish, Blueline: 14 lb., 6 oz.; Murrells Inlet; 1982

Triggerfish, Gray: 13 lb., 9 oz.; Murrells Inlet; 1989

Tripletail: 25 lb., 8 oz.; Mt. Pleasant; 1971

Tuna

 Blackfin: 30 lb.; McClellanville; 1989

 Skipjack: 25 lb., 14 oz.; Charleston; 1986

 Yellowfin: 241 lb., 12 oz.; Charleston; 1979

Tunny, Little: 29 lb., 7 oz.; Charleston; 1975

Wahoo: 108 lb., 8 oz.; Charleston; 1979

Weakfish (Summer Trout): 11 lb., 13 oz.; Parris Island; 1981

GEORGIA

Amberjack, Greater: 92 lb., 1 oz.; Artificial Reef "J"; 1975

Barracuda, Greater: 46 lb., 8 oz.; Savannah Snapper Banks; 1993

Bass, Black Sea: 5 lb.; Savannah Snapper Banks; 1981

Bluefish: 17 lb., 12 oz.; Artificial Reef "G"; 1980

Cobia: 88 lb., 12 oz.; Buoy "A" ESE of Tybee Island; 1985

Dolphin: 60 lb., 12 oz.; Gulfstream E. of Savannah Snapper Banks; 1991

Drum

 Black: 83 lb.; Village Creek, Glynn County; 1989

 Red (Channel Bass): 47 lb., 7 oz.; Artificial Reef "KC"; 1986

Flounder: 15 lb., 10 oz.; Jekyll Pier; 1990

Grouper

Gag: 34 lb., 8 oz.; 67 miles east of St. Simons Island; 1986

Warsaw: 252 lb.; 6.2 miles off Savannah in 150 feet of water; 1981

Jack, Crevalle: 35 lb.; Tybee Roads, Savannah River; 1977

Jewfish: 124 lb.; Savannah Snapper Banks; 1976

Ladyfish: 5 lb.; Off Cumberland Island; 1978

Mackerel

King: 63 lb., 8 oz.; Brunswick Snapper Banks; 1990

Spanish: 8 lb., 4 oz.; 5 miles east of Buoy YS; 1991

Marlin

Blue: 491 lb., 8 oz.; Gulf Stream off Brunswick; 1985

White: 49 lb., 12 oz.; Gulf Stream east of St. Catherines; 1986

Pompano, Florida: 4 lb., 8 oz.; Cumberland Island Beach; 1989

Runner, Rainbow: 17 lb., 12 oz.; Savannah Snapper Banks; 1984

Sailfish: 65 lb.; NOAA Buoy, Gulf Stream; 1981

Sea Trout, Spotted: 90 lb., 7 oz.; Christmas Creek; 1976

Shark

Black Tip: 131 lb.; Wassaw Channel; 1978

Bull: 455 lb.; STS Buoy, SSI Channel; 1978

Dusky: 272 lb., 8 oz.; STS Buoy, SSI Channel; 1978

Hammerhead: 770 lb.; Little Cumberland Island; 1973

Lemon: 375 lb.; St. Andrew Sound; 1974

Mako: 228 lb., 8 oz.; Off Savannah 45 FMS; 1975

Sandbar (Brown): 158 lb.; Jekyll Island Pier; 1979

Sand Tiger: 290 lb.; Ossabaw Island; 1977

Thresher: 116 lb.; Artificial Reef "C" (WR2); 1976

Tiger: 794 lb.; STS Buoy, SSI Channel; 1975

Sheepshead: 13 lb.; Lanier Bridge, Brunswick; 1977

Snapper, Red: 37 lb.; Savannah Snapper Banks; 1988

Snook: 10 lb., 2 oz.; Kings Creek, St. Simons Sound; 1990

Spadefish, Atlantic: 11 lb., 12 oz.; Artificial Reef "G"; 1981

Swordfish: 86 lb.; Gulf Stream 90 degrees east of Savannah; 1980

Tarpon: 139 lb.; Gould's Inlet, St. Simons Island; 1986

Triggerfish, Gray: 11 lb., 5 oz.; Savannah Snapper Banks; 1987

Tripletail: 28 lb., 7 oz.; S. Brunswick River; 1989

Tuna

Blackfin: 28 lb., 8 oz.; Gray's Reef; 1993

Yellowfin: 249 lb., 2 oz.; 130 degrees off WAS. Sea Buoy 300' DEP; 1980

Tunny, Little: 20 lb.; 135 degrees off WAS. Sea Buoy 35 out; 1973

Wahoo: 91 lb.; Savannah Snapper Banks; 1982

Weakfish (Summer trout): 6 lb., 8 oz.; Mouth of Troupe Creek; 1976

LOCATING CHARTER, PARTY, OR RENTAL BOATS

VIRGINIA

For information on charter boats, contact the Virginia Charterboat Association, P.O. Box 459, Deltaville, VA 23043, (804) 776-9850 or Virginia Saltwater Fishing Tournament, Suite 102, Hauser Building, 968 Oriole Dr., South Virginia Beach, VA 23451, (804) 491-5160.

NORTH CAROLINA

Detailed information and the most current list of charter and party boats may be obtained by calling the following numbers:

Greater Wilmington Visitors Bureau:
(800) 922-7117 in North Carolina
(800) 222-4757 in the eastern U.S.
(919) 762-2611 elsewhere

Southport/Oak Island Chamber of Commerce:
(919) 457-6964

Charter Services
(All area codes are 919.)

Carolina Beach

Flapjack Charters, 458-4362

Musicman Charters, 458-5482

Flo Jo Charters, 458-5454

The Adventuress, 458-5454

Fish Witch, 458-5855

Sea Filly, 458-6600

Bird Dog, 458-9345

Capt. Rick, 395-4458

Fired Up, 458-5172

Hooker, 458-8742

Poor Boy, 458-5373

Class Action, 458-3348

Lady Frances, 458-5228

Oregon Inlet Fishing Center

Erma Queen, 473-3345

Fish-N-Fool, 473-2027

Sea Whisper, 473-5759

Sinbad, 473-2398

Atlantis, 473-5710

Capt. B.C., 473-2348

Carolinian, 473-5224

Dare Devil, 473-2780

Dream Girl, 473-5157

Fight-N-Lady, 441-4016

Fintastic, 441-4151

First Crack, 473-3038

Fishin Frenzy, 441-8367

Gannet, 441-6292

Grand Slam, 473-2280

Gulfstream, 473-3012

Jo-Boy, 473-2427

Maddhatter, 441-4582

Marlin Fever, 491-8233

Miss Boo, 473-2774

Pelican, 441-3197

Pollyanna, 473-5082

Prime Time, 473-5913

Reelin', 473-5435

Right Hook, 473-2481

Sea Fever, 473-3386

Sea Witch, 441-1816

Sizzler, 473-5657

Smoker, 473-1934

Sportsman, 441-7295

Surfside, 473-2675

Tar Heel, 473-5791

Temptress, 441-7705

Wildfire, 473-5964

Crystal Coast Charter Boat Association

Abra-Ka-Dabra, 728-5020

Ashley Renaie, 728-3676

Bill Collector, 726-7650

Blue Marlin II, 728-7680

Calcutta, 393-8560

Captain Stacy VII, 247-7501

Fine Line, 247-6021

Four Wonders, 247-2034

Gale Anne, 247-3694

Kathi T., 223-5238

Laura J., 726-7641

Marlin Darlin, 726-4423

Offshore III, 729-2431

Priorities, 728-7847

Purrsuasion, 247-4070

Red Fin, 247-4148

Sea Hawk, 726-9876

Sea Mistress, 247-7501

Sea Wife III, 726-5670

Sea Wife IV, 726-4852

Sensation, 728-6571

Southwind, 825-2476

Sunrise, 726-9814

TailWalker, 633-1404

Tom 'N Jerry, 489-9688

SOUTH CAROLINA

South Carolina charter boats offer the average angler the opportunity to experience the thrills and excitement of deep-sea big game fishing. King mackerel, Spanish mackerel, wahoo, dolphin (fish), amberjack, and tuna are standard catch on a day spent trolling offshore. Sailfish, white marlin, swordfish, and the biggest prize of all, the blue marlin, also regularly figure into a day's catch.

These boats offer four basic types of fishing trips. The lowest priced, and one of the most popular, is the half-day trip, which usually concentrates on fishing for king and Spanish mackerel. Most of this angling is conducted 5 to 20 miles offshore.

On the full-day trips there are usually three options: mackerel fishing, Gulf Stream fishing, or blue marlin fishing. The mackerel trips are conducted in virtually the same area as the half-day trips and, while mackerel usually make up the bulk of the catch, little tunny, amberjack, jack crevalle, and even sailfish are commonly taken. The Gulf Stream trips are conducted further offshore, usually 30 to 50 miles, and normally produce larger fish. Dolphin, wahoo, king mackerel, barracuda, blackfin tuna, and yellowfin tuna are the most common gamefish taken, though these trips offer an excellent opportunity to pick up a billfish.

Blue marlin fishing is usually conducted beyond the continental shelf in the cobalt blue waters of the Gulf Stream. Because of the larger size and out-staning fighting qualities of these big gamefish, which may exceed 500 pounds, special tackle and bait are required for these ventures. Consequently, these trips cost more. While seeking blue marlin, these trips may produce excellent catches of wahoo, dolphin, and big tuna.

Some vessels are now offering night fishing trips for swordfish. This recently-discovered bonanza is sought at night in 200 to 300 fathoms (1,200 to 1,800 feet) of water, approximately 75 miles offshore. Trolling just before dusk and again early in the morning provides some diversity in the catch as night fishing usually produces either sharks or swordfish.

These vessels and their captains are licensed by the U.S. Coast Guard to carry up to six passengers. Charter boats are hired on a trip basis rather than on a fee-per-angler basis, like head boats. On a charter trip, all of the necessary bait and tackle are usually provided. Ice for holding the day's catch is also usually provided by the boat, but this should be checked before departure. The party chartering the boat is usually required to provide its own food and drinks unless other arrangements have been made beforehand. Charter boat captains are anxious to please their customers and will go out of their way to accommodate them.

Charter Services

Edisto Beach Marina, (803) 869-3505

Fripp Island Marina, (803) 838-5661

Outdoor Resort & R.V. Resort Yachtclub, (803) 681-3256

Palmetto Bay Marina, (803) 785-7131

Shelter Cove, (803) 842-7001

Sea Pines South Beach Marina, (803) 671-3577

Sea Pines Harbour Town, (803) 671-4534

Schilling Boat House, (803) 689-LURE

Head Boat Fishing

Head boat fishing has become popular among South Carolina anglers. Thousands of anglers enjoy the experience of deep-sea bottom fishing aboard these vessels each year. Black sea bass (blackfish), red porgy, vermilion snapper, red snapper, and a variety of groupers are present year-round and provide fast action to the angler venturing offshore to the blackfish or snapper banks. Experienced captains and crews assist the angler in every possible way to ensure a happy and successful trip. It is common for the angler's catch to exceed in value the price of the trip.

These vessels generally offer three different trips. The half-day sea bass (blackfish) trip is the most popular among anglers short on time or trying on their sea legs for the first time. Black sea bass, triggerfish, and porgies are the most common fish encountered on 5- to 15-mile offshore trips. Full-day black sea bass trips offer the angler a longer fishing period in areas 10 to 25 miles offshore. This area usually produces similar but more and larger fish. The third type of trip is the snapper-grouper or Gulf Stream trip, which is conducted in much deeper waters, (usually exceeding 80 feet), lying 25 to 40 miles offshore. Fish taken on these trips are consistently larger than those normally caught on the

other trips. Red porgies (silver snapper), vermilion snapper, red snapper, triggerfish, amberjack, and a variety of groupers provide the main action for anglers fishing the "snapper banks" of South Carolina.

Head boats carry from 30 to over 100 fishermen per trip and charge a set fee per angler. Captains are required to be licensed and each vessel is inspected by the U.S. Coast Guard. All of the necessary bait and tackle is supplied by the boat. Many of the snapper-grouper boats also have electric motor-driven reels available for a small additional charge. These vessels usually have a snack and refreshment center on board. Personal coolers are generally not allowed aboard these vessels due to limited space, but each boat does provide a fish box with ice. Head boats normally operate from April through November, although some boats are available year-round.

GEORGIA

Charter Services
(All telephone area codes are 912.)

AA Atlantic Coast Charters, Savannah, GA 31410, 897-4705, 656-8421

Action Charters, 117 Stafford Rd., Savannah, GA 31410, 897-7791

Amick's Deep Sea Fishing Inc., 6902 Samonetties Dr., Savannah GA 31410, 897-6759, 897-6270

B&D Marine, 300 Marina Dr., St. Simons Island, GA 31522, 638-7981

C. Wayne Davis Charters, Box 32, Darien, GA 31305, 832-4218

Captain C. Charters, 1000 Mallory St. #6, St. Simons Island, GA 31522, 638-7646

Captain Covington Charters, 19 Tidewater Rd., Savannah, GA 31406, 354-9651

Charter Fish Inc., Box 694, St. Simons Island, GA 31522, 638-7468

Chimney Creek Charters, Box 1336, Tybee Island, GA 31328, 786-9857

Chip Bright Charters, 206 Oak Rd., Brunswick, GA 31525, 264-6834

Coastal Adventures, General Delivery, Valona, GA 31332, 832-4926

Coastal Charters, 110 Bracewell Ct., St. Simons Island, GA 31522, 638-8228

Coastal Expeditions, 3202 E. Third St., Brunswick, GA 31520, 265-0392

Dan Druumond, 706 Oak Lane, Brunswick, GA 31525, 264-1733

D. Blackshear, 109 Demere Retreat Lane, St. Simons Island, GA 31522, 638-2512, 634-0706

Deep Sea Fishing, Box 336, Richmond Hill, GA 31324, 756-4573

Ducky II Charters, 402 Kelsall Ave., St. Simons Island, GA 31522, 634-0312

Gold Coast Charters, Rt. 1, Box 1934, Townsend, GA 31331, 832-4245

Happy Hooker Charters, 10A Hayes Ave., Jekyll Island, GA 31527, 635-2158

Hobo Enterprises, 9 Choctaw Rd., Brunswick, GA 31525-9265, 264-5735

Inland Charter, Box 11, N. First St., Sea Island GA. or 217 Westpoint Dr., St. Simons Island, GA 31522, 638-3611 ext. 520, 638-4261

Island Carters, Box 923, Brunswick, GA 31521, 261-0630, 638-8799

Island Dive Center, 107 Marina Drive, St. Simons Island, GA 31522, 638-6590

J.E. McVeigh Charters, Box 101, Waverly, GA 31565, 265-1465

J.Y.'s Charter Service, Box FFF, St. Mary's, GA 31558, 882-3996

Jeanne and Jim Pleasants, 310 Magnolia Ave., St. Simons Island, GA 31522, 638-9354

Jim Anderson, 800 Ash St., #A, Savannah, GA 31404, 232-2286, 233-1585

Joe Dobb's Charters, 10 Pennystone Retreat, Savannah, GA 31411, 598-0090

Kathy & Suzanne, Inc., 19 Seminole Rd., Brunswick, GA 31525, 267-1914

Kingfish Charters, Box 866, Woodbine, GA 31569-0866, 576-3460

Kip's Fishing Camp, Rt. 2, Box 2314, Townsend, GA 31331, 832-5162

Larry Kennedy, 511 Marsh Villa Rd., St. Simons Island, GA 31522, 638-3214

Maritime Charters, Box 2060, Tybee Island, GA 31328, 786-7379

Mike Evans Charters, 728 Pine Haven Circle, Brunswick, GA, 264-3807

Mike's Mistress, 507 Palmetto St., St. Mary's, GA 31558, 882-5133

Miss Judy Charters, 124 Palmetto Dr., Savannah, GA 31410, 897-3123

P.N. Patrick Charters, 619 Mackay Dr., Richmond Hill, GA 31324, 727-2694, 727-2215

Palmetto Coast, Box 536, Tybee Island, GA 31328, 786-5403

Ricky O. Smith, Rt. 11, Box 934, Brunswick, GA 31525, 264-3027, 264-9561

Saltwater Charters, 111 Wickersham Dr., Savannah, GA 31411, 596-1814

Savannah Charters, Box 1974, Tybee Island, GA 31328, 786-7507

Seawolf Charters, Box 3045, Jekyll Island, GA 31527, 635-2891

T.L. Kutrufis Charters, 101 Broadway, St. Simons Island, GA 31522, 638-2081

Trophy II Charters, 104 Sandy Way, Statesboro, GA 30458, 764-9071, 764-5118

Two Way Fish Camp, Rt. 10, Box 84, Darien Hwy., Brunswick, GA 31521, 265-0410

Vicki Ann Charters, 501 Beach Dr., St. Simons Island, GA 31522, 638-0001

Wendell Harper, 107 Boyd Rd., Brunswick, GA 31520, 264-4459

STATE AGENCIES

VIRGINIA

Virginia Marine Resources Commission Main Office:
2600 Washington Ave.
P.O. Box 756
Newport News, VA 23607
(804) 247-2200

499 Menchville Road
Newport News, VA 23062
(804) 877-1181

30 Jefferson Avenue
Newport News, VA 23707
(804) 247-2265

NORTH CAROLINA

District Offices of the Department of Marine Fisheries
Morehead City
(800) 682-2632 or (919) 726-7021
(Answers 24 hours)
Elizabeth City
(800) 338-7805 or (919) 264-3911
Wilmington
(800 248-4536 or (919) 395-3900
Washington
(800) 338-7804 or (919) 946-6481

SOUTH CAROLINA

Marine Resources Division of the South Carolina Wildlife and Marine Resources Department
P.O. Box 12559
Charleston, SC 29412
(803) 795-6350.

GEORGIA

Georgia Dept. of Natural Resources
Coastal Resources Division
1 Conservation Way
Brunswick, GA 31523-8600
(912) 264-7218

Coastal Georgia Regional Development Center
P.O. Box 1917
Brunswick, GA 31521
(912) 264-7363

University of Georgia
Marine Sciences Program
Ecology Building
Athens, GA 30602

Georgia Dept. of Industry, Trade, & Tourism
P.O. Box 1776
Atlanta, GA 30301
(404) 656-3545

University of Georgia
Marine Extension Service
P.O. Box 13687
Savannah, GA 31416
(912) 598-2496
FAX (912) 598-2302

The section of coast from Altamaha Sound, Georgia, to Fort Pierce, Florida, is part of a 400-mile-long incurvature that extends from Cape Romain, South Carolina, to Palm Beach, Florida. From Altamaha Sound to the mouth of the St. Johns River, Florida, the coast is bordered by a series of rather wide, irregularly shaped barrier islands. Broad estuaries, locally called sounds, which separate these islands are often deep and continuous with large coastal rivers draining great sections of the interior. Between the islands and the mainland are verdant saltmarshes, often miles wide, reticulated by meandering, brackish waterways. This complex of tidal water and wetlands constitutes one of the largest and relatively pristine coastal saltmarshes in the world.

South of the St. Johns River as far as Palm Beach, the coast is even, and were it not for the seaward projection of Cape Canaveral, it would be straight. Here the coastline is characterized by long, narrow barrier islands, behind which are narrow, shallow lagoons. Although these lagoons were formerly unconnected, they have been made continuous by the construction of the Intracoastal or Inland Waterway. Every 25 miles or so along the coast, narrow inlets connect this system of lagoons and waterways with the sea. Skirting many of the lagoons are saltmarshes and, in the extreme southern end of this section, mangroves. Only a few freshwater rivers and streams drain the interior along this part of the coast.

In this entire map section, there is little to relieve the nearly flat, sandy expanse of land, which is typical of the coastal plain. This plain is characteristic of the entire east coast south of about New York City. In Georgia, it extends over 150 miles inland, and in Florida, it covers the entire state. From the shore, it continues under the sea to form the gently sloping plateau of the continental shelf. The width of the shelf, which is about 80 miles off Altamaha Sound, progressively narrows to only 20 miles off Fort Pierce. Even though over most of its breadth the continental shelf is a plain of sand, scattered throughout are ridges and depressions as well as rocky reefs and outcroppings and coral heads. The reefs, often covered with live encrusting corals, tend to lie parallel to the 600-foot contour. Nearshore, the sediments have obscured most of the rock outcroppings. Proceeding seaward, the depressions and reefs become progressively more pronounced, attaining their maximum relief of 30 to 70 feet normally between the 180- and 300-foot contours. At the southern end of this map section, starting a few miles south of Sebastian Inlet, Florida, a nearly continuous rocky reef parallels the ocean shore and extends to Key West, Florida.

Scattered about the sea floor are known wrecks of well over 50 ships and many aircraft. Besides these, there are many artificial reefs—man-made obstructions placed along the ocean floor to enhance fishing.

2

Altamaha Sound, Georgia, to Fort Pierce Inlet, Florida

Georgia/Florida waters are loaded with a variety of species, such as this triggerfish, a colorful, thick-skinned fighter with an excellent taste. (JOHN PHILLIPS)

The hulls of sunken ships and the cargoes they carried, the broken and twisted wreckage of the aircraft, and the automobile bodies, tires, appliances, and other debris put down to form the artificial reefs provide shelter for fishes as well as surfaces for the attachment of sessile food organisms. Fishes tend to concentrate about these structures, just as they do around naturally occurring discontinuities of the bottom.

TIDES

Along the open seacoast of this section, high and low tides occur twice each day. Owing to peculiarities in the shape of the shoreline and in the configuration of the sea floor, tidal ranges vary considerably. Between Cape Hatteras, North Carolina, and Palm Beach, Florida, the shoreline forms a great incurvature that extends for over 600 miles and cuts 180 miles into the coast. It includes the 250-mile incurvature from Cape Hatteras to Cape Romain and the 400-mile incurvature from Cape Romain to Palm Beach. In the middle of the great incurvature, the sea floor slopes much more gradually than at either end. The combination of the shoreline's shape and the bathymetric configuration produces a funnel effect, causing tides to be highest near the middle and lowest at the ends. Thus, off Altamaha Sound, located near the middle of the incurvature, the tidal range is 7 feet. From there southward, the range progressively decreases to 6 feet at Fernandina Beach, Florida, to 5 feet at St. Augustine, Florida, to 4 feet at Daytona Beach, Florida, to 3½ feet at Cape Canaveral. From Cape Canaveral to Fort Pierce, the tidal range is

about 2½ feet. Tidal ranges in the sounds, lagoons, and waterways are often complicated, varying from several feet to only a few inches depending on their location, configuration, depth, and distance from the sea. The greatest range, over 8 feet, occurs in Georgia, several miles upstream from the mouths of the tidal rivers. The smallest range, less than a foot, occurs in Florida along various sections of the Intracoastal Waterway that are far removed from the influence of the sea, such as the stretch behind Flagler Beach, Mosquito Lagoon, and the north end of Indian River.

SEASONS AND WEATHER

The climate along this stretch of coast is mild with a warm season lasting over three-fourths of the year. Starting about December, temperatures fluctuate sporadically whenever cool continental air pushes down from the northwest and interrupts the otherwise pleasant mild weather. These winter fluctuations in air temperatures are the greatest of any time of the year. Winter storms are usually accompanied by strong, gusty northerly or swirling northeasterly winds. The most severe of these brings frost, sometimes even a trace of sleet. While fogs occur at any time of the year, they are most frequent during the cool season.

Spring is a rather short transitional period. The number of cold, stormy periods decrease, the winds moderate, and they become easterly and southwesterly. Then, sharp contrasts in temperature between the cool coastal water and the warm Gulf Stream water flowing northward result in the formation of heavy clouds offshore that often parallel the beach.

Summer is characterized by high temperatures, high humidities, and gentle winds. Air temperatures are usually warmer than 85°F during the day, and from June to September they commonly reach 90°F, sometimes even 100°F or more. As often happens along the coast during the day, high temperatures are reduced by winds blowing in from the sea. Indeed, the strong moderating effect of the sea on air temperatures along the shore results in somewhat cooler summers and warmer winters than in areas a few miles inland.

All anglers should be aware of the severe wind and lightning storms that commonly occur in early to midafternoon from June through September. Most storms form over the landmass and push offshore, posing a real threat to offshore boats. Many captains fish from first light to about 1:00 or 2:00 P.M., all the while listening carefully to VHF weather reports and reports from party boats with weather-watching radar.

With the warm season come hurricanes. Any time between May and November, these severe tropical cyclonic storms occasionally strike the coast. It is from August to October, however, that they are most common and intense. Sure signs of an approaching hurricane are the appearance of high, thin, feathery white clouds converging towards a point on the horizon; calm seas for several days with little or no wind but with long, heavy swells; a slight rise of the barometer followed by a continuous, usually rapid fall; and exceptionally clear water and increased feeding activity of fishes at the surface. When the strong and furious winds of a hurricane catch a vessel on the sea, they often cause it to break apart, to founder, or to strand on a shoal or beach.

Fall is a short transitional period from the pattern of summer to that of winter. The gentle southerly and westerly winds gradually become more variable, then shift to northerly and become progressively stronger. The weather, usually mild and dry, is interrupted by brief rainy periods followed by clear, cool days.

FISH MOVEMENT AND MIGRATION

An intense ocean current, the Gulf Stream, flows northward along this stretch of coast at 4 knots or more. It forms the boundary between the relatively cool, low salinity water lying alongshore and the warmer, saltier water of the Sargasso Sea. The Gulf Stream is 50 to 100 miles wide and a half mile deep at this point. Its name derives from the mistaken belief that its source is the Gulf of Mexico, more specifically, the Mississippi River and other rivers flowing into the Gulf of Mexico, and that it flows like a river or stream in the ocean. Actually, it would take over a thousand Mississippi Rivers, indeed, more than 30 times the combined flow of all rivers of the world, to equal the flow of the Gulf Stream. Nevertheless, the term Gulf Stream is now firmly established even though the Gulf of Mexico's contribution to it is insignificant.

The Gulf Stream, its western edge as close as 20 miles offshore, has an important influence on fish distribution. Its warm water carries tropical and subtropical pelagic species, including dolphin, king mackerel, blackfin tuna, bluefin tuna, yellowfin tuna, blue and white marlin, sailfish, and wahoo. Sargassum weed floating on the Gulf Stream's surface, often in long windrows, harbors entire communities of small pelagic animals, which include many larval and juvenile jacks, tunas, dolphins, mackerels, sailfish, marlins, and other important fishes. Bottom-dwelling species, including the groupers and snappers, occur along the sea floor where the deep water of the Gulf Stream touches bottom.

While the Gulf Stream's nearly constant water temperature and salinity would seem likely to provide a particularly favorable year-round habitat for fishes, relatively few of the 300 species occurring within this map section actually associate with the Gulf Stream. In comparison with coastal water, the Gulf Stream is much less fertile. Though the temperature and salinity of coastal water varies widely by season, fishes inhabiting it can stay in fairly constant environmental conditions simply by migrating. There are all manner of migratory habits among these fishes. Species such as the river herrings, shad, striped bass, and sturgeons move between the sea or estuaries and their upstream destinations in fresh water. Some species, among them tarpon, ladyfish, and snook, move from the open sea to estuaries where they spend the summer. Still others, e.g., the little tunny, migrate seasonally between shore or near the shore and the edge of the continental shelf or beyond. Fishes that live in the great depths of the ocean move between greater and lesser depths and perhaps between currents moving in differing directions.

What impels fishes to leave one area for another? What determines their destinations? How do they find their way? People who study fishes, and that includes fishermen as well as ichthyologists, are continually searching for answers to these questions—to discover natural laws to predict the behavior of fishes. One lesson we have learned about fishes is to be cautious about making absolute statements, for there have been too many occasions when predictions made on what had seemed to be firm grounds have not been fulfilled. Nevertheless, a few generalizations may be offered tentatively.

Many sea fishes of both northern and southern hemispheres tend to move toward their respective poles in spring and summer and toward the equator in fall and winter. Their movements are correlated to a considerable degree, though imperfectly, with water temperatures. Fishes move along the coast as temperatures change progressively from less favorable to more favorable levels. Each species concentrates within areas where the prevailing temperature best fits its particular requirements. Once a species finds an area where the temperature is suitable, its movements become dominated by other factors, such as the location and availability of food or suitable spawning grounds.

The migrants along this large section of coast begin their northward journey in the spring. Migration is usually most pronounced during March, April, and May as the surface water begins to warm. Most of the fishes sojourn here for only a few weeks and then continue on their way to more northerly summer destinations. They seem to arrive in waves. When one wave of fish overlaps another that had arrived earlier, as happens often, the cumulative effect makes for excellent fishing. During this spring migration, pelagic species often travel much closer to the surface than they do during their fall migration. By June, the surface water over nearly the entire shelf in this section has warmed to above 77°F. During this period and into the summer, the main bodies of tropical migrants, including pompano, tarpon, ladyfish, cobia, king and Spanish mackerel, move in from the south, dispersing along the entire area. They continue pushing their way north-ward, many traveling along the coast at least as far as the Chesapeake Bay. Some of these, as well as other species that follow routes farther offshore, often travel as far as southern New England or beyond.

In the fall, the southerly migration gets underway all along the coast. Then, while fishes that have been summering here move southward, others stream in from the north and, for a few weeks while the temperatures remain optimal for them, the migrants from the north pause here before resuming the journey to their more southerly wintering grounds.

During the winter, the average surface temperatures over the inner third of the continental shelf vary from about 54°F in Georgia to 68°F at Fort Pierce, Florida. These winter temperatures of the nearshore water along this stretch of coast are cooler than the summer surface temperatures over nearly the entire shelf between the Chesapeake Bay and southern New England. At the same time, the surface temperatures over the outer two-thirds of the shelf off Georgia and northern Florida, about 68°F to 73°F, are nearly the same as the summer temperatures between the Chesapeake Bay and southern New England. Consequently, temperate-water migrants, such as bluefish, whose movements seem to be strongly influenced by temperature, evidently remain out near the edge of the shelf during the winter or continue on to the Fort Pierce area where the nearshore temperature is also favorable.

Important though temperature may be, it is certainly not the only factor affecting fish movement. Recent studies have shown photoperiod to be important. A migration of a fish species may begin several days or even weeks before any change of temperature is evident. The approach of the spawning season probably provides a powerful impulse to begin moving towards a spawning area. The position of the sun may be an important influence on fish that are active during the day, for these species may be able to use the sun for navigating. This is probably true of the bluefin tuna, which, during some years, travels thousands of miles from the Caribbean Sea northward past Florida and Georgia and then eastward across the Atlantic Ocean to the coast of Norway. It is very likely that a combination of external as well as internal stimuli trigger migrations.

A striking feature of many sea fishes occurring in the estuaries and inshore along Georgia and northeastern Florida is that they are generally small. Because the inshore waters are shallow and turbid and their temperature and salinity fluctuate widely, they are unsuitable for larger and older fishes, which require deeper and more transparent water and more stable environmental conditions. The inshore water, however, is an ideal nursery for warm-temperate, subtropical, and tropical fishes. Many of these fish are spawned over the continental shelf or in the Gulf Stream. Drifting with cur-

rents, they somehow make their way to shore and into the protected water behind the barrier beaches. The young fish grow rapidly in this fertile estuarine water, so that some, (for example the pompano and tarpon), are ready to migrate out by the end of their first summer. Many others, among them spot, croaker, pigfish, and grunts, stay in the estuarine water throughout their first year or even longer. Eventually they move out and gradually take up the habits characteristic of adults of their species.

Any destruction of estuarine areas or even damage to them is deleterious to the plants and animals living there. The reclamation of saltmarshes for housing and industrial development and the channeling of shallow waterways for increasing numbers of boats have been generally destructive to marine life. Between 1954 and 1969, over 28,000 acres of tidal marshland have been destroyed in Georgia and along the east coast of Florida, most of it for real estate projects. In addition, during this same period, dredging and filling have destroyed over 36,000 acres of important shoal water habitats. Fortunately, this process is abating somewhat since the state began protecting the coastline through purchase and other means.

HISTORY

For over three centuries after the first Spanish forts were built, the coast along south Georgia and Florida remained sparsely populated. During the 1700s under British rule, many planters settled in Georgia where they lived on the mainland close along the large rivers, producing a valuable crop of rice. Because the coastal islands were vulnerable to invasion by pirates and, in time of war, to attack by warships, the planters provided themselves with some protection against these dangers by settling a few tenant farmers on the sea islands to warn their employers of imminent danger, to raise livestock, and to protect the game from poachers.

In Florida, many of the settlers were traders, located in isolated places, dealing mostly in furs, alligator hides, and bird plumes. While their occupations were diverse, the settlers living all along the coasts of Florida and Georgia depended to a considerable extent on the large system of interconnecting waterways for their food. Most of them had small boats from which they caught fish, shellfish, turtles, and so forth. Like the Indians, they found the waterways and the various rivers draining into them to be important spawning grounds for many species of fishes and feeding grounds for a great many more. They found shad, sturgeon, herring, and striped bass to be abundant in winter and spring during their spawning migrations up the Altamaha, Satilla, Ogeechee and St. Marys Rivers in Georgia and the St. Johns River in Florida. Mullet, spotted and gray sea trouts, southern kingfish, croaker, red and black drums, southern flounder, sheepshead, porgies, and bluefish were abundant in the saltwater of the sounds and along the beaches. Also, the sounds and creeks abounded in blue crabs, oysters, clams, turtles, and shrimps.

Unfortunately, the settlers lacked marketing outlets for seafood; hence, their harvest was limited to their personal needs. They had forgotten, or perhaps had never learned, the Indian's method of smoking fish, and their efforts to produce an acceptable salted product failed. Consequently, people came to believe that Southern fish were not amenable to curing processes. The only way Southern fishermen transported their catches to market was to keep them in livewells built into their fishing vessels.

A dramatic change took place in fishing after the Civil War. Many of the naval officers aboard Union ships blockading Southern ports discovered the excellent fishing and returned after the war. Then, common sights were smacks from Noank, Connecticut, sailing offshore for black sea bass and shad fishermen from Old Saybrook, Connecticut, setting their gill nets in the various rivers. These Northern fishermen introduced new and more efficient types of fishing gear and also the use of ice for keeping their fish fresh. Meanwhile, frequent steamship service to northern coastal cities and rail service to the interior opened new markets for fishery products. As railroads slowly pushed down Florida's east coast during the 1800s, important new fisheries became established.

Recreational fishing may have started earlier in the South than in other regions. Early explorers mention the merriment that Indians made as entire villages joined in collecting fish for a feast. The Spaniards who settled St. Augustine in 1565 often depended on seafood that they could catch locally, especially when their supply ships did not arrive on schedule. Like their countrymen at home, they probably fished for recreation. Not only did they use hooks and lines, but also the castnet, which they are credited with introducing into this country.

Until the late 1860s, most of the land within this map section was little more than a wilderness. Ten years later, St. Augustine and Fernandina Beach, Florida, had become winter resorts for thousands of visitors each year. Anglers fished in the mouth of the St. Johns River for red drum, locally called red bass, and spotted and gray sea trouts, also called speckled trout and yellowmouth trout. A few sailing vessels and steamers carrying pleasure-fishing parties, as they were called, made trips to the fishing grounds several miles away from shore to catch black sea bass and red snapper. New beach resorts, such as Daytona and Ormond, were developed to attract tourists from the North. By the turn of the century, railroads had pushed down the east coast and opened the vast expanses of the Indian River to anglers who fished out of the small settlements

of Eden, Titusville, Cocoa, Eau Gallie, Melbourne, Sebastian, and Fort Pierce. Palatial hotels of 300 or 400 rooms along Indian River became fashionable as wealthy sportsmen poured into this area to fish its water and hunt its game.

Throughout the first half of the 1900s, even as the various resorts became increasingly larger, most of the recreational fishing remained in the sounds and bays and within 5 miles of the ocean beaches. Besides the commercial snapper boats, only large charter boats piloted by skilled captains and a few large private boats fished far offshore. For the most part, anglers seemed to be content with the supply of fish in the sounds and along shore. Not only could they catch coastal species, such as spotted sea trout, red drum, and tarpon, but also those that occur a short distance offshore such as king mackerel, cobia, snappers, groupers, and little tunnys. During the mid-1950s, as high-powered outboard engines became common and larger boats were built to handle them, some of the inshore anglers began following the large charter boats farther and farther offshore. The catches of large king mackerel, sailfish, dolphin, barracuda, amberjack, and snappers they brought back to dock enticed other anglers to try, so that by the early 1960s, a considerable number of 16- to 22-foot boats, often with twin outboards, were fishing 15 to 20 miles offshore.

Sportfishing clubs greatly enhanced offshore fishing. Some of these instituted courses in boating safety, weather observation, rigging baits, and the techniques of angling. Experienced charter boat and commercial captains participated in these clubs. The clubs also have constructed artificial fishing reefs and a few of them, again with the cooperation of charter boat and party boat fishermen as well as commercial fishermen, have precisely located several dozen fishing grounds, marking them with specially numbered buoys.

Until recently, an angler in Georgia or Florida did not need a license to fish in salt or brackish water, but this has changed. There are also some saltwater regulations in place. In Georgia, there is a minimum size limit as well as a daily catch limit for striped bass and other species; in Florida, there are minimum size limits for bluefish, pompano, fluke, Spanish mackerel, spotted and gray sea trouts, red drum, snook, and others, with the list still growing. Florida also imposes limits on catches or possession of snook, sailfish, tarpon, and striped bass. Both states regulate the season, type of gear, method of capture, and catch limits of shrimps, oysters, and clams. In addition, Florida regulates fishing for spiny lobsters and stone crabs. Georgia requires a license to take shrimp for home consumption, sets a daily catch limit on blue crabs, and prohibits keeping egg-bearing blue crabs during a short period in the spring.

Detailed regulations for Georgia are found in Chapter

One, and for Florida later in this chapter. For the best information, obtain the most current copies of the fishing and shellfishing regulations from the following agencies:

Georgia: Department of Natural Resources, Coastal Resources Division, 1 Conservation Way, Brunswick, GA 31523-8600

Florida: Department of Natural Resources, 2510 Second Ave. North, Jacksonville Beach, FL 32250

ALTAMAHA SOUND TO NASSAU SOUND

LAND CONFIGURATION AND WATER DEPTH

Along the coast from Altamaha Sound to Nassau Sound and for a considerable distance into the interior, the land is low and nearly flat. Throughout most of the area it rises just a few feet above the high-water mark. Only in two locations within some 2 dozen miles of the sea are there landforms higher than 35 feet. Every 10 miles or so along the coast, a river system draining the interior works its meandering course to the sea. Aquatic vegetation bordering the rivers changes gradually from freshwater marshes along the upper reaches to salt-marshes about the estuaries. At the mouths of the rivers the saltmarshes broaden out and merge with each other, eventually forming a 3- to 6-mile-wide belt of rich, grassy wetland that parallels the coast. This belt is reticulated by a system of narrow salt and brackish waterways, locally called rivers, creeks, or dividings. These waterways ultimately connect with expanses of semienclosed saltwater, locally called sounds. Most of the waterways and sounds average 20 to 30 feet deep, though some carry depths of as much as 80 feet. Lying between the saltmarshes and protecting them from the action of the sea is a series of sandy barrier islands, locally called sea islands. These range from 6 to 15 miles long by a mile or two wide and are separated from each other by the sounds. The sounds connect directly with the open sea and serve as passageways for boats as well as fishes. The seaward side of the sounds is marked by sandy shoals that are either bars or tidal deltas extending out from shore some 4 or 5 miles. During heavy weather the shapes of these shallow areas are vividly outlined by the storm waves breaking on them.

The sea floor off this section, composed mostly of sand, slopes away from land at an average rate of only 3 feet a mile to the offshore limit of this map. The gradualness of the slope and the extensiveness of some shoals become evident to a boatman, who must sail up to 20 miles away from shore before finding depths as

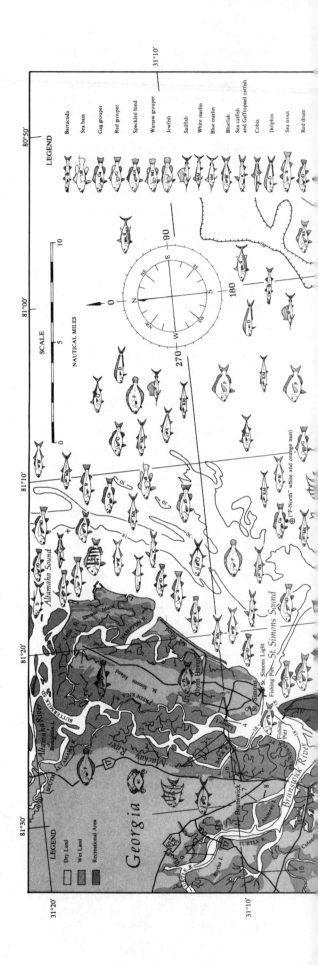

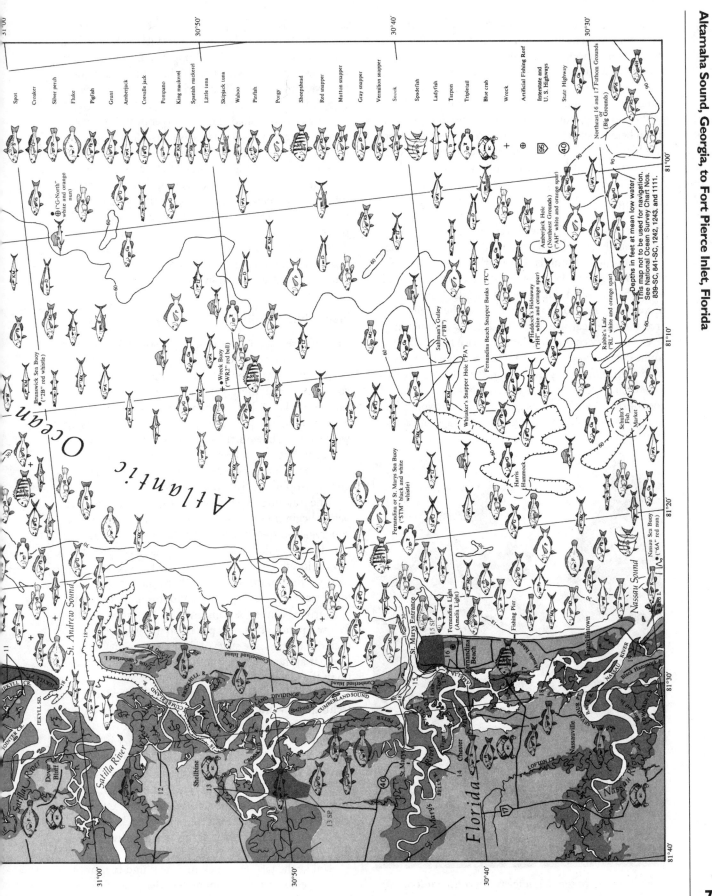

great as those within the sounds. Scattered over the floor are corrugations caused by sand ridges and depressions as well as rock outcroppings and coral heads. Close to shore the corrugations are low and the rocks generally obscured if not completely hidden by sediments. Along the offshore border of this map the offshore corrugations become higher, reaching a maximum height between trough and crest of 10 to 15 feet. It is here that fish tend to concentrate in greatest numbers; hence, the fishing is usually very good.

HISTORY

The first Europeans in the area settled along the mainland, usually on necks of dry land that run close to the river mouths and sounds. Since earliest times most of the population has been concentrated on the mainland or on the landward side of the sea islands. The settlers, principally agrarians, soon learned that they could "reclaim" the nearby marshes by ditching and making levees, thereby converting them into rice fields. The sounds and even the waterways between the marshes were deep enough to permit sailing vessels of the region to navigate, transporting to distant markets their cargoes of rice as well as crops grown in the interior. Even though the sounds provided good harborage and safe

During the warm months, anglers can catch adult tarpon weighing 100 pounds or more. (BOB MCNALLY)

sailing, it was a long trip to the open sea. Boats often sailed for 10 or 15 miles from their docks before crossing the ocean bar. Because of the long distances from population centers to the sea, most of the fishing was done in the rivers and sounds. The kinds of fishes sought by early fishermen were those ascending the various rivers to spawn, such as shad and sea sturgeon, and coastal migrants frequenting estuarine waters, such as sea trouts, red drum, and mullet. Later, shrimp became important, but fishing continued to be confined to estuarine waters. Recreational fishing subsequently followed the trend of commercial fishing so that most of the angling today is in the sounds. Even with high-powered boats and in good weather, it often takes anglers over half an hour to get to the ocean bar and nearly an additional three-quarters of an hour to get into water as deep as that in the sounds.

FISH AND FISHING

In many areas along the southeast coast the angler must travel miles from shore to find large gamefish, but the deep sounds along this portion of the Georgia–Florida coast hold one of the largest and most challenging adversaries found anywhere in the world. The tarpon is a wide-ranging fish providing sport for countless anglers worldwide. While other locations may be more famous as tarpon hot spots, the nearshore waters of the Altamaha, St. Simons, St. Andrew, and Nassau Sounds give up trophy size fish on a regular basis.

The traveling angler is well advised to hire a guide before beginning a quest for tarpon. These fish tend to congregate in specific areas, and the guide can transport you directly to the best spots that could take you many days to locate. Guides also know the channels and drains between the sandbars and mud flats, and that can save a lot of wear and tear on your boat bottom or lower unit.

Tarpon seem to be constantly on the move, but they follow a pattern that may put them in the same place each day at the same stage of the tide. This may be a sandbar at the mouth of the sound or a tidal creek well up in the saltmarsh.

Once you decide where to fish, the most productive technique is working a live bait from an anchored boat. A fish-finder rig will allow the tarpon to move off with the bait before he feels the weight of your terminal tackle. A Mustad Tuna Circle Hook provides a high hook-up ratio and is easily removed to release the fish.

Besides tarpon, there are plenty of other fish waiting to be caught in the sounds and in the ocean. One of the more abundant of these is the Spanish mackerel. While not as big as a king mackerel, this fish does live close to shore and can be taken on light tackle.

Unlike the tarpon, which may be found in murky water, the Spanish mackerel prefers clear water where he can easily see his prey. His main bill of fare consists of small fish that are best imitated by spoons and jigs measuring less than three inches. Trolling is the most productive technique because you can cover a lot of territory and keep the lures running at 5 to 6 knots, a speed that seems to attract a Spanish mackerel. If you do locate a school of tightly packed fish, it is possible to take them on metal lures, lead-head jigs and flies but the speed of your retrieve should be as fast as possible.

The setup for trolling spoons consists of a 1- to 3-ounce trolling sinker attached to your 20-pound running line with a ball bearing swivel. The spoon is tied directly to 30 feet of 15- to 20-pound line, which is attached to the trolling sinker with another ball bearing swivel. During the course of the day your leader will probably become twisted and should be replaced. I keep at least six rigs ready to go on leader spools to keep changing time to a minimum.

Tarpon and Spanish mackerel may be taken from the beach but you are more likely to catch spot, croaker, sea trout, flounder, and sea mullet. The barrier islands between the marsh and the ocean do provide some surf fishing opportunities but the inlets between these islands will be more productive. A list of piers and parks that offer access to these areas begins on page 105.

The live bottom, artificial reefs, and wrecks can be good locations for some serious bottom fish action. The red snapper and grouper are trophy fish out here but silver snapper, porgies, grunts, and black sea bass are more likely to fill the coolers of bottom fishermen.

What's In a Name?

The drum family is so called because of drumming sounds that most of its members produce. Fishes of other families, as well as the drums, make noises variously described as rumbles, growls, croaks, scrapes, and clucks. In some families, only one of the sexes makes noises. In the drum family, however, both sexes usually do. They do this by articulating dorsal and ventral patches of strong teeth located far back in the throat close to the swim bladder. The males also have special swim bladder muscles with which they can vibrate the bladder. Although kingfishers lack a swim bladder, they make faint rasping sounds of various tones with their teeth. Sounds produced by using the teeth tend to be high pitched, whereas those made by vibrating the swim bladder are generally of low frequency. Sonic activity of sea trouts usually increases in the breeding season, when congregations produce loud nocturnal choruses. It seems fishes produce noises for a variety of functions—to signal others of their own kind, to locate each other for courting, for warning, and also to discourage competition and intimidate potential enemies in defending a territory.

Cruising Florida's East Coast From Jacksonville to Miami

by Herb Allen

When planning an inside journey on the Intracoastal Waterway (ICW) or a voyage outside in the Atlantic Ocean, it's certainly more relaxing, rewarding, and logical to take it by intervals. It's been said that there's but one way to eat an elephant and that's a bite at a time. This aphorism can be equated to cruising Florida's east coast.

For our aqua safari, let's cast off in Jacksonville and cruise south via the ICW to Miami. In this exercise, we'll leave off spectacular side trips down

the St. Johns River, across the Okeechobee Waterway, and down through the scenic Florida keys.

Before departing Jacksonville, however, it's worth a delay to explore this interesting city, which historians tell us was first visited by Ponce de Leon in the 1500s while he searched for the legendary Fountain of Youth. Today, in addition to being a business center and home to a U.S. Navy base, Jacksonville boasts a lively resort community, beautiful white sandy beaches, dockage/marina facilities, excellent watering

holes, shops, and numerous historic sites.

Our first stop after leaving Jacksonville is St. Augustine, 18 miles to the south, said to be the oldest city in the United States. Here we can visit the restored Spanish village and experience what life in the Sunshine State was like 400 years ago. An old Spanish fort, Castillo de San Marcos, built in 1672, is an interesting site, as are several museums and some 33 historic buildings that date back to the colonial era. It's well worth allotting a little extra time to visit historic St. Augustine. Those who lay-over will find good dockage facilities at the Camachee Cove Yacht Harbor, Conch House Marina, the City Marina, and the Anchorage Motor Inn.

On to Daytona Beach

Leaving St. Augustine, ICW travelers will soon be in some deep but narrow and well marked channels that extend off and on all the way to the Indian River 80 miles south.

Stops at Fort Matanzas and Marineland are rewarding. Once a Spanish outpost and now a national monument, Fort Matanzas is an excellent place to unwind, relax, and soak up some history. A short distance south of the Matanzas Inlet is Marineland, the world's first oceanarium, established in 1939. More than 1,000 sea creatures, ranging from the common to the bizarre, live together in harmony and can be viewed close-up through underwater portholes. A convenient port of call, with laundry facilities, inexpensive dockage, and other amenities, Marineland's marina on the Waterway has 30 transient slips available. All have dockside power, beach access, and tennis court and pool privileges. To be sure of a space, call ahead for reservations by dialing (904) 471-0087, or Channel 16 on your VHF.

From here to a point just north of Ormond Beach, the Waterway broadens into a shallow lagoon called the Halifax River. This protected sector offers plentiful anchorages and marinas at Palm Coast and Flagler Beach, some of which can accommodate boats up to 165 feet in length.

Neighboring Ormond Beach is Daytona, with its numerous marinas including the Municipal Yacht Basin, the Daytona Marina, Howard Boat Works, and Seven Seas Marina.

For a good-sized city, Daytona tends to be a neat, laid back sort of place with plenty to see and do. The City of Daytona Beach recently upgraded its Municipal Yacht Basin by

adding 522 boat slips, a 10-acre park with a river garden, and more than 70,000 square feet of commercial space for retail shops, offices, and restaurants. In addition to its rich auto racing tradition (24 Hours of Daytona and the Daytona 500), the city has dog racing, jai alai, a profusion of reasonably priced hotels and motels, plus one of the nation's finest stretches of level, hard-packed beach where, during daylight hours, people can drive their vehicles.

Possible side trips for mariners include the Bulow Plantation Ruins, the wild and primitive Tomoka River, the 700-acre Tomoka State Park, and the Addison Blockhouse, which was built around the ruins of a burned-out 1807 cookhouse.

Daytona to Vero Beach

Next stop on our southbound journey is New Smyrna, a popular anchorage with adequate transient marina facilities including one at the Riverview Hotel, plus a limited number of slips at the Sea Harvest, Causeway Marina, and the New Smyrna Yacht Club. Those interested in a bit of sightseeing might want to take in the New Smyrna Sugar Mills, built in the 1800s out of coquina stones. It was destroyed by Seminole Indians in 1835.

Further along, just north of where the Banana River meets the Indian River and ICW, we find Cape Canaveral, the John F. Kennedy Space Center, Merritt Island and Cocoa Beach. Known as the Space Center, the area is well endowed with such stopover possibilities as the Indian Cove Marina, the Indian Harbour Marina, the Cape Marina, Westland Marine, Whitley Marine, Island Point Marina, Diamond 99 Marina, Tingley's Marina, Port Canaveral Marina, Skyline's Anchorage Yacht Basin, the Eau Gallie Yacht Basin, the Intracoastal Marina of Melbourne, and Melbourne Harbor Marine.

While in the area, visitors should certainly plan to visit the Space Museum. Also check out the Merritt Island National Wildlife Refuge, Port

Canaveral Jetty Park, the Canaveral Pier, and other points of interest.

Cruisers who have surfers aboard may want to stop near Sebastian and Sebastian Inlet, north of Vero Beach, which is considered one of the finest surfing sites on the east coast of the United States.

Visitors to Vero Beach, which marks the dividing line between the upper and lower reaches of the Indian River, will find transient berths at Summit Landings, Vero Beach Municipal Marina, the Riomar Bay Yacht Club, The Moorings, and Complete Yacht Services. We understand that the recently opened Center for the Arts, within walking distance of the municipal marina and the Vero Beach Yacht Club, is well worth a look-see.

Vero to Palm Beach

Between Vero Beach and Fort Pierce, 13 miles to the south, the ICW becomes quite broad and is dotted with numerous spoil islands that are home to nesting pelicans, cormorants, herons, and egrets. During the winter months, boaters are also likely to see quite a few manatees, especially in and around the warm water discharge at the Fort Pierce power plant.

Founded as a military base during the Seminole Wars, Fort Pierce is in the heart of the Indian River citrus country. It has excellent marina facilities for visiting and resident boaters, including the Pelican Yacht Club and City Marina.

Down the line, at Hutchinson Island, Jensen Beach, Stuart, and St. Lucie, cruisers will find some exceptional facilities including the Martin Memorial Hospital in Stuart, which accepts emergency patients at its own dock. Stuart also claims to be the Sailfish Capital of the World (with justification), but other regional locales are nothing to sneeze at either, especially during the winter months when spindlebeaks seem to outnumber tourists.

Travelers won't have far to look to

find a place to berth. To name a few: Pelican Yacht Club, Riverside Marina, and the City Marina in Fort Pierce; Frances Langford's Outrigger Resort and the Indian River Plantation at Hutchinson Island/ Jensen Beach; and Sailfish Marina, Mariner Cay Marina, David Lowe's Boat Yard, Pirate's Cove, and Charlie's Locker in the Stuart area.

Continuing south, cruisers will soon happen upon Hobe Sound (probably more exclusive than Palm Beach), passing by grand mansions and manicured lawns on the way to Jupiter, Lake Worth, and the Palm Beaches where the yachts seem to get longer and the marinas more opulent. A few possible stops in this stretch of the ICW include Loblolly Bay, Jib Yacht Club, Jupiter Marine, and the Bluffs Marina in Jupiter; Soverel Harbour, Harbour Point Marina, and the Old Port Cove Marina in North Palm Beach; Lake Park Marina, Cannonsport Marina, The Buccaneer, Sailfish Marina, Riviera Beach Municipal Marina, and the Cracker Boy Boat Works in Lake Worth; and the Spencer Boat Company, Flagler Marina, Palm Harbor Marina, North Palm Beach Marina, and the Australian/ Brazilian/Peruvian docks in the Palm Beaches.

Palm Beaches to Fort Lauderdale

A 40 or so mile jump to Fort Lauderdale winds mostly through a narrow landcut, spanned by some 20 bridges. Lined with waterfront homes, motels, condos, and high-rise apartments, this stretch gives an observer the sense of cruising down 5th Avenue in New York City. One municipality tends to merge with the next, and boaters might not even notice passing through such places as Lantana, Boynton Beach, Delray Beach, Boca Raton, Deerfield, and Pompano Beach before reaching Fort Lauderdale. Each of these towns offers its own attractions, though, so take your time through this stretch.

A delightful mix of older and newer homes is found at Delray, which was settled at the turn of the century by farmers and Japanese immigrants who raised vegetables and pineapples. The history and culture of this colony can be seen at the Morikami Museum. A big sidewalk arts festival is held here on the first weekend following Easter. Atlantic Avenue is a showcase for the arts, crafts, flowers and produce.

Boca Raton, literally translated as "mouth of the rat," is shown on 16th-century Spanish charts as Boca de Ratones and is said to have been inhabited by Blackbeard the Pirate. Those who would like to learn more about this and other local history can visit the Singing Pines Museum, thought to be the only unaltered wooden structure of its age in an area of expensive homes and shops.

Farther down the narrow, crowded, and often choppy ICW, boaters pass the communities of Deerfield Beach, Lighthouse Point, and Pompano, which offers fine dining and shopping opportunities, before blending into Fort Lauderdale. A center for recreational boating activities, Fort Lauderdale has 20,000 boats permanently anchored and, maybe, double that during the winter months. Nicknamed "The Venice of America," Fort Lauderdale has deep-water facilities and is home to many of the world's most luxurious yachts. It's also home to the annual Fort Lauderdale International Boat Show, the largest in-water event anywhere in the world. On-the-water restaurants are numerous and some shopping centers have their own docks on the ICW where skippers can tie up while dining, marketing, or browsing ashore.

Originally settled by the Tequesta Indians in about 1450 B.C. Fort Lauderdale has been under both Spanish and British rule at various times in its history. It started to grow up and out after Florida was admitted into the Union in 1845.

Dockage in this stretch can be found at the Lantana Boatyard, the Boca Raton Hotel and Club, the Lighthouse Point Yacht & Racquet Club, the Sands Harbor Hotel and Marina, Pier 66, Port Everglades, the Municipal Marina, Jackson Marine Sales, Harbour Towne Marina, and probably the ultimate of centers, Bahia Mar, to name a few.

On to Miami

Our final stop on this Florida east coast excursion is lusty, colorful, and sprawling Miami—a city still in search of its identity. A mix of high rises and slums, of new Cuban and old Cracker cultures, of kiwi and grits, Miami has frequently been described as "the world's most interesting city." When visiting Miami, be sure to allow ample time for sightseeing, shopping, and just plain gawking.

For the boater, Miami—like Fort Lauderdale—has complete offerings including outstanding cruising waters, plush dockage, balmy weather, and flamboyant watering holes. Some of the marina facilities here can aptly be described as "mind-blowing." Sunset Harbour, Williams Island, Turnberry Isle Yacht and Country Club, Maule Lake Marina, Miami Beach Marina, Waterways Marina, Fisher Island, Dinner Key Marina, the Biscayne Bay Marriott, Monty Trainer's Marina, Rickenbacher Marina, Crandon Park Marina, Mike Gordon's, and the Fontainebleau Dock are but a smattering of the facilities available.

For those planning to continue traveling south to the Florida Keys, or east to the Bahamas, Miami is a logical—and magical—spot to get recharged. ∎

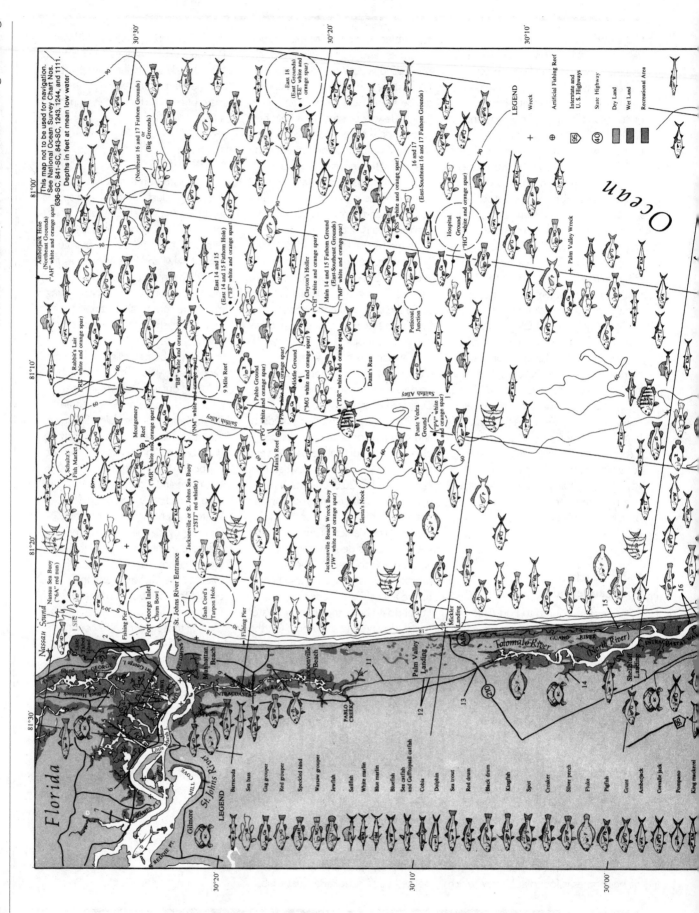

Florida

NASSAU SOUND TO MATANZAS INLET

LAND CONFIGURATION AND WATER DEPTH

The land along this stretch of coast, like that depicted on the previous map, is remarkably low and flat. Few landforms within a half dozen miles or so of the sea are higher than 25 feet. Indeed, the crests of the 5- to 10-foot sand dunes along the beaches are often the highest elevations for several miles.

The configuration of the coast changes dramatically at the mouth of the St. Johns River. For over 200 miles north of the St. Johns River the coast is characterized by a series of rather wide, irregularly shaped barrier islands, locally called sea islands. Separating these islands from each other are broad, deep bodies of salt and brackish water, called sounds. Between these islands and the mainland some miles away lie great expanses of saltmarsh that are reticulated by a system of meandering waterways. This complex of tidal water and wetland constitutes one of the largest coastal saltmarshes in the world.

For nearly 300 miles south of the St. Johns River the coast is characterized by long barrier bars, behind which are narrow, shallow lagoons. These lagoons, locally called rivers, extend for many miles along the coast. Although formerly a series of unconnected waterways, they have been made continuous in this section by construction of the Intracoastal Waterway, also called the Inland Waterway. Widely spaced inlets, which are usually shallow, connect the lagoons with the sea. Only a few streams of freshwater, such as the Matanzas River in this map section, drain into the lagoons.

The St. Johns River drains coastal northeast Florida as far south as Sebastian, a distance of over 200 miles. Consequently, there are no freshwater rivers of significant size south of the St. Johns. Because of numerous and intricate convolutions in the St. Johns River, water is carried over 400 miles from its source to the sea. However, the distance between the main river and the sea is usually less than 15 miles, rarely more than 30 miles. The St. Johns falls only a few feet over its entire course; hence, the current is quite sluggish and the tide reaches to Lake George, over 100 miles from the mouth.

Seasons of the Surf

by Bob McNally

It is never silent on the beach, never. Even when the tide is slack and the wind calm, there are special beach sounds. The roar of waves. The shrill calls of birds. And when fishermen are present, there is the slap of surf against human legs and the screech of reel drags as good fish take line.

These things and more endear surf fishing to a select few northeast Florida anglers, but there is no likely more overlooked fishing in that part of the state. That's curious, because Florida's First Coast has many miles of open, undeveloped beaches (some where automobiles still can be driven), and there are plenty of fish available. Yet competition among surf fishermen is minimal, at least compared to what's happening on offshore reefs and inshore creeks among the boating crowd. In fact, rarely do serious surf anglers run into anyone else during a typical day's fishing. Should one angler meet another, there is so much beach available that you easily can move to another prime surf fishing spot and not see another human carrying a fishing rod.

The roughly 150-mile span of coast from Fernandina Inlet at the Georgia state line south to Daytona Beach has some of the best, and most overlooked, surf fishing in Florida. Possibly the excellent beach fishing found in this area is overlooked only because so much other great fishing exists. There are many inlets to the ocean, and fishing is superb out of all those spots. In addition, hundreds of miles of inshore creeks, rivers, and the Intracoastal Waterway provide fishermen with a wealth of opportunities for catching flounder, redfish, sea trout, weakfish, black drum, sheepshead, ladyfish, jacks, bluefish, tarpon and other species as well. Public fishing piers, bridges, and jetties afford easy, good access to northeast Florida's abundant fish stocks. So even though plenty of open beach exists throughout the First Coast, great surf fishing is largely ignored—at least by the bulk of the region's fishermen.

Another factor is that surf fishing is not a traditional method of fishing in the region—at least not for most local anglers. Farther north in the Carolinas and farther south near Melbourne and Vero Beach, surf fishing is an accepted and very popular brand of marine angling. In northeast Florida, though, surf fishing isn't something every father teaches his kids (though it probably should be). In fact, many of the basics of surf fishing are completely foreign to area residents.

The surf intimidates some anglers because of the sheer size of the area available for fishing. A fisherman accustomed to casting around creek mouths, oyster bars, and pier pilings can be hard pressed to "read" the surf along a 10-mile beach to pinpoint prime spots.

For such fishermen it's important to understand that the surf holds a multitude of sportfish—from palm-size whiting, spots, and croakers; to mid-size flounder, Spanish mackerel, redfish, black drum, and bluefish; to big and fast citizens such as kingfish, cobia, sharks, outsize crevalle, and tarpon. All these species are migratory, and are available in the surf seasonally in different northeast Florida locales. Moreover, they have greatly varying habits, food preferences, etc. Thus a case can be made that it's almost impossible to fish incorrectly in the First Coast surf because, for one species or another, at the right time of year, just about any given beach spot can yield a good catch.

Still, as in all types of fishing, there are tips, tricks and shortcuts to northeast Florida surf angling success.

The most important part of beach fishing is choosing the right place to cast a lure or bait. An endless beach to your eye may all look the same. But to fish swimming parallel to it, the surf floor is a different place indeed. One of the keys to locating fish in the surf

Florida's First Coast has many miles of open, undeveloped beaches—and plenty of fish. (BOB MCNALLY)

is akin to finding hot spots for fish elsewhere in the offshore and inshore worlds. It's a pretty good bet that a surf area different from the surrounding beach will attract and hold fish. For instance, a subtle "point" of land jutting out along a beach almost always attracts fish and makes a prime surf casting spot. Few prominent, natural "points" exist in northeast Florida. But wherever there is an inlet, a point occurs on the beach just north and south of the cut, offering excellent surf fishing. One outstanding example is the beach just north of the St. Augustine Inlet—certainly one of the best surf fishing spots on the First Coast.

A beach area possessing large rocks, (like that found near Washington Rocks State Gardens south of Matanzas Inlet) or different bottom make-up than the surrounding region, typically offers superb surf fishing. These places have subtle, but important differences. For example, if a beach is made mostly of powder sand, but one area has an abundance of shells, that location will likely attract coast-running sportfish. One spot on the beach bearing a hard rock bottom nearshore may also make a region more appealing to fish. These places are especially productive when they're found in extensive beach areas that, otherwise, display no well-defined spot to attract and hold surf fish.

Man-made objects also form beach "structure" that attracts fish. Piers and riprap can be outstanding surf fishing sites. Any "break" or change in a beach or surf line also is noteworthy. Out-flow or intake "pipe," for example, can attract tremendous numbers of fish. The "pipeline" at Fernandina Beach, for example, is one of the best and most famous surf fishing spots in northeast Florida because it consistently offers good spring through fall sea trout, redfish, flounder, and jack fishing. A bit farther north are the jetties at the south side of Fernandina Inlet. On those jetties is a public fishing pier, which is accessed through Fort Clinch State Park. The beaches just south and north of the jetties and pier are outstanding surf fishing

spots for flounder, redfish, bluefish, jacks, Spanish mackerel, and marine panfish. The beach north and west of the jetties that extends below the overlook of Fort Clinch is prime for surf fishing, too. It's one of the best places I know for flounder and shark. Beach areas around northeast Florida inlets, sounds, and river mouths can offer terrific fishing. The mix of tide, current, and wave action, as well as the freshwater-saltwater exchange, attracts many marine species.

Beaches adjacent to inlet jetties are among the most unique and offer the best surf fishing. Many species of marine fish migrate parallel to the beach. Thus, an inlet jetty that extends far into the sea interrupts the usual path of sportfish. A man-made obstruction that migrating surf fish run into, jetties frequently hold or "jam" fish near the beach, like the south rocks at the St. Johns River mouth. Such "jams" also contain undulating bottoms due to currents the jetties create, and these sandbars and holes attract baitfish and sportfish.

Be observant when fishing the surf. Often, subtle factors are revealed that may draw fish within casting range of beach anglers. Any difference in water color along the surf deserves attention. The color change is caused by "something"—tide, current flow, sandbars—and it may hold surf fish. Likewise, watch for unusual tide rips or indications of abnormal currents along the beach. These things don't happen by accident, and they can attract sportfish. At Matanzas Inlet, a number of small, shifting sandbars act like fish-holding magnets, especially during falling tides. There's also a submerged, barely visible rock pile right in the middle of the inlet that's as sure a bet for catching redfish and sheepshead from the beach as any place I've ever fished. Only during the very lowest tides is the rock pile barely visible, but the fish know its there, and it's never failed to yield for friends and me when we cast to it. Matanzas Inlet sandbars, though, are easy to spot, and live mullet, shrimp, and jigs bounced

around them can yield anything from pompano in summer to bluefish in winter.

Watch for baitfish pods as they move along the beach because, simply, where there is food there is gamefish. Sometimes the ocean surface will ripple or appear "nervous" as a bait school moves along. At other times, bait, like mullet, can be seen jumping. Frequently, a pod of bait will appear as a dark ball the size of a car in clear surf water. In the warm months, menhaden (locally called pogies) often appear like a ball and are a major draw for most coast-cruising gamefish.

One morning some years ago while camping at Hannah Park with my wife, Chris, we arose early and walked to the beach. Hannah Park is located near Mayport, right on the coast just south of the mouth of the St. Johns River. The May sun was barely above the ocean and we were enjoying a quiet moment of calm water and low-flying pelicans. In fact, the pelicans were what first brought my attention to the tight school of menhaden boiling the water's surface only scant feet from the beach sand. Two or three pelicans dove into the water, and that's when I spotted the dark "ball" of menhaden, and the huge boils from feeding gamefish around them.

In a flash I was back to our tent and car, quickly retrieved a couple of rods, and in our first two casts with jigs we hooked up. I beached a 4-pound jack crevalle and Chris landed a 2-pound Spanish mackerel. During the next hour we landed about a dozen fish, including several more Spanish mackerel and a good 3-pound bluefish. Then the sun grew hot, the wind came up, and the sportfish disappeared. But the lesson serves as a good one for surf fishermen to watch for beach bait pods, and to be at the water's edge at first light—at least in summer.

Sometimes baitfish can't be seen. But diving birds and rolling porpoises indicate that bait is nearby, and that should always draw casts from surf fishermen. There are certain places

81

that seem to habitually attract and hold baitfish, and the south end of Amelia Island at Nassau Sound is one such spot. There are a series of undulating and constantly moving sandbars there and, for whatever reason, bait and gamefish frequent the area. Redfish, black drum, bluefish, flounder, whiting, and others are common catches there, as well as at the north tip of Little Talbot Island, which is at the south-side of Nassau Sound.

In angling, the most overlooked places to catch fish are often the best. And like the local lake, surf sportfish frequently relate to bottom structure that is not readily discernible to the average angler's eye. Since beach anglers can't use a fathometer to learn where the best "holes" and surf structures are located, anglers must rely on their eyes to tell them where prime fishing places are found. This is called "reading the surf," and it is among the most important and refined skills of First Coast beach anglers.

The whole key is learning how to look at water to determine where it's deep and where it's shallow. This is important because the better fishing usually lies in deeper areas. In many beach regions there is a trough or swash channel created by wave action. This trough or beach slough can change location and depth weekly, according to wind, tide, and season. As a rule, look for an offshore sandbar to locate these troughs. The incoming wave action will break over this bar, so there will be whitewater on it. Then, on the land side of the bar, the water will be deeper, so waves flatten and whitewater disappears until the waves strike the beach. This identifies a slough or swash channel between the sandbar and the beach, and this is where big fish hold.

Other hot spots for surf fishermen are offshore run-outs, which are cuts or passes through sandbars. These are the accesses or underway highways that allow gamefish to pass through the shallow offshore bars to dine in the deep sloughs or swash channels

near beaches. These run-outs can be found in much the same way that off-shore bars are located: by observing wave action and the color of surf water (with polarized sunglasses)—especially at low tide.

One misconception about surf fishing is that anglers must cast 300 feet to reach far offshore sloughs in order to catch fish. While distance casting is needed in some coastal areas for some species of fish, along the First Coast casts of 150 feet or less are all that are necessary to reach the best fishing places.

Virtually any type tackle can be used effectively in the northeast Florida surf. Even ultralight spinning gear can be used to cast lures and baits for bluefish, Spanish mackerel, and numerous marine panfish such as pompano, whiting, and croakers. A standard 7-foot medium-action spinning rod, and a reel holding 250 yards of 10-pound-test line will allow a surf fisherman to enjoy a great deal of sport. Still, there are times when surf fishermen must make long casts, and that's when a specialized 9- to 10-foot surf rod, having a quick action with plenty of backbone, is greatly appreciated. The rod should have large guides to allow easy flow of line through them for distance casts. A large-spool spinning reel also helps an angler get extra casting distance.

A wide variety of lures and natural baits can be used effectively in the First Coast surf. Productive lures run the gamut from surface plugs to jigs and heavy spoons. In fact, almost any lure that works in other types of saltwater fishing can be used in the surf.

Many different live and dead natural baits also work well for beach fishermen. Shrimp, mullet, menhaden, ballyhoo, squid, and fiddler crabs score well on surf sportfish. Most natural baits should be fished on the bottom with a simple sliding sinker, fish-finder rig. A pyramid-style sinker heavy enough to keep the bait in proper position on the surf floor is most practical.

When lures are used, beach anglers

hold their rods and reels during the cast-and-retrieve sequence. But when natural bait is employed, rods can be set down until a fish takes. Naturally, the more baits set out with different rods along a beach area, the more likely a strike. But wise surf fishermen never lay their expensive tackle in the sand, which can ruin the gear. Instead, they use a surf or sand spike, which is a rod holder that's easy to make from PVC pipe.

A 3-foot section of 3-inch diameter PVC pipe is used. One end of the PVC is cut at an acute angle with a saw to sharpen it, which allows easy insertion of the pipe in sand. About 1 foot from the opposite end of the PVC pipe a hole is drilled through the center, and a stainless steel bolt with nut is fitted through. This acts as a rod-butt stop when the surf rod is positioned in PVC pipe during fishing. A file can be used to round the edges of the PVC end so it doesn't scar fishing rods or their handles. Such sand spikes are quick and inexpensive to make, and they're impervious to saltwater. Thus, a number of rods with natural baits can be set out along a beach area, which maximizes an angler's chances to catch fish.

Spring and fall are peak times for surf action in the northeast. Summer is good, too, especially for tasty panfish such as croakers and pompano. Winter fishing is cold sport, but for hardy souls bluefish and whiting can be abundant, and big ones are available, especially in December and January.

For every First Coast surf fisherman, there is a season. ■

Make it Snappy, Group!

by Capt. Frank Bolin

After two months fishing the backwaters for trout, redfish, and flounder, Al Zamba was ready for a change. Zamba suggested that the time was right to fish the bottom for big grouper and snapper around the nearshore wrecks and reefs. Richard and Kenny Martin and I took the bait as Al described dropping live pinfish down to 20-pound-class grouper and snapper.

We put our plan together Wednesday afternoon. A cold front was predicted to arrive Friday, so Thursday seemed like a good bet. Traditionally, the day before a front passes is the best time for winter bottom fishing off the St. Augustine–Matanzas Inlet area. Kenny and I tackled the chore of catching pinfish, while Al and Richard tied bottom rigs.

Boarding Al's 23-foot *Kno-Better* early Thursday, we brimmed with excitement. With three dozen frisky pinfish in the livewell, we cleared the inlet and headed for our first destination, the Inner Plane Culverts. Pulling up, we quickly "jugged" the spot with a marker buoy. We anchored upcurrent to position the boat over the structure. On Richard's first drop, his rod bent double when a sow snapper inhaled the bait. Time flew for the next two hours as we hooked, fought, landed, and lost red snapper and gray grouper.

Flexibility is the key to getting in on the bite during the winter months. Strong winds and large seas often combine to make ocean fishing impossible from late December until February. Not only do the fish turn on the day before a front, it is also the most comfortable time to fish. Light southerly winds make running and anchoring easier.

Before heading offshore, we map

Ken Martin took this 27-pound genuine red snapper in 80 feet of water. (FRANK BOLIN)

out the spots we plan to fish. Our standard practice is to run out to numbers located in 80 to 90 feet of water and fish our way back to the inlet. This method lets us drop bait on as many as 10 spots and still get back before dark.

Al and I fish together often enough to experiment with new ways to make less work for ourselves. When bottom fishing, a good bottom machine is essential, preferably a color scope. We also carry a variety of marker jugs with different lengths of line to drop in different depths of water. A jug with 65 feet of line dropped in 60 feet of water is a more accurate mark than a jug with 80 or 90 feet of line.

I hardly ever drift a spot, because it scatters the fish. Snapper are noted for breaking from the school to follow drifted baits. Instead, position the boat so the bait drops directly

to the fish marked on the bottom machine.

Fishing for big grouper and snapper requires substantial gear. No wimpy rods or soft action tips allowed! When a snapper or grouper feels the hook, its first reaction is to head immediately for cover. A rod with backbone is necessary to handle the fish. Al and I use stiff, 40- to 80-pound-class rods with conventional guides, as do other local captains such as Bill Kerr, who runs *Bacchus*, and Bob Raduns, *Island Bait*'s operator.

The reel we commonly use for live-bait bottom bumping is the Penn 4/0, model 113H, spooled with 60-pound-test line. A standard star drag is fine, because we "hammer" it down as tight as it will go. These fish need to be muscled away from the structure quickly. One slip or pull of drag usually results in lost fish.

Making a live-bait rig is simple. Use either a figure-8 (two-wrap hangmans) or an improved clinch knot for all connections. First, tie the fishing line to a 1/0 ball-bearing swivel. Next, tie a short (18-inch) piece of 80-pound monofilament to the other end of the swivel. Thread this short length through an egg sinker of 4 to 8 ounces. Tie the line with the sinker to another 1/0 swivel. Rigging the sinker this way prevents it from riding up the fishing line on the drop. Finish off the rig by tying a 6- to 8-foot length of 80- or 100-pound-test monofilament to the swivel. Attach a strong live-bait hook to the business end of the leader.

A variety of hooks are good for live baiting. The most popular are forged Mustad hooks, models 531, 9175 SS, and 3467. Recommended hook size is 7/0 or 8/0 for the 531 and 9175 SS. Use size 1 with the 3467 series for smaller live baits.

All types of live baits will entice

grouper or snapper. The best live bait is a 4- to 6-inch pinfish. Live mullet, menhaden, cigar minnows, and grunts also produce fish. If you cannot catch live bait inshore, try using a feather rig to catch cigar minnows, threadfin herring, or Boston mackerel. Frank Timmons, captain of a local head boat, employs this technique with superb results.

If you get the time, come to St. Augustine and drop down a "livie." If you are lucky, a 20-pound gray grouper or sow snapper will put a bend in your rod and give you a workout. ∎

Local Experts

Some captains specifically target bottom from St. Augustine down to Matanzas Inlet. Call one of the following for more information or to book a trip.

Captain Bill Kerr, *Bacchus*, Camachee Cove Charters, (904) 825-1971

Captain Al Zamba, *Kno-Better*, Lion Charters, (904) 471-1841

Captain Bob Raduns, *Island Bait*, Island Bait Charters, (904) 829-6842

Captain Frank Timmons, *Sea Love II*, Sea Love Charters, (904) 824-3328

Official Artificials

The Ancient City Game Fish Association sets out artificial reefs that are proven fish attractors. Most of the local bait and tackle shops carry free maps of the reefs and wrecks, which include loran numbers. Some popular spots, all within 14 miles of the St. Augustine sea buoy, are listed below.

Inner Plane Culverts: 44873.4/ 61969.9

St. Augustine Shipwreck: 44818.8/ 61962.5

Pop Warner: 44960.0/62008.8

Nine Mile North: 44952.8/ 62025.5

Hoos On First?

by Herb Allen

Called "the fastest animal with fins" and "the poor man's marlin," the wahoo seems finally to have "arrived" in the high society of offshore anglers.

Until recently, the hoo was either a surprise or an added bonus for those trolling blue waters for billfish. Able to attain speeds of 50 to 60 miles per hour, the wahoo is normally caught on heavy gear designed to winch in blue marlin weighing 500 pounds or more. While the wahoo is known to grow to 150 pounds and heavier, most of those caught in tournaments or by accident will scale in the 20- to 40-pound range. When pitted against 50- to 130-pound tackle, the resulting "contest" is similar to matching a jalopy and a bulldozer in a demolition derby, the San Francisco 49ers against the Little Sisters of the Poor on the gridiron, or Hulk Hogan in a best two out of three falls rasslin' match with Pee Wee Herman.

Don't be surprised to see a mania for wahoo spread in coming years, especially in areas where marlin and sailfish have been severely depleted by longliners.

A member of the Scombridae tribe, the wahoo is related to various types of mackerel and is found in temperate waters throughout the world.

In recent years a wahoo constituency has blossomed in the Jacksonville/St. Augustine area, the Florida panhandle, off Louisiana and Texas, and in the Carolinas. They've always been popular throughout the Bahamas, California, Mexico, Florida's lower east coast, Hawaii, and Bermuda.

Although most offshore fishing tournaments include a wahoo division, there are only three annual events we're aware of that specifically target this speedster. All are held in Bimini during November and early December.

On Bimini, Capt. Bob Smith, who operates the *Miss Bonita II*, a 41-foot Hatteras, thinks that wahoo, pound-for-pound, are among the greatest of all saltwater challenges. He, more than any other person, has introduced the slugger as a viable alternative to billfish.

During his five decades of guiding sportfishermen, Smith has learned that the best months for wahoo are from mid-October through the end of March.

He prefers fishing an area from "The Pines" to north of the concrete ship where drop-offs from 150 to 400 feet are recorded. Fish bite better, Smith has found, when the water is clear and inky blue, and the tide is running either in or out.

The veteran charterboat skipper uses three lines when fishing for wahoo, on the theory that three are easier to control than four or five when turning sharply.

Ballyhoo with skirts are his preferred bait. The color of the skirt is unimportant, he says, because "all the fish sees are bubbles."

Smith's customers use his custom rods fitted with Fin-Nor 9/0 reels. His setup includes two lines running from the fighting chair and a third from either a port or starboard outrigger.

When trolling at about 10 knots, Smith will run his farthest line at about 225 feet back, while his chair lines will be positioned 150 and 75 feet behind the boat. The line at 150 feet will be fished three-feet deep, while the 75-foot line is weighted to run 15 feet beneath the surface. Generally, he uses wire lines of 50-pound test from the chair.

Don Strom of Boca Raton, president of Strom Engineering Company of Minneapolis, Chicago, Denver, and Tampa, probably has the highest percentage of first-place finishes in international wahoo fishing competitions than anyone. He has a few tricks of his own when going after this metallic or electric blue beauty with the prominent "tiger stripes" down its sides.

For one thing, he'll usually be seen trolling at a faster clip than anyone else in a tournament—11 to 13 knots, depending upon sea conditions. "From 70 to 80 percent of the wahoo I catch are taken on deep lines," says Strom. Because of this, the engineer/angler takes particular pains to see they are rigged just right. From the 80-pound Monel wire line spooled onto either an International or 9/0 Senator reel, he'll attach either one or two (depending upon the sea conditions and anticipated speed) 16-ounce cigar-shaped lead weights, a 30-foot shock cord made of 250 to 300-pound monofiliment line, a cable leader, and then his large, Tony Acetta Pet spoon. Ahead of the spoon he's likely to string a dozen or so beads of various colors that he buys in bulk at hobby shops.

Prior to a tournament, Strom will stretch his shock cords between two trees or dock posts for three days so they "coil up nice."

He'll usually use a black/red Moldcraft skirt that partially covers the spoon and, when using a ballyhoo bait

in conjunction with the rig, he'll protect it against wear and tear with Hawaiian Eye. He'll also up his odds by employing a trailing hook that is buried in the bait's tail.

The two deep lines, which get most of the action, will be sent back to the fourth or fifth wave, while his two outrigger lines "are so far back that I need binoculars to see if I've picked up weeds."

Before entering a tournament, Strom will have a dozen rigs made up for quick changes, as well as backup rods in case problems are encountered with those being used.

After finding fish, the angler will frequently switch to Plan B by taking in one of his tag lines so shorter turns can be made without fouling.

Plan C calls for slower trolling. "I usually troll fast because I want the fish to strike out of anger, instead of waiting for them to get hungry," said the skipper of the *Foxy Lady*, a 54-foot Boca Raton-based Striker that has seen action in many tournaments in Florida and throughout the Bahamas.

When getting his fish close-in to the transom, Strom recommends bringing it into the boat quickly. "This is important because of the wahoo's habit of violently shaking its head, which often results in it throwing the hook at the last minute," he explains. "Also, the longer you leave a fish in the water, the more chance it has of being mutilated by another wahoo or shark."

When fishing Bimini waters, Strom has found lots of fish on the island's lee, between Bimini and Sandy Cay. He also fishes Picket Rock and at Great Issac all the way to the bend and east to the pocket on the north side of the reef.

Drags on his Penn reels will be set lightly, at about three or four pounds. "We adjust our drags to the speed of the boat and will fine tune them while underway," said Strom.

When he feels a strike, the veteran keeps his boat running at between 11 and 13 knots for a spell before slowing down, to assure that the fish is solidly hooked.

While many offshore anglers along Florida's Atlantic coast or in the Gulf of Mexico may not cotton to Strom's heavy-tackle techniques, he has won the majority of wahoo tournaments he has entered and has never placed lower than fourth during the past 15 years.

While most wahoo-catching techniques involve trolling, some anglers have experimented with—and even developed—techniques for catching them on light tackle from an anchored boat, especially in those rare areas where schooling wahoo can be found on the surface, such as off St. Augustine, Key West, and the Marquesas.

When they find good structure, anglers start chumming. Once the wahoo rise to the surface, they cast artificials on 8- to 12-pound-test tackle. Just make sure that a quick-release anchoring system with a buoy line is aboard because, chances are, the hooked fish will have to be followed lest he dump the reel.

Many are now using downriggers or planers instead of lead weights and wire lines to get baits or lures down to the wahoo's strike zone. In such places as Australia, the Rapala, Bomber, and other minnow-type lures seem to be as popular as rigged baits, spoons or feathers. Down Under fishermen seem to prefer trolling at slower speeds than their counterparts in America and the Bahamas.

Hard metal jigs, such as the Newell Caster and the Ugly Jig, are often used to catch wahoo on head boats operating off the California coast, where an offshore trip of 400 miles or more is required to reach prime wahoo habitat. In Cabo San Lucas and other Mexican hot spots, live 4-inch anchovies are used.

Fishermen are often creatures of habit. But, wouldn't it be interesting to experiment and see if wahoo in Florida will take bass plugs as they do in Australia, or if a jig in Bimini waters might be as productive as the Pet spoon?

■

Port Canaveral Area Highlights

Port Canaveral offers many different types of fishing, including party boats for those who like to go offshore to fish for red snapper, grouper, triggerfish and an assortment of bottom dwellers. Port Canaveral has long been famous for its fine fleet of party boats and the excellent fishing they provide. Within the same port there is another type of fishing that has really captured the imagination of anglers from all over the world. With a fleet of offshore trolling boats numbering about 40, the Port Canaveral striking fish charters are second to none. Whether you want to make trips 120 miles offshore or fish the Gulf Stream in the 30- to 40-mile range, this is truly a prolific area that offers such fish as marlin, sailfish, wahoo, yellowfin tuna, blackfin tuna, kingfish, dolphin, and many other species in great abundance.

Fishing from the surf or 20 miles offshore, Port Canaveral is also a wonderful experience. This area is noted for the great cobia runs each year, along with tarpon, jack crevalle, kingfish, snook, Spanish mackerel and many, many more. Tarpon from 80 to 100 pounds are caught outside the surfline, and cobia in the 40- to 50-pound range are not uncommon to anglers using boats.

At the mouth of Port Canaveral is an area known as Jetty Park, which, along with its wonderful camping facilities and great beach, offers some of the best inshore fishing anywhere. Snook, sheepshead, bluefish, whiting, and other species are waiting to be caught.

Moving farther south you go back inside to the Indian and Banana Rivers and continue the excellent fishing found in the Merritt Island and Cocoa Beach areas. When you reach a landmark known as Dragon Point, the Indian and Banana Rivers merge and become the Indian River. From this point south the Indian River offers a variety of great fishing for trout, jack, redfish, ladyfish, and snook.

All area codes 407 except where otherwise noted.

Marinas
Harbor Towne Marina—267-6649
Kennedy Point Yacht Club and Marina—383-0280
Titusville Municipal Marina—269-7255
Westland Marine—267-1667
Abby Marina—453-0160
Lake Poinsett Marina—636-0045
Cape Marina at Point Canaveral—783-8410
Harbor Square Marina—453-2464
Indian Cove Marina—452-8540

Island Point Marina—452-0541
Jay's Harbor Lights Marina—453-6354
Mariner Square Marina—639-4228
Sunrise Marina—783-9535
Orange Cove Marina—783-8349
Tingley's Marina—452-0504
Whitly Marina—632-5445
Anchorage Yacht Basin—773-3620
Diamond 99 Marina—254-1490
Indian Harbour Marina—773-2468
Eau Gallie Yacht Basin—254-1786
Intracoastal Marina—725-0090
Melbourne Harbor Marina—725-9054
Pineda Point Marina—254-4199
Eau Gallie Yacht Club—773-2600
Palm Bay Marina—723-0851
Pelican Harbor Marina—725-4040
Bill's Discount Marina—724-5153
Miner's Marina Inc.—664-8500

Bait and Tackle Shops
Mim's Bait and Tackle—259-0600
Fish Tales and Surf Shop-267-1841
D & M Gun World—267-6480
The Fly Fisherman—267-0348
Hole 'n' The Wall Bait & Tackle—631-3268
Saltwater Concepts—784-9700
Terri's Tackle Shop—636-6511
Bwana's Tackle Locker—783-2912
Fishing and Diving Center—783-3477
Captain Jack's Tackle & Marine Supply—783-3694
Doc's Bait House—452-2288
Marty's Bait—868-0980
Goldstar Bait & Tackle—724-2566
Goode's Outdoor Shop—723-4751
Palm Bay Bait & Tackle—725-8819
Southland Bait & Tackle—722-3631
Pat's Bait & Tackle—722-9192
Satellite Bait & Tackle—773-6611
Surf Side Bait & Tackle—768-7929
Valkaria Discount Tackle & Marine—984-5385
Whitey's Bait & Tackle—724-1440
Wildcat Bait & Tackle—725-0370

Fish Camps
Lone Cabbage Fish Camp: 8199 Highway 520, Cocoa FL 32754; 268-2277
Camp Holly: 6901 W. Highway 192, Melbourne FL 32904; 723-2179
Honest John's Fish Camp: 750 Mullet Creek Rd. Melbourne FL 32951; 727-2923

(continued on page 87)

Poinsett Lodge Lake: Poinsett Rd. Melbourne FL 32926; 636-0045

Boat Ramps

Six Mile Creek, SR 46, Mims—one ramp

Port St. John Boat Ramp, US 1, Port St. John—two ramps

Marina Park, Marina Rd., Titusville—one ramp

Merritt Island National Wildlife Refuge, SR 3, Haulover Canal Recreational Center—one ramp

Ports End, Mullet Rd., Port Canaveral—one ramp

Central Park, Flounder St., Port Canaveral—three ramps

James G. Bourbeau Park, 8 miles west of US 11 on SR 520, Cocoa—three ramps

McFarland Park, Coquina Dr. and River Rd.—dock, one ramp

Constitution Bicentennial Park, SR 520, Cocoa Beach—two ramps

Ramp Road Park, 300 Ramp Rd., Cocoa Beach—two ramps

Kelly Park, 2550 N. Banana River Dr., Merritt Island—one ramp

Eau Gallie Causeway Park, SR 510, Melbourne—two ramps

Pollack Park, Main St., Palm Bay—one ramp

Front St. Park, 2200 S. Front St., Melbourne—one ramp

Coconut Point Park, A1A, Melbourne Beach—one ramp

Long Point Park, 9200 S. Highway A1A, Melbourne Beach—one ramp

First St. Boat Ramp, 4580 1st St., Grant—one ramp

Fishing Piers

Veterans Memorial Fishing Pier, SR 406, Titusville

Melbourne Beach Fishing Pier, Ocean Ave. South of Melbourne Causeway

Lee Wenner Park, SR 520, Cocoa—three piers

Cocoa Beach Pier, 401 Meade Ave., Cocoa Beach

Eau Gallie Fishing Pier, Mainland, Melbourne

Sebastian Inlet State Recreation Area, A1A, Melbourne Beach

MATANZAS RIVER TO MOSQUITO LAGOON

LAND CONFIGURATION AND WATER DEPTH

The coast along this section is a continuation of the one described in the previous maps. The land is low and nearly flat. The ocean shore is straight and interrupted only by a few inlets.

Matanzas River, located in the upper corner of this map, is a narrow, shallow, coastal lagoon draining a small section of the interior. Originally it emptied directly into the sea through the Matanzas Inlet, but later it was connected to Halifax Creek by a 7-mile-long canal to become part of the Intracoastal Waterway. Just south of Flagler Beach, the width of Halifax Creek suddenly broadens from several yards to nearly a mile and becomes Halifax River, a brackish and saltwater lagoon 20 miles long. Near Ponce de Leon Inlet the open watercourse of the Halifax River is interrupted by numerous closely spaced saltmarsh islands and becomes, in effect, a series of narrow, meandering waterways, locally called creeks. Although most of these creeks are very shallow, some are as much as 16 to 21 feet deep. South of Ponce de Leon Inlet this system of saltmarshes and tidal creeks broadens to become over 2 miles wide. This section is

called Mosquito Lagoon, even though it is still part of the Halifax River.

The most northerly occurring mangroves along the east coast are found within Mosquito Lagoon. Mangroves belong to a family of trees capable of living in saltwater as well as freshwater and even on dry land. They occur in tropical and semitropical areas around the world, their distribution being limited by killing frosts. As we proceed southward along the coast, mangroves appear near New Smyrna Beach mostly as scattered individuals or small clumps of bushlike trees among the cord grasses and rushes of the saltmarsh. Mangroves here are closely associated with certain marsh plants, which serve to hold sediments in place until the young trees become established. Farther south, however, where mangroves are the principal colonizing plants and dominate the shallow, protected coastal areas, they shield the shore from excessive erosion and, in fact, aid in building up the land. They do this by trapping sediments in a maze of prop roots that look like bracing stilts. These sediments slowly build up until eventually they rise above the high tide line. Then follows a succession of land plants that, in time and under favorable conditions, lead to the formation of a tropical forest.

For over 70 miles, from Matanzas Inlet to False Cape, just north of Cape Canaveral, the beach is straight and wide. Only Ponce de Leon Inlet, a narrow passage, breaks its continuity. For the most part, the beach is composed of white quartz sand, which, over the ages, has been carried from Georgia and the Carolinas by southward flowing shore currents. Most of east Florida's beaches lie upon rocky limestone deposits that themselves provide little quartz sand when decomposed by natural processes. Outcroppings of coquina, a rock formed of limestone-cemented shells appear frequently between Marineland and Flagler Beach. Detached blocks of coquina, as well as loose shell materials, are found on the beaches near these outcroppings. Enough shell material is mixed with the sand here to give the beach a golden cast. At Daytona Beach, the amount of shell diminishes, resulting in beach that is chiefly comprised of fine sand that packs hard, particularly when moist. This hard-packed sand and the width of the beach, as well as its gentle slope, make the beach suitable for auto racing.

The sea floor off this section is mostly of sand or sand-shell mixture. Rocky outcroppings occur at a few places in the surf. Some 10 miles or more seaward such outcroppings become a prominent feature of the sea floor. These offshore outcroppings tend to lie more or less in bands paralleling the 100-fathom contour. Rising only a few inches in some spots, several feet in others, and occasionally up to 25 feet, these areas are important gathering places for many kinds of fishes.

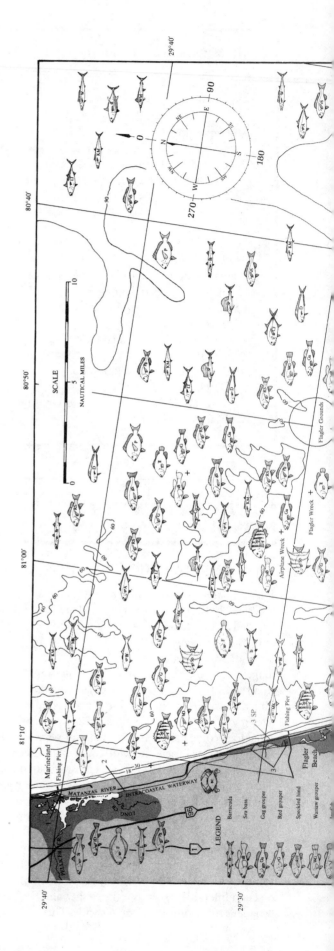

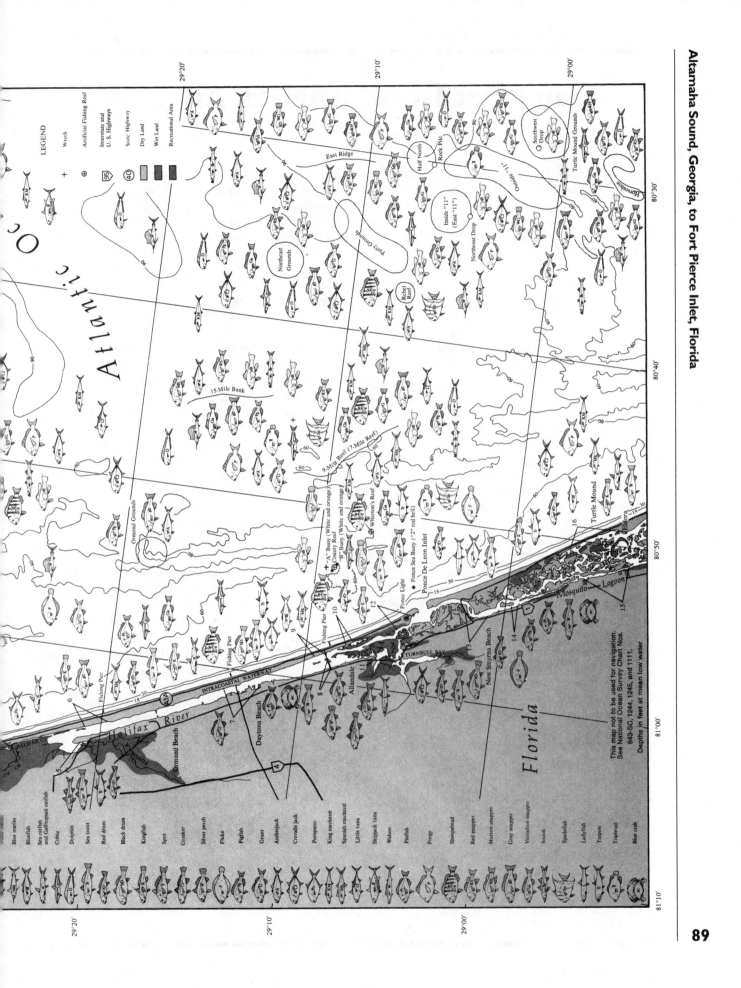

LEGEND

+	Wreck
⊕	Artificial Fishing Reef
95	Interstate and U. S. Highways
40	State Highway
	Dry Land
	Wet Land
	Recreational Area

Atlantic Oc

Atlantic O

Florida

Halifax River

Intracoastal Waterway

Daytona Beach

Ormond Beach

Ponce De Leon Inlet

Ponce Light

New Smyrna Beach

Turnbull Bay

Allandale

Mosquito Lagoon

Turtle Mound

Eldora

Fishing Pier

9-Mile Reef (7-Mile Reef)

15-Mile Bank

Ormond Grounds

Northeast Grounds

Party Grounds

East Ridge

Rebel Reef

Whirton's Reef

County Reef

"A" Buoy (White and orange)

"B" Buoy (White and orange)

Ponce Sea Buoy ("2" red bell)

Rock Pile

Half North

Inside "11"

(East "11")

Outside "11"

Northeast Drop

Southwest Drop

Turtle Mound Grounds

This map not to be used for navigation. See National Ocean Survey Chart Nos. 843-SC, 1244, 1245, and 1111. Depths in feet at mean low water

Blue marlin
Bluefish
Sea catfish and Gafftopsail catfish
Cobia
Dolphin
Sea trout
Red drum
Black drum
Kingfish
Spot
Croaker
Silver perch
Fluke
Pigfish
Grunt
Amberjack
Crevalle jack
Pompano
King mackerel
Spanish mackerel
Little tuna
Skipjack tuna
Wahoo
Pinfish
Porgy
Sheepshead
Red snapper
Mutton snapper
Gray snapper
Vermilion snapper
Snook
Spadefish
Ladyfish
Tarpon
Tripletail
Blue crab

89

Indian River Draws Anglers' Attention

by Herb Allen

Florida's anglers are ignoring some fine fishing prospects by failing to explore Florida's east coast between Daytona Beach and Titusville in general, and the Indian River in particular.

It had been a spell since we'd last had an opportunity to test these waters, so it was with more than a little enthusiasm that we hooked up with Kent Gibbens for a two-day river safari seeking trout, redfish, snook, tarpon, and anything else that couldn't resist our Cotee Jig and Spoon offerings.

Gibbens, who has plied these waters for nearly 50 years, is a former school teacher, a custom rod maker, fishing guide, and holder of three IGFA records including a 14-pound saltwater trout on 12-pound-test line; an 8-pound, 4-ounce sea trout on 6-pound test; and a burly 10-pound, 4-ounce redfish on 4-pound line. He's also a pro staffer for MirrOlure, DOA, and 12-Fathom, and serves on the FCA board of directors.

"Y'all came at the right time," said Gibbens as we loaded into his sleek skiff and headed east toward the Indian's mouth, where we were ambushed by several school-sized reds. These fish were lying along a rocky ledge in 3 feet of water that suddenly dropped off to about 8-foot depths. Our strikes came on a ¼-ounce gold Cotee Spoon which shimmied through the dark-colored water with a sexiness rivaling that of a Tarpon Springs belly dancer.

"I'd like to see if we can find some snook," said Gibbens. He cranked up and headed across the river to where he'd been doing well recently on snook lurking beneath several docks which jutted out into the water. For the linesiders, we switched to the ¼ Cotee Liv'Eye Action Jig with a motor-oil-colored Grub Tail. Our first few casts resulted in a pair of 3-pound trout, another rat red, plus a scrappy jack crevalle in the 4-pound class. Finally, on an outgoing tide, snook action picked up. Before the smoke cleared, we had landed and released about a dozen that would scale between 6 and 10 pounds each.

According to Gibbens, snook fishing here is good year-round. Trout and redfish are also active all year. "As we go into the winter months," he said, "trout tend to school up and hit live pigfish and streamer flies more than anything else. The best months for big, gator trout are from March through May, while those looking for tarpon in the river will probably do best in July and August, or off the beaches during the fall months."

He went on to say that snook in the 5- to 10-pound class are plentiful, and 15- to 20-pound fish are not uncommon. Gibbens prefers a high, outgoing tide for linesiders in the daytime, and fishes around the bridges at night, using jumbo shrimp for bait.

The Indian River provides excellent freshwater opportunities year-round for bass, speckled perch, and bream. "Freshwater, as well as saltwater fishermen, have other nearby hotspots too," said Gibbens. He pointed out that the Indian River is within about 20 miles of the St. Johns River, which is noted for its lunker largemouth, and Lake George, which is becoming famous for its striped bass.

During our trip, we saw many rolling tarpon but couldn't get any to hit. We also spotted numerous otters, manatees, porpoises, and a wide variety of bird life.

We hope to visit this piscatorial mecca again to take another shot at breaking one of Gibbens' records. ∎

Dolphin Are Tops on Florida's Atlantic Coast

by Herb Allen

Though the colorful and speedy dolphin is caught year round in offshore Atlantic and Gulf of Mexico waters, it's during the warmer spring and summer months that it is most bountiful. This is also the time when 80 percent of the saltwater anglers on Florida's Atlantic coast seek them out.

The dolphin isn't listed among prime targets for Florida's west coast contingent because they are often forced to travel 60 miles or more off-shore before reaching productive areas. Conversely, Florida east coasters frequently find this pelagic just 3 to 5 miles off the beach.

When in the mood, a voracious dolphin (also known as mahi mahi or dorado) swats just about anything that crosses its path. Live baits, strip baits, plugs, plastics, jigs, spinners, streamers—you name it and the dolphin will eat it most of the time.

One of the hottest dolphin rigs for trollers consists of a 6- to 8-foot length of 80-pound-test monofilament, a 5/0 to 8/0 hook (for use with 20-pound to 30-pound line), and a silver swivel. Those afraid of hooking kingfish, wahoo, barracuda, or other toothy critters can use wire instead of mono when making up a rig. Anglers using lighter tackle, or who prefer using lighter leaders, may want to drop down to 50-pound test. For hooks, a #3407 Mustad or a #254 Eagle Claw are ideal. Just be sure the hooks are plenty sharp.

With this rig trollers can employ a wide variety of live or strip baits, artificial lures, or combinations of both. Excellent live baits to use for slow trolling or drifting include pilchards, goggleyes and sardines. Strip baits, ballyhoo (baleo), or squid can be used plain or in conjunction with plastic trolling skirts. Green and yellow

When in the mood, a voracious dolphin will hit just about anything that crosses its path. (HERB ALLEN)

or pink and white seem to be preferred colors unless it's a dark, overcast day, in which case reds, blues, blacks, or purples are more productive.

Popular soft plastic lures include Moldcraft's Little Hooker and Little Bird, Dolphin Juniors, and Jelly Bellies.

When in a feeding frenzy, dolphin are likely to hit just about any lure in an angler's tackle box, including bass plugs, jigs of all types, and spinnerbaits. Perhaps the bestseller in hard plastic lures for dolphin is the Rattletrap with the treble hooks replaced with a single.

All types of streamer flies or chuggars will take dolphin that are within a wand waver's casting range.

A final tip: Always have one or two spinning rods rigged and ready for action because a school of dolphin will usually follow a hooked comrade to the boat. ∎

MOSQUITO LAGOON TO EAU GALLIE

HISTORY

In early March of 1513, Juan Ponce de León set out from Puerto Rico to claim what had been reported to be islands lying northward, and perhaps, as legend has it, to find a fountain having power to restore youth and strength to those who bathed in its water. For about two weeks he sailed along the eastern side of what is now the Bahama Islands, crossed the northernmost track sailed by Columbus on his historic 1492 voyage, and continued farther to the northeast. Three days after leaving the Bahamian island chain, he sighted a landfall. He spent a few days sailing along this new coast, looking for a safe harbor. Finding none, he ordered his three vessels to drop anchor off the beach and organized a landing party to put ashore in small boats. There on the sandy beach of what he believed to be a large island, probably near what is now St. Augustine, he conducted a short but solemn ceremony: planting the banner of the King of Spain, intoning in Latin a declaration of possession, and naming the new land *La Florida*. This was a most appropriate name, not only because of the florid vegetation along the shore but also because the discovery was made in the Easter season which, in Spain, is commonly called *Pascua Florida*, or Flowery Easter.

After returning to his ship, Ponce de León sailed north a short distance, then altered his course to the south. As he neared a cape of land on his southward course, strong currents buffeted his ships and impeded his progress, even though the winds were favorable and all the sails set. Ponce de León called this place *Cabo de Corrientes*, Cape of Currents. Subsequent Spanish explorers renamed it *Cabo de Canaveral*, Cape of Reeds. Either name aptly describes what we know today as Cape Canaveral, for not only is the prevailing current, the northward flowing Gulf Stream, strong off this point, but the dominant vegetation in the nearby marsh consists of salt grasses and reeds.

LAND CONFIGURATION AND WATER DEPTH

Cape Canaveral protrudes seaward more than 12 miles from the general trend of the coastline to form the most prominent feature along Florida's east coast. Built up of sand transported along the shore by southward flowing littoral currents, it is the only irregularity to break the otherwise straight line of coast between the St. Johns River and West Palm Beach, a distance of nearly 250 miles.

Cape Canaveral was probably formed over a very long time, as eddies breaking away from the Gulf Stream came close to the land and deflected southward-moving sediments in such a way as to cause them to be deposited offshore. Ocean waves breaking against these accumulated sediments redistributed them, building up a sandbar a few miles away from the mainland, parallel to the coast. As this bar increased in breadth as well as height, it developed into a barrier island, part of what is now Merritt Island. In time, a narrow strip of sand connected the northern end of Merritt Island to the mainland. What had been an open passage of ocean water became a semienclosed lagoon, which is now called Indian River. As more sediments accumulated off Merritt Island, a second bar was formed, which later became another barrier island of which Cape Canaveral is now a part. Again what previously had been a part of the ocean became a coastal lagoon, today's Banana River. Even today a third bar is forming parallel to the coast a few miles southeast of Cape Canaveral. In time this may become still another barrier bar with a coastal lagoon behind it.

Indian River is actually not a river, but a shallow lagoon or bay nearly 120 miles long and averaging less than 2 miles wide. Its average depth is about 5 feet, its greatest depth 17 feet. Indian River is connected with

Banana River by three passages—at its northern end by Banana Creek, at the south end of Merritt Island by a channelway, and, opposite Cape Canaveral, by a narrow, man-made canal. Banana River has almost the same average depth as Indian River. A man-made inlet, Canaveral Cut, connects both "rivers" with the sea. Of the six passages to the sea from Indian River, Canaveral Cut is by far the largest and deepest.

Beneath both rivers and their connecting waterways the bottom is hard and sandy. In some places the bottom is comprised of sandstone; in others, of limestone-cemented shells; in still others, of mud. But by far the most common and important bottom is sand. Extensive beds of turtle grass and other aquatic grasses grow on this generally firm bottom in the shallow water. These aquatic plants provide habitat for species on which local fish feed and produce shelter for the fishes themselves, especially juveniles.

MELBOURNE TO FORT PIERCE INLET

LAND CONFIGURATION AND WATER DEPTH

Indian River, a narrow, shallow saltwater lagoon, continues along this stretch of coast. For 15 miles, from Melbourne to south of Sebastian Inlet, this "river" is an open waterway averaging a mile and a half wide. Its mainland shore is sandy and nearly straight, its oceanside shore rather marshy and irregular. For the 12 miles from Sebastian Inlet to Vero Beach, a series of islands, some dry land and others marshy, reduces the width of this waterway to a half mile. For the 10 miles from Vero Beach to Fort Pierce, the waterway broadens to a little over a mile and both shores become irregular, marshy, and verdant with salt grasses, reeds, and mangroves. Just above Fort Pierce the waterway narrows slightly before broadening to a mile and a half; and again the shores become sandy.

The sandy ocean shore is continuous over the whole of this section except for Sebastian Inlet and Fort Pierce Inlet, both narrow passages cutting through the barrier beach. A break in the rocky reef off Vero Beach has apparently allowed storm waves to scour the sandy beach, creating an embayment a quarter mile deep by 2½ miles long. This is locally called Sea Cove. The beach here slopes so steeply where it meets the sea that depths of 15 to 20 feet are reached within casting distance of shore. Within Sea Cove, depths increase to over 30 feet and become continuous with the progressively deeper offshore water. A great variety of fishes gather here, drawn by a number of attractions, the most obvious being the relatively deep water, rich growth of bottom organisms, and strong tidal currents.

A happy Florida angler hefts a 65-pound amberjack taken inshore from a center-console boat. (HERB ALLEN)

Beginning a few miles south of Sebastian Inlet and continuing all the way to Key West, rocky reefs parallel the ocean shore. A short distance from shore along this stretch of coast are a few sandy shoals, the most important of which are Thomas, Bethel, Capron, and Pierce Shoals. Scattered throughout the continental shelf beyond these shoals are rock and coral outcroppings. These areas, commonly called reefs by fishermen, tend to become more rugged the farther they are from shore.

The Sun and Your Hide *by Vin Sparano*

The way fishing guides look and dress, especially in the warmer tropical climates, has changed a great deal over the years. Many older guides have deep, healthy looking tans. Unfortunately, they also have sagging skin and skin cancers on the backs of their hands, tips of their nose, edges of their ears and any other place that they have left unprotected in the hot sun year after year.

Younger guides now know better. On a recent trip to the Florida Keys, I saw guides with long pants, long-sleeved shirts, hats that protected their ears and neck, and even white cotton gloves as they poled their flats boats. They also coated their skin with sunscreens that blocked out damaging UV (ultraviolet) rays. They are well aware of the constant danger and harm that can come to them from the sun.

Not everyone is aware of this genuine health hazard from the solar system. The National Cancer Institute estimates 600,000 malignancies a year as a direct result of careless exposure to the sun. Of that number, close to 7,000 people will die from malignant melanoma, the most deadly skin cancer.

The sun is the bad guy, causing at least 90 percent of all skin cancers. Fortunately, the sun warns its victims with early symptoms. Those symptoms include those fashionable tans we see around town and which we usually ignore.

The sun produces two different types of UV rays, both harmful to the skin. Beta rays (UVB) can cause skin cancer. Alpha rays (UVA) cause both skin cancer and premature wrinkling of the skin. The easiest and most effective way of protecting yourself from these rays is through the use of a good sunscreen that is rated with a SPF (sun protection factor) of at least 15.

Even though sunscreens boast ratings of SPF 35 and higher, a rating of SPF 15 is all that is necessary for daily use in most cases. With a 15 SPF, a person can stay in the sun 15 times longer than without any protection at all.

Some doctors claim that regular use of an SPF 15 for the first 18 years of life may reduce the risk of skin cancer by 78 percent. For this reason, it's extremely important for parents to remember to keep small children out of direct sunlight, especially between 10:00 A.M. and 3:00 P.M., when the sun is strongest and inflicts most of the damage to skin.

Choose a waterproof SPF 15 sunscreen containing PABA and benzopheno (oxybenzone) to screen ultraviolet rays. Apply it liberally an hour or two before you go out in the sun, and reapply every two or three hours, especially after swimming and sweating. Some newer sunscreens are formulated to last all day, even after swimming. Read the manufacturers' claims carefully and take no chances.

Your skin type is also an important factor. If you're a Type I or II, meaning those with blonde hair, blue eyes, and/or fair skin, you will need more skin protection than others and you should be checked for skin cancer by a physician at least once a year. At the other extreme, is Type V and VI, which includes Middle Easterners, Indians, and Blacks, who will burn only after heavy exposure.

If you spend a lot of time in the sun, you should know about the types of skin cancers and how to detect them early. There are three kinds of skin cancers: basal cell, squamous cell carcinomas, and malignant melanoma.

Basal cell carcinoma is the most common skin cancer (about 80 percent) and is seldom deadly. It usually appears on the neck, head, face, and hands. It may be as small as a pinpoint or as large as an inch. It may also crust and bleed.

Squamous-cell carcinoma is the second most common skin cancer and looks like a raised pink wart. If left untreated, it can spread to other parts of the body.

Malignant melanoma is the least common but most deadly skin cancer. It usually appears quickly on the upper back or legs. It can be brown-black or multi-colored. Malignant melanoma grows fast and spreads to other organs.

If you spend a lot of time in the sun, check your skin regularly. Look at the back of your hands and your face. Look for scaly, rough patches of skin. Are there any white spots or red nodules with scales? If you see anything that looks suspicious, see your doctor. Most of the time, skin cancers are easily and successfully removed.

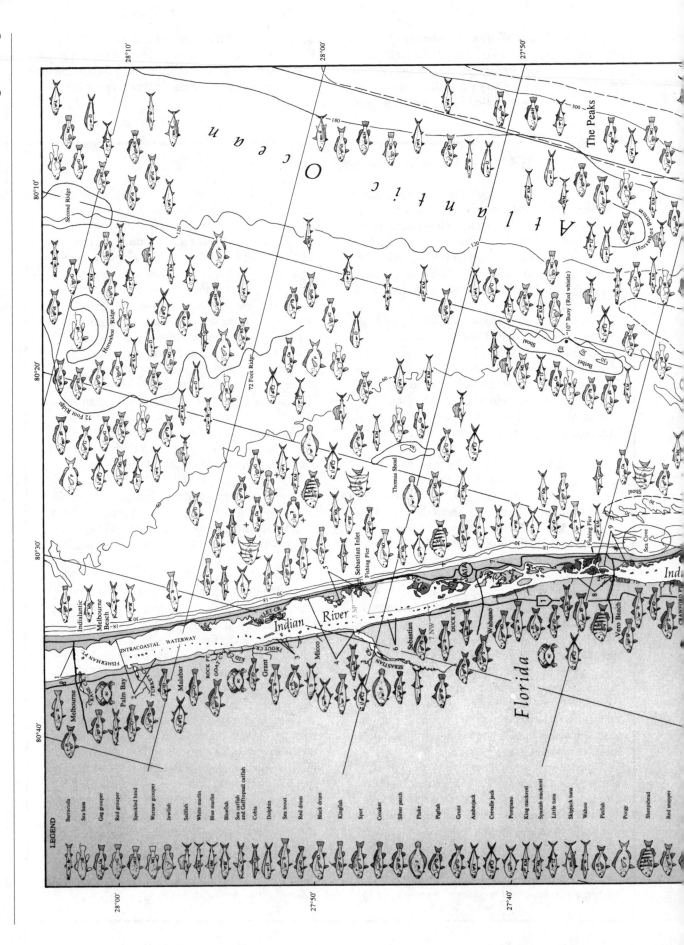

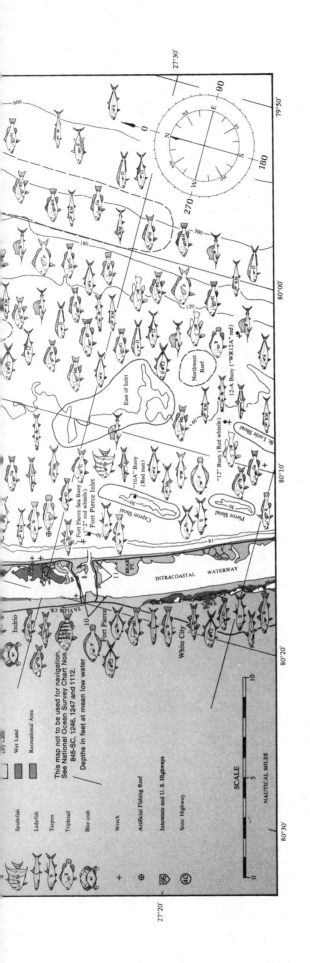

Sea trout can be caught just about anywhere in Florida's bays and backcountry waters. (HERB ALLEN)

Also scattered about the sea floor are wrecks of at least a dozen known vessels. The hulls of these vessels, many of them broken, twisted, and smashed, and the cargoes they carried are as effective as rocky outcroppings in providing shelter for fishes as well as surfaces for the attachment of sessile food organisms. The wreck of the *Amazone*, marked by the 12-A wreck buoy, is particularly well known among anglers as a gathering place for fishes, especially large pelagic species such as sailfish. This 1,300-ton Dutch freighter was torpedoed and sunk in May 1942.

FISHING REGULATIONS

What follows are abstracts of fishing regulations for Georgia and Florida. This information should be used for general purposes only. Regulations are constantly revised, and in some areas, local and federal restrictions apply as well. Because regulations change frequently, and because the regulations themselves are far more detailed than presented here, all anglers should contact the state agencies listed at the beginning and end of this chapter for current regulations, restrictions, and exemptions.

GEORGIA

For a discussion of Georgia's fishing regulations, turn to page 23.

97

FLORIDA

Don't forget that Florida requires anglers to possess a saltwater fishing license. Residents pay $11.50 for 10 days or $13.50 for one year. Non-residents can ante up $16.50 for seven days or $31.50 for one year. The Florida Marine Patrol does check! Call (904) 488-5757 to find out when certain species are out of season and for size and bag limits.

The following license exemptions apply in Florida:

- Any individual under 16 years of age.
- Any Florida resident fishing in saltwater from land or from a structure fixed to the land.
- Any individual fishing from a vessel issued a Vessel Saltwater Fishing License.
- Fishing aboard a vessel that has a valid Saltwater Products License. Only one individual may claim this exemption at any given time.
- Any resident 65 years of age or older.
- Any Florida resident who is a member of the Armed Forces while home on leave for 30 days or less, with valid orders in his/her possession.
- Any individual who has been accepted by the Florida Department of Health and Rehabilitative Services for developmental services or such services as provided as part of a court-decided rehabilitation program involving training in Florida's aquatic resources.
- Any individual fishing from a licensed fishing pier.

A Florida resident who is certified as totally and permanently disabled shall be entitled to receive, without charge from the county tax collector, a permanent saltwater fishing license.

A license is required for taking, attempting to take, or possessing marine fish. These include finfish species as well as marine invertebrates. Examples of finfish are sharks, trout, mackerel, rays, catfish, eels, tarpon, etc. Marine invertebrates include snails, whelks, clams, scallops, shrimp, crab, lobster, sea stars, sea urchins, etc.

The fees collected have been designated by the Legislature to be used specifically for improving and restoring fish habitats, building artificial reefs, researching marine life and its habitats, tightening enforcement, and educating the public about marine resources.

Minimum Size and Other Restrictions

Amberjack * (R): 28″ fork limit; daily bag limit of 3

Black Drum * (R): not less than 14″ or more than 24″ (total length); daily bag limit of 5; cannot possess fish over 24"

Sea Bass: 8″ total length; all sea basses

Billfish: Sailfish, 57″, Blue Marlin, 86″, White Marlin, 62″; daily bag limit of 1; species includes marlin, spearfish, and sailfish; cannot buy or sell

Bluefish: 10″

Bonefish: 18″ total length; daily bag limit of 1; cannot buy or sell; only one in possession

Cobia (Ling): 33″ fork; daily bag limit of 2

Dolphin: daily bag limit of 10; 20″ limit for sale

Red Drum (Redfish)*: not less than 18″ or more than 27″; season closed March, April, May; daily bag limit of 1; cannot buy or sell native redfish

Flounder: 11″

Grouper * (R): 20″ total length; daily bag limit of 5; includes yellowfin, red, black, nassau, gag, yellowmouth, scamp

Jewfish: prohibited harvest

King Mackerel (R): 12″; daily bag limit of 2; bag limit in Gulf-Atlantic fishery reduced when federal waters closed to all harvest

Spanish Mackerel * (R): 12″; daily bag limit of 5

Black Mullet (R): daily bag limit of 50 per vessel or person, whichever is less; mullet is not restricted west of the Ochlockonee River

Permit: no more than 2, 20″ or larger

Pompano *: 10″; sales greater than 20″ prohibited

Shad: daily bag limit of 10; hook and line only

Red Snapper * (R): 13″ total length; daily bag limit of 2; no more than 10 snappers aggregate of all snappers with a bag limit (includes schoolmaster, gray, lane, vermilion, and others)

Schoolmaster * (R): 10″ total length; daily bag limit of 5; see Red Snapper note above

Gray (Mangrove)* (R): 10″ total length; daily bag limit of 5; see Red Snapper note above

Lane * (R): 8″ total length; see Red Snapper note above

Vermilion * (R): 8″ total length; see Red Snapper note above

All other Snapper * (R): 8″ total length; daily bag limit of 10 aggregate of all snapper having a bag limit, includes blackfin, cubera, dog, mahogany, mutton, queen, silk, and yellowtail

Snook *: not less than 24″ or more than 34″; season closed January, February, June, July, and August; daily bag limit of 2; cannot buy or sell; snook stamp required

Tarpon: daily bag limit of 2; cannot buy or sell; requires $50 tarpon tag to possess or kill

Spotted Sea Trout (Spotted Weakfish)* (R): not less than 14″ or more than 24″; daily bag limit of 10

*Must remain in whole condition until landed ashore

(R): Restricted Species

Marine Mammals

Manatees or sea cows, porpoises, and whales are endangered species. All marine mammals or parts thereof are protected by both state and federal law. It is unlawful to take, kill, annoy, or molest a marine mammal. Report any harassment, distress, injury, or death of a marine mammal to the nearest Florida Marine Patrol office or call (800) DIAL-FMP.

Redfish, Black Drum, Pompano, Sea Trout

It is unlawful to take fish of these species with live or dead natural bait in conjunction with any multiple hook. Snatching is prohibited.

Snook

It is unlawful to take snook by any means other than hook and line, or with live or dead natural bait in conjunction with a treble hook. Snatching is prohibited.

Deadly Lures for Sea Trout

by Bob McNally

Having the right lures along can make a big difference in sea trout fishing success.

It's likely that every avid sea trout fisherman has at least some plastic-tail jigs in his tackle box. Indeed, few lures are so perfectly matched to a fish species as the "grub" jib is to the spotted sea trout. Some fishermen, in fact, state flatly that the grub jib was designed specifically for sea trout fishing—then the lure quickly gained a reputation for catching redfish, blues, mackerel, and myriad freshwater species, too.

Dozens of tackle companies manufacture plastic-tail jigs, and the bulk of them are good, especially ones made by well-established firms like Mann's, Mister Twister, Lindy, Cotee, Boone, and Bagley. Popular jig weights for sea trout are ¼- and ⅜-ounce, but some ½-ounce jigs also should be in every trout angler's tackle box for those times when fish are extra deep or when tides are particularly strong. Pink and brown probably are the most popular plastic-tail jig colors, since they most closely resemble the hues of shrimp, which is the hands-down favorite food of sea trout. White, yellow, green, silver, and combinations of those colors are commonly used for sea trout "grubs." A jig tipped with a whole, fresh shrimp is an outstanding taker of trout, too.

The "Gitzit" style plastic jigs also

Spotted sea trout are the most popular fish with Florida's anglers.
(BOB MCNALLY)

have been scoring well on sea trout in recent years. This interesting jig has numerous tentacles that make it resemble a small squid. Fished the same way as a grub jig, the Gitzit works wonders on sea trout, even though the lure was originally designed for freshwater bass.

Minnow-imitating plugs are excellent sea trout lures, and a healthy selection of different sizes, styles, weights and colors of such artificials belong in every sea trout angler's tackle box. MirrOlures are a mainstay of sea trout plug casters. Fast-sinking, slow-sinking and floating models are all good. Popular colors are red and white, blue and white, silver, and silver and blue. Sea trout on shallow flats have a passion for floating plugs, such as Bang lures, big Rebel minnows, Zara Spooks, and

Boone Zig-Zaggers. In addition, topwater chuggers and plugs with propellers fore and aft are important lure ingredients for any complete sea trout tackle box. Strader Tackle's School Teacher and Diamond Rattler are good topwater trout lures, too, and are especially popular with Gulf Coast anglers.

Sea trout can hold in deep holes, channels and canals, and at such times, deep-going lures are needed to ferret them out. Lipped diving plugs or crankbaits are not especially popular with sea trout fishermen, but the plugs are excellent for casting and trolling around deep sea trout structures. Trader Bay lures are especially good diving plugs for sea trout, designed expressly for this purpose by the company in Titusville, Florida, right on the Indian River, one of the most famous of all sea trout waters. Almost any type diving plug can be used for deep trout, but if working oyster bars and pilings, lures having tough lips are especially good because they withstand the rigors of bumping off hard bottom better than ones with plastic lips.

The new Hot Flash sinking plug is gaining a reputation as a deadly taker of trout. It has a body size and shape identical to a pinfish. The lure is best worked slow and deep. It is built tough, and sea trout have a passion for it. It comes in a wide variety of hot lure colors, and lots of trout over 10 pounds have fallen to this unique lure.

The Heddon Sonar is more like a metal jig than a plug, but no matter how it's classed, it's an outstanding sea trout artificial when jigged in deep holes. Small Hopkins, Krocodile, and Kastmaster spoons are good additions to a trout tackle kit for those times when trout are feeding deep on small, shiny minnows.

On shallow grass flats, gold and silver spoons score well on sea trout. The Johnson Sprite is a favorite of many anglers, and the new Rebel Arrowhead spoon is being well received by sea trout fishermen. (It's deadly on redfish, too.)

Sea trout are excellent targets for fly fishermen when the fish are in shal-low, clear water. Small yellow, white, pink, and green bucktail or saddle-hackle streamers, popping bugs, and sliders in the same colors all score well on trout. Shrimp-fly patterns intended for bonefish are excellent for sea trout, too, though they're rarely employed by fly-rodders after trout. ∎

Different Lines for Different Conditions

by Lefty Kreh

I guess almost every fly fisherman knows that there are many different kinds of line. There are double tapers, levels and weight-forwards. Cortland Line Company makes more than 350 different kinds and sizes of fly lines, and Scientific Angler has an even larger inventory. Why are there so many kinds of lines? Obviously, the companies aren't going to produce them unless there are good reasons—and they sell.

First, double taper lines, which taper to a small point on each end, are useful in saltwater fishing only to build shooting tapers, often called shooting

heads. I can't think of any other good applications for them. Level lines are also used very little in saltwater. They do work well for the shooting line, which is attached to the shooting taper head. A caution here is that two commercial level fly lines are produced by some manufacturers for use as shooting lines. One is rather weak, about 12- to 15-pound test. This is often weaker than the leader tippet, and during the heat of battle the line can part, losing the shooting head, leader, and fish. The stronger shooting line will measure .027 or larger, and usually is so marked on the container.

All of the other kinds of fly lines used by anglers in saltwater are of the weight-forward design. Within this design are many types of fly lines. Used in the right situations they are deadly, but if they are used for something other than what they are designed for, they often handicap the fly fisherman.

Let me give one quick example. Consider bonefish tapers. These are lines designed for anglers who wait until a bonefish is within 35 or 40 feet of the boat before they make a cast. If used for this purpose, they work exceedingly well. The lines are designed so that a great deal of the weight is concentrated well forward in the line. This allows the angler to hold much of the heavier weight-forward portion of the line outside the rod guides. With a quick backcast the angler can come forward and shoot his fly to a bonefish close by.

I find this same line to be a poor one for distance casting. When a forward cast is made, the line is straight until the rod stops. Then the line folds over and unrolls toward the target. The bonefish taper has an extra-thin running line to allow distance on short casts, but when the line is extended and you come forward and stop, this thin line doesn't support the rest of the line well as it unrolls. This causes a wobbly, jerky presentation. The bonefish taper, then, is excellent for short cast, but should be avoided for longer cast.

The right fly line helped Lefty Kreh land this nice barracuda. (LEFTY KREH)

Shooting tapers are the best lines when distance is critical or desirable. The heavier head, attached to super-thin shooting line, allows you to throw over a great distance. For many saltwater fishing situations, though, the shooting head is not a good line to use. One good example is bonefishing. Few bonefish ever travel far in a straight line. They zigzag across the flats as they feed. It is extremely difficult to pick up a shooting head for a backcast if much of the limp, thin shooting line is outside the rod tip.

On windy days many anglers tend to switch to a heavier line. That's a good idea when fishing where casting distances are short. If you are using an 8-weight rod and the wind picks up, switch to a number 9 line and, at short distances, you'll be able to better load the rod. Use the opposite technique if you are forced to make *long* cast into a stiff breeze. If you use a line one size heavier, and many anglers do, you hamper your casting. If you handle a long line and want to cast a greater distance into the wind, use one line smaller than the rod calls for. For example, when using an 8-weight rod,

switch to a number 7 line. You should extend slightly more line than you would normally carry outside the rod when false casting. This will put the proper bend in the rod. A heavier line would cause the rod to bend too deeply and cause you to throw wider loops, which won't go as far. If you extend, for example, an extra 10 feet, you are that much closer to the target on the cast. The lighter line, when extended a bit more than normal for its size, allows the rod to flex properly, so you can throw good, tight loops. The thinner line will also penetrate the wind better.

To give you an idea of how specialty lines can help you do better under certain fishing conditions, let's look at two lines especially designed for giant tarpon fishing. Clear monofilament lines, often called slime lines because they are slippery and sometimes difficult to handle, are great when tarpon have been hard-fished and have become wary. The clear line, attached to a clear monofilament leader, gives the tarpon less to see and they spook less on the presentation. Orvis has developed a special giant

tarpon line that is very effective. It is a floating line that has a clear monofilament 10-foot front end. If you add a conventional leader of 5 to 8 feet, you are able to present to the tarpon a fly with 15 to 18 feet of clear leader and line between it and the regular floating line. The advantage of this line is that if an imperfect cast is made ahead of the school of tarpon, and you'd like to wait a bit, you can. A slime line or another slow-sinking line will descend well below the level of the tarpon in the water column. But the Orvis special clear tip line is supported by the floating line behind it. This gives the angler more time to wait until the fish are close, when a proper retrieve can be started.

The examples given here are simply to make fly fishermen aware that there are good reasons why manufacturers produce so many lines. Each manufacturer has a catalog listing its lines, and in many cases stating why specially-made lines are produced. Many anglers would enjoy the sport more, and catch more fish, if they used lines designed for particular fishing conditions. ■

Florida's Redfish Roundup

by Doug Olander

If you think Florida flats fishing means bonefish, you'd better think again. Thanks to their prevalence around the entire state, their generally increasing abundance under decommercialization and very strict sport laws, and the sky-rocketing interest in catching them, *redfish* are Number One.

Like no other state, Florida offers diverse opportunities to catch reds year-round. In top redfish areas all around the Sunshine State, though, September and October stand out as prime time for reds.

The fall fishing peak is common to

all of the state's various redfish hot spots, but the differences in fishing for reds among these areas is striking. *How* you'll fish for reds, in what conditions, and for what size fish vary considerably depending upon where you go.

What's your preference? Fishing deep channels or oyster bars? Sight casting shallow grass flats in clear water or blind-casting into muddy mangrove shorelines? Trying for 30-pound monsters or casting into huge schools of smaller "rat" reds? Stalking reds under a bright, hot sun or anchoring up at dusk? You can do it all in the fall in Florida.

This roundup explains what each area offers and how to fish it.

Flamingo/Upper Florida Bay: Pink Tails On Grass Flats

"Fall is definitely the best time of year," explains flats guide Capt. Paul Tejera. "We can consistently sight-fish for reds all day, usually in water anywhere from 6 inches to 2 feet."

About 20 flats guides based in the upper Keys, like Tejera, make the 30- to 45-minute run through the backcountry to the Flamingo area where school reds prowl. Tejera, who's been fishing the area for 20 years and guiding full-time for the past 10, says, "I often have to fish shallower for tailing reds than I do for tailing bonefish. Fly fishing for reds is very big and growing here."

According to Tejera, the largest schools of reds start showing up in September and remain at least through October—until cold fronts bring stiff winds. Most Flamingo flats reds will range from 6 to 9 pounds. Expect a wider range of sizes when fishing the channels, from "rat" reds of 12 inches to the rare 14-pounder.

Tejera says reds are plentiful. "Last year during the fall Redbone Tournament, in one day all redfish records for the five-year event were broken—one boat caught 32 on artificials. Unfortunately, I went bonefishing that day," he adds.

Most fly and light-tackle guides who fish Flamingo either run from the upper Keys or trailer from Miami. Expect to pay in the vicinity of $325 for a full day for the boat.

Here are several redfish guides who fish upper Florida Bay: Paul Tejera, (305) 595-2707; Rob Fordyce, (305) 238-9399; John Donnell, (305) 852-3749; and Rick Murphy, (305) 233-0615. For other guides and area information call the Flamingo Chamber of Commerce at (813) 695-3941 and the Islamorada Chamber of Commerce at (305) 664-4503.

Canaveral's Banana/Indian Rivers: Shallow Water, Monster Reds

"[This] is the only place in the state to go for really big redfish inshore," says state biologist and redfish expert Mike Murphy. "We were amazed to catch 200 or 300 20-pound redfish in our nets (for tagging fish)." A year later, the state re-netted many of the same fish. Fish of that size are spawners, and Murphy says this is the only area where they spawn inshore and get so big.

Reds over 20 pounds are common for guides like Capt. Troy Perez, who

An angler works mangroves on a low tide with a soft-bodied jig.
(DOUG OLANDER)

specializes in fly- and light-line/artificial fishing. In the last seven years of guiding he's tagged and released over 1,000 reds. Most of these fish were *too large* to fit within the legal 18- to 27-inch window. Another successful redfish guide who fishes the Indian River and Mosquito Lagoon, Capt. Shawn Foster of Cocoa Beach uses lures and blue crab chunks to entice larger redfish. His biggest shallow-water red to date: 55 pounds.

Unlike many fisheries, this one seems to get better and better. "When I grew up, I never saw redfish tailing in huge schools in the Banana and Indian rivers [as we do now]—schools of 100 to 200 or more fish, *never*." The good news is that besides such schools of trophy-sized reds, "we're also starting to catch more 18- to 21-inch fish," says Perez. Recently he caught 44 fish from one little area on the flats, all 3 to 7 pounds. "That was a first." Foster agrees. "I'm seeing lots of 3- to 7-pound fish that I'd never seen before this year in the area, and it's good to see."

While much of this is sight-fishing, the water is not crystal clear and larger fish are likely to be along dropoffs in 3 to 6 feet of water. But a mass of big reds offers trained eyes what Perez calls "the glow"—"because nothing else looks like it; that's just what it is, a big pink area in the water." Also, guides like Perez and Foster spend much of their time watching for subtle surface wakes from the broad shoul-

ders of big reds cruising just below.

Canoeists and wade fishermen can take advantage of a rare, pristine stretch of the Banana River just north of State Highway 528. Expect to pay $300 or more for a day of guided fishing here. Full-time redfish guides include: Troy Perez, (407) 631-4841; Shawn Foster, (407) 784-2610; and Frank Catino, (407) 777-2793. For other guides and area information call the Merritt Island Chamber of Commerce at (407) 459-2200.

Pensacola Pass: Anchor Up for Bull Reds

Some of the state's biggest redfish invade the current-swept waters of Pensacola Pass every fall. "They're too big to keep, so I tag them and let them go," says Col. Allan Davis of Gulf Breeze, who's tagged over 2,000 reds during this fall fishery since 1986.

While redfish abundance seems to be up or stable in most areas, Davis has noted a definite drop here. He has tagged as many as 500 in a single year but last year tagged just over 200. He suspects much of that decline has to do with purse seiners now netting tons of menhaden outside the pass. "I used to get all the bait I needed with one throw of the castnet," he says, but it's no longer so easy.

On the other hand, "It's still great fishing for reds." Davis now uses traps to get his menhaden, which are the bait of choice for this relatively deep-water fishery. Shrimp and crabs also work well.

Davis anchors toward dusk on the shelf or bar just inside the pass, about 150 feet from the beach, and fishes the slope from 8 feet to about 28 feet. He anchors so his bait drifts up the inside edge of the bar on an outgoing tide, and down the same edge on the flood.

When a school moves through, multiple hookups are common, Davis says. He's caught reds here up to 35 pounds and has heard of them closer to 45. With fish that size in heavy currents and other boats around, Pensacola Pass is not the place to fish light tackle for reds (though at times, big schools of much smaller reds up inside the bay on tidal flats make fly fishing productive).

There is no fleet of Pensacola redfish guides, but a Pass fishing trip can be set up with Capt. Bob Gray at Gray's Tackle, (904) 934-3151. Expect to pay $200–$250 to fish the Pass for reds. Capt. Jimbo Mador of Pt. Clear, Alabama, also fishes the pass ((205) 928-8557). For other guides and area information call the Pensacola Chamber of Commerce at (904) 438-4081.

Ten Thousand Islands and Everglades National Park: Full of Reds—and Surprises

"September is peak time, all right: On a good day, you can do a redfish on every fourth cast," says Capt. John Glorieux, who has guided the southwest Florida waters beyond Chokoloskee for years. In the fall, he fishes only redfish—and only here.

"There are definitely more redfish around the area now and I see more schools of bigger reds," he reports. Probably nowhere in the state is there more of such intricate, unspoiled habitat to explore. "You could spend a lifetime [fishing] here and [still] come around a corner and find a new creek."

Much of Glorieux's action is around the outermost points of Gulf oyster bars. On higher, flooding tides, he moves in along with the feeding reds to cast toward the shore. The waters here are dingy and lack shallow flats, so sight casting is rare. Glorieux often actually chums up reds with live threadfin herring. "As the tide goes out . . . , I move to outer points, put a stake in, and start chumming (live threadfin)." This local take on the "bait-and-switch" routine does offer fly casters a shot at boiling reds, which are plentiful here if not enormous, averaging 3 to 12 pounds.

But most of his fishing is with plugs—MirrOlures, a 55M or 65M—or ¼-ounce jigs in chartreuse, white, or yellow tipped with shrimp. Surprises

also await beneath the surface, since Glorieux often hooks several snook in a day as well as baby jewfish, tarpon, jacks, 'sail cats, ladyfish, and more.

Several good local guides are available through tackle shops or through Outdoor Resorts ((813) 695-2881, ask for Kenny Brown). Most fish bait. Light-tackle artificial enthusiasts may want to contact Glorieux at (407) 575-9450. A day of guided fishing for reds here will run $250 to $300. (Muddy water and loads of heavy-duty oyster bars make these waters tricky for private boaters who don't know the area, by the way.) For other guides and area information call the Everglades Chamber of Commerce at (813) 695-3941.

Pine Island Sound— Hunt and Stalk in Crystal Clear Waters

"What we call Pine Island Sound is, along its east side, a continual shallow water flat about 15 miles long, anywhere from one-quarter mile to two miles wide with lush green grass flats, sandy bars, potholes, oyster bars— perfect redfish habitat."

Capt. Mike Rehr of nearby Sanibel is a skiff guide who specializes in fly fishing and light-tackle casting—and thinks he has the ideal spot for it. He also thinks fall is a great time for reds.

"We catch them here all year, but, yes, September, October and into November is when we see large schools of big spawners that move into the bay from the open Gulf." Rehr believes these are specific schools and he knows their movements. "Using the tides, I can pinpoint within 200 yards where they're likely to be in the fall." And that pays off: he cites one angler who landed redfish 16 of 22 casts, all to tailing fish.

Reds aren't the only spawners at this time. "The Florida round-winged stingray start to spawn, also," Rehr says. "As these big rays skim the grass, they spook up crabs, shrimp and the like. Redfish travel with them to capitalize on this 'traveling deli.' At times, it'll look

like a crown of tails sticking up around a settled-in stingray and that's a great target for fly or light tackle." Rehr says by October it's not unusual to spot several rays moving over the flats in the same area—surrounded by so many 8- to 12-pound redfish that "the waters glow orange! It's a sight to make a fisherman weak in the knees."

Among the redfish guides working the Pine Island Sound area for fall reds are: Rehr, (813) 472-3308; Phil O'Bannon of Boca Grande, (813) 964-0359; and Dave Gibson of Ft. Myers, (813) 466-4680. Most charge $325 to $350 or so a day for their boats. For other guides and area information call the Pine Island Chamber of Commerce at (813) 283-0888.

Cedar Key: Fall Redfish Is King

Cedar Key's abundant oyster bars and grass flats had always offered an abundance of redfish, at least until the mid-1980s. But in the 1990s, since the red became a tightly-managed sport fish, "Without a doubt, redfishing has really improved here."

Jim Dupre of Gainesville guides fly and light-tackle anglers in these out-of-the-way waters just south of the Suwannee River mouth. He echoes what guides from around the state are reporting: "There are definitely more big schools now; I've seen schools of fish [in the distance] where the water just turns red—schools of several hundred fish."

Cedar Key reds are typically in the 7- to 10-pound range; much more rarely do 20-pounders haunt these shallow Gulf waters—and those typically fall to live-baiters, Dupre says. But there's a thrill in casting into huge schools. At such times, "They'll eat literally whatever you want to throw at them."

Dupre, who makes the short drive from his Gainesville home, has been fishing here for a decade. He can be reached at (904) 371-6153. Bill Roberts is a local guide who fishes various methods: (904) 543-5690.

A day of guided fishing around Cedar Key will run about $200 to $250. For other guides and area information call the Cedar Key Chamber of Commerce at (904) 543-5600. The Tackle Box in Gainesville is also a good information source: (904) 372-1791.

Northeast Florida: Pick Your Inlet

From settings pristine to urban, inlets dominate the coast around Jacksonville. Fishing the deep water here may lack the glamour of shallow-water fly casting, but it's one of the best areas in the state to tangle with big bull reds.

"Lots and lots of really big fish start coming in the fall," says Bob McNally, author of *Fishermen's Knots, Fishing Rigs, And How to Use Them*, who lives in the area and has probably fished these reds—and written about it—more than anyone. Reds in the 20-pound range are commonplace and McNally sees many over 30 pounds at this time of year.

As in many other areas, it seems to be getting better and better up here. "A good friend, Art Ginn of Palatka, is 74 and has fished around Matanazas and the Crescent beaches all his life and... this is *the best* redfishing he's seen."

The northernmost of the state's inlets, Fernandina, offers big jetties with lots of places to fish and few anglers. The mouth of the Nassau River (Nassau Sound) also offers exceptional fall action, according to McNally. Other good bets: the mouth of the St. Johns River (Mayport, Jacksonville Beach), Fort George Inlet and, to the south, St. Augustine and Matanzas inlets.

Most inlet enthusiasts such as McNally work a "fish-finder" rig: a slip sinker of an ounce or so on the main line above a short leader with a sliding float rig to keep the bait near the bottom as it floats out with the tide.

When runs of mullet pour in through the inlets, "Bait is everywhere and you can see redfish just hammering it!" At such times, particularly, McNally casts plugs like Bagley's Finger Mullet or Zara Spooks. Up in the saltmarshes,

which, north of Jacksonville, are extensive, such lure can be sight cast. Despite the dark, tannin-stained water, visible tails and wakes make sight fishing part of the mix.

Mostly private boaters take advantage of fall reds here. John Dryssen of Jacksonville Beach (904-261-4053) guides in the lower St. Johns. Larry Miniard of Palm Valley (904-285-7003) works the St. Augustine area and fishes fly. McNally says Carl Middleton of Fernandina Beach (904-285-7003) can help anyone who wants to fish the area for fall reds find a guide. For other guides and area information call the Jacksonville Chamber of Commerce at (904) 366-6600.

Homosassa/Crystal River: Salt Creeks and Spoil Banks

"In the mid '80s, redfish here were in real trouble. We caught mostly 'rat reds' of 10 to 12 inches," says Frank Schiraldi,

who's been guiding anglers to redfish here for about 25 years. Today, however, it can be a problem finding a fish under 27 inches to keep, Shiraldi says.

"Here, from the time the moon makes full in August, through September, October and even into November, redfish are active. Schools of spawners offshore hit the flats hungry and well above 27 inches for the most part," according to Schiraldi.

Some of the best shallow-water fishing is during the high-incoming through high-outgoing tide, when those who know their way around can follow the reds up into shallow intertidal areas. Just north of Crystal River, you can find fall reds in most tides and conditions—at the spoil banks, one of Schiraldi's favorite fishing grounds.

"It's wonderful habitat for reds," he says of the structure created when a channel was dredged from the nuclear power plant above town.

Return of the Redfish

The numbers don't tell the whole story, but they offer a pretty good place to start. More Florida redfish were caught in 1984 than any other year: 2.1 million in all. In 1986, the state decommercialized redfish (making them illegal to sell as a food fish). At the same time, it reduced the recreational limit dramatically, to one fish per day, and instituted a complete seasonal closure. The result: fewer than 200,000 redfish taken in succeeding years.

Today, the harvest is only a bit more than this, according to the Florida Marine Research Institute's most recent red drum assessment report. Yet fishermen are catching many more redfish, testament to a return to levels of earlier abundance thanks to a predominantly catch-and-release fishery.

Once Florida's redfish begin to mature (at three years, 26 to 27 inches), they move offshore and

become less significant in the sportcatch, according to the state's Department of Natural Resources redfish expert, biologist Mike Murphy. The majority of Florida's sportcaught reds are immature fish of one to two years (12 to 22 inches).

Redfish not only grow quickly, they keep growing. "Redfish as old as 60 years have been found in the northern part of their range," Murphy says. Florida fish have been aged to at least 25 years.

Tight restrictions have helped redfish populations rebound, but any near-term liberalization of sport limits for Florida anglers is unlikely since the legal size window of 18 to 27 inches (much larger fish are rare in most areas) targets immature fish. "This is an inshore fishery based on immature animals," says Murphy, adding that taking too many will allow the stock no chance to replenish itself.

Tackle Tips for Florida Reds

As you might figure, with so many different habitats in different areas for an opportunistic feeder like the red, lots of bait and lures work. But there are some common themes.

One seems to be color: chartreuse. That's the color more guides cite than any other as a best bet for flies. Red and white comes in a close second.

Fly tackle shouldn't be too beefy. Keys guide Paul Tejera suggests a 9-weight rod with 8- to 12-pound tippet and a 40-pound shock tippet.

Many guides enjoy sharing the thrill of a big redfish attacking such surface plugs as Zara Spooks, particularly since their underslung mouths make for extra fireworks as they try to nail the lure. When tossing surface lures, the larger the school, the better.

Small bucktail jigs are widely if not universally popular for Florida reds. At least one guide insists that reds are sight feeders and tipping the jig with shrimp is unnecessary, while a guide working a different part of the state insists that reds' keen sense of smell makes a shrimp-tipped jig much more appealing. Some guides suggest very small jigs such as Hildebrandt's Tin Foiler when spooky reds are in very shallow water.

Gold, generally weedless, spoons are widely popular—and remain one of the top choices in some central Florida areas, on both coasts.

When they're hungry, redfish aren't reluctant feeders. "My theory is that as long as you present something to them when they're tailing—because then you know they're feeding—and they're not spooked, they'll eat it," says Tejera.

Fish where the spoil edges drop off, in a few feet of water, Schiraldi suggests. The large rocks create great cover for reds, which feed along the south side during the outgoing tide and the north side on the incoming, or anywhere the tide runs around a point.

While schools in shallow water may spook when one of their members is hooked, he says, "If you get a fish on and keep it on (in the deep water of the spoil canal), these fish may act like school dolphin: I've had 200 to 300 reds rise up behind one hooked fish that way."

Although tarpon and Homossassa are synonymous, there are a number of guides who know the fall redfish scene.

Some of them, along with Schiraldi (904-795-5229), are Mike Locklear (904-628-4207), Roger Bachelor (904-795-6444), and Earl Waters (904-628-0333). Expect to pay about $200 or a bit more per day. For other guides and area information call the Homosassa Chamber of Commerce at (904) 628-2666. ■

FISHING ACCESS

GEORGIA

The following list of shore access for Georgia includes only those counties from Altamaha Sound to the Florida border (Glynn and Camden counties). For a list of access to the north of the Sound, see page 47. Information concerning Georgia's artificial reefs begins on page 49.

Fishing Piers

Glynn County

Back River Fishing Piers
I-95 at Exit 6 (US 17). North on US 17 for 9.1 mi. to Torras Causeway. East on causeway 1.5 mi. to Back River Bridge. Parking area on left.

Jekyll Island Pier
I-95 at Exit 6 (US 17). North on US 17 for 5 mi. Right on Jekyll Causeway (GA 50), 6.3 mi. Left on Beachview Dr., 4.3 mi., right at Clam Creek Rd. Pier and parking area at end of road.

Blythe Island Regional Park
I-95 at Exit 6 (US 17). South on US 17 for 0.6 mi. to GA 303. North on GA 303 for 3.6 mi. to park sign. Turn right into park, drive 1.4 mi. to pier.

Little River Catwalk
I-95 at Exit 6 (US 17). North on US 17 for 9.1 mi. to Torras Causeway. East on causeway 2.3 mi. to Little River Bridge. Parking area on right.

Mackay River Fishing Piers
I-95 at Exit 6 (US 17). North on US 17 for 9.1 mi. to Torras Causeway. East on causeway 2.3 mi. to Mackay River Bridge. Parking area on right.

St. Simons Island Pier
I-95 at Exit 6 (US 17). North on US 17 for 9.1 mi. to Torras Causeway. East on causeway for 4.0 mi., bear right on King's Way. Drive 5.7 mi. to Mallory St. Turn right, drive 0.2 mi. to pier.

Bank or Surf Fishing

Glynn County

Gould's Inlet

I-95 at Exit 6 (US 17). North on US 17 for 9.1 mi. to Torras Causeway. East on causeway 6.3 mi. Causeway becomes Demere Rd. Left at East Beach Causeway, drive 0.3 mi. Bear left on Bruce Dr. at Coast Guard station. Road dead-ends at inlet parking area.

St. Andrew Picnic Area

I-95 at Exit 6 (US 17). North on US 17 for 5 mi., right on Jekyll Causeway (GA 50) 6.1 mi. to Riverview Dr., Jekyll Island. Turn right, drive 2.3 mi. Right at radio tower into parking area.

Camden County

Crooked River State Park

I-95 at Exit 2 (GA 40). East on GA 40 for 3.6 mi. to King's Bay Rd., then north for 2.1 mi. to GA Spur 40. Left on GA Spur 40 for 4.2 mi. to end of road beyond park entrance.

Boat Ramps

Glynn County

Blythe Island Regional Park (912) 261-3805

Jekyll Island Historic District Wharf 1 Pier Rd., Jekyll Island, (912) 635-2891

Camden County

Crooked River State Park

I-95 at Exit 2 (GA 40). East on GA 40 for 3.6 mi. to King's Bay Rd., then north for 2.1 mi. to GA Spur 40. Left on GA 40 for 4.2 mi. to end of road beyond park entrance.

Dark Entry Creek Boat Ramp

GA 40 west of St. Marys

Harriett's Bluff Boat Ramp

I-95 at Exit 3 (Harriett's Bluff Rd.). East for 5 mi., right at Harriett's Bluff sign. Drive 0.4 mi., turn right onto Crooked River Dr. for 0.3 mi. Parking area on left.

Satilla River Waterfront Park

I-95 at Exit 4 (GA Spur 25). West on GA Spur 25 for 2.5 mi. to US 17. North on US 17 for 0.7 mi. Fishing dock entrance on right at Park sign.

St. Mary's Boat Ramp

I-95 at Exit 2 (GA 40). East on GA 40 for 8.8 mi. to waterfront. Right at waterfront pavilion, drive 0.1 mi. Parking area on left.

St. Mary's Waterfront Pavilion

I-95 to Exit 2 (GA 40). East on GA 40 for 8.8 mi. GA 40 dead-ends at fishing dock.

Marinas

Glynn County

(Brunswick, St. Simons, Jekyll and Sea Islands)

Blythe Island Regional Park, 261-3805

Brunswick Landing Marina, 262-9264

Brunswick Marina, 265-2290

Credle's Fish Camp, 261-3805

Golden Isles Marina, 634-1128

Hampton River Club Marina, 638-1210

Jekyll Harbor Marina, 635-3137

Jekyll Island Historic Marina, 635-2891

St. Simmons Island Marina, 638-9146

Taylor's Fish Camp, 638-7690

Troupe Creek Marina, 264-3862

Two-Way Fish Camp, 265-0410

Village Creek Landing (rental boats only), 634-9054

Camden County

Hickory Bluff Marina, 262-0453

Ocean Breeze Marina, 264-1239

FLORIDA

Atlantic Coast Launch Ramps

What follows is a listing of Florida launch ramps from the Georgia border to Fort Pierce Inlet. For a listing of launch ramps from Fort Pierce Inlet south, see page 155.

Duval County

Ft. George State Park Ramp on Hecksher Drive

Municipal Marina Ramp at 901 Gulf Life Drive on the St. Johns River, Jacksonville

Dunn Avenue Ramp on the Trout River, Jacksonville

Riverview Avenue Ramp on the Ribault River, Jacksonville

Blanding Blvd. Ramp on Cedar Creek, Jacksonville

Ortega Farms Blvd. Ramp on Fishing Creek, Jacksonville

Beach Blvd. Ramp on Big Pottsburg Creek, Jacksonville

1st Ave. North Ramp, at back of Beach Marine on the Intracoastal Waterway, Jacksonville

New Berlin Road Ramp on the St. Johns River, Jacksonville

West End Ramp on Arlington Road, Jacksonville

Burt Manrell Park Ramp on Broward Road, Jacksonville

Ramp at the north end of Rogero Road, Jacksonville

Clark's Fish Camp Ramp, Mandarin

A1A Ramp on the St. Johns River, Mayport

St. Johns County

A1A Ramp at Crescent Beach

Guana Dam Ramp on S.R. A1A at Ponte Vedra

St. Augustine Boating Club Ramp, 3 miles north of St. Augustine on A1A

A1A North Ramp on Vilano Beach Causeway, St. Augustine

Butler Beach Ramp, 8 miles south of St. Augustine on A1A

Flagler County

Flagler Beach Bridge Ramp on the ICW at Flagler Beach

Flagler Beach State Park Ramp

Artesia Road Ramp on the ICW, 4 miles south of Marineland on A1A

Volusia County

Seabreeze Bridge Causeway Ramp at Daytona Beach

Tomoka Park Ramp at Daytona Beach

South Beach Street Ramp at Daytona Beach

Edgewater City Ramp

Lighthouse Point Marina Ramp on A1A, north of Ponce Inlet

New Smyrna Causeway Ramp

Ormond Beach Causeway Ramp

Port Orange Causeway Ramp

Turtle Mound Ramp, 6 miles south of New Smyrna Beach on A1A

Brevard County

Tingley's Fish Camp Ramp on the Barge Canal

Sykes Creek Ramp on the Cocoa Beach Causeway

Indian River Ramp on the Cocoa Beach Causeway

520 Ramp on the Cocoa Beach Causeway

Dania Ramp, N.E. 8th Ave. and 4th Street

Eau Gallie Causeway Ramp

Ballard Park Ramp, east of US 1 & 5, on the Eau Gallie River

Honest John's Fish Camp Ramp on A1A at Melbourne Beach

Melbourne Causeway Ramp

Kelly Park Ramp on the Banana River at Merritt Island

Funtime Marina Ramp on the Banana River, 520 Causeway, at Merritt Island

Allenhurst Fish Camp Ramp, north of Haulover Canal at Merritt Island

Neptune Marina Ramp on US 1 at Micco

Palm Bay Marina Ramp on US 1

Mosquito Lagoon Ramp, north of Haulover Canal, at North Merritt Island

Port Canaveral Ramp

Port St. John Ramp on US 1

Titusville Park Ramp on SR 402, on the west shore of the Indian River

Parrish Park Ramp on SR 402, east of the bridge in Titusville

Titusville City Yacht Basin Ramp

Marina Yacht Basin Ramp in Titusville

Indian River County

Inlet Marina Ramp at Sebastian

May's Marina Ramp at Sebastian

Sebastian Inlet Park Ramp

Vero Beach Municipal Ramps in Vero Beach

St. Lucie County

Avenue C Ramp on Indian River Drive in Fort Pierce

Seaway Drive Ramp, ½-mile east of South Bridge on A1A

Melaleuca Drive Ramp, south on A1A in Fort Pierce

Ft. Pierce City Ramp on North 2nd Ave

St. Lucie Country Club Ramp at Port St. Lucie

White City Ramp

State Parks with Fishing Access

The following Florida state parks, listed here from the Georgia border to Ft. Pierce Inlet, offer saltwater fishing access. See Chapters Three and Four for more state parks with fishing access.

Anastasia, St. Augustine Beach, off SR A1A off US 41

Faver-Dykes, 15 mi. south of St. Augustine, east of US 1

Flagler Beach, Flagler Beach, off SR A1A

Fort Clinch, Fernandina Beach, off SR A1A

Fort Pierce Inlet, 4 mi. east of Fort Pierce, off SR A1A, SR 703

Little Talbot Island, 17 mi. northeast of Jacksonville, off SR A1A, 98

St. Lucie Inlet, Port Salerno, accessible by boat on ICW

Sebastian Inlet, Sebastian Inlet, SR A1A

Tomoka, 3 mi. north of Ormond Beach, off N. Beach St.

Washington Oaks, 3 mi. south of Marineland, off SR A1A

FISHING RECORDS

GEORGIA

Georgia fishing records appear on pages 61 and 62.

FLORIDA

Conventional Tackle

Amberjack: 142 lb.; Islamorada; Feb. 1979

Barjack: 4 lb., 2 oz.; Key West; Oct. 1984

Barracuda: 67 lb.; Islamorada; Jan. 1949

Bass, Black Sea: 5 lb., 1 oz.; Panama City; July 1956

Bass, Striped (saltwater): 33 lb., 2 oz.; Tallahassee; Feb. 1989

Bluefish: 22 lb., 2 oz.; Jensen Beach; March 1973

Blue Runner: 7 lb.; Fort Lauderdale; Nov. 1990

Bonefish: 15 lb., 6 oz.; Islamorada; Dec. 1977

Bonita, Atlantic: Vacant

Catfish
Gafftopsail: 8 lb., 12 oz.; Stuart; Feb. 1991
Hardhead: 1 lb., 4 oz.; Charlotte Harbor; July 1988

Cobia: 103 lb., 12 oz.; Destin; April 1980

Croaker: 3 lb., 12 oz.; Pensacola; Sept. 1992

Dolphin: 77 lb., 12 oz.; Fort Pierce; April 1985

Drum
Black: 93 lb.; Fernandina Beach; March 1957
Red: 51 lb., 8 oz.; Sebastian Inlet; August 1983

Flounder: 20 lb., 9 oz.; Nassau County; Dec. 1983

Grouper
Gag: 71 lb., 3 oz.; Destin; July 1991
Nassau: 3 lb., 4 oz.; Key Largo; Nov. 1984
Red: 39 lb., 8 oz.; Port Canaveral; June 1991
Warsaw: 436 lb., 12 oz.; Destin; Dec. 1985
Yellowfin: 34 lb., 6 oz.; Key Largo; Dec. 1988

Grunts, Margates, Sailors Choice: 11 lb., 4 oz.; Tavernier; Feb. 1985

Hind, Speckled: 42 lb., 6 oz.; Destin; Oct. 1987

Hogfish: 19 lb., 8 oz.; Daytona Beach; April 1962

Jack, Crevalle: 51 lb.; Lake Worth; June 1978

Jack, Horse-eye: 24 lb., 8 oz.; Miami; Dec. 1982

Jewfish: 680 lb.; Fernandina Beach; May 1961

Ladyfish: 4 lb., 10 oz.; Jupiter; March 1991

Mackerel
Cero: 15 lb., 8 oz.; Key West; Nov. 1984
King: 90 lb.; Key West; Feb. 1976
Spanish: 12 lb.; Fort Pierce; Nov. 1984

Marlin
Blue: 980 lb., 8 oz.; Destin; June 1985
White: 161 lb.; Miami Beach; March 1938

Permit: 51 lb., 8 oz.; Lake Worth; April 1978

Pompano
African: 50 lb., 8 oz.; Daytona Beach; April 1990
Florida: 8 lb., 1 oz; Flagler Beach; March 1984

Runner, Rainbow: 17 lb.; Key West; April 1987

Sailfish, Atlantic: 116 lb.; Miami Beach; May 1989

Sawfish: 545 lb.; Naples; April 1958

Scamp: 25 lb., 4 oz.; Port Canaveral; Nov. 1991

Sea Trout, Spotted: 15 lb., 6 oz.; Jensen Beach; May 1969

Shark
Blacktip: 152 lb.; Sebastian; Oct. 1987
Bull: 486 lb.; Key West; April 1978
Dusky: 764 lb.; Longboat Key; May 1982
Hammerhead: 991 lb.; Sarasota; May 1982
Lemon: 397 lb.; Dunedin; April 1977
Mako: 911 lb., 12 oz.; Palm Beach; April 1962
Spinner: 190 lb.; Flagler Beach; April 1986
Thresher: 544 lb., 8 oz.; Destin; Sept. 1984
Tiger: 1,065 lb.; Pensacola; June 1981
White: 686 lb.; Key West; April 1981

Sheepshead: 15 lb., 2 oz.; Homosassa; Jan. 1981

Snapper
Cubera: 116 lb.,; Clearwater; July 1979
Gray: 17 lb.; Port Canaveral; June 1992
Lane: 6 lb., 6 oz.; Pensacola; April 1991
Mutton: 27 lb., 6 oz.; Madeira Beach; Sept. 1989
Red: 46 lb., 8 oz.; Destin; Oct. 1985
Yellowtail: 8 lb., 8 oz.; Fort Myers; July 1992

Snook: 44 lb., 3 oz.; Ft. Myers; April 1984

Spearfish, Longnose: 61 lb., 8 oz.; Islamorada; April 1981

Spot: Vacant

Swordfish: 612 lb., 12 oz.; Key Largo; May 1978

Tarpon: 243 lb.; Key West; Feb. 1975

Tripletail: 32 lb.; Apalachicola Bay; July 1988

Tuna
Bigeye: 167 lb.; Miami Beach; Jan. 1957
Blackfin: 38 lb.; Islamorada; May 1973
Bluefin: Vacant
Skipjack: 31 lb., 8 oz.; Miami Beach; Jan. 1949
Yellowfin: 211 lb.; Islamorada; Jan. 1972

Tunny, Little: 27 lb.; Key Largo; April 1976

Wahoo: 139 lb.; Marathon; May 1960

Weakfish: 10 lb.; Port Canaveral; Dec. 1987

Fly Fishing Tackle

Amberjack: 103 lb., 12 oz.; Key West; Jan. 1977

Barjack: Vacant

Barracuda: 37 lb., 12 oz.; Key West; Dec. 1978

Bass, Back Sea: Vacant

Bass, Striped (saltwater): Vacant

Bluefish: 18 lb.; Miami Beach; April 1983

Blue Runner: 3 lb., 14 oz.; Fowey Rock; July 1987

Bonefish: 14 lb., 6 oz.; Islamorada; Sept. 1985

Bonita, Atlantic: Vacant

Catfish, Gafftopsail: 7 lb., 8 oz.; Port Canaveral; Dec. 1989

Catfish, Hardhead: 1 lb., 3 oz.; Pompano Beach, Dec. 1992

Cobia: 78 lb.; Key West; Feb. 1982

Croaker: Vacant

Dolphin: 24 lb., 8 oz.; Key West; May 1987

Drum, Black: 50 lb., 4 oz.; Merritt Island; July 1986

Drum, Red: 31 lb.; Titusville; Feb. 1990

Flounder: Vacant

Grouper, Gag: 9 lb., 4 oz.; Key West; Feb. 1978

Grouper, Nassau: Vacant

Grouper, Red: Vacant

Grouper, Warsaw: Vacant

Grouper, Yellowfin: Vacant

Grunts, Margates, Sailors Choice: Vacant

Hind, Speckled: Vacant

Hogfish: Vacant

Jack, Crevalle: 34 lb.; Pensacola; Aug. 1992

Jack, Horse-eye: 3 lb., 6 oz.; Key West; Aug. 1987

Jewfish: 356 lb.; Islamorada, March 1967

Ladyfish: 4 lb., 5 oz.; Titusville; Oct. 1985

Mackerel, Cero: 9 lb.; Key West; Dec. 1991

Mackerel, King: 51 lb., 4 oz.; Key West; Feb. 1987

Mackerel, Spanish: 3 lb., 10 oz.; Key West; Dec. 1987

Marlin, Blue: Vacant

Marlin, White: 68 lb.; Fort Pierce; Dec. 1972

Permit: 32 lb., 4 oz.; Key West; May 1986

Pompano, African: 33 lb., 8 oz.; Palm Beach; Dec. 1968

Pompano, Florida: 6 lb., 8 oz.; Cocoa Beach; Jan. 1978

Runner, Rainbow: 8 lb., 10 oz.; Key West; Jan. 1980

Sailfish, Atlantic: 55 lb., 8 oz.; Palm Beach; Feb. 1980

Sawfish: Vacant

Scamp: Vacant

Sea Trout, Spotted: 12 lb., 7 oz.; Stuart; March 1984

Shark, Blacktip: 80 lb., 8 oz.; Marathon; Oct. 1992

Shark, Bull: 389 lb., 4 oz.; Key West; March 1980

Shark, Dusky: Vacant

Shark, Hammerhead: 154 lb.; Key West; March 1993

Shark, Lemon: 288 lb., 8 oz.; Key West; March 1978

Shark, Mako: Vacant

Shark, Spinner: Vacant

Party boats abound throughout Florida and offer anglers an easy, inexpensive way to tap the state's marine fishing.
(BOB MCNALLY)

Shark, Thresher: Vacant

Shark, Tiger: 61 lb., 12 oz. Key West; Feb. 1992

Shark, White: Vacant

Sheepshead: 6 lb., 5 oz.; St. Petersburg; Nov. 1989

Snapper, Cubera: Vacant

Snapper, Gray: 9 lb., 8 oz.; Key West; Dec. 1986

Snapper, Lane: Vacant

Snapper, Mutton: 17 lb.; Key West; May 1990

Snapper, Red: Vacant

Snapper, Yellowtail: Vacant

Snook: 28 lb., 8 oz.; Stuart; July 1972

Spearfish, Longnose: Vacant

Spot: Vacant

Swordfish: Vacant

Tarpon: 188 lbs; Homosassa Springs; May 1982

Tripletail: 21 lb., 2 oz.; Port Canaveral; April 1988

Tuna, Bigeye: Vacant

Tuna, Blackfin: 34 lb., 3 oz.; Islamorada; Dec. 1977

Tuna, Bluefin: Vacant

Tuna, Skipjack: Vacant

Tuna, Yellowfin: Vacant

Tunny, Little: 18 lb., 8 oz.; Key West; June 1985

Wahoo: 28 lb., 12 oz.; Key West; April 1982

Weakfish: Vacant

STATE AGENCIES

GEORGIA

For a listing of Georgia agencies, see page 66.

FLORIDA

State of Florida
Department of Natural Resources
2510 Second Ave. North
Jacksonville Beach, FL 32250
(904) 359-6580

Florida Marine Patrol
Marjory Stoneman Douglas Building
3900 Commonwealth Blvd.
Talahassee, FL 32399
(904) 488-8978

Florida Marine Fisheries Commission
2540 Executive Center Circle West
106 Douglas Building
Tallahassee, FL 32301
(904) 487-0554

Florida Division of Tourism
126 Van Buren
Tallahassee, FL 32399-2000
(904) 487-1462

State Boating Safety Coordinators
Florida Marine Patrol
3900 Commonwealth Blvd.
Tallahassee, FL 32399-3000
(904) 488-5757

Party Boat Fishing—Good, Better, and Best

by Ross Parsons

Three words to describe Florida party boat fishing in late fall and winter are good, better and best. On 90 percent of the daily trips made by the 60- to 90-foot boats, from dozens of ports, anglers discover party boat time means great times. They're inexpensive, they'll put you on fish, and they're available statewide.

Regulars on these boats are apt to take a variety of reef fish, ranging from hand-size grunt and sea bass to grouper topping 30 pounds. Bonus action involves dolphin or billfish rising to bait free-lined behind the drift boats. On some boats the basic fare is doubled, but so is the length of the trip. From Jacksonville to the Keys on the Atlantic side, and Pensacola to Fort Myers on the Gulf Coast, the big party, head, or drift boats are an angler's best and most economical introduction to blue water fishing in Florida.

Research Pays Off

The sharpest looking vessel won't guarantee you the biggest or best fish. Smart anglers will check several vessels during docking and unloading, questioning disembarking anglers while the trip is still fresh in their minds. Party boat regulars are a good source to determine which boat will please you, while local marinas can alert you to a skipper's professional reputation. Recommendations from tackle shops you trust also make sense. Don't step aboard an unfamiliar vessel with no knowledge of its cleanliness, nautical safety, and crew's attitude for your first party boat outing.

Spot the regulars by their custom rods and fish-filled coolers. Ask them about specific tackle needs in place of the standard rental rod and reel for a leg up toward enjoying the fishing when you do head out. Specific needs vary with geographical regions and target fish for the day, but a 7-foot rod, 4/0 reel and 40-pound-test line will cover 90 percent of your action. Add wire leader material for toothy critters, heavy monofilament to avoid breakoffs over rocky reefs, and an assortment of hook sizes and sinker weights to supplement the boat's offerings. Some veterans supply their own live bait, such as goggle-eye or shrimp, and a moderate investment along these lines can make a big difference.

Trophies and world records have been landed on Florida party boats, but a boat ride, with a chance to collect a fresh seafood dinner, is a more realistic goal. The price is right, and the fish are usually hungry, so check the yellow pages, give 'em a call, and get out there fishing!

Northeast Coast

At the top of the peninsula on the east side, drift boats sail from Jacksonville, seeking the 50- to 70-foot deep Hammer Grounds, where red grouper, red snapper and sea bass are the quarry. Red snapper are the fish preferred by anglers who leave from St. Augustine or Daytona Beach to work the Spawning Grounds. Also available are the fall runs of king mackerel, involving all-day trips on twin-diesel boats, manned by captains who chart their "secret spots" to insure anglers are satisfied after spending eight hours with rod and reel in hand.

East-central Florida waters, just south of Cape Canaveral, offer hot spots including wrecks as shallow as 40 feet, where amberjack and cobia are the prime targets, as well as the famed Inshore Grounds, in 60 to 120 feet of water, which hold red and black grouper plus large red snapper.

For the most up-to-date information on party, charter, or rental boats, call the chamber of commerce or the state agency with jurisdiction in the area you are interested in visiting (see below).

Master Guides

What follows is an alphabetical listing of some of northeast Florida's Master Guides, including addresses and telephone numbers. For a list of southern coast guides, see Chapter Three. Chapter Four contains a list of Gulf Coast guides.

Capt. Frank Catino, 468 St. John's Dr., Satellite Beach, FL 32937, (407) 777-2793

Capt. Eric Ersch, 171 Norwood Ave., Satellite Beach, FL 32937, (407) 779-9054

Thurman Green, 845 35th Ave., Vero Beach, FL 32960, (407) 567-7468

Capt. Dennis Hammond, 945 Barbra Ln., Rockledge, FL 32955, (407) 632-7686

Tom Pierce, 432 Perch Ln., Sebastian, FL 32958, (407) 388-0911, Key West (305) 294-6098

Grady Warren, 4921 Jackman Ct., Jacksonville, FL 32216, (904) 737-2071 or 268-7233 (H)

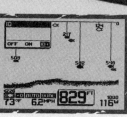
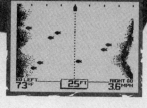

GET...

SCHRADE TOUGH

... AND GET A GRIP ON A FILLET KNIFE THAT'S A KEEPER !

Built Schrade Tough, this Old Timer® Safe-T-Grip™ was designed by fishermen for fishermen. The 147OT Pro Fisherman sports a super-sharp 7 1/2" Schrade+ stainless steel blade. The Sure grip handle is ergonomically designed for easy, safe, and comfortable use. Comes with a weather-resistant ballistic cloth sheath. Get your hand around the Pro Fisherman from Schrade... It's a Keeper!

Est. 1904

SCHRADE CUTLERY®
Built To Last A Lifetime.

Made in U.S.A. © 1995 Imperial Schrade Corp., 7 Schrade Court, Ellenville, N.Y. 12428

3

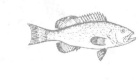

St. Lucie Inlet to the Dry Tortugas, Florida

The section of Florida from St. Lucie Inlet to the Dry Tortugas is the southernmost coastline in the United States. Two small islands just off Key West, Woman Key and Man Key, are the extreme southern land points and lie only 60 miles from the geographical boundary of the tropics, the Tropic of Cancer.

A remarkable feature of the land along this section is its flatness; elevations within a 10-mile-wide strip bordering the coast rarely exceed 25 feet. Throughout the Everglades that cover practically the southern third of the Florida peninsula, few points rise higher than 18 or 19 feet. Even these heights seem lower than they actually are, for they occur far inland within this nearly flat, frequently flooded region and they slope almost imperceptibly seaward at the rate of only two inches per mile.

From St. Lucie Inlet south to Miami Beach, a distance of 85 miles, the mainland is bordered by long, straight, narrow, sandy barrier islands behind which are narrow lagoons. Although many of these lagoons were formerly unconnected, they have been made continuous by construction of the Intracoastal or Inland Waterway. This waterway connects with the sea by narrow inlets that occur at intervals of a dozen miles or so. Skirting the lagoons are dense stands of mangroves, at least along those areas that have not yet been filled or bulkheaded for real estate development. Although there are only a few small rivers and streams of fresh water in this section, there are over a half dozen large, man-made canals draining vast areas of the interior. During rainy periods, especially when hurricanes strike, these canals empty huge volumes of sediment-laden fresh water into the lagoons, thus changing them from salt water to nearly fresh, and blanketing the bottom with a mucky silt.

South and west of Miami Beach, the coast is characterized by a narrow chain of low, mostly rocky islands, which begins at Virginia Key and ends 190 miles away at the Dry Tortugas. These islands are the Florida Keys. They are basically remnants of a once-living coral reef formed many thousands of years ago when the level of the sea was much higher than it is today. A series of shallow, semienclosed bays and sounds, nearly all of them bordered by mangroves, lies between the Florida Keys and the mainland. The largest of these, Florida Bay, is a broad expanse of water over which are scattered some 150 mangrove-covered islands.

The continental shelf in southern Florida is narrower than anywhere else on our eastern seaboard. Between Palm Beach and Miami Beach, the 600-foot contour lies only three to four miles from the beach; even along the Florida Keys where the shelf is broader, it is only 10 miles away. An important feature of this narrow shelf is a series of submerged reefs paralleling the ocean beach. Although remnants of these reefs can be traced along most of Florida's east coast and as far north as Cape Hatteras, North Carolina, they are most sharply defined and best known from about Palm

Beach to Key West. Like the foundation material of the Florida Keys, these reefs are the remains of massive coral growths that flourished thousands of years ago. Three distinct series of reefs are recognizable, and they are believed to have formed in response to changes in sea level caused by the periodic advances and retreats of continental glaciers. The shallowest, which fishermen call the First Reef or Inside Reef, runs close along the beach in about 10 to 20 feet of water. The next, called the Second Reef or Outer Reef, runs along the 60-foot contour. The last one, called the Third Reef or Deep Reef, runs roughly along the 120-foot contour. From St. Lucie Inlet to near Fowey Rocks, a shoal area just south of Miami Beach, the reefs are rocky structures, many of them covered with encrusting corals, sea fans, sponges, and a few with reef-building corals. Beginning at Fowey Rocks and continuing all the way to the Dry Tortugas, the reefs are composed mostly of living, reef-building corals. These are most abundant along the Second or Outer Reef, which is, in fact, a barrier reef of the same type as the Great Barrier Reef in Australia, the greatest living coral structure in the world.

The structure of a coral reef consists of a calcareous frame of interlocking skeletons of animals, most of them belonging to a class of invertebrates, the corals, which are related to jellyfishes and anemones, and of plants belonging to an order of calcareous red algae. The calcareous algae, the corals, and some invertebrate animals other than the corals, such as bryozoa, secrete the lime that provides their framework and cements the reef, holding it together and protecting it from destruction by wave action. Coral reefs develop where water temperatures during the year usually do not fall below 64°F, and they flourish where the average annual water temperature ranges between 72°F and 75°F. The most highly developed coral reefs of the Atlantic occur in southern Florida, around the islands of the Caribbean and the West Indies, in Bermuda, along the coast of South America to about Rio de Janeiro, and in the Gulf of Guinea off West Africa.

A large variety of marine organisms are called corals. Some are soft-bodied with little evidence of skeletal material. Others, such as the sea fans and sea feathers, have horny axial skeletons that often branch into slender stems. Still others are the stony or true corals that have skeletons of calcareous or stony material. These include the builders of coral reefs. A typical coral reef colony is composed of myriad individuals interconnected by a network of nerve and nutritive canals and existing in a calcareous matrix that provides protection and support. While the individuals, called polyps, are usually minute, the colonial masses they form may be quite large, some reaching several feet in diameter and weighing thousands of pounds.

If examined closely at night when fully expanded and feeding, an individual polyp is seen to have a cylin-

Flats guides can usually put you in front of big tarpon; then it's up to the angler to bring this silver jumper to the boat. For fly fishermen, there is no greater challenge.
(HERB ALLEN)

drical body that is attached to its limestone shelter at one end and free at the other. The free end has a mouth surrounded by tentacles armed with stinging cells, called nematocysts. These capture the polyp's food, consisting of minute animals of the plankton community, called zooplankton.

The great masses of coral seen growing on the ocean bottom develop chiefly by division of the polyps. A coral colony may enlarge into a great mass by branching and budding, grow out sideways into convoluted and flower-shaped lobes, or grow upward into tubular spires. Colonies originating by this asexual method form a single sexually produced polyp consisting largely of calcareous secretions of which only the surface is occupied by living substance. The growth rate of corals varies by species and is greatly influenced by environmental conditions. For the massive, slow-growing types, it may be only about one-fourth inch each year; with the faster growing, branching types, it may be as much as four to eight inches annually.

Single-celled algae grow within nearly all reef-building corals. Although their function has been much debated by scientists, the algae are never used as food by the corals. These two dissimilar organisms are probably mutually benefited by their close association. The algae benefit by utilizing the carbon dioxide as well as the nitrogenous and phosphorous wastes given off by the corals. The corals benefit by receiving oxygen that the algae produce during the day and by having their waste products removed.

113

Charter boats with skilled captains and mates, like the Catch 22 *out of Bud and Mary's Marina in Islamorada, can almost guarantee trophy catches, such as this big bull dolphin.* (FLORIDA KEYS TDC)

From off the Dry Tortugas to St. Lucie Inlet, the Gulf Stream flows northward at 3 to 5 knots. Its width is 40 to 70 miles, its depth is half a mile. This great ocean current forms the boundary between the relatively cool, somewhat low-salinity water lying alongshore and the warmer, saltier water of the Sargasso Sea. It was originally believed that the rivers flowing into the Gulf of Mexico, especially the Mississippi, combined to form the source of the Gulf Stream, which was often analogized to a river or stream in the ocean. Actually, the Gulf Stream does not originate at a point but is part of the general circulation of surface water in the North Atlantic Ocean.

TIDES

Along the east coast between St. Lucie Inlet and Key Largo, the two successive daily tidal cycles are of equal amplitude. Here the difference between high and low water is about 2½ feet. Along the rest of the Florida Keys, at the entrance to the Gulf of Mexico, there is a flood and an ebb of tide twice daily, as along the east coast, but they are peculiar in being markedly unequal. During most of the time, one of the daily high tides is twice as high as the other and one of the low tides twice as low as the other. This phenomenon is especially char-

acteristic of the tides at Key West, where the tidal range varies between ½ and 2½ feet.

Tidal ranges in the lagoons, sounds, and bays vary between a few feet and a few inches depending on their distance from the influence of the sea. The tidal range is usually about a foot near inlets; it may be only a few inches in lagoons located midway between the various inlets, and in northeastern Florida Bay where the tidal flow is hampered by the shallowness of the bottom and aquatic vegetation. In parts of Florida Bay the wind direction and velocity often have more influence than the tide on the rise and fall of the water level.

SEASONS AND WEATHER

The climate along this stretch of coast is subtropical to tropical. The temperatures are warm almost throughout the year and the humidity high. This part of Florida is in the belt of the Northeast Trade Winds, the dependability of which made this a popular route for sailing vessels. These winds are interrupted only during the short winter season as occasional cold waves accompanied by northwest winds push down from the Arctic. Air temperatures then plummet to about 40°F but soon return to their normal winter range in the low 70s. Throughout the rest of the year, daytime air temperatures normally range from the high 70s to the low 90s. The rainy season occurs over a 6-month period from May to October. Then, squalls and thunderstorms are frequent, sometimes with gale-force winds. Occasionally hurricanes strike. These severe tropical cyclonic storms, most frequent and intense from August to October, produce huge tides and waves. The resulting floods and heavy winds can wreak terrible damage to boats and docks, as well as to shore settlements.

REGULATIONS

Most anglers in Florida need a license to fish in salt or brackish water. There are saltwater regulations, too. There are minimum size limits for bluefish, pompano, fluke (locally called flounder), Spanish mackerel, spotted and gray sea trouts, red drum (locally called redfish), and snook. Also, there are possession limits or catch limits for snook, sea trout, redfish, bonefish, sailfish, tarpon, and striped bass. Florida regulates the season, type of gear, method of capture, and catch limits of shrimps, spiny lobsters (locally called crawfish), stone crabs, oysters, and clams. Regulations also exist for spearfishing and for netting mullet. For a copy of the fishing and shellfishing regulations, write to the Florida Marine Patrol, Marjory Stoneham Douglas Building, 3900 Commonwealth Blvd., Tallahassee, FL 32399; (904) 488-5757.

Turn to page 97 in Chapter 2 for a more detailed description of Florida's fishing regulations.

Sailing Along On Florida's Atlantic Coast

by Herb Allen

Labeled by author Jim Bob Tinsley as a "Swashbuckler of the Open Seas," the sailfish is considered by many to be the most glamorous and precious booty in the blue water treasure chest. Scores of hearts have skipped more than a beat or two when encountering sails basking or feeding on the surface.

When hooked, this fish often explodes in a series of sky-groping leaps. It'll greyhound, tail-walk, twist, tug, turn, bend, curl, roll, spin, arch, and sound in a frenzied quest to disengage.

Although sailfish have come under intense scrutiny since the 1920s and 30s by the angling and scientific communities, many questions about their migratory patterns, growth rates, feeding habits, and spawning rituals remain unanswered. Even today, veteran fishermen are often divided regarding the manner in which the fish will strike a bait, what enticements are best, and the requirements for optimum tackle.

What is not known about sailfish frequently surpasses what is.

For example, it's been assumed for decades that pelagic Atlantic and Pacific sailfish were distinct subspecies of the family *Istiophoridae*, because the Pacific variety "grows larger." Based upon current taxonomy, some scientists are now suggesting that the Atlantic and Pacific genres are not only one in the same, but that Atlantic residents can reach much larger sizes than previously thought. Other scientists dispute this theory.

Various studies made by biologists indicate that East Coast sailfish will average between 30 and 50 pounds, with a 100-pounder being rare. On the West Coast, a longer and heavier Pacific sail weighing 100 pounds won't draw a second look. Like most other species in fishdom, the female grows larger than the male.

When hooked, the majestic sailfish often explodes in a series of sky-groping leaps. (BOB MCNALLY)

A quick scan of the current International Game Fish Association (IGFA) record book confirms that Pacific sailfish do seem to grow quite a bit larger than the Atlantic variety. The all-tackle mark for the Pacific sail is an impressive 221 pounds, while the Atlantic standard-bearer is 128 pounds. A comparison of line-class records from 2- to 80-pound test reflects the same size discrepancy.

Pursuing sails for sport, recreation, or commercial purposes is a rather recent development. The first commercial hook-and-liners brought some into Key West in 1884. Presumably a recreational angler, a gentleman by the

name of Mr. Armes, is described as having caught a sailfish off the Hotel Royal Palm in 1898 or 1899 in the 1902 publication "Where, When, and How to Catch Fish on the East Coast of Florida."

Offshore pioneer Capt. Charlie Thompson may have been the first charter boat skipper to regularly fish for the gamester. He is known to have put a party onto sailfish in March, 1901, off Soldier Key. In another early memorandum, Thompson is said to have guided John Martin to a sail catch off Miami in 1904.

Charles Frederick Holder, a top angler of his day, took his first sailfish in the early 1900s off Loggerhead Key. James P. Hall of New Jersey and Miami Beach caught one of the first on rod and reel in 1906, while trolling in the Gulf Stream off Palm Beach.

The drop-back technique is thought to have been developed by Capt. Bill Hatch in 1915. Hatch also contrived the first strip bait, while Capt. Jimmy "Cotton Thread" Jordan's "brightly colored rubber ball" is said to be the first teaser used to bring sailfish close in to the boat.

The first sailfish tournament ever held took place at the Long Key Fishing Club in 1925, where Capt. Hatch brought in 113 fish during the five-week event. The remainder of the field, consisting of 13 boats, combined for 106.

Capt. George Farnsworth of California first introduced kite fishing to the United States in 1905. Capt. Tommy Gifford is said to have used kites designed by early IGFA record holder Harlan Major in the late 1920s in Florida waters. Gifford is also credited with developing the modern outrigger in 1933.

Baits used at the turn of the century included grunts, porgies, spots, and other small fishes weighing up to one-half pound. Hatch's bonito and dolphin strip baits of the 1920s are still used today, but have been expanded to include the bellies of barracuda, whip ray, and mackerel. Whole baits now being used include mullet, goggle-eyes, ballyhoo, blue runners, flying fish, sardines, squid, and pilchards.

Names used for sailfish in other parts of the country and the world include swordfish, bayonetfish, spikefish, spindlebill, spindlesnout, Jumping Jack, Ballerina of the Bounding Main, and Blue Water Greyhound. The Chinese refer to it as a birdfish, sailing fish or sailor fish, while a writer in the 1600s called it a sea-wood-cock, an allusion to the woodcock's long bill.

Basic sailfish colors are blue, purple, and silver, with variations in shade and density. A series of 15 to 20 cross bands or vertical stripes decorate the body of most specimens. Their colors will change with the mood of the fish, as well as with prevalent food, light, and water conditions.

When a sailfish is fighting or excited, it is said to be "lit up." Its color appears much deeper than usual and its light blue tail edge and its pectoral and dorsal fins often glow like neon, but fade immediately after the fish is boated.

The most striking feature of the sailfish is the large, fanlike anterior dorsal fin that begins at the nape of its neck, occupies more than half of its back, and is nearly twice its body depth. The membrane is thin, similar to parchment, and is reinforced with long, flexible rays about an inch apart that radiate from the backbone. This sail can be raised or folded away in the manner of an Oriental fan.

When hooked, there's no telling what a sailfish may do. It has an amazing assortment of tricks and maneuvers. Anglers are well advised to keep slack out of their lines, keep their rod tips up, and set the reel's drag system at less than one-half of the line's breaking strength.

Joe Contillo, who works with the National Oceanic and Atmospheric Administration (NOAA) in its billfish program, is one of many who still feel the Atlantic and Pacific sail are separate and distinct species. "The same condition holds true for blue marlin," he points out. "Pacific blues average out quite a bit larger than the Atlantic variety."

While studies are ongoing to determine if, in fact, there is a taxonomic difference between the species, scientists are in general agreement that sailfish are circumtropical and occur in warm waters throughout the world, ranging roughly from latitude 30-degrees south to latitude 30-degrees north, "with occasional stragglers beyond these limits."

G.L. Voss says sailfish distribution is extended during long, hot summers with prevailing southerly winds. He also points out that the densest concentra-tions in western Atlantic stocks are found closer to land masses, perhaps due to the influence of the Gulf Stream.

Throughout its various ranges, a large segment of the sailfish population is thought to be year-round. However, pronounced seasonal variations in abundance and distribution have been documented. In other words, some fish migrate while others stay at home.

A 1973 study showed that Brazilian longliners caught sailfish all year long, but that catches were larger and over a broader area from October through March than from April through September. In the Caribbean and Gulf of Mexico, the greatest abundance occurs from April through September, while Florida's southeast coast sees a dramatic increase during the winter months.

Voss states that sailfish distributions along the east coast of Florida appear to be affected by wind and temperature. "In the summer," he said, "there is a diffusion of sailfish to the northward correlated with a northward extension of warm water. These same fish are driven southward to congregate in schools off the Florida coast with the beginning of cold weather and northerly winds."

If every egg spawned by female sailfish survived to reach maturity, it's doubtful there would be any room left in the sea for other species. In 1953, Voss determined that western Atlantic specimens spewed between 2.3 and 4.7 million eggs. In 1971, one study found 19.5 million eggs in a single East African sailfish.

Young billfishes are all quite similar in their early development, thus making identification between marlins and sailfish difficult. As the fish rapidly grow into juveniles, they begin displaying prominent pterotic and preopercular spines, a beak-like snout, and a very dark pigmentation. When a billfish reaches 10 mm total length, its large dorsal fin begins to take shape, as does its long bill.

In its juvenile and adolescent

phases, a sailfish's diet will consist mainly of fish larvae and copepods. As it grows, its meals become more varied and sophisticated, graduating into shrimp, crustaceans, squid, and a potpourri of diminutive fishes.

Except for humans, the sailfish has few natural enemies. Scattered reports of attacks by dolphins, sharks, and killer whales upon free-swimming sailfishes are probably the exception rather than the rule, scientists agree.

Some sailfish are known to migrate for long distances. The Woods Hole Oceanographic Institution Cooperative Gamefish Tagging Program once tagged a fish off Cape Hatteras, North Carolina, that was later recovered in waters off Surinam on the northern coast of South America, more than 1,000 miles away. So far, no transatlantic or transequatorial movements for sailfish have been documented.

Currently, the scientific community is zeroing in on methods to determine the age of sailfish. NOAA's Eric Prince and Dennis Lee point out that age and growth research is an important component of fishery science. "In order to assess the well-being of an entire population of fish, it's often necessary to separate catch or landing statistics by age, so each year-class can be followed through the fishery as they get older," said Prince and Lee. "In this way, assessment models can be used to determine the health or general status of each component of the population and management recommendations can be adjusted accordingly."

One of the approaches used by NOAA scientists to determine age and growth rates of fish is analogous to the method used to estimate the age of trees. The number of concentric rings in the trunk of a tree generally represents its age, (i.e. one ring is equal to one calendar year of life). The spacing between these rings is proportional to the rate of growth for that particular year; the larger the spacing, the faster the rate of growth. In temperate regions, faster growth usually occurs in summer and slowest growth in winter.

"In much the same manner," say Prince and Lee, "the age and growth rate of fishes are estimated by counting concentric rings or growth bands which form in their skeletal tissues, such as spines, fin rays, vertebrae, scales, or inner ear bones called otoliths. One problem in using this approach," they said, "is that the time span between the formation of those rings in skeletal structures needs to be determined. This is referred to as validating the accuracy of age determination methods, and it is a critical part in our aging study."

There was a time when biologists thought the life span of sailfish was three or four years. They've now revised this figure sharply upward based upon a tagging and recapture program that has enlisted the help of tournament sponsors and commercial fishermen. One sailfish tagged and released in 1973 off Islamorada was taken nearly 11 years later off Boynton Beach. It was estimated to have weighed 40 pounds at the time of release, and weighed 54 pounds when caught again in 1984. How old was this fish in 1973 when caught the first time? Good question.

Perhaps one day soon, providing we still have a billfishery left to study, scientists will be able to accurately determine the age of these fish.

One thing that can be concluded from various figures accumulated by biologists in recent years is that the number of sailfish being caught by recreational anglers is steadily declining. For example, the number of Fish Hooked-Per-Hour-Of-Effort (HPUE) in the northern Gulf of Mexico declined tremendously from .047 in 1976 to .007 in 1986. Off Florida's east coast, the figures are more drastic, falling from an HPUE 1977 high of nearly .090 to a dismal .005 in 1986.

As far back as the early 1960s scientists confirmed that heavy commercial longlining can devastate a bill fishery, not to mention such bottom feeders as grouper, snapper, amberjack, etc. One study, off Central America, showed a hook rate of 10.6 sailfish per

100 hooks in 1964. The following year the rate dropped to 9.5, and in 1966 it dipped to 5.8 fish per 100 hooks. Another survey, made off Kenya between 1958 and 1968, showed that even though the catch and the catch-per-unit effort (CUE) remained relatively stable, there was a sharp decline in the mean weight of fish caught.

The Japanese longlining fishing effort for sailfish probably peaked out in the Atlantic in the mid-60s when more than 97 million hooks were fished, resulting in a catch of at least 118,000 billfish, including sails. The catch per 10,000 hooks rose from 39.0 in 1959 to a high of 189.0 in 1967.

While the Japanese longline effort in our waters is down today, domestic operations are up and, unfortunately, the end is not yet in view. Shortsighted federal rulemakers twiddle their thumbs and ignore the obvious fact that our saltwater fishery is being sacrificed on the alter of greed.

An even more ominous threat to the billfishery—and everything else that swims—is the relatively new, efficient, and deadly drift net that kills indiscriminately. An abomination that is proliferating at an alarming rate, drift nets could prove to be fatal for all finny inhabitants of offshore waters worldwide, say knowledgeable fisheries biologists.

As usual, federal authorities charged with management planning show little or no interest in implementing constraints on destructive gear utilized by a selfish and thoughtless commercial industry that very conceivably could transform productive seas into arid aqua-deserts. ■

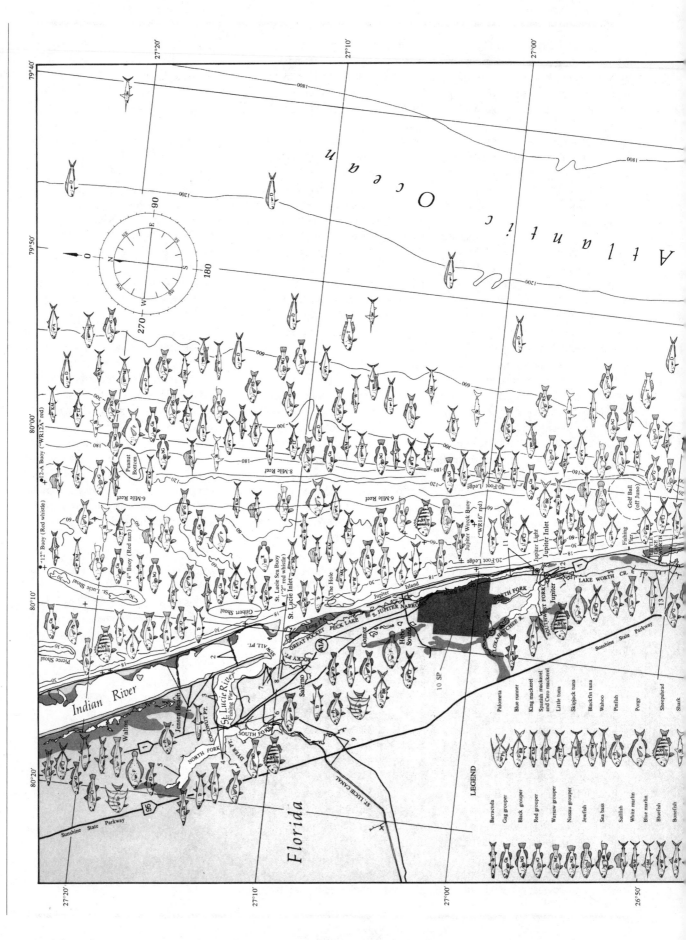

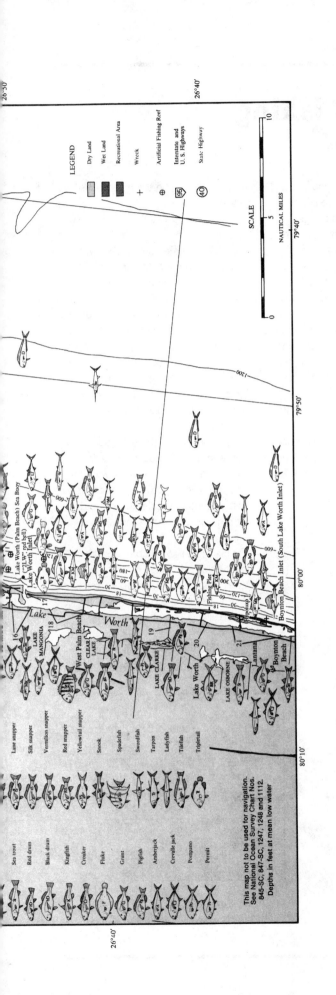

ST. LUCIE INLET TO BOYNTON BEACH INLET

LAND CONFIGURATION AND WATER DEPTH

The land along this section, like that of all Florida's east coast, is uniformly low and flat. Within two dozen miles of the sea, few landforms rise more than 25 feet. Indeed, man-made structures jutting above the otherwise low, tree-lined horizon are what arrests our attention as we view the coast from a boat offshore.

The Indian River

Indian River, a narrow, shallow, coastal lagoon, ends along this section. It began over 100 miles up the coast behind Cape Canaveral and now terminates where the North Fork and South Fork of St. Lucie River connect to the sea by way of St. Lucie Inlet. Until about the middle of the 1800s, Indian River south of Cape Canaveral was connected to the sea in only two places. One, which no longer exists, was Indian River Inlet, located about a mile north of Fort Pierce; the other was Jupiter Inlet at the southern end of the Indian River. During the second half of the 1800s, St. Lucie Inlet was blasted and dug through a narrow point of the beach. This passage eventually captured most of the flow of water between the sea and the lagoon and, as St. Lucie Inlet became a larger and more important passage for boats, people gradually came to think of it as being the southern end of Indian River.

The Gulf Stream

The dominant current along this stretch is the Gulf Stream, flowing northward at 1 to 5 knots. Off Palm Beach, the western edge of its tropical blue water, locally called the inside edge, ordinarily sweeps along the outermost reef, but because of the Gulf Stream's undulating course, it may even touch the beaches at times. The inside edge of the Gulf Stream closely follows the 120-foot contour along southeastern Florida, and, as the continental shelf broadens north of Palm Beach, the Gulf Stream gradually moves farther away from land.

Mad Man Fishing

by Herb Allen

Jerry Metz calls his snook fishing technique, "Mad Man Fishing."

Metz is a veteran Cotee Master Guide who operates on and around the St. Lucie River, and a respected teacher of local public and private fishing classes.

He mainly targets linesiders during the daylight hours, around docks, with light tackle. "People have called me nuts, and maybe they're right," mused Metz. "But I get plenty of strikes, have lots of fun, and even manage to catch a few."

Metz uses anything from 4- to 8-pound-test line. He suggests that smaller fish are fairly easy to move away from the pilings. Metz describes larger, legal-sized snook as "oh man

fish" because by the time you can say, "Oh man, nice fish," they've cut him off on barnacle-encrusted pilings.

But that doesn't discourage him.

When in his own boat, a small, canoe-like craft, he chases big snook under a dock and, with the reel in free spool, lets the fish take its own course through the pilings. Sometimes it works, sometimes it doesn't. Either way, it's both enjoyable and challenging to an angler who has caught literally tens of thousands of snook in three decades.

Metz determines the bite by the moon's position on the horizon.

"Fish eat something every six hours and majorly every 12 hours," said the West Palm Beach expert. "When the

moon is resting on the horizon, fish get active."

Metz fishes almost exclusively with ¼-ounce Cotee Liv'Eye Action Jigs, often with a green Super Grub with gold and red metal flake. To his light monofilament, the Mad Man rigs with 18 inches of double line tied with an Albright Special knot to three feet of 25-pound leader material.

For snook, he likes docks with an average water depth of four to six feet.

"If there is a large boat tied up or hung on davits, there'll probably be a hole beneath where snook lay up," he stresses.

According to Metz, the tide direction is immaterial, just so long as the water is moving. "Fish will always lay into the tide," he says. "The idea is to cast a jig into the tide under the dock, let it hit bottom, and then work it out."

Placing a jig well up under the dock involves a technique known as skipping. With a side arm cast, Metz tosses it at near water level so it bounces off the surface like a smooth stone skipping across a pond.

During his favorite fall months, Metz often finds two or three fish at each dock. The largest he's landed lately on such tiny tackle was a 15-pounder.

When fishing from a larger boat that's unable to navigate beneath a dock and between pilings, he will nose the craft near the structure and flip a Cotee Jig into likely spots, just as a bass angler will flip plastic worms into small weed openings or dense obstructions.

Next time you're fishing on the St. Lucie River and see a bearded guy hanging around boat docks, it'll probably be the "Mad Man," Jerry Metz, doing what he likes best. ■

In the time you can say "Oh man, nice fish," a snook can cut you off.
(HERB ALLEN)

Medley in Hobe Sound

by George Poveromo

That could be redfish!" said Capt. Steve Anderson, throttling his trolling motor and giving chase to the school of mullet that had suddenly turned skittish. Somewhere under the dark water, a predator—or predators—had moved onto the flat, and was now stalking the nervous school of bait.

"Cast when you can reach the school," the guide instructed. I did, and quickly found myself cupping the spool of my spinning reel, trying to stop whatever it was from reaching the channel. The fish stopped short of the deep water, but continued a series of short, powerful runs as I eased it toward the boat on the 8-pound line. Eventually Anderson was able to slip a net under the fish, adding yet another chunky red to an already impressive season's tally. Before the redfish encounter, we had caught and released dozens of small snook, plus lots of big ladyfish, mangrove snapper, jack crevalle, a couple of trout, and a small barracuda.

We were plugging the shallow coves along the west bank of the Intracoastal Waterway (ICW) in Hobe Sound, Florida, between Stuart and Jupiter. Anderson favors this stretch of waterway because of the diversity of gamefish and lack of fishing pressure. It's overlooked by many local anglers because of the productive fishing nearby in Jupiter's Loxahatchee River and Stuart's St. Lucie River.

With the inshore attention focused on the more popular river systems, Anderson rarely contends with more than a handful of anglers along "the strip"—a section of the ICW running between marker 32 at the northern end and marker 42 to the south. That's fine with him. Having fished this area for nearly 20 years, he has fine-tuned his strategies to produce a variety of inshore species. The

Herb Allen with a hefty redfish caught on a jig. (HERB ALLEN)

action can be fast-paced, perfect for kids who grow impatient between strikes and light-tackle enthusiasts. Anderson has even developed a strong fly fishing clientele who seek snook, ladyfish, and redfish.

One of Anderson's specialties is catching redfish, a gamefish that's not too common locally. Although he doesn't specifically target them, because of the abundance of other species, he does average one fish per trip between February and March. Redfish usually reveal their whereabouts by chasing mullet up onto the flats, forcing them to school up and dart about erratically.

Anderson's strategy is to sneak up on a school of nervous mullet and cast a gold-flake Cotee shad-tail jig to the outskirts of the school. The jig's pulsating tail provides a lifelike action, and it should be retrieved slowly and steadily as soon as it hits the water. If any redfish are around, the jig rarely gets far.

On first glance, the western side of Hobe Sound's Intracoastal Waterway appears to be simply a vast expanse of shallow mud and grass. What most anglers don't know, however, is that this relatively shallow bottom has a network of hidden troughs that run along the shoreline. In January and February, scores of small snook ambush bait from these channels and depressions, which average about a foot deeper than the surrounding bottom. Some of the best troughs run parallel to the mangrove-lined banks. To fish them, Anderson factors in the wind and current before positioning himself for a quiet drift down the flats, using an electric trolling motor to hold him near the better points along the way. Anderson fan-casts into and along the troughs, letting the lure sink for a second or two before beginning the retrieve.

Most ICW snook range between 12 and 18 inches—but there are lots of them! During the peak season, a

121

Charter Information

Capt. Steve Anderson knows the ICW extremely well. Fishing from his 18-foot Hewes flats skiff, *Still Water*, he also scouts the Loxahatchee River for big jack crevalle and snook, the Jupiter Inlet and nearby beaches for summer snook, and the nearshore waters and reefs for bonito, jacks, barracuda, African pompano, and cobia. He can also arrange specialty trips for shad fishing in the Titusville region. His expertise is light-tackle and fly fishing. Anderson can be reached at (407) 744-3630.

good angler can commonly release between one dozen and two dozen snook in a four-hour period. Count on the bigger ones to weigh around five pounds, although Anderson's largest Hobe Sound flats snook weighed 17 pounds, 6 ounces.!

The gold-flake jig Anderson favors imitates the local bait inhabiting the grass beds, such as finger mullet, mojarra, pinfish, and pilchards. It's a breeze catching several types of fish by fan-casting this relatively small lure. Anderson uses about 18 inches of 20-pound-test monofilament for a leader, connecting it to a short (one-foot) Bimini loop with a small barrel swivel. The leader is upgraded to 25-pound test for ladyfish and bluefish. Be sure to change the leader after every lady or blue, no matter how little it has been abraded.

Voracious predators that emerge from the channels to annihilate bait on the flats, "chopper" bluefish in the three- to six-pound class are abundant between December and March. These fish can be chummed up from the channel with glass minnows (live ones produce best) and caught on topwater plugs and flies. Sometimes the blues are so aggressive that they'll chomp a

hooked ladyfish in half! On a good morning, Anderson catches a half-dozen bluefish while he's variety fishing. If a client wants to pursue them specifically, he'll anchor upwind or upcurrent of a sandy patch off the ICW channel and wait for the blues to chase bait off the flat. As long as there's bait in the area, the bluefish should be around.

As mentioned, this section of the ICW yields trophy-sized ladyfish, some as heavy as six pounds. Here, the strategy shifts from the flats to the channel, where ladyfish weighing between two and four pounds are thick between November and March. On a slick-calm morning, ladyfish can often be seen rolling like tarpon on the surface. When they're on top, they'll explode on small surface plugs such as the Tiny Torpedo. Otherwise, they're suckers for jigs, spoons, and flies.

Anderson has two methods of catching ladyfish. On 2-, 4-, or 8-pound spinning tackle, he uses a pink bone-fish-style jig with a white head and 20 inches of 25-pound mono leader. He casts the jig along the channel edges in about eight feet of water and allows it to sink. With quick, sharp jerks of the rod tip, he sweeps the jig off the bottom and lets it free-fall a foot or so. As long as the jigging action is fast, the ladies will strike. They tend to belt the jig primarily on the fall.

Fly fishing can also be productive on the ICW. Anderson covers the surface with a popper during the morning. When the wind kicks up, he switches to an intermediate sinking line with a six- to eight-pound tippet and uses either a Clouser Minnow or a Steve's Death Bomb fly (a hot-pink, double-skirted fly).

The trick to catching ladyfish on a fly is to let the line sink to the bottom (a 10 count is sufficient) and strip it quickly three or four times before allowing it to sink again. Drawing strikes requires hard, sharp strips. As with jigs, ladyfish usually attack a fly on the fall.

Mangrove snapper also cruise the flats and congregate around the channel markers. If you're serious about

catching legal-sized (12-inch) fish, anchor on the outside of the channel marker and use a piece of shrimp on a No. 6 hook tied directly to an 8-pound-test outfit. About two feet up the line, add a ¼-ounce sinker and a small barrel swivel.

Anderson has found that the best action occurs when the boat is stationary. Sometimes he'll anchor off the bow and stern to hold his boat in position. He gives the fish about 30 minutes to turn on before trying another piling. The fish seem to school up and feed best around the full moon in January and February. As an added bonus, black drum averaging around three pounds appear like clockwork around Super Bowl weekend.

Since the Hobe Sound stretch can also be fished in rough weather because of the mangroves (the exception being a hard east wind, when there's no protection), it's a great winter option. The biggest drawbacks are the long runs from Jupiter and Stuart, and the no-wake manatee zones.

Even so, the effort is worth it, especially if you're after some fast action with a variety of species. Whether you're a light-tackle buff, a fly fisherman, or just want some good fishing to get you through the winter, give this stretch of the ICW a try. You won't be disappointed. ∎

BOYNTON BEACH INLET TO GOVERNMENT CUT, MIAMI BEACH

LAND CONFIGURATION

A chain of long, low barrier sandbars that separates the open ocean from the shallow tidal lagoons and the mainland begins near the mouth of the St. Johns River and ends 300 miles to the south at Miami Beach. Most of the sand composing these barrier bars has come from farther north. Since far back in geological time, sediments have been carried down the various rivers of what we know as Georgia, South Carolina, and North Carolina, and have been deposited in the sea. Although a large amount of quartz sand, among the most resistant of the accumulating sediments and also the heaviest, has remained close to shore, prevailing nearshore currents have been strong enough to transport it southward. In northeastern Florida, the continuous addition of sand from the north makes ocean beaches wide and the dunes behind them relatively high. In southeastern Florida, in contrast, the continental shelf is very narrow. There the sand that might otherwise be used in building the beaches continually slips away into the abyss of the ocean so that the beaches are at most only a few hundred feet wide, and, in the few places where dunes exist, they are very small.

Behind the barrier bars lies a narrow, semienclosed waterway. What was formerly a series of unconnected lagoons, rivers, lakes, and creeks bordered by mangroves has been blasted, dug, and dredged into a continuous brackish-water canal that serves as a passage for boats. This is the Intracoastal or Inland Waterway. Bulkheading and building along this part of the waterway is so extensive that most of the shallow flats and aquatic vegetation that had formerly provided habitat required by many shore fishes has become greatly reduced. Consequently, very few fishes are able to live in this waterway.

Reefs

The most striking feature of this narrow shelf is a series of three rocky reefs paralleling the ocean beach. The shallowest, called the First Reef by fishermen, runs close along the beach in about 10 to 20 feet of water. The next, called the Second Reef, is ½ to 1½ miles from shore in about 60 feet of water. The deepest, called the Third Reef, is 1½ to 2½ miles farther at a depth of about 120 feet. Although remnants of these reefs, especially the Third Reef, can be traced along most of Florida's east coast and as far north as Cape Hatteras, North Carolina, they are most sharply defined and are best known by fishermen from about West Palm Beach to Key West.

FISH AND FISHING

A large variety of fishes reside among the coral heads, shelves and ledges of eroded coral rock, and the coral rubble strewn over the bottom. Many of these species find shelter and food among the communities growing on the ancient reefs, including calcareous algae, sponges, sea fans, seaweeds, and sea grasses. The Gulf Stream's western edge sweeps past the Third Reef, affording favorable conditions for many species of pelagic fishes. By knowing the habits of each species and the depth of water it prefers, an angler can vary his fishing location and technique and be able to determine fairly accurately what he will catch.

A diverse array of fishes occurs along the ocean beaches and the First Reef. Among these are a number of species that are often referred to as shore fishes. These include members of the drum family, especially the sea trouts and kingfishes, locally called whiting. In general, these species are not as abundant along here as in more northern areas where the continental shelf is broader. Nevertheless, sea trouts and king whitings as well as other members of their family are quite common among the sea grasses growing in shallow sandy places protected from the waves by outcroppings of the reef. Other shore fishes, including pompano and ladyfish, migrate seasonally along the coast, feeding as they move. Tarpon occur mostly in the shallow water along

Jack crevalle are frequent visitors to inshore reefs along the Florida coast. (HERB ALLEN)

123

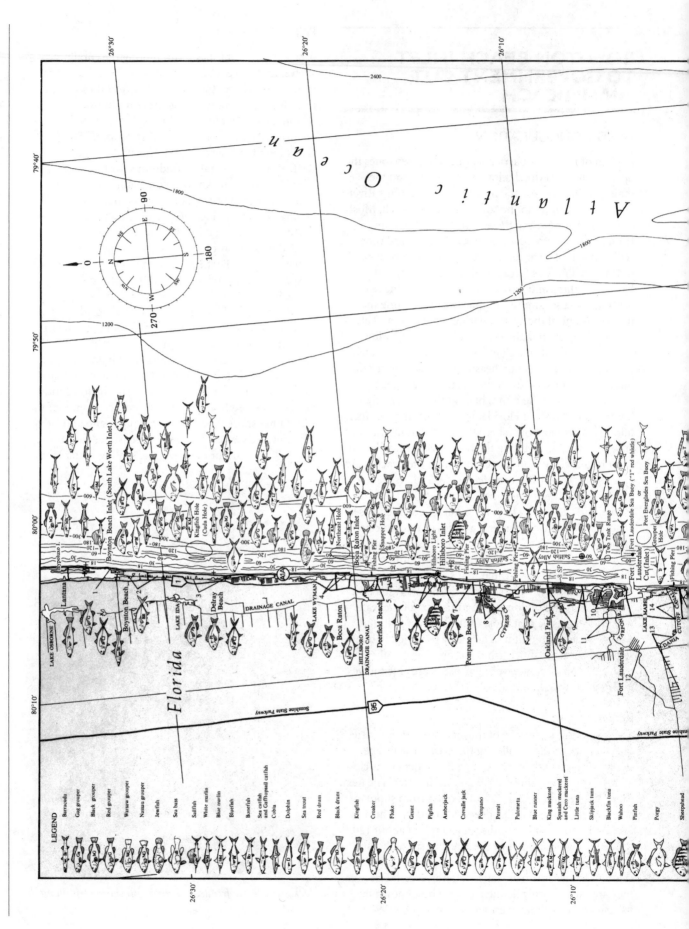

the ocean beaches and the First Reef, except during their seasonal migrations out beyond the Third Reef. Snook occur in the surf along this stretch of coast, especially during summer. The young of deep-dwelling groupers and snappers are also common in this shallow water as are the young of grunts, crevalle jack, and blue runner. Barracuda, cobia, and, at times, even large sharks are common just off the First Reef. One of the common fishes occurring in shallow water here is the Spanish mackerel. While some are as far off as the outside edge of the Second Reef, by far the great majority stay inshore of the Second Reef within the coastal water, which fishermen call green water.

The principal habitat of many adult groupers and snappers begins along the edge of the Second Reef, usually in depths of 60 to 90 feet. Here are found the large gag, black, red, and Nassau groupers and the mutton and gray snappers. Even though these species, like most other reef dwellers, are relatively stationary, many move into shallower water during warm months and back into deeper water during the cold months. Warsaw groupers occur in the shallow water along the First Reef but reach their largest sizes in the deep water about the Third Reef. Here, too, in the deep water of the Third Reef occur the vermilion, red and silk snappers, as well as the largest size jack crevalles, blue runners, and amberjacks.

Large king mackerel often occur near the bottom of the Third Reef, sometimes even in depths of 300 feet or more. Like many other members of the mackerel and tuna family, large individuals remain in deeper water, staying close to the bottom, and are more solitary than the smaller ones. While most of the king mackerel concentrate between the offshore edge of the Second Reef and the western edge of the Gulf Stream, small individuals sometimes school with Spanish mackerel of similar size, usually in the shallow water of the First Reef.

Most of the sailfish concentrate in the same general area as king mackerel. Some of the sailfish are in the Gulf Stream or oceanic water, which fishermen call the blue water, but most seem to concentrate along the boundary where the green inshore water meets and mixes with the blue offshore water. Although sailfish venture far offshore during their seasonal migrations, especially in the fall, they generally remain relatively close to land and are certainly less oceanic than their relatives, the white and blue marlins. White marlin occur most often between the Third Reef and the Gulf Stream edge. They are usually more concentrated closer to the Third Reef in fall and winter, and somewhat farther offshore in the spring and summer. Blue marlin occur over deeper water than do white marlin. It is unusual to find them in as close as the Third Reef, most being offshore in the Gulf Stream beyond the 300-foot contour.

Dolphins are another oceanic species occurring

commonly in the blue water. Even though they are closely associated with warm ocean currents, dolphins often concentrate along the interface of the Gulf Stream and the green coastal water. At the surface along this convergence of water masses are long windrows of drifting seaweed, principally sargassum. Fishermen call these weed lines. Animal life, notable both for the numbers of organisms as well as the diversity of species, thrives about this floating weed. Weed line inhabitants include pelagic crabs, shrimps, and sea slugs, as well as young triggerfishes, tilefishes, puffers, flying fishes, jacks, and scads. Large pelagic fishes, especially dolphins but also white marlin, little tunny, and king mackerel, gather about this drifting sargassum community to feed.

GOVERNMENT CUT, MIAMI BEACH, TO KEY LARGO

LAND CONFIGURATION AND WATER DEPTH

Like the rest of Florida's coast, the mainland here is monotonously low. From Miami to Homestead, for example, only a narrow limestone ridge rising slightly more than 10 feet above sea level separates the coast from the nearly 50 miles of extremely flat, wet prairie, covered largely by sawgrass and stunted trees, that make up a large part of the Everglades.

Dense stands of mangroves line most of the mainland shore here except in places where people have filled them for housing lots, businesses, and boat docks, or have otherwise destroyed them to gain easy access to the water. The mangroves growing in dense, low forests thrive on the salt-impregnated soil in areas often flooded by tide, and they extend into the shallow bays and sounds.

The Florida Keys, which begin in this section at Virginia Key, separate Biscayne Bay and the other shallow bays and sounds, including Florida Bay, from the sea. Locally called the Keys, they are a rather narrow chain of low, rocky islands that extend southwestward in a sweeping, 190-mile arc from Miami Beach to Loggerhead Key in the Dry Tortugas.

The Upper Keys, that is from Virginia Key to about Big Pine Key, consist of an ancient coral reef formed many thousands of years ago when a warm sea covered this entire area to a depth of 60 to 120 feet. The rise of these Keys above the water resulted from changes in sea level and by the natural upward growth of coral. Over the years, currents have cut narrow passageways between them. The shores of the Upper Keys are mostly of sharp, craggy coral and limestone or of dense mangrove stands which are especially abundant along the

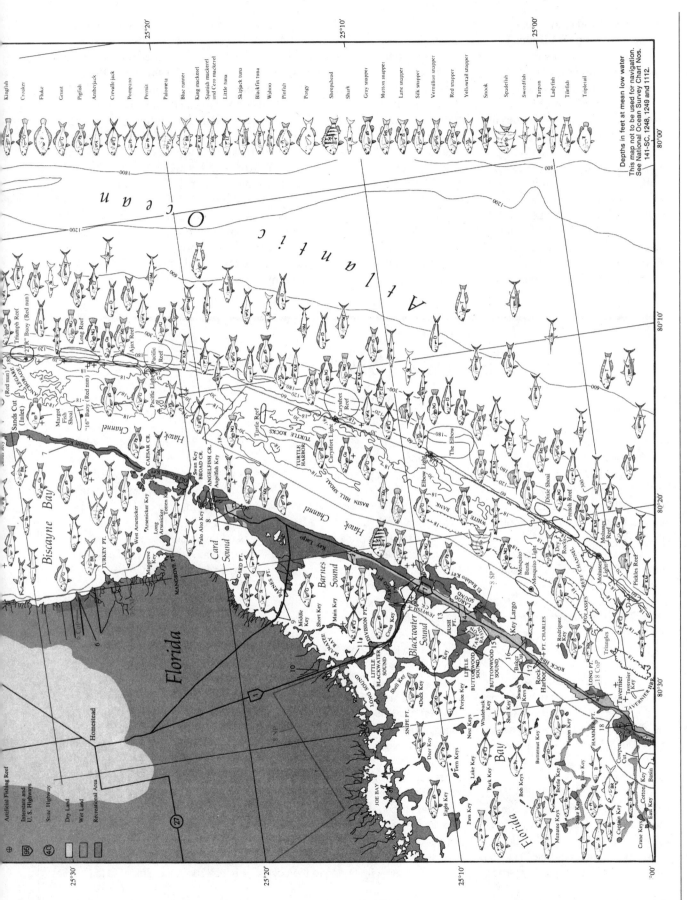

Kingfish
Croaker
Fluke
Grunt
Pigfish
Amberjack
Crevalle Jack
Pompano
Permit
Palometa
Blue runner
King mackerel
Spanish mackerel and Cero mackerel
Little tuna
Skipjack tuna
Blackfin tuna
Wahoo
Pinfish
Porgy
Sheepshead
Shark
Gray snapper
Mutton snapper
Lane snapper
Silk snapper
Vermillion snapper
Red snapper
Yellowtail snapper
Snook
Spadefish
Swordfish
Tarpon
Ladyfish
Tilefish
Tripletail

Depths in feet at mean low water
This map not to be used for navigation.
See National Ocean Survey Chart Nos.
141-SC, 1248, 1249 and 1112.

Artificial Fishing Reef
Interstate and U.S. Highways
State Highway
Dry Land
Wet Land
Recreational Area

Florida

Biscayne Bay

Atlantic Ocean

protected Florida Bay side. Few sandy beaches exist along here except at Virginia Key and Key Biscayne.

The series of rocky reefs that began near Sebastian Inlet, 120 miles farther north, continues off here. The distance these reefs extend seaward increases progressively from 3 miles off Miami Beach to 6 miles off Plantation Key. The reefs form the continental shelf along this part of the coast.

Starting from the Keys and proceeding seaward, the sea floor gradually dips to 20 feet in about a mile and a half. A mile farther out it rises to a depth of about 6 feet in a series of rocky and coral reefs, which is locally called the Second or Outer Reef. Southward of about Fowey Rocks to the Dry Tortugas, this reef consists largely of living corals that are arranged in such a way as to form a barrier reef. It is a miniature of the Great Barrier Reef, which extends more than a thousand miles along the Australian coast. The area between the Keys and the Outer Reef is a more or less protected lagoon, called Hawk Channel, which extends all the way to Key West. Because of various rocky and sandy shoals, Hawk Channel is clearly defined only by aids to navigation. On its floor, large beds of turtle grass alternate with rocky areas rich in growths of corals, sponges, anemones, sea fans, and the attached stages of sargassum weed. These rocky areas are called patch reefs or patches and are favorite gathering places for fishes. A mile or two beyond the Outer Reef, the sea floor slopes abruptly to about 120 feet, the Third or Deep Reef. This reef consists of rocky outcroppings with growths of live corals, sponges, sea fans, and other attached forms. Seaward from here, the sea floor, which consists of silt, sand, and rock rubble, descends down to a depth of half a mile. This is the bottom of the Florida Straits.

Florida's Silver Prince

by Jody Moore

Whether it is from the banks of a residential canal or from the deck of a tricked out guide boat deep in the backcountry of Florida's Everglades, baby tarpon are accessible to a fly rodder of any means in South Florida.

Baby tarpon are classified as fish between 2 to 40 pounds. You can find them in the most unlikely of places, as well as where you might expect to find them. Tarpon are euryhaline species. They can live in freshwater or saltwater. Groups of small fish can be found rolling in freshwater canals or golf course lakes miles form the ocean.

"Rolling" describes fish that come to the water's surface to expose their heads as they gulp down air. Tarpon have a lung-like gas bladder allowing them to breathe in waters with low oxygen content. This ability allows tarpon to live in areas where other predator fish can't survive, avoiding competition for food or harassment. Some say that when tarpon roll they don't feed. This is simply not true. My friends and I have caught many rolling tarpon.

I agree with Zane Grey, who said, "As long as they so obligingly roll on the surface in plain sight just so long do they make their beauty mine."

My first experience fishing in Florida was with baby tarpon. I had just moved to South Florida for my first job out of college and was living in an apartment in North Miami Beach. A canal ran along the side of the apartment complex and, one day after work, I fished that water. I assumed the canal was completely fresh and that bream lived there. Armed with one of my grandfather's bamboo fly rods and a couple of popping bugs, I set out to tangle with some bluegills. My first cast landed near some overhanging mangrove branches. A mangrove-covered shoreline should have clued me in to the absence of bream. I popped the bug a couple of times and almost immediately noticed five torpedo-shaped shadows move out from underneath the mangroves and suspend themselves below the pattern. I thought these were some large black bass tracking my fly. I popped the bug

while one fish broke from the pack and ascended. As the fish rose, I recognized a tarpon. The tarpon struck the fly. A quick, explosive take and turn-tail tug broke the four-pound leader I was using. I fumbled to tie on another popper. In what seemed like forever, I tied on a new popper and made an identical presentation. Again, shadowy shapes appeared. Another strike, another lost fly. I decided to quit losing flies and find someone who knew about these fish.

I found Bob Kay, a South Florida fly-tying legend. Bob was working at a now-defunct Fort Lauderdale fly shop. He listened to my tale with amusement. He told me to use an abrasion tippet of at least 30 pounds. He also revealed the most productive of baby tarpon flies, the yellow Marabou Muddler.

Then Bob introduced me to Steve Kantner. Steve is the only walk-in fly fishing guide in South Florida, also known as the "Land Captain." Bob convinced Steve to take me to one of the local spots, the Griffin Road Canal.

Maybe that day has become more fantastic in my mind with time, but on that particular day as far as the eye could see up and down the canal, tarpon rolled, waked, and crashed bait. I hooked a 20-pounder that immediately took to the air and popped my leader, teaching me the hard lesson about bowing to a jumping tarpon. For years after, I walked the banks of many canals and spillways confirming the effectiveness of the yellow Marabou Muddler.

Once at the Griffin Road Canal, I hooked a 60-pound tarpon. Being under-gunned with a nine-weight, I fought the fish for nearly two hours and purposely broke him off when the sun set and it got too dark to see. That fish had me running up and down the bank trying to keep up with him. For several days afterward, my palm bore the hatchmarks of first-degree burns inflicted by the reel's rim drag.

The canal system in South Florida is bisected by lock systems known locally as spillways. These spillways and canals were put in place 50 years ago to control flooding from the Everglades and deposit fresh water into the ocean. This juncture has created a unique feeding zone for tarpon. When a spillway opens, a fast current is created that rivals any swollen Rocky Mountain stream. The current sweeps small bream and shiners over the falls. Once on the other side, they tumble, disoriented, in the swirling eddies and are easy targets for baby tarpon. It is amazing that amidst all this turbulence, a baby tarpon can pick out a small Marabou Muddler Minnow dashing across the surface.

Spillways usually become active in the summer, when thunderstorms flood the Everglades and force open the spillways. Some of the best fishing is when the gates of the spillway are wide open during the height of a thunderstorm. Many times, thoroughly drenched, I have run to the shelter of my jeep to escape lightning. Other times, overwhelmed by the opportunity for a great bite, (and during one of my more foolhardy moments), I have weathered a lightning storm to catch baby tarpon.

Jody Moore displays a baby tarpon taken on a black Marabou Muddler in the Everglades. (JODY MOORE)

Most of the time, though, I have sat dripping wet in a stiflingly humid car and watched the undaunted Steve Kantner cast away while lightning crashed all around him.

The fly rodder, for some strange reason, has the advantage when fishing for baby tarpon at spillways. Many times my friends and I have out-fished fellow anglers who are using plugs, jigs, and even live shiners. Some of these guys, who would easily qualify for the ranks of Dixie's finest, don't look favorably on being out-fished by a "playboy" fly fisherman. They volley stares of disgust and mutter surly remarks when I land a fish on fly.

The Tamiami Trail Canal is another easily accessible walk-on spot that holds plenty of baby tarpon. This is hallowed ground trod upon by fly fishing greats like Homer Rhodes, Joe Brooks, Charles Waterman, Lefty Kreh, Chico Fernandez, and Flip Pallot. Here the fly fisherman reigns simply because he can present a fly that best resembles the size and color of bait fish in the area. Spin-casters and plug-rodders just can't compete because there isn't an artificial bait small enough that will cast any dis-

tance. Most of the flies we use are tied on #4s and #2s. Small bonefish patterns with tan or brown kip tail and a grizzly hackle wing work very well. Small Marabou Muddlers and Dahlberg Divers in yellow, tan, and black are frequently used patterns. Mike Conner's Glades Minnow is a deadly pattern and truly matches the hatch in that area.

The canals in Key Largo also have resident populations of baby tarpon. During the spring run of the big boys, these same canals are the prowling grounds for fish up to 100 pounds. Zane Grey Creek on Long Key bears the famous author's name because of his enthusiasm for fishing the baby tarpon there.

The tidal creeks and residential canals and lakes on Florida's west coast from Naples to Tampa Bay are home to baby tarpon. The fish have no worry, really, because the retirees of west Florida believe if you can't eat them, they're not worth catching.

For the boater or the angler who can hire a guide, the possibilities for baby tarpon are almost endless. Again, though, for reasons that are a mystery to me, tarpon here are not a highly sought after quarry. Big tarpon on big tackle take precedence in the fly angling hierarchy. So do other species in the area such as snook, redfish, and bonefish. A baby tarpon matched with the proper tackle provides almost the same excitement as its older siblings—and with a lot less strain and wear.

The Everglades that fringe the coastal tip of Florida provide a timeless and awe-inspiring backdrop for fly fishing baby tarpon. To see baby tarpon rolling in a backcountry tidal creek bordered by a thick wall of mangroves void of any sight or sound of man will send you back in time. The local Tequesta and Caloosa Indians saw the same scene 2,000 years before the Spanish arrived. It is a scene that existed a million years before that.

There is no easy formula for finding baby tarpon in the backcountry. One coastal tidal creek may be full of them while a creek just 100 yards away may never show a fish. A backcountry creek will hold fish one year but not the next, only to be revisited the following year. Some of the creeks deep in the backcountry that are directly fed by the water flow of the Everglades hold lots of bronze-colored tarpon stained by the tannic acid in the tea-colored water in which they swim. During the summer months, they are on the flats of Snake Bight out of Flamingo or cruising the western shoreline of Biscayne Bay. A few select islands around Big Pine Key of the lower Keys shelter baby tarpon with their mangrove canopies. Bridge and dock lights of Florida's vast Intracoastal Waterway, fished during the dark hours of night, are another place to find baby tarpon.

Finding some of these spots is tough without the helpful knowledge of an experienced guide. You find some spots by accident when exploring new territory, while others are revealed to friends under the oath of strict secrecy.

Those who know where, when, and how to find baby tarpon guard their knowledge. I once talked with two old men at a sportfishing show. We were talking about the great fishing of the Everglades in the area of Chokoloskee. Our conversation was going along quite well as we discussed various spots and techniques for redfish and snook. One of the gentlemen absently mentioned jumping and catching some baby tarpon on a recent trip. I asked where. The joviality ceased, the conversation stumbled and became awkward. They forgot exactly where that particular spot was. They looked for a way to bow out of the conversation, then walked away. I had committed the greatest offense in the circle of baby tarpon fishermen: I asked, "Where?".

Flies, on the other hand, are not held so closely to the breast. If you don't know where to go, the best fly isn't going to help. Tarpon have a distinct upturned mouth with a projecting mandible that make the fish suited for top-water flies. The yellow Marabou Muddler, designed by Dan Gapen in

1948 for Ontario trout, has proved its deadly effectiveness on baby tarpon. Its spun deer-hair head and the shape of the head places the Muddler Minnow just below the surface film to push a small V-wake.

Coupled with an undulating marabou tail, this resembles a vulnerable baitfish that juvenile tarpon find irresistible. Ninety percent of the baby tarpon I have caught were taken on yellow Marabou Muddlers. A black Marabou Muddler is a real killer in low light. I have fished it way past sunset when darkness made it impossible to see my presentation, much less the fly. Only a hard tug and the sound of a leaping fish let me know that a fish was on.

Other spun deer-hair head patterns, such as Dahlberg Divers and sliders, substitute well in the absence of a Muddler Minnow. These top-water patterns work best when tarpon are rolling in a relaxed manner and it is apparent that they are staying close to the surface. When tarpon display this type of behavior, they are affectionately referred to as "happy" fish.

Another pattern introduced to me by Steve Gibson is a weighted Tarpon Bunny. It has a chartreuse or olive green rabbit strip tail with a black rabbit strip collar, a few strands of crystal flash, and painted lead eyes. The same pattern with a bright blue collar and a white tail is also effective. Covering the lead eyes with five-minute epoxy is a trick that will protect the painted eyes as well as give the pattern a little extra weight. Take this pattern out of the box when the fish are in deep water and heading straight back to the bottom upon completing their roll. To indicate tarpon hanging deep, look for a fast roll and a quick flip of the tail. An intermediate or slow-sinking line is essential here.

Other effective patterns include miniature renditions of typical Keys-style tarpon patterns. Cockroach patterns tied on #2 hooks, in the regular or bendback style, are popular. Hi-ties with white bucktail, black thread, and a bit of silver Flashabou also work.

Tarpon like to strike a moving fly. Short, erratic strips coupled with a few long, swimming strips seem to work best. Avoid methodic, uninteresting strips. If the fly's movement is not interesting to you, it won't interest the tarpon. If the fish are working a strong current, such as at a spillway, fish it like a trout stream. Cast upstream, mend the line so as not to allow the fly to move faster than the current, and present the fly where the current is strongest. We know how far we can cast. If you cast the whole line, the mid-part of the line falls where the current is strongest and creates a belly in the line that drags the fly, creating an unrealistic presentation. Once the fly line straightens itself and the fly is facing the current, give the fly a few short strips and let it drop back. Repeat this process until you get a strike, or until you lose confidence in the presentation.

A strip strike is the most effective form of setting the hook. For years, I set the hook by lifting the rod tip. Having switched to the strip strike method, I have drastically increased my hook-up-to-strike ratio.

Some of my most fantastic strikes from any fish have been provided by juvenile tarpon—like the time a fish inhaled a fly as it simultaneously sky-rocketed out of the water. Another fish on the Tamiami Trail tracked my Muddler Minnow for several long seconds. It finally took the fly in a flash of angry silver and left a boil on the surface that would compete with any toilet flush. More than once a fish has cleared the water as it dove for a surface fly. Most strikes are the "take and turn" variety that nearly jerk the rod out of my hand. Never is a strike dull or anticipated with baby tarpon.

Once the fish is on, prepare to bow to a jumping fish. Even if the tackle is matched properly, without bowing, these fish can pop a leader in the air or throw a hook just as easily as their older siblings can. The "down and dirty" fighting technique also should be applied for a quick fight with little strain and wear to the fish. These fish will eventually grow up to be much bigger in our lifetime and it would be nice to catch them again when they weigh 100 pounds.

A 9-weight outfit would be my first choice for these fish. Most of the baby tarpon that are caught are between three and ten pounds, but it is not uncommon to hook into a 60- to 70-pound fish in the same water. Most fish are caught on top-water flies so, naturally, a floating line would be used. Only in the case of deep swimming fish, surf, or a very strong current is a sinking line needed.

The leader system, simply enough, is a scaled down version of a big-game tarpon leader. A class tippet of 10 to 12 pounds can be connected to a 30- to 40-pound abrasion tippet. A perfection loop know works best because it allows a floating fly to swing back and forth and allows a sinking fly to react like a jig as it is stripped through the water.

I am fanatical about baby tarpon. Maybe I love them because they were my first saltwater fish on fly. They were also much bigger than any of the sunfish and bass I pulled out of the

creek that runs behind my boyhood Louisiana home. Maybe it is the anticipation they cause from their rolling. Their willingness and preference to take a top-water fly qualifies them for my affection. Maybe it is their vicious strike. Maybe their tough fight. Maybe their acrobatic display. I know it is all of the above, plus the satisfaction of having caught such an ancient and noble fish with a form of angling that transcends all others. ■

Cash in on Florida's Fishing Opportunities

by Herb Allen

A good case can be made that Florida's recreational fishery is the state's second largest industry—right up there behind tourism.

Consider this: A late-1970s study by the University of Florida indicated that 3.5 million residents go fishing two or more times per year. The University study concluded that recreational fishing annually contributes $5 billion to the state's economy.

In 1980, Florida's Division of Tourism released figures showing that of the 70 million visitors to the state that year, 18 million went fishing at least once while here.

Any way you cut it, recreational fishing is a large slice of Florida's economic pie.

On any fall weekend, except during a hurricane, there'll be many more anglers wetting lines in the Gulf of Mexico or off the Atlantic coast than will be in the grandstands at every high school, college, and professional football game throughout the state combined.

What can they expect to catch?

Aside from bass, bream, catfish, chain pickerel, and speckled perch in our freshwater ponds, lakes and rivers, more people will be trying for saltwater trout than for any other species. Caught year-round, these trout (no relation to freshwater trout caught up north and out west) are usually found on grass flats and will bite on both live bait (shrimp, sardine minnows, etc.) and such artificial lures as top-water plugs, diving-crank baits, and bottom-bumping jigs. They'll also hit a fly rodder's streamer or popping bug. Best tides for trout include the last hour of an incoming and the first 90 minutes of an outgoing. While most will weigh between one and three pounds, there might be a few scaling between five and ten.

Redfish, known in Yankeeland as channel bass, usually weigh in the neighborhood of two to three pounds. However, there are enough pulse-quickening 10- to 15-pounders around to keep an angler on the edge of his or her boat seat. Though rare, a few reds tipping the Toledos at between 25 and 50 pounds are caught each year in Florida waters. Live shrimp, spoons, Reel Magics, and artificial jigs fished near oyster bars on a falling tide, or in a deep channel—particularly during the cooler months of the year—will usually produce strikes if any reds are around.

Few fish produce more pure angling excitement than snook. While a few of these linesiders do scale on the plus side of 30 pounds, most caught in the Sunshine State are between 5 and 15 pounds.

At times, a snook will hit just about any kind of live or artificial bait within reach, while at other times, it will turn up its nose at the choicest offerings. Generally, the best time to fish for snook in bays and rivers, along our mangrove shorelines, or in our passes is on a dropping tide.

The tarpon—often called the "poor man's gamefish"—is king in tropical and subtropical waters. It's active in the spring, summer, and early fall months throughout the state and year-round in Biscayne Bay and the Keys. Every year, tarpon tournaments attracting hundreds of anglers are held in Tampa, St. Petersburg, Sarasota, and Boca Grande. Numerous fish weighing more than 100 pounds each are caught and released. Each tournament will boast of two or three entries weighing more than 150 pounds and, in May of 1973, a fish weighing 218 pounds was landed off Davis Island, within rock-throwing distance of

131

downtown Tampa. St. Petersburg school teacher Rick Wotring landed an International Game Fish Association (IGFA) world record in the 80-pound-test line category.

In shallow water, it's not unusual to get from six to a dozen leaps from this powerful foe as it battles furiously to throw your hook. In deeper waters, such as those found in Boca Grande Pass, they will generally jump two or three times before going deep to slug it out.

Tarpon are caught from bridges, piers, small boats, and, frequently, by waders. Not the least bit picky in their eating habits, they will inhale dead baits on the bottom, live baits (pinfish, grunts, etc.), and just about any lure in a well-stocked tackle box, ranging from a top-water Zara Spook to a bottom-bouncing Cotee Liv' Eye Action Jig. The bulk of this feeding action will take place soon after the beginning of an outgoing tide.

Spanish mackerel and kingfish are prime angler targets on both Florida coasts. Spanish mackerel often go on feeding frenzies, striking just about any live bait or artificial lure they see. King-fish, found in offshore waters ranging from 30- to 120-foot depths, are hard-

fighters that will also hit a wide variety of live baits and artificials.

The number one target of offshore bottom anglers is the grouper, a bruiser found around rock piles, reefs, and wrecks in anywhere from 35 to 150 feet of water. Although not spectacular battlers, grouper will average between 8 and 20 pounds each and are an excellent main course on any dinner table.

Those lucky enough to find an off-shore wreck are likely to meet up with an amberjack, one of the most powerful and explosive fish that swims. These fish grow to 50 pounds or more and will leave even veteran fishermen with a bad case of the shakes.

Although billfish (sailfish, blue and white marlin) are plentiful in offshore Gulf waters due west of Clearwater and St. Petersburg, fishing for them often requires a large boat and a run of 100 miles or more to reach them. On Florida's east coast, the trio is a staple.

Chamber of Commerce folks don't like people to talk or write about sharks. However, there are plenty around in bays and offshore waters, resulting in increased angler attention for those who have discovered that on a rod and reel, the predator is an excellent

gamester. In addition, more and more people are discovering that shark meat is a viable menu choice.

In one three-day shark fishing tournament held in the summer of 1983, seven monsters weighing between 800 and 1,100 pounds were brought into port and placed on the scales.

This brief outline of fishing possibilities only skims the tip of the fin. Along both Florida coasts, anglers will find dozens of other species ready, willing, and able to put a bend in a rod, including silver trout by the "blue-zillions," whiting, pompano, sheepshead, drum to 50 pounds and more, ladyfish, jack crevalle, flounder, bluefish, and cobia, to name a few. Off the beaches—in deeper water—there's bonito, barracuda, dolphin, jewfish scaling more than 500 pounds, permit, tuna, red snapper, scamp, dolphin, and red grouper.

We'd suggest that if you have a hankering to challenge one or more of these piscatorial gamesters that you release all fish not destined for the dinner table so the next generation can enjoy the same fun and excitement. ∎

Baffling Barnacles, a Bane or Blessing?

By Herb Allen

Anyone who has seen a boat's bottom, or a pier, dock, or bridge piling on Florida's Atlantic or Gulf Coast has seen the barnacle.

Seen? They'd be hard to miss since scientists estimate that waters in some areas of the Sunshine State contain as many as 2 billion barnacles per square mile. Heck, it seems that at least half that number can be found on my boat's hull at any given time.

Betcha didn't know, however, that the barnacle eats with its feet and pro-

duces a glue that has twice the strength as the epoxies used in spacecraft. Also, did you know this small, intriguing creature that measures in the neighborhood of a quarter inch is kin to lobsters, crabs and shrimp?

Of the more than 1,500 species of barnacles seen throughout the world, many call Florida home.

This crustacean, usually seen on pier pilings as clumped or crusty formations, begins life as a triangular shape with bristly appendages, one eye, and a

pair of antennae. It quickly evolves into a two-sided, bi-valved shell with three eyes and six pairs of legs, which aid the animal as it swims about searching for an object on which to attach itself.

Once it finds a suitable home, the barnacle turns over on its back, cements itself to the surface, and secretes an armored shell of calcium carbonate plates that protect its soft inner parts. It then loses its eyes and, glued upside down at its head, stays put for the remainder of its life cycle, which may span anywhere from three to seven years.

The soft body within the shell plates is itself enclosed in a sac and resembles a small shrimp with six pair of feathery legs that literally kick food into its mouth.

Most species of barnacles are hermaphroditic, having both male and female reproductive organs, but are rarely self-fertilizing. In warmer climes, a barnacle may spawn three or four times per year, producing up to 15,000 eggs per pop. Fertilized eggs are then brooded within the protective sac for about 10 days before hatching as free-swimming, microscopic larvae.

Barnacle larvae are a major food source for many plankton-feeding marine animals. Several species of fish will feed on adult barnacles as well, including the triggerfish, which sucks the crustaceans from their shells, and sheepshead, which crush the shell in powerful jaws and eat the soft flesh inside. In many parts of the world, particularly South America and Asia, barnacles are also eaten by humans.

Larger barnacles frequently provide homes or refuges for tiny fish such as blennies.

Medical researchers have found that the cement holding a barnacle in place is thinner than a single coat of auto lacquer, yet has a shear strength of more than 7,000 pounds per square inch. This glue is but slightly softened at 662°F (lead melts at 620°F), and will not crack or peel even at temperatures of 380°F below zero. An adhesive of such strength, reasons the medical profession, may someday prove a boon to dentists in making tooth repairs and to orthopedic surgeons in mending broken bones.

Now, if only we could discover a way to keep these little critters from attaching themselves to the bottom of my boat, we'd save a bundle in hull scraping, painting, and refinishing costs. ■

A Guide to the Keys

by Capt. Jim Sharpe

The Florida Keys are a string of low, emerald green islands extending westward from the tip of the panhandle, with the Gulf of Mexico and Florida Bay on the north, and the Atlantic Ocean on the south.

U.S. Highway 1, the oldest highway in America, is the tie that binds these islands and is called the Overseas Highway. The highway extends 120 miles across 37 bridges connecting the island groups of Key Largo, Islamorada, Marathon, the Lower Keys, and Key West. Everything in the Keys is located by mile markers, small green signs at the shoulder of the road along the length of this highway.

The Florida Keys offer the greatest variety of backcountry and offshore gamefishing found anywhere in the world. Many species are year-round residents. (See the chart on page 142 for annual species abundance.)

In addition, the Keys have one of the largest living barrier reefs in the world, offering an endless variety of water sports. Each island in the Keys has unique flora and fauna. Many pro-vide refuge to endangered species, including the American bald eagle, the saltwater crocodile, and the miniature key deer.

A frequent Islamorada fisherman, former President George Bush, recognized the uniqueness of the Keys. In January 1990, Bush signed into law the National Marine Sanctuary Bill, creating a management plan for the 2,700 square miles of islands, coral reefs, and marine resources of the Keys, considered to be one of the crown jewels of the nation.

Visiting the Keys is an American odyssey full of surprises. The main reason people come to the Keys is to fish; there are presently 146 fishing world records held in the Keys, more than any other single location in the world. The Keys boast more world-class fishing tournaments than any other area in the world. If you're talking about "world-class sportfishing," you're talking about the Florida Keys. Each segment of the Keys' chain has its own special attraction for fishermen.

Key Largo: Gateway to the Keys

For most travelers, a trip to the Florida Keys begins in Miami on the Florida Turnpike, winding through the rich farmland of southern Dade County. When you reach US Route 1, look for the famous green and white mile markers (MM) along the side of the road; they will help in determining your location wherever you travel in the Keys.

Your first taste of the Keys will be across 18 scenic miles of Everglades. You may see roseate spoonbills, osprey, and cranes feeding in tidal pools along the highway—or perhaps glimpse a bobcat or alligator before arriving on the first and largest key, Key Largo.

Entering Key Largo, there is a sign, "Careful, Crocodile Crossing." This is no joke. Northern Key Largo is home to the American saltwater crocodile, an endangered species, and also the more common alligator. It's not too unusual to observe these reptiles crossing the roadway.

Along the north side of the island, a gentle transition takes place as the

133

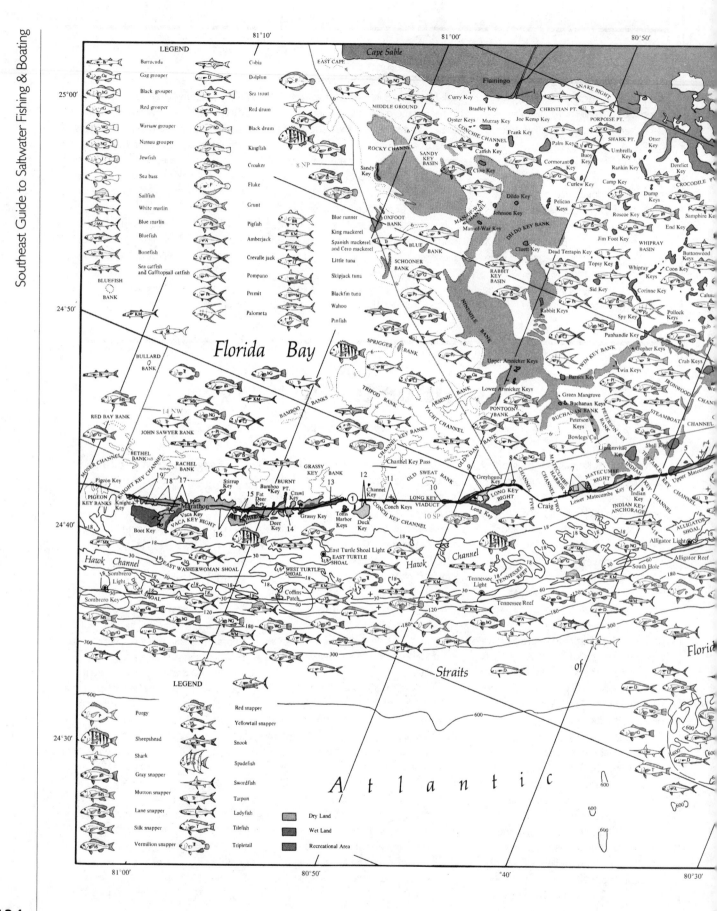

LEGEND

Barracuda		Cobia	
Gag grouper		Dolphin	
Black grouper		Sea trout	
Red grouper		Red drum	
Warsaw grouper		Black drum	
Nassau grouper		Kingfish	
Jewfish		Croaker	
Sea bass		Fluke	
Sailfish		Grunt	
White marlin		Pigfish	
Blue marlin		Amberjack	
Bluefish		Crevalle jack	
Bonefish		Pompano	
Sea catfish and Gafftopsail catfish		Permit	
		Palometa	

Blue runner	
King mackerel	
Spanish mackerel and Cero mackerel	
Little tuna	
Skipjack tuna	
Blackfin tuna	
Wahoo	
Pinfish	

LEGEND

Porgy		Red snapper	
Sheepshead		Yellowtail snapper	
Shark		Snook	
Gray snapper		Spadefish	
Mutton snapper		Swordfish	
Lane snapper		Tarpon	
Silk snapper		Ladyfish	
Vermilion snapper		Tilefish	
		Tripletail	

Dry Land

Wet Land

Recreational Area

Florida Bay

Atlantic

Straits of Florida

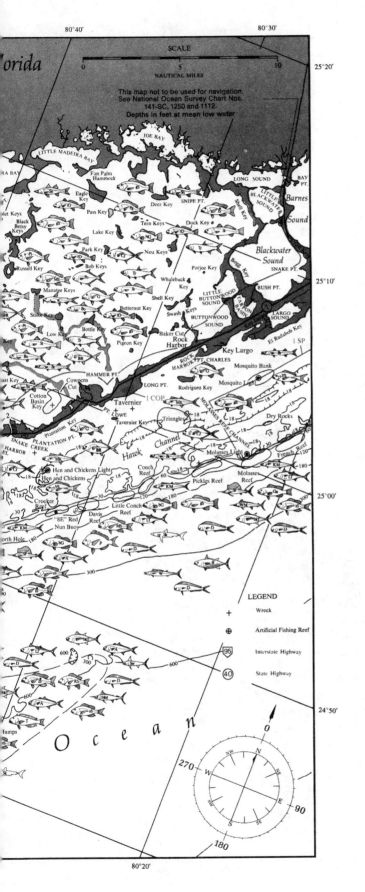

Florida Everglades, the "River of Grass," joins the Ten Thousand Islands. Together they blend into the shallow mangrove island-lined Florida Bay. Numerous small marinas, campgrounds, and motels dot the northern shoreline. This area is a haven where you can observe exotic birds and animals while enjoying the spectacular fishing in this unusual marine environment.

Key Largo is perhaps the only place in the world where you can stay in a fine hotel, motel, or campground, fish along mangrove-studded islands, observe bird life and raccoons scurrying along the bank, land a trophy snook, tarpon, or redfish, and perhaps catch a glimpse of a saltwater crocodile and alligator all in the same day.

Along the south side of the island lies the Atlantic Ocean, where the blue Gulf Stream waters flow within sight of the island. These cobalt waters teem with barracuda, shark, wahoo, kingfish, tuna, sailfish, and marlin—to name just a few of the natives that bite.

Onboard one of the many offshore sportfishing boats, the angler can expect to capture wahoo, dolphin, and sailfish in a single outing. Deepwater marinas offer full facilities to accommodate large and small sportfishing boats, as well as charter fishing boats for anglers preferring to capitalize on the talents of local charter boat captains and guides. There are a number of professional guides and captains who offer the experience and all the fishing equipment necessary to capture local gamefish.

Islamorada: The Purple Isle

Islamorada was called the purple island by the early Spanish sailors because of its lush purple flowering native plant called Bougainvillea. Today, Islamorada is called the "Fishing Capital of the World," and offers an abundance of backcountry and offshore sportfishing.

Along the shoreline, a number of waterfront motels and restaurants offer sunset celebrations of fine food and drink. Stories of the one that didn't get away can be told here.

The north side of the island faces Florida Bay, a clear, shallow bay dotted with thousands of mangrove islands, flats, and seagrass beds. In this area, light-tackle anglers can enjoy some of the finest bonefish, tarpon, trout, shark, and permit fishing from powerful, shallow-draft backcountry boats as they are poled along the flats and seagrass beds. Light spinning tackle or fly tackle can be used to sight cast to any of the many gamefish found on the shallow flats.

The south side of the island faces the Atlantic Ocean and offers big-game fishing for wahoo, dolphin, shark, sailfish, and marlin. Several world-class marinas offer offshore charter boats, party boats, and backcountry boats complete with experienced captains and guides.

Big-game fishing in the nearby Gulf Stream uses live bait such as ballyhoo or pilchards cast with light 12-pound-test spin tackle. Trolling with artificial lures or bait along the

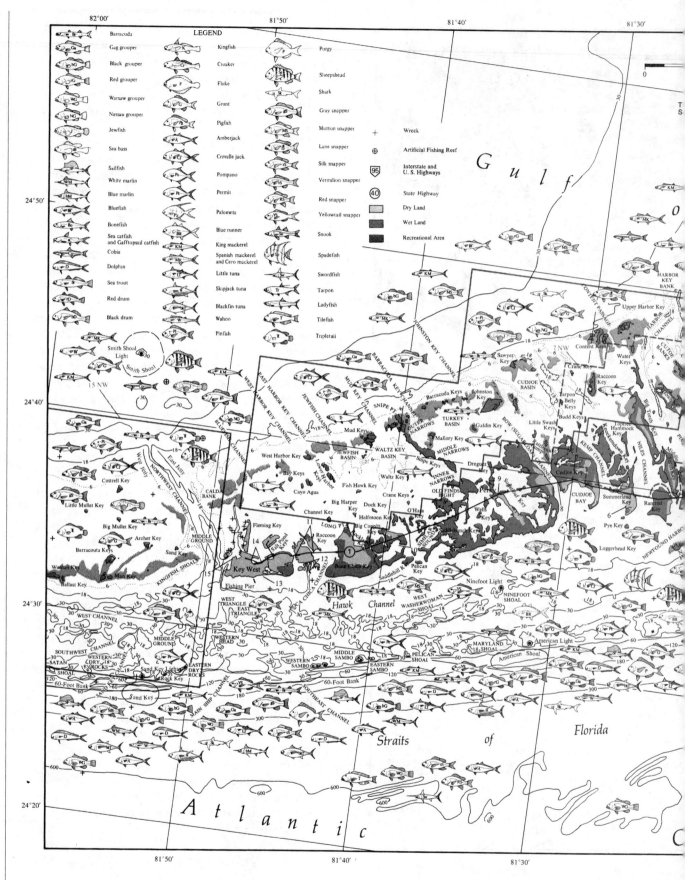

LEGEND

Barracuda		Kingfish		Porgy	
Gag grouper		Croaker		Sheepshead	
Black grouper		Fluke		Shark	
Red grouper		Grunt		Gray snapper	
Warsaw grouper		Pigfish		Mutton snapper	
Nassau grouper		Amberjack		Lane snapper	
Jewfish		Crevalle jack		Silk snapper	
Sea bass		Pompano		Vermilion snapper	
Sailfish		Permit		Red snapper	
White marlin		Palometa		Yellowtail snapper	
Blue marlin		Blue runner		Snook	
Bluefish		King mackerel		Spadefish	
Bonefish		Spanish mackerel and Cero mackerel		Swordfish	
Sea catfish and Gafftopsail catfish		Little tuna		Tarpon	
Cobia		Skipjack tuna		Ladyfish	
Dolphin		Blackfin tuna		Tilefish	
Sea trout		Wahoo		Tripletail	
Red drum		Pinfish			
Black drum					

+ Wreck
⊕ Artificial Fishing Reef
95 Interstate and U.S. Highways
40 State Highway
Dry Land
Wet Land
Recreational Area

Gulf of

24°50'

24°40'

24°30'

24°20'

Smith Shoal Light

Smith Shoal

15 NW

Northwest Channel

Cottrell Key

Little Mullet Key

Big Mullet Key

Archer Key

Barracouta Keys

Woman Key

Man Key

Ballast Key

West Channel

Southwest Channel

Satan Shoal

Western Dry Rocks

Sand Key Light

Rock Key

Sand Key

60-Foot Bank

Main Ship Channel

Middle Ground

Sand Key

Calda Bank

Middle Ground

Fleming Key

Key West

Fishing Pier

West Triangle

East Triangle

Western Head

Western Sambo

Middle Sambo

Eastern Dry Rocks

Raccoon Key

Boca Chica Key

Hawk Channel

West Washerwoman Shoal

Eastern Sambo

60-Foot Bank

Southeast Channel

Saddlehill Key

Pelican Key

Ninefoot Light

Ninefoot Shoal

Pelican Shoal

Maryland Shoal

American Light

American Shoal

Straits of Florida

Atlantic

Johnston Key Channel

Barracuda Keys Channel

West Harbor Key Channel

East Harbor Key Channel

Jewfish Channel

Snipe Pt. Channel

Mud Keys

West Harbor Key

Bay Keys

Cayo Agua

Channel Key

Big Harper Key

Little Harper Key

Duck Key

Halfmoon Key

Fish Hawk Key

Crane Keys

Waltz Key

Snipe Keys

Waltz Key Basin

Jewfish Basin

Lower Harbor Keys

Middle Narrows

Inner Narrows

Old Finds Bight

O'Hara

Wells Key

Outer Narrows

Turkey Basin

Mallory Key

Galdin Key

Barracuda Keys

Johnston Key

Cudjoe Basin

Content Keys

Sawyer Key

Crane Key

Water Keys

Raccoon Key

Tarpon Belly Keys

Budd Keys

Little Swash Keys

Johnston Key

Cudjoe Key

Cudjoe Bay

Summerland Key

Ramrod Key

Pye Key

Loggerhead Key

Newfound Harbor

Kemp Channel

Niles Channel

Big Torch Key

Cutter Banks

Harbor Key Bank

Upper Harbor Key

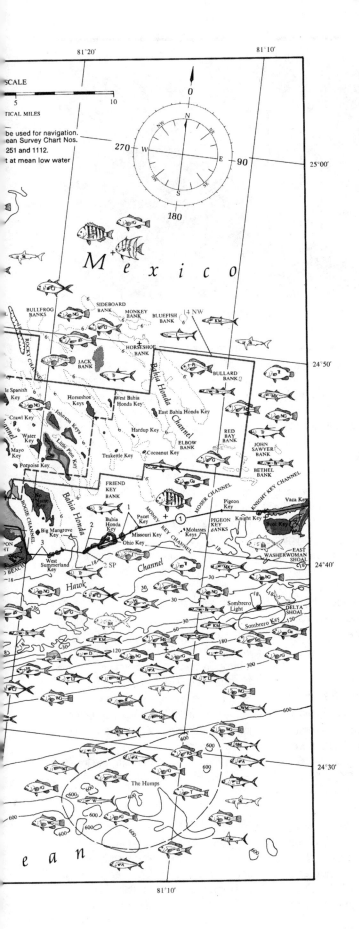

outer reefs or offshore weed lines will produce a variety of gamefish depending on the time of year.

Located offshore of Islamorada and Marathon are several areas known as the "Humps." These sea mounts rise several hundred feet above the bottom, offering exciting fishing for dolphin, tuna, amberjack, and a variety of sharks, including the mako and great white shark.

Marathon: Home of the Seven Mile Bridge

Traveling south along the Overseas Highway from Islamorada, you begin to encounter the first of a series of large bridges—Channel Two, Channel Five, Long Key, and Tom's Harbor Bridge. You've probably noticed by now that the north side of the highway is more of a gulf than a bay, with islands visible close to the Keys and large expanses of water beyond as the islands dotting Florida Bay give way to the deeper, more open Gulf of Mexico.

Marathon is a small island town at the foot of the famed Seven Mile Bridge. It is best known for its friendly natives, unobstructed sunsets, offshore big-game fishing, and explosive tarpon fishing around the bridges.

Here in the Middle Keys, the waters of the Gulf of Mexico mix with the Atlantic Ocean right under the bridges. The water in the Gulf is deeper than that in the Florida Bay. It is heavily laden with baitfish and crustaceans spawned in the seagrasses of the Bay and carried by strong currents under the bridges into the ocean where tarpon, snook, jack crevalle, and many other gamefish await.

Marathon offers a fleet of world-class captains and guides with all the knowledge and equipment to engage the willing angler in an epic battle with one of the biting natives.

Flats fishing for bonefish, tarpon, and permit surrounds the island. Guides experienced in fishing the big tarpon leave earlier in the morning to castnet live mullet or other live baitfish. Live baits are floated near the bridge, using 12- to 20-pound spinning tackle. Battling a tarpon 100 pounds or more is a challenge every angler should experience.

Offshore big-game fishing is excellent in the Gulf Stream lying just to the south. The ocean side of Marathon offers deep reefs for yellowtail, grouper, and snapper. Beyond the reef in the cobalt blue waters of the Gulf Stream, kingfish, wahoo, tuna, marlin, and sailfish offer big game angling at its best.

Lower Keys: Home of the Key Deer

Leaving Marathon, we cross the Seven Mile Bridge and touch down briefly on Sunshine Key and Bahia Honda Key before crossing the scenic Bahia Honda Bridge. This beautiful, laid-back area is characterized by small island campgrounds nestled on white sand beaches and some of the best tarpon fishing anywhere in the world.

Crossing the Spanish Harbour Bridge brings us to Big

Seven Mile Bridge is the longest of 43-bridges that comprise the 113-mile Overseas Highway in the Florida Keys.

Pine Key. Here the sign reads "Endangered Key Deer, Drive Deerfensively." Big Pine Key, a large, pine-studded island located midway between Marathon and Key West, is one of several islands called the Lower Keys. A herd of several hundred small key deer, the size of large dogs, live on this island. The key deer is an endangered species protected by law. They are often seen crossing the highway where the speed limit is reduced to protect them.

The Lower Keys comprises several islands, extending west toward the southernmost city of Key West. They are Big Pine, Little Torch, Summerland, Cudjoe, and Sugarloaf Keys. In this area, hundreds of mangrove islands, flats, and wash channels extending north into the Gulf of Mexico, offer the angler perfect conditions for light-tackle fishing for tarpon, bonefish, and permit.

The Great White Heron Preserve is located in this area and many marine bird rookeries are found on the islands.

Accommodations in the Lower Keys include secluded campgrounds, motels, several marinas, and even an island retreat with Tahitian huts that can only be reached by boat.

Offshore fishing is excellent in this area. The angler has the option of traveling north into the Gulf of Mexico to fish on a shipwreck for cobia, permit, shark, and snapper, or south into

the Atlantic Ocean to angle for sailfish, marlin, dolphin, or wahoo. Marlins weighing up to 665 pounds have been caught in the waters of the Lower Keys and Key West.

The world-famous Wall lies 20 miles south offshore of the Lower Keys and Key West. It's here that the ocean bottom plummets from 1,000 feet straight down to depths of 2,000 feet, forming a dramatic undersea wall. The northerly flow of the Gulf Stream flows over the bottom, forcing bait and nutrients to the surface and attracting giant blue marlin, wahoo, sharks, dolphin, and tunas. The Wall is one of the most productive marlin grounds in North America, only a one-hour run from the Lower Keys and Key West docks.

Key West:
The Southernmost City

The Overseas Highway ends at Key West, although the emerald green islands continue 30 miles to the west, terminating with Marquesas Key. Some 70 miles to the west of Key West is the Fort Jefferson Monument on Dry Tortugas, the westernmost boundary of the new Florida Keys Marine Sanctuary.

Key West is a quaint city dating back to the early 1800s when ship builders built the wooden houses that line the narrow streets. The home of Ernest Hemingway is a Key West

attraction, as are several watering holes where Hemingway sipped a cold beer and recounted stories of the big marlin in the Florida Straights between Cuba and the Keys. A number of big-game fishing tournaments in Key West still honor the tradition of *The Old Man and the Sea.*

Key West is surrounded with big-game fishing: islands and flats for light-tackle angling lie to the west; to the north, the Gulf of Mexico offers spectacular wreck fishing for cobia, permit, and barracuda; and to the south, the Atlantic Ocean offers dolphin, wahoo, sailfish, and marlin. In Key West you can literally catch a tarpon in the shadow of your hotel in the morning, catch a permit before noon, then fight a sailfish in the Gulf of Mexico in the afternoon on the outgoing tide.

After a day of sportfishing, Duval Street offers quaint shops, Jimmy Buffet Burgers, or a cold beer in one of Hemingway's old haunts. Air transportation is available from Marathon or Key West daily to accommodate the interstate and international traveler.

In Summary

The Keys are a unique blend of islands connected by the Overseas Highway and surrounded by flats, seagrass beds, gulfs, bays, and oceans. The Keys offer the greatest variety of year-round sportfishing found anywhere in the world. The fact that more world records are held in the Keys than any other single area of the world is the best recommendation. Whether you seek a 500-pound blue marlin offshore or a 5-pound bonefish on the flats, the fabulous Florida Keys have it all.

Key Attractions
MM 107

The first Key accessible by car after leaving Miami offers a cornucopia of things to do and see. There's sightseeing, the best fishing in the world, scuba diving, snorkeling, boating, sunbathing, history lessons, golfing, fine dining, camping, exploring, skiing, sailing, and the list goes on.

The Ocean Reef Club controls the northern end of Key Largo and offers everything any well-equipped town could offer, including the hotel, two excellent golf courses, tennis, croquet, restaurants, charter boats, and luxurious atmosphere and service.

As you head south, Best Western Suites at Key Largo offers dock space outside each handsome suite. Each two-floor suite has a screened patio and a full kitchen. The Holiday Inn Resort and Marina has every amenity and every watersport you could want, dock space, launching ramp, marina, glass-bottom boat tours, and dive packages. Marina Del Mar Marina and Resort is within the boundaries of John Pennekamp Coral Reef State Park and adjacent to Key Largo National Marine Sanctuary. They have a deep-water marina to accommodate guests arriving by boat and can offer you a rental boat if you didn't bring one. They have rooms, suites, a fitness center, Coconuts (an award-winning restaurant), tennis, dive and fish packages, and more.

There are at least 35 other hotels, motels, and resorts in Key Largo, running the gamut from the Sheraton Key Largo Resort to the Calusa Camp Resort with space for tents and RVs.

Pennekamp Park is the only park of its kind in the United States. Located at MM 102.5, Pennekamp offers 120 square miles of coral reefs, seagrass beds, and mangroves for your diving, fishing, boating, and camping pleasure. The Key Largo Undersea Park has underwater trails to follow while snorkeling and even has the Jules Undersea Lodge—an underwater hotel five fathoms down in the park lagoon. It has great service and an unbelievable view at all hours. And if you like marine life, stop by Dolphins Plus, a dolphin research center specializing in rehabilitating handicapped children through play with the dolphins. Call (305) 451-1993 for an appointment to swim with the dolphins.

Farther south at MM 92.5 is the smaller Harry Harris Park, providing facilities for fishing, barbecue, softball, biking, and swimming.

There are loads of dive operators throughout Key Largo and Stephen Frink's Photographic Service can supply divers with the means to take superb underwater photos during their stay.

Some other attractions worth seeing are the Caribbean Shipwreck Museum with its incredible collection of real sunken treasure (MM 102.6) and the Bluewater Tackle Shop (MM 100.5), a huge fascinating stop for anyone needing fishing gear.

Key Largo has some of the finest dining anywhere. Many restaurants even offer to take your own fresh catch of the day and prepare it in any number of savory, mouth-watering ways. The Fish House Restaurant serves up some of the best-tasting fish dishes anywhere in the continental U.S., and don't forget The Quay, Snooks Bayside, and The Italian Fisherman. Also, the folks come down from the Ocean Reef Club at the head of Key Largo to eat at the Crazy Flamingo at Garden Cove Marina.

—Dean Travis Clarke

MM 88

Islamorada exists for the sportfisherman. Home of some of the great legends of fishing, such as Jimmy Albright and Billy Pate, Islamorada has been the training ground for many of the top captains and anglers now setting records and opening new fishing grounds around the world.

The Purple Isle is especially known for offshore fly fishing. There are probably more experienced big-game fly fishing crews here than anywhere in the world. The World Wide Sportsman tackle shop displays the mount of the first blue marlin ever caught on fly, and is among the most comprehensive all-around tackle stores anywhere. (Proprietor George Hummell is former President Bush's personal fishing guide.) A new tackle shop, Orvis' Islamorada Outfitters, caters particularly to fly fishermen, and Islamorada is home to the expertly staffed Florida Keys Flyfishing School.

The Islamorada area extends 26 miles from Tavernier Creek to the Long Key Bridge, encompassing Plantation Key, Windley Key, Upper and Lower Matecumbe, and Long Key.

Mile Marker 88 is both the address and the name of a nationally famous gourmet restaurant.

Just a short way farther south, the major charter marinas are visible on the ocean side from US Route 1. The first, at MM 84.5, is the Holiday Isle Resort, home of the world-famous Tiki Bar. The most high-profile of Islamorada's resorts, the Holiday Isle Marina, is home to all three types of Keys guides: offshore charter, backcountry skiffs, and Robbie's party boats.

At the southern tip of the island, across from Papa Joe's landmark restaurant, Bud 'n Mary's preserves the real laid-back Keys style, and docks some of the island's most prestigious captains and guides. Look here for offshore, backcountry, and party boats.

Other private resorts and marinas also boast fishing charters or guides. Just north of Islamorada is Plantation Yacht Harbor, mostly accommodating larger visiting boats. Around the corner from Holiday Isle are wedged the smaller charter boats of Abel's Marina.

On the bay side as you travel south, you won't miss the sign for the Lorelei Restaurant and home of some

139

of the island's specialized backcountry guides.

In the middle of Islamorada, elegant Cheeca Lodge books charters from their own guide list and provides exceptional service and amenities.

For those who want to stay out of town, the Caloosa Cove Marina and Safari Lounge is an isolated option a few miles to the south.

Although nearly everyone who comes to Islamorada fishes, the other amenities are not neglected.

For entertainment, the Theater of the Sea has marine mammal shows, educational wildlife exhibits, and a dolphin swim program. Cheeca Lodge sports a nine-hole golf course, and several dive shops provide excellent diving and snorkeling. Specialized Keys-related shopping is found at H.T. Chittum's, the Artist's Village, and numerous small boutiques. For kids, Cheeca Lodge has an environmentally oriented camp program.

State historical and botanical attractions include Indian Key State Botanical Site and Lignumvitae State Botanical Site, accessible only by boat. The Windley Key Quarry State Park shows how the Keys were formed, for those with geological interests. A unique underwater state park is the San Pedro Underwater Archaeological Preserve, a Spanish treasure ship sunk in 18 feet of water, accessible by glass-bottom boat or snorkeling. Information on all of the above is available from the Long Key State Recreation Area (305) 664-4815.

—*Albia Dugger*

MM 63

"Do it all in Marathon," reads the official guide book of the Marathon Chamber of Commerce. A quick look at what's available locally seems to bear this out: There are more than 50 resorts and motels, five campgrounds, 11 dive shops, numerous shopping centers and restaurants, a large public beach, a nine-hole golf course, and ecologically oriented sites like the Museum of Natural History and the Dolphin Research Center. Add to this more than 50 backcountry and off-

shore captains to choose from and the convenience of an airport with connections to Miami and Key West, and you have the ingredients for a "Do It All" destination.

Due to its central location, Marathon offers perhaps more types of fishing than can be found anywhere in the Keys, including the world's largest fishing pier—the old Seven Mile Bridge. Primarily a residential fishing community, Marathon combines low-key atmosphere with all the conveniences of a bigger city.

The "Heart of the Florida Keys," the Marathon area stretches between the two longest Keys bridges, Long Key Bridge and the famous Seven Mile Bridge, from MM 53 to MM 47.

Past the fishing village of Conch Key is a world-class, West Indies-style island resort, the 60 acres of Hawk's Cay Resort and Marina (MM 61), with residences, fine restaurants, and charter boats.

On Grassy Key, the fascinating Dolphin Research Center (MM 59) promotes educational programs as well as scientific research, and conducts in-water "dolphin encounters" with visitors by appointment.

An oceanside causeway (MM 53.5) leads to the Key Colony Beach Marina and a par-three public golf course.

The Marathon Airport (MM 51.5) not only connects the Middle Keys with the world, but provides aerial tours by helicopter or seaplane.

Marathon itself is a bustling metropolis on Vaca Key, named for the West Indian sea cow, or manatee. A major project of the Land and Sea Trust recently purchased the 64-acre Crane Point Hammock Estate (MM 50), where the new Museum of Natural History of the Florida Keys is now located. The museum includes sea life exhibits and a children's museum. Outside the museum, visitors can walk the nature trails to become acquainted with the plants and trees of the native Florida hammocks.

A landmark of the Florida Keys, the Faro Blanco (White Lighthouse) Marina

and Resort (MM 48), home of The World Class Angler tackle shop, has several restaurants, lounges, and an Olympic-size swimming pool, as well as charter fishing.

Across the island on the ocean side, the scenic Sombrero Resort (MM 50) is a full-facility resort with a championship golf course available to guests. Sombrero Beach itself is one of the few public beaches maintained by Monroe County. Another popular family resort is the Buccaneer (MM 48.5) at the south end of Marathon.

—*Capt. Buddy LaPointe*

MM 40

The Lower Keys are truly a world away in attitude and lifestyle. Unlike the more developed areas of the Keys, the Lower Keys retain their natural, unhurried air and wilderness feel.

Enjoyment of nature is this region's theme, conveyed by several protected wilderness areas. Indeed, the Great White Heron National Wildlife Refuge encompasses all of the Lower Keys on the north side of US Route 1, from the lower end of the Seven Mile Bridge to just above Key West.

In the Lower Keys, nature lovers find plenty to love. At the top of the Lower Keys, Bahia Honda State Recreation Area (MM 37), with its mile-long natural sand beach, is one of the most beautiful in the Keys, with camping areas, marina, and picnic grounds.

The Looe Key National Marine Sanctuary (pronounced Loo Key) at MM 37 is a 5.3-square-mile area of spectacular coral and diverse marine life, protected by federal law. Activities that damage the ecosystem, such as anchoring near coral, are restricted, but hook and line fishing and other nondestructive uses are encouraged.

The largest and most developed of the Lower Keys, the island of Big Pine Key itself, with its dense pine woods and fresh water, is unlike any of the other Keys. Its very rock formation, not of coral origin, sets it apart from its northern limestone neighbors.

The National Key Deer Refuge (MM 30) on Big Pine Key is one of the last strongholds of this tiny endangered mammal. Once reduced to fewer than 50 animals, the key deer population has now stabilized around 300. The deer are frequently seen near or on the highway, and care should be exercised when driving in key deer territory. Feeding key deer is detrimental to their survival and is illegal.

Watson's Hammock, within the refuge, is a nature preserve with a variety of native plants and animals. Also inside the refuge is a popular spot for encountering large alligators, called the Blue Hole.

South of Big Pine Key, Coupon Bight is an aquatic preserve, an area of exceptional natural beauty and fragility, set aside by the State of Florida to be protected in its natural condition—an area of clear tropical waters dedicated to recreation, contemplation, research, and education.

Fishermen will find marinas, boat rentals, and charters scattered throughout the Lower Keys, both backcountry and oceanside. Accommodations range from fishermen's cottages to elegant bed and breakfasts, waterfront villas, or conventional motels. Sugarloaf Lodge on Sugarloaf Key has its own airstrip, marina, and porpoise pool. For truly four-star, isolated luxury, try Little Palm Island, a resort on its own island at MM 28.5. In fact, they say it all with their telephone number: (800) GET-LOST. At the other end of the spectrum, and in keeping with the area's natural theme, there are more oceanfront campgrounds in the Lower Keys than in any resort area in Florida.

—Albia Dugger

MM 1

Key West is a world unto itself. It is exotic, mysterious, fantastical, and artistic. There is no other place on earth quite like it. It has accommodations for every taste. At last count, 151—from large, beautiful luxury hotels like the Hyatt Key West, the Marriott Casa Marina, and the Pier House, to campgrounds like Boyd's, Jabour's, and Leo's. While each has something to recommend it, Key West's most interesting

accommodations are its guest houses and vacation rentals. Many are restored conch houses with terrific history and are filled with beautiful furniture, art, and ambiance.

One of the best times of year to be a tourist in Key West is around Halloween. This is the time of the weeklong Fantasy Fest, culminating in the most outrageous Halloween Costume Parade you will ever see. Not even Carnival in Rio or Mardi Gras in New Orleans comes close. It is extraordinary.

Besides the people themselves, there's lots to see in Key West. The Audubon House and Gardens are typical of the architecture and style of the early 1800s, when Audubon himself stayed in Key West sketching birds of the area. There are also tours, such as the Conch Tour Train, Old Town Trolley, and the Glass Bottom Boats. And of course, no trip to Key West would be complete without a visit to Ernest Hemmingway's house, where he lived and wrote some of his best and most famous works between 1931 and 1940. Then there are all of the art |galleries, fabric stores, shell markets, original jewelry design shops, boat and seaplane tours, and the crowning touch of each and every day in Key West—sunset at Mallory Dock.

Enjoy the carnival atmosphere of jugglers and street performers and Key West's resident bagpiper, who all speed the sun on its way into the ocean.

—Dean Travis Clarke

Marinas, Charters, Accommodation and Facilities

These codes indicate services available at the following establishments in the Florida Keys:

C= Charter Boats, G= Guide Skiffs, P= Party Boats, R= Boat
(Telephone area code for all numbers is 305.)

Key Largo
Bill's Bait & Tackle—C, G, P, R, MM 99.5, 451-0531

Bluewater Tackle—C, G, MM 100.5, 451-5875
Club Nautico—R, MM 100, 451-4120
Garden Cove Marina—C, MM 106.5, 451-4694
Gilbert's Motel & Marina—C, MM 107, 451-1133
Italian Fisherman—C, G, R, MM 104, 451-3726
Holiday Harbour—C, G, P, R, MM 100, 451-3661
Kona Kai Bayfront Resort—C, G, MM 97.8, 852-7200
Perdue-Dean, Ocean Reef Club— C, G, R, SR 905, 367-2661
Tavernier Creek Marina—G, MM 90.5, 852-5854
Yellow Baithouse—C, G, MM 101.7, 451-0921

Islamorada
Abel's Marina—C, G, MM 84.5, 664-8456
Bud 'n Mary's—C, G, P, MM 79.5, 664-2461
Caloosa Cove Marina—C, MM 73.5, 664-4455
Club Nautico—R, MM 79.5, 664-2409
Holiday Isle Marina—C,G,P, MM 84, 664-2321
Lorelei Yacht Basin—G, MM 82.5, 664-4338
Papa Joe's Marina—C, G, MM 79.5, 664-5005
Smuggler's Cove Marina—C, MM 85, 664-5564
Tavernier Creek Marina—G, MM 90.5, 852-9022
Whale Harbor Docks—C, G,P, MM 83.5, 664-4511

Marathon
Captain Hook's Marina—C, G,R, MM 53, 743-2444
Hawks Cay Marina—C,G, R, MM 61, 743-9000
Key Colony Beach Marina—C, G,R, MM 54, 289-1310
Marathon Days Inn Marina—C, G, MM 54, 289-0222
Tournament Bait and Tackle—C, G, P, MM 52.5, 743-8105
The World Class Angler, Faro Blanco Resort—C, G, MM 47.5, 743-6139

Species Abundance Chart

Species	Best Season(s)	Species	Best Season(s)
Amberjack	March through May, September	Permit	October
Blue Marlin	April through November	Sailfish	January through May, August through December
White Marlin	February and March, May through July		
Bonefish	August through October	Shark	September and October
Cobia	January	Snapper	July
Dolphin	March through October	Blackfin Tuna	Feb. through April, Oct. through Dec.
Grouper	October	Yellowfin Tuna	Jan. and Feb., July and Aug., Oct. through Dec.
Kingfish	January through April, November and December	Wahoo	January through April, August through December

Lower Keys

Dolphin Marina—C, G, R, MM 28.5, Little Torch Key, 872-2685

Helicon Charters—G, Pickup/Dropoff, 745-2800

John and Dot's Bait and Tackle—C, G, R, MM 30, Big Pine Key, 872-9872

Looe Key Reef Resort and Dive Center—C, MM 27.5, Ramrod Key, 872-2215

Neredi Charters—G, MM 28.5, Little Torch Key, 872-4317

Outcast Charters—G, MM 27.5, Ramrod Key, 872-4680

T.J.'s Sugarshack Rentals and Charters—C, G,R, MM 17, Sugarloaf Key, 745-3135

Key West

A&B Marina—C, G, Front Street, 294-2535

Club Nautico—R, 717-C Eisenhower Dr., 800-338-7161

Murray Marine—C, G, MM 5, 296-9555

Galleon Marina—C, G, R, 619 Front St., 292-1292

Garrison Bight Marina—C, G, R, 294-3093

Harborside Motel & Marina—C, G, R, 294-2780

Key West Municipal Marina—C, G, P, 292-8167

Key West Seaport—C, G, 631 Greene St., 292-1727

Oceanside Marina—C, G, 5950 Peninsular Ave. 294-4676

Fishing Information

Don't forget that Florida requires anglers to possess a saltwater fishing license. Residents pay $11.50 for 10 days or $13.50 for one year. Non-residents can ante up $16.50 for seven days or $31.50 for one year. The Florida Marine Patrol does check. Call (904) 488-5757 to find out when certain species are out of season, for size and bag limits, and for current licensing information.

For more details on Florida's fishing regulations, see pages 97-99.

Special Publications

A User's Guide to the Florida Keys, also available in Spanish, is a 48-page text on Florida Keys land and marine flora and fauna. Published by the Land and Sea Trust, the text is designed to quickly orient visitors to the environment. It is available at bookstores or from the Trust (P.O. Box 536, Marathon, FL 33050; (305) 743-3900) for $3.95.

Another way to learn about Key Largo is by ordering the Chamber of Commerce's 28-minute video. It's not as good as the famous Lauren Bacall, Edward G. Robinson, Humphrey Bogart movie named Key Largo, but you'll learn more from it.

The Marathon Fishing Guides Association Fishing Brochure provides information on over 50 charter boats, ranging from backcountry skiffs to the large offshore sportfishermen, including the types of fishing each captain does and a seasonal listing of when certain species are available. Write to Marathon Guides Association, P.O. Box 65, Marathon, FL 33050.

Travel and Accommodations

Key Largo Chamber of Commerce
105950 Overseas Highway
Key Largo, FL 33037
(305) 451-1414
(800) 822-1088

Islamorada Chamber of Commerce
P.O. Box 915
Islamorada, FL 33036
(305) 664-4503

Marathon Chamber of Commerce
3330 Overseas Highway
Marathon, FL 33050
(305) 743-5417

Heart of the Florida Keys Information Center
7434 Overseas Highway
Marathon, FL 33050
(800) 441-7991

Lower Keys Chamber of Commerce
P.O. Drawer 511
Big Pine, FL 33043
(305) 872-3580
(305) 872-2411

Key West Chamber of Commerce
P.O. Box 984
Key West, FL 33041
(305) 294-2587 ■

Backcountry: Fishing the Fabulous Flats

by Capt. Buddy LaPointe

It's eight in the morning and already the cloudless spring sky indicates another beautiful Florida Keys day. Stretching before you, dotted by mangrove islands and winding channels, are tantalizing shallow-water sand and grass flats that you hope will produce the fish of your dreams. Positioned on the casting platform of a backcountry skiff, spinner or flyrod in hand, you await the arrival of your fish. Perhaps you're seeking the elusive gray ghost—the bonefish, or the silver king of the flats—the majestic tarpon. Or perhaps you're enjoying the multitude of small gamefish that prowl the sea grass beds for food.

In prime-time tarpon season, you'll need to make advance reservations with your guide, as the backcountry specialists are called. They are a specialized group of fishermen with finely tuned, distinctive shallow-draft boats, rigged with low platforms, electric motors, and the traditional 20-foot fiberglass poling pole to sneak silently and safely into the shallows.

This huge area north of the Florida Keys is Florida Bay. It averages two to three feet in depth, and merges with the Everglades and other national parks and the Gulf of Mexico. Because the channels are often nothing more than prop ditches, and usually unmarked, it is rare for anyone to venture into this country without a guide. Also, the ecology here is exceedingly fragile and vulnerable to damage from boats. The guides jealously guard their territory against damage brought about by ignorant boaters.

The Backcountry Trip

In the strictest sense, a backcountry trip is an expedition north from the Keys into the wilderness of uninhabited Keys and mangrove shorelines of Florida

No matter where you fish on the flats chances are excellent you'll catch barracuda. (VIN T. SPARANO)

Bay. These trips are highlighted by beautiful scenery, plentiful bird life, and, for the most part, superb fishing. It is a true get-away-from-it-all trip. The term "backcountry fishing" is also used in a broader sense to cover the various types of fishing done by a backcountry guide, including fishing the flats and channels in the nearby waters of the inhabited Keys.

Not surprisingly, a special breed of boat was developed to deal with the many varieties of fishing encountered by the Florida Keys guides. The backcountry flats skiff averages 16 to 20 feet in length and has a very shallow draft (drawing 10 to 12 inches with the motor tilted up), so that it can fish (or run) in very shallow water.

A platform is positioned above the motor of most skiffs to provide the captain maximum visibility as he poles his skiff quietly across the flats in search of fish. The rest of the boat is constructed with fishing in mind—

flow-through livewells, excellent storage areas for rods and other gear, raised bow area for casting, and gunwales wide and sturdy enough to walk on. The backcountry skiff is, in effect, a clutter-free, highly mobile, casting platform.

Your Guide

The Florida Keys backcountry fishing guide is a truly colorful subject; an intriguing blend of knowledge, determination, and enthusiasm (allowing for the occasional gesture of despair). The backcountry guide is not only called upon to be highly proficient at finding and catching fish, but must also be able to impart that knowledge in instructions to his anglers.

There is probably no other area in the realm of charter fishing that requires a guide to be so "plugged in" to the conditions around him. Knowing which tide to fish for a given species is not enough. Your guide must know which hour in the tide to fish, as well as the effects of water temperature, wind speed and direction, cloud cover, moon phase, barometric changes, and a host of other variables.

The guide combines the offices of businessman, entertainer, teacher, and diplomat in sufficient proportion not only to catch his anglers some fish, but to transform a good percentage of those anglers into return clients. Good guides are the true masters of their art. The rest are still learning. (See below for tips for locating and hiring a guide.)

Types of Fishing

One of the truly wonderful problems a skiff guide faces each morning is deciding what fish to target and what techniques to employ. Usually the guide will listen to an angler's piscatorial preferences, make an assessment of an angler's skills, and then make a recommendation for a plan of action.

For instance, he may recommend fishing the flats if his angler has the ability to sightcast. Bonefish, permit, tarpon, redfish, barracuda, and shark are the most commonly sought flats species. The epitome of flats fishing involves stalking "tailing" fish (fish that show their tails above the surface of the water as they busily root crustaceans out of the bottom). On a calm day it is possible to

see tailing fish several hundred yards away. The anticipation that builds as you quietly approach such a fish or school of fish can make you want to explode. Such fish are very spooky, so a perfect presentation is required.

Occasionally, novice anglers want to catch a bonefish, even if their casting skills are not what they need to be. In such a case, the guide will often dice up about a dozen live shrimp and toss them into a flat where the current will carry the scent. Several live shrimp are then cast into the same area where the diced

shrimp were tossed. Bonefish react very well to this approach; many a rookie angler has been rewarded with his "bone" through the use of this method.

Another option a guide may choose is backcountry fishing in Florida Bay. These trips are captivatingly scenic, and provide first-rate fishing for trout, snapper, snook, tarpon (ranging from juveniles to giants), pompano, black drum, ladyfish, sheepshead, and shark.

Normally it is the mangrove-covered shorelines, deep-cut channels, and hidden backwater creeks that get the

Backcountry Target Species

Species	Best Time and Techniques
Barracuda	Year-round; sightcasting on flats or blindcasting channel edgers with light to medium spinning or plug-casting tackle. Live bait very effective. Good artificials include tube lures, plugs, and spoons. Excellent beginner fish for flyrod.
Bonefish	Year-round but avoid severe cold fronts and midsummer days after 11 A.M. Best April through June and October through December; sightcasting on flats with light spinning tackle; live shrimp best, small jigs good. Good target on flyrod.
Permit	March through June; sightcasting on flats with light- to medium-weight spinning tackle; small live blue crabs best; large live shrimp and jigs good; highly sought prize on flyrod.
Redfish	March through April, October through December; sightcasting on flats with light spinning tackle with live shrimp or shrimp-and-jig combination; blindcasting jigs, plugs, and weedless spoons into potholes on flats or along channel edges; Everglades National Park is best area.
Shark	Year-round but winter cold snaps may empty flats; sightcasting on flats with spinning plug or fly tackle suited for shark's size; live or fresh dead bait best but will take a variety of artificials (including fly) in spite of poor eyesight.

Species	Best Time and Techniques
Snapper	Year-round; still fishing or bottom fishing with live shrimp in channels, potholes, and around coral heads (Lower Keys); can be caught blindcasting with jig tipped with shrimp.
Snook	April through June, September through November; blindcasting with spinning or plug-casting tackle near bridges or in backcountry around points, deep-cut shorelines, channels, or potholes. Jigs and plugs good, jig and shrimp combo excellent.
Tarpon	March through June, October through November; drifting with live bait (mullet or pinfish) on 20- to 30-pound spinning or conventional tackle near bridges or in backcountry channels; on oceanside or backcountry flats, sightcasting with large live shrimp, crab, or artificials (plug, jig, or worm combo); excellent on fly (10- to 12-weight rod).
Trout	Winter months; blindcasting with light spinning or plug-casting tackle; fish backcountry channel edges, deepwater flats, especially mullet muds with jig and shrimp combo or shrimp under a popping cork.

bulk of angling attention. However, flats fishing opportunities also exist out in the backcountry, especially for redfish.

In the spring, many guides make a specialty out of a third type of fishing, live bait tarpon fishing. Done primarily around the bridges or in the deepwater channels of the backcountry, this style of fishing is probably the best for putting customers with only modest angling skills onto a really big fish. The hotbed of prime season activity seems to be the Middle Keys (Islamorada and Marathon), but some great early-season activity can be found in Key West Harbor, and even some of the smaller, lesser known bridges and channels throughout the Keys can be great producers.

Where to Fish

Where you decide to do your backcountry fishing is pretty much a matter of personal preference. Excellent oceanside flats exist throughout the entire chain of the Keys from North Key Largo to Key West. In addition, another area of flats starting about two miles west of Key West runs for about 15 miles west to the Marquesas Keys, and offers some excellent fishing for tarpon and permit.

As for the backcountry, three national parks provide great fishing potential. Biscayne National Park covers the North Key Largo area; Everglades National Park runs from Key Largo through Islamorada to a point just northeast of Marathon; and the Great Blue Heron National Wildlife Refuge runs from a point just northwest of Marathon all the way to Key West.

Your Choice

If you like the challenge of stalking and then making a finesse presentation to a great gamefish, if you enjoy the feeling of really being "on the water," if you appreciate the concept of having a guide customize your trip to meet your needs, then a backcountry charter is for you. Spend a day with a skiff guide in the Keys backcountry and the fish may not be the only thing that gets hooked. ■

Helpful Hints for Hiring a Backcountry Guide

1. In some parts of the Keys, a fleet of backcountry skiffs may be visible from the road. This would be an obvious starting point to inquire about a charter, but keep in mind that some parts of the Keys won't have charter docks with highway exposure. In this case, local tackle shops are a good place to start your search. Many motels allow captains to display their business cards and brochures in the front office. The local Chambers of Commerce also provide such information. If a guides' association exists in the area, they will usually have a brochure listing the local captains.

2. Once you have located a captain, be sure to communicate with him either in person or by phone. It's important he knows what you want and has some idea of your angling ability (don't fib). It's also important to develop a rapport with your guide before you go out, perhaps even before you book the trip. If you don't feel comfortable talking with him, you certainly aren't going to feel comfortable together all day in an 18-foot boat.

3. Unless it's a spur-of-the-moment decision, expect to leave a deposit to secure the trip (varying from $50 up to half the charter price).

4. Although many guides will take three anglers, do yourself a favor and keep it to two. Going alone with the guide, if you can afford it, is the best—an 18-footer can get mighty small with four passengers (guide included).

5. Remember, you're not going on an air-conditioned cabin cruiser. Be sure to bring a hat, a powerful sunscreen, and polarized sunglasses (to help you see fish through the water's surface glare). Also, if you are planning on sight fishing the flats, don't wear brightly colored or dark clothing. You'll look like an aid to navigation on the casting platform, which will scare all the fish! Light blue, teal green, light gray, and khaki are good choices as they reflect less light and provide less contrast against the sky.

6. Be flexible if the weather forces you from your original game plan. Most guides are very good at fishing the conditions, that is, choosing a method of fishing that will best suit the weather conditions, seasonal availability of fish, and an angler's skill level. When in doubt, heed the advice of your guide.

7. Although May and June are prime season for most backcountry gamesters, an excellent fall run of tarpon occurs from October through December, along with good snook fishing at the bridges, and great bonefishing and redfishing on the flats. Not only is there less fishing pressure in the fall, but the motel rates are often at their lowest.

8. Regarding boat traffic and fishing pressure, try, if possible, to book your trip during a weekday rather than a weekend.

Party Boats: There's Economy in Numbers

By Capt. Walt Mason

Party boats, or head boats, are those big charter boats that take a lot of fishermen out for a per-person (by the head) fee. The crews that run these boats are knowledgeable and try to make the experience as much like a personal charter as possible.

In the Florida Keys, there are boats that go out for a half-day (four hours either in the morning or afternoon), a full seven-hour day, a five-hour night trip, or a long-range Marquesas and Tortugas trip, far past the end of the Overseas Highway.

Typical prices (as of this writing) are $22 to $25 for a half-day, $40 for a full day, and $30 to $35 for a night trip. Prices for long-range trips vary.

Half-days: Half-day trips are good for the novice fisherman and those who want a short day's exposure to sun and weather. Half-days are great for beginners and young children.

Full-Days: Full-day boats are generally for more experienced fishermen who can take a full day's exertion. The advantage to a full-day boat is if the fish aren't biting in one area, the captain has more freedom to move around and fish more spots. Also, only full-day boats have the time to catch live bait, which is the best ammunition for bottom fishing, especially on calm days when a live bait puts out a "hum."

Night Trips: Night trips are romantic. Lots of young people on their honeymoons go for this one. They are also good for people who don't like the sun. It's usually calm and cool, especially in the summer, and shallow-water snappers, like mangroves, feed better at night. During the dark of the moon, fishing will be shallow; on bright nights, deeper.

Snapper fishing is great from late spring to early fall. Night fishing is particularly good for snappers on days when the water is clean and clear. Then snappers are caught more easily at night because they rely more on smell than sight to feed—groupers and kings, too. Night fishing has a different style and a different feel. I recommend all fishermen try it.

The Depths

Shallow: Most Keys party boats fish at anchor. On rough days when the water is muddy, generally in fall through spring when water temperature drops in the bay and fish move to the patches, they will fish shallow or patch reefs. Cero and Spanish mackerel are caught on the surface, and mutton, mangrove snapper, yellowtail, groupers, porgy, and sheepshead are caught on the bottom.

Reef: The reef itself, 55 to 120 feet deep, is fished year-round, and is especially good at night from May through September. The reef teems with cero, king mackerel, sailfish, bonito, yellowtail, mutton snapper, big groupers, and even occasional tuna and wahoo.

Deep Ledges: In fall and winter, deep-ledge fishing in 130- to 200-foot depths is hot. This is where big king mackerel, muttons, vermilion and lane snappers, large porgy, mangrove, silk, and genuine red snappers are caught.

The Wrecks: Gamefish concentrate on wrecks such as The 220, the Haitian, and many others, especially in the summer when shallow waters get hot and the grouper move to cooler waters. Wreck fishing is especially good on boats that catch live bait (like the *Gulf Lady*). Big amberjack, smoker kings, 50- to 60-pound grouper, and blacktip sharks are great on the wrecks in the fall.

Fishing Conditions

Conditions that affect the catch include weather, wind and current direction, and the number of people on the boat.

It's easier to catch fish with fewer people aboard. The more lines there are in the water, the more lead each must use to prevent tangles. Fishing without weights, as in yellowtailing, can't be done successfully if there are more than 30 people fishing. Generally, fishermen on the bow of the boat will use the heaviest weights, decreasing as you get farther back on the boat.

The closest part of the boat to the wreck or the reef is the preferred spot for large groupers. Muttons will wander on the outskirts of the chum slick. Larger fish are caught away from the crowd, at the bow or the stern. Smaller fish are caught all around the boat.

Smoky water conditions can allow more people to fish successfully, and overcast days are also good. Fish bite well when it's rough, but you should avoid going out if winds are in excess of 20 miles per hour.

The most important key to success is following instructions. When fishing 60 to 200 feet down, remember that mono stretches. When using a sliding sinker rig, wind down tight before striking a fish. When using a large bait, a short drop-back is needed first. Wind till the rod bends over before striking a bottom fish.

Success will vary depending on conditions and the type of fishing. Consult with the crew.

Fishing Tips

Hooking the bait: When dropping the bait to the bottom, think of a bullet—the pointed end goes down first. Hook the bait through the smallest or pointed end. Thread the bait onto the hook several times to cover the shank well, leaving the point of the hook exposed.

Dropping the bait: Don't let the bait down too fast—it will wrap around the

The Boats

The best way for the novice to choose a party boat is to go to the dock the day before and talk to people who are coming in from a trip. Ask them if the crew was courteous. Did they work hard to catch fish? Did they move if the fish weren't biting? Did they circulate among the fishermen and try to be helpful? Most of all, ask the fishermen if they had a good time. Word of mouth is the best recommendation.

Most head boats are associated with the larger marinas along the Keys. Locations are at Mile Markers (MM) found all along U.S. Highway 1. The telephone area code is 305.

Key Largo: Starting at the north end of Marina del Rey (MM 100) are the *Sailor's Choice* (451-1802), a half-day boat, and the *Captain Jack III* (451-4425), a full-day boat.

Key Largo is close to the Gulf Stream and has strong currents. The area has excellent black grouper and yellowtail snapper fishing.

Islamorada: Islamorada has three full-day party boats: At Holiday Isle Marina, Robbie's Dock, you'll find the *Capt. Winner II* (664-8498), specializing in yellowtail and reef fishing. The *Caloosa* (852-3200) at Whale Harbor also specializes in yellowtail and reef fishing. At Bud 'n Mary's Marina (MM 79.8), the *Gulf Lady* (664-BOAT) specializes in live-bait bottom fishing and surface fishing. All generally fish at anchor.

Half-day boats in Islamorada include the *Miss Tradewinds* at Whale Harbor (664-8341) and the *Captain's Lady* at Robbie's, Holiday Isle (664-4196). Both specialize in yellowtail and bottom fishing.

Marathon: Two party boats fish out of the Marathon Lady docks (MM 53; 743-5580). The half-day *Marathon Lady* fishes shallow reefs for yellowtail and mangrove snapper.

The full-day boat fishes the reef for both king mackerel and bottom fish. There are no full-day trips over the summer; instead, night trips are scheduled for snapper.

The *SS Winner Queen* (743-6969) fishes out of Marathon in the winter only. They offer day trips for grouper, snapper, and yellowtail, and schedule long-range trips to the Tortugas south of Key West. Two-day trips are $170, three-day trips $200.

Key West: Key West has two full-day party boats, with one running seasonal night trips, and one half-day. The *Gulfstream III* (296-8494) runs full-day trips every day except Mondays, and *Can't Miss* (296-3735) runs full-day trips daily, Labor Day through Memorial Day, and evening trips the rest of the year.

Capt. John's Greyhound V (296-5139) is a half-day boat, fishing in both mornings and afternoons.

line and make a tangled mess. Let the bait all the way down. The bait should lay flat on the bottom.

Getting Started

Party boat fishing is fun and easy to do. You just come to the dock and buy a ticket. Sometimes you can make reservations for stern spots, which are preferred by yellowtail and king fishermen.

Introduce yourself to the captain and mate. Be sure to have your tackle checked, or rent some.

Choose your spot by placing your tackle. Fishing spots on the rail may be numbered, or there may be a string or rod holders. Positions are first come, first served.

Stow your gear and familiarize yourself with the boat. Read all the safety notices posted. Locate the heads and find out how they operate.

Get friendly with the crew. They can be very helpful. Tell them if you are a novice and need any special instruction.

Relax and enjoy the ride out. It will take 20 minutes to an hour, depending on where the captain decides to fish, and whether you stop to catch live bait.

Wait for the boat to anchor and the captain's instructions to begin fishing.

Tackle

All party boats rent rods—about $3 is standard. Some sell rigs, but terminal tackle (hooks, sinkers, leaders, and swivels) are usually provided. If you bring your own rod, make sure it's in good condition with new, good quality line—and find out if the boat carries extra rods on board, just in case. Here's the gear used for the most common species:

Surface: Surface rigs are free drifting lines with little or no weight. Yellowtail snapper call for 12- or 15-pound spin-

ning gear with low visibility pink or gray line and no leader. Other surface fish like kings or wahoo need 20-pound spinners with light mono or wire leaders.

Bottom: Bottom tackle ranges from 20-pound spin to 50-pound conventional, with matching leader and hook. The standard bottom rig is the SOB (Shrimp—or Strip—On the Bottom) with a light leader. Snapper will take a 30- to 50-pound leader with a 1/0 to 5/0 hook. Groupers call for a 40- to 125-pound leader and 5/0 to 9/0 hooks. All bottom rigs use a sliding egg sinker with a barrel swivel below.

What to Bring

Each party boat has different amenities. Some have air conditioning and an enclosed cabin. Some have TV and microwave ovens. Most provide room for small coolers, while some have communal coolers. Some even sell snacks. All provide bait and chum. Be sure to ask about the facilities on the boat.

To be prepared, besides your fishing tackle, you should bring a windbreaker jacket, a floppy hat, and sunblock. Don't forget your still camera or video camera. Fairweather fishermen should ask about the sea conditions before boarding. If you have a tendency toward seasickness, get scopolamine patches or other preventives from your doctor, and take as directed, well in advance.

Mates

The mate on the party boat is your most valuable asset. He or she should provide information on the tackle and how to use it. They recommend rigs and bait, give tackle instructions to novices, and tie tackle and leaders. Depending on the service, a mate should earn a 10 to 20 percent tip. Cleaning fish at the dock is extra; there is either a set fee or a separate tip for the service.

Summary

There are many advantages to fishing on a party boat. They are inexpensive and a fun way to take your family fishing. There is lots of camaraderie, and fishing stories from around the world are exchanged. Of course, there is the down side: One angler hooked into a circling bonito can tangle 23 other lines—but that, too, is a part of your special Florida Keys fishing experience. ■

MARQUESAS TO THE DRY TORTUGAS

LAND CONFIGURATION AND WATER DEPTH

The small groupings of islands known as the Marquesas Keys and the Dry Tortugas mark the southern end of the Florida Keys. The Marquesas Keys, locally called the Marquesas (Mar'key ses), are some 20 miles east of Key West and 70 miles southeast of the nearest point of the mainland, Cape Sable, Florida. The Dry Tortugas lie some 60 miles from Key West, and are actually 20 miles closer to Cuba than to Florida's mainland. The only inhabitants on these two island groups are a caretaker and his family on Garden Key in the Dry Tortugas.

The Marquesas are a group of low, mangrove-covered islands that lie upon a shallow bank of calcareous sand. The islands themselves are the exposed

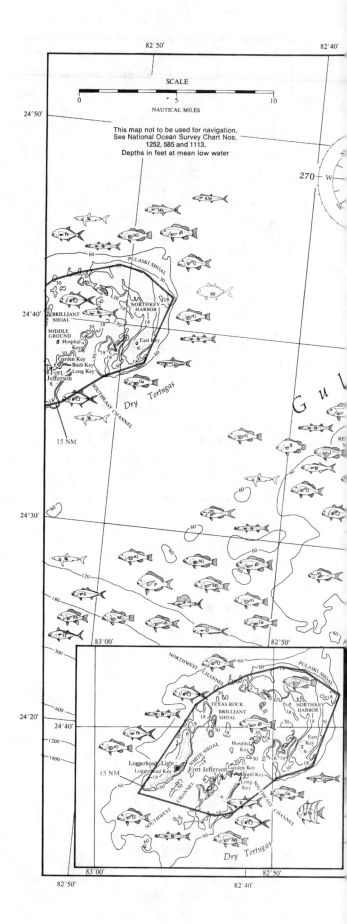

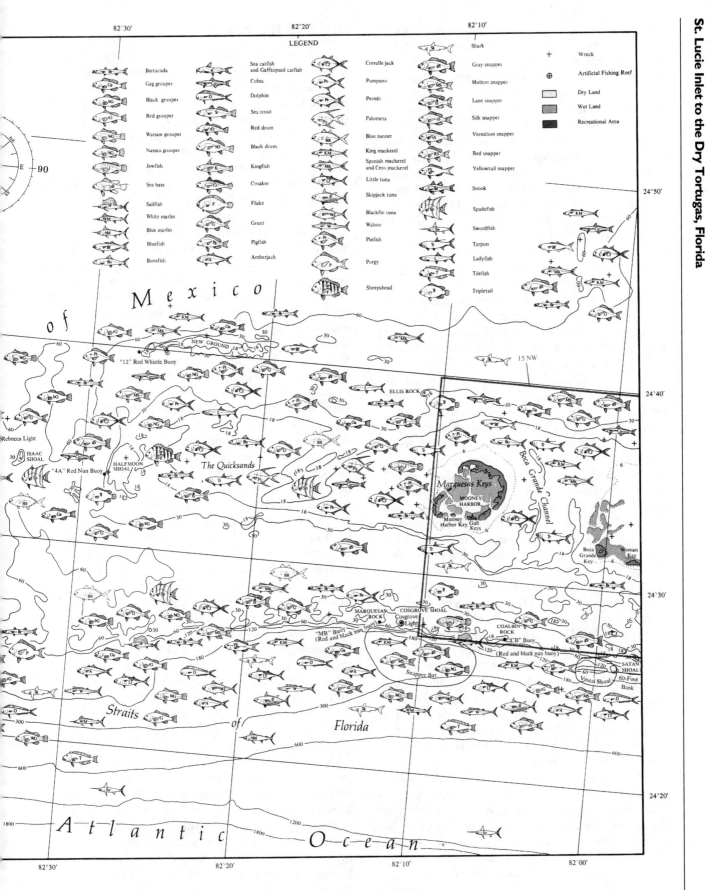

LEGEND

Barracuda
Gag grouper
Black grouper
Red grouper
Warsaw grouper
Nassau grouper
Jewfish
Sea bass
Sailfish
White marlin
Blue marlin
Bluefish
Bonefish

Sea catfish and Gafftopsail catfish
Cobia
Dolphin
Sea trout
Red drum
Black drum
Kingfish
Croaker
Fluke
Grunt
Pigfish
Amberjack
Sheepshead

Crevalle jack
Pompano
Permit
Palometa
Blue runner
King mackerel
Spanish mackerel and Cero mackerel
Little tuna
Skipjack tuna
Blackfin tuna
Wahoo
Pinfish
Porgy

Shark
Gray snapper
Mutton snapper
Lane snapper
Silk snapper
Vermilion snapper
Red snapper
Yellowtail snapper
Snook
Spadefish
Swordfish
Tarpon
Ladyfish
Tilefish
Tripletail

+ Wreck
⊕ Artificial Fishing Reef
Dry Land
Wet Land
Recreational Area

part of a narrow sand strip that forms the rim of an approximately 3-mile-wide continuous circle. Within the rim is a sheltered lagoon having depths as much as 10 feet. This circle of islands surrounding the lagoon looks superficially like an atoll such as are common in the South Pacific Ocean, but unlike the Pacific atolls, which are composed almost entirely of coral or coral debris, the Marquesas are composed of calcareous sands that are not of coral origin. Apparently these sands have been cast up by waves and the circular shape formed by the actions of tidal currents and wind. Although the sand strip of the Marquesas is nearly continuous, the sea cuts through in a number of places, forming nearly a dozen islands of various sizes.

The shallow bank of calcareous sand continues westward of the Marquesas to form the 30-square-mile area known as the Quicksands, perhaps so named because of the loose sand bottom into which heavy objects sink. Depths there range from 2 to 20 feet, and average about 10 feet. Halfmoon Shoal marks the western end of the Quicksands. During winter months, large numbers of king mackerel gather off here and also just north of here in the area that commercial fishermen call No Man's Land. A few hundred yards away from the Quicksands the water deepens to about 50 feet, but in less than a half dozen miles it shoals abruptly to form the New Grounds to the north and Isaac Shoal and Rebecca Shoal to the west. Beyond Rebecca Shoal, the water deepens to 100 feet or so and forms a 12-mile-wide strait that is used by coastal ships bound from the east coast to the west coast of Florida. The Dry Tortugas form the offshore side of this strait.

The Dry Tortugas are a group of small, low islands scantily vegetated and surrounded by extensive shoals. The islands and shoals, like the Marquesas, are atoll-shaped and surround and shelter a central lagoon. Unlike the Marquesas, the Tortugas are a true atoll composed of calcareous material derived mostly from living corals. In all of the Dry Tortugas there are only about a hundred acres of land. Were the sea level to drop by only six feet, well over 5,000 acres would be exposed. The islands and shoals are constantly changing shape in response to storms and currents. In 1513, when Juan Ponce de Leon first saw these islands and named them for the large catch of sea turtles he made (*tortuga* being Spanish for turtle), there were 12 to 15 islands. Today only eight remain.

The central lagoon of the Tortugas is about 50 feet deep and is connected to the sea by three principal channels that are at least as deep. Both the channels and the lagoon have luxuriant growths of corals and sea fans as well as other attached organisms. The channels are often lined along their sides with an abundance of corals. One of the most impressive growths in the lagoon is White Shoal, with sides rising nearly vertically 60 feet above the bottom.

FISH AND FISHING

Of the more than 500 species of fishes living in this area, barracudas are among the most common and easiest to identify. The almost cylindrical body, long pointed head, large mouth, sharp teeth, and silvery sides are obvious marks that distinguish barracudas from other fishes. They are of a family that includes some 20 species, all members of a single genus distributed in tropical, subtropical, and warm-temperate waters around the world. Four species occur along the Florida coast, the northern and southern sennets, guaguanche, and the great barracuda.

The great barracuda, distinguished by conspicuous black blots on the rear part of the body, is a major predator, a favorite subject of lurid stories of attacks on people, and an acceptable gamefish. Caught on light tackle, barracuda often make a series of spectacular jumps similar to those of sailfish. The great barracuda is perhaps the most widely distributed species of the family, only its absence from the eastern Pacific keeping it from being distributed around the world. It spends much of its life nearshore, though large ones may be found traveling far offshore—one was taken some 900 miles east of Bermuda. In the western Atlantic, the great barracuda's reported range extends from Cape Cod to southern Brazil. Along our east coast, its numbers decrease rapidly north of about Palm Beach, Florida, and few are seen alongshore north of Cape Canaveral, Florida. Even so, large adults are common on offshore wrecks and reefs to about Cape Hatteras, North Carolina.

Mature females produce several batches of ripe eggs from April to about August. The eggs are probably cast and fertilized in open water. From spring until mid-September, the young come close to shore, usually into depths of less than 10 feet, along beaches, about nearshore obstructions and mangroves, in grass beds, or in the brackish water of estuaries. Some take shelter under floating seaweeds. At this age, they may gather into small groups of as few as 10 to 30 or as many as thousands, and prey on small fishes, including killifishes, sardines, anchovies, silversides, gobies and young puffers, needlefishes, snappers, parrotfish, and mojarras. As they grow larger, they move into deeper water where they find larger prey.

Although great barracuda 10 to 30 inches long are fairly gregarious, each individual seems to keep domain over its own territory from which it excludes others of the group. It will leave its territory only briefly to catch a passing fish. However, when schools of small fish such as silversides, halfbeaks, or sardines come inshore with the flood tide, the barracuda abandon their territories to make the attack. As great barracuda get larger, they become less gregarious; and when they get to be about three feet long, they usually travel alone or in groups of two or three. As they become larger, they take larger

Clean Water and Boat Care—There is a Connection

- Shun products that remove stains or make your boat shine—they can be very toxic and may kill marine life if washed overboard.
- Rinse and scrub your boat with a brush after each use to minimize use of soap.
- Use, or make sure your boatyard uses, the least damaging bottom paints available. Pesticides in these paints prevent barnacles, seaweed, and other fouling organisms from growing on boat bottoms, but can be harmful to valuable marine life. Incidentally, tributyltin (TBT) is banned nationally for non-aluminum boats less than 82 feet.
- Scrape and paint your boat away from the water; catch scrapings in a drop cloth and dispose of them at an official hazardous waste collection, or have your marina do so.
- Copper-only paints generally provide adequate protection over a full boating season. Scrubbing the bottom periodically extends the useful life of the paint, and there are formulas available that do not lose effectiveness during storage over the winter.
- Use a paste of equal parts salt and flour, with enough white vinegar to moisten, to clean brass, copper, and bronze. Rub on, rinse with water, dry.
- Mix 1 tablespoon white vinegar in 1 pint water to clean boat windows.

prey, such as groupers, mackerel, dolphin, sailfish, wahoo, and various tunas.

Very little is known about the migrations of great barracuda. Beginning about their third year, they travel seasonally. In summer, some seem to go northward in coastal waters or in the Gulf Stream; others go far out over deep water. In fall they return to their winter habitats along the south Florida coast. Many spend the winter about the Keys, both along the edge of the Outer Reef and in holes along the flats.

In some localities, great barracuda weighing over three pounds are occasionally poisonous to eat. The poisoning, called *ciguatera* in the Caribbean region, is technically known as ichthyosarcotoxism. Symptoms may include nausea, vomiting, acute diarrhea, metallic taste in the mouth, tingling sensations in the skin, cramps in the extremities, aching muscles and joints, scalding urination, and sometimes convulsions. A few severe cases have led to coma and even death. This poisonousness does not result from spoilage, but probably is a property of the flesh that develops after the great barracuda has fed on prey such as trunkfishes and puffers, which are generally poisonous in tropical waters. The same effect might result from eating invertebrates that have fed on poisonous algae. Fish poisoning is a phenomenon of tropical seas around the world affecting many fishes of coral reef communities.

FISHING REGULATIONS

For a discussion of Florida's fishing regulations, including saltwater licensing, see pages 97-99.

Bad Weather Bones

by Capt. Buddy LaPointe

Well, I guess this front is going to ruin our bonefishing today," said my chagrined angler, as we stood together on the dock staring into the windswept expanse of Florida Bay. His disappointment was well founded, as he had traveled a pretty fair distance from the extreme northern portion of the world (Wisconsin or Michigan or someplace) down to the tropical climes of the Florida Keys in order to escape— you guessed it—cold windy weather.

A January cold front had torn through the Keys the day before, and the high pressure system that had built in behind it was pummeling us with a 20 knot (and gusting) wind. Furthermore, temperatures had dropped from the mid-seventies down to the upper-fifties, (which is bone-chilling if you live here year-round).

However, it was not the air temperature that concerned us, but rather the corresponding drop in water temperature on the flats. Although this was to be his first trip with me, my prospective angler was no slouch when it came to knowing his quarry, or the conditions under which they are normally caught. Not only had he been catching bonefish for years in both the Keys and the Bahamas, but he had also devoured just about every piece of literature ever written on the subject. So when I suggested that conditions looked just about right for applying deep-water, wintertime tactics to catch bonefish, it came as no surprise that the look I got from him ranked somewhere between shock and suspicion. I'm sure he thought he was about to get "hustled."

The Norm

If you were to ask a handful of dedicated bonefishermen to briefly describe the sport they so dearly love, they would probably create a scenario similar to the following:

Picture yourself standing on the casting platform of a shallow-draft "battle-ready" skiff that was specifically designed to take an angler into extremely shallow water where bonefish are found. Having already run 45 minutes from the dock, you are now located on some remote backcountry flat staring ahead into a mirrored sea and sky that seem to meet together as one. You are surrounded by a peacefulness and tranquillity that only the early morning hours of the Florida Keys backwaters seem to be able to produce.

The waters before you are anything but tranquil, though, as the transparent shallows are teeming with life. Schools of glass minnows scurry about trying to avoid predators of all types, while horseshoe crabs ramble across the bottom in their own businesslike manner. Several majestic white herons wade the shallows up ahead, while an occasional tern or gull swoops and dips for a meal on the surface. Every few minutes a large stingray or small shark swims past the boat with an agenda all its own.

Yet, as wondrously synchronized as the environment is, you refuse to allow yourself to be distracted, choosing instead to focus on the task at hand—locating some bonefish. The level of anticipation and excitement building within you over the prospect of meeting with the legendary "Gray Ghost" of the flats is just indescribable.

At the other end of the skiff, perched upon his poling platform, is your guide, deeply tanned from his many years of fishing out on these sun-soaked flats. He is a picture of concentration and proficiency, silently poling his skiff while intensely searching the broad expanse of flats before him for telltale signs that might give away the presence of a bonefish. Some of those "clues" might come in the form of "nervous water" (small ripples on the surface that are out of sync with the ripples from the wind), a noticeable wake (caused by a single moving fish), or a "push" (a moving bulge in the water caused by a school of moving fish). Small patches of discolored water can also give away a school of feeding bonefish as they stir up bottom sediments. The one sign that both angler and guide long to see is what could arguably qualify as the prettiest sight in all of flats fishing—the exposed waving silver tail of a bonefish as it roots out crustaceans from the shallow grass flat.

Finding a bonefish is only the first of many challenges. It must next be approached with the utmost of stealth or it will "spook," as bonefish are very much aware of their own vulnerability

Captain Buddy LaPointe poles his boat from the bow on a bonefish flat in the Florida Keys. (VIN T. SPARANO)

when they feed within the shallow confines of a flat. Once the fish is within range, an angler is then called upon to make nothing less than a perfect cast to his quarry; too close and the fish will bolt for the safety of deep water—not close enough and it'll never see the bait.

If the angler is lucky enough to hook up, he must now subject his tackle to what is perhaps the fastest, most powerful run by any fish in shallow water. Its first dash for freedom frequently covers over 100 yards, and its second run nearly rivals that of the first. Large bonefish are tough, cagey fighters, and possess a level of endurance that would make the Energizer Bunny look like a slug.

After the angler finally does catch and release that bonefish (whether it be his first or his fiftieth), he is filled with both satisfaction and awe, knowing he has just experienced one of those defining moments in the life of a fisherman. The entire process transcends the term sport, and becomes nothing less than an art form. If perchance this procedure has taken place with a fly rod, then the intensity of the experience seems magnified tenfold.

This is classical bonefishing at its best, a game of absolute precision and, to many, the epitome of catch and release angling. Yet not all bonefishing is done in this manner. Conditions such as high winds, heavy cloud cover, or higher stages of the tide warrant a change in tactics. If an angler's casting skills aren't up to snuff for sight casting to spooky "tailers," another tack must be tried. Keys area guides have perfected a method whereby the boat is staked out or anchored on a section of flat along which bonefish are known to travel. A handful of diced-up shrimp is then tossed behind the boat. Once the smell of the "chum" wafts down current from the boat, the bonefish simply swim through the "chumline" and follow it to its source. Then an angler can make an easy downwind cast to the fish (if he didn't already have the bait laying in the chumline in the first place). Countless anglers have

caught their first bonefish using this very method.

A Break with Tradition

Both of these styles of bonefishing are based on the presumption that there will be bonefish on the flat. However, when water temperatures dip below a certain point (about 70°F for the Keys) bonefish will leave the flats for the sanctuary of deeper, warmer water. Although everything you've ever read about the subject states that blustery winter cold fronts are not synonymous with good bonefishing, there is, in fact, a very good chance of catching bonefish provided you're willing to make a radical departure from normal tactics. Savvy Keys guides have been using this method for years to find fish for their winter clients.

Make no mistake—fishing for bonefish in cold water is not to be confused with normal sight casting on a flat. First of all, you are fishing "blind," casting not at a particular target, but rather into a general area. Secondly, you are not even up on a flat per se; you'll be fishing in water ranging from about four to six feet, but sometimes as deep as 10 feet. Finally, rather than spending the day charging around the backcountry of Florida Bay, efforts are concentrated just off the ocean-side flats from Key Biscayne all the way down to Key West. These flats provide bonefish with quick access to deeper, warmer water during a cold snap. Because the ocean side is basically a lee shore during the north winds of a cold front, anglers reap the benefit of relatively comfortable fishing conditions in even a 20-knot wind.

Locating the Fish

Two Marathon area flats guides who have made deep-water bonefishing a way of life during the coldest months of winter are Capt. Albert Ponzoa of the *Always Late*, and Capt. Barry Meyer aboard the *Magic*. Both consistently produce bonefish on days when many

captains don't even bother to leave the dock. Says Capt. Meyer, "The cruddier the weather the better... I like a stiff cold wind out of the north, but I do prefer a day or two *after* the leading edge of the front has gone through... that way the precipitation has all moved out, the skies are fairly clear, and the fish have settled down from being run off of the flats."

"The first order of business when it comes to finding cold-water bones is to locate a *mud*," says Capt. Ponzoa. These *muds* are a discoloration in the water caused by sediments being stirred up by fish rooting around on the bottom for food. "The mud may be the size of a my boat, or it may be as large as a house, but I'll spend a good deal of time hunting for a mud before we ever wet a line. And sometimes it's possible to get fooled; what looks like a good bonefish mud, may turn out (after fishing it) to be a patch of muddied water created by a deep draft boat that came through 20 minutes before. Even a stingray can chum up a sizable area of bottom, making you think you've found a *hot* mud. I'll invest about 20 minutes on a mud... if we haven't hooked a bone by then, I'm out of there."

Some days the fish will lie right off the edge of the flat and the muds will be in four to six feet of water. At times during extreme cold, you may have to work them in water as deep as 8 to 10 feet! Typically, bonefish are more likely to mud on deep water grass than on large expanses of white sand, because the grass holds crustaceans better. Some guides feel its darkness absorbs some heat from the sun, making dining all the more comfortable for the bones.

Fishing a Mud

Once a mud is located, care is taken not to disturb the bonefish in it. The general rule is to cut the engine 75 to 100 yards upwind of it and then pole or drift in toward it. The boat is then

153

staked out with the push pole, or if it's fairly deep, the anchor is quietly slipped over the side.

Once the boat is positioned several boat lengths upwind of the mud, the next order of business is to chum. "I like to dice up about a dozen and a half shrimp and toss them out behind the boat to help concentrate the fish in one area," says Capt. Ponzoa. "Then I'll add more as needed. When things get busy and we're hooking up regularly, I'll really pour it on to keep the bonefish close by." You can really go through some shrimp in the course of a trip. Both guides bring no less than twelve dozen live shrimp per trip, and when things are hot they sometimes have to duck in to the nearest marina for more.

In terms of how to catch those deep-water bonefish once they're located, the two captains differ somewhat in their technique. Capt. Meyer likes to use a whole shrimp Texasrigged so to speak (see diagram) on a 2/0 sliced shank hook with a split shot just above the knot. He likes his clients to cast into the mud just beyond the point where the chum was tossed in, and slowly twitch and retrieve the shrimp along the bottom. Capt. Ponzoa, on the other hand, prefers the use of an ⅛- or ¼-ounce brown, tan, or pink jig sweetened with a thumbnail-size piece of shrimp. He likes it worked in that same slow twitch and retrieve fashion.

For tackle, both prefer 8- to 10-pound line on a light 7-foot spinning rod. The reels must hold at least 200 yards of line and have drags that are *silky smooth*.

Both guides are quick to add that fly fishing for these deep-water bonefish can be quite productive. Although many would balk at the idea of trying to sling a fly line around in a 20-knot wind, it's really not as bad as it sounds, as all of the casting will be made to a point that is only a couple of boat lengths directly downwind. A 9- or 10-weight outfit is about right for these conditions, and although an angler can get away with a floating line with a long

leader and weighted fly, a much more effective presentation can be made with an intermediate flyline (the slow sinking mono core lines are an excellent choice). Both guides like the Clouser minnow with heavy lead eyes to help it get down. Ponzoa finds the chartreuse and white color scheme tied on a #2 hook to be particularly effective for this pattern. The retrieve on a fly, (once it's been allowed to sink), should be in 4- to 6-inch *ticks* spaced about two seconds apart. The fly should be fished deep enough so that an angler can occasionally feel it hang momentarily in the turtle grass.

When asked about problems that can come up, both captains are quick to point out that boat traffic along the edge of the flat can occasionally be a real source of frustration, especially on weekends. According to Capt. Meyer, "Most people have no idea how many fish they are blowing out of muds as they roar by in their boat along the edge of the flat. They either don't see the mud or else don't equate the mud with fish. Mostly it's from boaters that just don't realize what we're trying to do out here."

Hooking a large bonefish while staked out on a productive mud presents another problem (albeit a pleasant one). Because of the deeper water and the wind, trying to pole the boat after a "reel screamer" isn't very effective, and starting the motor would spook the fish in the mud. "Sometimes," says Capt. Ponzoa, "you just have to cross your fingers and hope your angler can turn the fish before you run out of line. When you've got over 100 yards of 8-pound test out there attached to a large, fast-moving bonefish, plenty can go wrong. Seafans, lobster trap lines, and floating seaweed are just some of the things the line can get hung up in when you've got a lot of line out... It's a classic *Catch 22* predicament!"

One item that these two guides disagree on is the best time of day to fish. Whereas Capt. Meyer finds his best action between the hours of

11:00 A.M. and 3:00 P.M. (the warmest hours of the day), Capt. Ponzoa feels confident about fishing any part of the day, as long as the wind and tide flow are lined up in the same direction.

Just what kind of action can you expect from winter bonefishing? Both captains have posted some pretty impressive numbers considering the conditions. Capt. Ponzoa's best day last winter was landing 15 out of 22 bonefish hooked. Capt. Meyer's best day in the past couple of winters was a whopping 21 out of 25! Although these two examples are extremes, it does demonstrate what kind of potential is out there off the edge of the flat during those cold fronts. For a figure that might be more representative of an average day, both captains report regular catches of a half dozen bonefish or more per trip, with a lot of days producing better than 10. The bonefish themselves average about four to five pounds, although on Capt. Meyer's aforementioned "crush" day, he had four fish in the 10- to 12-pound bracket. Double-headers are frequent when you find a hot mud, and the furious action, though usually short-lived, can at times be similar to bailing schoolie dolphin on a weed line. "I've taken as many as 12 to 15 fish out of one mud," says Ponzoa. "On days like that you barely have time to look up, what with netting and releasing fish, baiting jigs, dicing and tossing chum and such."

From time to time, those winter muds will also produce some surprise guests, the most welcome of which is the feisty permit. Though they are loners at this time of the year and not of the size that will be around in the spring, these 10- to 15-pound permit do have a way of livening things up for an angler. Other bonus catches include small tarpon, pompano, mutton and mangrove snapper, jack crevelle, big blue runners, and sharks.

Conclusion

Interestingly enough, not everybody enjoys fishing "blind" for bonefish in deep water. No doubt, some anglers addicted to the thrill of the hunt will never be happy targeting bonefish by any other means than shallow-water stalking and sight casting. Some purists might even carry it one step further, feeling that catching a bonefish without first seeing and stalking it somehow

dishonors the fish and the sport (like catching an Atlantic salmon on an earthworm suspended under a bobber). The purpose of this article is not to quibble over preferences, but rather to demonstrate that a viable fishery exists in the Keys for bonefish even during the cold fronts that often make

up a good portion of the weather in December, January and February. Far from being the death knell of productive bonefishing, winter cold snaps can provide fast and fairly consistent action for those willing to vary their tactics to suit the demands of the existing weather conditions. ∎

SOUTH FLORIDA FISHING ACCESS

LAUNCH RAMPS

What follows is a list of Atlantic Coast launch ramps from St. Lucie Inlet through the Keys. See pages 106 and 177 in Chapters Two and Four for other Florida ramps.

Martin County

Hobe Sound Ramp, 4 blocks south of Hobe Sound Bridge on the ICW

Palm City Bridge Marina Ramp

Sand Sprite Park Ramp in Salerno

Stuart Ramp on US 1 at Frazier Creek

Pruitt's Camp Ramp in Stuart

Lyons Bridge Ramp in Stuart

Martin Marine Center Ramp in Stuart

Jensen Beach Causeway Ramp

Palm Beach County

Palmetto Street Bridge Ramp on the ICW at Boca Raton

Boynton Beach Ramp on U.S. 1 at N.E. 20th Ave

Delray Beach Ramp at S.E. 10th and S.E. 7th Ave

June Park Ramp, ½-mile north of PGA Blvd. on Ellison Wilson Road, ¼-mile south of US 1 Bridge on ICW, west of US 1

Lantana Avenue Bridge Ramp on ICW in Lantana

Foster Park Causeway Ramp on Blue Heron Blvd. at Riviera Beach

Curry Park Ramp, 25th St. at Flagler Drive, in West Palm Beach

Broward County

S.W. 7th Ave. and S.W. 4th St. in Fort Lauderdale

S.E. 15th St. and 14th Ave. in Fort Lauderdale

2nd St. and 14th Ave. in Hollywood

Dade County

Snapper Point Ramp on the Goulds Canal in Goulds

Homestead Bayfront Park Ramp in Homestead

Matheson Hammock Ramp in Miami

Crandon Marina Ramp in Miami

Watson Park Ramp on McArthur Causeway in Miami

Dinner Key Marina Ramp at Seminole Park in Miami

79th Street Causeway Ramp in Miami

Sunrise Park Ramp in Miami

Haulover Park Ramp on Miami Beach

79th Street Ramp in North Bay

Monroe County

Harry Harris Park Ramp at Tavernier

Tavernier Creek Ramp at the Oceanside Bridge in Tavernier

STATE PARKS WITH FISHING ACCESS

The Florida state parks listed here, from the St. Lucie Inlet to the Keys, offer saltwater fishing access. See pages 107 and 180 in Chapters Two and Four for more state parks with fishing access.

Bahia Honda, Bahia Honda Key, off US 1

Fort Zachary Taylor, Key West

Hugh Taylor Birch, Fort Lauderdale, off SR A1A

John D. MacArthur Beach, N. Palm Beach on Singer Island, via SR 703

John U. Lloyd Beach, Dania, off SR A1A

John Pennekamp Coral Reef, Key Largo, off US 1

Long Key, Long Key, off US 1

Oleta River, N. Miami on Sunny Isles Blvd., off US 1

Oscar Scherer, 2 mi. south of Osprey, off US 41

Perdido Key, 15 mi. southwest of Pensacola, off SR 292

Capt. Pat Casey, Islamorada B & T, P.O. Box 514, Mile Marker 81.6, Overseas Hwy., Islamorada, FL 33036, (305) 664-4578 or 9348

Capt. Greg Koon, P.O. Box 8023, 312 Holly Ave., Port St. Lucie, FL 34985, (305) 442-8558

Capt. Paul Tejera, 4201 S.W. 87th Ave., Miami, FL 33165, (305) 388-1747

Tom Ryan, 141 S.W. 24th Ave., Boynton Beach, FL 33435, (407) 737-6292

Capt. Gregg Gentile, shipping address, Michael Wertheim, MD, c/o Evelyn Gentile, 509 Riverside Dr., Suite 200, Stuart, FL 34994, (407) 878-0475 (H)

FISHING RECORDS

For a list of Florida records for both conventional and fly tackle, see page 108.

MASTER GUIDES

A comprehensive list of Florida master guides appears on pages 181 and 182.

Capt. Jerry Metz, 415½ Lakewood Rd. E., West Palm Beach, FL 33405, (407) 547-9337

STATE AGENCIES

A listing of various Florida agencies with jurisdiction over the state's saltwater fishing appears on page 111.

The Gulf of Mexico produces 40 percent of the commercial fish yield in the United States and a major portion of its shrimp fishery. It provides critical habitat for 75 percent of America's migratory waterfowl. Its coastal wetlands comprise about half the national total. Offshore oil and gas from the western Gulf account for 90 percent of all U.S. production. With these figures in mind, is it any wonder that the Gulf of Mexico is considered to be a national treasure?

Florida's Gulf Coastline has historically been a mecca for recreational anglers throughout the nation and around the world who travel here for a crack at a monstrous blue marlin, a speedy bonefish, a rampaging snook, or a hurdling tarpon. Inshore and backcountry anglers today enjoy increasing numbers of channel bass (redfish). Because of recent protective measures, those trolling off the Gulf beaches are once again catching kingfish and Spanish mackerel in substantial numbers. In deeper waters, bottom fishermen continue to swing impressive-sized grouper and snapper over the transom. And those plying the "blue waters" of the Loop Current and continental shelf regularly catch billfish, wahoo, and tuna.

For several decades, particularly from the end of World War II until 1980, the Gulf and its adjacent coastal land masses were set upon by despoilers of every ilk, including greedy land developers and an unthinking commercial fishing industry intent on wiping out anything that swam. These environmental rapists, aided and abetted in part by oblivious elected officials, reigned supreme for years in the Sunshine State until growing opposition in the form of sportfishermen and conservationists finally yelled, "Enough!"

During the 1994 general election, Floridians went to the polls and voted overwhelmingly (72 to 28 percent) to ban all nets from the state's waters. On the Gulf Coast, this means nine miles from shore; on the Atlantic coast, three miles from shore. One exception to this new constitutional amendment, which went into effect on July 1, 1995, is the hand-thrown castnet which can still be used to take baitfish and mullet.

This ban, when combined with reasonable limits placed upon all hook and line fishermen (recreational and commercial), more attention being paid to sane home and industrial development, a drastic reduction in dredge and fill projects, and a conspicuous reduction in the amount of pollutants entering Gulf waters, should result in an immediate and drastic increase in Florida's fish populations.

4

Florida's Gulf Coast

This pompano may weigh only two or three pounds, but it makes up for its size on light tackle and on the dinner table. It's a favorite target for surf and other land-based fishermen. (JOHN PHILLIPS)

LAND CONFIGURATION AND WATER DEPTH

In the Gulf, three physiographic features are prominent: a shoreline bordered by coastal plains and mountains; a surrounding, generally wide, continental shelf; and a large, deep, off-central basin.

The general shape of the Gulf of Mexico is oval, resembling a huge pit with a wide, shallow rim (continental shelf) grading into relatively steep sides (continental slope) that drop from 100 to 1,700 fathoms.

The maximum width of the Gulf is about 1,000 miles in an east-west direction and roughly 500 miles on a line from Pensacola to the tip of the Yucatan Peninsula. The total area of the Gulf of Mexico is about 600,000 square miles. Its total tidal shoreline, including all the bays, inlets and other features, is over 17,000 miles long. Of this lengthy shoreline, 1,553 miles are sandy beach (much of it on barrier islands), some 1,370 miles are barrier islands, and the remainder is a profusion of topographical features that include beach ridges, keys, barrier reefs, pocket harbors, coastal bays, lagoons, marshes, bayous, and mangrove forests.

The submerged continental shelf is nearly continuous around the entire Gulf basin. Any list of interesting areas would certainly include the drowned limestone shelves (or karst region) on the northwestern Florida coast, the great mangrove ridge of the Ten Thousand Islands, and the many springs that produce either fresh or saline waters near the continental shelf, such as those found on a deep-sea limestone platform off Destin, Panama City, and Pensacola.

TIDES AND CURRENTS

There are three types of tides in the Gulf of Mexico: diurnal (with one high and one low tide per day); semidiurnal (two generally equal high and low tides per lunar day); and mixed diurnal (two unequal high and two unequal low tides per day). In some areas, such as the northwestern coast of Florida and in the Sanibel Island area of south Florida, there often may be just one tide per lunar day.

Gulf tidal ranges on peninsular Florida are usually from 2 to 4½ feet, higher than in other Gulf states where they average one to two feet, except during periods of strong onshore winds, tropical storms or hurricanes.

The three most important factors affecting the climate and weather patterns of the Gulf of Mexico are the Bermuda High, hurricanes, and sea surface temperatures which range from an average 84°F in the summer months to 65°F or less during the colder periods.

Gulf Coast ecosystems include Florida Bay which, features extensive mangrove swamps and islands, seagrass beds, and mudflats bordered by the Everglades National Park; the Ten Thousand Islands from Cape Sable to Cape Romano, which is a complex mangrove swamp and island coastline with tidal channels and reticulated oyster bars; the central barrier coast from Cape Romano to Tarpon Springs, which consists of sandy beaches backed by coastal lagoons, marsh, and mangrove swamps; the Big Bend limestone coast from Tarpon Springs to Lighthouse Point, which has rugged, shallow shoreline, a rocky bottom, extensive oyster bars, and seagrass beds; and the Florida Panhandle. From Apalachicola to Cape San Blas, the coast is marked by a barrier-enclosed coastline, smooth sandy beaches, shallow muddy bays, and sparse sea grass. From Cape San Blas to Pensacola and beyond to Mobile Bay, features include extensive barrier island coast and dune systems, along with white sand high-energy beaches.

The Caribbean current enters the Gulf of Mexico through the Yucatan Channel to form the Loop Current, which rotates clockwise in the Gulf. This current dominates the surface circulation pattern on Florida's Gulf Coast. The Loop Current varies seasonally. It influences currents on the continental shelf, and probably generates the nearly permanent eddy centered over the western Gulf in addition to numerous minor migratory loops.

It occupies a band 90- to 150-kilometers wide and travels at one to four knots, transporting 25- to 30-million cubic meters of water per second. This flow is one-third that of the Gulf Stream in the Atlantic and 1,000 times greater than runoffs discharged into the Gulf of Mexico by the Mississippi River and sundry smaller streams.

Exiting from the Gulf through the Florida Straits,

the Loop Current then merges with the Gulf Stream. In the nearshore area of Florida's coastline, there's a predominating northward, counterclockwise current drift prevailing most of the year which is driven by the Loop Current and modified by the wind.

At the shelf edge off the southern half of the Florida Gulf Coast, upwelling generally occurs along the outer margin of the Loop Current, bringing cooler, nutrient-rich waters to the surface.

Offshore anglers in Florida carefully monitor the position of the Loop Current, which varies year to year. Off Tampa Bay, for example, the Loop Current sometimes approaches to within 75 miles of shore. In other years, a boater may have to travel 110 miles or more offshore before reaching it.

Loop Current waters often dictate where fishermen find such piscatorial plums as blue marlin, white marlin, sailfish, dolphin, wahoo and other coveted "blue water" species.

Between shore and the continental shelf is an area loosely defined as "The Middlegrounds," where the rocky and reef-covered bottom slopes from 100 feet or more out to the shelf. Here, anglers find other deep-water rewards, including several varieties of grouper, along with barracuda, amberjack, kingfish, an occasional sail, sharks, snapper, tuna, and bonito.

Generally, fishermen from Tarpon Springs to the Carrabelle area must travel great distances to reach the Middlegrounds. Depending upon where you cast off, a trip ranging between 50 and 75 miles is required.

Rock and reef areas between the blue water and coastline also contain grouper and mackerel in 40- to 150-foot depths in areas ranging from Tampa Bay, south to Naples.

A "one-foot-per-mile" rule is in effect in Gulf waters from Tarpon Springs north to the Big Bend area. In other words, you can be fishing in only 15 feet of water and be 15 miles offshore.

Although there are exceptions, most grouper activity takes place in these west-central to north Florida waters in depths ranging from 40 to 125 feet. Here too are found Spanish mackerel, bluefish and kingfish during the spring, summer and fall months.

SHORELINE MARSHES AND GRASSES

Near the shoreline of the Florida Gulf, saltmarshes occupy intertidal coastal areas of low energy and gentle slope. In the eastern Gulf they cover vast areas. From Tarpon Springs northward to Port St. Joe, the shoreline exhibits distinct zonation, with saltmarsh grass forming the outer band. Saltmarshes are productive in terms of photosynthesis, and they contribute critical habitat to the coastal fishery. It's here that tarpon, snook, redfish, and trout often roam in great numbers and are readily accessible to the sportfishing community.

The eastern Gulf supports diverse underwater flora. Benthic algae flourish from the intertidal zone to depths of 200 meters. Five species of sea grass are also characteristic. The three most abundant inshore species are turtle grass, manatee grass, and shoal grass. These grasses grow from the lower intertidal zone out to depths of 10 to 20 meters and may occupy several thousand square miles of the inner continental shelf. The other two species, *Halophila bailllonis* and *H. engelmannii*, occur in greater depths (to 70 meters), although they also grow in a few shallow water areas.

MANGROVES

Four species of mangroves are native to the eastern Gulf of Mexico: red, black, white, and buttonwood.

Mangroves are characterized by an ability to grow in the saline, waterlogged soils of the intertidal zone or on its edge.

In the southern part of the eastern Gulf, centered in the area of the Ten Thousand Islands, stands one of the greatest mangrove forests of the western Hemisphere. Red, white and buttonwood mangroves generally reach their northern limit between Port Richey and Cedar Key, but the black mangrove is continuous around the Bend, all the way to Pensacola and beyond.

Mangroves exhibit zonation, with reds at the edge of the sea, blacks in a second band, and whites and buttonwoods as a land-side fringe.

Until laws were passed in the 1970s, development and dredge and fill projects were responsible for the elimination of more than half of Florida's mangrove shorelines. It's estimated that Tampa Bay today has but 15 percent of the mangrove "forests" of the pre-1950 era.

In addition to providing nursery vicinages for hundreds of species of inshore and offshore fry, mangrove shorelines are famous for attracting snook, trout, and redfish. They also tend to accumulate debris, especially organic matter, and to build up the land. What's more, this priceless gift of nature serves as a windbreak, offers protection from storms, and contributes in one way or another to the welfare of every living marine animal that swims, flies, or crawls on the Gulf Coast.

DESTRUCTIVE ELEMENTS

Storms and hurricanes are the most powerful natural threats to the eastern Gulf Coast. Wind, flooding and storm surges are shown to have caused extensive damage to coastal areas over the years. These destructive elements have taken a toll on beaches, vegetation, development, and freshwater supplies.

Dredge and fill operations, combined with waterfront devolvement, are the eminent artificial environmental factors that have devoured the Gulf's formerly pristine status. Literally millions of coastal acres of

You'll have to travel, but blue marlin are plentiful off the Florida Panhandle. (HERB ALLEN)

original habitat, including grass beds, marsh areas, and wetlands have been lost to the bulldozer and dredge, particularly during the heavy construction years from the late-1950s through the mid-1980s.

While local, county, state, and federal restrictions on this type of environmental damage has restricted operations of waterfront developers since the 80s, the Gulf Coast still isn't "out of the woods." Despite increased permitting regulations, developers still defile thousands of acres of natural shoreline, mangroves, marine habitat, and grasses annually. Industrial pollution and sewage contamination on the eastern Gulf Coast coexist generally with large communities and industrial concentrations. Even though strident advances in anti-pollution decrees appear to have turned the tide of source contamination, and many communities report better water quality now than 10 years ago, pollutant-associated fish kills still occur in Tampa Bay, Pensacola Bay, and other major Gulf Coast waterways.

Finally, beach erosion caused by wind and wave action is a natural environmental problem exacerbated by human development patterns, particularly in more developed areas such as Pinellas, Sarasota, Manatee, Escambia, Santa Rosa, and Bay counties.

ATMOSPHERE

The waters of the Gulf are a major influencing factor on the weather phenomena for a large portion of the United States, as well as parts of Central America and related island land masses.

Climatically, Florida's peninsula encompasses three zones: subtropical, tropical and temperate. However, it is generally characterized by a subtropical high-pressure belt which extends over or near the Gulf throughout the year.

The atmospheric circulation patterns of the eastern Gulf of Mexico are relatively simple. The period from March through September is characterized by a general clockwise circulation pattern related to the areal position in the western portion of the Bermuda high-pressure cell.

From October through February a western anticyclonic cell separates from the Bermuda high and is nearly stationary off the central Gulf, resulting in the flow over the eastern Gulf being predominately from the northwest and north.

Wind and waters respond generally to the seasonal changes in these atmospheric circulation patterns.

Local weather and cloudiness are strongly influenced by diurnal heating and cooling patterns of adjacent land areas. Precipitation is almost entirely in the form of rain and drizzle. Snow rarely occurs, even in the northern coastal area, but fog is a frequent visitor to Florida's Gulf Coast.

Thunderstorms are a major factor throughout the entire eastern Gulf of Mexico. The Tampa Bay area ranks first nationally in fatal lightning encounters.

GEOLOGICAL FACTORS

The four geological formations constituting the eastern Gulf of Mexico are: 1) the Florida Platform and Escarpment, 2) the Alabama–Mississippi Coastal Plain, Continental Shelf and DeSoto Slope, 3) the Mississippi Fan, and 4) the Yucatan Bank and the sills between Yucatan, Cuba and Florida.

The western boundary of the Florida Platform is relatively precipitous in its lower portions, whereas the upper slope is more gentle or is terraced. The DeSoto Slope westward from the DeSoto Canyon to the Mississippi Fan is a normal continental slope dipping at an angle of about two degrees.

On shore, all of the estuaries of the eastern Gulf of Mexico are drowned portions of former river valleys. These estuaries are the principal catchment basins for sediments carried by their rivers and, in some cases, for offshore sediment carried shoreward by tidal currents.

Accumulation of oysters and other mollusk shells contributes significantly to estuary structure. At estuary margins, saltwater marsh grass and the different genera of mangroves are commonly present in the more tropical areas.

MARINE LIFE

The marine mammal population of the Gulf of Mexico consists almost entirely of several whale and dolphin species. However, there are two other groups represented: a nearly extinct population of seals and sea lions, plus an expanding number of manatees.

In general, few large whales and only two species of dolphin—the Atlantic bottlenose and the spotted dolphin—are of any real significance on Florida's Gulf Coast.

All of these mammals have a similar life history. The young (almost invariably only one) are born alive after a gestation period of approximately a year, or in some cases up to 16 months. The calf is ready to swim immediately and can keep up with its mother who, along with other nearby females in a herd, defends her young against predators.

Marine mammals enjoy long life expectancies and are quite social. All marine mammals on Florida's Gulf Coast, except manatees, are carnivorous, the bulk of their diet consisting of fish. Manatees (also called sea cows) feed exclusively on vegetation.

Varied saline habitats along the Gulf Coast of Florida support large populations of numerous species of birds. In all, some 400 avian species have been recorded in or flying over the eastern Gulf of Mexico. A few of the more common species enjoyed by bird watchers on the Gulf coast include loons, cormorants, herons, egrets, ibis, roseate spoonbills, ducks, eagles, osprey, rails, coots, plovers, sandpipers, gulls, terns, and skimmers.

Major habitats of birds found in the eastern Gulf consist of open Gulf waters, coastal Gulf waters, open beach areas, brackish marshes, coastal mudflats, sheltered saltwaters, and mangrove forests.

Open waters, defined as the deeper waters of the Gulf starting at about 10 km from shore and extending seaward, are home to truly pelagic birds. Coastal waters, extending roughly 10 km out from shore, support numerous species of birds, especially those that feed on fish.

Open beaches are defined as the wave-washed coastal strand and the sand dunes immediately behind. Beaches are home to numerous shore birds including sea gulls and pelicans.

If you've got a boat on the Gulf, you're close to gamesters like this big barracuda. (HERB ALLEN)

Salt and brackish marshes are tidal areas which support, among other species, rails, sparrows, ducks, and numerous shore birds. Coastal mudflats are devoid of attached vegetation and flood during high tides. These mudflats are frequented by feeding shore birds and many types of ducks.

Sheltered saltwaters are the saline embayments surrounded on most sides by land and protected from winds. Mangrove forests are described in earlier sections of this book.

FISH AND FISHING

Among the world's oceans, the Gulf of Mexico is said to be second only to the Peruvian coast in terms of fishery production. This is due, say scientists, to vast quantities of nutrient-rich materials supplied to eastern Gulf Coast waters by numerous tributaries including the Mississippi River.

Unfortunately, the Gulf's abundance has attracted commercial fishing fleets from throughout the world. They have ravished the fishery, pushing some species nearly to extinction.

Since the early 1980s, Florida's recreational anglers have become increasingly militant and have forced reluctant or timorous legislators to enact some sane conservation measures.

Now that Florida has a commercial net ban, the angling outlook has grown increasingly bright. Since recent harvest restrictions were placed upon snook, redfish, kingfish, Spanish mackerel, and tarpon, these species have rebounded dramatically. Still on the troubled and stressed list are trout, mullet, grouper, and snapper (due to commercial longline and fish trap operations), as well as numerous baitfish populations including sardines.

Currently, however, a sad situation has been reversed to the point that an angler visiting the Gulf Coast of Florida can do so in full expectation of enjoying a quality fishing experience, especially if he is seeking out a trophy tarpon, redfish, or snook.

FISHING REGULATIONS

For a discussion of Florida's fishing regulations, including saltwater licensing, see pages 97–99.

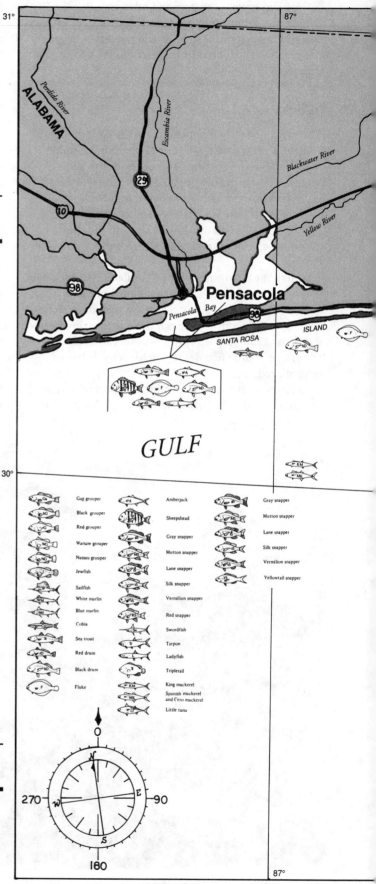

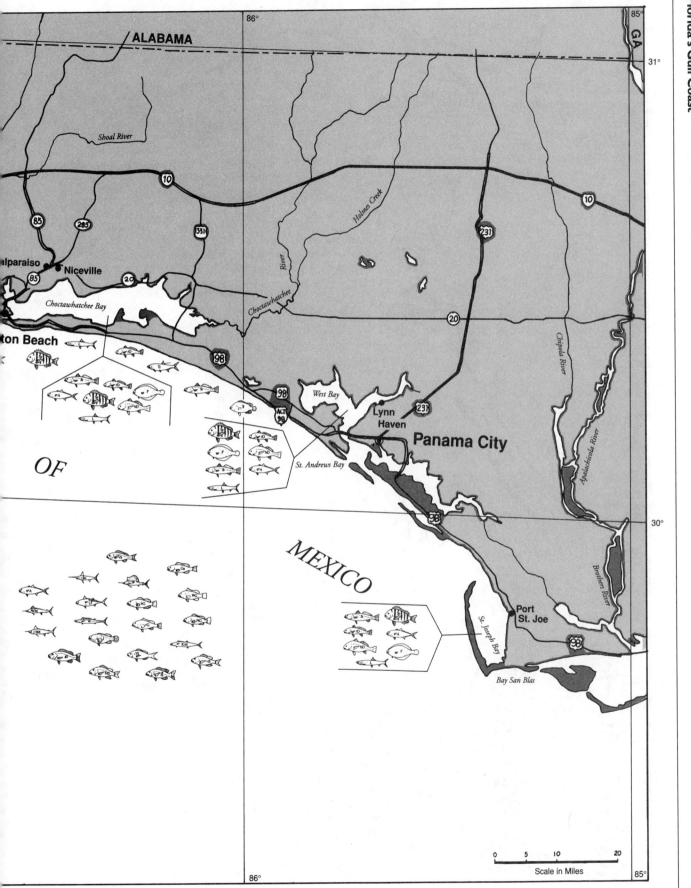

ALABAMA

GA

Shoal River

85

285

331

10

Holmes Creek

231

10

alparaiso ● Niceville

85

20

Choctawhatchee Bay

River

Choctawhatchee

20

Chipola River

ton Beach

98

West Bay

Apalachicola River

98

ALT 98

Lynn
Haven

231

Panama City

St. Andrews Bay

OF

MEXICO

Brothers River

Port
St. Joe

St. Joseph Bay

98

Bay San Blas

86°

85°

31°

30°

0   5   10   20

Scale in Miles

86°

85°

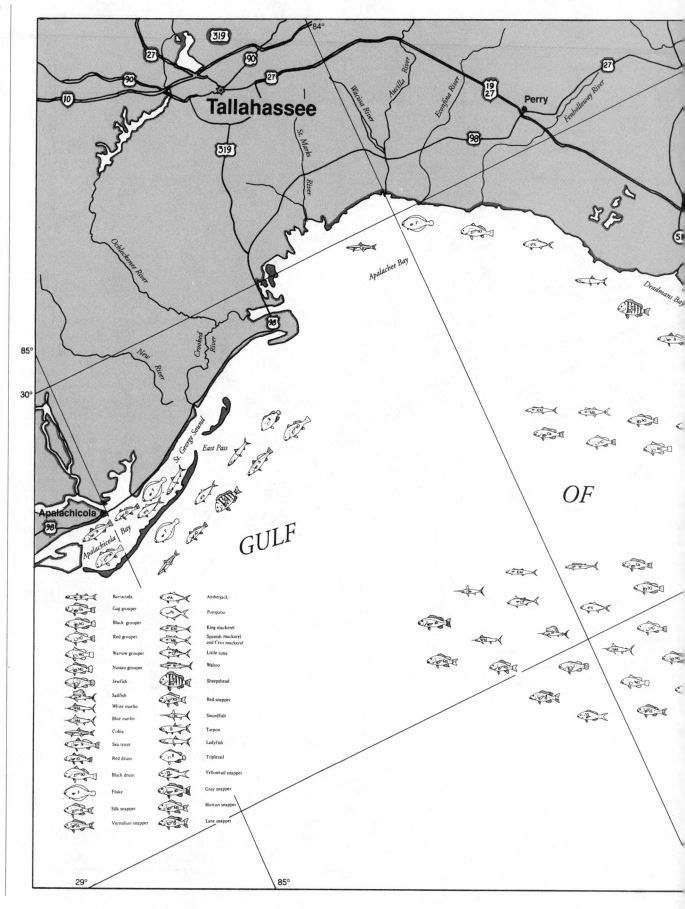

GULF

OF

Tallahassee

Perry

Apalachicola

Apalachee Bay

Deadmans Bay

St. George Sound

East Pass

Apalachicola Bay

Ochlockonee River

New River

Crooked River

St. Marks River

Wacissa River

Aucilla River

Econfina River

Fenholloway River

84°

85°

30°

85°

29°

85°

Barracuda
Gag grouper
Black grouper
Red grouper
Warsaw grouper
Nassau grouper
Jewfish
Sailfish
White marlin
Blue marlin
Cobia
Sea trout
Red drum
Black drum
Fluke
Silk snapper
Vermilion snapper

Amberjack
Pompano
King mackerel
Spanish mackerel and Cero mackerel
Little tuna
Wahoo
Sheepshead
Red snapper
Swordfish
Tarpon
Ladyfish
Tripletail
Yellowtail snapper
Gray snapper
Mutton snapper
Lane snapper

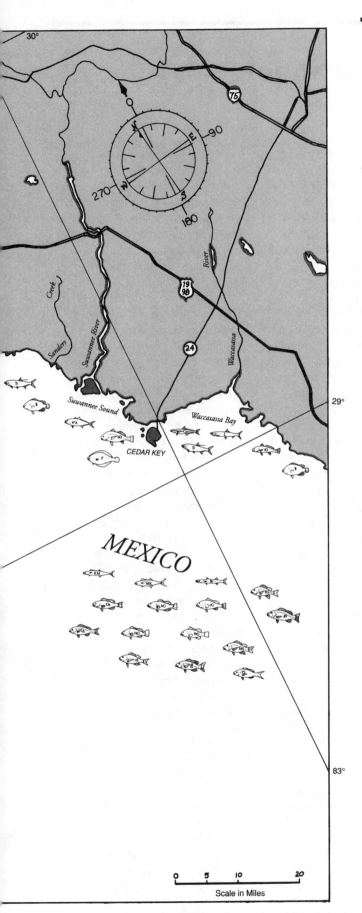

Tide and Current Are Key Elements to Saltwater Fish Success

by Herb Allen

Those mythical 10 percent of the fishermen who catch 90 percent of the fish depend upon several factors for their success, not the least of which is attention paid to tides and currents.

Most experienced Florida saltwater anglers jockey in waters less than eight feet in depth on a rising or falling tide. A moving flow of water is vital to their success.

Under normal weather conditions, the bulk of small marine life will be found in shallow water and near grassy cover, rocks, and other obstructions that offer protection from predators. Isn't it logical that larger gamefish will also be found near this food supply?

One rule of thumb is to fish two hours on a rising tide to the high tide stand, and another two hours on a falling tide, especially in bays, tidal rivers, and shallow grass flats out from shore. This "two plus two" situation takes in the period when waters are highest and currents are usually more pronounced.

Keep in mind, however, there are days when an incoming and high tide may vary in length, sometimes by as much as four hours or more. These diurnal tide days can be dismal due to a lack of moving water. A long high tide stand with little or no water movement does not create optimal fishing conditions.

Currents are particularly important in shallow water because they carry food scents for considerable distances. Nearly all fish species, including sharks, redfish, trout, tarpon, and snook, use their noses to zero in on food sources. If this weren't true, how do you suppose they could find a meal in murky water where visibility is reduced to mere inches?

In dusky or dim water it's often advantageous to use chum or some type of hook additive such as Cotee's Pro-Bait to help fish find the lure. When putting out a chum line, it's best to do so from an anchored boat. Drifters or those moving through an area with an electric motor are probably better off adding a hook scent of some type.

Though it's generally accepted that a rising or high falling tide is best, anglers can also score when the tide is low or slack by fishing channel dropoffs and deeper holes where gamefish retire until they can move back onto grassy flats where food is abundant. ■

Sawgrass Snook

By Bill AuCoin

Just north of Tarpon Springs on Florida's west coast, an angler will notice the Gulf of Mexico shoreline vegetation change from mangrove to sawgrass. Guides used to tell you that the sawgrass creeks were good habitat for trout and redfish. If you wanted to catch a snook, they said, you would have to fish south of the mangrove line. Otherwise, the water was just "too cold" for snook.

The guides have a different line now. The last winter freeze here was in December, 1989. After four no-freeze, no-fish-kill winters, *Centropomus undecimalis* has decided that the creeks and bayous of sawgrass country are a fine place to live and feed and spawn. Until the next winter freeze kills or frightens off this sizable splinter population, the snook seem to be happy in the sawgrass, too.

The saltmarsh sawgrass starts in Hudson, Florida, in Pasco County, and defines the Gulf shoreline almost all the way north to the Panhandle. Though snook are caught as far north as the Panhandle, the best populations of catchable snook are south of the Chassahowitzka National Wildlife Refuge, near the Citrus–Hernando county line. This is a maze of saltmarsh punctuated on the chart with names like Bird Island, Raccoon Point, Fiddler's Point, Two Man Creek, Fillman's Bayou, Oyster Creek, Rocky Creek, Salt Springs Run, Hope Bayou, Long Granny Creek, and Hammock Creek. On the road map, look for towns (and launching ramps) in New Port Richey, Hudson, Aripeka and Bayport.

Ron Taylor, a snook biologist with Florida's Department of Environmental Protection in St. Petersburg, estimates that the population of snook on the west coast of Florida has at least doubled since the hard Christmas freeze

of 1989. He points out that it is natural for some of those snook to seek new areas where there is less competition with other snook. "Animals look for greener pastures, areas with fewer predators, or less competition; that seems to be the case whether you're talking buffalo or fish," said Taylor.

Those are the snook that are now giving sawgrass anglers a good time almost all year long, but especially when the water cools in the fall, in late September, October and November, and again when it warms in the spring, particularly late April, May and June. In one five-day period in late April, just prior to the full moon, Capt. Dennis Royston, of Hudson, and his clients boated and released more than 100 snook up to 26 pounds, all in the sawgrass of Pasco and Hernando Counties. Snook will feed heavily again from late September through December, particularly in front of the tall seasonal tides of the new and full moons of September and October. "You can hear those big guys way up there in the creek crashing bait and making a commotion," said Royston. "Nothing holds 'em back when they're hungry." They'll be lethargic in January and February but start to feed again in March.

Royston has found the best sawgrass snook fishing to be on the first one-third of the outgoing tide. He poles his clients upcurrent. Look for breaks in the sawgrass, tiny passes where the outgoing tide can squeeze through. Snook will be hunkered tight against a stand of sawgrass, waiting to ambush bait being swept out with the tide. One snook that was just under the two-foot limit jumped my red and yellow MirrOlure, a floater-diver, in one such cut in Fillman's Bayou north of Hudson.

Spawning is believed to take place near the mouths of the larger sawgrass

creeks and bayous, especially in April, May, June, and July. Taylor says the snook will forage the sawgrass for food in the early part of the day, but they probably don't stray too far from the spawning area so they can return to the spawning ritual in the afternoon. After the spawn, Taylor believes, the snook move further back into the low-salinity sawgrass backcountry and probably stay there the rest of the year, safely away from predators.

Snook can often find comfortable water in the cul-de-sacs or near an underwater, freshwater spring, which will empty 72°F water into the surrounding area. One day in January, when the water temperature on the flats was 51°F, the water temperature in Fillman's Bayou was 63°F, an indication of the existence of a freshwater spring somewhere near.

Obviously, you need a boat that does not draw much water. You'll be fishing tidewater that, in many cases, at extreme low tide, is just wet sand and mud. You need a pole and an electric motor. You can drift, too, of course, but lure fishermen will want to cast to the side of the boat, not in front of it, so that the lure swims with the current; that's because the fish will be looking into the current for their food.

Wade fishing is very productive, particularly if you have spotted fish and want to fish the area carefully and thoroughly. Just anchor the boat well away from the fish. Put on wading shoes—old high-top sneakers are fine—and do the stingray shuffle until you get into casting range. The longer the cast the better; these are spooky fish.

This is light tackle fishing—generally spinning tackle with 8-pound line and a 2-foot, 30-pound monofilament leader. You're tossing lead-headed jigs (⅜-ounce), floater-diver and topwater propeller plugs, and the new cigar-shaped plastic baits with a channel for making your exposed hook weedless. Red and white, red and yellow, and gold are good colors. Fish weedless when you want to cast into areas with floating sawgrass or into pockets of open water surrounded by sawgrass.

Royston, who regularly guides clients into sawgrass creeks, has identified the following patterns:

- The openings between stands of sawgrass are obvious ambush points.
- Potholes, when you can find them, will hold snook. They like to rest on the warm sand, tucked up against and hiding next to the grass.
- Just like water in the mangroves, the tide that sweeps around stands of sawgrass will carve out deeper channels. The snook use these "swash channels" for traveling and as holding areas for feeding.
- Cul-de-sacs are the tiny, dead-end bays that send you off in another direction. Before you leave, make a long cast across the mouth and up either shoreline. These are good areas to fish in the colder months. The water is warmer for two reasons: There is less current and the bottom is often black, so it holds the heat of the day longer.
- The snook are below matted sawgrass, in the shade, waiting to pounce on anything that tries to crawl on that tangled carpet. The trouble is, there aren't many lures weedless enough to fish it. A Texas-rigged plastic worm (no lead) will do it. So will one of those cigar-shaped plastic baits. I tossed a Cotee Reel Magic black pearl and walked it across the matted sawgrass. I had five strikes in one cast.
- Those oyster beds at the mouth of the creek more often hold

Captain Dennis Royston with a snook that moved into sawgrass country in recent years. (BILL AUCOIN)

redfish, but snook will sometimes swim with the reds and beat them to the bait. Throw a gold, weedless spoon tipped with a chartreuse plastic teaser.

There are two major problems that sawgrass creek anglers have to contend with—getting in and getting out. The oyster bars that guard the entrances to these creeks can chew up your prop or the bottom of your boat. Also, if you don't leave a creek in time, a falling tide can leave your boat without enough water to float. For these two reasons, and to help locate and catch the fish, hiring a fishing guide is probably smart.

Boat Ramps
Hudson Beach in Pasco County
Anclote Park, at the mouth of the Anclote River in Holiday
Nick's Park, one block west of US 19 in Port Richey, on the Cotee River
State Route 50 at Bayport on the Weeki Wachee River

Citrus County Road 480, Chassahowitzka National Wildlife Refuge

Tackle and Bait
One Stop, Holiday, on US 19; 813-842-5610
Salonika Bait and Tackle, 6205 Ridge Road, Port Richey, (813) 849-6377
Pete's Corner Store, Old Dixie Highway, Hudson, (813) 868-2607

Places to Stay
Holiday Inn, Weeki Wachee, (813) 596-2007
Best Western, Holiday, (813) 937-4121
Budget Inn, New Port Richey, (813) 848-3487
Comfort Inn, (813) 842-6800
Comfort Inn, (813) 863-3336
Days Inn, Port Richey, (813) 863-1502
Econo Lodge, Port Richey, (800) 424-4777

Fishing Guides
Capt. Dennis Royston, (813) 863-3205 ∎

Amberjack Grow Big in Florida

By Herb Allen

One February several years ago, while fishing 140-foot depths out from Tarpon Springs, Jay Ramsey caught the largest amberjack I ever saw.

It weighed in at a bulky 120 pounds, only 35 pounds shy of the then IGFA all-tackle world record taken off Bermuda in 1981. Even Ramsey, who had caught literally hundreds of big amberjack in three decades, had to stop and catch his breath following this high noon duel in the Gulf of Mexico.

When grouper or red snapper aren't biting, this tenacious tackle-destroyer often saves a Waltonion's day.

For example, on another trip not many years ago with Cotee Master Guide Bill Miller aboard his *Double Trouble*, Tampa ad man Howard Hilton, astronaut Wally Schirra and this author went offshore in search of grouper. "If we can't find any grouper on this trip," said Miller, "I'll guarantee that we'll catch plenty of amberjack."

He was right. We met more amberjack that day than we could handle. It wasn't unusual to see a bend in every rod at once. We all gave out after several hours of frenzied activity, except Schirra, who maintained a furious all-day pace until it was time to up anchor and head to port. Miller was reluctant to leave because the astronaut was having so much fun.

However, what's enjoyable for some is agony to others.

Back in the early 60s, Ms. Marva Allen of Dunedin went on her first saltwater safari out from Panama City in the Panhandle area of north Florida. Everything went fine that day until she hooked a 75-pound amberjack that refused to budge. It took Ms. Allen nearly an hour before she was able to land the monster, and 25 years elapsed before she again ventured onto saltwater.

Anyone who has battled this member of *Scombridae* knows the amberjack is one of the most tenacious of foes.

Found in waters throughout the world, this pelagic is particularly abundant throughout the eastern Gulf of Mexico from the Tampa Bay area to Pensacola, and all along Florida's Atlantic coast from Jacksonville to Key West. It usually hangs out around offshore wrecks, reefs, and other bottom structure.

It'll strike fast and will generally dive for the bottom, where it often cuts an angler's line on rocks, reefs, or submerged obstructions. Usually, the amberjack hits near the bottom. However, it sometimes surfaces, especially when responding to a chum line, and can be taken on lighter tackle including fly rods. It'll grab live baits, dead baits, strip baits, some artificial lures, and a wide variety of jigs ranging in weight from one to eight ounces.

Anglers pursuing this bruiser, which is caught year-round in Florida's offshore waters, would be wise to employ sturdy tackle, such as a 40- to 60-pound grouper or tarpon outfit. For deep jigging, a 5½ stand-up rod with 30- to 50-pound mono will work fine. Fly rodders might consider an 8½- to 9-foot, 10- to 12-weight rod with a floating or sinking tippet, and a reel holding at least 200 yards of 20-pound Dacron backing.

Recent steps to protect this gamefish from exploitation have resulted in the establishment of a three-fish bag limit and a minimum size restriction of 28 inches.

As table fare, this fish doesn't rate high marks with many. However, those who marinate the filets overnight in French dressing, then cut the filets into small, thin "fingers" and deep-fry them as they would grouper or snapper, will find them to be quite tasty. Amberjack is also appetizing when smoked. A tip: when fileting, be sure to trim off the dark, red meat, which tastes a mite strong.

Whenever you're offshore and have an opportunity to square off against one of these powerful adversaries, don't hesitate. The amberjack is a true gamester and worthy foe. Just be sure that you've eaten your Wheaties before lowering a bait or jig. ■

Grouper Lively in Skinny Water

by Herb Allen

A genuine "gee whiz" fishing adventure unfolded recently when Cotee Master Guide Jim Bradley took Capt. Everett Antrim and me in tow for a grouper safari into the Gulf of Mexico aboard his 25-foot Mako, *Big Daddy*.

It wasn't surprising that we'd catch grouper with Capt. Bradley at the helm. He's known for catching fish even when they have lockjaw. What was astonishing, however, was where we caught them and what was used to get the job done. Would you believe... eight feet of water on Reel Magic, the weedless plastic lure developed by Roland Martin at Lake Okeechobee for largemouth bass?

First item on the agenda after leaving Bradley's dock on the beautiful Weeki Wachee River was to load up the livewell with bait—not just any live bait. Bradley gets it in two sizes: small for chumming, large for hook use. From the shallow flats, where two throws of a baitcasting net filled an oversized livewell almost to overflowing, it was but a short hop to one of the skipper's secret grouper spots.

After precisely gauging the wind direction and tidal flow, Bradley lowered an anchor to enable his boat to drift near the shallow, horseshoe-shaped rock pile that was clearly visible jutting two feet from a sandy bottom. "It's important not to let the boat drift over the spot," Bradley explained. "In shallow water, the boat and the on-board commotion will spook the fish."

Positioned at the stern, Bradley began to launch smaller white bait overboard, which drifted toward the target rocks. Before long, we all saw grouper leaving the rocks and venturing into open water, where they began slamming into the chum line with the gusto of lumberjacks diving into stacks of steaming pancakes. One dandy-sized

You don't necessarily need deep water to bag grouper. This angler also brought in a tail-less snook. (HERB ALLEN)

gag grouper was so eager to cash in on this bonanza that it actually cleared the water in a leap similar to that of a soaring tarpon!

Both Bradley and Antrim, known far and wide as "Mr. Trout," cast larger white bait into the chum line on bare hooks and 17-pound-test line, while I opted to test out artificials in the form of the Reel Magic lure on 6- and 8-pound-test lines.

Every cast (emphasis on EVERY) produced a strike or a hookup.

They weren't peewees either. While many of the grouper measured just under the legal limit, an equal number measured on the plus side of 20 inches. Several weighing between 6 and 14 pounds went into the ice chest. All the others were released.

Before long, schools of toothy Spanish mackerel, kingfish, and other Waltonian delights cut into the chow line. Their arrival quickly encouraged us to add about 18 inches of 50-pound monofilament leader material to prevent cutoffs.

In bygone days it was common to catch keeper grouper in shallow water on both Florida coasts. As the human population has grown throughout the Sunshine State, anglers have had to search in progressively deeper waters for these tasty bottom dwellers, which have graced many dinner tables and appear on most seafood restaurant menus.

Bradley, who can be contacted by calling (904) 596-5639, proved to me that shallow-water grouper fishing is still a possibility. And, perhaps, we proved to him that as many—or more —grouper can be caught on artificial lures. Providing, of course, that you have plenty of live bait aboard to use as chum. ∎

Way Down on the Suwannee River

By Herb Allen

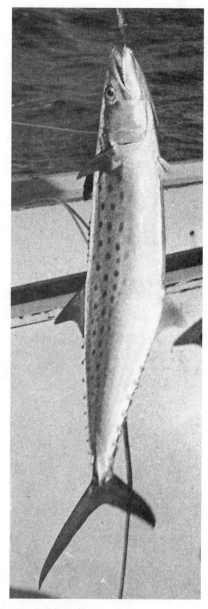

Spanish mackerel are but one of the many delights available to anglers in the unspoiled waters where the Suwannee River enters the Gulf of Mexico. (HERB ALLEN)

It's a whole new ball game up there," enthused Capt. Jim Bradley, describing the area where the Suwannee River enters the Gulf of Mexico.

"This is the way Florida was 50 years ago," said the Cotee Master Guide, following his return from one of his quarterly trips to Suwannee. "We fished there for a week and seldom saw another boat."

With Bradley on this safari was another Cotee Master Guide, Capt. Everitt Antrim, along with Mate Kevin Scarborough and Tampa's Eric Coppin.

Leaving from his home base of Weeki Wachee, Bradley made the two-hour run to Suwannee by boat. He and his party stayed at Angler's Resort in the wee community of Suwannee.

Similar to other areas along Florida's upper Gulf Coast, Suwannee has clear water, hundreds of square miles of shallow grass flats, and oodles of fish.

Near shore and in the backcountry, trout and redfish are plentiful. "Lots of tarpon too," Bradley added, "but, nobody fishes for them."

In 40-foot depths, anglers find big, black grouper just about everywhere. "We sometimes have a problem getting to the grouper because amberjack, ranging from 20 to 70 pounds, grab baits before they reach the bottom," he said. "In all the years I've been fishing, I've never seen so many amberjack. It's not unusual to see them by the acres on the surface, and I'll guarantee they'll hit just about anything you throw at them." Large schools of barracuda are seen on the surface, too.

Adding to this list of piscatorial delights are snapper by the "blue zillions," cobia, jewfish, kings, Spanish mackerel, and grunts ranging in weight from two to three pounds each.

"There's no big trick to accumulating a limit of whatever you're fishing for," Bradley continued. "However, you'd better use heavier gear when going for grouper and amberjack because 30-pound blacks and 60-pound amberjack are not uncommon."

For reef fishing, Bradley and Antrim recommend 50-pound outfits. Antrim pointed out that he got broke off several times and wished he had stepped up to 80-pound gear for some of the fish that he was unable to control.

This group used fresh-caught live bait whenever possible. "However," added Bradley, "Cotee jigs and spoons also took plenty of fish when we'd run out of bait."

Both guides agreed that this quiet, laid-back area of Florida is the perfect spot for R & R. "You'll not find friendlier, more accommodating or helpful people anywhere than at Suwannee," they stated.

Nor, apparently, will you find a greater abundance or a wider variety of cooperative fish.

While neither Bradley nor Antrim even mentioned the freshwater possibilities in the Suwannee River itself, many insiders agree that the river is home to a great number of largemouth bass weighing in excess of eight pounds, bushels of scrappy panfish, scallops by the tubs, and blue crabs everywhere.

For those who'd like to explore the Suwannee area, Bradley can be contacted by calling (904) 596-5639, while Antrim can be reached by dialing (813) 868-5747. ■

A Mighty Big Little River

by Herb Allen

As rivers go, the Chassahowitzka doesn't compare in size to the St. Johns or the St. Lawrence. It's certainly not as long as the Mississippi, nor as wide as the Amazon. But, from the standpoint of pure, unadulterated beauty and tranquility, the Chassahowitzka certainly outshines any of the aforementioned giants and most smaller ones as well.

Bounded on the north and south by heavily wooded areas, the river begins modestly at a little community just off U.S. Highway 19, with a spring pouring millions of gallons daily into a shallow river bed.

As it continues its short westward trek, the river swells with additional gin-clear water gushing forth from the subterranean aquifer until it reaches the brackish estuary areas of the 30,500-acre National Wildlife Refuge which was established in 1943 by the U.S. Department of the Interior.

A winter home for migratory waterfowl, the Refuge is also home to several rare, endangered, or threatened species including the brown pelican, wood ibis, bald eagle, and Florida black bear.

For those driving north or south along U.S. Highway 19, the place is easy to miss. Located about seven miles south of Homosassa and about 10 miles north of Weeki Wachee, the Chassahowitzka is bordered at its beginnings by homes. Further along, permanent residential abodes give way to houseboats anchored to shoreline trees and cabins built on stilts.

In the freshwater portions of the river, anglers can take a shot at largemouth bass and several varieties of bream. During the winter months, the river offers excellent fishing for trout, drum, sheepshead, redfish, and mangrove snapper.

As you move into brackish waters, you'll be rewarded with migrating redfish, an occasional snook, and trout. In the spring, summer, and early fall, there'll be redfish on high tide at nearly every outside point.

During the spring and summer months, tarpon invade the area in substantial numbers. Anglers in the nearby Homosassa flats have set numerous tarpon records in recent years.

When reaching Homosassa Bay, anglers will connect with most of the saltwater gamefish species peculiar to this section of the Gulf of Mexico.

During the waterfowl season, hunters can bag ducks after obtaining a special permit at Refuge headquarters. Bird watchers and photographers can enjoy the scenery and abundant wildlife year-round.

Chassahowitzka has a couple of excellent restaurants, a smattering of small, clean "mom and pop" motels, the Chassahowitzka River Lodge, a grocery store and a post office. The Lodge has a launching ramp, rental boats, and canoes.

A word of warning: The river is quite shallow in spots and full of rocks. Also, don't get caught in a remote area during a falling tide. ∎

Cold-Weather Grouper

by Herb Allen

Why is it that the best offshore bottom fishing opportunities often occur during the coldest, most miserable time of the year?

Regardless of what Chamber of Commerce types may say, winters in Florida can often be bone chilling, especially on the water. Several winters ago, for example, I saw ice forming along shorelines in the Panhandle after a cold front blasted in from Yankeeland on Christmas Day and sent thermometers plunging into the teens.

Whenever the thermometer dips to holy mackerel lows, I can count on a call from Dr. Hugh Harmon proposing an offshore grouper safari. One such call came as things were beginning to thaw a bit, but it was still in the high 30s just before dawn. "We're leaving the dock at 4:00 A.M.," he said without preamble. "Be there."

Let's face it. Anything starting at 4:00 A.M. is a loser. Through the years I've found that the high point of any day beginning at that hour is when you roll out of bed. From then on, it's downhill.

"You're nuts," screamed Miss Marva (my first wife), when I announced my scheme for the following day. "Anybody crazy enough to go out in weather like this deserves to freeze their you-know-what. Just don't wake me up when you leave."

"She's right," I said to myself soon after shutting off the alarm at 3:15 the following morning and putting coffee water on. "(Expletive deleted),"

I mumbled, "it's even too early for the morning paper delivery."

The Dunedin dentist already had the engines humming on his 45-foot *Mother Lode* when I stumbled aboard at four on the dot. At that point his engines were the only warm things this side of Kingston, Jamaica.

"Anybody else going along?" I asked, making ready to cast off the bow and stern lines. "No, you're the only one I could get," he replied, confirming what is generally accepted to be my intelligence quotient.

Because of the chill factor, we decided to forgo catching live bait. On this day we would do or die with frozen sardines already in the bait box.

Harmon, one of the better grouper fishermen on Florida's Gulf Coast, punched in some numbers on his Loran-C unit after we rounded the north end of Anclote Key and headed on a northwest course intended to put us in 42 feet of water off Homosassa. Bucking a 15- to 20-mile-per-hour blow straight out of the north, choppy seas, and a wind-chill factor that felt like 50 below zero, the numb (which rhymes with dumb) "dynamic duo" finally arrived at the predetermined spot just as Mr. Sun broke over the horizon.

Fortunately, the Molar Mauler has a black book filled with productive numbers for all seasons of the year. We were in the January through March mode on this trip.

"I'm marking fish down there," Doc said, scanning the scratches on his electronic depth recorder.

"I hope they're not too cold to bite," I answered, ready to lower the anchor.

That question was answered the moment Harmon dropped his frozen sardine to the bottom. He was greeted with a formidable strike. "Bingo," he yelled while straining to move a big fish up and away from the rocks. "Looks like we found our spot on the first try."

I didn't have time to reply because just as he was swinging a dandy 15-pounder over the rail, my rod began bucking and bending into the shape of a horseshoe. After some huffing and puffing, I was able to bring in a matching 15-pounder.

We both used heavy 8-foot grouper rods, Penn reels, 60-pound line and 90-pound monofilament shocker leaders. A 5/0 hook and 8 ounces of lead rounded out our rig.

It was one of those days when you could do nothing wrong. All we needed to do was send the frozen sardine offering to the bottom, reel up a crank or two, and get braced for a thundering strike.

Things continued like this all morning. Often a hot hole plays out after a few fish are removed, but today was different. These fish, all running between 10 and 20 pounds each, stayed with us and showed no inclination to quit. Early on we had our pair of keepers in the fish storage box aboard the *Mother Lode*, but kept fishing just for the fun of it.

(continued on page 175)

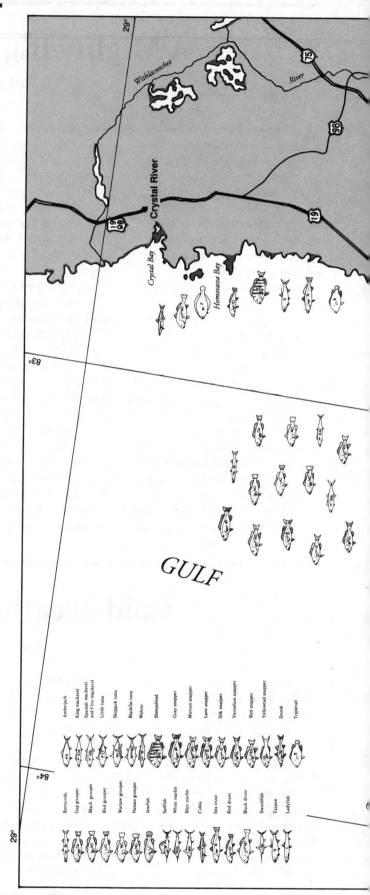

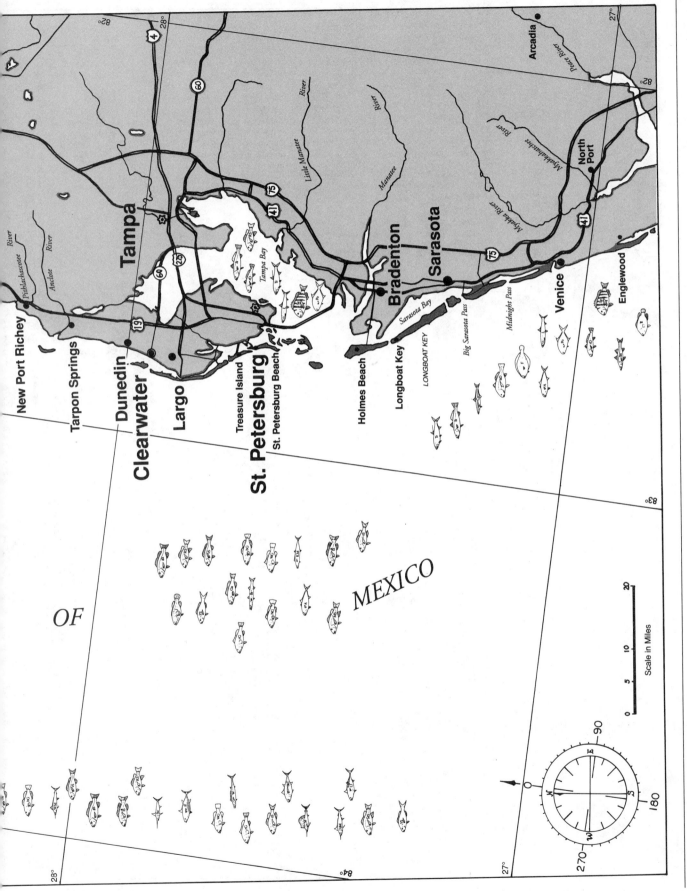

GULF OF MEXICO

New Port Richey
Tarpon Springs
Dunedin
Clearwater
Largo
Treasure Island
St. Petersburg
St. Petersburg Beach
Holmes Beach
Longboat Key
LONGBOAT KEY
Big Sarasota Pass
Midnight Pass
Venice
Englewood

Tampa
Bradenton
Sarasota
North Port
Arcadia

Tampa Bay
Sarasota Bay

Pithlachascotee River
Anclote River
Little Manatee River
Manatee River
Myakka River
Myakahatchee River
Peace River

Scale in Miles
0 5 10 20

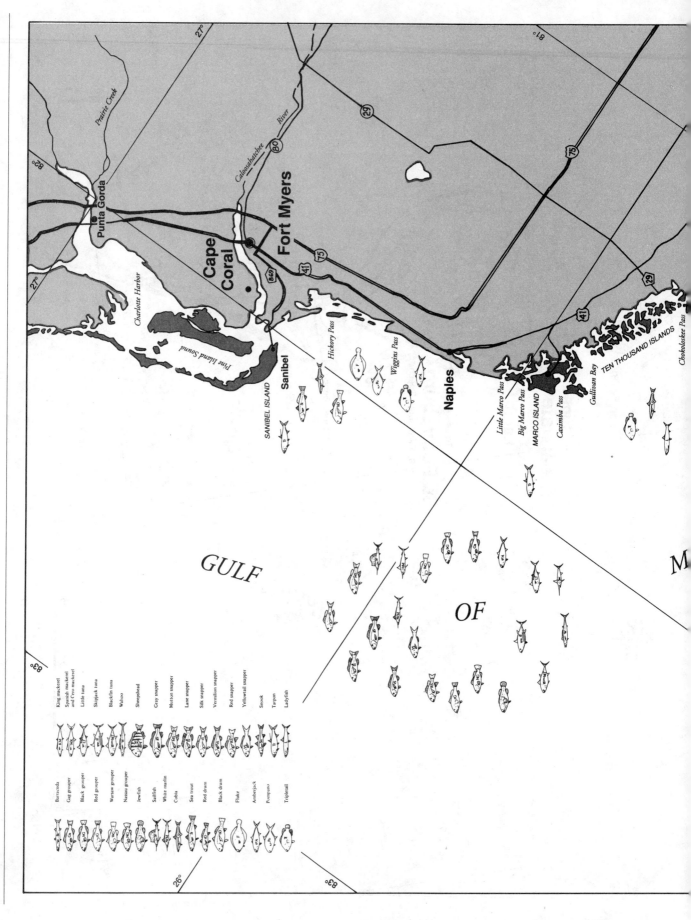

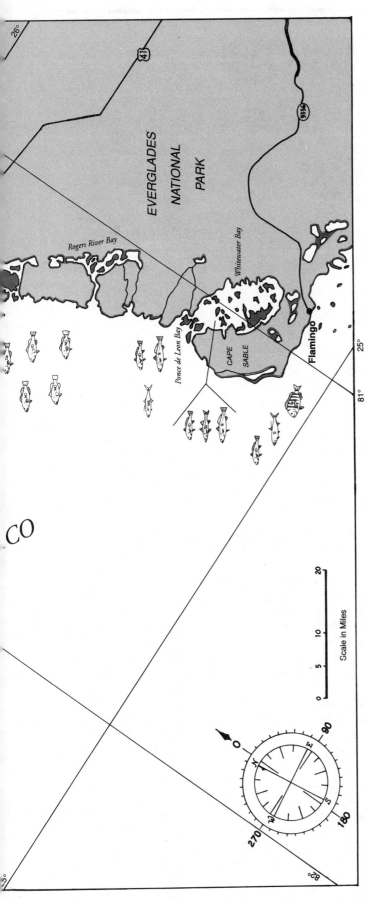

"A heckuva note," Harmon remarked as we raised the anchor at about high noon. "Imagine, leaving a good hole with the fish still biting like there's no tomorrow."

"Just keep in mind there'll be other trips," I replied. "Only next time, let's pick a colder day."

"It might be cold and nasty," he said, bundling up for the return trip, "but it sure beats pulling teeth."

"When you're pulling teeth, you're at least doing it in a warm office," I shot back.

Fortunately, winter isn't the only time you can catch grouper on the Gulf Coast. It's a year-round proposition, though you'll want to work different areas depending upon the time of year.

Usually, from late December through the end of March or into early April, anglers can find fish relatively close in. It's not unusual during this period to locate medium and large-sized gamesters in waters ranging in depth from 35 to 55 feet.

As water temperatures rise, however, black and red grouper tend to migrate into deeper haunts where, apparently, they're more comfortable. During the late summer and fall months, don't be surprised if you have to travel 40 to 80 miles or more offshore before zeroing in on your target.

As recently as 20 years ago, grouper could consistently be caught close to shore year-round. Due to increasing recreational and commercial pressure from folks equipped with more sophisticated electronics and fishing gear, those days are probably gone forever.

Experienced anglers—particularly those with good loran numbers—can still make excellent hauls in the Gulf's deeper areas, providing they have the time and trappings to devote to the effort.

They may even be able to do so the easy way—when the weather is decent—instead of following the example of Dr. Hugh Harmon and a frigid scribe who, it seems, do their best when the weather is at its worst.

It's a grim way to make a living—but someone has to do it. ∎

Sheepies Are Aqua Thieves

By Herb Allen

A sheepshead is as adept at stealing bait as a pickpocket is at lifting wallets.

It's also been said that an angler must set the hook just *before* the fish bites.

While these statements may be a bit of an exaggeration, certainly many anglers have experienced the frustration of examining an empty hook after reeling in to check their bait.

You can often sense sheepie by sight, rather than by feel. When the line twitches or begins to move, set the hook hard.

Many successful sheepshead enthusiasts on both the Atlantic and Gulf Coasts of Florida fish straight down near barnacle-encrusted pier pilings or over rock piles, favorite haunts of the "convict fish," so named because of its stealth and the seven dark bands encircling its lightly-colored body. Other likely spots include bridge pilings, oyster bars, jetties, submerged debris, logs, or shipwrecks.

Sheepshead tend to become more active during a high tide change, and many veteran anglers suggest that a faster current contributes to a feeding spree.

By using a bell-type sinker or a baited jig head, an angler can quickly lower his bait to the bottom where these fish seem to gather in greater abundance. Due to a hard mouth, it's best to keep your 3/0 or 4/0 hook razor sharp when trying for these dandies.

Since it's often necessary to quickly move the fish away from pilings or obstructions, try using monofilament line in the 12- to 20-pound class. A short piece of heavier shocker leader might be employed as protection against sharp dentures.

The most popular bait in Florida waters is a fiddler crab. Other successful offerings used by sheepshead buffs throughout Florida include shrimp, sea worms, sand fleas, oysters, minnows, and cut bait. Cotee's recently introduced Natural Bait is drawing increasingly rave reviews. Chumming with scraped barnacles and broken clams frequently draws the fish to a specific area.

A sheepie is not shy. If you haven't had action within a few minutes after dropping bait in one particular spot, move to another. They'll either hit right away or not at all.

Once hooked, the sheepie is a hard, durable battler that'll make powerful underwater runs. A 5-pounder is a worthy adversary for those using light tackle, while a 10-pounder is guaranteed to make the heart skip a beat or two. Also, those going after sheepshead often claim an added bonus by catching redfish, trout, snook, whiting, and drum, which frequent the same aqua environment.

Although common throughout the Sunshine State year-round, the sheepshead becomes more active when water temperatures cool down, from mid-October through March.

A member of the porgy family—a species which also includes the mangrove snapper—sheepshead generally average between one and three pounds. However, a few might be on the plus side of 10 pounds. Deep-fried or baked, sheepshead filets taste great.

The fish gets the name "sheepshead" because of its flat, protruding teeth, which give its face a sheep-like look. In addition to its stripes, the sheepie can be distinguished from the porgy by a rounded rather than a forked tail. ∎

Here's The Point

by Herb Allen

There are several great places remaining along Florida's Gulf Coast where, seemingly, time stands still and anglers continue to enjoy fast finny action as our forefathers did.

Located in Franklin County, about 50 miles south of Tallahassee, Alligator Point is a long, narrow spit of land, just wide enough to accommodate one road running down its center.

Although we've had opportunities to wet a line out from Alligator Point a few times during the past three decades, one trip particularly stands out in our memory.

It was mid-June, 1972, when we—along with writer Vic Dunaway, his two sons, Danny and David, and local angler Dennett Jackson—tested our skills against a potpourri of piscatorial adversaries.

What made this safari memorable is that it was timed just one day before Hurricane Agnes zeroed in on the east coast.

Fishing from a 19-foot Robalo near Dog Island Reef, Danny and David, then 18 and 16 respectively, connected simultaneously on their first casts. Danny brought a dandy three-pound trout into the boat and ice chest, while David landed and released a frisky, trophy-sized five-pound ladyfish.

We continued drifting the lush grass flats, tossing Salty Dog Jigs, a precursor to the now famous Cotee Liv'Eye Action Jig, and, by actual count, landed a two- to four-pound spotted trout on every third cast.

Leaving the trout, we hopped over to Marker 26 in Apalachee Bay, where we were met by a large school of cobia (known in these parts as ling). While these were not large as cobia go, many tipped the Toledos in the 10- to 15-pound class which, on 6-pound tackle, these were formidable fish. Before long, some hefty brutes put in an appearance. We were unable to keep these 50- to 60-pounders away from the marker and were continually cut off.

When one cobia is hooked, others will follow it around, giving other anglers a shot at hooking up. In this respect, cobia are similar to dolphin. So long as you keep one in the water, others in the school won't be far off.

With the exception of snook, just about everything that swims in the Gulf of Mexico can be found here, including bull redfish, tarpon (in summer), trout, cobia, Spanish mackerel, kingfish, marlin, sailfish, bonito, wahoo . . . you name it.

Even better, an angler is not covered up by other boats. It's not uncommon to fish all day and not see another fisherman.

On Alligator Point itself, there is a marina, a couple of small restaurants, and grocery stores. The Point boasts of a nice, uncrowded beach, and the limited number of residents and weekend property owners from Tallahassee are mostly good Ol' Cracker folks. Overnight accommodations can be found in nearby Panacea. Anglers are advised to trailer their own boats.

Although tucked away off the beaten path, visiting Alligator Point is well worth the effort. Fishing is good year-round, with the late spring, summer and early fall months probably best, if for no other reason than the Panhandle of Florida often gets chilly in winter.

We're looking forward to another visit here in April or May when those big cobia show up.

If you arrive before us, leave a few. ∎

FISHING ACCESS

GULF COAST BOAT LAUNCHING RAMPS

Every large or small community on Florida's Gulf Coast will probably have one or more public ramps where a fisherman can launch his boat free of charge.

In addition, most fish camps and many marinas dotting the coastline have private ramps where, for free or for a small fee, an angler can jump off on an aqua safari to nearby fishing grounds.

Each Gulf Coast county is listed here, starting in Escambia and traveling southward to Monroe County, with a sampling of available ramps.

Escambia
Ft. Pickins State Park Ramp on Santa Rosa Island
Bayou Grande Ramp at Navy Point
17th Ave. Ramp, rear FHP Office in Pensacola
Bayview Park on Bayou Texar in Bayview
Ski Jump Road on Bayou Texar in Bayview
Pensacola Beach Ramp
Sanders Beach Ramp on Pensacola Bay

Santa Rosa

Bagdad Ramp at the end of Forsyth Street

Holley Ramp at East River Bridge

Dickerson City Ramp, 12 miles south of Bagdad

Milton Ramp at City Park, Munson Hwy. and Broad St.

Navarre Beach Ramp at Wayside Park

Old Navy Boat Dock Ramp in Milton

Blackwater River Bridge Ramp in Milton

McMillan's Fish Camp Ramp at Mulat

Jim's Fish Camp Ramp, Escambia Fill, Pace

Brown's Fish Camp Ramp, Escambia Fill, Pace

Pete's Seafood & Camp Ramp, Escambia Fill, Pace

Floridatown Picnic Area Ramp in Pace

Bill's Seafood Ramp on Ward Basin

Driskell's Fish Camp Ramp on Ward Basin

Causey's Fish Camp Ramp on Ward Basin

Okaloosa

Cinco Bayou Bridge Ramp, Hwy. 85

East Pass Marina Ramp in Destin

Destin Marina Public Ramp

Ramp next to Island Marina, US 98, at Ft. Walton Beach

Niceville Park Ramp on Boggy Bayou

Okaloosa Island Ramp at the east end of Brooks Bridge on US 98

Valpariso Ramp at Lions Park on Boggy Bayou

Walton

Choctawhatchee Ramp, south of US 331 Causeway

County Park Ramp, head of Basin Bayou, Choctawhatchee

State Park Ramp on SR 20, Choctawhatchee

Nick's Lodge Ramp, Choctawhatchee

Marsh Fish Camp Ramp, Choctawhatchee

Basin Bayou Ramp, Choctawhatchee

Western Lake Ramp at Grayton Beach

Santa Rosa Ramp at the head of Hogtown Bayou

Bay

Wayside Park Sound Ramp, end of Bailey Bridge in Lynn Haven

Overstreet Ramp, 5 mi. north of Mexico Beach on Hwy. 386

Hollanday Motel Ramp on US 98 East at Mexico Beach

Bob George Park Ramp at Milleville

Gulf Marine Ramp, 1500 East US 98, Panama City

Harby Marina Ramp, 1961 East US 98, Panama City

Glen Bridge Ramp on East 4th St. at Watson Bayou, Panama City

Ethridge Marina Ramp at 112 A 3rd Court, Panama City

Tyndall AFB Park Ramp, east end of Dupont Bridge, Panama City

St. Andrew Marina Ramp, 3000 W. 19th St., Panama City

Carl Gray Park Ramp at the east end of Hathaway Bridge on US 98, Panama City

Treasure Island Marina Ramp at Grand Lagoon on Thomas Drive, Panama City

St. Andrews State Park Ramp in Panama City

Phillips Inlet Ramp, West Hwy. 98, Panama City

West Bay Bridge Ramp, Hwy. 79, Panama City

Gulf

Port St. Joe City Pier Ramp

Magnolia Landing Ramp, Wewahitchka

Chipola Park Ramp, Chipola

Fish Hatchery Ramp east of SR 71

Franklin

Alligator Harbor Ramp at Linton Landing on US Hwy 98

Carrabelle Ramp next to Carrabelle Coast Guard Station

St. George Island Ramp at the southwest end of toll bridge

Wakulla

St. Marks River Bridge Ramp at Newport

Trade Winds Pier Ramp in Ocklockonee

Tarpon Marina Ramp on the Ocklockonee River

Shield Marina Ramp on St. Marks River

Shell Island Fish Camp Marina on the St. Marks River

Shell Point Marina Ramp on the St. Marks River

Taylor

Horseshoe Ramp at Horsehoe

Steinhatchee Public Ramp in Steinhatchee

Keaton Beach Public Ramp

Dixie

Suwannee Public Ramps (2) at Suwannee

Levy

Cedar Key Public Ramp

Shell Mound County Ramp

Waccasassa County Ramp

SR 40 Ramp at Yankeetown

Cracker Town Ramp at Yankeetown

Citrus

Knox Bait House Ramp in Crystal River

McRae's Bait House Ramp in Homosassa

Hernando

Bayport County Ramp

Pasco

Norfleet's Camp Ramp at Aripeka

Cape Clay Ramp in Hudson

Hudson Marina Ramp on Hudson Beach Road

Signal Cove Ramp in Hudson

Main Street Ramp at High Bridge in New Port Richey

Port Richey Ramp

Sunset Landing Ramp in Port Richey

Pinellas

Bellair Beach Causeway Ramp

Seminole Street Ramp in Clearwater

High & Dry Marina Ramp on Clearwater Beach Causeway

Marina Sixty-Six Ramp on Clearwater Beach Causeway

Boatel Marine Ramp on Clearwater Beach

Dunedin Marina Ramp on SR 480

Gulfport Yacht Basin Ramp at 46th St. & 29th Ave

Indian Springs Marina Ramp at Indian Rocks Beach

America Gas Station Ramp on Gulf Blvd., Indian Rocks Beach

Kool's Marine Ramp in Madeira Beach at 150-25th St. East

Medeira Beach Marina Ramp

Speckled Trout Fish Camp Ramp on SR 584, Ozona

Al's Fish Camp Ramp on SR 584, Ozona

Seashore Marine Ramp on SR 584, Ozona

George's Fish Camp Ramp on SR 584, Ozona

Storm Harbor Marina Ramp on Klosterman Rd., Palm Harbor

Palm Harbor Fishing Lodge Ramp on Alt. US 19

Blind Pass Marina Ramp on St. Petersburg Beach

Maximo Park Marina, 6800 34th St. South, St. Petersburg

O'Neil's Boat Basin Marina, North end of Sunshine Skyway, St. Petersburg

Maximo Moorings Marina, 4700 South 34th St., St. Petersburg

Big Bayou Ramp, 6th St. & 37th Ave., St. Petersburg

Gandy Bridge Marina Ramp on Gandy Blvd., St. Petersburg

Modern Marine Ramp, 120 13th Ave. S.E., St. Petersburg

Embree Marine Service Ramp, 201 16th Ave. South, St. Petersburg

George's Boat Basin Ramp on Gandy Blvd., St. Petersburg

Weedon Bridge Ramp on Weedon Drive, St. Petersburg

Smack's Ramp at Crisp Park, 35th Ave. & 1st Street North, St. Petersburg

Coffeepot Ramp, 31st Ave. & 1st Street North, St. Petersburg

South Yacht Basin Ramp, 1st Ave. South, St. Petersburg

Ft. DeSoto Park Ramps on US 19 South, St. Petersburg

Municipal Park Ramp on Whitcombe Bayou, Tarpon Springs

Treasure Island Marina Ramp

Johns Pass Marina Ramp

Hillsborough

Giant's Camp Ramp on the Alafia River & Hwy 41, Gibsonton

Bahia Beach Resort Ramp at Bahia Beach

Cockroach Bay Ramp at the end of Cockroach Bay Road

American Legion Hall Ramp at Port Tampa

Commongood Park Ramp at Ruskin

Shell Point Fish Camp Ramp at Ruskin

Simmons Park Ramp at Ruskin

Baycrest Ramp in Tampa

Public Ramps on Courtney Campbell Causeway, Rt. 60, Tampa

Salty Sol Fleischman Ramps, at east end of Gandy Bridge, Tampa

Interbay Marina Ramp, 4323 S. Westshore Blvd., Tampa

Dawson's Fish Camp Ramp on Gandy Blvd., Tampa

Ballast Point Ramp, Tampa

Highway 41 Ramp in the Roadside Park, South of Little Manatee River Bridge, Tampa

Manatee River Bridge Ramp, Tampa

Seabreeze Pier Ramp on the 22nd St. Causeway, Tampa

Davis Island Ramp on Davis Island, Tampa

Lowry Park Ramp on North Blvd. & Sligh Ave., Tampa

Williams Park Ramp on the Alafia River and Hwy. 41, Gibsonton

Manatee

North Point Marina Ramp, 412 Pine Ave., Anna Maria

Bayou Marine Ramp on Bay Blvd., Anna Maria

Trailer Estates Marina Ramp, 2302 Penn Ave., Bradenton

Marshall's Marina Ramp on Hwy. 64, Bradenton

Perico Island Marina Ramp on Manatee Ave., Bradenton

Cortez Marina Ramp in Cortez

Anderson's Marina Ramp in Cortez

Turner's Tackle Shop Ramp in Cortez

Holmes Beach Airport Ramp

Up-Island Marine Supply Ramp in Holmes Beach

Manatee River Ramp at Ft. Homer Rd. and Manatee River

Longboat Key Marina Ramp

Longboat Key Pass Ramp

Terra Manna Sport Center Ramp on Snead Island

Gus Landing Ramp on Snead Island Cutoff

Snead Island Boat Works Ramp

Fisherman's Cove Ramp on Hwy. 19 at Terra Cia

Sarasota

County Island Ramp on Blackburn Road, Sarasota

Municipal Yacht Club Ramp at Casey Key

Main Street Ramp in Osprey

City Island Ramp in Sarasota

Municipal Auditorium Ramp in Sarasota

Turtle Beach Ramp, Sarasota

Sarasota City Ramp

The Landings Ramp, Sarasota

Sarasota Pass Ramp at Sarasota Pass & Rt. 54

Municipal Yacht Club Ramp in Venice

Charlotte

Beach Road Ramp in Englewood

Port Charlotte Beach Yacht Club Ramp

Punta Gorda Ramp at the South end of the bridge

Lee

Bonita Beach Ramp off Bay View Drive, Bonita Beach

Orange River Ramp at Rt. 80, Ft. Myers

City Boat Ramp on Edison Drive, Ft. Myers

Lee County Boat Ramp at Matlacha

Dewey's Marina Ramp at Sanibel

Collier

Naples City Dock Ramp

Bayview Park Ramp, Naples

Boat Haven of Naples Ramp on 5th Ave. South

Brookside Marina Ramp, Naples

Bay Marina Ramp on River Point Drive, Naples

Bayview Ramp on 5th Ave., Naples

Port of the Islands Resort Ramp, 20 miles east of Naples on Hwy. 41 (Tamiami Trail)

Monroe

Bahia Honda State Park Ramp

Old Wooden Bridge Marina Ramp on Big Pine Key

Little Blackwater Sound Ramp on Cross Key

Mid-Key Ramp on Cudjoe Key

Bow Channel Ramp on Cudjoe Key

Little Torch Marina Ramp on Little Torch Key

Mid-Key Ramp on West Summerland Key

STATE PARKS WITH FISHING ACCESS

The following Florida state parks offer saltwater fishing access. See pages 107 and 155 for more state parks with fishing access.

Collier-Seminole, 17 mi. south of Naples, off US 41

Delnor-Wiggins Pass, 6 mi. south of Bonita Springs, County Road 901 off US 41

Grayton Beach, Grayton Beach, off SR 30A S.

Henderson Beach, Destin, on US 98W

Honeymoon Island, Dunedin, SR 586 west from US 19A

Koreshan, Estero, off US 41

Rocky Bayou, Fred Gannon, 5 mi. north of Niceville, on SR 20

St. Andrews, 3 mi. east of Panama City Beach, off SR 392

St. George Island, 10 mi. southeast of Eastpoint, off US 98

St. Joseph Peninsula, Near Port St. Joe, off CR 30, west of US 98

Wakulla Springs, Edward Ball, Wakulla Springs, off SR 267 and 61

FISHING RECORDS

For a listing of Florida records for both conventional and fly tackle, see page 108.

LOCATING PARTY, CHARTER, OR RENTAL BOATS

For a general introduction to finding charter, party, or rental boats in Florida, turn to page 110 in Chapter Two.

WEST COAST

Florida's west coast provides a shallow, sloping bottom which forces serious anglers to book all-day trips if oversized grouper and snapper are the target. Half-day outings for sea bass and other bottom fish are available through marinas berthing the big drift boats, but longer trips are the mainstay in the area.

Panhandle drift boat skippers out of Destin head for the southeast grounds to fish 90 feet of water for grouper and snapper. They also work the 350-foot depths of Mingo Ridge for some oversized Warsaw grouper.

The Apalachicola Bay area is seldom frequented by drift boats, due to the distance from most sportfishing ports. Grouper, Spanish mackerel, flounder and grunt are available in depths as shallow as 10 feet, extending out to 90 feet of water, but this part of the Gulf is the domain of private boat operators rather than party boats, despite the excellent angling opportunities.

Moving to the area between Cedar Key and Tarpon Springs, drift boats range over the Middlegrounds, where 70 to 150 feet of water offer the best black and red grouper, red snapper, and scamp activity in the Gulf.

TAMPA BAY AREA

Although captains out of the Clearwater–St. Petersburg–Tampa Bay triangle know dozens of productive small reefs, where close-to-home fishing ranges from good to excellent, most skippers head for the massive fishing site known as The 27's, west of Clearwater. With depths as shallow as 50 feet, but pocked by holes where depthfinders ping solid at 600 feet, the largest red snapper and black grouper of the year traditionally come from this area. Fishing southwest Florida requires a choice between short runs to nearby shallow reefs, where sea bass are the predominant species, or full-day journeys to the Sand Ridges, where 250-foot depths provide snapper and grouper in the 10-pound range.

The three keys to enjoying a fall or winter Florida drift boat trip are determining how much time, money and effort you choose to spend. Check with local skippers for half-day outings, or prepare to get up in the middle of the night and expect it to be just as dark when you return home. Your ticket usually covers the trip, tackle suitable for the fish you're chasing, and the correct bait.

GULF COAST MASTER GUIDES

A list of other Florida master guides appears on page 156.

Boca Grande. Capt. Ron Jones, (813) 625-2494

Boca Grande to Tampa Bay. Capt. Jerry Sloan, (800) 328-5686

Tampa Bay, Gulf beaches. Capt. Tom. Tamanini, (813) 581-4942

Homosassa/Crystal River. Capt. Al Kline, (904) 628-5381

Chokoloskee. Capt. Dan Prickett, (813) 695-4573

Boca Grande. Capt. Cookie Diaz, (813) 653-0435

Chokoloskee. Capt. John Carlisle, 1-800-952-6597

St. Petersburg. Capt. Larry Blue, (813) 595-4798

Everglades City. Capt. Cecil Oglesby, (813) 695-2910

Marco Island. Capt. Jay Peeler, (813) 642-1342

Naples/Ten Thousand Islands. Capt. Glenn Puopolo, (813) 353-4087

Marco Island. Capt. Glenn Andrews, (813) 394-8959

Marco Island. Capt. Ron Morris, (813) 394-6322

Naples. Capt. Pete Villani, (813) 455-2334

Anna Maria. Capt. Ben Webb, (813) 778-7647

Pinellas Park. Capt. Charlie Walker, (813) 546-7257

Naples. Capt. Wayne Maahs, (813) 261-7045

Cortez. Capt. Scott Moore, (813) 778-3005

Crystal River. Capt. Frank Schiraldi, (904) 795-5229

Hudson. Capt. Everet Antrim, (813) 868-5747

Tampa. Capt. Charley Cleveland, (813) 935-0214

Sarasota. Capt. Pete Greenan, (813) 923-6095

Clearwater. Capt. Richard Howard, (813) 446-8962

Venice. Capt. Addison Gilbert, (813) 485-2584

Cedar Key. Capt. Abbie Napier, (904) 543-5511

Inverness. Capt. Roger Johnson, (904) 344-5765

Boca Grande. Capt. Ken Shannon, (813) 497-4876

Lakeland. Capt. Phil Chapman, Florida Game & Fish Commission, (813) 646-9445 (H), 648-3202 (W)

Sarasota. Capt. Ed Hurst, (813) 925-1871

Homosassa. Capt. Mike Locklear, (904) 628-4207

St. Petersburg. Capt. Paul Hawkins, (813) 894-7345, answering service 825-2882

Naples. Capt. Mark Ward, (813) 775-9849

Englewood. Capt. Mike Sweeterman, (813) 475-7256

Port Charlotte. Les Hill, (813) 743-6622

Naples. Glenn Puopolo, (813) 353-4807

Crystal River. Jackie Bryant, (904) 746-2880 or 563-3846

Sarasota. Jonnie Walker, (813) 922-2287

Tampa. Capt. Bill Miller, (813) 935-3141 or 251-4866

Terra Ceia. Capt. James Wood, (813) 722-8746

Naples. Capt. Tod Geroy, (813) 455-7761

Boca Grande. Capt. Van Hubbard, (813) 697-6944

Brooksville. Capt. Don Ebbealce, (904) 796-8282

Oldsmar. Bill Hernandez, (813) 786-5543

Oldsmar. Dennis Dube, (813) 786-5543

Destin. Mike Conley, (904) 837-9523

Clearwater. Michael Faust, 1699 Woodridge Drive

Mexico Beach, Alan Duke, (904) 648-4015

Naples. Ray Bearfield, 640 10th Street S.

Spring Hill. Capt. Jim Bradley, (904) 596-5639

Hudson. Capt. Dennis Royston, (813) 863-3204

Holiday. Capt. Ed Peters, (813) 934-7587 or 844-9084

Tarpon Springs. Gene Struthers, (813) 937-5938

Tarpon Springs. Michael Duclon, (813) 942-3639

Sarasota. Rick Grassett, (813) 366-8095

Panama City. Mike Ware, (904) 785-6216

Tampa. Dave Markett, (813) 962-1435

STATE AGENCIES

A listing of various Florida agencies with jurisdiction over the state's saltwater fishing appears on page 111.

 5

Commonly Caught Species, Including an Angler's Guide to Sharks

ATLANTIC BONITO, *Sarda sarda*. Bonito. SIZE: To 15 lbs; average 2–4 lbs; over 7 lbs unusual. HABITS: Pelagic, schooling and migratory. These rapid swimmers occur in continental shelf water. They feed mainly at or near the surface and often jump clear of the water when in pursuit of prey. FISHING METHODS: Caught at or near the surface by trolling in water warmer than 65°F; some by casting, jigging, and chumming from boats. Most are caught incidentally while fishing for other pelagic fishes. BAITS: Feathers, spoons, plugs, jigs, strip bait, feather-strip bait or skirt-strip bait combination, and cut fish.

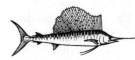

ATLANTIC CROAKER, *Micropogon undulatus*. Croaker, hardhead. SIZE: To 5 lbs; average 1–3 lbs; over 3 lbs unusual. HABITS: These bottom feeders occur on mud, sand, shell, or coral bottom and around rock jetties or wrecks in salt and brackish water; a few in nearly fresh water. Spawned offshore in depths to 300 ft, the young move inshore and spend their first year of life in shallow estuaries. As growth proceeds they gradually move seaward. Adults migrate inshore during the spring to water warmer than 61°F. FISHING METHODS: Most are caught from a few feet below the tide line to depths of 30 ft by bottom fishing, chumming, live-lining, and jigging from shore or boats. BAITS: Shrimp, soft or shedder crab, clams, worms, and cut fish. A few are caught on small jigs and weighted bucktails.

ATLANTIC SAILFISH, *Istiophorous platyperus*. Sailfish. SIZE: To over 141 lbs in the Atlantic Ocean; average 25–35 lbs; over 70 lbs unusual. HABITS: Pelagic and migratory. Occur in continental shelf water usually in depths over 40 ft, but they occasionally venture close enough to shore to be taken from ocean piers. Travel in small groups or singly. Sailfish usually feed more in midwater and near bottom than at the surface. FISHING METHODS: Trolling and live-lining from boats. A few are caught from shore. BAITS: Strip bait, feather-strip bait or skirt-strip bait combination, whole rigged ballyhoo or mullet, and live bait. Some caught on feathers, spoons, skirts, and plugs.

ATLANTIC SPADEFISH, *Chaetodipterus faber.* Spadefish, angelfish, porgy, moonfish. SIZE: To 16 lbs; average 1–3 lbs; over 10 lbs unusual. HABITS: They aggregate in salt water on sand, shell, coral, or rock bottom and around buoys, wrecks, rock piles, bridge abutments, pilings, jetties, and breakwaters. During warm months most occur inshore of the 90 ft bottom contour; during cold months some retreat further offshore. FISHING METHODS: Bottom fishing from boats or shore. BAITS: Clams, worms, shrimp, crabs, and cut fish.

BLACK DRUM, *Pogonias cromis.* Drum. The young have 4 to 6 broad, black bars on their sides, which disappear with age. SIZE: Barred fish average 1–3 lbs and large fish 10–20 lbs; over 45 lbs unusual. HABITS: Occur in large aggregations during spring migration, but usually solitary during fall. Feed on any type of bottom but prefer mussel, clam, or oyster beds. Also live around breakwaters, jetties, pilings, bridge abutments, and piers. FISHING METHODS: Bottom fishing and chumming from shore or boats for large fish; these methods plus casting artificial lures for small fish. BAITS: Shrimp, clams, soft or shedder crab, squid, and cut fish; also spoons, jigs, and weighted bucktails.

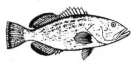

BLACK GROUPER, *Mycteroperca bonaci.* Blackfin grouper. Sometimes miscalled gag grouper. Usually distinguished from other groupers by the large, dark rectangular-shaped blotches arranged in rows on the body. SIZE: To over 100 lbs; average 3–7 lbs; over 30 lbs unusual. HABITS: Occur in depths of 400 ft or more on high relief bottom of coral and rocks encrusted with living organisms, or around wrecks. Small fish occur both inshore and offshore. As they grow larger, they tend to remain offshore. FISHING METHODS: Bottom fishing, live-lining, jigging, or trolling near bottom from boats. BAITS: Whole or cut fish, crabs, spiny lobsters, shrimp, and live pinfish, grunt or snapper; also strip bait, feather-strip bait combination, spoons, plugs, jigs, and weighted bucktails.

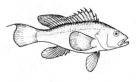

BLACK SEA BASS, *Centropristis striata.* Sea bass, blackfish, common bass, humpback bass. Small ones taken in estuaries are called black Willies. See rock sea bass. SIZE: Average 1–3 lbs; over 4 lbs unusual. HABITS: Gregarious, year-round

residents occurring on rock, coral, or shell bottom and around wrecks, pilings, wharves, rock jetties, or breakwaters. They are most common from a few feet below the tide line to about 180 ft; some to 450 ft or more. They attain their largest size and greatest abundance on offshore grounds. FISHING METHODS: Most are caught in depths from 60 to 120 ft by bottom fishing from drifting or anchored boats. Small ones are taken from shore by bottom fishing. BAITS: Squid, clams, crabs, worms, shrimp, and cut fish.

BLACKFIN TUNA, *Thunnus atlanticus.* Tuna. SIZE: To over 40 lbs; average 7–10 lbs; over 22 lbs unusual. HABITS: These rapid, pelagic swimmers occur usually near the surface between the 100- and 600-ft bottom contours. They often form large, dense schools with many thousands of individuals. FISHING METHODS: Trolling, casting, and live-lining from boats. BAITS: Feathers, strip bait, feather-strip bait or skirt-strip bait combination, spoons, jigs and plugs; also rigged ballyhoo and mullet, or small live fish.

BLACKLINE TILEFISH, *Caulolatilus cyanops.* Tilefish, gray tilefish. See tilefish. SIZE: To 35 lbs; average 5–12 lbs; over 25 lbs unusual. HABITS: These bottom dwellers occur in depths of 200 to 1,000 ft or more, on mud, sand, shell, or rock bottom favoring areas with high relief. At times they will swim a short distance off the bottom to feed. FISHING METHODS: Most are caught from boats by bottom fishing with wireline in depths of 450 to 750 ft. BAITS: Whole or cut fish, squid, clams, shrimp, and crabs.

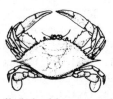

BLUE CRAB, *Callinectes sapidus.* Crab, blue claw crab. Males are called Jimmies, females sooks, and those bearing eggs, sponge crabs. Crabs about to shed their shells are called shedders or peelers. Immediately after shedding their shells, they are called soft crabs. Size is usually expressed as the width of the shell across the back measured from spine tip to spine tip. SIZE: To 10 inches; average 5–6 inches; over 9 inches unusual. HABITS: Occur on mud, sand, sand-shell, and gravel bottom, in salt, brackish and sometimes freshwater. Especially abundant in estuaries and the mouths of streams or rivers around sea grass. During warm months crabs frequent shallow water; during cold months they seek deep water and may embed in mud. Active in water warmer than 50°F. Check state laws governing size limit and the taking of egg-bearing females. FISHING

METHODS: Hand lines or crab traps from shore or boats. BAITS: Whole and cut fish or scrap meat.

 BLUE MARLIN, *Makaira nigricans*. See white marlin. Distinguished from white marlin by having the tips of the dorsal and anal fins pointed and, except for very small fish, the lateral line is inconspicuous. White marlin have rounded dorsal and anal fin tips and the lateral line is conspicuous. SIZE: To over 1,700 lbs in the Atlantic Ocean; Pacific marlin over 2,000 lbs are reported; average 250–300 lbs; over 600 lbs unusual. HABITS: Pelagic and migratory. Occur in oceanic and continental shelf water from the surface to depths of at least 300 ft. Travel in small groups or singly. Most are taken near the surface between the 300- and 600-ft bottom contours. FISHING METHODS: Trolling, kite fishing, and live-lining from boats. BAITS: Whole rigged squid, Spanish mackerel, mullet, striped bass, eel, and ballyhoo; also strip bait, feather-strip bait combination, and live fish. Some are caught on artificial lures.

 BLUE RUNNER, *Caranx crysos*. Runner, hardtail, jack. SIZE: To over 4 lbs; average 1–2 lbs; over 3 lbs unusual. HABITS: Pelagic and schooling, occurring throughout the water column. Spawned offshore, the young move inshore along the beaches into estuaries and over shallow reefs. Adults frequently occur around pilings, bridge abutments, and buoys. FISHING METHODS: Casting, jigging, live-lining, chumming, trolling, and bottom fishing from boats or shore. BAITS: Shrimp, cut fish, and small live fish; also weighted bucktails, plugs, spoons, jigs, and streamer flies. Most blue runners are used as bait for large fish.

 BLUEFISH, *Pomatomus saltatrix*. Blues. Small ones called snapper blues, cocktail blues, or sour blues. SIZE: Average ¾ to 1¼ lbs; over 3½ lbs unusual. HABITS: Pelagic, schooling, and migratory. Bluefish occur throughout the water column in temperatures warmer than 55°F. They often concentrate around inlets, shoals, wrecks, and artificial reefs. Large fish (12 to 15 lbs) are sometimes caught offshore. Abundance fluctuates from year to year. FISHING METHODS: Casting, bottom fishing, live-lining, and jigging from shore; these methods plus trolling from boats. Most bluefish are caught within 6 miles of shore in water of 65°-76°F. Check state regulation on size limit. BAITS: Shrimp, mullet, cut fish, and live fish; also spoons, feathers, weighted bucktails, jigs, and plugs.

 BONEFISH, *Albula vulpes*. Silver ghost, phantom. SIZE: To over 20 lbs; average 4–6 lbs; over 12 lbs unusual. HABITS: These inshore fish occur singly, in groups, or in schools from the tide line to depths of 40 ft. They often feed by rooting in the bottom of sand and grass flats; this feeding action is called "tailing" or "mudding." FISHING METHODS: Chumming, live-lining, and casting from boats or while wading in shallow water. Most bonefish are caught in depths of ½ to 10 feet. BAITS: Shrimp, crabs, clams, conch, sand bugs, and squid; also weighted bucktails, feathers, plugs, and streamer flies.

 CERO MACKEREL, *Scomberomous regalis*. Mackerel, often miscalled Spanish mackerel. Distinguished from Spanish mackerel by having scaled pectoral fins, and their sides marked with stripes and spots, the spots being below the lateral line and in rows. Spanish mackerel have scaleless pectoral fins, and the spots on their sides are irregularly distributed. Distinguished from king mackerel by the lateral line sloping downward gradually under the second dorsal fin. In the king mackerel, the lateral line slopes dramatically after the second dorsal. SIZE: To over 25 lbs; average 2–4 lbs; over 13 lbs unusual. HABITS: These pelagic fish occur along ocean beaches and the Keys from shore to depths of 100 ft or more in water warmer than 67°F. More solitary than Spanish mackerel, cero do not usually form large schools. FISHING METHODS: Live-lining, casting, trolling, jigging, and bottom fishing from boats. Some are caught from shore by casting, live-lining, and bottom fishing. BAITS: The same as for Spanish mackerel.

 COBIA, *Rachycentron canadum*. Crab-eater ling, lemonfish, black salmon, sergeant fish. SIZE: To 120 lbs; tackle record 110 lbs; average 15–25 lbs; over 65 lbs unusual. HABITS: Pelagic and migratory. Cobia occur both offshore and inshore, often in inlets and estuaries. They usually occur singly or in small groups and are often around buoys, wrecks, floating debris, and with schools of other fish, sea turtles, and large rays. FISHING METHODS: Bottom fishing, live-lining, casting, and chumming from shore; these methods plus trolling from boats. BAITS: Whole spot, eel, and shedder crab or cut fish; also spoons, plugs, and large weighted bucktails.

 CREVALLE JACK, *Caranx hippos*. Jack, common jack, jack crevalle, crevalle. SIZE: To over 70 lbs; average 2–4

lbs; over 10 lbs unusual. HABITS: Pelagic, schooling and migratory. These rapid swimmers occur in salt and brackish water; sometimes in coastal rivers to nearly fresh water. Small fish are common in shallow estuaries. As they grow larger, they tend to move offshore into deeper water. FISHING METHODS: Casting, live-lining, chumming, and bottom fishing from shore; these methods plus trolling from boats. BAITS: Feathers, spoons, plugs, jigs, weighted bucktails, and bucktail flies; also live or cut fish and shrimp.

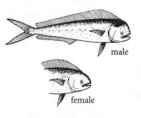

DOLPHIN, *Coryphaena hippurus*. Small ones called school dolphin, feather dolphin, and grasshoppers; large males called bulls and large females called cows. SIZE: To 85 lbs; average 3–7 lbs; over 45 lbs unusual. HABITS: Pelagic, schooling and migratory. These rapid swimmers occur near the surface in water warmer than 70°F. Although dolphin occasionally venture close enough to shore to be caught from ocean piers, they usually occur offshore of the 60-ft bottom contour. They often gather under floating debris, seaweed, and buoys. FISHING METHODS. Trolling, casting, live-lining, chumming, and kite fishing from boats. BAITS: Feathers, spoons, jigs, plugs, weighted bucktails, strip bait, feather-strip bait or skirt-strip bait combination, and whole rigged ballyhoo, mullet, squid, or Spanish mackerel; also live fish.

GAFFTOPSAIL CATFISH, *Bagre marinus*. Sail cat, top cat, catfish. SIZE: To 6 lbs; average 1–2 lbs; over 3 lbs unusual. HABITS: These inshore fish occur on any type of bottom in salt and brackish water, some in nearly fresh water. Although primarily bottom feeders, they sometimes pursue prey to the surface. Unlike sea catfish, gafftopsail catfish strike artificial lures. More active during night than day. FISHING METHODS: Bottom fishing or casting from shore or boats. BAITS: Shrimp, crabs, cut fish, and squid; also weighted bucktails, plugs, and streamer flies.

GAG GROUPER, *Mycteroperca microlepis*. Grouper. Distinguished from most other groupers by the gray color with no distinctive markings and by the slightly forked tail. SIZE: To 50 lbs; average 2–5 lbs; over 15 lbs unusual. HABITS: Occur to depths of 400 ft on any type of bottom but concentrate around rock or coral outcrops and wrecks. Small fish occur both inshore and offshore; large fish usually in water deeper than 60 ft. FISHING METHODS: Most are caught by bottom fish-

ing in depths of 120 to 240 ft, some by jigging from boats. BAITS: Shrimp, squid, clams, cut fish, and live fish; also weighted bucktails and jigs.

GRAY SEA TROUT, *Cynoscion regalis*. Gray trout, summer trout, trout, sea trout, yellow-fin trout, yellow-mouth trout, weakfish. Fish less than 3–4 lb called pan trout. See silver sea trout. Distinguished from spotted sea trout by having the dark blotches on its back often arranged in rows, but no round, dark spots on second dorsal fin and tail. In contrast, spotted sea trout have round, dark spots on upper half of body, second dorsal fin, and tail. SIZE: Average ½ to 1 lb; over 2 lbs unusual. HABITS: Occur throughout the water column in salt and brackish water to depths of at least 90 ft. Although found over any type of bottom, they favor sandy areas. FISHING METHODS: Bottom fishing, live-lining, casting, chumming, and jigging from shore; these methods plus trolling from boats. Most are caught a few feet off the bottom in depths of 4 to 45 ft. In North Carolina, most are caught in sounds, bays, and inlets. Although anglers usually do not take them during winter, gray sea trout are along the beaches and in the open ocean. In South Carolina, they are caught in both estuaries and along the ocean beaches to depths of 60 ft. BAITS: Spinners, spoons, plugs, jigs, and weighted bucktails. Also shrimp, squid, silversides, mullet, soft or shedder crabs, worms, clams, cut fish, and killifish.

GRAY SNAPPER, *Lutjanus griseus*. Snapper, mangrove snapper, mango snapper. SIZE: To 20 lbs; average 1–2 lbs; over 7 lbs unusual. HABITS: These bottom feeders aggregate on or a few feet above mud, sand, gravel, coral, or rock bottom in salt and brackish water; sometimes in fresh water. Although abundant in shallow water, especially around mangrove roots, they also occur in channels, cuts, or holes, on high relief rock or coral outcrops, and around wrecks in depths to 120 ft. FISHING METHODS: Bottom fishing, live-lining, chumming, and casting from shore; these methods plus trolling near bottom from boats. BAITS: Cut fish, shrimp, clams, conch, crabs, and live fish; also weighted bucktails, jigs, plugs, feathers, strip bait, and streamer flies.

GREAT AMBERJACK, *Seriola dumerili*. Amberjack, jack hammer. An extremely hard-fighting foe, the amberjack is plentiful around deeper offshore wrecks and reefs year-round. SIZE: To over 180 lbs; average 20–30 lbs; over

100 lbs unusual. HABITS: Schooling and migratory. These swift swimmers occur in oceanic and continental shelf water from the surface to depths of at least 600 ft. Although great amberjack may occur anywhere in the water column, they often concentrate over high relief rock or coral bottom and around wrecks or buoys. FISHING METHODS: Trolling, bottom fishing, jigging, chumming, and live-lining from boats. Anglers catch many large amberjack while fishing for snappers and groupers in depths of 150 to 300 ft. BAITS: Live and dead fish; also strip bait, plugs, spoons, feathers, and jigs.

GREAT BARRACUDA, *Sphyraena barracuda*. Barracuda, cuda. SIZE: Average 10–15 lbs; over 40 lbs unusual. HABITS: Pelagic and migratory. Occur offshore, sometimes inshore, and over any type of bottom. Barracuda often concentrate around wrecks or rock and coral bottom with high relief. Most are taken near the surface in water from 50- to 120-ft deep and temperatures warmer than 70°F. FISHING METHODS: Trolling, casting, and live-lining from boats. Usually taken as an incidental fish while trolling for other species. BAITS: Spoons, strip bait, feathers, plugs, and live fish.

GULF KINGFISH, *Menticirrhus littoralis*. Whiting, surf whiting, silver whiting, king whiting, bullhead whiting, kingfish. Miscalled sea mullet, gray mullet, and mullet. Distinguished from southern kingfish by the absence of any dark markings on its silvery body, and by its pale gill cavity. In contrast, southern kingfish have dusky bars on back and sides, and a dark gill cavity. This sleek, migratory and audacious gamester is one of the more popular angler goals. SIZE: To 3 lbs; average 1 lb; over 2 lbs unusual. HABITS: Gulf kingfish prefer saltier water than southern kingfish. Although a few occur within sounds or bays, most remain along sandy beaches of the open ocean and near the outside mouths of sounds. FISHING METHODS and BAITS are the same as for southern kingfish.

JEWFISH, *Epinephelus itajara*. Spotted jewfish, spotted grouper. Distinguished from other groupers by the short dorsal spines, dark spots, and rounded tail. The young have five dark bars on each side that disappear with age. SIZE: To over 800 lbs; average 30–60 lbs; over 250 lbs unusual. HABITS: Although some occur in depths of 100 ft or more, most are inshore of the 70-ft bottom contour. Favor wrecks, ledges, caves, jetties, and deep holes near bridge abutments. Small ones more

active than large ones. FISHING METHODS: Bottom fishing from shore or boats. Small ones take artificial lures. BAITS: Crabs, spiny lobster, live or dead fish, and clams; also jigs, plugs, and feathers.

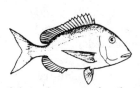

JOLTHEAD PORGY, *Calamus bajonado*. Porgy. Small fish do not possess the characteristic blunt head. Except for the sheepshead, this is the largest fish in the porgy family occurring along the southeastern coast. SIZE: To over 17 lbs; average 1–2 lbs; over 10 lbs unusual. HABITS: These bottom feeders occur in depths of at least 150 ft on mud and sand bottom, but prefer the high relief provided by coral or rock outcrops. Often around wrecks or rubble. FISHING METHODS: Bottom fishing from anchored or drifting boats. BAITS: Shrimp, clams, squid, cut fish, and crabs.

KING MACKEREL, *Scomberomorus cavalla*. Kingfish, kings. King mackerel have scaled pectoral fins and the lateral line dips downward abruptly under the second dorsal fin. In contrast, Spanish mackerel have scaleless pectoral fins and the lateral line slopes downward gradually under the second dorsal fin. SIZE: Spring-run fish average 6–8 lbs, fall-run fish 15–20 lbs; over 40 lbs unusual. HABITS: Pelagic, schooling and migratory. King mackerel occur over any type of bottom in salt water warmer than 67°–69°F. They often congregate over wrecks, high relief rock or coral bottom, and around buoys. Although some occasionally venture close enough to shore to be caught from ocean piers, most occur offshore of the 50-ft bottom contour. FISHING METHODS: Most are caught by trolling from boats 5 to 15 miles offshore, some by casting or live-lining from shore or boats. Fishing is especially good around the various capes. BAITS: Spoons, feathers, strip bait, feather-strip bait or skirt-strip bait combination, and plugs; also whole rigged mullet or ballyhoo, and live fish.

LADYFISH, *Elops saurus*. Skipjack, ten-pounder. For forceful strikes, aerial acrobatics and fast runs on light tackle, nothing matches a ladyfish. SIZE: To 9 lbs; average ¾ to 1¼ lbs; over 4 lbs unusual. HABITS: These schooling fish occur throughout the water column over any type of bottom in salt and brackish water; some in fresh water. They often congregate along the edges of deep holes or channels within shallow estuaries; also in inlets. FISHING METHODS: Bottom fishing, casting, jigging, live-lining and chumming from shore; these methods plus trolling from boats. Most are caught within a mile of ocean beaches and in inlets and estuaries. BAITS: Shrimp, small crabs, and cut fish; also weighted bucktails, jigs, plugs, spoons, spinners, streamer flies, and feathers.

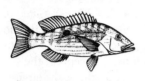

LANE SNAPPER, *Lutjanus synagris*. Snapper, spot snapper, redtail snapper. SIZE: To 3 lbs; average 1–2 lbs; over 2 lbs unusual. HABITS: These bottom feeders occur on mud, sand, coral, or rock bottom. Although reported to depths of 1,300 ft, they are abundant over shallow reefs and in estuaries, especially in cuts and passes and around bridges, abutments, piers, and pilings. FISHING METHODS: Bottom fishing, chumming, and live-lining from boats and shore. BAITS: Shrimp, cut fish, and squid; also small weighted bucktails.

LITTLE TUNNY, *Euthynnus alletteratus*. Bonito, false albacore, rum jugs. Miscalled albacore. SIZE: To 26 lbs; average 6–10 lbs; over 20 lbs unusual. HABITS: Pelagic, schooling, and migratory. These rapid swimmers occur in salt water warmer than 65°F. They travel in groups varying from three or four individuals to schools of many thousands. Although they occasionally venture close enough to shore to be caught from ocean piers, little tunny usually occur offshore of the 30-ft bottom contour. FISHING METHODS: Most are caught by trolling and casting from boats; some by casting from shore. BAITS: Feathers, strip bait, feather-strip bait or skirt-strip bait combination, spoons, jigs, and plugs.

MUTTON SNAPPER, *Lutjanus analis*. Snapper, muttonfish. SIZE: To 25 lbs; average 4–8 lbs; over 15 lbs unusual. HABITS: Occur from a few feet below the tide line to depths of 300 ft or more on mud, sand, coral, or rock bottom, favoring rock or coral outcrops encrusted with live organisms. Although usually bottom feeders, they sometimes pursue prey into midwater. FISHING METHODS: Bottom fishing, chumming, live-lining, and jigging from boats. A few caught by slow trolling near bottom. BAITS: Cut fish, squid, shrimp, and live fish; also weighted bucktails, jigs, and plugs.

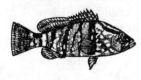

NASSAU GROUPER, *Epinephelus striatus*. Grouper. Distinguished from other groupers by the dark blotch on the narrow part of the tail and the dark bars on the head and body. SIZE: To 55 lbs; average 2–4 lbs; over 20 lbs unusual. HABITS: Occur from the shore to depths of at least 200 ft on high relief bottom of coral and rocks or around wrecks. Small fish occur from shallow to deep water. As they grow larger, they tend to remain in deep water. FISHING METHODS: Bottom fishing from shore or boats. Small fish are caught by casting, jigging, or trolling near bottom. BAITS: Cut fish, squid, shrimp, spiny lobster, and live fish; also weighted bucktails and feathers.

NORTHERN KINGFISH, *Menticirrhus saxatilis*. Whiting, king whiting, bullhead whiting, roundhead, kingfish, Carolina whiting. Miscalled sea mullet, Virginia mullet and mullet. This fish is the least abundant of the three species of kingfish along the southeast coast. Distinguished from the southern kingfish by having eight, sometimes nine, soft anal rays, the largest spine of the first dorsal fin in adult fish reaches far beyond the origin of the second dorsal fin, and the dark, oblique bars along the side form a V just behind the head. In contrast, southern kingfish have seven, rarely eight, soft anal rays, the longest spine of the first dorsal fin in an adult reaches just beyond the origin of the second dorsal fin, and the obscure, oblique bars along the side do not form a V just behind the head. Coloration of the northern kingfish and the dark inner lining of the gill cover are characteristics that separate this fish from the Gulf kingfish. See Gulf kingfish. SIZE: To 3 lbs; average 1 lb; over 2 lbs unusual. HABITS, FISHING METHODS and BAITS are the same as for southern kingfish.

PALOMETA, *Trachinotus goodei*. Gafftopsail pompano, longfin pompano. Distinguished from other Atlantic coast pompanos by having four narrow, dark bars on their sides. SIZE: To 3 lbs; average ½ to 1 lb; over 1 lb unusual. HABITS, FISHING METHODS and BAITS are the same as for pompano.

PERMIT, *Trachinotus falcatus*. Great pompano. Small ones sometimes called round pompano. Distinguished from pompano by having one spine and 17 to 21 soft rays in the second dorsal fin. Pompano have one spine and 22 to 27 soft rays. SIZE: Average 5–10 lbs; over 35 lbs unusual. HABITS: These bottom feeders occur from the tide line to depths of 100 ft or more. Although they occur in shallow flats and reefs, they frequent holes and cuts along the edges of these shallow areas. Permit sometimes feed near sharks and rays rooting in the bottom. Spawned offshore, the young move inshore and subsequently spend most of their lives in shallow water. FISHING METHODS: Bottom fishing, casting, live-lining, chumming, and jigging from boats, shore, and while wading. Most permit are caught in water warmer than 66°F and depths of 4 to 12 ft. BAITS: Live crabs, shrimp, and bait fish, also conch and clams. Some are caught on weighted bucktails, plugs, and streamer flies.

PIGFISH, *Orthopristis chrysoptera*. Grunt. Often miscalled hogfish and sailors choice. Distinguished from white grunt by having a small mouth with no bright color inside, and by its body scales above the lateral line being about the same size as those below. In contrast, white grunt have a large mouth with an orange-red lining, and the body scales above the lateral line are larger than those below. SIZE: To 2 lbs; average 1 lb; over 1 lb unusual. HABITS: Occur in salt and brackish water on sand or mud bottom and around wrecks, piers, jetties, or bridge abutments. Although common in estuaries, inlets, and along ocean beaches, they also occur offshore to depths of 100 ft or more. Pigfish usually feed within a few feet of bottom. FISHING METHODS: Bottom fishing and jigging from shore or boats. Although pigfish are plentiful, they are not highly sought. Most are caught incidentally with other bottom fishes. BAITS: Shrimp, crabs, squid, worms, clams, mussels, and cut fish; also small weighted bucktails and jigs. Pigfish are often used as live or cut bait for other fishes.

PINFISH, *Lagodon rhomboides*. Bream, salt water bream. Miscalled sailors choice. SIZE: To 2 lbs; average 1–2 lbs; over 2 lbs unusual. HABITS: Occur in silt, brackish and, a few, in nearly fresh water. Small fish remain all year in shallow estuaries, especially those abounding with sea grasses. Large fish spend the warm months in shallow estuaries but move offshore during cold months to spawn. Feed on or near bottom. FISHING METHODS: Bottom fishing from shore or boat. Most are caught incidentally with other bottom fishes. BAITS: Small pieces of cut fish, worm, clams and shrimp. Pinfish are often used as live or dead bait for other fishes.

POMPANO, *Trachinotus carolinus*. This fish is more commonly referred to as the pompano than any of its other Atlantic coast relatives. See permit and palometa. SIZE: To 8 lbs; average 1–2 lbs; over 3 lbs unusual.

HABITS: Schooling and migratory. Pompano are caught within a few miles of the ocean beaches and in bays as well as the connecting inlets. Adults move offshore, some as far as 60 miles, to spawn. They feed on, or a few feet off, sand and mud bottom in water warmer than 65°F. Many die when trapped in water colder than 60°F. FISHING METHODS: Bottom fishing, casting, live-lining, chumming, and jigging from shore; these methods plus trolling from boats. BAITS: Shrimp, sand bugs, cut fish, and clams; also small weighted bucktails, jigs, and feathers.

RED DRUM, *Sciaenops ocellata*. Channel bass, drum, red bass, spot bass, sea bass. Names often vary with size. Fish to 5 lbs called puppy drum or spottail bass, those to 15 or 20 lbs called yearling drum or school bass and reef bass, and those larger than 15 or 20 lbs called bull drum, big reds or channel bass. A powerful foe on lighter tackle, the redfish is once again one of the more popular gamefish. SIZE: Small fish average 2–4 lbs and large fish 15–20 lbs; over 50 lbs unusual. HABITS: Occur in brackish and salt water on mud and sand bottom, especially near shoals and shellfish beds. Small ones occur in shallow estuaries; large ones are around inlets and within 6 miles of the coast. However, during migrations large fish usually travel near the surface between 5 and 20 miles offshore. Although red drum occur offshore during the winter, many remain within 6 miles of the beach and in sounds or bays on sand and sand-shell bottom. During spring migrations, schools occur near the surface along the shore, but usually beyond the breakers; during summer and fall, schools and large solitary fish occur near bottom within the breakers. FISHING METHODS: During spring most are caught by trolling and casting from boats, during summer and fall by bottom fishing and casting from shore and boats. Check state regulations on size and catch limits. BAITS: Jigs, feathers, and weighted bucktails; also soft or shedder crab, shrimp, squid, clams, and cut mullet, spot, herring, or menhaden.

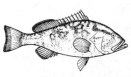

RED GROUPER, *Epinephelus morio*. Grouper. Distinguished from most other groupers by the edge of membranes between the dorsal spines being slightly curved or nearly straight. In most other groupers they are deeply notched. SIZE: To 50 lbs; average 4–6 lbs; over 25 lbs unusual. HABITS: Occur to depths of at least 900 ft sometimes on smooth sand or mud, but most frequently on high relief bottom consisting of rock and coral or wrecks encrusted with living organisms. FISHING METHODS: Bottom fishing from anchored and drifting boats. Some caught by jigging or trolling near bottom. BAITS: Squid, shrimp, crabs, cut fish, and live fish; also weighted bucktails, jigs, and feathers.

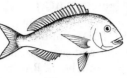

RED PORGY, *Pagrus sedecim*. Pink porgy, rose porgy, strawberry porgy. Miscalled silver snapper and Charleston snapper. SIZE: To over 13 lbs; average 2–5 lbs; over 8 lbs unusual. HABITS: These bottom feeders occur on high relief rock or coral bottom in depths of 30 to 400 ft. FISHING METHODS: Bottom fishing from anchored or drifting boats. BAITS: Cut fish, squid, clams, and worms.

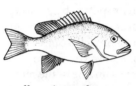

RED SNAPPER, *Lutjanus aya*. Snapper, Daytona red snapper, American red snapper. Common names vary with size. Starting with the smallest size and progressing to the largest, they are called: spot snappers or rats, chicken snappers, snappers, sow snappers, and mules. SIZE: To 40 lbs; average 5–8 lbs; over 25 lbs unusual. HABITS: These bottom feeders aggregate on or a few feet above mud, sand, gravel, coral, or rock bottom to depths of 800 ft or more. They often congregate on high relief rock or coral outcrops encrusted with living organisms. Most occur beyond the 60-ft bottom contour. FISHING METHODS: Bottom fishing from anchored or drifting boats. BAITS: Squid, cut fish, shrimp, and crabs.

ROCK SEA BASS, *Centropristis philadelphica*. Sea bass, blackfish, sand bass. Distinguished from black sea bass by having six or seven broad vertical bars or stripes on back and sides, and a distinct black spot at base of last three dorsal spines. Black sea bass have no vertical bars or stripes and no large distinct spot. SIZE: To 1 lb; over 1 lb unusual. Most anglers make no distinction between rock sea bass and black sea bass. HABITS, FISHING METHODS and BAITS are the same as for black sea bass.

SCUP, *Stenotomus chrysops*. Porgy, sea porgy, southern porgy (formerly considered a separate species, *S. aculeatus*). SIZE: Average ½ to 1 lb; over 1 lb unusual. HABITS: These gregarious fish occur on mud, sand, gravel, coral, or rock bottom and around pilings, wrecks, or rubble in depths of at least 200 ft. Usually near bottom during daylight but move towards mid-depths at night. FISH-

ING METHODS: Bottom fishing, live-lining, and chumming from shore and boats. BAITS: Shrimp, clams, squid, worms, cut fish, and small crabs.

SEA CATFISH, *Galeichthys felis*. Sea cat, catfish. SIZE: To 3 lbs; average ½ to 1 lb; over 1½ lbs unusual. HABITS: These shallow-water shore fish aggregate on any type of bottom. Although small ones occur in both salt and brackish water, large ones are almost always in salt water. More active during night than day. FISHING METHODS: Bottom fishing from shore or boats. Most are caught incidentally while fishing for other species. BAITS: Shrimp, crabs, cut fish, and squid.

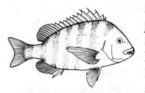

SHEEPSHEAD, *Archosargus probatocephalus*. Sheephead. SIZE: To 30 lbs; average 2–4 lbs; over 10 lbs unusual. HABITS: Aggregate in salt and brackish water on sand, shell, gravel, or rock bottom and around bridge abutments, jetties, breakwaters, rock piles, and wrecks. Feed on or near bottom from a few feet below the tide line to depths of at least 100 ft. FISHING METHODS: Many are caught by bottom fishing and chumming from boats or shore, some by jigging from boats or shore. BAITS: Crabs, clams, shrimp, and sand bugs; also small jigs and weighted bucktails.

SILK SNAPPER, *Lutjanus vivanus*. Snapper, yellow-eyed snapper, silky snapper, golden-eyed snapper, chicken snapper. SIZE: To over 15 lbs; average 1–3 lbs; over 6 lbs unusual. HABITS: These deep-water bottom feeders usually occur in depths of 200 to 800 ft. FISHING METHODS: Bottom fishing from drifting or anchored boats. BAITS: Shrimp, cut fish, squid, and live fish.

SILVER PERCH, *Bairdiella chrysura*. Perch, yellowtail, sand perch. Distinguished from spot by having no dark shoulder spot and a nearly square tail. In contrast, spot have a dark shoulder spot and a slightly forked tail. SIZE: To 1 lb; average ½ lb; over ½ lb unusual. HABITS: Occur in salt and brackish water on mud, sand, shell, and especially on sandy-mud bottom with sea grass. Adults may migrate a short distance offshore during winter, but young fish remain inshore year-round. FISHING METHODS: Bottom fishing from shore; this method plus live-lining and chumming from boats. Usually taken incidentally with other fishes. BAITS: Worms, shrimp, clams, soft crab, and cut fish; also small weighted bucktails.

SILVER SEA TROUT, *Cynoscion nothus*. Trout, silver trout, sand trout. Distinguished from gray sea trout by having a rounded tail and nine (sometimes eight or ten) anal fin rays. Gray sea trout have slightly forked tails, and 11 or 12 anal fin rays. Distinguished from spotted sea trout by having no round, dark spots on the upper half of its body, second dorsal fin, and tail. SIZE: To 2 lbs; average 1–2 lbs; over 1½ lbs unusual. HABITS: Occur in salt and brackish water over any type of bottom to depths of 60 ft. Other habits of silver sea trout are similar to gray sea trout. FISHING METHODS: Bottom fishing, jigging, live-lining, and chumming from boats and shore. BAITS: Shrimp, squid, clams, and cut fish; also small weighted bucktails and jigs.

SKIPJACK TUNA, *Katsuwonus pelamis*. Oceanic bonito, bonito, striped egg. SIZE: To 45 lbs; average 5–9 lbs; over 20 lbs unusual. HABITS: Pelagic, schooling and migratory. These rapid swimmers usually occur near the surface in continental shelf and oceanic water warmer than 63°F but offshore of the 90 ft bottom contour. FISHING METHODS: Most are caught by trolling near the surface 5 to 20 miles from shore. Also caught by casting from boats. BAITS: Feathers, strip bait, feather-strip bait or skirt-strip bait combination, spoons, jigs, and plugs.

SNOOK, *Centropomus undecimalis*. A snook is prized for its delectability as table fare. SIZE: To over 55 lbs; average 3–7 lbs; over 30 lbs unusual. HABITS: Occur throughout the water column in salt, brackish, and fresh water from a few feet below the tide line to depths of 60 ft or more. They often congregate around inlets and passes, favoring those with rock jetties, pilings, and bridge abutments. FISHING METHODS: Most are caught in estuaries and within ¼ mile of the coast by casting, live-lining, and bottom fishing from shore; these methods plus trolling from boats. Check state regulations on size and daily limit. BAITS: Live shrimp, mullet, pinfish, croaker, pigfish, and crabs; also plugs, feathers, spoons, weighted bucktails, jigs, spinners, and streamer flies.

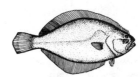

SOUTHERN FLOUNDER, *Paralichthys lethostigma*. Southern fluke, flounder, southern flounder. Distinguished from northern fluke by having 8 to 11, (usually 9 or 10), gill rakers on the lower limb of the first gill arch. In contrast, northern fluke have 13 to 18, (usually 15 or more), gill rakers on the lower limb of the first gill arch. SIZE: To over 13 lbs; average 1–2 lbs; over 6 lbs unusual. HABITS: These bottom feeders live on mud, sand, and sand-shell bottom. They occur in salt and brackish water and often ascend freshwater streams or rivers for a considerable distance. During warm months many occur near the shore in shallow estuaries. During cold months they move into deeper water. FISHING METHODS: Bottom fishing from shore; this method plus chumming, live-lining, and trolling near bottom from boats. Night spearing, called gigging or floundering, is commonly done either while wading or from boats. Check state regulations on size limit. BAITS: Killifish, squid, mullet, clams, worms, and cut fish. A few are caught on jigs, spinners, and weighted bucktails.

SOUTHERN KINGFISH, *Menticirrhus americanus*. Whiting, king whiting, bullhead whiting, round-head, kingfish, Carolina whiting. Miscalled sea mullet, Virginia mullet, mullet. See Gulf kingfish and northern kingfish. SIZE: To 3 lbs; average 1–2 lbs; over 1 lb unusual. HABITS: These bottom feeders aggregate on any type of bottom but adults favor sand or sand-shell along the beaches and around the mouths of sounds. Most occur in salt and brackish water warmer than 50°F, from the tide line to depths of 40 ft, some to 180 ft in the ocean. FISHING METHODS: Bottom fishing, chumming, and jigging from shore and anchored or drifting boats. BAITS: Shrimp, worms, cut fish, squid, clams, mussels, silversides, and small crabs; also small jigs and weighted bucktails.

SPANISH MACKEREL, *Scomberomorus maculatus*. Mackerel. Distinguished from king mackerel by the scaleless pectoral fins and the lateral line sloping downward gradually under the second dorsal fin. King mackerel have scaled pectoral fins and the lateral line dips downward abruptly under the second dorsal fin. Spanish mackerel frequently swim among kingfish schools. See cero mackerel. SIZE: To 12 lbs; average 1–2 lbs; over 5 lbs unusual. HABITS: Pelagic and schooling. Occur throughout the water column to depths of 80 ft in water warmer than 67°F. Spanish mackerel will pursue bait-fish through inlets into estuaries. FISHING METH-

ODS: Casting, live-lining, bottom fishing, jigging, and chumming from shore; these methods plus trolling from boats. Most fish are caught within 2 miles of the beach and in or around inlets. Check state regulations on size limit. BAITS: Spoons, feathers, strip bait, weighted bucktails, plugs and jigs; also live shrimp or live fish and cut fish.

SPECKLED HIND, *Epinephelus drummondhayi*. Grouper, Kitty Mitchell. Distinguished from other groupers by being dark red or yellow-brown, densely covered with small white spots, and by the edge of the tail being nearly straight. SIZE: To 50 lbs; average 6–10 lbs; over 30 lbs unusual. HABITS: These bottom dwellers occur on rock or coral bottom and around wrecks to depths of 300 ft or more. FISHING METHODS: Bottom fishing from anchored or drifting boats. BAITS: Cut or whole fish, squid, and shrimp.

SPOT, *Leiostomus xanthurus*. Small fish taken in the spring called white-eyes; large fish taken in the fall called yellowfins. See silver perch. SIZE: To 2 lbs; over 1 lb unusual. HABITS: These gregarious bottom feeders occur on mud, sand, or sand-shell bottom in salt and brackish water; a few in fresh water. Spawned offshore in depths to 500 ft, the young move inshore and spend their first year of life in shallow estuaries. As they get older, they migrate offshore during fall and inshore during spring. FISHING METHODS: Bottom fishing from shore; this method plus chumming from boats. BAITS: Shrimp, worms, clams, soft crab, and cut fish.

SPOTTED SEA TROUT, *Cynoscion nebulosus*. Speckled trout, winter trout, trout. Fish less than 1 lb called school or pan trout, large ones called gator trout, winter trout. It is probably the most sought-after fish in the Gulf of Mexico because of its easy accessibility to a majority of Gulf Coast anglers. This member of the weakfish family can be caught from bridges, piers, shorelines, seawalls, and beaches, as well as by small boaters fishing in bays, rivers, and inlets everywhere. See gray sea trout and silver sea trout. SIZE: Average 1–2 lbs; over 6 lbs unusual. HABITS: Occur in salt and brackish water, particularly the shallow water of estuaries and along ocean beaches. Although favoring sandy areas, especially around sea grass beds, they occur over any type of bottom in water warmer than 50°–54°F. FISHING METHODS: Casting, bottom fishing, jigging, chumming, and live-lining from shore; these methods

plus trolling from boats. In North Carolina, most are caught along the ocean beaches and in inlets. In South Carolina, they are caught both along the ocean beaches and in estuaries. BAITS: Plugs, weighted bucktails, jigs, and spoons; also shrimp, silversides, mullet, killifish, and soft or shedder crab.

STRIPED BASS, *Morone saxatilis*. Rock, rockfish. SIZE: Average 1–2 lbs; over 25 lbs unusual. HABITS: Anadromous. North of Core Banks, North Carolina, adults are migratory and occur in fresh, brackish, and salt water. South of Core Banks, striped bass are resident and occur in fresh and brackish water, seldom in salt water. They occur throughout the water column over any type of bottom. FISHING METHODS: Casting, jigging, and live-lining from shore; these methods plus trolling from boats. BAITS: Weighted bucktails, jigs, plugs, and spoons; also worms, shrimp, cut fish, pork rind, and live fish.

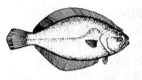

SUMMER FLOUNDER, *Paralichthys dentatus*, northern fluke, flounder, summer flounder. See southern fluke. SIZE: Average 1–3 lbs; over 12 lbs unusual. HABITS: Found in shallow bays, flats, estuaries, and passes during the cooler months, and in deeper passes and along rock jetties in the summer. Flounder make excellent mealtime entrees and will hit all types of small natural baits, bucktails, and jigs with enthusiasm. Live on mud, sand, sand-shell, or gravel bottom and around wrecks. Although most occur in salt and brackish water, some ascend fresh water streams. During warm months they usually occur within bays and sounds in depths of 40 ft or less; during cold months they retreat to deeper ocean water, some to depths of 150 ft or more. They usually feed near bottom but will pursue prey to the surface. FISHING METHODS: Bottom fishing from shore; this method plus chumming, live-lining, and trolling near bottom from boats. Night spearing, called gigging or floundering, is a common practice, done either while wading or from boats. BAITS: Killifish, squid, silversides, clams, worms, and cut fish; also spinners, jigs, and weighted bucktails.

SWORDFISH, *Xiphias gladius*. Broadbill swordfish. SIZE: Average 125–225 lbs; over 300 lbs unusual. HABITS: Pelagic and migratory. Occur in oceanic and continental shelf water from the surface to depths of 2,100 ft or more. They often congregate over high relief rock and coral outcrops beyond the 600-ft bottom contour. FISHING METHODS: Most are caught incidentally while fishing for groupers or snappers. A few are caught while surface trolling and live-lining. BAITS: Live grouper or snapper and whole squid, Spanish mackerel, or eel.

TARPON, *Megalops atlanticus*. Silver king, sprat. Anything you've ever heard about the magnificent fighting qualities of the silver king is probably true. SIZE: To over 350 lbs; average 20–50 lbs; over 150 lbs unusual. HABITS: Pelagic and migratory. Occur over any type of bottom in salt and brackish water, sometimes in fresh water. Although during migrations some are 10 miles or more offshore, they usually occur in estuaries, inlets, and within 3 miles of ocean beaches. Tarpon feed mainly at night in water warmer than 66°F. FISHING METHODS: Live-lining, chumming, and casting from shore; these methods plus trolling from boats. BAITS: Live mullet, spot, pinfish, croaker, kingfish, shrimp, crabs, squid, and cut fish; also spoons, plugs, weighted bucktails, and bucktail flies.

TILEFISH, *Lopholatilus chamaeleonticeps*. Colorful tilefish. Distinguished from the blackline tilefish by having a fleshy, finlike flap in front of the dorsal fin. Blackline tilefish lack this flap. SIZE: To 50 lbs; average 8–15 lbs; over 30 lbs unusual. HABITS, FISHING METHODS and BAITS are the same as for blackline tilefish.

TRIPLETAIL, *Lobotes surinamensis*. SIZE: To over 30 lbs; average 4–8 lbs; over 20 lbs unusual. HABITS: Occur from the surface to the bottom in depths of a few to 200 ft or more. These fish usually occur singly or in small groups. Small ones enter inlets and estuaries; large ones tend to remain in the ocean. Tripletail frequent buoys, floating debris, wrecks, and underwater obstructions. FISHING METHODS: Bottom fishing, jigging, casting, and live-lining from boats; a few are taken by these methods from shore. BAITS: Shrimp, cut fish, clams, crabs, squid, and live fish; also weighted bucktails, jigs, and plugs.

VERMILION SNAPPER, *Rhomboplite aurorubens*. Snapper, beeline snapper, California red snapper. SIZE: To over 9 lbs; average 1–3 lbs; over 5 lbs unusual. HABITS: These bottom feeders aggregate on mud, sand, gravel, coral, or rock bottom in depths of 90 to 350 ft. They often concentrate on high relief rock or

coral outcrops and wrecks, especially if encrusted with living organisms. FISHING METHODS: Bottom fishing from anchored or drifting boats. BAITS: Squid, cut fish, shrimp, and clams.

WAHOO, *Acanthocybium solanderi*. The movable upper jaw, large number of dorsal fin spines (21–27) and the slightly forked tail distinguish the wahoo from other mackerels. SIZE: To over 150 lbs; average 20–30 lbs; over 75 lbs unusual. HABITS: Pelagic and migratory. These rapid swimmers occur in oceanic and continental shelf water beyond the 100-ft bottom contour. They usually swim in small groups or singly, and they often concentrate over high relief rock or coral bottom and wrecks. FISHING METHODS: Trolling and live-lining from boats. Never abundant, wahoo are taken incidentally with other pelagic fishes. BAITS: Whole rigged Spanish mackerel, squid, mullet, and ballyhoo, or live fish; also spoons, feathers, and strip bait.

WARSAW GROUPER, *Epinephelus nigritus*. Grouper, black jewfish. Miscalled jewfish and black grouper. Distinguished from most other groupers by 10 dorsal spines (instead of 11) and the end of the tail having a nearly straight edge. SIZE: To 500 lbs; average 20–30 lbs; over 300 lbs unusual. HABITS: Occur to depths of 400 ft or more, especially on high relief bottom consisting of rock, coral, or wrecks encrusted with living organisms. Although usually near bottom, they may occur halfway to the surface. FISHING METHODS: Bottom fishing, jigging, or deep trolling from boats. BAITS: Squid, cut fish, shrimp, clams, crabs, and live fish; also spoons, feathers, and plugs.

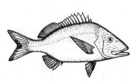

WHITE GRUNT, *Haemulon plumieri*. Grunt, common grunt, red-mouthed grunt. Distinguished from pigfish by its large mouth having an orange-red lining and by its body scales above the lateral line which are larger than those below this line. In contrast, pigfish have small mouths with no bright color inside, and their body scales above the lateral line are about the same size as those below. SIZE: To 4 lbs; average 1 lb; over 2 lbs unusual. HABITS: Occur in salt and brackish water on mud, sand, rock, or coral bottom and around wrecks, piers, jetties, or bridge abutments. Although common in estuaries, inlets, and along the beach, they occur offshore in depths of 100 ft or more. They usually feed within a few feet of bottom. FISHING METHODS: Bottom fishing and jigging from shore or boats. BAITS: Shrimp, crabs, worms, clams, and cut fish; also small weighted bucktails and jigs.

WHITE MARLIN, *Tetrapturus albidus*. Distinguished from blue marlin by having the tips of the dorsal and anal fins rounded, as well as a conspicuous lateral line. In the blue marlin the tips of the dorsal and anal fins are pointed and, except in very small fish, the lateral line is inconspicuous. SIZE: To over 161 lbs; average 40–60 lbs; over 90 lbs unusual. HABITS: Pelagic and migratory. Occur in oceanic and continental shelf water but, during warm months, some come close to shore into depths as shallow as 60 ft. Travel in small groups or singly. Most are taken near the surface in water warmer than 70°F between the 100- and 600-ft bottom contours. FISHING METHODS: Trolling and live-lining from boats. BAITS: Strip bait, feather-strip bait or skirt-strip bait combination, and whole rigged eel, squid, ballyhoo, mullet, or Spanish mackerel; also live bait. Some caught on feathers, skirts, and plugs.

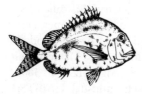

WHITEBONE PORGY, *Calamus leucosteus*. Porgy. Miscalled silver snapper. SIZE: To over 5 lbs; average ½ to 1 lb; over 3½ lbs unusual. HABITS: These bottom feeders occur on mud, sand, and rock bottom, especially those with high relief, and around wrecks in depths of 30 to 300 ft. Small ones sometimes found inshore of the 30-foot contour. FISHING METHODS: Bottom fishing from anchored or drifting boats. Most are caught in depths of 90 to 150 ft. BAITS: Shrimp, cut fish, squid, and clams.

YELLOWTAIL SNAPPER, *Ocyurus chrysurus*. Yellowtail. SIZE: To 6 lbs; average 1–2 lbs; over 3 lbs unusual. HABITS: These schooling fish occur in mid-water from a few feet below the tide line to depths of 150 ft or more. Although in the Keys they sometimes occur in the backcountry on shallow flats, most remain over ocean reefs. FISHING METHODS: Live-lining, chumming, casting, and jigging from boats. Some are caught by these methods from shore or by trolling from boats. Most are caught by chumming and live-lining at night. BAITS: Shrimp, crabs, and cut fish; also small jigs, weighted bucktails, and plugs.

AN ANGLER'S GUIDE TO SHARKS

After years of being considered something of a second-class gamefish, sharks have attracted the attention of anglers looking for good sport, tough fights, and the thrills that come with gaffing a thrashing catch you've just pulled alongside. Few gamefish can equal the spectacular leaps and swift runs of the mako, and many other shark species are recognized and appreciated for their own special challenges.

Only a few individuals of even the most vicious species of shark ever pursue and attack man, but there is little doubt that all sharks will defend themselves when molested. Not only their teeth, but their rough hides and powerful tails can inflict painful wounds. The fisherman or swimmer who carelessly handles, spears, or otherwise provokes a shark invites injury.

All sharks found off the eastern U.S. are edible. Small sharks and any shark not intended for the dinner table should be tagged and released. According to biologists, makos under 300 pounds are probably immature fish and have not yet spawned.

HOW TO IDENTIFY A SHARK

It is difficult to identify the various species of sharks that inhabit Atlantic coastal waters, and that's where this guide comes in.

The first step is to establish that the fish is in fact a shark. A shark has:

- 5 to 7 paired gill openings located at least partly on the side of the head
- a skeleton composed entirely of cartilage
- jaws, teeth, and paired fins
- a body shape that is typically torpedolike (with the exception of the flattened angel shark)
- a skin, because it's covered with minute toothlike scales similar to the texture of sandpaper.

These features help distinguish sharks

- from lampreys, which lack paired fins and true jaws
- from skates and rays, in which the body is flattened and the gill openings are entirely on the undersurface of the body
- from bony fishes, which have only one pair of gill openings
- from whales and porpoises, which lack gills and scales.

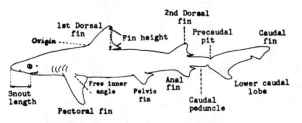

General identifying characteristics of a shark.

Once you're sure that the fish is a shark, the next step is to see how it differs from other sharks. Sharks are distinguished by shape, by size, and often by the presence or absence of the anatomical features shown in the following illustrations. The position and relative size of fins, gill openings, and eyes are important. Each illustration is accompanied by a description that emphasizes these characteristics; an outline drawing of each species is shown on a grid background. It's important to note that the grid divisions show *percentage of total length*, not actual measurements. For example, the drawing of the spiny dogfish shows that its tail is generally about 20 percent of its total length. But a spiny dogfish might be about 4 feet long, while the Greenland shark pictured just above it might be more than 20 feet long.

Species that might cause confusion are shown together to point out differences. To identify your specimen, find an illustration that it resembles, read the distinguishing characteristics, and make your identification. It's important to note that the drawings show only typical examples of each species; an individual shark will not look exactly like the drawing since body proportions vary with size.

A more dependable method is to use the Identification Key that follows on page 206. This key offers a series of alternative descriptions that leads, by successive choices, to the correct identification.

See the following pages for shark descriptions.

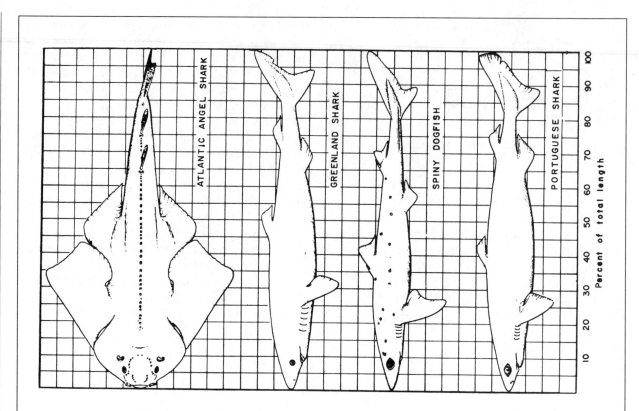

Atlantic Angel Shark—*Squatina dumerili*

Distinctive characters: The flattened, skate-like appearance separates this from all other sharks in our area. Distinguished from skates and rays by its sharp teeth and the fact that its gill slits are partly on the side of the body.
Color: Gray above, tinted with red on head and fin margins; white below.
Maximum size: 4 to 5 feet. **Size at birth:** Unknown.
Range: New England to Jamaica.
Remarks: Found in depths of a few feet to several hundred fathoms. Feeds on flatfish, skate, crustaceans, and snails. Most common in summer along middle Atlantic coast (North Carolina to Delaware) but seldom abundant anywhere within its range.

Greenland Shark—*Somniosus microcephalus*

Distinctive characters: Lacks anal fin. The absence of dorsal spines sets this species apart from the next two.
Color: Brown to gray to black below and above; the back and sides sometimes with indistinct dark bands or whitish spots.
Maximum size: 21 feet. **Size at birth:** Unknown.
Range: Both sides of the Atlantic in arctic and subarctic waters; found south to Cape Cod.
Remarks: A cold-water species abundant along the Greenland and Labrador coasts, occurring in New England waters only as a stray. Seldom taken in waters warmer than 50°F. It feeds on a wide variety of fishes, seals, and carrion.

Spiny Dogfish—*Squalus acanthias*

Distinctive characters: Lacks anal fin. Distinguished from the Greenland shark by the presence of dorsal spines, and from the Portuguese shark by the position of the pelvic fins in relation to the second dorsal.
Color: Slate colored above, pale gray to white below; young specimens with white spots scattered on body.
Maximum size: 4 feet. **Size at birth:** 6½ to 13 inches.
Range: Worldwide in temperate and subarctic latitudes.
Remarks: One of our most common sharks found inshore and to depths up to 100 fathoms. It feeds on smaller fishes, squid, worms, shrimps, and jellyfish. The spines are mildly poisonous.

Portuguese Shark—*Centroscymnus coelolepis*

Distinctive characters: Lacks anal fin. Distinguished from the Greenland shark by the presence of dorsal spines, and from the spiny dogfish by the position of the pelvic fins in relation to the second dorsal.
Color: Dark brown above and below.
Maximum size: 3 feet 8 inches. **Size at birth:** About 9 inches.
Range: Both sides of the North Atlantic; reported as far north as Grand Banks in the western Atlantic. Southern limit of distribution unknown.
Remarks: Evidently a deep-water species as it has not been reported from waters less than 180 fathoms. Little is known of its habits.

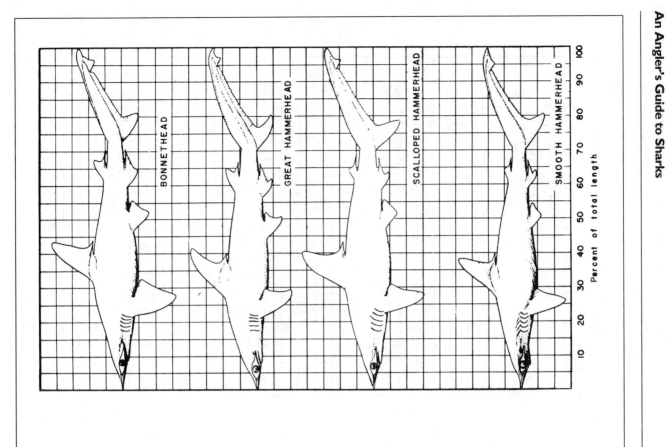

Percent of total length

BONNETHEAD

GREAT HAMMERHEAD

SCALLOPED HAMMERHEAD

SMOOTH HAMMERHEAD

Bonnethead (Shovelhead)—*Sphyrna tiburo*

Distinctive characters: Differs from other hammerheads in having a shovel- (not hammer-) shaped head.

Color: Gray or grayish brown above, paler below; no fin markings.

Maximum size: 6 feet. **Size at birth:** About 12 inches.

Range: Abundant in tropical and subtropical Atlantic. Found regularly as far north as North Carolina, and as a stray to southern New England.

Remarks: Occurs chiefly in shallow water, often in bays and estuaries. It feeds largely on crabs, shrimps, and small fish.

Great Hammerhead—*Sphyrna mokarran*

Distinctive characters: Head indented at midline as in *Sphyrna lewini* (see below), but the corners of the mouth are about opposite the rear margin of the head; both upper and lower teeth are serrated (saw-edged).

Color: Small specimens brownish gray above and paler below. The dorsals, both caudal lobes, and upper surfaces of the pectorals are dusky toward the tips. Larger specimens are dark olive above and pale olive below.

Maximum size: 15 feet. **Size at birth:** About 28 inches.

Range: Possibly worldwide in tropical and subtropical seas. Details of distribution in Atlantic unknown; reported as far north as North Carolina.

Remarks: Most specimens recorded offshore. Nothing is known of its diet.

Scalloped Hammerhead—*Sphyrna lewini*

Distinctive characters: Head indented at midline as in the great hammerhead, but the teeth are smooth-edged and the corners of the mouth are behind the rear margin of the head (see above). In the smooth hammerhead (see below) the midline of the head is rounded.

Color: Light gray above shading to white below, the pectorals tipped on their lower surfaces with black.

Maximum size: 13 feet. **Size at birth:** About 17 inches.

Range: Tropical and warm-temperate Atlantic. Not uncommon in New Jersey waters during the warmer months.

Remarks: This shark is found both inshore and offshore, where it feeds largely on stingrays, skates, and other bottom fishes.

Smooth Hammerhead—*Sphyrna zygaena*

Distinctive characters: Head rounded at midline; teeth of young are smooth-edged, but may become slightly saw-edged in adults. The rear tip of the second dorsal is farther from the base of the tail when compared with the hammerhead (*lewini*) above.

Color: Deep olive or brownish gray above, paler on sides, grayish white below; fins of same color as back with tips dusky.

Maximum size: 14 feet. **Size at birth:** About 20 inches.

Range: Tropical to warm-temperate belts of Atlantic; north commonly to southern New England and as stray to Massachusetts Bay.

Remarks: Occurs far out at sea as well as close inshore. Its diet consists of stingrays, smaller sharks, shrimp, crabs, and squid.

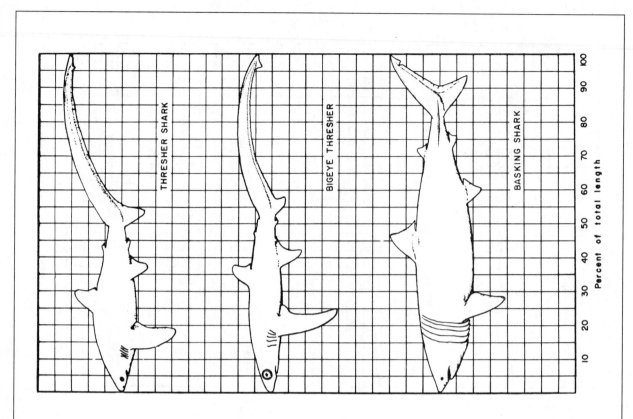

THRESHER SHARK

BIGEYE THRESHER

BASKING SHARK

Percent of total length

Thresher Shark—*Alopias vulpinus*

Distinctive characters: The enormously elongated tail sets the thresher apart from all other Atlantic sharks, except for its close relative, the bigeye thresher (see below).

Color: Back and upper sides vary from brown, through shades of gray to nearly black, becoming white below; lower surface of snout in front of nostrils and the lower surface of pectorals may be of same hue as upper sides.

Maximum size: 20 feet. **Size at birth:** 30 to 49 inches.

Range: In warm temperate and subtropical latitudes. Reported more frequently from southern New England than elsewhere along our east coast.

Remarks: Pelagic species, most often seen at least a few miles offshore. It feeds most commonly on mackerel, bluefish, shad, menhaden, herring, bonito, and squid. Uses tail to group schooling fishes in a tight circle during feeding.

Bigeye Thresher—*Alopias superciliosus*

Distinctive characters: Set apart from *A. vulpinus* (above) by its much larger eyes, longer snout, first dorsal being closer to the base of the tail, and in having only 10 or 11 teeth on a side in each of its jaws (about 20 in *vulpinus*).

Color: Dark gray or brown above, back and upper sides gray or brown; freshly caught specimens may show blue-green iridescence on upper surface of head and body. Rear margin of first dorsal, pectorals, and pelvics dusky.

Maximum size: 18 feet. **Size at birth:** 30 to 43 inches.

Range: Only a few specimens recorded; occurs in both tropical and temperate waters.

Remarks: Extremely large eyes suggest that it is chiefly a deep-water species, but specimens have been seen or caught near the surface. Squid and pelagic fishes are included in its diet. Little is known of the habits of this uncommon shark.

Basking Shark—*Cetorhinus maximus*

Distinctive characters: The combination of a crescent-shaped tail, enormously long gill openings, long gill rakers, and numerous minute teeth sets the basking shark apart from all others.

Color: Grayish brown to slaty gray or nearly black above; underside may be same color or lighter than the back, sometimes with a triangular white patch under the snout and two pale bands on the belly.

Maximum size: 45 feet. **Size at birth:** 5 to 6 feet.

Range: Has been reported in the Gulf of Maine and off northeastern shores. Only one report farther south than North Carolina. In the past, there have been numerous reports of basking sharks off Massachusetts and on occasion off New York and New Jersey.

Remarks: Basking sharks often gather in schools and swim sluggishly near the surface. In the winter it is assumed they retire to deeper water. Their diet consists of plankton which they sift out of the water by means of their gill rakers.

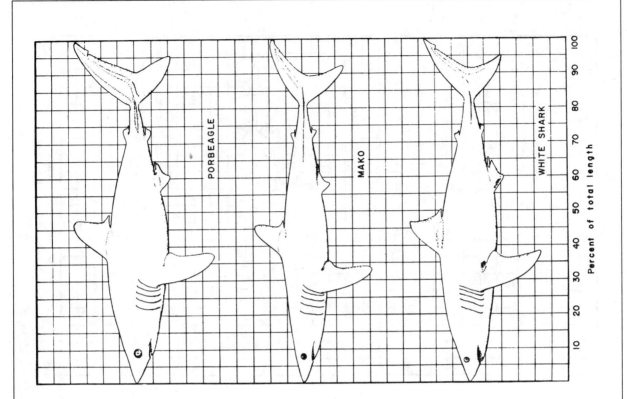

PORBEAGLE

MAKO

WHITE SHARK

Percent of total length

Porbeagle (Mackerel Shark)—*Lamna nasus*

Distinctive characters: Flattened caudal peduncle and crescent-shaped tail. Easily separable from the mako and the white shark by its teeth and by the presence of 2 keels on the caudal fin.

Color: Dark bluish gray above, changing abruptly on the lower sides to white; pectoral fins are dusky on outer half or third, the anal fin white or slightly dusky.

Maximum size: 10 feet. **Size at birth:** About 29 inches.

Range: Northern Atlantic, perhaps as far south as South Carolina.

Remarks: Found inshore as well as offshore, but more abundant in deeper water (40 to 70 fathoms). The porbeagle preys largely on schools of mackerel, herring, and pilchards, following their migrations; also on such groundfish as cod, hake, cusk, flounders, and squid.

Mako—*Isurus oxyrinchus*

Distinctive characters: Flattened caudal peduncle and crescent-shaped tail. The mako is separable from both the porbeagle and the white shark by its teeth and more slender form; also by the relative position of the second dorsal and anal fins.

Color: Deep blue-gray above when fresh caught, but appearing cobalt or ultramarine blue in the water; snow-white below; dirty gray on the lower surface of the pectoral fins.

Maximum size: 12 feet. **Size at birth:** Unknown.

Range: An oceanic species of the tropical and warm-temperate Atlantic; Gulf of Maine to Brazil.

Remarks: Strong-swimming, pelagic shark, known to leap from the water under natural conditions and when hooked. It is a fisheater, preying upon schools of mackerel, herring, and squid. It is considered to be the only natural enemy of the broadbill swordfish.

White Shark—*Carcharodon carcharias*

Distinctive characters: Flattened caudal peduncle and crescent-shaped tail. The large, triangular, saw-edged teeth and more rearward position of the anal fin (relative to the second dorsal fin) separate the white shark from the porbeagle and the mako.

Color: Slaty brown, dull slate blue, leaden gray, or even almost black above, shading to dirty white below; may have a black spot in the axil of the pectoral; the dorsals and caudal darker along rear edges.

Maximum size: 36½ feet. **Size at birth:** About 50 inches.

Range: Widespread in tropical, subtropical, and warm-temperate belts of all the oceans.

Remarks: Occurs both inshore and offshore. The white shark feeds often on large prey which it devours practically intact, as illustrated by the presence of other sharks (4 to 7 feet), as well as sea lions, seals, sturgeons, and tuna in the stomachs of some specimens. The white shark is credited with numerous attacks on man in tropical and temperate waters the world over and has thus been given the name "maneater."

Note: 1st upper and lower tooth of each jaw illustrated above.

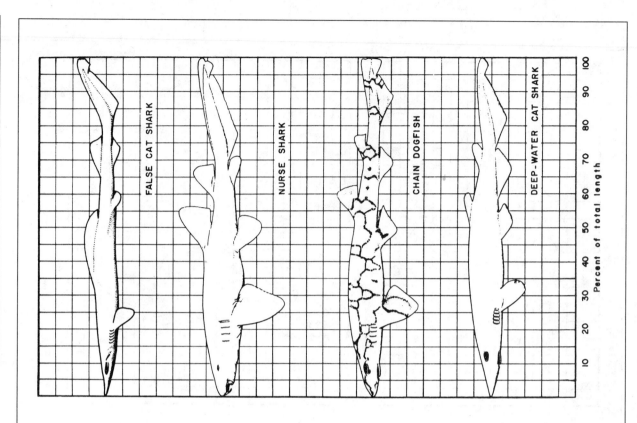

FALSE CAT SHARK

NURSE SHARK

CHAIN DOGFISH

DEEP-WATER CAT SHARK

Percent of total length

False Cat Shark—*Pseudotriakis microdon*

Distinctive characters: Separable from all other Atlantic sharks by the great length of its first dorsal fin.

Color: Uniformly dark brownish gray; darkest on the front margins of fins.

Maximum size: At least 9 feet 8 inches. **Size at birth:** Little known; one female contained embryos 2 feet 9 inches long.

Range: Both sides of the Atlantic, but rarely taken anywhere. Specimens reported from Spain, Portugal, Iceland, New York, and New Jersey.

Remarks: One of the larger deep-water sharks. Most captures have been made in depths of 164 to 807 fathoms, but two specimens (New York and New Jersey) were taken in shallow water. Little is known about its food, size at maturity, or habits.

Nurse Shark—*Ginglymostoma cirratum*

Distinctive characters: Set apart from all other sharks of the western Atlantic by the long barbel on the margin of each nostril and the deep groove connecting the nostril with the mouth.

Color: Yellowish to grayish brown, darker above than below. Small specimens may have dark spots on body or brown crossbars on the fins; adults may or may not retain these markings.

Maximum size: 14 feet. **Size at birth:** About 11 inches.

Range: Common in Caribbean and southern Florida with migrations to North Carolina. Occurs as stray to Rhode Island.

Remarks: Appears chiefly inshore, often in water as shallow as 2 to 10 feet. Sometimes travels in schools and feeds mainly on shrimps, squids, crabs, and small fish.

Chain Dogfish—*Scyliorhinus retifer*

Distinctive characters: Most obviously separated from other sharks by its chainlike color pattern.

Color: Dark reddish brown above, yellowish below, with a very characteristic pattern of sooty black stripes which branch out to form irregularly shaped polygons.

Maximum size: 2½ feet. **Size at birth:** 2 to 3 inches.

Range: Offshore (40 to 125 fathoms) from New York to North Carolina.

Remarks: Lives close to bottom on outer part of the Continental Shelf; seldom if ever strays into shoal water. This is the only common shark on the middle Atlantic Coast which lays eggs; they are described as amber colored, about 2 inches long, ¾ inch wide, with a long tendril at each corner. Little is known of its life history and diet.

Deep-Water Cat Shark—*Apristurus profundorum*

Distinctive characters: Size and position of dorsal fins, large anal fin, and presence of gill rakers protruding from rounded gill openings separate this unusual shark from all other sharks of this region.

Color: Grayish brown above and below.

Maximum size: Unknown; largest specimen measured about 20 inches.

Size at birth: Unknown.

Range: Definitely known only from Continental Shelf off Delaware Bay.

Remarks: Little is known of the habits of this rare species, but the uniform coloration above and below suggest a deep-sea habitat.

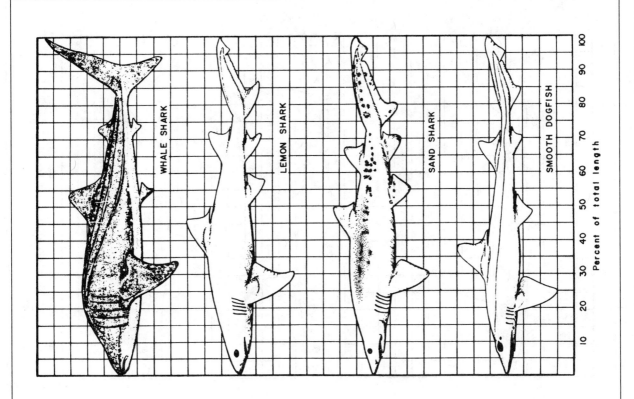

WHALE SHARK

LEMON SHARK

SAND SHARK

SMOOTH DOGFISH

Percent of total length

Whale Shark—*Rhincodon typus*

Distinctive characters: Unique because of its great size and spotted color pattern; its mouth is at tip of snout; prominent ridges on the sides of the body.
Color: Dark gray to reddish or greenish brown and sides; marked with round white or yellow spots and a number of white or yellow transverse bars; white or yellow below.
Maximum size: 45 feet. **Size at birth:** Unknown.
Range: All tropical oceans; reported as far north as Long Island.
Remarks: This offshore species is the largest living fish known to man. It does not bear its young alive, but deposits egg capsules. Its diet is composed mainly of plankton and small fishes.

Lemon Shark—*Negaprion brevirostris*

Distinctive characters: Both dorsal fins triangular and of nearly the same size; distinguished from the sand shark by its blunt snout and by the position and shape of its anal fin, and from the smooth dogfish by its sharp teeth.
Color: Yellowish brown to bluish gray above; white to yellowish below.
Maximum size: About 11 feet. **Size at birth:** About 25 inches.
Range: Occurs regularly from Brazil to North Carolina and as a stray to New Jersey.
Remarks: The diet of this inshore species is not well known; it probably feeds on skates, rays, and a variety of small fishes.

Sand Shark—*Carcharias taurus*

Distinctive characters: Both dorsal fins triangular and of nearly the same size as in the lemon shark (see above) and in the smooth dogfish (see below); easily distinguished from the lemon shark by its more pointed snout, and from the smooth dogfish by its sharp, pointed teeth and more rearward position of the first dorsal fin.
Color: Gray-brown above becoming grayish white below; in some specimens darker spots cover the posterior section of the trunk.
Maximum size: 10 feet 5 inches. **Size at birth:** About 36 inches.
Range: Gulf of Maine to Florida.
Remarks: One of our most common large sharks during the summer months. The diet of this inshore species includes black drum, bluefish, butterfish, eels, flatfishes, menhaden, and others; reported to travel in schools and surround other fishes.

Smooth Dogfish—*Mustelus canis*

Distinctive characters: Both dorsal fins triangular and of nearly the same size. Separated from the lemon and sand sharks (see above) by the position of the first dorsal fin, and from all sharks in this region by its minute, flat, pavementlike teeth. Sometimes confused with the spiny dogfish (see p. 8) from which it is distinguished by the presence of an anal fin and the absence of dorsal spines.
Color: Gray to brown above and grayish white below.
Maximum size: 5 feet. **Size at birth:** About 13 inches.
Range: Cape Cod as far south as Uruguay.
Remarks: One of our most abundant sharks. Preys primarily on crabs, but also on lobsters and small fishes.

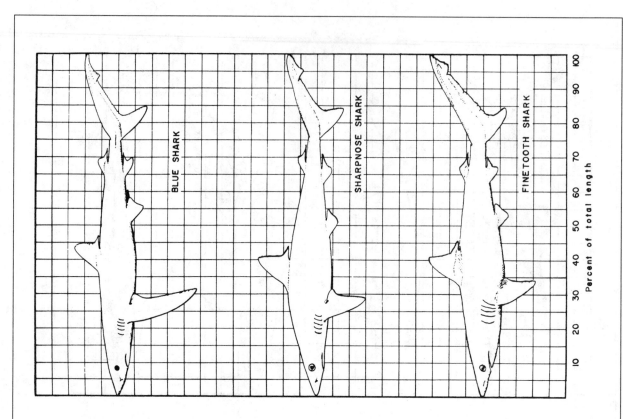

Blue Shark—*Prionace glauca*

Distinctive characters: Distinguished from other western Atlantic sharks by the combination of a long pointed snout, a long sickle-shaped pectoral fin, and its blue color.

Color: Blue on upper surface, shading to pure white below.

Maximum size: 12 feet 7 inches. **Size at birth:** About 21 inches.

Range: Worldwide in tropical and temperate seas; common along the northeastern United States during warmer months.

Remarks: Reputedly the most numerous of the large oceanic sharks; it is the one with which sperm whalers were most familiar, and the one around which many superstitions about sharks have developed. Its diet includes herring, mackerel, other small fishes, squid, and garbage.

Atlantic Sharpnose Shark—*Scoliodon terraenovae*

Distinctive characters: Distinguished by its smooth-edged, curved teeth which are similar in both jaws; also by the presence of well-developed labial furrows around corners of the mouth. Differs from the closely related finetooth shark (see below) by its teeth and by the origin of the second dorsal fin which is located over the MIDDLE of the anal fin.

Color: Brownish to olive gray above; white below.

Maximum size: 3 feet. **Size at birth:** 10¼ to 16 inches.

Range: Found on both sides of tropical and subtropical Atlantic. Occasionally strays northward to Canada, but it is uncommon north of the Carolinas.

Remarks: This is a shallow-water species that feeds on small fishes, shrimps, and mollusks.

Finetooth Shark—*Aprionodon isodon*

Distinctive characters: Distinguished by its smooth-edged straight teeth which are similar in both jaws; also by the presence of well-developed labial furrows around corners of the mouth. Differs from the sharpnose shark (see above) by the origin of the second dorsal fin which is located over the ORIGIN of the anal fin.

Color: Bluish gray above, shading to gray on sides; white below.

Maximum size: 4 feet or more. **Size at birth:** Unknown.

Range: Tropical species, the majority having been recorded from Florida and the coasts of the Gulf of Mexico. Occasionally strays northward along the east coast of the United States during summer months.

Remarks: Apparently an inshore species which feeds on a variety of small fishes.

Note: Fourth upper and lower tooth of each jaw illustrated above.

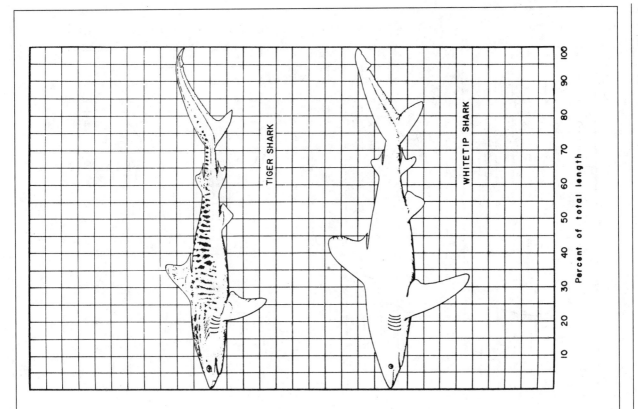

TIGER SHARK

WHITETIP SHARK

Percent of total length

Tiger Shark—*Galeocerdo cuvieri*

Distinctive characters: A low lateral ridge on each side of the caudal peduncle; the short blunt snout and the distinct notch in the rear margin of the teeth distinguish this shark from all others.

Color: Gray or grayish brown, darker above than on sides and belly; small specimens up to about 5 or 6 feet long are marked on back with darker spots, often fusing irregularly into oblique bars on sides and fins. Markings may fade with growth.

Maximum size: 30 feet. **Size at birth:** About 19 inches.

Range: Worldwide in tropical and subtropical seas; not uncommon along New Jersey coasts during warmer months.

Remarks: Occasionally taken far out at sea but more often in coastal waters. Stomach contents of tiger sharks have included squids, horseshoe crabs, stingrays, sharks, and many other fishes, turtles, birds, sea lions, and a remarkable assortment of such garbage as carrion, lumps of coal, tin cans, boards, and empty sacks.

Whitetip Shark—*Pterolamiops longimanus*

Distinctive characters: Set apart from similar species by the broadly rounded first dorsal fin, short snout, white-tipped fins, and rear tip of the anal fin reaching nearly to the lower precaudal pit.

Color: Varying from grayish brown to light gray or pale brown above, and yellowish or dirty white below. In adults the dorsal and pectoral fins are often, but not always, white-tipped. Black-tipped fins are reported on embryos and young specimens.

Maximum size: 12 to 13 feet. **Size at birth:** About 27 inches.

Range: Tropical and subtropical Atlantic, occasionally to Cape Cod.

Remarks: A pelagic species usually found near the surface in offshore waters where the depth exceeds 100 fathoms. Its diet includes squids, dolphin, mackerels, other small schooling fishes, and garbage.

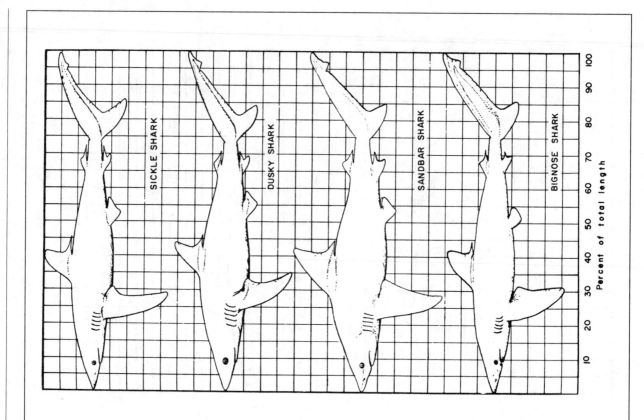

Sickle Shark—*Carcharhinus falciformis*

Distinctive characters: Distinct ridge along back between dorsal fins as in the sharks below, but separable from similar ridged-back species by the longer pelvic fins and the longer free tip of its second dorsal fin. Also, the sickle shark has a smaller eye than the dusky shark, and its first dorsal fin is not as high as in the sandbar shark and is placed farther back.
Color: Black to gray above, grayish white below.
Maximum size: 10 feet. **Size at birth:** Unknown.
Range: Common in the tropical belt of the western North Atlantic; strays northward to Cape Cod in the summer.
Remarks: An offshore species; its diet probably consists of various small fishes and squids.

Dusky Shark—*Carcharhinus obscurus*

Distinctive characters: Distinct ridge along back between dorsal fins. Distinguished from the sickle shark (above) by its shorter pectoral fins, larger eye, and shorter free tip of its second dorsal fin; separable from the sandbar shark (below) by the size and position of its first dorsal fin; and from the bignose shark by its shorter snout.
Color: Lead gray, bluish, or copper above, white below.
Maximum size: 11 feet, 8 inches. **Size at birth:** 38 to 48 inches.
Range: Common in inshore and offshore waters along east coast of United States from Cape Cod to Florida.
Remarks: One of the most common sharks in New Jersey waters. Feeds primarily on bottom fishes including searobins, skates, headfish, and flatfish.

Sandbar Shark (Brown Shark)—*Carcharhinus milberti*

Distinctive characters: Distinct ridge along back between dorsal fins; separated from similar species by its larger first dorsal (vertical height exceeds 10% of shark's total length—less than 10% in sickle, dusky, and bignose sharks), also the first dorsal is further forward in relation to the pectoral fins.
Color: Gray to brown above. Paler below. Fin margins slightly darker.
Maximum size: 7 feet 8 inches. **Size at birth:** About 25 inches.
Range: Common in inshore and offshore waters along east coast of the United States from Cape Cod to Florida.
Remarks: This is the most common large shark reported from New York–New Jersey coastal waters. Adult females enter bays in this area to give birth to their young. Large males are seldom taken and probably remain farther offshore. Its diet is similar to that of the dusky.

Bignose Shark—*Carcharhinus altima*

Distinctive characters: Distinct ridge along back between dorsal fins. This little-known species has a snout length about equal to the width of the mouth (in the sickle, dusky, and sandbar sharks, the length of the snout is less than the width of the mouth).
Color: Grayish brown above, sides a lighter tint; belly dirty white.
Maximum Size: 9 feet. **Size at birth:** About 25 inches.
Range: Reported only from subtropical waters of the western North Atlantic; might occur in local offshore waters as a stray.
Remarks: An offshore species which rarely occurs in depths of less than 50 fathoms. Little is known of its habits.

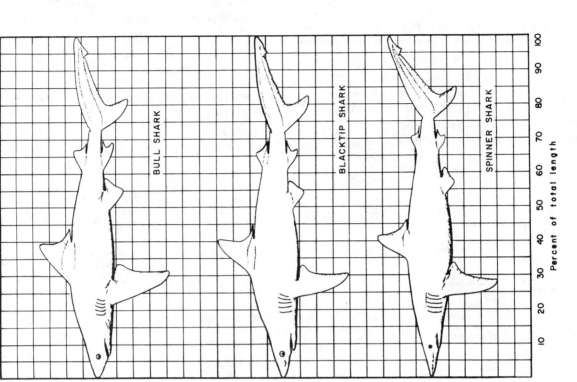

BULL SHARK

BLACKTIP SHARK

SPINNER SHARK

Percent of total length

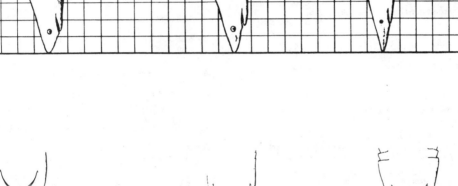

Bull Shark (Cub Shark)—*Carcharhinus leucas*

Distinctive characters: Lack of ridge along back between dorsal fins separates this from similar species on the preceding page. Absence of black-tipped fins and a snout which is broadly rounded and shorter than the distance between the nostrils separate the bull shark from the blacktip and spinner (see below).

Color: Gray above and white below; lower tips of pectorals sometimes dusky.

Maximum size: 12 feet. **Size at birth:** 28 inches.

Range: Common in tropic waters, strays to Long Island.

Remarks: A sluggish heavy-bodied inshore species, known to enter estuaries and travel up rivers. Feeds on various fishes, other sharks, and garbage.

Blacktip Shark—*Carcharhinus limbatus*

Distinctive characters: Lack of ridge along back between dorsal fins; fins conspicuously tipped with black; differs from the bull shark (above) by its longer snout, and from the spinner (below) by its larger eyes (horizontal diameter ⅓ the length of first gill opening) and more forward position of its first dorsal fin.

Color: Gray or ashy blue above, pure white or whitish below; sides with a light wedge-shaped band beginning near the pectoral fins and gradually widening rearward to the pelvic fins where it merges with the white on the belly.

Maximum size: 8 feet. **Size at birth:** 23 to 26 inches.

Range: Southern New England to Brazil, occurring as a stray north of Cape Hatteras, N.C.

Remarks: An active, swift-swimming shark often seen in schools at the surface. It has a habit of leaping from the water and spiraling through the air before falling back into the sea. Feeds on squid, butterfish, menhaden, and other fishes.

Spinner (Large Black-tipped) Shark—*Carcharhinus maculipinnis*

Distinctive characters: Lacks ridge on back between dorsal fins; fins conspicuously tipped with black; differs from the bull shark (above) by its longer snout, and from the blacktip by its smaller eyes (horizontal diameter ¼ the length of first gill opening) and more rearward position of the first dorsal relative to the pectorals.

Color: Similiar to that of the blacktip shark.

Maximum size: 8 feet. **Size at birth:** Unknown.

Range: Tropical and subtropical western Atlantic; may stray north of Cape Hatteras.

Remarks: Has the same jumping and spinning habit as the blacktip shark. Little known of its life history and food habits. Probably feeds on squids and small fishes.

IDENTIFICATION KEY

The following key is a series of paired descriptive statements that give contrasting characteristics. Each pair offers two choices; choose the one that best describes the shark you are examining. That selection either names the shark or refers you to another pairing, or couplet. As successive choices are made, the characteristics become more specific. For example, in identifying the smooth hammerhead, your path would be 1B to 2B to 5A to 6B to 7A. Just remember to always begin at the beginning and follow every step until you reach your identification.

Adapted from Anglers' Guide to Sharks of the Northeastern United States *published by the U.S. Department of the Interior.*

1
A. Body flattened; pectoral fins broad and winglike = **Atlantic Angel Shark**
B. Body rounded, torpedo-shaped. *Go to couplet 2.*

2
A. Anal fin absent. *Go to couplet 3.*
B. Anal fin present. *Go to couplet 5.*

3
A. Spine in front of each dorsal fin. *Go to couplet 4.*
B. No spine in front of either dorsal fin = **Greenland Shark**

4
A. Origin of second dorsal fin behind the pelvic fins = **Spiny Dogfish**
B. Origin of second dorsal fin over the pelvic fins = **Portuguese Shark**

5
A. Head expanded sideways like shovel or hammer. *Go to couplet 6.*
B. Head not expanded sideways like shovel or hammer. *Go to couplet 9.*

6
A. Head shovel-shaped = **Bonnethead**
B. Head hammer-shaped. *Go to couplet 7.*

7
A. Front margin of head not notched at midline = **Smooth Hammerhead**
B. Front margin of head notched at midline. *Go to couplet 8.*

8
A. Free rear tip of second dorsal fin shorter than the vertical height of the fin = **Great Hammerhead**
B. Free rear tip of second dorsal fin longer than vertical height of the fin = **Scalloped Hammerhead**

9
A. Tail about as long as entire length of body. *Go to couplet 10.*
B. Tail much less than length of body. *Go to couplet 11.*

10
A. Rear tip of first dorsal fin terminates in front of pelvic fins = **Thresher Shark**
B. Rear tip of first dorsal fin extends at least as far as the pelvic fins = **Bigeye Thresher**

11
A. Keel or ridge on sides of caudal peduncle. *Go to couplet 12.*
B. No keel or ridge on sides of caudal peduncle. *Go to couplet 17.*

12
A. Keel a weakly developed ridge; caudal peduncle nearly round; lower lobe of tail less than half as long as upper lobe. *Go to couplet 13.*
B. Keel strongly developed; caudal peduncle flattened; lower lobe of tail ⅔ as long as upper lobe. *Go to couplet 14.*

13
A. Origin of first dorsal fin about opposite rear margin of pectorals; body gray, often with irregular dark bands or spots = **Tiger Shark**
B. Origin of first dorsal fin well behind pectorals; body blue, no dark bands or spots = **Blue Shark**

14
A. Gill slits long—extend almost full height of head and nearly meet on under side of head = **Basking Shark**
B. Gill slits shorter—do not extend full height of head or very far on under side of head. *Go to couplet 15.*

15
A. Second keel below and to rear of main keel; teeth with two small auxiliary points at their base = **Porbeagle**
B. Second keel absent; teeth without auxiliary points at base. *Go to couplet 16.*

16
A. Edges of teeth smooth — **Mako**
B. Edges of teeth serrated (saw toothed) = **White Shark**

17
A. Base of first dorsal fin at least 4 times the height of fin = **False Cat Shark**
B. Base of first dorsal fin much less than 4 times the height of the fin. *Go to couplet 18.*

18
A. Origin of first dorsal fin over or behind origin of pelvic fins. *Go to couplet 19.*
B. Origin of first dorsal fin well in front of origin of pelvic fins. *Go to couplet 21.*

19
A. Origin of first dorsal fin over origin of pelvic fins; a long barbel on each nostril = **Nurse Shark**
B. Origin of first dorsal fin well behind origin of pelvic fins; barbels absent. *Go to couplet 20.*

20
A. Irregular chain-like markings on side of body = **Chain Dogfish**
B. No chain-like markings on sides of body = **Deep-Water Cat Shark**

21
A. Mouth at tip of snout = **Whale Shark**
B. Mouth not at tip of snout. *Go to couplet 22.*

22
A. First and second dorsal fins about equal in size. *Go to couplet 23.*
B. First dorsal fin much larger than second dorsal fin. *Go to couplet 25.*

23
A. All 5 gill openings in front of pectoral fins = **Sand Shark**
B. Last 1 or 2 gill openings over or behind origin of pectoral fins. *Go to couplet 24.*

24
A. Origin of anal fin opposite CENTER of second dorsal fin; teeth flat, blunt (pavement-like) = **Smooth Dogfish**
B. Origin of anal fin opposite ORIGIN of second dorsal fin; teeth pointed and sharp = **Lemon Shark**

25
A. Origin of second dorsal fin about opposite CENTER of anal fin = **Atlantic Sharpnose Shark**
B. Origin of second dorsal fin about opposite the ORIGIN of anal fin. *Go to couplet 26.*

26
A. Maximum length of pectoral fin as great as or greater than distance from tip of snout to last gill opening; fins often white at tips =**Whitetip Shark**
B. Maximum length of pectoral fin less than distance from tip of snout to last gill opening; fins without white tips. *Go to couplet 27.*

27
A. Edges on both upper and lower teeth smooth =**Finetooth Shark**
B. Edges of upper teeth finely to strongly serrated; lower teeth smooth or serrated. *Go to couplet 28.*

28
A. A low but distinct mid-dorsal ridge present in the skin between first and second dorsal fins. *Go to couplet 29.*
B. Mid-dorsal ridge absent. *Go to couplet 32.*

29
A. Length of free rear tip of second dorsal fin more than twice as long as vertical height of the fin =**Sickle Shark**
B. Length of free rear tip of second dorsal fin less than twice as long as vertical height of the fin. *Go to couplet 30.*

30
A. Origin of first dorsal fin behind free inner angle of pectoral fin =**Dusky Shark**
B. Origin of first dorsal fin over or forward of free inner angle of pectoral fin. *Go to couplet 31.*

31
A. Distance from front of mouth to tip of snout less than width of mouth =**Sandbar Shark**
B. Distance from front of mouth to tip of snout about equal to width of mouth =**Bignose Shark**

32
A. Distance between nostrils greater than distance from front of mouth to tip of snout =**Bull Shark**
B. Distance between nostrils less than distance from front of mouth to tip of snout. *Go to couplet 33.*

33
A. Vertical height of first dorsal fin much greater than distance between tip of snout and eye; first gill opening less than 2½ times as long as horizontal diameter of eye; edges of lower teeth finely serrated =**Blacktip Shark**
B. Vertical height of first dorsal fin about equal to distance between tip of snout and eye; first gill opening more than 4 times as long as horizontal diameter of eye; edges of lower teeth smooth =**Spinner Shark**

Part Two

Fishing and Boating Techniques and Gear

6

Tackle

A host of saltwater gamefish—from half-pound snapper bluefish to 40-pound yellowtails to bluefin tuna weighing nearly half a ton—draw millions of fishermen to the briny each year. They stand in crashing surf and on jetties and piers, and they sail for deeper waters aboard boats of almost every description.

Because of the great differences in weights of saltwater fish, it is important for the fisherman to be armed with balanced tackle that is suited for the particular quarry he is after. Just as the freshwater muskie angler wouldn't use bluegill tackle, the person who's trolling for, say, blue marlin wouldn't use a jetty outfit designed for striped bass.

Balanced tackle—in which rod, reel, line, and other items are all in reasonable proportion to one another—is important for a number of reasons.

For one, a properly balanced outfit—for example, a 9-foot surf rod with a good casting reel and 15- to 25-pound-test line—is a joy to use. Conversely, if you substituted a 5-foot boat rod for the 9-footer in the above outfit and tried to cast, you would soon be turning the air blue. Besides the casting advantage, properly balanced gear makes hooking and playing a fish easier and more effective.

There is still another reason for using balanced tackle. Every fisherman, beginner and expert alike, who tosses or trolls lure or bait in the salt has a chance to sink a hook into a record-size gamefish. The rules of the International Game Fish Association, keeper of the official records of marine gamefish, require that any fish submitted for a record be caught on tackle that is "in reasonable proportion . . . to the line size."

Let's take a detailed look at the various kinds of conventional saltwater gear and how to match up the component parts.

TROLLING REELS

Trolling is the method of fishing in which a lure or bait is pulled along behind a moving boat. It is also a method in which the reel is of paramount importance.

Saltwater trolling reels are sometimes designated by a simple and yet not completely reliable numbering system. This system employs a number followed by a diagonal (/) and then the letter "O" (pronounced "ought"), which merely stands for "ocean." The numbers run from 1 to 16, with each one representing the line capacity of the reel. The higher the number, the larger the reel's line capacity.

It should be noted, however, that these numbers are not standardized—that is, one manufacturer's 4/O trolling reel may have a smaller capacity than another maker's 4/O. A prospective reel buyer would do well to check manufacturers' catalogs to make sure of a reel's line capacity.

Trolling reels are the heavyweights among saltwater reels. Weighing from 18 ounces (for the 1/O size) up to nearly 11 pounds (for the 16/O), they are designed primarily for handling the largest of gamefish (sailfish, marlin, bluefin tuna, swordfish) but are also effective for bluefish, stripers, channel bass, albacore, dolphin, and the like.

These reels have no casting features (such as anti-backlash devices), since their sole function is trolling. Spools are smooth-running, usually operating on ball bearings. The reels are ruggedly built and, of course, corrosion resistant. Unique features include lugs on the upper part of the sideplate for attachment of a big-game fishing harness worn by the fisherman, a U-shaped clamp for more secure union of rod and reel, and, in the largest reels, a lug-and-brace arrangement for extra rigidity.

TROLLING REELS AND LINE CAPACITIES (In Yards)

LINES	REELS									
	1/0	2/0	3/0	4/0	6/0	9/0	10/0	12/0	14/0	16/0
20-lb. mono-filament	350	425								
30-lb. mono-filament	200	275	375							
36-lb. mono-filament				350	600					
45-lb. mono-filament				275	500					
54-lb. mono-filament				200	400					
72-lb. mono-filament					350	500	850			
90-lb. mono-filament						400	600	800	1100	1400
108-lb. mono-filament						300	500	600	1000	1200
20-lb. Dacron	225									
30-lb. Dacron	200	275	350	450						
50-lb. Dacron			200	250	400					
80-lb. Dacron				150	250	400	650	800	1050	1250
130-lb. Dacron						300	450	550	850	1000

The Penn International 80 is typical of a modern trolling reel. Built for 80-pound-test line, the reel has a side lever drag system. A reel of this size is preferred for giant tuna, billfish, sharks, and other big fish. (PENN REEL)

By far the most important feature on a trolling reel is the drag. If a reel is to handle the sizzling runs and line-testing leaps of fish weighing hundreds of pounds, its drag must operate smoothly at all times. And the drag must not overheat or it may bind, causing the line to break.

In most reels the drag is of the star type and consists of a series of alternating metal and composition (or leather) washers. Some quite expensive trolling reels have not one but two drag controls. One is a knob-operated device that lets you preset drag tension to a point below the breaking strength of the line being used. The other is a lever, mounted on the sideplate, that has a number of positions and permits a wide range of drag settings, from very light up to the safe maximum for the line in use. This lever, when backed off all the way, throws the reel into free-spool.

Trolling-reel spools can be graphite composites or made of metal, usually either machined bronze or anodized aluminum, and range in width from 1⅝ inches (for the 1/O size) to 5 inches (for the 16/O).

Some trolling reels are designed especially for wire and lead-core lines. They have narrow but deep spools and extra-strong gearing.

Other features of trolling reels include a free-spool lever mounted on the sideplate, a single oversize handle grip, and gear ratios ranging from 1.6:1 to as high as 5:1.

TROLLING RODS

Big-game trolling rods have the strength and fittings to withstand the power runs and magnificent leaps of such heavyweights as marlin, sailfish, and giant tuna. The great majority of these rods are of fiberglass and graphite construction.

Almost all blue-water rods have a butt section and a tip section—that is, they seldom have ferrules fitted midway along the "working length" of the rod. In most rods the tip section is about 5 feet long, while butt lengths vary from 14 to 27 inches, depending on the weight of the tip. Standup fighting rods are smaller. Tip sections are usually designated by weight, ranging from about 3 ounces to as heavy as 40 ounces, depending on the line being used and the fish being sought.

Trolling rods are rated according to the line-strength classes of the International Game Fish Association. The eight I.G.F.A. classes are: 6-pound line, 12-pound (line testing, when wet, up to and including 12 pounds), 20-pound (line testing, when wet, more than 12 pounds and up to and including 20 pounds), 30-pound (line testing, when wet, more than 20 pounds and up to and

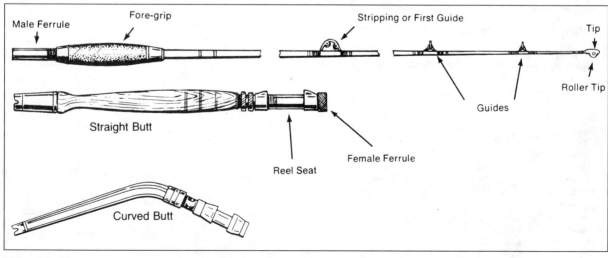

Typical trolling rod construction: designed for strength.

HOW TO MATCH UP OFFSHORE TROLLING TACKLE

This table is meant only as a general guide aimed at helping you put together, in proper balance, the basic elements of a bluewater trolling outfit tailored for fish of a particular weight category. Specific conditions—and your ability and personal preferences—should also be considered.

SPECIES OF FISH	REEL	ROD (Tip-Section Weight, in oz.)	LINE (Lb. Test)
Striped bass, dolphin, wahoo, yellowtail, king-fish, salmon, barracuda, tarpon, school tuna	1/0 to 3/0	3 to 9	12 to 30
Atlantic sailfish, Pacific sailfish, white marlin	3/0 to 6/0	6 to 18	30 to 50
Striped marlin	4/0 to 9/0	6 to 20	30 to 80
Black marlin, blue marlin, swordfish, sharks	6/0 to 14/0	9 to 30	30 to 130
Giant bluefin tuna	9/0 to 16/0	16 to 30	50 to 130

including 30 pounds); 50-pound, 80-pound, 130-pound, and 180-pound.

No rod used in catching a fish submitted for an I.G.F.A. record can have a tip length of less than 5 feet. In the 12-, 20-, and 30-pound classes, a rod's butt length can be no more than 18 inches. In the 50- and 80-pound classes, butt length can be no more than 22 inches. In the 130- and 180-pound classes, butt length can be no more than 27 inches.

The fittings on trolling rods include strong, high-quality guides. The first guide above the reel (called the stripping guide) and the tip guide are of the roller type (either single-roller or double-roller). The middle guides, usually numbering four or five, are of the ring type and are made either of heavily chromed stainless steel or of tungsten carbide (carboloy), which is the most durable material. In some rods all of the guides are rollers. Most roller guides have self-lubricating bearings that can be disassembled for cleaning.

Other features of trolling rods include extra-strong, locking reel seats, and gimbal fittings in the end of the butt that enable the rod to be fitted into a socket on a boat's fighting chair or into a belt harness worn by the fisherman.

CASTING AND BOAT REELS

Conventional (revolving-spool) reels in this category are widely used by saltwater fishermen who cast lures and baits from piers, bridges, jetties, and in the surf, and by sinker-bouncers (bottom fishermen) in boats. Actually an outgrowth and refinement of freshwater baitcasting reels, these reels fill the gap between those freshwater models and big-game trolling reels.

Many surf and jetty casters, especially those who are after big fish, prefer a conventional reel (and rod) over a spinning outfit because the conventional rig is better able to handle heavy lures and sinkers. And a vast majority of bottom fishermen lean toward the revolving-spool reel.

Conventional reels designed for casting have wide, light spools (a heavy spool makes casting difficult) of either metal or a synthetic, and gear ratios ranging from 2:1 to 4½:1. Weights range from about 12 to 22 ounces. In most models the drag is of the star type and there is a free-spool lever mounted on the side-plate. Some of these reels have level-wind mechanisms.

Line capacities range from about 250 yards of 12-pound-test monofilament to 350 yards of 36-pound-test mono. For most surf, jetty, and pier situations, 250 yards of line is sufficient.

A few of these reels have a mechanical brake, magnets, or a thumbing device to help prevent the spool from overrunning during a cast and causing a backlash. In most models, however, as in freshwater baitcasting reels, thumb pressure against the spool is required to control the cast.

Conventional reels designed for deep-sea bottom fishing are quite similar to the casting models but are somewhat heavier and have narrower, deeper spools. They also have larger line capacities and can take heavier lines.

CASTING AND BOAT RODS

In choosing a conventional casting rod, more so than with boat (bottom-fishing) rods, the type of fishing to be done and the fish being sought are critical factors. For casting in the surf, for example, the rod must be long enough so that the fisherman can make lengthy casts and hold the line above the breakers. A rod for jetty use, on the other hand, need not be so long. And if you'll be fishing mainly from piers and bridges, you'll need a rod with enough backbone to lift hefty fish from the water and up over the rail.

However, the beginning fisherman can get a casting rod that will handle most of the situations he'll be facing. A good choice would be one that is 8½ to 9 feet in overall length, of tubular fiberglass (rather than solid fiberglass), and has a rather stiff tip. The stiff tip of a conventional rod lets the angler use a wide range of lure weights and enables him to have more control over big fish.

Conventional casting rods are available in lengths from about 8 to 11½ feet and even longer. A few split-bamboo models are still kicking around the beaches, but most are now made of fiberglass, graphite, Kevlar, or a combination thereof. Recent developments in graphite show that rods of this material can carry an exceptionally wide range of lure weights. In tests, weights of 18 ounces were cast with graphite rods. A majority of these rods are of two-piece construction, breaking either at the upper part of the butt or about midway up the working length of the rod.

These rods are distinguished by the number and arrangement of their guides. In most models, there are only three or four guides, including the tip guide, and all are located in the upper half of the tip section. Why this arrangement? Because these rods are stiffer than most others, fewer guides are required to distribute the strain along the length of the rod. The guides are bunched near the tip because that's where most of the bend occurs when a fish is being played.

Conventional casting rods have sturdy salt-resistant reel seats, usually of anodized aluminum, and butts of hickory, other sturdy woods, cork, or synthetics.

Boat, or bottom-fishing, rods, as their name implies, are designed for noncasting use aboard boats—party boats, charter craft, and private boats. They are also used on piers and bridges, in situations in which lure or bait is simply dropped down to the water.

Boat rods are considerably shorter than casting rods, running from about 4½ to 6½ feet in overall length, with a good length being about 6 feet. Their shortness makes them highly maneuverable, a factor of more than a little importance aboard a crowded party boat, and makes it easier to handle, say, a 30-pound cod while trying to remain upright on a pitching deck.

As with most other modern rods, boat rods are mostly of fiberglass construction, with a growing number of graphite models available. For saltwater angling, most are one-piece. The number of guides on a boat rod depends on length, but there are seldom more than five. Some of these rods, designed for large fish, have a roller tip. Other boat-rod features are similar to those of casting rods.

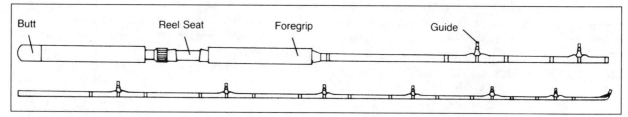

A typical surfcasting rod usually measures from 8 to 14 feet in length and is designed to cast lures and sinkers from 1 to 4 ounces.

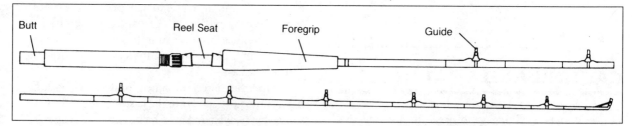

A typical boat rod usually has a stiff action. It measures from 5 to 7 feet and is generally designed for noncasting use, such as on party boats and charter craft.

HOW TO MATCH UP SALTWATER CASTING TACKLE

This table is meant only as a general guide aimed at helping you put together, in proper balance, the basic elements of a saltwater casting outfit tailored for fish of a particular weight category. Specific conditions—and your ability and personal preferences—should also be considered.

SPECIES OF FISH	REEL	ROD TYPE & LENGTH (In Feet)	LINES (Lb. Test)	LURE WEIGHTS (Ounces)
Small stripers, bluefish, weakfish, snook, bonefish, redfish, salmon, pompano, jacks	Light (with star drag)	Popping 6 to 7	8 to 15	½ to 1
Stripers, big bluefish, school tuna, albacore, bonito, salmon, dolphin, wahoo	Medium	Medium-action 6½ to 8	12 to 30	¾ to 3
Channel bass, black drum, tarpon, dolphin, big kingfish, sharks	Heavy	Heavy-action 7 to 8½	18 to 50	1½ to 5
Surf species (bluefish, stripers, drum, channel bass, etc.)	Squidding (Surf-casting)	Surf 8 to 11½	18 to 45	1½ to 6

HOW TO SET DRAG

Drag is what keeps a fish from breaking your line. That sounds simple, but fishermen sometimes lose big fish because they do not know or understand a few basic facts about the drag on their reel.

Many anglers, for example, tighten their drag when a big fish makes a long run and strips off a lot of line. This is wrong. The drag should actually be lightened, because a lot of line in the water as well as a smaller spool diameter will increase the drag. Unfortunately, the reaction of most fishermen is to tighten the drag and stop the fish. Often the result is a lost trophy.

Drag is the resistance of a reel against the fighting pull of a fish, and drag is set at a strain the line can endure without breaking. The drag mechanism usually consists of a series of metal (stainless steel, aluminum, or chromed brass) and composition (leather, cork, plastic, fiber) washers. The washers are stacked, alternating metal and composition, and the friction between the surface areas of the washers creates "drag."

When an angler tightens the drag on his reel, he compresses these washers, creates more friction, and increases drag. Conversely, when he backs off the drag, he lessens friction and lightens drag.

If the size of a fish was the only factor in setting drag, the job would be easy. But there are other consid-erations, such as the friction of the line against the rod guides, resistance of the line being pulled through the water, and the amount of line remaining on the reel spool after a long run.

In addition, not all drags are created equal. They should be smooth, but many are sticky and jerky. In fact, it often takes as much as double the force of the drag setting to get the drag moving. For example, a drag set at 5 pounds may actually take up to 10 pounds of pull before the drag starts moving. It's obvious, therefore, that if you're using 8-pound-test line you should set your drag at about 2 pounds to allow for "starting your drag."

The amount of line on your spool is another factor affecting drag. When the outside diameter of line on your spool is reduced by half, the drag tension is dou-bled. For example, if your drag is set at 2 pounds with a full spool, it will be increased to 4 pounds when a fish makes a long run and strips off half your line.

Long, fast runs will also generate friction and heat between drag washers. This will frequently tighten a drag and add even more tension.

It's also important to remember that a rod held at about 45 degrees will add about 10 percent to the drag you get with the rod pointed directly at the fish. This

215

You can set the drag on your reel even if you're alone. As Jerry Gibbs demonstrates, fill a bucket with sand, hook a fish scale to the handle and lift with your rod until the scale indicates the correct setting. The accompanying table shows the correct settings for various weight lines.
(VIN T. SPARANO)

increased drag is due to friction between your line and the rod guides. If the rod is held at about 90 degrees, drag will increase about 35 percent of the initial setting.

This is why it is important to lighten the drag and, when possible, point the rod at the fish when it is about to be netted or gaffed. If you hold your rod high and keep a tight drag, a sudden lunge by a fish could break your line. But point the rod tip at the fish and the line will run off the spool more easily, even with the same drag setting.

This technique of lowering the rod is also used when handling thrashing or jumping fish, such as tarpon and marlin. Lowering the rod will lighten drag tension and "cushion" the line from the shock of a jumping fish, a move called "bowing." It's part of the technique that makes it possible to land 100-pound tarpon on 10-pound line.

Taking all the above factors into consideration, how does an angler set his drag so that he can feel reasonably

secure when he hooks a trophy fish? The first step is to determine the minimum and maximum range of drag for the various pound-test lines (see accompanying table). By minimum drag, I mean "starting drag," the amount of pull needed to get the drag moving. If the minimum drag seems light for the pound-test line, remember that there will be other factors increasing your drag beyond this setting, such as rod angle, spool diameter, and amount of line in water. Maximum drag means the heaviest setting you should use while fighting a fish. Never go beyond the maximum for your line class.

Let's take 12-pound-test line and see what factors come into play. Minimum drag is set at 4 pounds, but 8 pounds of pull will likely be required to get that drag started. If the angler holds his rod at 45 degrees or higher, he can add another 10 percent, which brings the drag to 9 pounds. To this figure we also have to add water resistance or line drag, which varies according to amount of line in the water, line diameter, and speed of the fish. With 12-pound line and a fast fish, it can amount to as much as 2 pounds, which brings us up to 11 pounds of drag on our 12-pound line. With only 1 pound of drag to spare, a big fish would likely break the line. It's obvious that you're far better off with a very light drag setting.

Range of Drag

Line	Mininum Draw (lbs.)	Maximum Drag (lbs)
6-lb.-test	1½	4
8-lb.-test	2	5
10-lb.-test	3	6
12-lb.-test	4	8
20-lb.-test	6	12
30-lb.-test	8	15
50-lb.-test	12	25
80-lb.-test	20	40
130-lb.-test	30	50

The first step is to set your drag at the minimum setting. This is easily done at dockside with a reliable fish scale and the help of a friend. Run your line through the guides and tie it to the scale. Ask your friend to hold the scale and back off about 30 feet. Tighten your drag and begin to apply pressure as you would when fighting a fish. Now adjust the drag so that it comes into play when the scale reads the correct minimum drag weight. For example, if you're using 12-pound line, the drag should begin to slip when you apply enough pressure to pull the scale indicator to the 4-pound mark.

Now, with your drag set at 4 pounds, slowly tighten your drag until it comes into play at 8 pounds, which is

Jerry Gibbs, Outdoor Life *fishing editor, puts pressure on a 30-pound-test outfit while Vin Sparano, editor of both the Northeast and Southeast editions of the* Guide to Saltwater Fishing & Boating, *checks the indicator on a fish scale to set drag. Gibbs here is applying 26 pounds of pressure; note the bend in the rod.* (VIN T. SPARANO)

the maximum setting. Note how many turns of the star drag or spool cap are required to bring your drag to maximum setting. Play with the drag, setting it back and forth from 4 to 8 pounds. Do this several times and get the feel of the resistance and pressure you're putting on the line. With enough practice, you'll be able to safely lighten and tighten the drag while fighting a fish.

An easier technique is to leave your drag set at the minimum setting and use your hand or fingers to apply more drag. This is a method many anglers use and it works well. You can practice with your buddy and the scale. With drag at the minimum setting, cup your hand around the spool (assuming you're using an open-face spinning reel), grip it so that the drag does not slip, and apply just enough pressure to pull the scale indicator to the maximum figure. Practice this technique and you'll soon be able to bear down on a fish and gain line without even touching the drag knob.

As mentioned above, you can also cup your hand around the spool of an open-face spinning reel to apply more drag. With conventional reels, use your thumb against the spool and hold the lines against the rod. Make sure you lift your finger when a big fish begins a run, or else you'll get a bad line burn.

Learn to combine this hand technique with "pumping" and you will be able to land big fish on light lines. Pumping a big fish in is not difficult. Let's assume you're using an open-face spinning reel with a light drag. Put your hand around the spool, apply pressure, and ease your rod back into a vertical position. Now drop the rod tip and reel in the slack. Repeat the process and you'll

eventually have your fish at boatside. Always be ready, however, to lower the rod tip and release hand pressure from the spool when you think the fish is about to make a run. When he stops, you begin to pump once again.

One last point: At the end of the day, back off the drag and release all pressure on the washers, or they will lose their physical characteristics and take a set. If this happens, the drag will become jerky and unpredictable. If the washers do take a set, replacing them is then the only solution.

CARE AND REPAIR OF FISHING TACKLE

There's more than a germ of truth in the old saying, "A fisherman is no better than his tackle." Of course, that has also been said of quarterbacks!

Seriously, though, it pays in more ways than one to keep your gear in good working order. For one thing, proper maintenance can add a good many years to the working life of rods, reels, and other tackle on which hard-earned money has been spent. And legions of fishermen have discovered, to their chagrin, that unoiled reels can "freeze up," neglected rods can snap, and rusty lure hooks can give out—just when that lunker comes along.

The following tackle-care tips should help to prevent such problems.

KEEP YOUR TACKLE TUNED

I get a pain in the pit of my stomach whenever I look in someone's car trunk and see a couple of fishing rods bouncing around with a tire iron and jumper cables. The same thing happens when I see rods leaning against garage walls and reel drags screwed down tight when not in use. All of these things will wreck tackle. Fishing tackle today is not cheap, and you should learn how to protect your investment.

Today's rods, for example, are designed for long life, but they still require some basic maintenance to keep in good working order. This is especially important for salt-water fishermen. Even the best of tackle can't withstand the corrosive action of salt. Here are the steps that you will need to keep your rod in good shape:

1. Wash the rod, including the guides, thoroughly with soap and fresh water; rinse it with hot water and then let it dry thoroughly. This step should be taken after each use.

2. Clean the guides and ferrules well and give them a very light coating of grease to help prevent oxidation of the metal. I know a charter captain who scrubs all the roller guides with a tooth-brush after every trip.

3. New graphite rods usually need nothing more than periodic washing, but I still wax my rods at least once a season with a good car wax.

4. Check the guide wrappings. If they start to look thin or worn, rewrap them. Don't wait until the threads start to unravel. You may not have this problem, however, if you give the wrappings a coat of varnish each season. Two thin coats are better than one. To avoid bubbles in the varnish, apply it with a finger or a pipe cleaner.

5. When you're not using the rod, store it flat or upright without any weight on the tip. If you lean a rod against a wall, it may develop a set or permanent bend. Never store a wet cork-handled rod in a case. Mildew will form on the cork.

Reels are probably the most important piece of fishing gear and probably the most expensive. If you don't want them to fail when you're fighting a big fish, follow this checklist:

1. I rinse off my reels after every trip, and I use lots of soap. Dry your reels thoroughly and oil sparingly.

2. Most important, release drag tension to eliminate fatigue in your drag system.

HOW TO WRAP GUIDES

1. Start by wrapping over the end of the thread toward the guide so thread end is held down by the wrapping. Using the tension from whatever type tension device you are using to hold the wrapping tight, continue to turn the rod so that each thread lies as close as possible to the preceding turn.

2. About 5 to 8 turns from the finish of the wrap, insert the loop of tie-off thread. (This can be 6 inches of heavier thread or a fine piece of nylon leader material.) Finish the wrap over this tie-off loop.

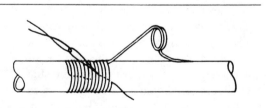

3. Holding wrap tightly, cut the wrapping thread about 4 inches from your rod. Insert this cut end through the tie-off loop. Still holding onto the wrapping thread, pull cut off thread under the wraps with tie-off loop.

4. With a razor blade, trim cut-off end as close as possible to the wrap. With the back of a knife or your fingernail, push wrapping up tight so that it appears solid, and none of the rod or guide shows through.

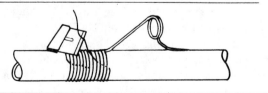

3. Clean internal gears, but don't attempt to break down the reel completely. More than once, I've had to return a reel to a manufacturer because I couldn't put it back together.

4. If you're not going to use a reel for awhile, give it a light coat of oil and store it in a cloth bag that will allow air to enter and escape. I store reels in Ziploc bags, but I never seal the the bags completely.

ROD-WRAPPING TRICKS OF THE TRADE

Guides and Tension: Guides should be purchased in matched sets to assure uniformity. Feet of guides should be dressed with a file to a fine taper. Next sight your rod; you will note a slight bend, or offset. Apply guides opposite the bend; this will bring it into a straight position. Guides should be affixed with snug wrapping tension, so that you may sight after wrapping and make slight guide adjustments before applying color preserver. Do not wrap guides to the absolute breaking point of the thread. Remember, 10 or 20 wraps of thread exert very heavy pressure on feet of guides. It is possible to damage a blank by wrapping too tight.

Threads: Sizes 2/O to E are most commonly used. Size 2/O or A for fly, casting, or spinning rods. Size E for the heavier freshwater spinning or saltwater rods. Naturally the finer size 2/O thread will make a neater job, but, being lighter, it is not quite as durable.

Trim: You may trim the basic color of your wrap with 5 to 10 turns of another color thread. This is done just as outlined in instructions for basic wrap.

Color Preserver and Rod Varnish: Good color preserver has plastic in it, and should be quite thin in order to penetrate the wrappings. Good-grade varnish is essential to durability of finish. A brush may be used to apply both the color preserver and rod varnish; however, air bubbles are usually present when a brush is used. To maintain a smooth finish, make certain these bubbles are out. A very satisfactory method of minimizing air bubbles is to apply both the color preserver and rod varnish with your index finger. Usually color preserver can be worked in with index finger. This will prevent any shading of the wrapping color.

SELECTING THE TIP TOP AND OTHER GUIDES

In building rods, you get what you pay for; don't skimp on guides, especially for saltwater rods.

Guides are made of various metals, including hardened stainless steel, chrome (or chrome-plated Monel), agate, and tungsten-carbide, with the carbide types being the most durable. Roller guides for heavy saltwater fishing are usually made of stainless steel, Monel, or nickel alloy.

The rod-builder should note that the guides are available in sets tailored to particular rod types and lengths.

SELECTING ROD FERRULES

Ferrules are jointlike devices inserted along the working length of a fishing rod that enable the rod to be dismantled into two or more sections. Ferrules are generally made of metal (nickel, brass, or aluminum), fiberglass, graphite, or a synthetic.

A ferrule set consists of two parts, the male ferrule and the female ferrule. The male section should fit snugly into the female section.

SPACING OF ROD GUIDES

Whether you are building a fishing rod from scratch or refinishing an old favorite, you must pay close attention to the placement of the guides along the working length of the rod.

Putting too many or too few guides on a rod, or placing them improperly, may detract from proper rod action and put undue strain on the line and the rod.

The following chart gives the correct number of guides—and exact spacing measurements—for most spinning, baitcasting, spincasting, and fly rods.

ROD GUIDE DIAMETERS

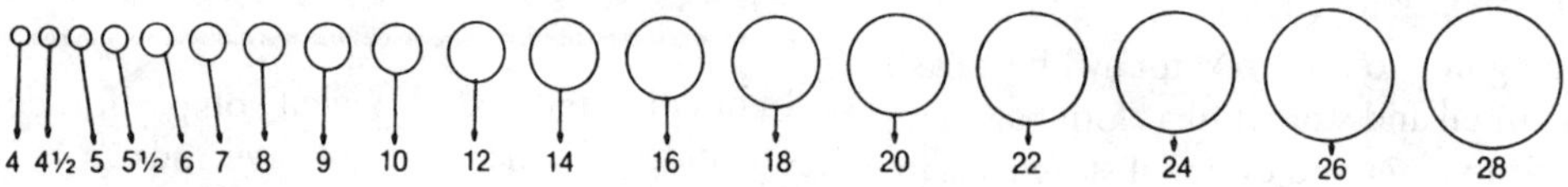

4 4½ 5 5½ 6 7 8 9 10 12 14 16 18 20 22 24 26 28

ACTUAL SIZES OF TIP GUIDES IN 1/64"

TYPES OF ROD GUIDES

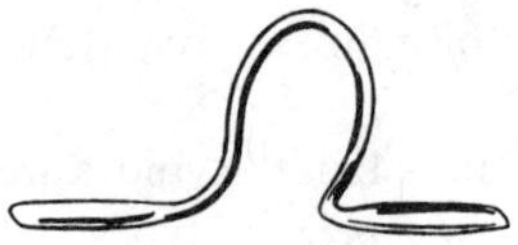

Snake (Fly Rod)

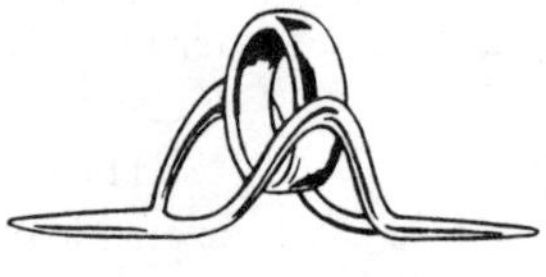

Ring (Baitcasting/Spincasting)

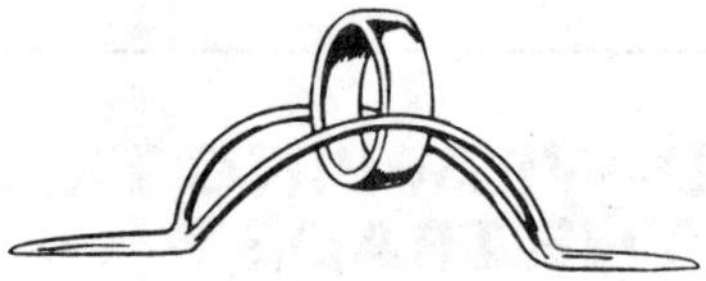

BRIDGE (Baitcasting Spincasting)

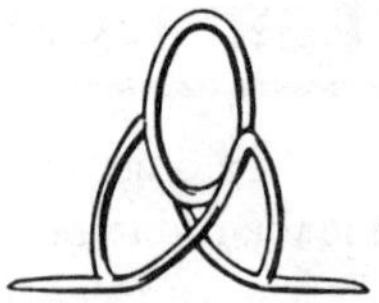

Spinning

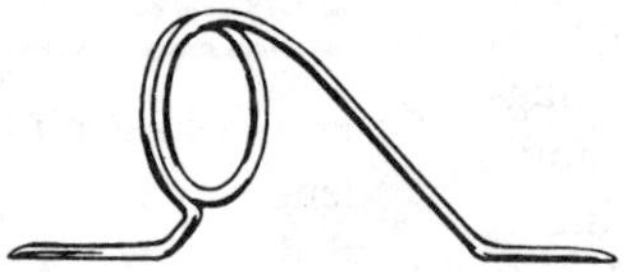

Loop or Foulproof (Spinning)

Roller (Big Game)

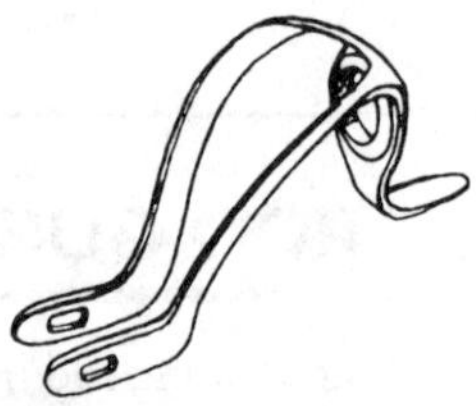

Fuji (Big Game)

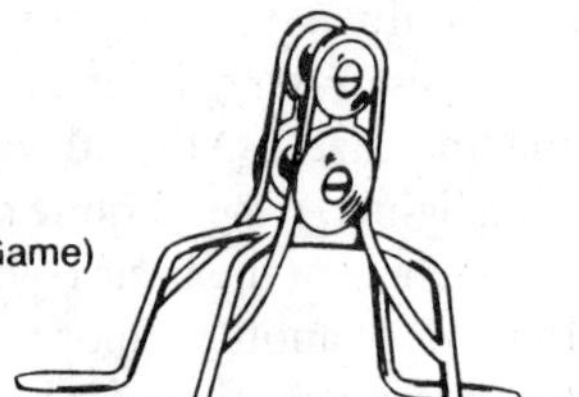

Roller (Big Game)

TYPES OF ROD TIPS

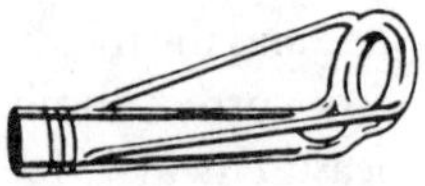

Ring with Support
(Spinning, Baitcasting, Spincasting)

Fly Rod

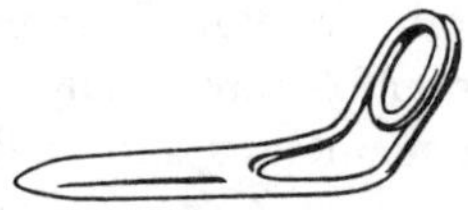

Foulproof (Spinning)

Fuji (Big Game)

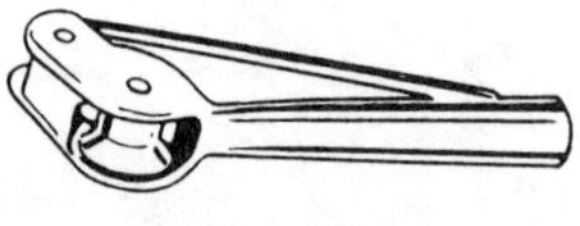

Roller (Big Game)

SUGGESTED GUIDE SPACING TABLE

All measurements are from tip of rod down. Figures indicate measurements at the guide ring.

Rod Length & Type	Lure-Weight Range	Fly-Line Weights	1st	2nd	3rd	4th	5th	6th	7th	8th
Spincasting, Baitcasting										
5½-ft.	⅛ to ⅓ oz.		4½"	12"	23"	36"				
6-ft.	⅛ to ⅜ oz.		4	10	18	28	40			
6-ft.	¼ to ¾ oz.		4	8¼	13	18	24½	32⅛	42	
6-ft.	⅜ to 1¼ oz.		3½	7½	12	17⅜	23⅝	31⅞	42½	
6-ft. 4-in.	¹⁄₁₆ to ¼ oz.		4	10	18½	28½	41			
6-ft. 4-in.	⅜ oz.		4	10	18½	28½	41			
6-ft. 4-in.	⅛ to ½ oz.		4	10	18½	28½	41			
6-ft.	⅜ to ⅝ oz.		4	10	18	28	40			
6-ft. 4-in.	¼ to ⅝ oz.		4	10	18½	28½	41			
Fly Rods										
5-ft. 5-in.		5 F, 6 S	5	13	25	40				
6-ft.		5 F, 6 S	3	7½	12	17¾	25	33	42½	
7½-ft.		6 F, 7 S	6	13	21	30	41½	60		
7-ft. 8-in.		6 or 7 F, 7 S	6	13	21	30	43	62		
8-ft.		6 or 7 F, 7 S	6	13	21	30	41	52	66	
8-ft.		7 F, 7 S	6	13	21	30	40	53	66	
8-ft.		7 or 8 F, 7 or 8 S	6	13	21	30	41	53	66	
8½-ft.		7 or 8 F, 7 or 8 S	6	13	21	30	40	56	73	
8½-ft.		7 F, 7 S	6	13	21	30	40	56	73	
8½-ft.		8 or 9 F, 8 or 9 S	6	13	21	30	40	56	73	
9-ft.		7 or 8 F, 7 or 8 S	5	11	18	26	35	45	58½	73
9-ft.		8 or 9 F, 8 or 9 S	5	11	18	26	35	45	58½	73
10-ft.		9 or 10 F, 9 or 10 S	6	13	22	32	43	54½	66½	80½
Spinning Rods										
6-ft.	up to ¼ oz.		5½	15½	27½	40½				
6-ft.	up to ⅜ oz.		3½	10	19	29¼	41½			
6½-ft.	¹⁄₁₆ to ¼ oz.		3½	8½	15	23	33	46		
6½-ft.	⅛ to 1 oz.		5	10⅜	16⅜	23⅜	31⅞	44		
6½-ft.	⅛ to ⅜ oz.		3½	8½	15	23	33	46		
7-ft.*	¹⁄₁₆ to ⅜ oz.	5 or 6 F, 6 S	4	10	18	27½	38½	52½		
7-ft.	¹⁄₁₆ to ⅜ oz.		4	10	18	27½	38½	52½		
6½ ft.	¼ to ⅝ oz.		3½	8½	15	23	33	46		
7-ft.	up to 1½ oz.		4	10	18	27½	38	51		

F = Floating   S = Sinking   * = Combination spin/fly rod

7 Lines, Leaders, and Hooks

LINE TYPES

No fisherman is stronger than the line that connects him and his quarry. Fishing lines are made of a wide variety of natural and synthetic materials and as a result differ widely in their characteristics and the uses to which they can be put. No two types of lines, for example, have the same degree of elasticity, abrasion resistance, water absorption, weight, and diameter.

Let's take a look at the physical characteristics of the various lines and the uses for which they are best suited.

MONOFILAMENT (SINGLE-STRAND NYLON)

By far the most widely used fishing line today. It is suitable for everything from blue-water trolling to surf casting to freshwater spinning, and it is the universal material for leaders in both fresh water and salt because of its near-invisibility in water. It is extremely strong and light for its diameter, and it absorbs very little water (3 to 12 percent of its own weight). About the only drawback of monofilament is its relatively high rate of stretch (15 to 30 percent when dry, 20 to 35 percent when wet). For that reason it is not the best choice for such uses as deep-water bottom fishing, in which large fish must be reeled up from considerable depths.

DACRON

A DuPont trademark for a synthetic fiber that is made into a braided line. It is nearly as strong as monofilament but does not stretch as much (about 10 percent). It has virtually the same characteristics whether wet or dry. Its visibility in water is greater than that of monofilament. Dacron's widest uses are as trolling line or for deep jigging.

LINEN

A braided line made from natural fibers and rated according to the number of threads, with each thread having a breaking strength of 3 pounds (6-thread linen has a breaking strength of 18 pounds, 15-thread tests 45 pounds, and so on). This material absorbs considerable water and is stronger when wet. Linen line is subject to deterioration and is heavy and bulky. Very little linen fishing line is made or used today, but because of its negligible stretch and good abrasion resistance it is still preferred by some big-game fishermen.

Braided Fishing Line

by Vin Sparano

The new braided fishing lines sound great the first time we see and hear about them. These lines have small diameter, minimum stretch, and good knot strength. The new braided lines get a high score on two out of three. If you want to use a braided line, you better listen to some sound advice on knots.

There are more than a dozen manufacturers of braided lines, and they all claim their lines are three times as strong as monofilament of the same diameter. This means, of course, that you can get three times as much line on your reel. The smaller diameter also means easier casting with lighter lures. So far, so good.

Braided lines have a stretch factor of less than 5 percent. Monofilament has a stretch factor of about 25 percent, depending on the manufacturer. Minimum stretch is a big deal in fishing. It means sensitivity and fast hook-ups. I've used braided lines on blackfish, a bottom feeder that's tough to hook and keep out of the rocks. The Stren Kevlar braided line worked as predicited. I could feel the hits, and setting the hook was almost instant. The braided line seemed to hold well against the rocks.

So where's the rub with braided lines? It's in the knots! With braided lines, you may only get about 75 percent knot strength, and that's only if you use the right knot. With monofilament, you can get nearly 100 percent with the right knot. Unless you take certain precautions tying knots, the strength-to-diameter ratio of braided lines isn't such a big deal.

Berkley, a line manufacturer that has done a great deal of research on the new braided lines, admits that knots may be the weak link. Good knots are difficult to tie. They are tough to cinch up tight, and they tend to slip.

After considerable research, Berkley recommends the Palomar Knot and the Trilene Knot. The Palomar and Trilene knots are used to tie fishing line to swivels, snaps, hooks, and lures. It's extremely important to wet braided lines before cinching the knot tight. Also, take care to keep the wraps from crossing over one another, and double the length of the tag line.

Stren has another answer to the knot problem in braided lines. This company recommends a glue called Stren Lok-Knot. A drop or two of this adhesive will literally weld a poorly tied knot and eliminate slippage. Stren feels so strongly about the strength of Lok-Knot that it even recommends it for totally knotless connections.

Braided lines have a lot going for them, including small diameter, minimal stretch, and the sensitivity to transmit the slightest nibble. Learning to tie and use the right knots should eliminate any knot problem.

Remember to double the tag end. In fact, it's wise to double braided line before tying any knot. Braided lines are also sharp and hard. Joining braided lines with monofilament may not be suuch a good idea, though further testing may prove otherwise. ■

Palomar Knot

The Palomar Knot is a general-purpose connection used in joining fishing line to swivels, snaps, hooks and artificial lures. The double wrap of line through the eyelet provides a protective cushion for added knot strength.

1. Double the line and form a loop three to four inches long. Pass the end of the loop through hook's eye.

2. Holding standing line between thumb and finger, grasp loop with free hand and form a simple overhand knot.

3. Pass hook through loop and draw line while guiding loop over top of eyelet.

4. Pull tag end of line to tighten knot snugly and trim tag end to about 1/4".

Trilene ® Knot

The Trilene Knot is a strong, reliable connection that resists slippage and premature failures. This knot can be used in joining line to swivels, snaps, hooks and artificial lures. The knots unique double wrap design and ease of tying consistently yields a strong, dependable connection.

1. Run end of line through eye of hook or lure and double back through the eye a second time.

2. Loop around standing part of line 5 or 6 times. Thread tag end back between the eye and the coils as shown.

3. Tighten knot with a steady, even motion without hesitation. Trim tag end leaving about 1/4".

Care of Lines

Check each line for cracking, aging, wear, and rot. If the entire line is no longer serviceable, discard it. If one end has taken all the use, reverse the line. Fly lines tend to crack at the business end after considerable use. If the cracking is confined to the last foot or so, clip off the damaged section or, if the line is a double-taper, reverse it. If the damage is more widespread, replace the line.

Check particularly for nicks and other weak spots in monofilament, and test its breaking strength. If it's weak, replace it.

With braided line, check for dark spots, signifying rot, and test the breaking strength. Replace if weak.

LEAD-CORE

This type of line is made by sheathing a flexible lead core in a tightly braided nylon sleeve. It's suitable for deep trolling in both fresh and salt water, and is especially useful for quickly getting a bait or lure down deep without bulky, heavy sinkers or planers. It's color-coded in 10-yard segments for precise depth control.

WIRE

These lines, too, are designed for deep trolling in both fresh and salt water. They're made of stainless steel, Monel (nickel alloy), bronze, or copper. Wire is popular for downrigger fishing, but because it's heavy enough to sink on its own, it's also used without downriggers and in many cases eliminates the need for a cumbersome drail weight or planer. Since it has no stretch, the angler can jig the rod and give movement to a bait or lure. However, wire is somewhat tricky until a fisherman

FISHING LINE TROUBLESHOOTING CHART

Symptoms	Possible Causes	Recommended Cures
Unexplained line breaks under low stress loads.	a. Nicks or abrasion. If smooth surface and shiny, failure may be line fatigue.	a. Strip off worn line or retie line more frequently.
	b. If surface dull, faded and fuzzy, failure due to sunlight or excessive wear.	b. Replace line.
	c. Wear or stress points on guides and/or reel.	c. Replace worn guides.
Line usually sticky and stretchy.	Line stored in area of high heat. Line damaged by chemicals.	Replace line and change storage areas.
Line has kinks and flat spots.	a. Line spooled under excessive tension.	a. Use lower spooling tension. Make one final cast and rewind under low tension.
	b. Line stored on reel too long without use.	b. Strip out and soak last 50 yards in water.
Excessive curls and backlashes.	Using too heavy mono for reel spool diameter.	Use a more flexible mono or one with a lower pound test or smaller diameter.
Mono stiff and brittle; dry, powdery surface.	Improper storage in either wet or too warm conditions.	Replace line and change storage area.
Line looks good, but losing too many fish.	Faulty or improperly set reel drag. Using too light a break strength for conditions.	Check reel drag. Lubricate or replace washers. Refill with line of higher break strength.
Reel casts poorly.	Not enough line on spool or line is too heavy for reel.	Fill spool with additional line. Use lighter, more limp monofilament.
Line is hard to see.	Line has faded due to excessive exposure to sunlight. Using wrong color line.	Replace line. Switch to high visibility line.

Chart courtesy Berkley, Inc.

This chart was designed to help you quickly find and correct line troubles when you can least afford to have them— on the water. Keep this handy chart in your tackle box.

gets used to it. Kinks can develop, causing weak spots or possibly cutting an unwary angler's hand. Wire line is generally available in a wider range of test weights than lead-core line.

Wire leaders, usually sleeved in plastic, are widely used to prevent line-cutting when fishing for such toothy battlers as pike, muskellunge, and many saltwater species.

LEADERS

There are two basic leader materials, wire and monofilament (single-strand nylon).

Wire leaders—either piano wire (high-carbon or stainless steel) or braided wire—are used generally to protect the line from sharp underwater obstacles and from the teeth, gill plates, and other sharp appendages of both freshwater and saltwater fish.

Some wire leaders, particularly the braided type, are enclosed in a "sleeve" of nylon, which prevents the wire strands from fraying and eliminates kinking.

Some monofilament leaders perform a similar function. Called shock tippets, they are short lengths (6 feet or shorter in most cases) of strong monotesting up to about 100 pounds depending on the size of the fish being sought. Shock tippets protect the line from sharp objects and sharp teeth, but they are also able to withstand the sledgehammer strikes of large fish.

The main purpose of most monofilament leaders, however, is to provide an all-but-invisible link between the end of the line and the lure, bait, or fly. In spinning and spincasting, a leader is seldom necessary, for the line itself is monofilament.

Recommended Leader Strength for Various Species

Mangrove or Gray Snapper	8-pound test
Bonefish	6- or 8-pound test
Tarpon, baby (under 20 pounds)	8-pound test
Tarpon, big (over 20 pounds)	12-pound test
Channel Bass (Redfish)	10-pound test
Striped Bass (to 10 pounds)	8-pound test
Striped Bass (over 10 pounds)	12-pound test
Jack Crevalle	10-pound test
Horse-Eye Jack	10-pound test
Ladyfish	8-pound test
Snook	12-pound test
Spotted Seatrout	10-pound test
Barracuda	12-pound test

Deepwater Fish, by Chumming or Sighting

Dolphin	10-pound test
Mackerel	10-pound test
False Albacore	10-pound test
Bonito	10-pound test
Grouper	10-pound test
Yellowtail	10-pound test
Bermuda chub	10-pound test

Special Leaders For Fish That Might Bite Or Fray Through Leader

Bluefish	10-pound test with 12 inches #4 wire leader added
Sailfish	12-pound test with 12 inches 80-pound-test nylon added
Marlin	12-pound test with 12 inches 100-pound-test nylon added
Tarpon	12-pound test with 12 inches 100-pound-test nylon added
Tuna	12-pound test with 12 inches 100-pound-test nylon added
Barracuda	12-pound test with 12 inches #5 wire leader added
Sharks	12-pound test with 12 inches #5 or #7 heavier wire leader added

HOOKS

Modern hook design and manufacture has come a long way since the first Stone Age bone hooks dating back to 5000 B.C. Today's fishhooks come in hundreds of sizes, shapes, and special designs. They're hardened and tempered, then plated or bronzed to meet special specifications. Some are thin steel wire for use in tying artificial flies; others are thick steel for big-game fish that prowl offshore waters. Avoid stainless steel hooks if you plan to catch and release.

There is no such thing as an all-purpose hook. Fishermen must carry a variety of patterns and sizes to match both tackle and size of fish being hunted. Let's start from the beginning by learning the basic nomenclature of a typical fishhook, illustrated in the accompanying drawing. Even the various parts of a typical fishhook may vary in design to meet certain requirements. There are sliced shanks to better hold bait on the hook, forged shanks for greater strength in marine hooks, tapered eyes to reduce weight of hooks used in tying dry flies, and so on.

225

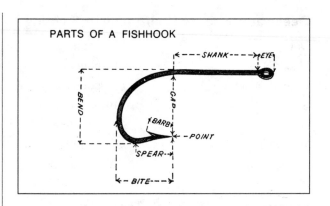

PARTS OF A FISHHOOK

SHANK — EYE
BEND
GAP
BARB
SPEAR — POINT
BITE

HOOK WIRE SIZE

The letter X and the designations "Fine" or "Stout" are used to indicate the weight or diameter of a hook. For example, a 2X Stout means the hook is made of the standard diameter for a hook two sizes larger, and a 3X Stout is made of the standard diameter for a hook three sizes larger.

When we go to lightweight hooks, the designations are reversed. For example, a 2X Fine means that the hook is made of the standard diameter for a hook two sizes smaller, and so on.

Obviously, the angler seeking the big fish should lean toward the stout hooks, which are not apt to bend or spring when striking the bigger saltwater fish.

SHANK LENGTH

The letter X and the designations "Long" or "Short" are used to specify shank length of a hook. The formula for determining shank length is similar to that used for wire sizes. A 2X Long means the shank of the hook is the standard length for a hook two sizes larger, and a 4X Long for a hook four sizes larger. A 2X Short is a hook that has a shank as short as the standard length of a hook two sizes smaller, and 4X Short for a hook four sizes smaller, and so on.

Picking a hook with the correct shank length depends on the type of fishing you plan to undertake. A short-shank hook is preferred for baitfishing, since it can be hidden in the bait more easily. The long-shank hook is at its best when used for fish with sharp teeth. A bluefish, for example, would have a tough time getting past the long shank and cutting into the leader. Long-shank hooks are also used in tying streamers and bucktails.

HOOK SIZE

Attempts have been made to standardize hook sizes, but none has been very successful. The problem has been that a hook actually has two measurements—the gap and the length of the shank, both of which vary from pattern to pattern.

Only by studying the various patterns and sizes in the accompanying charts can an angler become sufficiently familiar with hook patterns to pick the right hook for the job.

As a guide, refer to Natural Saltwater Baits on page 240, and note the hook sizes recommended for various species of fish. Match those recommendations with the hook sizes on these pages and compare the differences. With this information, it is not difficult to choose the correct size hook for your type of fishing.

HOOK CHARACTERISTICS

In addition to size and shank length, there are other characteristics of hooks to consider when selecting a hook for a specific purpose. The barb, obviously, is a critical part of the hook. A short barb is quick to set in the mouth of a fish, but it also gives a jumping fish a greater chance of dislodging it. A long barb, on the other hand, is more difficult to set but it also makes it a lot tougher for a fish to shake it loose.

So what guidelines should an angler follow? Let's list some basic recommendations. The all-round saltwater fisherman can't go wrong by using the O'Shaughnessy, Kirby, Sproat, or Siwash patterns. And if you happen to have some Salmon hooks, they're perfectly all right to use with a wire leader for barracuda and other too thy fish.

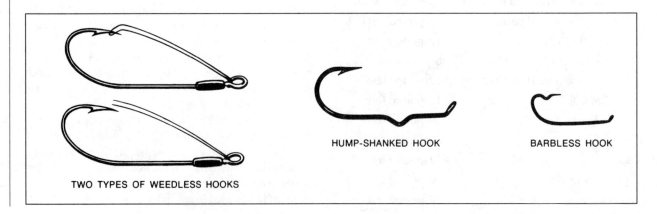

TWO TYPES OF WEEDLESS HOOKS

HUMP-SHANKED HOOK

BARBLESS HOOK

HOOK PART VARIATIONS

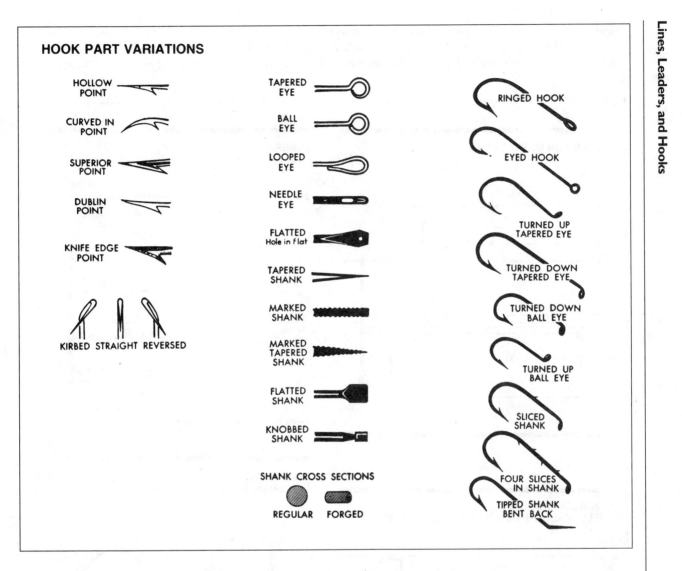

HOLLOW POINT

CURVED IN POINT

SUPERIOR POINT

DUBLIN POINT

KNIFE EDGE POINT

KIRBED   STRAIGHT   REVERSED

TAPERED EYE

BALL EYE

LOOPED EYE

NEEDLE EYE

FLATTED Hole in flat

TAPERED SHANK

MARKED SHANK

MARKED TAPERED SHANK

FLATTED SHANK

KNOBBED SHANK

SHANK CROSS SECTIONS

REGULAR   FORGED

RINGED HOOK

EYED HOOK

TURNED UP TAPERED EYE

TURNED DOWN TAPERED EYE

TURNED DOWN BALL EYE

TURNED UP BALL EYE

SLICED SHANK

FOUR SLICES IN SHANK

TIPPED SHANK BENT BACK

If you're a flounder fisherman, you'll find that the Chestertown and Carlisle patterns are your best bet. The long-shanked Chestertown makes it especially easy to unhook flounders, which may well be a primary reason for using them when fishing for these flatfish.

If you're a baitfisherman, use the sliced shanked Mustad-Beak or Eagle Claw patterns. Those extra barbs on the shanks do a good job keeping natural baits secured to the hook.

Fishermen can also become confused when they see hooks with straight-ringed eyes, turned-up eyes, and turned-down eyes. This should not present a problem. If you're replacing hooks on lures or attaching hooks to spinners use a straight-ringed eye. If you're tying short-shanked artificial flies, pick the turned-up eye, which will provide more space for the hook point to bite into the fish. The turned-down eye is the best bet for standard flies and for baitfishing, since it brings the point of the hook closest to a straight line of penetration when striking a fish.

Curved shanks also lead to some confusion. Without getting into specific details, let's say simply that a curved shank, curved right or left, has its place in bait-fishing. The offset point has a better chance of hitting flesh when a strike is made.

When you are casting or trolling with artificial lures or spinners, however, the straight-shanked hook is a better choice, since it does not have a tendency to spin or twist, which is often the case with curved-shanked hooks.

Below and on upcoming pages, you will find various styles of hooks. In most cases, the smallest and largest of hooks in these styles are shown, with intermediate hook sizes indicated by means of horizontal lines and corresponding hook numbers. To match the name and size of an unknown hook, just compare yours to the drawings. (CHART CONCEPT BY JEFF FITSCHEN)

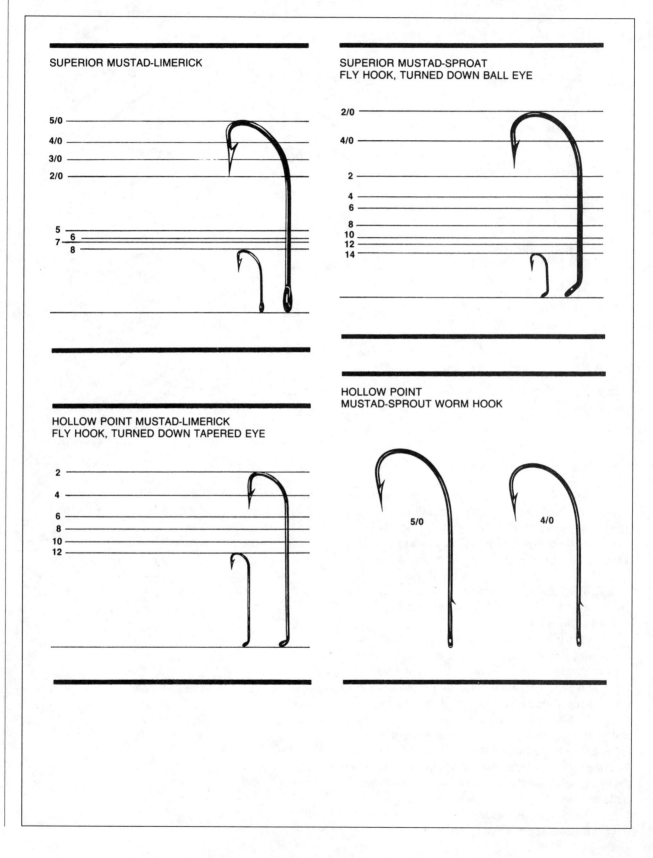

SUPERIOR MUSTAD-LIMERICK

5/0
4/0
3/0
2/0

5
7 6
8

SUPERIOR MUSTAD-SPROAT
FLY HOOK, TURNED DOWN BALL EYE

2/0
4/0

2
4
6
8
10
12
14

HOLLOW POINT MUSTAD-LIMERICK
FLY HOOK, TURNED DOWN TAPERED EYE

2
4
6
8
10
12

HOLLOW POINT
MUSTAD-SPROUT WORM HOOK

5/0

4/0

SUPERIOR MUSTAD-CARLISLE

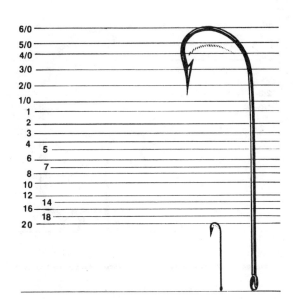

HOLLOW POINT MUSTAD-WIDE GAP HOOK

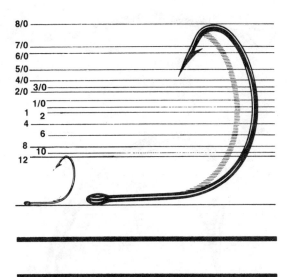

SUPERIOR MUSTAD-ABERDEEN
CRICKET HOOK

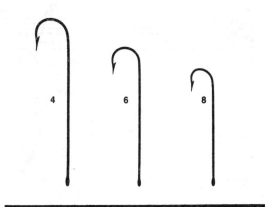

SUPERIOR MUSTAD-O'SHAUGHNESSY

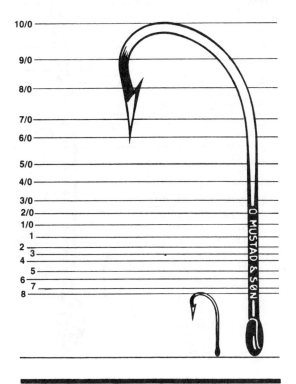

229

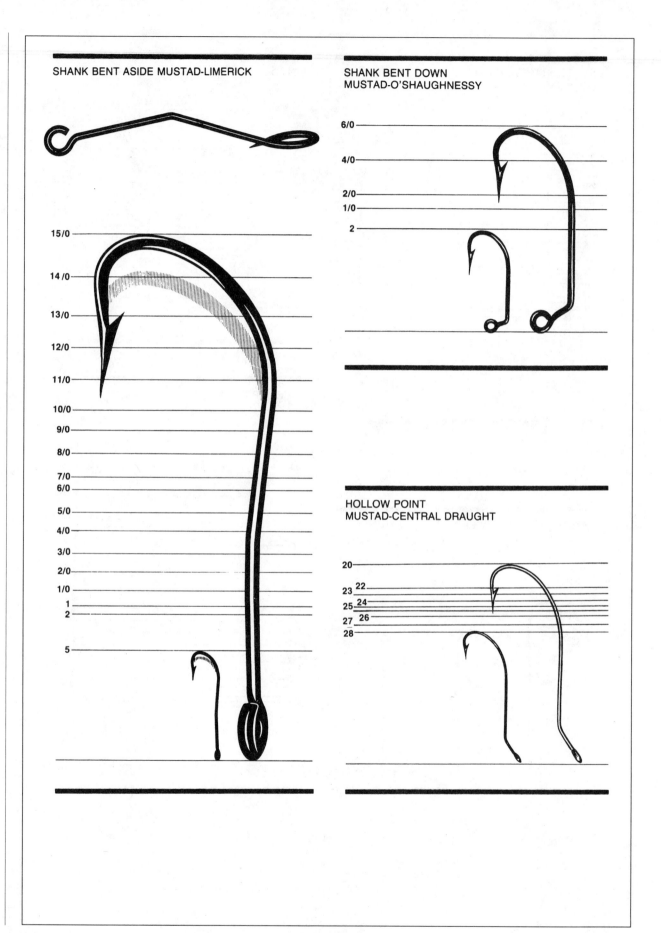

SHANK BENT ASIDE MUSTAD-LIMERICK

SHANK BENT DOWN
MUSTAD-O'SHAUGHNESSY

6/0

4/0

2/0
1/0

2

15/0

14 /0

13/0

12/0

11/0

10/0

9/0

8/0

7/0
6/0

5/0

4/0

3/0

2/0

1/0

1
2

5

HOLLOW POINT
MUSTAD-CENTRAL DRAUGHT

20

23 22
25 24
27 26
28

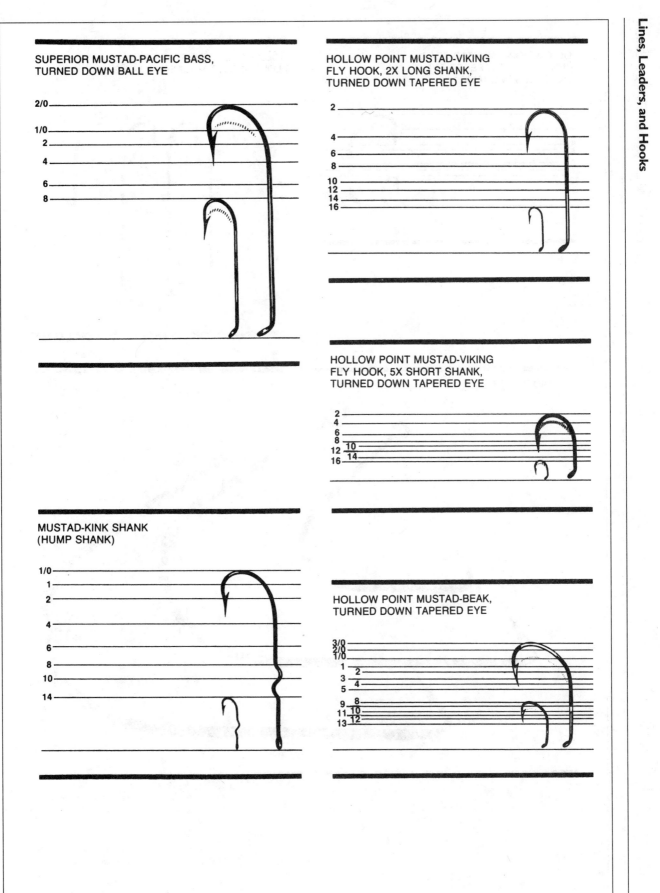

SUPERIOR MUSTAD-PACIFIC BASS,
TURNED DOWN BALL EYE

2/0
1/0
2
4
6
8

HOLLOW POINT MUSTAD-VIKING
FLY HOOK, 2X LONG SHANK,
TURNED DOWN TAPERED EYE

2
4
6
8
10
12
14
16

HOLLOW POINT MUSTAD-VIKING
FLY HOOK, 5X SHORT SHANK,
TURNED DOWN TAPERED EYE

2
4
6
8
12 10
16 14

MUSTAD-KINK SHANK
(HUMP SHANK)

1/0
1
2
4
6
8
10
14

HOLLOW POINT MUSTAD-BEAK,
TURNED DOWN TAPERED EYE

3/0
2/0
1/0
1 2
3 4
5
9 8
11 10
13 12

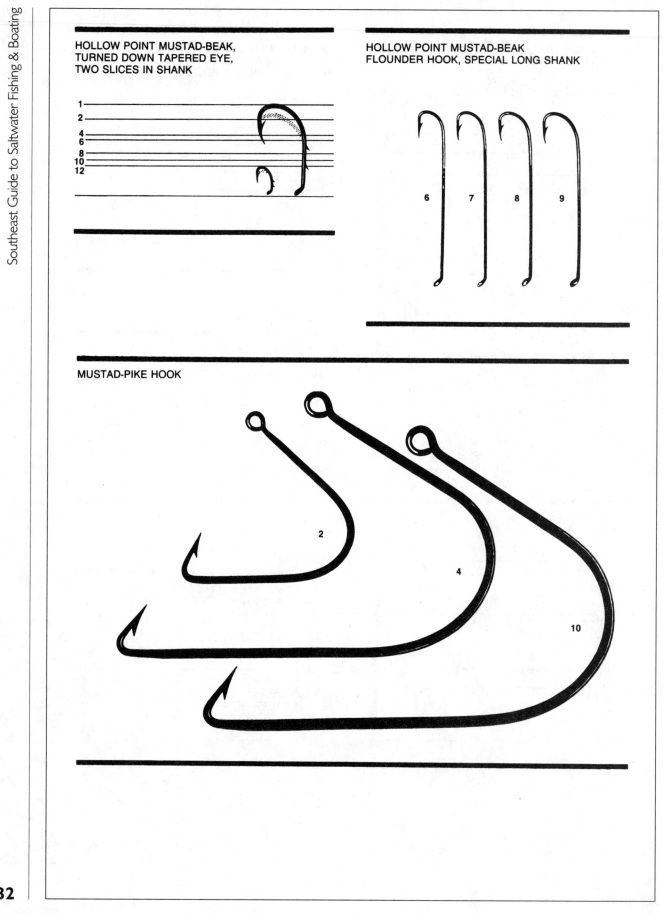

HOLLOW POINT MUSTAD-BEAK,
TURNED DOWN TAPERED EYE,
TWO SLICES IN SHANK

HOLLOW POINT MUSTAD-BEAK
FLOUNDER HOOK, SPECIAL LONG SHANK

MUSTAD-PIKE HOOK

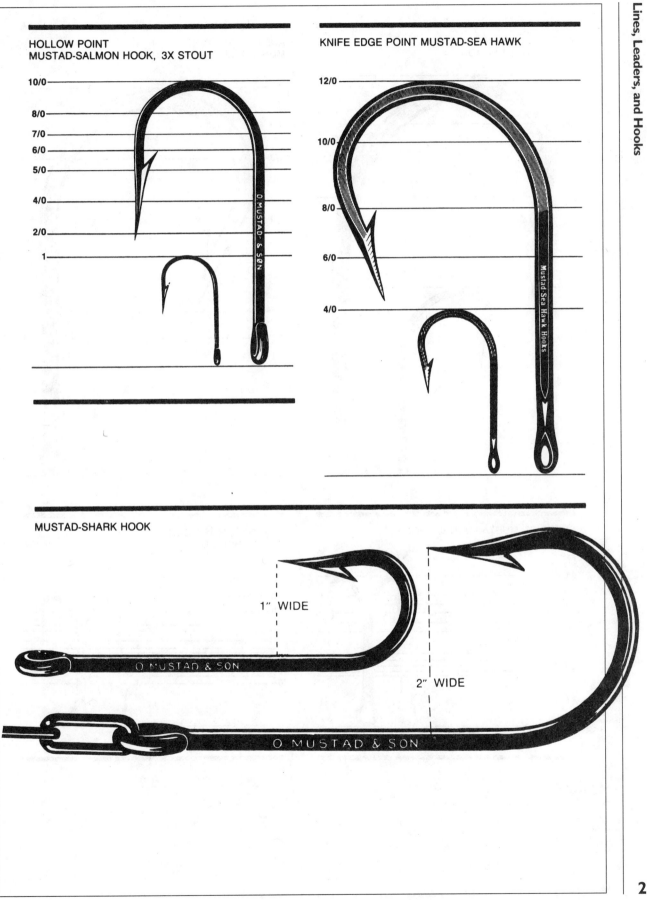

HOLLOW POINT
MUSTAD-SALMON HOOK, 3X STOUT

10/0
8/0
7/0
6/0
5/0
4/0
2/0
1

KNIFE EDGE POINT MUSTAD-SEA HAWK

12/0
10/0
8/0
6/0
4/0

MUSTAD-SHARK HOOK

1" WIDE

2" WIDE

O MUSTAD & SON

O MUSTAD & SON

233

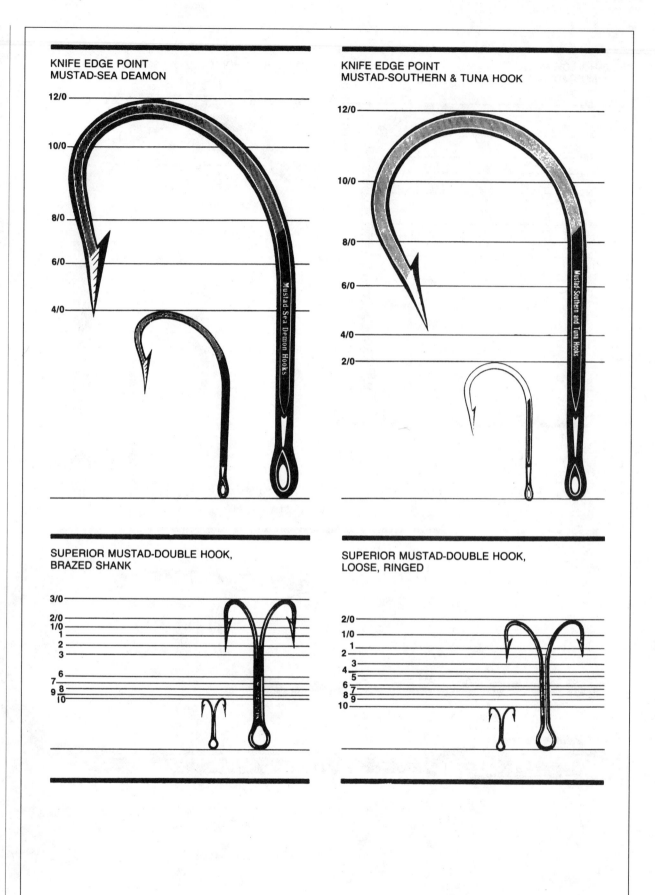

KNIFE EDGE POINT
MUSTAD-SEA DEAMON

12/0
10/0
8/0
6/0
4/0

Mustad-Sea Demon Hooks

KNIFE EDGE POINT
MUSTAD-SOUTHERN & TUNA HOOK

12/0
10/0
8/0
6/0
4/0
2/0

Mustad-Southern and Tuna Hooks

SUPERIOR MUSTAD-DOUBLE HOOK,
BRAZED SHANK

3/0
2/0
1/0
1
2
3
6
7
8
9
10

SUPERIOR MUSTAD-DOUBLE HOOK,
LOOSE, RINGED

2/0
1/0
1
2
3
4
5
6
7
8
9
10

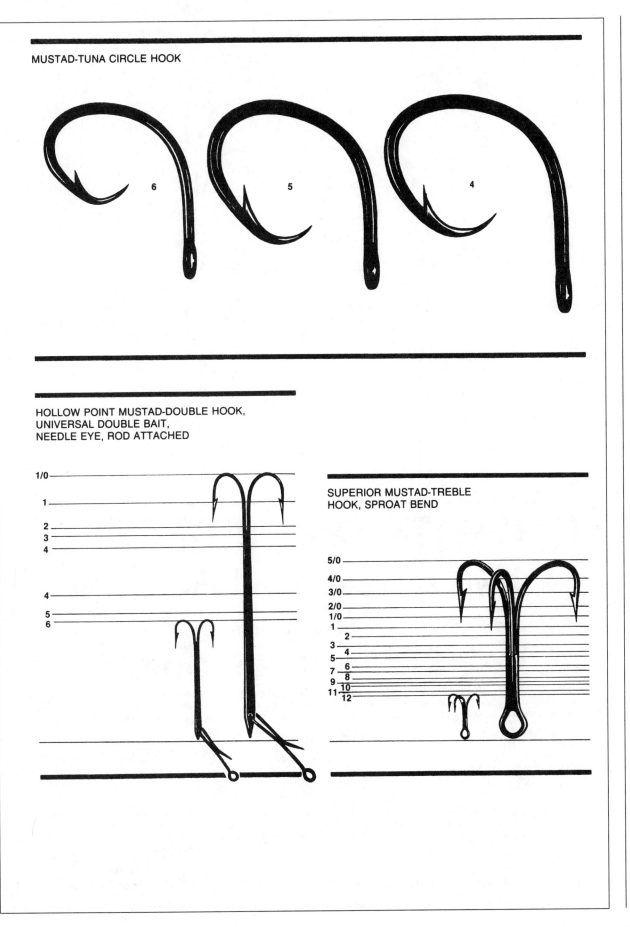

MUSTAD-TUNA CIRCLE HOOK

HOLLOW POINT MUSTAD-DOUBLE HOOK,
UNIVERSAL DOUBLE BAIT,
NEEDLE EYE, ROD ATTACHED

SUPERIOR MUSTAD-TREBLE
HOOK, SPROAT BEND

235

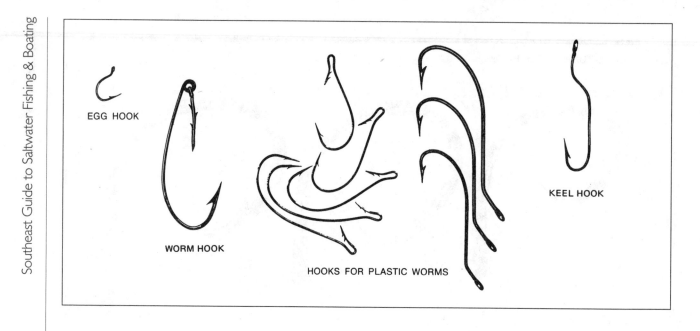

EGG HOOK

WORM HOOK

HOOKS FOR PLASTIC WORMS

KEEL HOOK

Natural baits are no less important in salt water than they are in fresh water. That fact is well known to anyone who has seen a school of ravenous bluefish slash viciously into a horde of spearing, mossbunkers, or the like.

What natural saltwater baits should you use and when? Those are questions that only time and experience can help you answer accurately. Generally, you will find that it pays to use any bait that is prevalent when and where you are fishing. A few discreet questions at a bait shop in the fishing area will go a long way toward helping you choose a productive bait.

How you rig a saltwater bait can be a vital factor. The primary consideration in rigging most baits is to make them appear as lifelike as possible, whether they are to be trolled, cast out and retrieved, or bounced on the bottom. The upcoming drawings show proven ways to prepare and rig the most popular baits used in salt water.

HOW TO CATCH BAIT AND KEEP IT FRESH

Anglers are often puzzled if they have to catch and keep something other than a dozen worms for a day's fishing. Catching the various baits and keeping them alive and kicking is not difficult.

SEA WORMS

Sea worms, such as blood- and sandworms, are delicate and should be kept in damp seaweed. If they are to be kept for a week or so, spread them out in seaweed and keep them refrigerated. Blood- and sandworms are enemies and should be kept separate. Use a wood partition to divide your bait box into two compartments.

MINNOWS

There are several ways to collect minnows: minnow trap, drop or umbrella net, minnow seine, or the cast net. Remember, saltwater fishing requires saltwater minnows.

Caution: A fishing license is usually required to take bait in fresh water, and many states set limits on the number of baitfish that may be kept. Check the fishing regulations of your state before netting or trapping.

The minnow trap requires the least skill to use. It works on the principle that a small fish will swim into the funnel-like openings after food and be unable to find its way out. For bait, you should wet oatmeal or cornmeal and roll it into balls the size of golfballs.

8

Baits and Lures

A minnow seine is fun to use and an effective way to collect bait. A 20-foot net is about right for beginners. Two fishermen wade about 100 feet from the beach and sweep the net along the bottom toward shore. Bait will be trapped and carried up on shore. (VIN T. SPARANO)

The meal will break up gradually in the trap and provide bait for long periods.

The best place to set the trap is in shallow water near a dock or boathouse. On streams, set it near the head or side of a pool where the current is slow.

The drop or umbrella net, which measures 36 by 36 inches, gets more immediate results but may be more difficult to use. Lower it into the water just deep enough so that you can still lift it fast.

A drop or dip net can be used from any dock or bulkhead. Most nets are 36 by 36 inches. Lower it in the water just deep enough so that you can lift it fast. Sprinkle bread crumbs over the net. When minnows gather to fed on the crumbs, lift the net fast and collect your bait.

Sprinkle breadcrumbs over it and let them sink. When minnows begin to feed on the crumbs, lift the net fast. With practice, you'll make good hauls every time.

A minnow seine not only produces a lot of bait, but is fun to use, especially in bays and tidal rivers. A seine is usually 4 feet high and anywhere from 10 to 50 feet long, with lead weights along the bottom and floats on top. A 20-footer is a good size for most purposes. Seining is easy. Two people carry the seine about 100 feet from shore or until depth hits 4 feet or so. Keeping the weighted end of the seine on the bottom, the people sweep toward shore. The seine will belly out, catching everything in its path and carrying bait up on shore, where it can be picked up.

The cast net is one of the most useful tools of both the freshwater and saltwater angler because he can use it to get the bait that he can't buy, and to obtain forage baitfish native to the water that he's fishing—which is the best bait to use under most circumstances.

A few states prohibit the use of cast nets, or restrict sizes or materials. Again, check the fishing regulations of your state before netting.

Monofilament nets, because their nylon strands are stiff, open better than nets made of braided threads. Mono nets also sink faster and are less visible after they're thrown into the water. Generally, they catch more fish, but they're also more expensive.

Cast nets are available in various sizes and types. Experts throw 16-foot and larger nets, but anglers who would only use them occasionally are better off getting one that measures 8 to 10 feet. Bridge nets, popular in the Florida Keys, are short nets with extra lead weights around the bottom. When the net is dropped off a bridge into deep water, its added weight allows it to sink quickly and hold baitfish before they dive.

(continued on page 244)

NATURAL BAITS FOR SALTWATER FISH

SPECIES OF FISH	NATURAL BAITS AND LURES	RECOMMENDED METHODS	HOOKS
Albacore	Feather lures	Trolling	7/0
Amberjack	Strip baits, feathers, spoons, plugs	Trolling, casting	6/0 to 9/0
Barracuda	Bait fish, plugs, feathers, spoons	Trolling, casting	1/0 to 8/0
Bass, California kelp	Sardines, anchovies, clams, mussels, sea worms, shrimp	Trolling, casting, still-fishing	1 to 1/0
Bass, channel	Mullet, mossbunker, crab, clam, spoons, plugs	Casting, still-fishing, trolling	6/0 to 10/0
Bass, giant sea	Cut bait, mullet, mackerel, sardines	Still-fishing, trolling	12/0 to 14/0
Bass, sea	Squid, clam, sea worm, crab, killie	Drifting, still-fishing	1/0 to 5/0
Bass, striped	Sea worm, clam, eel, metal squids, plugs, jigs, live mackerel	Casting, trolling, drifting, still-fishing	2/0 to 8/0
Billfish (sailfish, marlin, swordfish)	Balao, mackerel, squid, bonito, strip baits, feathered jigs	Trolling	4/0 to 12/0
Bluefish	Rigged eel, cut bait, butterfish, plugs, spoons, feathers	Trolling, casting, drifting, still-fishing	3/0 to 8/0
Bonefish	Cut bait (mainly sardine and conch), flies, plugs, spoons	Casting, drifting, still-fishing	1/0 to 4/0
Bonito	Feather lures, spoons	Trolling	4/0 to 6/0
Codfish	Clam, crab, cut bait	Still-fishing, drifting	7/0 to 9/0
Croaker	Sand bugs, mussels, clam, sardine, sea worm	Still-fishing, casting,	1/0 to 6/0
Dolphin	Bait fish, feather lures, spoons, plugs, streamer flies	Trolling, casting	2/0 to 6/0
Eel	Killie, clam, crab, sea worm, spearing	Still-fishing, drifting, casting	6 to 1/0
Flounder, summer	Squid, spearing, sea worm, clam, killie, smelt	Drifting, casting, still-fishing	4/0 to 6/0
Flounder, winter	Sea worm, mussel, clam	Still-fishing	6 to 12 (long-shank)
Grouper	Squid, mullet, sardine, balao, shrimp, crab, plugs	Still-fishing, casting	4/0 to 12/0
Grunt	Shrimp, crab, sea worm	Still-fishing	2 to 1/0
Haddock	Clam, conch, crab, cut bait	Still-fishing	1/0 to 4/0
Hake	Clam, conch, crab, cut bait	Still-fishing	2/0 to 6/0
Halibut	Squid, crab, sea worm, killie, shrimp	Still-fishing	3/0 to 10/0
Jack Crevallé	Bait fish, cut bait, feathers, metal squid, spoons, plugs	Trolling, still-fishing, casting, drifting	1/0 to 5/0
Jewfish	Mullet, other bait fish	Still-fishing	10/0 to 12/0
Ladyfish	Killie, shrimp, flies, spoons, plugs	Trolling, casting, still-fishing, drifting	1/0 to 5/0
Ling	Clam, crab, cut bait	Still-fishing	4 to 2/0
Mackerel	Bait fish, tube lures, jigs, spinners, streamer flies	Trolling, still-fishing, casting, drifting	3 to 6
Perch, white	Sea worm, shrimp, spearing, flies, spoons	Still-fishing, casting	2 to 6
Pollack	Squid strip, clam, feather lures	Still-fishing, trolling	6/0 to 9/0
Pompano	Sand bugs, jigs, plugs, flies	Trolling, casting, drifting, still-fishing	1 to 4
Porgy	Clam, squid, sea worm, crab, mussel, shrimp	Still-fishing	4 to 1/0
Rockfish, Pacific	Herring, sardine, mussel, squid, clam, shrimp	Still-fishing, drifting	1/0 to 8/0
Snapper, mangrove	Cut bait, shrimp	Trolling, still-fishing, drifting	1/0 to 6/0
Snapper, red	Shrimp, mullet, crab	Trolling, still-fishing, drifting	6/0 to 10/0
Snapper, yellowtail	Shrimp, mullet, crab	Trolling, still-fishing	4 to 1/0
Snook	Crab, shrimp, bait fish, plugs, spoons, spinners, feathers	Casting, drifting, still-fishing	2/0 to 4/0
Sole	Clam, sea worm	Still-fishing	4 to 6
Spot	Crab, shrimp, bait fish, sea worm	Still-fishing	8 to 10
Tarpon	Cut bait, bait fish, plugs, spoons, feathers	Trolling, casting, drifting, still-fishing	4/0 to 10/0
Tautog (blackfish)	Clam, sea worm, crab, shrimp	Still-fishing	6 to 2/0
Tomcod	Clam, mussel, shrimp	Still-fishing	6 to 1/0
Tuna, bluefin	Mackerel, flying fish, bonito, squid, dolphin, herring, cut bait, feathered jigs	Trolling	6/0 to 14/0
Wahoo	Bait fish, feather jigs, spoons, plugs	Trolling, casting	4/0 to 8/0
Weakfish	Shrimp, squid, sea worm	Still-fishing, casting, drifting, trolling	1 to 4/0
Whiting, northern	Sea worm, clam	Still-fishing, drifting, casting	4 to 1/0
Yellowtail	Herring, sardine, smelt, spoons, metal squids, feather lures	Trolling, casting, still-fishing	4/0 to 6/0

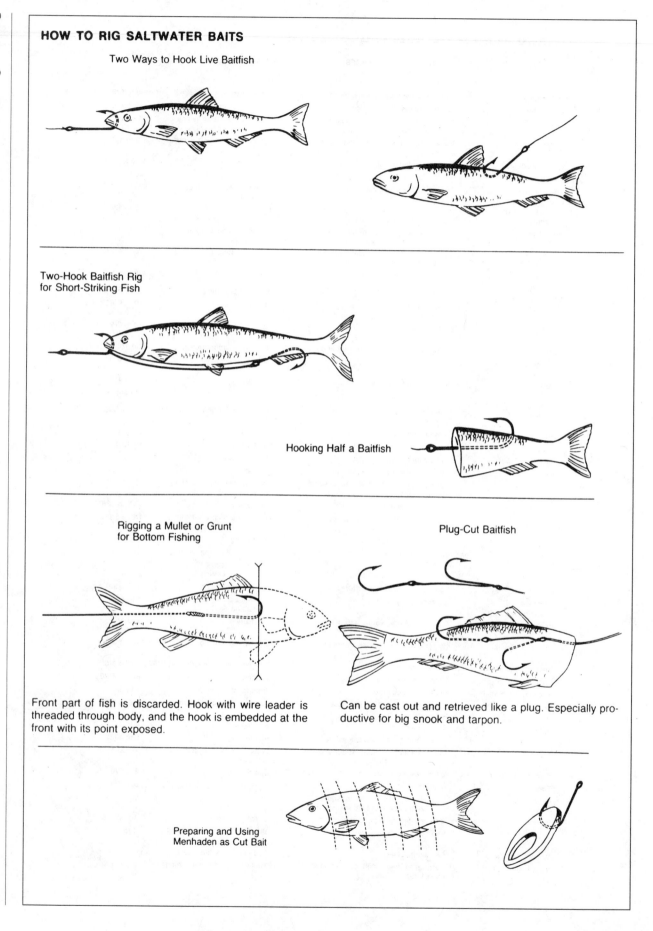

HOW TO RIG SALTWATER BAITS

Two Ways to Hook Live Baitfish

Two-Hook Baitfish Rig
for Short-Striking Fish

Hooking Half a Baitfish

Rigging a Mullet or Grunt
for Bottom Fishing

Plug-Cut Baitfish

Front part of fish is discarded. Hook with wire leader is threaded through body, and the hook is embedded at the front with its point exposed.

Can be cast out and retrieved like a plug. Especially productive for big snook and tarpon.

Preparing and Using
Menhaden as Cut Bait

Hooking a Whole Crab

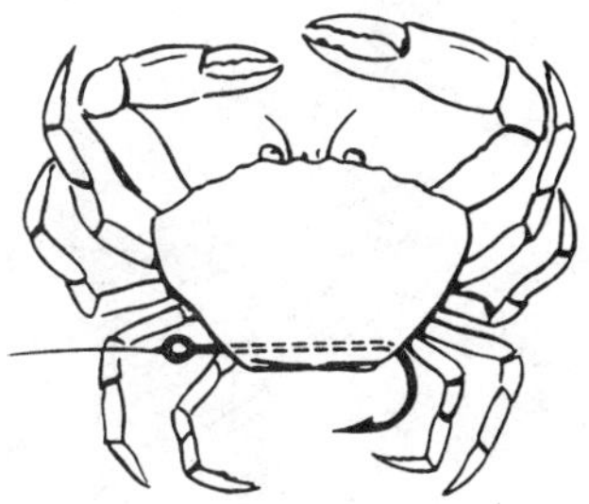

Hooking Half a Crab

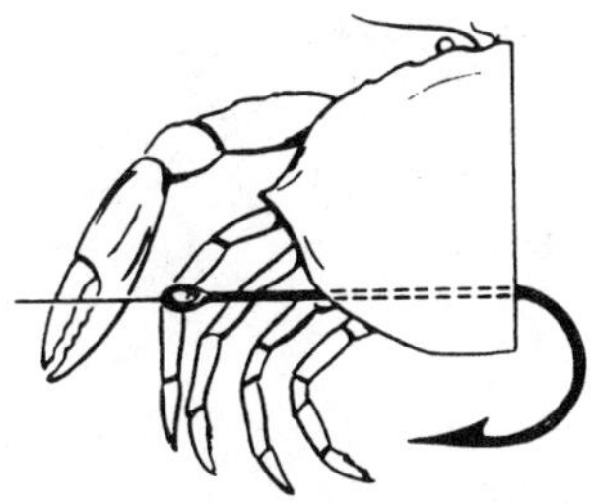

Rigging a Dead Soft-Shell Crab

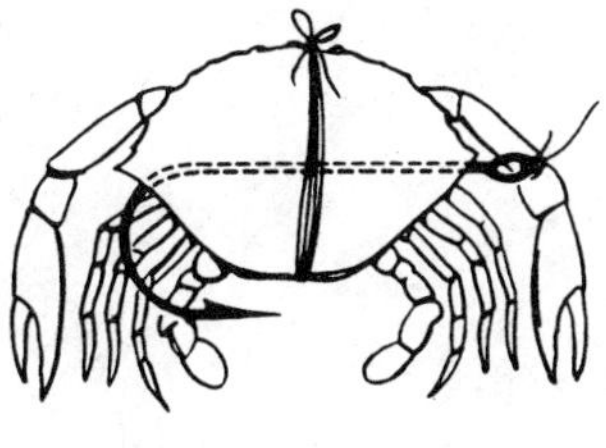

Hooking a Sand Shrimp

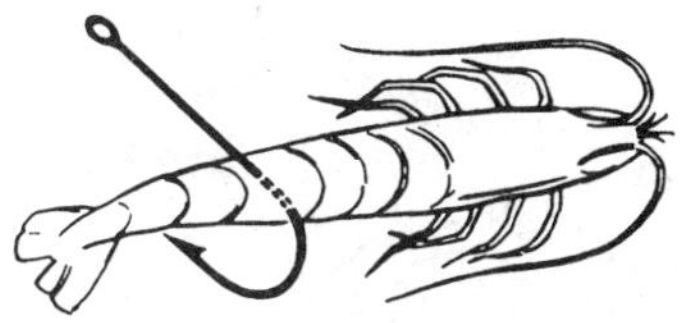

Rigging a Single Shrimp

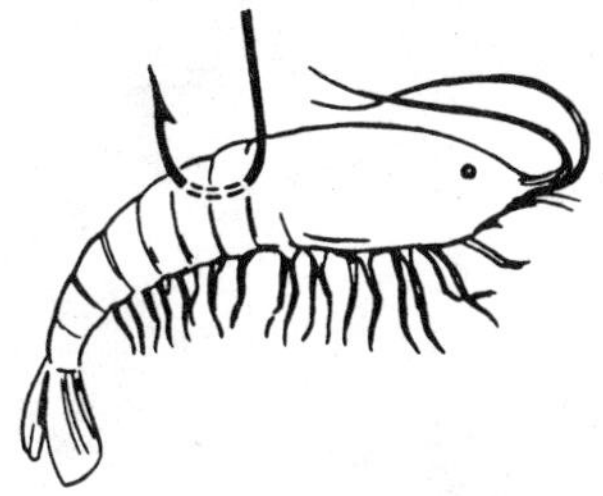

Rigging Two Shrimp
on Single Hook

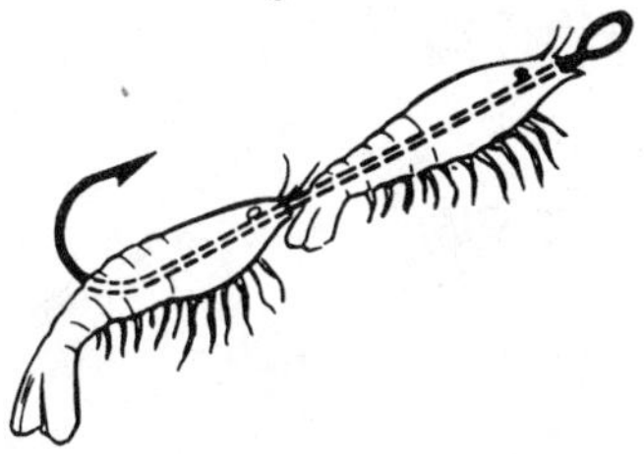

Hooking a Sandworm
or Bloodworm

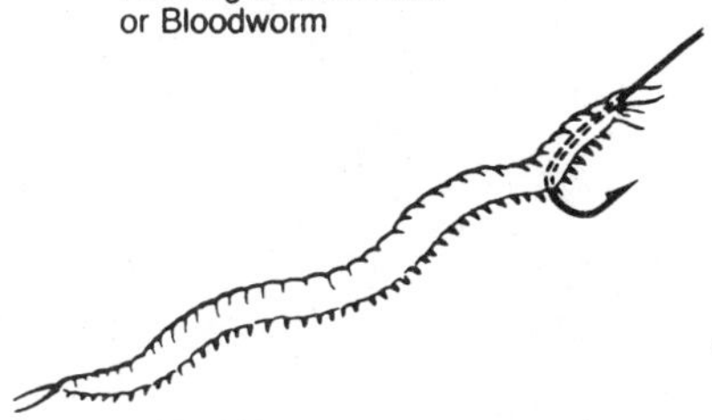

Mooching Rig with Keel Sinker

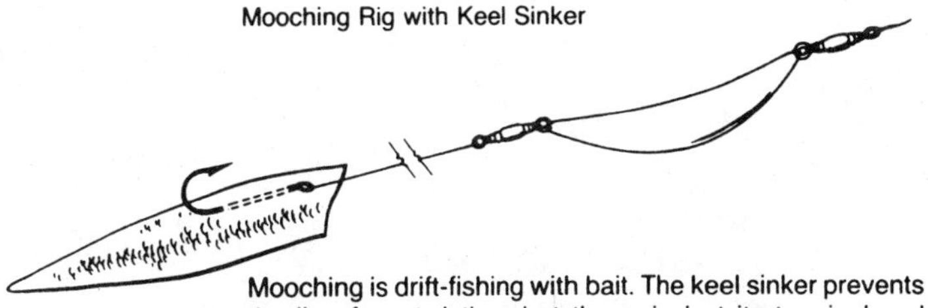

Mooching is drift-fishing with bait. The keel sinker prevents the line from twisting, but the swivel at its terminal end permits the bait to spin.

SALTWATER BAIT RIGS

Rigging a Whole Unweighted Eel

Hooks are attached to light chain or heavy monofilament, or they can be attached to linen line.

Rigging an Eelskin with Metal Squid

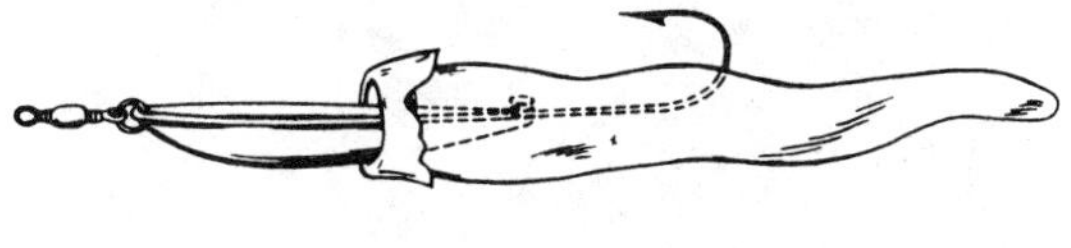

To a Montauk or Belmar-type metal squid, a ring is attached, onto which the eelskin is tied.

Rigging an Eelskin with Plug

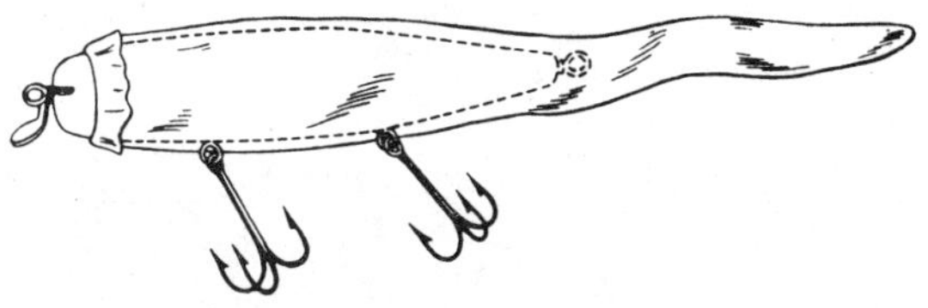

Eelskin is slipped over the plug, whose tail treble hook has been removed. Bottom treble hooks protrude as shown, and skin is tied on at the plug's head.

Two Ways to Hook a Live Eel

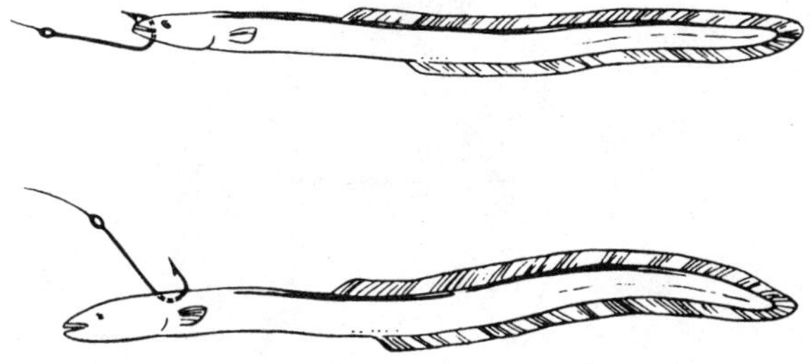

241

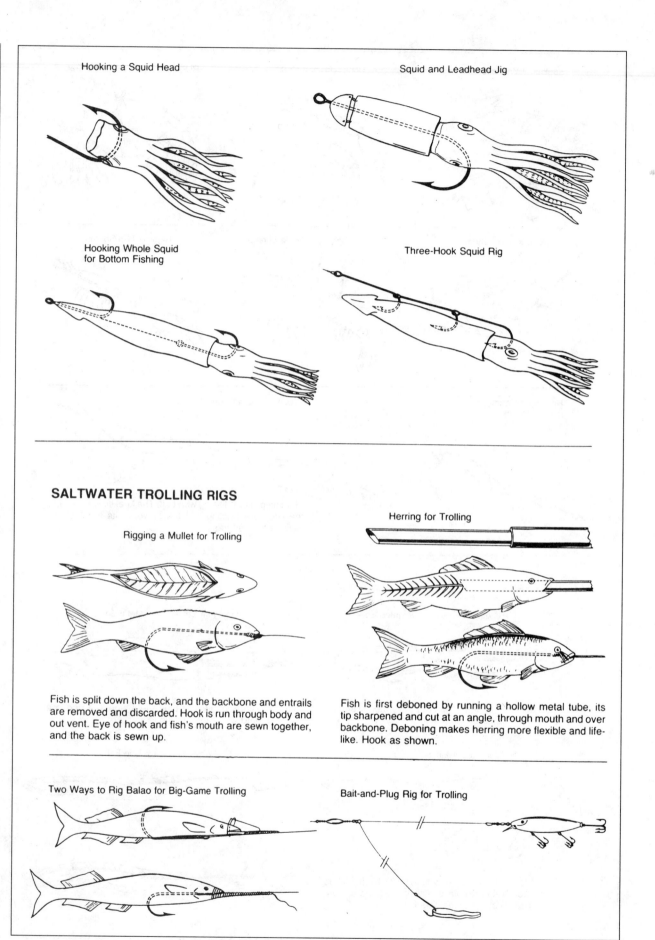

Hooking a Squid Head

Squid and Leadhead Jig

Hooking Whole Squid
for Bottom Fishing

Three-Hook Squid Rig

SALTWATER TROLLING RIGS

Rigging a Mullet for Trolling

Herring for Trolling

Fish is split down the back, and the backbone and entrails are removed and discarded. Hook is run through body and out vent. Eye of hook and fish's mouth are sewn together, and the back is sewn up.

Fish is first deboned by running a hollow metal tube, its tip sharpened and cut at an angle, through mouth and over backbone. Deboning makes herring more flexible and life-like. Hook as shown.

Two Ways to Rig Balao for Big-Game Trolling

Bait-and-Plug Rig for Trolling

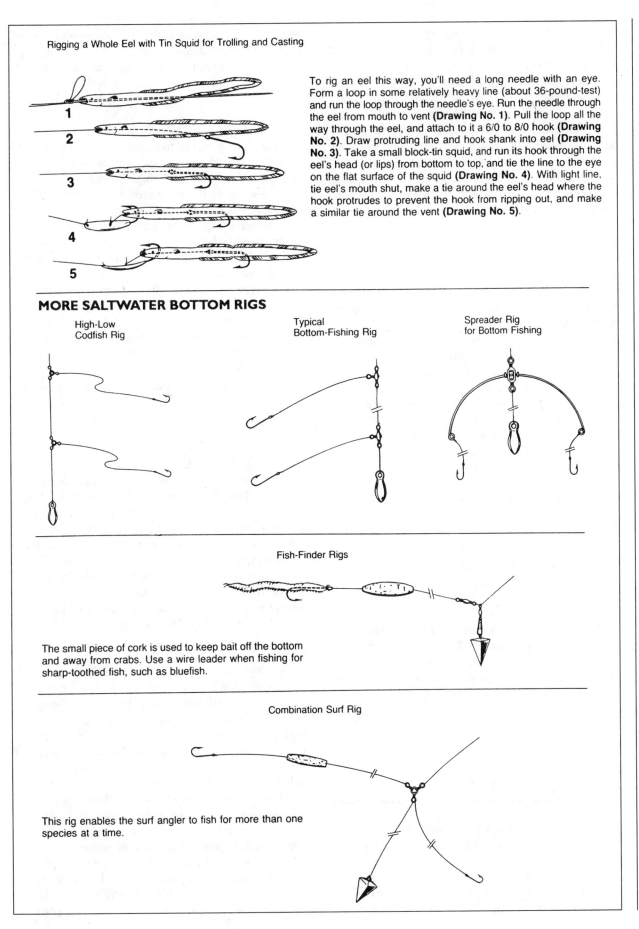

Rigging a Whole Eel with Tin Squid for Trolling and Casting

To rig an eel this way, you'll need a long needle with an eye. Form a loop in some relatively heavy line (about 36-pound-test) and run the loop through the needle's eye. Run the needle through the eel from mouth to vent **(Drawing No. 1)**. Pull the loop all the way through the eel, and attach to it a 6/0 to 8/0 hook **(Drawing No. 2)**. Draw protruding line and hook shank into eel **(Drawing No. 3)**. Take a small block-tin squid, and run its hook through the eel's head (or lips) from bottom to top, and tie the line to the eye on the flat surface of the squid **(Drawing No. 4)**. With light line, tie eel's mouth shut, make a tie around the eel's head where the hook protrudes to prevent the hook from ripping out, and make a similar tie around the vent **(Drawing No. 5)**.

MORE SALTWATER BOTTOM RIGS

High-Low
Codfish Rig

Typical
Bottom-Fishing Rig

Spreader Rig
for Bottom Fishing

Fish-Finder Rigs

The small piece of cork is used to keep bait off the bottom and away from crabs. Use a wire leader when fishing for sharp-toothed fish, such as bluefish.

Combination Surf Rig

This rig enables the surf angler to fish for more than one species at a time.

243

A plastic bucket is the best storage container for a net. All nets should routinely be rinsed with clean water and cleared of debris.

The proper gripping technique is just as important as the method you use to throw the net. If you're right-handed, you should coil the throwing line and loop it in your right hand. Stretch the net full-length, and grab the net two-thirds of the way down with your left hand. Then bring your right hand (which is still holding the coils) just below your left hand and grasp the net, with your thumb pointing outward. Reach down to the bottom of the net with your left hand, pick up the weighted line at the bottom of the net, and drape the inside of the net over your right shoulder.

Gather about two-thirds of the net in your left hand, and with your feet pointing in the direction in which you'll throw the net, rotate the upper half of your body to the right. You're now ready to cast—just throw the net straight out in front of you.

The next problem is keeping the minnows alive and fresh. The water must be aerated to keep enough oxygen in the bucket for survival, and this can be done in several ways. Water can be aerated by battery-powered devices. You can also aerate the water manually with a tin can. Scoop up a canful of water and pour it back into the bucket from a height of 2 feet. Doing this a dozen times every 15 minutes should provide sufficient oxygen for a couple of dozen minnows.

Bait water must be kept at a constant temperature. In summer, add ice cubes to the water before transporting them. As the ice melts, it will cool the water and add oxygen. Take care, however, not to cool the water too fast.

It is important to avoid abrupt temperature changes, which will kill minnows.

If you plan to troll, keep bait in a bucket designed for trolling. This bucket, built to float on its side, will take water at an angle and aerate it.

If you're stillfishing, use the traditional bucket, which is actually two buckets. The outer bucket is used when transporting minnows. When you start fishing, lift out the insert and lower it into the water. The insert, which floats upright, is vented so that water is constantly changed.

ARTIFICIAL LURES

Fishing with bait is enjoyable, certainly, but there's something about fooling a fish with an artificial that gives most anglers a special charge.

A neophyte fisherman who visits a well-stocked sporting-goods store or tackle shop is confronted with a bewildering array of plugs, spoons, spinners, jigs, flies, bugs, and others. Some artificials look like nothing that ever swam, crawled, or flew, and yet they catch fish.

Let's look at each type of artificial and see how and why it works and how it should be fished.

PLUGS

Plugs are lures designed to imitate small fish for the most part, though some plugs simulate mice, frogs, eels, and other food on which gamefish feed. Plug action—meaning the way it moves when retrieved by the angler—is important and is something on which manufacturers expend much money and time. Many plugs, particularly the divers, are known as crankbaits because every crank of the reel handle imparts some sort of diving or darting action.

The type, size, and weight of the plug you select is determined by the fish you are after and the kind of fishing outfit you are using. The charts, found elsewhere in this book, on how to match up various kinds of fishing tackle will help the beginner choose the right weight plugs.

There are five basic types of plugs: popping, surface, floating-diving, sinking (deep-running), and deep-diving.

Popping
These plugs float on the surface and have concave, hollowed-out faces. The angler retrieves a popping plug by jerking the rod tip back so that the plug's face digs into the water, making a small splash, bubbles, and a popping sound. Some make a louder sound than others. This sound is especially attractive to some inshore saltwater species, such as striped bass and bluefish. Most popping plugs (and most other plugs) have two sets of treble hooks. Popping plugs are most productive when the water surface is calm or nearly so. They should usually be fished very slowly.

Surface
These plugs float on the surface, but they can be fished with various kinds of retrieves and create a different kind of surface disturbance than poppers do. Designed with an elongated, or bullet-shaped, head, they create surface disturbance by various means, including propellers (at the head or at both head and tail), a wide metal lip at the head, and hinged metal "wings" just behind the head. They can be twitched so that they barely nod, retrieved steadily so that they chug across the water, or skimmed across the top as fast as the angler can turn his reel handle. The proper retrieve depends on the lure's design and, of course, on the mood of the fish. It's best to try different retrieves until you find one that produces. Good saltwater surface plugs include the MirrOlure (float model), which is good for small species, and the Zara Spook.

The Rapala Magnum is typical of deep-running saltwater plugs. It measures 9 inches and weighs 3½ ounces. Plugs of this type are effective on both inshore and offshore fish.

Floating-Diving

These plugs are designed to float when at rest and dive when retrieved. Some float horizontally while others float with the tail hanging down beneath the surface. They are made to dive by an extended lip at the head. The speed of the retrieve determines the depth of the dive. The faster the retrieve, the deeper the dive. Most of these plugs have a side-to-side wobbling action. An erratic retrieve—dive, surface, dive, surface—is often productive, and these plugs are also effective when made to swim just above a submerged weed bed, rock pile, and so on. Good saltwater floater-divers include the Thinfin Silver Shad and larger models of the Rebel Shiner and the Creek Chub Darter.

Sinking (Deep-running)

These plugs sink as soon as they hit the water and are designed for deep work. Some sink slower than others and can be fished at various depths, depending on how long the angler waits before starting his retrieve. Most of these plugs have some sort of wobbling action, and some fairly vibrate when retrieved. Some have propellers fore and aft.

These plugs are excellent fish-finders: the fisherman can start by bouncing them along bottom, and if that doesn't work, he can work them at progressively shallower depths until he finds at what depth the fish are feeding.

The Boone Needlefish has taken its share of striped bass, bluefish, and weakfish in bays, off jetties and from the surf. The Boone T.D. Special is good for salt water at any depth and has proved useful on New Jersey's striped bass. The MirrOlure (sinking model) is a big lure that casts easy and sinks fast. The shiny-sided plug draws strikes from striped bass, bluefish, tarpon, snook, barracuda, and similar inshore species.

Deep-Diving

These plugs may float or sink, but all are designed with long and/or broad lips of metal or plastic that cause the plugs to dive to depths of 30 feet or more as the angler reels in. As with other diving plugs, the faster the retrieve, the deeper the dive. Most of these lures have some sort of wobbling action. They are ideally suited for casting or trolling in deep lakes and at the edges of dropoffs, and they work best in most waters when the fish are holding in deep holes, as fish usually do during the midday in July and August.

Good diving plugs for saltwater include the Atom and the Rebel for casting or trolling, the Creek Chub Surfster for surf casting, and the Stan Gibbs Darter for nearly all inshore species.

SPOONS

Spoons are among the oldest of artificials. If you cut the handle off a teaspoon, you'd have the basic shape of this lure.

Spoons are designed to imitate small baitfish of one kind or another, so flash is an important feature in many of these lures. Most spoons have a wobbling side-to-side action when retrieved.

Many spoons have a silver or gold finish, while others are painted in various colors and combinations of colors. Most have a single free-swinging treble hook at the tail; others have a single fixed hook. Weedless arrangements are becoming more and more popular on both types.

Here are some good saltwater spoons:

Cop-E-Cat: Big mackerel-finish spoon has action similar to the well-known Dardevle, except it is designed for casting and trolling in coastal waters. Trolled deep on wire line it will take bluefish. When it is cast from surf or boat it will take stripers.

Seadevle: Similar to the Cop-E-Cat, except slimmer, this spoon is built for saltwater casting and trolling. Large sizes will get strikes from stripers, bluefish, yellowtails. Small models will catch mackerel, pollack.

Reed R.T. Flash: Well-designed spoon that can be cast, trolled, jigged. Good lure in coastal waters for tinker mackerel, snappers, weakfish, kingfish. Trolled off shore with wire line or trolling lead, it takes bigger inshore species.

Wob-L-Rite: A heavy brass spoon, easy to cast far distances. Wobbles on steady retrieve or can be jigged. Good choice for deep jigging reef species or surf and boat casting.

Tony Accetta Spoon: Available in various sizes, this spoon has proven itself in coastal waters. Usually rigged with pork rind strip, it is an effective trolling and casting lure for nearly all inshore game fish.

SPINNERS

Spinners, like spoons, are designed to imitate baitfish, and they attract gamefish by flash and vibration. A spinner is simply a metal blade mounted on a shaft by means of a revolving arm or ring called a clevis. Unlike a spoon, which has a wobbling action, a spinner blade rotates around the shaft when retrieved.

Good saltwater spinners include the Willow Leaf, particularly effective when trolling blood or sandworms for striped bass, and the Indiana Double-Blade, a multipurpose spinner rig that can be cast or trolled. The Indiana has been used on party boats drifting cut bait along the bottom for fluke and flounder.

JIGS

Generally speaking, a jig is any lure with a weighted head (usually lead), a fixed hook, and a tail of bucktail (though not always), feathers, nylon, or similar material. Jigs are made in sizes of $\frac{1}{16}$ ounce to 6 ounces and even heavier, and they will take just about any fish that swims in fresh water and salt. Jigs imitate baitfish, crustaceans, and other gamefish forage. In some jigs, the hook rides with the point up, to minimize the chance of snagging.

Jigs, and related lures, take many forms. Here's a look at the most popular types.

Bucktail jigs, such as this Hopkins model, will catch fish at nearly any depth. Cast the jig, let it sink to the bottom, then jig the lure to the surface until you determine the depth at which the fish are feeding. Jigs are sometimes more effective when tipped with cut bait, shrimp, or a plastic worm.

Feathered Jig

Often called Japanese feathers, this jig is commonly used in saltwater trolling and casting. It consists of a heavy metal head with eyes. Through the head runs a wire leader, to the end of which the hook is attached. Running from the head down to the hook is a long tail, usually of feathers. A plastic sleeve covers the feathers for about half their length.

Bonito Jig

Similar to the feathered jig but smaller and having a fixed hook embedded in the metal head. Line is tied to ring on head. Used for saltwater trolling and casting.

Bucktail Jig

Consists of a lead head, embedded hook, and trailing tail of bucktail. Head has ring to which line is attached. Head is painted, with the most popular colors being white, red, yellow, and combinations of those colors. The most popular member of the jig family, bucktail jigs are used on a wide variety of freshwater and saltwater gamefish, especially striped bass, bluefish, and many other bottom-feeders.

Bullet Bucktail Jig

Same as standard bucktail jig except that head is bullet-shaped, coming to a blunt point.

Metal (Block-Tin) Squids

Falling under the general category of jigs are these lures, which are used mostly in salt water for striped bass, bluefish, and the like. Made to resemble baitfish, they have a long, narrow body of block tin, stainless steel, chrome, or nickel-plated lead and either a single fixed hook or a free-swinging treble hook, with or without a tail of bucktail. Most metal squids range in length from 3 to 6 inches. All have bright finishes, usually silvery; in some the finish is smooth, while others have a hammered finish that gives a scalelike appearance. Among the most popular metal squids are types such as the Hopkins (which has a hammered finish; a long, narrow, flat body; and a free-swinging treble hook), the diamond jig (four-sided body, treble hook), and the sand eel (long, rounded, undulating body). A strip of pork rind often adds to the effectiveness of metal squids.

Jig and Eel

Consists of a small metal squid onto which is rigged a common eel, either the real McCoy (usually dead and preserved) or a plastic artificial. These rigged eels range in length from about 6 inches up to a foot or longer. The jig and eel is a deadly combination for striped bass, big snook, redfish, and sea trout. Best retrieve depends on various conditions, but usually a slow, slightly erratic swimming motion is best. Good saltwater jig-and-eel rigs include the Hopkins Swimming Tail, the

Hopkins Shorty ST, the Block Tin Squid, and the Diamond—the mainstay of East Coast deep jiggers.

How do you fish a jig? Most jigs—except the jig-and-eel combination and those designed for trolling—should be retrieved with sharp upward jerks of the rod tip so that they look like fleeing darting bait. Most jigs have little action of their own (though some are designed to wiggle when retrieved), so the angler must impart fish-attracting motion.

Diamond Jig: The mainstay of East Coast deep jiggers. Simple in design, it takes stripers, blues, mackerel, cod, pollock, and similar species. Frequently used in conjunction with one or more surgical tube teasers attached one foot or so above the jig.

Block-Tin Squid: An old favorite, with a pork rind strip, has proven itself a good casting and trolling rig for stripers, bluefish, and other inshore species.

SALTWATER TROLLING LURES

Here are a number of saltwater trolling lures that have proved effective:

Artificial Eel: With lead head and double hooks, weighing six ounces and measuring 18 inches, it's the heaviest artificial eel made. Excellent for big striped bass and other large saltwater gamefish.

Barracuda Jig: A rig more commonly known as Japanese feathers, it is basically a trolling lure for offshore work on billfish, tuna, albacore, and bluefish.

Tony Accetta Pet Spoon: Big with a single fixed hook, this type of lure is more commonly known as a bunker spoon. It can be trolled with large strip of pork rind or an eel. One of the most effective lures for striped bass.

Leisure Lures' Plastic Squid: With long wire leader running through body and attached to single hook, this rig is designed for offshore trolling for billfish, tuna, albacore, bluefish, and similar species.

Plastic Trolling Lures: A variety of soft and hard-headed ones for canyon and offshore fishing. All are effective for marlin, sailfish, tuna and other bluewater species.

Umbrella Rig: A fishing lure with four wire arms, each supporting two or three surgical-tube lures. A single tube is trailed from the center. Designed to imitate a school of sand eels or baitfish, the umbrella rig is extremely effective on the East Coast for saltwater fish, especially bluefish. The umbrella rig is always trolled.

Care and Repair

Take a close look at your tackle box. It probably represents a bigger investment than your rods and reels. Saltwater lures, for example, cost as much as $30 or so. I fill a bucket to the top with soapy water and drop all the lures I've used in it. Swab them around for a few minutes, then rinse them off with a hose. Let them dry before you put them back in the tackle box or canvas bag.

Examine all hooks on lures and discard rusty hooks and all lures that are beyond repair. A soft-wire soap pad can restore a finsish on plugs, spoons, and spinners. If the hooks are rusty or broken, replace them. It's a good rainy-day project.

Don't leave rusty gear in your tackle box. Rust seems to be contagious. If you see rusty stuff, either clean it or throw it away.

The Candy Man

by Jerry Gibbs

You ask why a six-foot-three, 260-pound Marine Vietnam vet is frolicking in a rose garden? I'll tell you my theory—but first you should know that this is one extraordinary rose garden, the kind that compels passersby to stop their cars and wander, drawn like hummingbirds to the incredible burst of color vibrating from trellises of climbers and intricate topiaries of bush plants. Men, it seems, relate to this even more strongly than women. The garden is outside the landmark Shady Rest Restaurant on Route 9 in Bayville, New Jersey, a beautiful rococo device that draws intrigued visitors into the restaurant. It's a tender trap because the food, which centers on sea fare and pasta, is very good.

The garden, I think, reflects its owner's insatiable infatuation with color, patterns and creative design—abundantly evident inside, as well. Like a bowerbird, Bob Popovics, the ex-Marine turned restaurateur, has created in his Shady Rest a small haven evocative of his passion for fish and the art of angling. Giant aquariums of exotic fish species line the walls. There are handsome fish carvings behind Plexiglas, a gemlike fly-tying display and an exquisite hand-crafted net, the twin of which was presented to former President Bush. Although there's no denying Popovics' passion for angling artifacts that have been elevated to artforms, anglers know his fascination with color, design and fine craftsmanship through the man's own work. It is for his unique, tradition-breaking fly patterns that Bob Popovics has stormed to prominence in the modern angling world. It happened quickly.

In 1970, newly married and back in Seaside Park, New Jersey, after his stint with the First Marine Air Wing Division in Danang, Popovics and his pals Butch Colvin and Jim McGee were into hot bluefish one day, when Bob glanced over his shoulder. "I suddenly saw these bright, thick lines going out like party streamers and realized they were fly lines. I'd never tried it, always wanted to, and told Butch. Within the week he and his dad, Cap, had me in front of Cap Colvin's tackle shop, casting over the street. I got excited right away.

"Soon after, it was my birthday, and Butch came to our house to watch the Ranger-Bruins hockey game. In a cardboard beer flat, he had an old vise, tools, bucktails, feathers. He said 'Happy Birthday!' I told him, 'Ah, Butch, I can't do that; look at these big hands.' He said, 'You're going to learn between periods.' I liked it right away—and then I went crazy over it. Butch made me keep an open mind. There was no tradition in saltwater fly tying. 'We've not been told things we can't do,' he said. 'There's always a way, so do it.'"

Popovics did exactly that, first collaborating with Colvin on a method to produce big extended-body streamers that imitate menhaden (mossbunker), then going on to create an entire family of patterns that hold no traditional allegiance to construction or materials. Go back to the '60s, though, and you'd have no hint that a cult of Popfleye (as he calls his creations), and Popovics enthusiasts were destined to burst onto the fishing scene. Back then there was no

Bob Popovics, creator of the hard-bodied Candy flies, works over a school of breaking stripers in Barnegat Inlet, New Jersey.
(VIN T. SPARANO)

rose garden, and the restaurant was called the Shady Rest Pizza Parlor and Cabins. Although he'd always worked in the family business, young Popovics had just finished schooling as a computer programmer when the invitation from the Marine Corps arrived: "Why don't you join us," it read, "you don't have to go right away. . . ."

"Fifteen minutes after reading the invite, I went and signed up, and my mother said, 'Oh, God, why the Marines?' Well, it's what I wanted to do."

You have little doubt he has always done just that. Bob is a hands-on, can-do kind of guy with a quixotic artistic flare. A natural leader, he draws a loyal circle of friends now, as he did back in the Corps when stress-reducing R&R took the form of friendly wrestling free-for-alls—the usual drill was several buddies trying to take down big Bob. But there were serious times, too. Popovics' smile vanishes with the memory of pulling a recruit through a personal crisis during an endless night of shelling. "I had to knock him down," he says softly, "then sit on him all night."

As a kid living a block from the Delaware River in Trenton, New Jer-

sey, he'd always fished some. When the family moved to Seaside Park, Bob sometimes joined his surf-fishing father. "I liked it, but I wasn't truly affected by it until I came back from the service," he says. "It wasn't until Alexis and I married that I got wild about it. It was a social thing somehow; all the friends I met—it was all around fishing."

In 1970, there was still much for Bob to learn. Along with fly tying, Butch Colvin began showing Popovics the intricacies of fishing Barnegat Bay. By 1978, computer programming a fast-fading memory, Bob and Alexis became full owners of the Shady Rest and the ceaseless demands of the restaurant business.

Happily, peak restaurant season corresponds with slow fishing periods. "From Memorial Day to Labor Day it's a relentless seven-days-a-week run in the heat at the restaurant," he'll tell you. "After that, we get a migration of mullet that coincides with the migration of people leaving the shore, and that starts the fall fishing season."

Bob fishes locally or up in Martha's Vineyard or maybe a trip out of the country from fall into December, when it's back to the Shady Rest for Christmas season. January through March, he bounces between the restaurant and personal fly-tying appearances. And always, he is plotting new fly patterns based on need, not the orgasmically wild and often purposeless creations of some nonfishing tiers. The simple, durable Candy flies for which he may be best known, are typical.

Tired of losing good flies to the teeth of bluefish, Bob built a creation with a fishform epoxy head that creates a tooth-impervious shield over tying thread and synthetic wing material from shank to hook bend. To prove the pattern's durability, he caught 30 blues on one Candy before retiring it. A chewed epoxy head, he found, can be restored to new with a light coat of Sally Hansen's Hard-As Nails. Eventually, the epoxy head Candies evolved into a family of flies that suggest a variety of forage forms. Many spin fishermen use them as teasers ahead of their plugs.

A shorter version of his big off-shore fly came after a frustrating late-season day in the surf with bass feeding on rainfish (bay anchovies). "There were bass that looked 40 pounds, but we couldn't get them to eat. That night, I realized I'd thrown everything at them but something big. I came up with a slightly downsized version of my offshore Big Boy. At first light the next morning, with a raw north wind going, I took a 12-pound fish on the new pattern. My hands were so cold I couldn't take out the hook. The next fish just annihilated the fly. My hands were so cold I couldn't control the reel. I think it was the biggest bass I've ever had on, and I blew it. But the Cotton Candy fly was born!"

The stuff that seals your bathtub figured in another of Bob's break-through patterns. It is silicone that coats a fleece head, soft and squishy-feeling.

"I loved soft-plastic baits for fresh-water bass," Bob tells me. "These are like that. After it cured I threw the first one in the water. It floated. What a great mullet imitation waking on the surface, I thought. Squeeze the trapped air from the head and the fly sinks. So many ways to fish it. Rub on a little fresh silicone to fix the tears from fish teeth. I call them Siliclones."

The new flies have obvious fresh-water application for pike, muskies, bass, but more was yet coming. Exhausted from his creative high with the Siliclones, Popovics felt he'd hit the wall with new patterns, but friend Ed Jaworowski wouldn't let him rest. "What we need is a real swimming fly," Jaworowski insisted.

"Well, my friend Sal Ribarro had been fooling around with hard lips to make flies swim—even tried women's artificial fingernails. I'd messed with other kinds of hard lips before, but they're tough to pull from the water. But now I had silicone, and the next day I had the fly."

I want to know about the lip and

Bob says, "Oh, yeah, the Poplips. It's really a Siliclone with one extra step—a fleece beard covered with silicone to make a lip that bends back a little on the pick-up. That makes it easier casting than a hard lip. But they swim . . . man, the first time I saw one go, I just started chuckling.

At a table in the Shady Rest, we're joined by Sal Ribarro and Bob's police officer pal Lance Erwin, who relates how the Poplips fly is supreme during conditions that would also favor swimming plugs—easy swells, gentle currents. Because the lip digs in, swells or wind don't ruin the retrieve, as can happen with normal streamers.

There are so many more patterns. What's his favorite? "I like the Surf Candy a lot, and the Siliclones," Bob thinks aloud. "But maybe the Banger. It is the Banger. I've never had to create another popper after that!"

Bob leaps from the table for the kitchen and returns with a pizza, which he has made himself. He places it on the table, watching, pleased.

"He won't let anybody else make the pizza when he's got friends," Sal says. It turns out to be wonderful pizza.

When the Salt Water Fly Rodders of America disbanded about 1978, local flyfishers had no real home. Popovics' reputation was growing, and by 1987 he was regularly receiving calls from strangers with technical questions, and local anglers began visiting his home on Tuesday nights for informal tying sessions.

"From a handful of guys, we were getting more than 50 people in the house. There'd be people tying, standing in the hallway, crowded in the bathroom, waiting on the steps for a chance at the vises. I said, 'Ah well, we've got a problem. We've got to start a club.'"

The Atlantic Salt Water Fly Rodders was born in April 1992. At a recent count, there were 177 members. An average of 100 members attend summer meetings centered on tying and casting clinics.

The Shady Rest is festive and busy at this evening hour. Non-angling din-

ers gaze happily at the saltwater exotics staring back at them behind aquarium glass. Others admire the bonito and sailfish carvings, the tarpon and snook dioramas. At the bar, big screen images come from the TV via projector. Not just ball games: At Christmas, there's a sing-along tape and jigs and reels on St. Patrick's Day.

In this bright place, everyone seems to be having a good time. It's the Popovics rich talent for attraction, just as the man's fascinating fly creations continue drawing enthusiasts from across the United States—including, not insignificantly, the fish.

Many of Popovics' flies—including the Siliclones, Candies, Cotton Candy and Ultra Shrimp, plus a kit to produce the Bangers—are available through Umpqua Feather Merchant dealers. For those nearest you, contact the company at Box 700, Glide, OR 97443 (503-496-3512).

Popovics fly patterns are included in the following books: *Salt Water Fly Tying* by Frank Wentink; *Flies for Bass & Panfish* by Dick Stewart and Farrow Allen; *Flies for Saltwater* by Dick Stewart and Farrow Allen; *Saltwater Fly Patterns* by Lefty Kreh; *A Fly-Fisher's Guide to Saltwater Naturals and Their Imitation* by George V. Roberts Jr. ■

9

Rigs

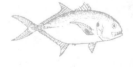

SWIVELS, SINKERS, FLOATS

The items of fishing gear covered here are various components of the rigs shown previously. These accessories are as important as links in a chain, so buy the best you can afford. A well-constructed snap swivel of the correct size, for example, won't literally come apart at the seams under the surge of a good strike.

Swivels come in many forms and sizes, but basically a swivel consists of two or three round metal eyes connected in such a way that each eye can rotate freely and independently of the others. Swivels perform such functions as preventing or reducing line twist, enabling the angler to attach much more than one component (sinker and bait, for example) to his line, and facilitating lure changes.

Sinkers, like swivels, come in many shapes and weights. Usually made of lead, they are used to get a bait (or lure) down to the desired depth.

Floats are lighter-than-water devices that are attached to the line. They keep a bait at a predetermined distance above the bottom and signal the strike of a fish. Floats are usually made of cork or plastic and come in many forms.

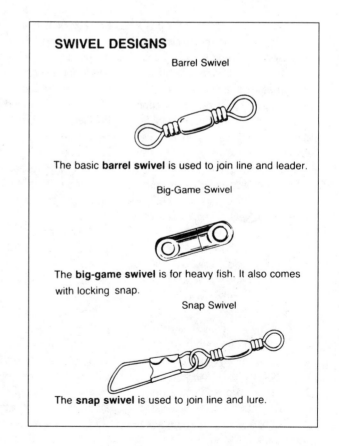

SWIVEL DESIGNS

Barrel Swivel

The basic **barrel swivel** is used to join line and leader.

Big-Game Swivel

The **big-game swivel** is for heavy fish. It also comes with locking snap.

Snap Swivel

The **snap swivel** is used to join line and lure.

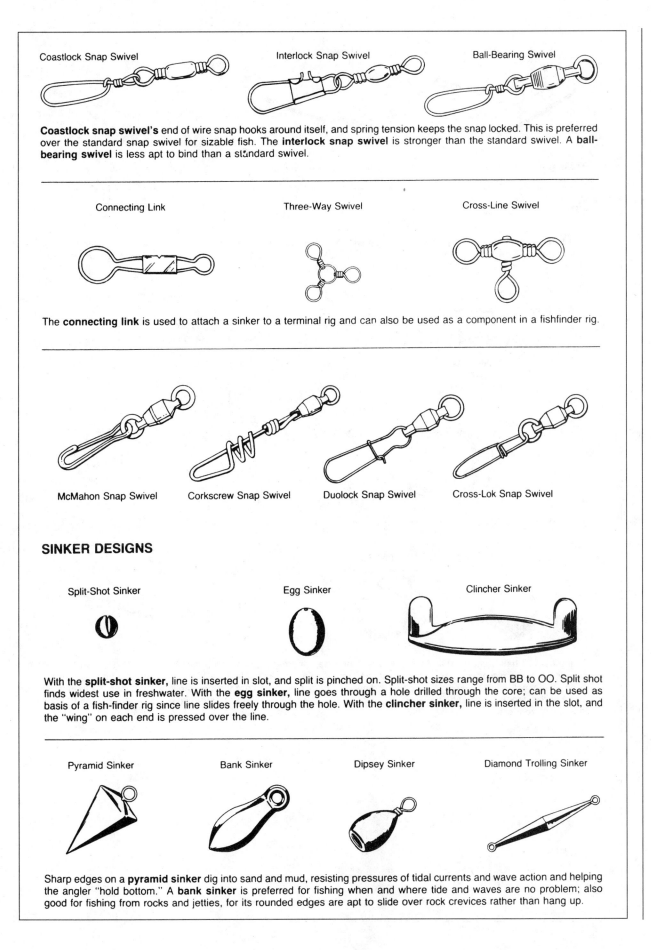

Coastlock Snap Swivel

Interlock Snap Swivel

Ball-Bearing Swivel

Coastlock snap swivel's end of wire snap hooks around itself, and spring tension keeps the snap locked. This is preferred over the standard snap swivel for sizable fish. The **interlock snap swivel** is stronger than the standard swivel. A **ball-bearing swivel** is less apt to bind than a standard swivel.

Connecting Link

Three-Way Swivel

Cross-Line Swivel

The **connecting link** is used to attach a sinker to a terminal rig and can also be used as a component in a fishfinder rig.

McMahon Snap Swivel

Corkscrew Snap Swivel

Duolock Snap Swivel

Cross-Lok Snap Swivel

SINKER DESIGNS

Split-Shot Sinker

Egg Sinker

Clincher Sinker

With the **split-shot sinker,** line is inserted in slot, and split is pinched on. Split-shot sizes range from BB to OO. Split shot finds widest use in freshwater. With the **egg sinker,** line goes through a hole drilled through the core; can be used as basis of a fish-finder rig since line slides freely through the hole. With the **clincher sinker,** line is inserted in the slot, and the "wing" on each end is pressed over the line.

Pyramid Sinker

Bank Sinker

Dipsey Sinker

Diamond Trolling Sinker

Sharp edges on a **pyramid sinker** dig into sand and mud, resisting pressures of tidal currents and wave action and helping the angler "hold bottom." A **bank sinker** is preferred for fishing when and where tide and waves are no problem; also good for fishing from rocks and jetties, for its rounded edges are apt to slide over rock crevices rather than hang up.

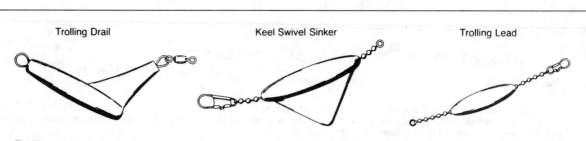

Trolling Drail   Keel Swivel Sinker   Trolling Lead

Trolling drail eliminates line twist, gets bait down deep. **Keel swivel sinker,** used for trolling, eliminates line twist.

TROLLING DEVICES

The trolling planer is a heavily weighted device with metal or plastic "wings" that permit trolling at considerable depths. The bait-walker sinker keeps the bait moving near the bottom but not dragging on the bottom. The downrigger assembly shown has a terminal rig with cable, cannon ball, and multi-bead release.

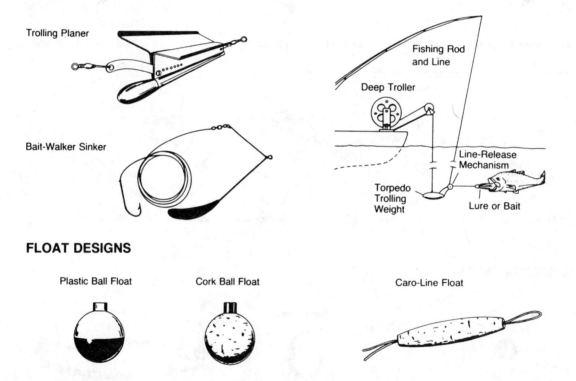

Trolling Planer

Bait-Walker Sinker

Fishing Rod and Line

Deep Troller

Line-Release Mechanism

Torpedo Trolling Weight

Lure or Bait

FLOAT DESIGNS

Plastic Ball Float   Cork Ball Float   Caro-Line Float

In the **plastic ball float,** a spring-loaded top section, when depressed, exposes a small U-shaped "hook" at the bottom into which line is placed. Releasing the top section reseats the "hook" holding the line fast. The **Caro-line cork float** has a doubled length of line running through it lengthwise. The fishing line is run through the loop, and then the loop is pulled through the cork body, seating the line. The Caro-line float is generally used in surf fishing to keep a bait off the bottom and away from crabs.

KNOTS

Anyone who aspires to competence as a fisherman must have at least a basic knowledge of knots. Most anglers know and use no more than half a dozen knots. However, if you fish a lot, you are sure to run into a situation that cannot be solved efficiently with the basic ties. The aim of what follows is to acquaint you with knots that will help you handle nearly all line-tying situations.

All knots reduce—to a greater or lesser degree, depending upon the particular knot—the breaking strength of the line. Loose or poorly tied knots reduce line strength even more. For that reason, and to avoid wasting valuable fishing time, it is best to practice tying the knots at home. In most cases, it's better to practice with cord or rope; the heavier material makes it easier to follow the tying procedures.

It is important to form and tighten knots correctly. They should be tightened slowly and steadily for best results. In most knots requiring the tyer to make turns around the standing part of the line, at least five such turns should be made.

Now let's take a look at the range of fishing knots. Included are tying instructions, the uses for which each knot is suited, and other information.

BLOOD KNOT

Used to connect two lines of relatively similar diameter. Especially popular for joining sections of monofilament in making tapered fly leaders.

1. Wrap one strand around the other at least four times, and run the end into the fork thus formed.

2. Make the same number of turns, in the opposite direction, with the second strand, and run its end through the opening in the middle of the knot, in the direction opposite that of the first strand.

3. Hold the two ends so they do not slip (some anglers use their teeth). Pull the standing part of both strands in opposite directions, tightening the knot.

4. Tighten securely, clip off the ends, and the knot is complete. If you want to tie on a dropper fly, leave one of these ends about 6 to 8 inches long.

STU APTE IMPROVED BLOOD KNOT

Excellent for joining two lines of greatly different diameter, such as a heavy monofilament shock leader and a light leader tippet.

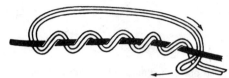

1. Double a sufficient length of the lighter line, wrap it around the standing part of the heavier line at least five times, and run the end of the doubled line into the "fork" thus formed.

2. Wrap the heavier line around the standing part of the doubled lighter line three times, in the opposite direction, and run the end of the heavier line into the opening, in the direction opposite that of the end of the doubled line.

3. Holding the two ends to keep them from slipping, pull the standing parts of the two lines in opposite directions. Tighten the knot completely, using your fingernails to push the loops together if necessary, and clip off the ends.

DOUBLE SURGEON'S KNOT

Used to join two strands of greatly unequal diameter.

1. Place the two lines parallel, with ends pointing in opposite directions. Using the two lines as a single strand, make simple overhand knot, pulling the two strands all the way through loop, and then make another overhand knot.

2. Holding both strands at each end, pull the knot tight and clip off the ends.

IMPROVED CLINCH KNOT

Used to tie flies, bass bugs, lures, and bait hooks to line or leader. This knot reduces line strength only slightly.

1. Run the end of the line through the eye of the lure, fly, or hook, and then make at least five turns around the standing part of the line. Run the end through the opening between the eye and the beginning of the twists, and then run it through the large loop formed by the previous step.

2. Pull slowly on the standing part of the line, being careful that the end doesn't slip back through the large loop and that the knot snugs up against the eye. Clip off end.

DOUBLE-LOOP CLINCH KNOT

Same as Improved Clinch Knot except that line is run through eye twice at the beginning of the tie.

TRILENE® KNOT

Used in joining line to swivels, snaps, hooks and artificial lures, the Trilene Knot is a strong, all-purpose knot that resists slippage and premature failures. It is easy to tie and retains 85–90 percent of the original line strength. The double wrap of monofilament line through the eyelet provides a protective cushion for added safety.

1. Run the end of the line through the eye of the hook or lure and double back through the eye a second time.

2. Loop around the standing part of the line five or six times.

3. Thread the tag end back between the eye and the coils as shown.

4. Pull up tight and trim the tag end.

SHOCKER KNOT

Used to join two lines of unequal diameters.

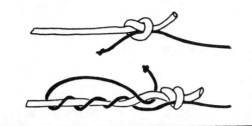

JANSIK SPECIAL KNOT

This is a terminal-tackle connecting knot that is popular with muskie anglers.

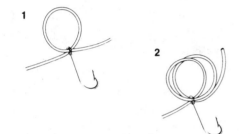

1. Run about 5 inches of line through eye of hook on lure; bring it around in a circle and and run it through again. **2.** Make a second circle, parallel with the first, and pass end of line through eye a third time.

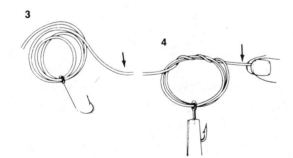

3. Bend standing part of line (identified by arrows) around the two circles. Bring tag end around in a third circle and wrap it three times around the three parallel lines. **4.** Hold hook, swivel, or lure with pliers. Hold standing line with other hand and tag end in teeth. Pull all three to tighten.

ARBOR KNOT

The Arbor Knot provides the angler with a quick, easy connection for attaching line to the reel spool.

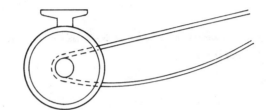

1. Pass line around reel arbor.

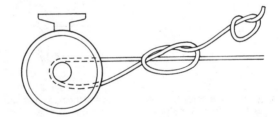

2. Tie an overhand knot around the standing line. **3.** Tie a second overhand knot in the tag end.

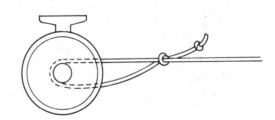

4. Pull tight and snip off excess. Snug down first overhand knot on the reel arbor.

MULTIPLE CLINCH KNOT

Used to join line and leader, especially in baitcasting. This knot slides through rod guides with a minimum of friction.

A loop is tied in the end of the line. Then leader is run into the loops, around the entire loop four times, and then back through the middle of the four wraps.

DOUBLE IMPROVED CLINCH KNOT

Same as Improved Clinch Knot except that line is used doubled throughout entire tie.

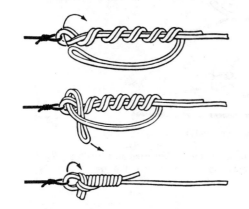

PALOMAR KNOT

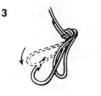

1. Pass line or leader through the eye of the hook and back again to form 3- to 5-inch loop. **2.** Hold the line and hook at the eye. With the other hand, bring the loop up and under the double line and tie an overhand knot, but do not tighten.

3. Hold the overhand knot. With the other hand, bring the loop over the hook. **4.** Pull the line to draw the knot to the top of the eye. Pull both tag end and running line to tighten. Clip tag end off about ⅛ inch from knot.

KING SLING KNOT

This offers the angler an easy-to-tie end loop knot that is used primarily as a connection for crank baits. This knot allows the lure to work freely, making it more lifelike, and resulting in more strikes.

1. Insert tag end of line through artificial bait so that it extends 8 to 10 inches.

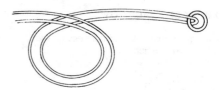

2. Hold the tag end and the standing line in your left hand, and form a loop.

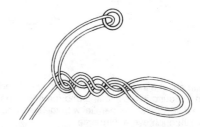

3. With the bait in your right hand make four turns around the tag end and the standing line above the loop.

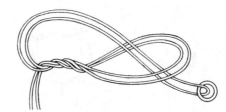

4. Bring the bait down and through the loop.

5. To tighten, hold line above the bait at desired loop length and pull the tag end and the standing line at the same time. **6.** Trim the tag end.

DOUBLE SURGEON'S LOOP

This is a quick, easy way to tie a loop in the end of a leader. It is often used as part of a leader system because it is relatively strong.

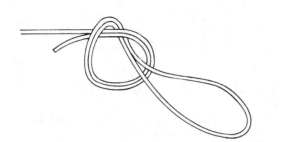

1. Double the tag end of the line. Make a single overhand knot in the double line.

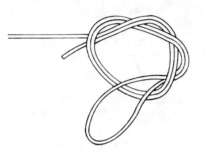

2. Hold the tag end and standing part of the line in your left hand and bring the loop around and insert through the overhand knot again.

3. Hold the loop in your right hand. Hold the tag end and standing line in your left hand. Moisten the knot (don't use saliva) and pull to tighten.

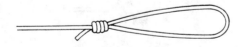

4. Trim off the tag end.

WORLD'S FAIR KNOT

An easy-to-tie terminal tackle knot for connecting line to swivel or lure.

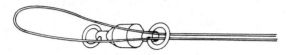

1. Double a 6-inch length of line and pass the loop through the eye.

2. Bring the loop back next to the doubled line and grasp the doubled line through the loop.

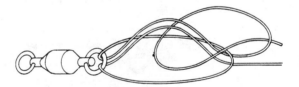

3. Put the tag end through the new loop formed by the double line.

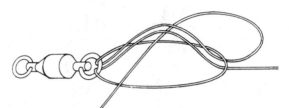

4. Bring the tag end back through the new loop created by Step 3.

5. Pull the tag end snug, and slide the knot up tight. Clip the tag end.

PERFECTION LOOP KNOT

Used to make a loop in the end of line or leader. Make one turn around the line and hold the crossing point with thumb and forefinger **(Drawing 1)**. Make a second turn around the crossing point, and bring the end around and between loops *A* and *B* **(Drawing 2)**. Run loop *B* through loop *A* **(Drawing 3)**. Pull upward on loop *B* **(Drawing 4)**, tightening the knot **(Drawing 5)**.

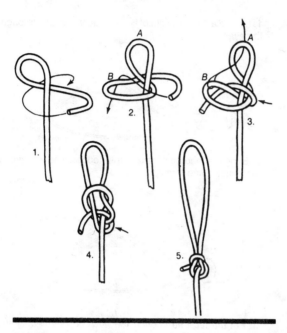

TUCKED SHEET BEND

Joins fly line and leader when leader has an end loop.

TURLE KNOT

Used to tie a dry or wet fly to a leader tippet. Not as strong as the Improved Clinch Knot, but it allows a dry fly's hackle points to sit high and jauntily on the surface of the water.

1. Run end of leader through eye of hook toward the bend, and tie a simple overhand knot around the standing part of the line, forming a loop.

2. Open the loop enough to allow it to pass around the fly, and place the loop around the neck of the fly, just forward of the eye.

3. Pull on the end of the leader, drawing the loop up tight around the neck of the fly.

4. Tighten the knot completely by pulling on the main part of the leader.

DROPPER LOOP KNOT

This knot is frequently used to put a loop in the middle of a strand of monofilament.

1. Make a loop in the line and wrap one end overhand several times around the other part of the line. Pinch a small loop at point marked X and thrust it between the turns as shown by the simulated, imaginary needle.

2. Place your finger through the loop to keep it from pulling out again, and pull on both ends of the line.

3. The knot will draw up like this.

4. Finished loop knot.

OFFSHORE SWIVEL KNOT

1. Slip loop of double-line leader through the eye of the swivel. Rotate loop ½ turn to put a single twist between loop and swivel eye.

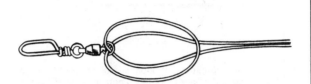

2. Pass the loop with the twist over the swivel. Hold the loop end, together with both strands of double-line leader, with one hand. Let the swivel slide to the other end of the double loops now formed.

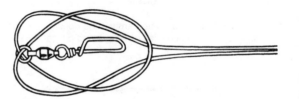

3. Still holding loop/lines, use other hand to rotate swivel through center of both loops. Repeat at least five times.

4. Continue holding strands of double-line leader tightly, but release the end of the loop. As you pull on swivel, loops of line will begin to gather.

5. To draw knot tight, grip the swivel with pliers and push the loops toward eye with fingers, still keeping strands of leader pulled tight.

THE UNI-KNOT SYSTEM

The Uni-Knot System consists of variations on one basic knot that can be used for most needs in freshwater and saltwater. The system was developed by Vic Dunaway, editor of *Florida Sportsman* magazine and author of numerous books. Here's how each variation is tied, step by step.

A. TYING TO TERMINAL TACKLE

1. Run line through eye of hook, swivel, or lure at least 6 inches and fold it back to form two parallel lines. Bring the end of the line back in a circle toward the eye.

2. Turn the tag end six times around the double line and through circle. Hold double line at eye and pull tag end to snug up turns.

3. Pull running line to slide the knot up against the eye.

4. Continue pulling until knot is tight. Trim tag end flush with last coil of the knot. This basic Uni-Knot will not slip.

B. LOOP CONNECTION

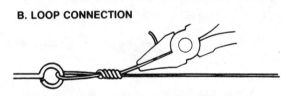

Tie the same basic Uni-Knot as shown above—up to the point where coils are snugged up against the running line. Then slide knot toward eye only until the desired loop size is reached. Pull tag end with pliers to tighten. This gives a lure or fly free, natural movement in the water. When fish is hooked, knot slides tight against eye.

C. JOINING LINES

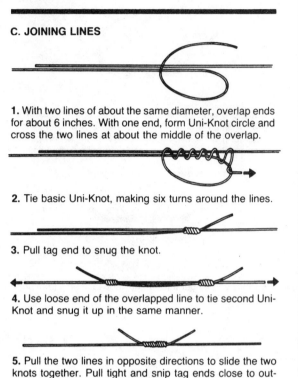

1. With two lines of about the same diameter, overlap ends for about 6 inches. With one end, form Uni-Knot circle and cross the two lines at about the middle of the overlap.

2. Tie basic Uni-Knot, making six turns around the lines.

3. Pull tag end to snug the knot.

4. Use loose end of the overlapped line to tie second Uni-Knot and snug it up in the same manner.

5. Pull the two lines in opposite directions to slide the two knots together. Pull tight and snip tag ends close to outermost coils.

D. JOINING LEADER TO LINE

1. Using leader no more than four times the pound-test of the line, double the end of line and overlap with leader for about 6 inches. Make Uni-Knot circle with the doubled line.

2. Tie a Uni-Knot around leader with the doubled line, but use only three turns. Snug up.

3. Now tie a Uni-Knot with the leader around doubled line, again using only three turns.

4. Pull knots together tightly. Trim tag ends and loop.

E. JOINING SHOCK LEADER TO LINE

1. Using leader of more than four times the pound-test of the line, double the ends of both leader and line back about 6 inches. Slip line loop through leader loop far enough to permit tying Uni-Knot around both strands of leader.

2. With doubled line, tie a Uni-Knot around doubled leader, using only four turns.

3. Put finger through loop of line and grasp both tag end and running line to pull knot snug around leader loop.

4. With one hand, pull long end of leader (not both strands). With the other hand, pull both strands of line (as arrows indicate). Pull slowly until knot slides to end of leader loop and slippage is stopped.

F. DOUBLE-LINE SHOCK LEADER

1. As a replacement for Bimini Twist or Spider Hitch, first clip off amount of line needed for desired length of loop. Tie the two ends together with an overhand knot.

2. Double the end of the running line and overlap it 6 inches with knotted end of the loop piece. Tie a Uni-Knot with the tied loop around the double running line, using four turns.

3. Now tie a Uni-Knot with the doubled running line around the loop piece, again using four turns.

4. Hold both strands of double line in one hand, both strands of loop in the other. Pull to bring knots together until they barely touch.

5. Tighten by pulling both strands of loop piece (as two arrows indicate) but only main strand of running line (as single arrow indicates). Trim off both loop tag ends, eliminating overhand knot.

G. SNELLING A HOOK

1. Thread line through the hook eye for about 6 inches. Hold line against hook shank and form Uni-Knot circle. Make as many turns as desired through loop and around line and shank. Close knot by pulling on tag end.

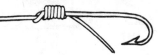

2. Tighten by pulling running line in one direction and hook in the other. Trim off tag end.

LOOP KNOT

Tie overhand knot in line, leaving loop loose and sufficient length of line below loop to tie rest of knot. Run end through hook eye and back through loop in line, and then tie another overhand knot around standing part. Pull tight.

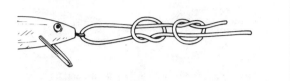

DAVE HAWK'S DROP LOOP KNOT

Used to attach lure to line or leader via a nonslip loop that will permit freer lure action than would a knot snugged right up to the eye of the lure.

1. Tie overhand knot about 5 inches from end of line, pull tight, and run end through the lure eye.

2. Bring end back parallel with standing part of line, bend end back toward lure, and then make two turns around the parallel strands.

3. Slowly draw the knot tight, and then pull on the lure so that the jam knot slides down to the overhand knot.

END LOOP

Used to form a loop in the end of a line.

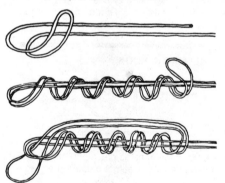

BUFFER LOOP

Used to attach lure to line or leader via a nonslip loop.

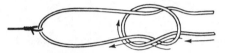

1. Tie simple overhand knot in line, leaving loop loose and leaving end long enough to complete the knot, and then run end through eye of lure.

2. Run end back through loose loop, and make another overhand knot, using end and standing part of line.

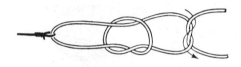

3. Tighten overhand knot nearest to lure eye, and then tighten second overhand knot, which, in effect, forms a half hitch against first knot.

4. Finished knot.

BIMINI TWIST

Used to create a loop or double line without appreciably weakening the breaking strength of the line. Especially popular in bluewater fishing for large saltwater fish. Learning this knot requires practice.

1. Double the end of the line to form a loop, leaving yourself plenty of line to work with. Run the loop around a fixed object such as a cleat or the butt end of a rod, or have a partner hold the loop and keep it open. Make 20 twists in the line, keeping the turns tight the line taut.

2. Keeping the twists tight, wrap the end of the line back over the twists until you reach the V of the loop, making the wraps tight and snug up against one another.

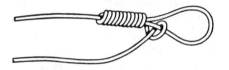

3. Make half hitch around one side of loop and pull tight.

4. Then make a half hitch around the other side of the loop, and pull this one tight.

5. Now make a half hitch around the base of the loop, tighten it, clip off excess line at the end, and the Bimini Twist is complete.

HAYWIRE TWIST

Used to tie wire to hook, lure, or swivel, or make loop in end of wire.

Run about 4 inches of the end of the leader wire through the eye of the hook, lure, or swivel, and then bend end across standing part of wire as in **Drawing 1**. Holding the two parts of the wire at their crossing point, bend the wire around itself, using hard, even, twisting motions. Both wire parts should be twisted equally **(Drawing 2)**. Then, using the end of the wire, make about 10 tight wraps around the standing part of the wire **(Drawing 3)**. Break off or clip end of wire close to the last wrap so that there is no sharp end, and job is complete **(Drawing 4)**.

SPIDER HITCH

Serves same function as the Bimini Twist. But many anglers prefer the Spider Hitch because it's easier and faster to tie—especially with cold hands—and requires no partner to help, nor any fixed object to keep the loop open. And it's equally strong.

1. Make a long loop in the line. Hold the ends between thumb and forefinger, with first joint of thumb extending beyond your finger. Then use other hand to twist a smaller reverse loop in the doubled line.

2. Slide your fingers up line to grasp small reverse loop, together with long loop. Most of small loop should extend beyond your thumb tip.

3. Wind the doubled line from right to left around both thumb and small loop, taking five turns. Then pass remainder of doubled line (large loop) through the small loop.

4. Pull the large loop to make the five turns unwind off thumb, using a fast, steady pull—not a quick jerk.

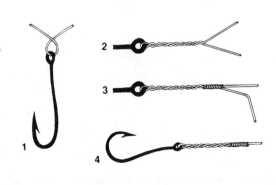

5. Pull the turns around the base of the loop tight and then trim off the tag end.

10

Saltwater Fishing Techniques

WATER TEMPERATURE AND FISH

There is no doubt left in anglers' minds of the importance of water temperature and its direct bearing on the activities of fish. Water temperature will tell you where the fish gather and where they feed at various times of the year.

It is a scientifically proven fact that every species of fish has a preferred temperature zone or range and it will stay and generally feed in this zone.

Taking temperature readings of water is not difficult, whether you use a sophisticated electronic thermometer or an inexpensive water thermometer lowered into the water on a fishing line. One electronic thermometer has a probe attached to a cable that is marked at regular intervals, so depth and temperature can be read simultaneously.

The inexpensive water thermometers can also do the job, and many also indicate depth by inserting a water pressure gauge in the thermometer tube. With these thermometers, allow at least 30 seconds to 1 minute for a reading. Also, the fishing line attached to it should be marked off in regular intervals, say 5 feet, so you can determine just how deep you are lowering the thermometer in the water.

The accompanying Preferred Temperature Table shows popular saltwater gamefish and baitfish and their preferred temperature zones. Look up the fish you are seeking and the water temperature it prefers. Then begin taking temperature readings from the surface on down, at 5-foot intervals, until you locate the correct zone and depth. Concentrate your efforts at that depth and you'll soon come to discover how important this water temperature business is.

SALTWATER GAMEFISH

Species	Lower Avoidance	Optimum	Upper Avoidance
Albacore (Thunnus alalunga)	59°	64° (17.8 C)	66°
Amberjack (Seriola dumerili)	60°	65° (18.3 C)	72°
Atlantic bonito (Sarda sarda)	60°	64° (17.8 C)	80°
Atlantic cod (Gadus morhua)	31°	44°–49° (6–8 C)	59°
Atlantic croaker (Micropogon undulatus)			100°
Atlantic mackerel (Scomber scombrus)	45°	63° (17 C)	70°
Barracuda (Sphyraena barracuda)	55°	75°–79° (24–26 C)	82°
Big-eye tuna (Thunnus obesus)	52°	58° (14.4 C)	66°
Blackfin tuna (Thunnus atlanticus)	70°	74° (23.3 C)	82°
Black marlin (Makaira indica)	68°	75°–79° (24–26 C)	87°
Bluefin tuna (Thunnus thynnus)	50°	68° (20 C)	78°
Bluefish (Pomatomus saltatrix)	50°	66°–72° (19–22 C)	84°
Blue marlin (Makaira nigricans)	70°	78° (26 C)	88°
Bonefish (Albula vulpes)	64°	75° (23.9 C)	88°
Dolphinfish (Coryphaena hippurus)	70°	75° (23.9 C)	82°
Fluke or summer flounder (Paralichthys dentatus)	56°	66° (18.9 C)	72°
Haddock (Melanogrammus aeglefinus)	36°	47° (8 C)	52°
Horn shark (Heterodontus francisci)		75° (24 C)	
Kelp bass (Paralabrax clathratus)	62°	65° (18.3 C)	72°
King mackerel (Scomberomorus cavalla)	70°		88°
Opaleye (Girella nigricans)		79° (26.1 C)	86°
Permit (Trachinotus falcatus)	65°	72° (22.2 C)	92°
Pollock (Pollachius virens)	33°	45° (8.3 C)	60°
Red drum (Sciaenops ocellata)	52°	71° (22 C)	90°
Red snapper (Lutjanus blackfordi)	50°	57° (13.8 C)	62°
Sailfish (Istiophorus platypterus)	68°	79° (26 C)	88°
Sand seatrout (Cynoscion arenarius)	90°	95° (35.0 C)	104°
Sea catfish (Arius felis)			99°
Skipjack tuna (Euthynnus pelamis)	50°	62° (16.7 C)	70°
Snook (Centropomus undecimalis)	60°	70°–75° (21–24 C)	90°
Spotted seatrout (Cynoscion nebulosus)	48°	72° (22 C)	81°
Striped bass (Morone saxatilis)	61°	68°	77°
Striped marlin (Tetrapturus audax)	61°	70° (21 C)	80°
Swordfish (Xiphias gladius)	50°	66° (19 C)	78°
Tarpon (Megalops atlantica)	74°	76° (24.4 C)	90°
Tautog (Tautoga onitis)	60°	70° (21 C)	76°
Weakfish (Cynoscion regalis)		55°–65°	78°
White marlin (Tetrapturus albidus)	65°	70° (21.1 C)	80°
White sea bass (Cynoscion nobilis)	58°	68° (20.0 C)	74°
Winter flounder (Pseudopleuronectes americanus)	35°	48°–52° (9–11 C)	64°
Yellowfin tuna (Thunnus albacares)	64°	72° (22.2 C)	80°
Yellowtail (Seriola dorsalis)	60°	65° (18.3 C)	70°

SALTWATER BAITFISH

Species	Lower Avoidance	Optimum	Upper Avoidance
Atlantic silverside (Menidia menidia)			90°
Atlantic threadfin (Polydactylus octonemus)			92°
Bay anchovy (Anchoa mitchilli)		82° (27.8 C)	92°
California grunion (Leuresthes tenuis)	68°	77° (25.0 C)	93°
Gulf grunion (Leuresthes sardina)	68°	89° (32 C)	98°
Gulf menhaden (Brevoortia patronus)			86°
Pacific silversides such as jacksmelt and topsmelt (Atherinopsis sp)	72°	77° (25 C)	82°
Rough silverside (Membras martinica)			91°
Skipjack herring (Alosa chrysochloris)	72°		84°
Spot (Leiostomus xanthuras)			99°
Tidewater silverside (Menidia beryllina)			93°

Mark Sosin's Top Tips for Chumming Reefs and Wrecks

Chumming is becoming more popular every year as *the* tactic to attract—and catch—game fish that lurk around bottom structure.

Chumming ranks as one of the most effective ways to locate and attract fish that live around reefs and wrecks. Almost every species, from billfish to bottom dwellers, responds enthusiastically to a free dole of tasty tidbits.

But successful chumming is more than merely hanging a frozen block of ground-up fish over the side or simply tossing a handful of chunks behind the boat. Those skippers who chum on a daily basis have honed this technique into an art form. Here are some of their key tactics.

Choosing the Spot

Position is everything, whether you are anchoring near underwater structure or drifting a reef line. To be effective, the chum must reach the fish. A near miss doesn't count. You'll often see top captains such as Bouncer Smith of Pembroke Pines, Florida, and Ken Harris of Key West move their anchor four or five times before they begin to chum.

The trick is to calculate the lie of the boat in relation to the target and the force of the current. There must be a flow of water, and you have to be on the upcurrent side of the structure. How *far* upcurrent is the primary question. Picture an inclined plane from the stern of the boat to the submerged structure. Chum will follow this route as it sinks. A strong current reduces the angle of the plane, carrying the chum much farther before it reaches the bottom. The opposite is true as the water slows. Your job is to anchor over a spot that assures the chum will reach bottom right at the

structure. If it doesn't, the results may be frustrating.

Drifting involves more than a random approach. Learn to position the boat so that wind and current will take it over the structure you want to fish. You may find fish at a certain depth along the reef, and should therefore concentrate on that zone. One approach is to work from shallow to deep; another is to drift parallel to the edge of the reef, where predators prowl.

If the boat is being pushed too fast, fish may find the chum long after you are out of range, particularly if you are using live chum. Capt. David Doll of Fort Lauderdale remedies this by using sea anchors and even his engines to help control the drift rate.

Types of Chum

Personal preference, availability, and even the species you target determine the type of chum you should use. Options range from frozen blocks of ground-up fish to chunks to shrimp-boat bycatch to live bait, and, in some cases, even ground-up lobster heads.

No matter what type of chum they use, most reef and wreck anglers will also hang a mesh bag of block chum over the side. Ken Harris is an exception. He pursues large individual fish, and relies on shrimp-boat bycatch or live bait to attract them. The ground chum attracts swarms of smaller fish that he would rather not have in his slick.

Researchers report that the sound of smaller fish feeding frequently attracts larger predators. That's why block chum can be effective in many situations. Capt. Tom Greene of Lighthouse Point, Florida, insists on sweetening any slick with small goodies, such as glass minnows. Capt. Neil Grant of Sunshine Key, Florida, feels that live

glass minnows flashing in the water creates an important visual attraction.

Over a reef, ground chum often tempts ballyhoo and speedos (frigate bonito). On the back side of the reef, you'll usually find mackerel and little tunny in the chum slick. If you do raise these species, it pays to net or catch some and then put them out as bait.

Work the Water Column

When trying to pull fish out of deeper water or when working the entire water column, David Doll has a neat trick. He puts a heavy weight on the end of some stout line and ties several mesh bags of chum to the line, staggered at various depths.

When targeting some bottom species, Tom Greene attaches a 10-pound sash weight to the end of a garden hose, lowers it to the bottom, and then pumps water through the hose with an extra bilge pump or salt water washdown. The water stirs up the bottom, much as a ray would, which attracts species that feed on bottom-dwelling critters.

Some veterans make chum containers that hold a handful of small baitfish. The device has a sinker and a trip mechanism. The first load of baitfish is released near the bottom. Subsequent drops are let go at higher and higher levels. This helps to bring game fish to the surface.

Commercial yellowtail fishermen mix their chum with sand so it will sink quickly. They then make chum balls with the sand, put the hooked bait in the middle, and wrap the fishing line around the outside. The ball is placed in the water carefully and dropped a measured distance. By lifting on the rod, you unwind the line and break the ball at the depth you want. This puts out a small cloud of chum with your bait in the middle. It's a deadly technique, but your boat won't be a pretty sight at the end of the day.

Chumming Rhythm

"I develop a rhythm when I chum," says Ken Harris, "and the fish quickly adjust to it. You must be consistent with that rhythm and keep the slick going at the same pace, no matter how busy you are aboard the boat."

The majority of skippers caution against over-chumming. Bouncer tosses in a fresh chunk or two at about the time the last pieces drift out of sight.

Harris talks about being stingy. He puts out far fewer pieces of chum than the number of big fish might be able to see. This stimulates competition.

A steady stream of chum keeps the fish well back in the slick. When you follow a slower rhythm, the fish tend to swim closer to the source, hoping to find the next piece before a competitor does.

The same theory holds when chumming with live bait, such as pilchards. Fish are extremely sensitive to feeding activity, even if they don't find something every time. The sound of a few predators crashing live bait causes the others to hang around for the next handout.

Mesh Size

Professional skippers who use frozen blocks of chum pay attention to the mesh size of their chum bags. This determines how fast the chum will be dispersed. As an example, a bag with ½" mesh should release a seven-pound block of chum in 30 to 40 minutes. Smaller mesh will lengthen the process.

Those who target yellowtail want to create a cloud of chum, and therefore opt for much larger mesh sizes. Some anglers buy landing-net replacement bags with one-inch or two-inch mesh, string a line around the top, and make their own chum bags.

Coastal tackle shops sell blocks of frozen chum. You certainly have the option of grinding your own and freezing it in various size containers. Understand from the beginning that it's a messy job. That's why most captains buy their chum already frozen. Besides, many spouses don't appreciate chum in their food freezers.

David Doll does suggest, however, that you freeze any small baitfish you don't use on a trip. These make wonderful chunks for a future adventure. That includes offshore baits, such as ballyhoo, which can also be cut into chunks.

People Food and Pet Food

When fishing for bottom species over reefs, some anglers use both people food and pet food as chum. Capt. Penny Banks has his own recipe. He cooks five-gallon buckets of macaroni, which he then ladles into the water for yellowtail and snappers. Corn has become a staple in some areas, either used alone or mixed with natural chum for yellowtails. Raw oats and cooked oatmeal find favor with some, while others beef up their chum with bread.

Aboard some boats, bulk bags of dog food are laced with menhaden oil and then used in place of other types of chum. Dog food does not have to be refrigerated. Cans of cat food contain acceptable chum for some species. A number of different scents (in addition to bunker oil) and fish attractants can be used to enhance artificial chum or natural chum.

How to Hook a Bait

Chumming and fishing the slick should be tailored to specific species. If you are using chunk baits, make sure each piece is trimmed neatly, and insert the hook in one corner. When that doesn't work, try burying the hook, so most of it is hidden in the bait. My own preference is to use relatively small hooks. I don't want the weight of the hook to make the bait sink more quickly than the natural chum, and therefore miss the concentration of fish. The same theory applies when using whole, small, dead fish as bait. Place the hook carefully and strategically.

With live bait, Bouncer Smith has a system that makes sense. His first choice is to place the hook low in the body near the head. With a pilchard, for example, the hook is inserted right under the pectoral fins. When you pull on the line, it forces the bait to dive deeper, which should put it right in the strike zone.

When the current slows, Bouncer hooks the bait low and near the tail so that it will swim away from him when he tightens the line. In a strong current, the bait is hooked near the dorsal fin. The secret, according to Bouncer, is to place the hook in an off-center position so the fish has trouble swimming. This causes it to send out more distress vibrations, which attracts predators.

How to Fish a Chum Slick

Fishing a chum slick seems simple enough, but it takes a bit of practice to do it right. All you're trying to do is put the bait where the fish are and make it appear the same as the free-drifting chum. If your boat is anchored, the current is carrying the chum away at a given rate and it is sinking at the same time. The bait must follow this same path, because the fish are going to be somewhere along the chum trail.

The technique involves pulling slack line off the reel before you put the bait in the water. As the current starts to carry the bait away from the boat, watch the line. Just before it becomes taut, strip some more slack line into the water. If you allow the line to tighten, the bait will stop drifting and rise in the water column, away from the chum line. Fish become suspicious of any morsel that rises or stops in the current.

When you first start chumming, fish tend to appear well back in the slick. Therefore it makes sense to drift your bait a long distance before reeling in and starting again. Sometimes it takes a while to attract anything, so be patient.

If the fish get finicky and stop feeding, Ken Harris recommends you stop fishing for a while and just chum.

By watching the line, you can also detect a strike before you feel it. As soon as the line moves faster than the current, you'll know a fish has picked up the bait. In some instances, you may want to lower the rod tip and wait for the line to come tight before setting the hook. Other times, it makes sense to reel rapidly until you feel the fish on the other end.

With live bait, the tactics change. You can hold a live bait stationary in the slick, because it continues to swim around. Unless the fish are chasing everything to the surface, you may want to put a small sinker ahead of the live bait to force it deeper.

If you are chumming and drifting, David Doll recommends that you cover the water column. He likes to fish baits at various depths and distances from the boat. Some of his rigs will have sinkers, while others won't. It's a matter of experimenting until he finds the setup that works.

Light Lines

Fish can suddenly become fussy feeders. Leader diameter, hook size, bait type, or any number of other factors may convince them to ignore the standard rigs. We once ran some crude experiments on a school of yellowtail that were visible behind the boat.

Unless we offered them a bait on six-pound line with no leader, they refused to bite. You could put two identical tidbits side by side and they would always turn down the one fished on heavier line.

When the fish get selective, skippers like Bouncer Smith and Tom Greene switch to very light lines and smaller baits and eliminate leaders. For toothy critters, such as king mackerel, they use long-shanked hooks, which help somewhat in preventing bite-offs. A few fish may be lost in the process, but it beats getting skunked. Tom may even use a fresh water bass hook designed for plastic worms, since it has a long shank and bait-holder barbs.

Fishing Artificials

Chumming provides the perfect setting for fishing artificial lures. You have the option of standing ready until some oversized predator suddenly appears in the slick, or you can simply work a lure blindly. You can allow some soft plastic baits that resemble the chum to drift back without imparting any motion. Most artificials, however, work best when cast and retrieved through the chum. To be effective, you have to get the lure down to the fish or pick a time when your quarry is aggressive enough to hit something on the surface.

Leadheads let you work different depths. If you choose a swimming plug, make sure it will dive down to the same level as the chum. On active fish, try a topwater chugger. It represents a smaller baitfish feeding on surface chum. In a slick, the big guys often ignore the chum and feed on the smaller species that are feasting on the handouts. Keep in mind, however, that even sailfish and marlin will ingest chunks of dead fish from time to time.

Retrieves should be somewhat erratic with lures, and the speed should match the preferences of the targeted species. If you're after king mackerel, try a fast retrieve. Cobia, on the other hand, might prefer a slower presentation.

Most fly fishermen now prefer to dead-drift their flies back in the chum slick, unless they spot a specific fish to cast to. It's a technique that's proven extremely successful. Prior to 1966, I had never heard of this method. Fishing over a reef in Bermuda for yellowfin tuna back then, I watched the fish refuse a moving fly over and over. Finally, it occurred to me to let it drift naturally with the chum. The closest tuna to the fly picked it up instantly.

Chumming combines the very basic approach of establishing a food source for fish with more sophisticated subtleties. The difference in results can usually be traced to small details rather than major mistakes. Professional captains who chum successfully on a daily basis stick with a game plan and refuse to cut corners. Follow their suggestions and you'll also enjoy some exciting days over the wrecks and reefs. ■

Reading the Ocean

by Ed Jaworowski

Locating fish in the ocean constitutes the angler's first order of business, surpassing tackle choice, fly selection or technique in importance. Fly anglers in particular, because of the limited effective range of their tackle, need all the help they can get to improve their odds in a seemingly endless sea; shore-based anglers even more so.

Several facts compound an already difficult chore. First, most ocean gamefish don't have homes. Their movements are largely determined by the movement of the food supply and tides. Second, their habits are greatly affected by the physical makeup of the areas in which they feed. This primer will remove some of the mysteries of tides and structure. Reading the ocean, like reading a trout stream, is an indispensable skill for the salt water angler and the first requirement for salt water anglers.

Tides represent the single biggest difference between freshwater and saltwater fishing. Though gamefish may temporarily take up residence around structure—inlets, seawalls, rock jetties, sand bars and the like—they will invariably move on with the next tide, following migrating food forms that also obey tidal influences. Any angler who hopes to score with any consistency in the salt must have at least a rudimentary knowledge of the way tides work. However subtle, tidal movements establish what amount to the equivalent of freshwater rivers. Here are some of the basics and suggestions on how to fit it all into your fishing.

The gravitational pulls of the moon and, to a lesser degree, the sun, cause ocean waters to move, building higher in some areas while getting lower in others. As a rule, a section of coast will experience two high tides and two low tides in each 24- to 25-hour period. A low will follow a high every six to six and one-half hours. Each day the highs and lows will therefore occur about an hour later than the previous day. This also means that at a given time and day each week, the tide will be nearly the exact opposite from what it was the previous week. If you had good fishing on the incoming tide on Saturday morning at daybreak, remember that you will have the opposite tide the following Saturday at the same time.

During different times of the month tides also vary. When the new moon (the darkest time of the month) and the full moon occur, expect the highest highs and lowest lows. Such tides are called "spring tides." It means during the six hours of tidal flow between the highs and lows you will note faster flows and stronger pulls. During the first and last quarters of the moon the tides are weaker, current flows slower and differences less great——lower highs and higher lows. Such tides are called "neap (or nip) tides."

Here's a typical scenario. If the new

Striped bass fishing at dusk along a rocky Martha's Vineyard beach.
(ED JAWOROSKI)

moon occurs on the 1st of the month and the full moon about two weeks later, on the 15th, you will experience the highest and lowest tides and strongest pulls at those times of the month (stronger over the full moon). During the week preceding each of those phenomena tides wax stronger, waning each successive day following. During the weeks of the first and last quarters (approximately the 8th and 22nd) the tides will be gentler. Also, on any given day, if a high tide occurs at 6:00 A.M. expect the next low around noon and the next high 6 to 7:00 P.M.

The change of water level from high to low will also vary with geographic locale. Consider the Atlantic coast. On Florida flats, only a few inches may separate low tide from high tide, particularly during the neap tide periods. On the Bay of Fundy, Nova Scotia, on the other hand, there may be more than a 25-foot difference; the flooding tide comes in so quickly that a man walking rapidly can't outpace it. Mid-Atlantic coastal states commonly show four- to six-foot tidal variations. As a rule, tide variations diminish closer to the equator.

Tide tables are approximations based upon a couple of dozen factors, in addition to time of month, time of day and moon phase, and changes in some of these may alter the predicted times. Other contributing factors affecting fish behavior are wind, weather,

light intensity, bait availability, barometric pressure, currents. The wind is one of the strongest. A strong and persistent wind following the waves can make a high tide occur much earlier than predicted and reach much higher onto the shore. Obviously, when blowing against the tide, it can have the opposite results, actually holding the ocean back. I've seen 150 yards of a New Jersey beach exposed when it should have been under a few feet of water, totally because of a strong northwest wind.

Changes in atmospheric pressure will affect the water. Low barometric pressure will allow the surf to rise higher and develop more violent wave action. We've all seen what happens to the ocean during a hurricane, a period of very low barometric pressure.

All this data may seem confusing to the newcomer to saltwater fishing but it's really no more so than learning about freshwater insect hatches or differences in fly dressings. On the other hand, knowledge of tides can be more important than either of those concerns; if you fish where there is no water or can't get to the feeding grounds, you're not apt to catch many fish.

Here is a random list of additional ideas for the angler to consider.

- When you plan to fish an area, consider how the tide will affect the water there. During times of strong tidal flow, bait will be caught and forced to collect in rips around jetties and inlets; the bait can't swim against the flow.

- During spring tides, high waters will flood grass beds in the bays and tear loose a lot of eel grass and other vegetation. The effect is less during neap tide periods. Grass buildup is generally also greater the closer you fish to an inlet.

- One change of tide can dirty the water or can clear a surf, by bringing or removing grass or cloudy water.

- Usually, more whitewater tends to develop when the tide is dropping. It tends to disappear on a rising tide.

- My experience has been that tides are less a factor when fishing farther from shore. Inshore, moving water, whether incoming or outgoing, is nearly always superior to the static water you get at flood or ebb tide. A moving tide tends to concentrate bait; static water allows it to disperse.

- Great changes in water temperature can affect fishing. If deeper offshore water is cooler, a strong tide may move it inshore, displacing the shallower warmer water and turn fish off.

- Know the contour of the beach you fish. When the tide drops, gamefish will make every effort to get out to deeper water rather than risk being cut off by a sand bar. If the bar is a hundred yards from shore, the fish will be out of range at low tide. If you can't wade to the bar, plan on fishing the area closer to shore at higher tide, when the fish can get over the bar.

- Note that the times of the highs and lows along the coast will be approximately the same along the beach for many miles.

Back on the bays, estuaries and creeks, however, tides may be two, three or four hours different. Tide tables will tell you how to make the necessary adjustments. Get a tide table for the area you are considering fishing. Bait and tackle shops will carry them. You can also consult local newspapers. Learn how to read the tables and consider them a basic part of your equipment.

As with tides, learning to read structure will increase your odds dramatically. Even when the arrival of bait and favorable tides indicate the likelihood of gamefish in the area, narrowing the possible spots demands some skill in recognizing structure and understanding why some spots are more likely to be productive than others.

Like freshwater bass, stripers gravitate to rocks, weeds, and bars. Bluefish often feed close to underwater lumps, ridges or wrecks. Snook hide among mangroves, weakfish seek out bottom depressions or jetties and false albacore like rips and strong flows. All these gamefish regularly position themselves where structure will concentrate food, making it easy to locate, ambush or trap. Just what constitutes structure?

Basically any bottom formation or contour (like a sand bar or drop-off), rocks, wrecks, bridge and pier pilings, weeds, even waves. Structure may be natural or artificial, temporary or permanent. One of the most obvious forms of structure is the jetty or groin, usually a man-made, rocky finger jutting out from the beach. Jetties cause waves to break, loosening shellfish and organisms on which the fish feed. They also provide places for forage fish to hide as well as causing and directing currents. The biggest mistake you can make when fishing from jetties is to cast out and away. Nearly all feeding takes place close to and among the rocks. Cast parallel to the rocks and smack your offerings down right in the foaming water. Rubber-headed Siliclone flies are especially deadly in this situation.

All kinds of pilings also give shelter to bait. Some are best fished from a boat and most produce best at night, so scout out your spots at day. It's amazing how bold fish become in the dark, swimming around boat docks and harbors they would never approach in daylight. Look for older pilings, as new piers and docks haven't yet developed encrustations that provide food for the chain. White perch, weakfish and stripers particularly like docks, piers and bridges. At night, they lie on the edge of the shadows and assault bait attracted to lights shining on the water. You are very apt to see and hear surface activity then. I've taken scores of small stripers all around the piers and terminals in New York Harbor, the East River and the Brooklyn waterfront!

Many back bays are marked by sod banks, grass covered islands and cutouts of land laced by narrow streams. Fish take up position any place a smaller flow dumps water into a larger area. If you can walk the sod banks (some are mucky and nearly impossible to walk), stay back from the edge. Not only might it give way, you could spook the fish, which like to hang under the overhang and rush out to snatch bait. A small boat, even a cartopper with a small outboard is adequate to fish among the sod banks in many areas. Nautical charts of the areas you plan to fish provide invaluable assistance in locating channels, holes and dropoffs and bars.

Some oceanfront structure is obvious. Reading other forms requires more experience. Look first at the contour of the beach. Is it pretty straight, north-south, or scalloped out with indentations and cuts? Straighter beaches generally don't attract bait so well. They have fewer points to obstruct wave flow and form holes and pockets, thus fewer ambush points. Storms and heavy wave action may create new holes and sand bars—or destroy them. Routinely check out and explore the beaches you want to fish. They can change in short order. Also take note of the slope of the beach. Flatter beaches have less bottom structure, hence less cover for fish. Steeper beaches allow bait to move closer to the shore.

Bars running parallel to the beach

commonly draw fish, yet some provide great fishing on the inshore side, while others are fishless. The difference usually depends on breaks in the bar. If you see white water breaking over a bar within 100 or 200 yards of the shore, forming a deep trough close to the beach, check to see if there are any cuts (marked by darker colored water) through which fish can get back to the safety of deeper water. Without such cuts, fish have little opportunity to get over the bar, usually only for the brief periods of high water and then generally only at night.

On the other hand, fish will stay and feed in deep troughs close to the beach right through low water, so long as they have the opportunity to get back beyond the bar through a cut or channel. Thick weed masses also serve as structure. They form slack pockets in the current where bait can hide and fish can feed, just like weed beds in a smallmouth stream. A drift over a bay

or ocean bottom with an electronic depth finder/fish locator is a real eye opener. Fish will register in the tiniest of pockets or holes, more so if they can hide behind vegetation anchored to the bottom. However, even clear bottoms can hide fish in depressions; waves and currents flow over them.

Finally, waves themselves sometimes represent a form of structure. Surf turbulence can conceal gamefish stalking forage. An understanding of how wave action works shows how this can be so. As a wave moves toward the shore, the water particles swirl down and back up in a circular path, equal in diameter to the height of the wave. For example, as a three-foot wave moves toward the shore, the water particles near the surface go down and around in a three-foot clockwise pattern, nearly returning to their starting position as the wave itself rolls along. Sand particles, grass and other suspended matter are also

moved around by this turbulence. A striped bass can readily move into striking range concealed by this mass of confusion and visual disturbance.

Incidentally, you can estimate the depth of water on a bar over which a wave breaks. Normally a wave breaks when it reaches a depth equal to its own height up to one and a half times its height. Thus, a four-foot wave will break when it runs into bottom interference four to six feet down. The most effective way to fish a turbulent surf is to let your fly wash around on a semi-slack line, simulating the naturals which lose much their ability to swim in the strong currents.

Reading an ocean is fascinating and challenging. As with all fishing, the more you understand the environment in which the fish feed, in the long run, the more fun you will have and the more successful you will be. ■

Salt Water Sportsman's Guide to Releasing Fish

by Tom Richardson

Gather round, you skeptics, we've got news for you. Released fish *do* survive. Problem is, many anglers simply don't know how to release a fish properly. There's a lot of confusion, not to mention controversy, about what to do. Today we're going to set the record straight.

Before we get into the best ways to release specific species, there's a few general rules that apply across the board. Much of the following was gleaned from a fact sheet entitled "Guidelines To Increase Survival of Released Sport Fish," written by Cornell University researchers Mark Malchoff, Michael Voiland, and David

MacNeill. It's is an excellent source of information for anyone interested in proper catch-and-release procedure, and can be obtained by sending $1 (ppd.) to the Media Services Resource Center—Fish, Cornell University, 7 Business and Technology Park, Ithaca, NY 14850.

Stress and wounding, say the authors, are the two major causes of angling mortality in fish. Stress is most often caused by "vigorous physical exertion (which) causes lactic acid to accumulate in the fish's muscles as a result of fighting the rod and reel. If the animal is able to restore its blood acid (pH) level to pre-stress or normal lev-

els, normal physiological processes return and the fish may live to fight another day. In some cases, blood chemistry balance is not restored and the fish may die—perhaps as long as 72 hours after the catch.

"Since the amount of lactic acid generated is directly proportional to the duration and intensity of muscular activity, a quick retrieve and capture of the fish would thus tend to lessen muscular exertion and metabolistic stress." In other words, the quicker you can get the fish to the boat and release it, the better its chances of survival. This would certainly seem to refute the idea that light tackle is more "sporting."

Hook wounds were listed as the second major cause of fishing mortality. The researchers found that wounds to the gill and stomach areas were the most deadly. Intermediate mortalities were caused by injury to the lower jaw, isthmus (the triangular "throat" section connecting the head and body), and eye regions. Finally, hooks imbedded in the snout, the upper jaw, the corner of the mouth, and the cheek caused the lowest level of mortality. The pamphlet also states that baited hooks were more likely to cause serious injuries than lures, and that the use of barbless hooks and single hooks, being easier to remove, cause less out-of-water stress (oxygen deprivation, excess handling) than barbed hooks or treble hooks. Also important is the type of metal the hook is made of. For instance, some hooks erode faster than others, and there is some evidence that tin/cadmium hooks may poison the fish if left embedded in the tissue.

Other causes of physical stress include the removal of protective slime, low salinity, high and low water temperature, depressurization, and internal injury caused by rough handling. These factors, alone and in combination with physical exertion, can increase mortality.

General recommendations are also given in the Cornell pamphlet concerning the best way to release fish. For example, the authors say not to remove the fish from the water if at all possible, and recommend the use of hook-removal devices, such as needle-nose pliers and J-shaped dehookers. Also important is minimizing the time a fish spends out of the water: if a hook is difficult to remove, it's better to cut the line or leader as close to the mouth as possible rather than struggle with the fish. Do not touch the gills or soft underbelly, and if you must handle the fish, always do so with wet hands or wet gloves to keep the protective mucous coating intact.

Additional tips include covering a fish's eyes with a wet cloth or towel to calm it down, placing the fish on a soft, wet surface (i.e., foam or carpeting) if it

A quick fight and a quick release, with a minimal amount of handling, is the best way to ensure a fish's survival.

has to be brought aboard, and releasing the fish with a headfirst plunge from several feet above the water if it appears healthy after capture.

I found that almost all of the above recommendations were shared by the fishermen and biologists I interviewed for this article. Let's take a look now at how these experts practice release on some specific species.

Releasing Striped Bass

If there's anyone qualified to answer questions on how to release striped bass, it's Captain Al Anderson of Point Judith, Rhode Island. During his 27 years as a charter captain, Anderson has released a total of 3,102 fish. A few days before I spoke with him, Anderson had tagged and released his 1,700th bass for the American Littoral Society and had recently learned of the 70th recapture of stripers he's tagged.

Anderson, who began tagging striped bass in 1967, has a finely honed method of tag and release. "First, we recognize very quickly if the fish is a keeper or not," he says. "If it looks undersized, or just barely legal, we land the fish with a (soft cotton) net. Then we lift it out of the water and place it on the wet, carpeted deck where a

saltwater hose is kept running. This helps keep the fish's protective slime from being rubbed off. Then we quickly place a wet towel over the fish's head to calm it down."

Anderson makes sure he has his yardstick and tagging equipment ready to go, so he won't waste valuable time. If the angler wants a picture taken, he'd better be ready to shoot. "If the cameraman isn't ready, too bad," says Anderson. "That fish goes right back in the water."

After the fish has been measured and tagged, Anderson releases it by dropping it headfirst, "like a torpedo," from three or four feet above the water. This is to give the fish a head start and get water flowing through its gills. The entire process, from the time the fish is brought aboard to the time it's released, takes roughly 15 to 20 seconds—quick and efficient with a minimal amount of handling.

Remember that Anderson only removes the fish from the water to tag it or to remove a hard-to-reach hook. If you aren't going to tag your fish, try to keep it in the water to give it oxygen and reduce the risk of slime removal caused by handling. Bringing the fish onboard can also result in internal injury if it's allowed to flop around violently. (How many times have you fumbled a slippery fish and sent it skittering across the deck?)

Schoolie stripers that have been hooked in the lip can be safely released by lifting them out of the water by the leader and using a J-shaped dehooker to extract the hook. With this device, you never have to touch the fish, and it only spends a few seconds out of the water. Large fish should not be lifted out of the water by the leader.

Incidentally, the J dehooker is also the preferred method among many charter captains for releasing bluefish. It's convenient, not only because you avoid handling the fish, but also to avoid the sharp teeth. After you get the hang of using the J dehooker, it's unbelievable how fast you can release a fish and get back in the action.

Striped bass that have been fought to exhaustion, as often happens in surf fishing or when using light tackle, have to be treated more carefully. If possible, do not take an exhausted fish out of the water to remove the hooks. For instance, it's poor practice, in Anderson's opinion, to drag a surf-caught fish onto the beach, where a lot of slime can be rubbed off and where sand can irritate the gills. If the hooks are difficult to remove on a severely exhausted fish, cut the line or clip the hook from the lure rather than wrenching it out and handling the fish excessively.

It's also important to revive an exhausted fish before letting it go, even if it takes quite a while. Holding the fish's lower jaw with your thumb and supporting its body with your other hand, revive the fish by gently "swimming" it back and forth in the water so that oxygen can wash over the gills. "You know the fish is reviving when it bites down on your thumb and shakes its head," says Anderson. Anderson recalls catching bass from the rocks along Narragansett Bay and letting the fish recover in a small tidal pool before sending it back out into the surf. It would be interesting to see if letting an exhausted bass recover in a large livewell might not also be beneficial.

As previously mentioned, water temperature and salinity can affect fishing mortality. This was proved with striped bass in experiments conducted by Keith Lockwood at the University of Maryland. Using hook-caught bass, Lockwood and his associates discovered that the higher the water temperature and the lower the salinity, the lower the survival rate. Therefore, stripers that are caught during periods of hot weather, such as in summer, or in rivers and estuaries where salinity is lower, should be handled with much greater care.

King Mackerel

Randy Gregory, a technician with the North Carolina Department of Marine Fisheries (NC-DMF), uses many of the same release techniques as Anderson, except that his specialty is king mackerel. Gregory, who says the NC-DMF tagged and released roughly 1,500 kings last year, agrees that when it comes to a successful release, time is of the essence. "If you keep a king mackerel out of the water for more than a minute," he says, "you would probably cut its chances of survival by 50 percent. If it takes more than 30 seconds to remove the hook, cut the line."

Like Anderson, Gregory says it's best not to remove the fish from the water if you know you're going to release it. Try to remove the hooks over the side of the boat or clip the line close to the hook if it can't be reached. "Handle them as little as possible," he says. "King mackerel have really soft skin and a lot of slime, which serves as protection against bacteria and parasites. When you break the integrity of that coating, it allows bacteria to grow and the fish has to work harder to replace the slime."

As for removing the hook, Gregory warns not to rip it out of the fish, even if this seems like the quickest and easiest way to get it out. If the hook, or hooks, are lodged very deep, tearing them out could cause severe internal injury, especially to the delicate gill area. Since so much blood courses through the gills, tearing them could cause the fish to bleed to death, or the blood could attract predators.

When Gregory has to bring a fish onboard to tag it, he likes to place it on a wet surface, such as in his specially designed king mackerel trough that's filled with wet foam. Like Anderson, he folds a wet towel over the fish's head and body to calm it down and to keep the skin moist. Holding the fish upside down by its tail also has a calming effect, he says. Any time Gregory has to handle a fish, he makes sure that his hands or gloves are wet to protect the slime. After the tagging has been completed, Gregory releases the fish using the head-first-plunge method—"almost like you're chucking a spear," he says.

According to Gregory, one of the best methods for bringing a king aboard is with a tail rope, since it doesn't harm any organs or remove a lot of slime; however, he admits it may take some practice to master the device. Because king mackerel are so fast, you have to place the rope loop around the head of the fish first. That means the loop has to be passed around the rod and reel and down the line. When the loop is parallel with the eyes, quickly cinch it shut and it should end up around the tail after the fish shoots forward. If you decide against using a tail rope, then netting the fish is preferable to lifting it by the leader, especially if it's a "smoker."

Gregory and the North Carolina DMF are working to get more North Carolina anglers involved in the tagging program. The DMF actively recruits the help of sport fishermen through tournaments and lectures, and last year the number of kings released by anglers rose to around 300. For more information, call Gregory at the NC-DMF, (919) 726-7021.

Billfish

But what about releasing bigger game, such as billfish? To find out, I spoke with John Jolley, former head of the State of Florida's East Coast Marine Lab. From 1970 to 1980, one of the lab's primary missions was assessing the stocks of Atlantic sailfish in the western North Atlantic, and Jolley and his team collected and tagged hundreds of specimens. Although Jolley's current job involves the assessment of a different stock, the Wall Street kind, he still tags and releases sailfish whenever he has the time to go fishing.

Jolley says that a quick fight and a quick release, with a minimal amount of handling, is the best way to ensure survival. The longer a fish is fought, the more exhausted it will be and the longer it will take to recover, thus making it susceptible to predation. Using 20-pound-test tackle, Jolley says he's usually able to bring a fish to the boat within 20 minutes, without backing down. If the fight reaches the 30-minute mark, he advises putting on some extra pressure and/or backing down to get the fish in.

Jolley tries to avoid touching the fish at all during the release. In fact, he never even bills the fish, because he says this can cause injury when the fish slams against the side of the boat. He also says not to cram the stomach back inside the mouth if the sailfish has everted it during the fight; the fish will swallow it later. With the boat moving slowly forward, he grabs the leader, wraps the fish in, and clips the leader next to the mouth, leaving the hook in the fish. By doing this, the fish maintains its forward momentum and usually swims off with plenty of vigor. Only if the fish appears to be completely exhausted and begins to float belly up does Jolley advise grabbing its bill and swimming it along beside the moving boat.

While Jolley takes exceptional care to release his sailfish, he realizes that all of them may not make it, particularly those that have sustained injury to the eye. But at the same time he points out how tough these fish really are. "Survival is actually higher than we once thought," he says, and offers the example of a badly injured sailfish he had once tagged and released. The fish had suffered severe eye damage and was bleeding from the gills. Even worse, it was brought aboard so it could be fitted with a sonic tag. Jolley was sure the fish would sink to the bottom and die; however, he and his crew tracked the sail for six hours before it was finally eaten by a shark.

To Bill or Not to Bill

Salt Water Sportsman's, George Poveromo has also released his share of sailfish, a lifetime total estimated at 300. However, Poveromo differs from Jolley in that he prefers to bill the fish, primarily for safety reasons. He argues that a billfish, especially if it's brought in quickly and is still green, can pose a real threat to the person handling the leader if it decides to greyhound or jump next to the boat.

When Poveromo leaders a billfish to the boat, he does so very gently to avoid causing any internal injuries if the hook has been swallowed. "The worst thing you can do is manhandle a fish to the boat or try to snap-jerk the leader to break it," which he says is practiced by some tournament anglers who want to get back in the action quickly. While Poveromo is leadering the fish, he's always prepared to drop the leader if it makes a last-ditch run. After getting the fish next to the boat, he grabs the thick base of the bill, keeping his thumbs opposed, so the fish can't snap the bill by thrashing. This positioning also gives him more leverage to control the fish. When he's got control, he looks to see where the hook is located and then removes it with his pliers. If the hook is lodged too deeply to reach, he clips the leader next to the mouth.

Throughout the process, the boat is kept slowly moving forward to maintain the flow of water through the mouth and over the gills. After he removes the hook, Poveromo holds the fish in the water until he feels it swimming under its own power, then gives it a little shove forward to get it going. A little trick he uses is to reach back and give the fish a quick squeeze on the base of its tail, which causes the sailfish to shoot ahead quickly. This reaction may be a flight instinct used to escape an attacking predator, and seems to be enough to get a sluggish fish moving under its own power.

Poveromo releases white marlin the same way as sails, but he says that blue marlin have to be handled with a little more caution due to their size and the type of rigs used. If double-hook rigs are used, he always checks to see where the hooks are embedded *before* he grabs the bill. The last thing you want is a 12/0 hook through your hand and a green marlin threatening to take off at boatside. Poveromo also says he makes every attempt to remove a double-hook rig, since the loose hook could actually wire the fish's mouth shut by later swinging around, causing it to drown.

Like many other big-game fishermen, Poveromo believes that trolling lures are better suited for catch and release than natural bait, since they're less likely to be swallowed and lodge in a critical area. Trolling lures rigged with single hooks, which are becoming increasingly popular, are even better for release.

Both Poveromo and Jolley agree that a billfish should never be lifted up by the gill plate or bent over the gunwale to remove a hook or have a picture taken. More importantly, the fish should never be brought onboard, which could result in internal injuries, allow lots of slime to be removed, and cause severe trauma. Keep in mind that a billfish's (or any fish, for that matter) body is designed to be supported by water, and that removing it from that medium can compress and damage the organs.

Sharks

The same holds true for sharks, especially big sharks, according to Jack Casey, a biologist with the National Oceanographic and Atmospheric Administration in Narragansett, Rhode Island. Casey says that large sharks may actually be more susceptible to injury than small ones if removed from the water or retrained with a tail rope or gaff. (Aquarium cases, in which large sharks were injured while being transported from one tank to another, support this.) Allowing a shark to bang against the side of the boat or roll itself tightly in a leader can also cause internal damage.

Still, Casey is quick to dispel the myth that released sharks don't survive. "That notion," he says, "is a bunch of bull." For evidence he points to NOAA's extensive shark-tagging program, which began in 1962. To date, over 100,000 sharks have been tagged and released in the NOAA program, most of them by sport fishermen. So far, Casey's department has recorded a four-percent (over 4,500) return rate on the tagged fish.

Over the years, Casey has seen many healthy sharks with four or five old hooks in their jaws. He's also recorded plenty of recaptures of sharks released from commercial long-lines, and told me that several sharks in the program had been recaptured over three times!

When it comes to gut-hooked fish, Casey admits that the returns have been fewer, although he's seen recaptured sharks that have survived with hooks lodged in their gullets. The problem is that many times a swallowed hook increases the risk of infection. Because of this, he believes the use of stainless steel hooks may be more harmful than other hook types, since they are extremely slow to erode. To avoid gut-hooking, Casey advocates setting up on the fish quickly after it has taken the bait, so it doesn't have time to swallow the hook.

Finally, Casey recommends leaving the hook in the fish by cutting the leader close to the mouth. Again, the main objective is to get the fish in quickly and release it. Unless you've had some practice at it, trying to wrench the hook out of a shark's mouth can only cause more trauma. And considering the value of sharks as a game fish, hooks are cheap.

Shallow-Water Game Fish

Fly fishermen and light-tackle inshore enthusiasts pay attention: Paul Tejera has some advice to offer. During his nine years as a light-tackle guide in South Florida and the Keys, Tejera has gained a lot of experience in releasing shallow-water game fish. In fact, he estimates that 90 percent of the fish his clients catch are released.

To give a fish its best chance of survival, Tejera tries to keep it in the water at all times. He says using a net can rub off lots of slime and bringing the fish in the boat can only cause further injury through oxygen deprivation and by allowing the fish to flop around.

"With bonefish, I try not to bring them in the boat at all," says Tejera. With permit, he says you can lift the fish briefly out of the water by its caudal peduncle to remove the hook. This reduces slime removal.

Since most of Tejera's clients use light tackle, the fish are usually exhausted by the time they are brought to the boat. Therefore, he doesn't advocate the method of dropping the fish headfirst to release them. "You really have to spend a lot of time with them and make sure they've recovered," he says. Tejera's method is to hold the fish by the tail and swim it gently back and forth. In some cases he'll let the fish swim off a little ways and then grab it by the tail again and continue to revive it. He'll do this several times until he feels confident that the fish will be able to make it on its own.

Tejera stresses the importance of making sure a flats fish is completely recovered before its allowed to swim off on its own, otherwise it's a prime target for sharks. A released fish will instinctively head for the deeper water beyond the flat to seek safety; ironically, that's where sharks usually wait to pick off weak and injured fish.

Reds Are Tough, Snook Aren't

"Redfish," Tejera says, "are tough. I don't worry as much about them as the other species. In fact a lot of times the redfish will stay alive in your livewell all day long. They're one of the easiest species to release safely."

Tough they may be, but they're not immune to sharks. In fact, Tejera warns *anglers* to be careful of barracuda and sharks while reviving a fish. He points to the unfortunate case of a fisherman who spent several weeks in the hospital after a large barracuda sliced his arm while attacking a red he was releasing.

In regards to survival rates following release, A.G. Woodward, a fisheries biologist with the Georgia Department of Natural Resources, offers this encouraging data. Between 1988 and 1989, 513 sub-legal, hook-caught redfish were

placed in tanks and observed for a minimum of two weeks. Of the 394 mouth-hooked reds, 92 percent survived. Fish that had been hooked in the gill and throat exhibited a 68 percent survival rate and the 52 gut-hooked fish had a survival rate of 47 percent.

With only five months of open snook season and strict size limits, anglers in southern Florida should certainly be aware of how to release these valuable game fish successfully. Particularly important is water temperature—not so much high temperature (as with striped bass), but low. Tejera says that snook caught during periods of cold weather have to be handled very carefully. Usually these fish are heavily stressed by the low water temperatures to begin with and may not be able to recover from a lengthy battle on light tackle. Handle these fish as little as possible, always keep them in the water, and make sure they're able to swim off vigorously, otherwise they could end up as shark bait, too.

As for the practice of lipping a healthy snook caught in optimum water temperatures, Tejera says that he doesn't have any evidence that it's harmful to the fish. "At least you're not touching the gills or rubbing off any slime when you do that," he says. "What usually happens, though, is that the person will lift the snook up to remove the hook or take a photo and the fish will shake. Then, of course, the person immediately drops the fish. That's worse than if you used a net and didn't drop the fish."

Releasing Tarpon

When it comes to tarpon, Tejera speaks out strongly against the common practice of lip-gaffing. "My latest project," he says, "is getting people not to lip-gaff. Usually, you will rip six to eight inches of jaw membrane before the hook catches around the hard lip cartilage." And for what? To get back the fly or lure? Consider yourself lucky enough to get the fish to the boat in the first place, and cut the line.

Another practice Tejera believes should be stopped, even though he used to do it himself, is the ceremonial removal of a trophy scale from the tarpon's back. Tejera says that he's seen some tarpon with big clumps of growth where a scale has been removed.

To revive a tarpon, Tejera grasps it firmly by the lower lip and swims it back in forth, keeping the fish facing into the current. He'll also raise the tarpon's head to give it a gulp of air once and a while, "since that's what they do naturally." Again, Tejera stresses the importance of making sure a tarpon that's exhausted after being fought on light tackle has completely recovered before it's allowed to swim off. "The fish that are hurt the least are the ones caught near the bridges on heavy tackle: there the fight may last five minutes. It's the fly-rodders that really exhaust them the most."

And an exhausted tarpon, Tejera says, is a prime target for hammerhead sharks. "Where you find tarpon," he warns, "There's always a hammerhead lurking nearby. And a tired tarpon is a hammerhead's favorite meal. If a fish is bleeding, it's automatically dead." To make sure a tarpon is able to make it on its own, Tejera has spent up to 20 minutes reviving it. "I've even gone into the water to revive a fish that's really exhausted," he says. Uh, what about those hammerheads, Paul?

Pacific Salmon

Although Tony Floor, spokesman for the Washington State Department of Fisheries, admits that the Northwest hasn't been very forward-thinking when it comes to catch and release, he says that anglers—particularly salmon anglers—had better start getting used to it. "Due to a recent downward spiral in native coho salmon stocks," he says, "anglers are going to be required, like it or not, to release the native fish."

Floor admits that it's going to cause a lot of controversy. However, he was quite confident that it's the only answer. "The next step down from

here is putting native cohos on the Endangered Species List, and we want to avoid that at all costs." Anglers will likely be required to release all native cohos, but may keep hatchery fish, which can be identified by the one missing ventral fin that was removed prior to release from the hatchery.

For those who want to get used to releasing fish, there's no need to wait. Jump right in and get some practice! Floor recommends obtaining some sort of dehooking tool, such as a pair of needlenose pliers or a J-shaped dehooker. Try to keep the fish in the water while you remove the hook and handle the fish as little as possible. If you have to handle the fish, only do so with wet hands, and be particularly careful not to touch the gills. The proper way to hold a salmon is by grasping the caudal peduncle (base of the tail) with one hand and gently cupping the other hand under the belly, just behind the gills. If the hook is deeply embedded and you can't get to it, cut the line near to the mouth. Another quick way to release a jaw-hooked salmon without touching it is to grab the hook with a dehooking tool, lift the fish out of the water, and twist the hook so the salmon simply falls into the water. If the hook has been removed quickly, and the salmon is not exhausted from the fight, it will usually zip right off.

If you're not confident with your dehooking abilities and need to bring the fish aboard, Floor recommends using a cotton-mesh net rather than one made of nylon, since cotton removes less slime and scales. In fact, anglers may be *required* to have a cotton-mesh net and some sort of dehooking tool on board their vessel in the future.

Sport fishermen in Washington have been required to use barbless hooks now for ten years. In fact, many expert salmon anglers now *prefer* them to barbed hooks, since they penetrate easier. As far as Floor knows there haven't been any studies on treble hooks versus single hooks. However,

he says that trebles are "hellish on the head and mouth areas," and feels that barbless singles give the fish the best chances of survival.

Deep-Water Bottom Fish

Finally, we come to the most controversial issue of them all: how to release deep-dwelling reef and bottom fish. Although the jury's not out yet on this one, initial studies offer some encouraging data. For instance, several studies involving red snapper caught off the Gulf Coast oil rigs in water approximately 100 feet deep showed a very high rate of survival if the fish had no hook injuries and weren't eaten on the way back to the bottom. In fact, most of the snappers had no problem returning to the bottom on their own. Some of the snappers were kept in cages on the bottom and observed for several days after release with no ill effects observed.

The bad news is that fish caught in depths over 100 feet showed a rapid increase in mortality after being observed in cages, and many of the "free-released" fish weren't able to return to the bottom because of the buoyancy caused by expanded stomach gas. It appears that the deeper the water, the higher the mortality due to injuries caused by decompression.

What about the practice of deflating the fish's abdomen so it can return to the bottom? According to Ron Schmied, special assistant for NMFS's Southeast Regional Office, and who also put together a video on how to release fish called *Pass it On* with *Salt Water Sportsman's* Senior Editor Mark Sosin, deflating a fish is better than leaving it floating on the surface, where it's susceptible to predation and exposure to the sun. It's the same principle as leaving the hook in a gut-hooked fish: sure, it isn't the ideal situation, but at least the fish has a chance.

Another biologist who advocates abdomen deflation is Dr. Ray Wilson of the University of South Florida. Wilson is currently studying hook-caught groupers (red, gag, and scamp) taken from South Florida's offshore reefs, and has found that release survival is relatively high if the fish are taken in less than 200 feet of water. Here the process of decompression and recompression doesn't seem to affect survival. Any deeper than 200 feet, however, and decompression injury becomes a factor and survival rate rapidly decreases.

"Don't have the attitude that you're throwing away a good fish," Wilson says, regarding a common misconception shared by many bottom fishermen. If you can get the fish in quickly so it's not completely exhausted, and deflate (aspirate) the abdomen (not the swim bladder, which is destroyed when the fish is brought to the surface), the fish has a good chance of surviving. Wilson recommends using a clean hypodermic needle (around 14 gauge) to deflate the abdomen, because it has a hole in the center that allows the gas to bleed off. Naturally, you need to remove the back of the syringe for it to work. If you can't obtain a needle, a *clean* ice pick, bait-stitching needle, or a debarbed hook will work in a pinch. Later, the puncture hole will heal.

"Remember," says Wilson, "that the only thing you're doing by deflating the abdomen is assisting the descent—so the fish is no longer buoyant. Some fish do have the energy to overcome that buoyancy." If a fish is still fighting hard when you get it to the boat, first see if it's able to descend on it's own. If not, then you should aspirate the abdomen.

The best way to deflate, or aspirate, a grouper is to turn the fish over on its back and insert the needle (or other device) on either side of the centerline just forward of the anus. (Many people confuse the large bulbous sac protruding from the mouth of a grouper or snapper as the swim bladder. This is actually the stomach of the fish that has been everted by the expanding gas and should not be punctured.) Then gently massage the gas out of the abdomen

General Rules for Safe Release

- Bring the fish to the boat quickly.
- Keep the fish in the water if possible. Always keep large fish, such as billfish and sharks, in the water.
- Small fish can be lifted from the water briefly and the hook removed with a dehooking tool.
- Cut the line or leader as close to the mouth as possible if the hook is difficult to remove.
- Use single, barbless hooks. Change trebles to singles on plugs or clip off two of the barbs on a treble to maintain balance.
- If you have to handle the fish, only do so with wet hands to keep the protective mucous coating intact.
- Don't touch the gills.
- Minimize time kept out of water.
- Lay the fish on a wet surface if it has to be brought onboard.
- Cover the fish's head with a wet towel to calm it.
- Take time to revive an exhausted fish.
- Deflate (aspirate) bottom fish only if they are unable to descend on their own.

and return the fish to the water. If the fish appears to be too exhausted to swim, Wilson says you can keep it in a live well just long enough for its breathing to return to normal. Groupers are surprisingly hardy, I was interested to learn, and have a fairly good chance of surviving if returned to the water in under three minutes. Some red grouper have been kept out of the water for up to five minutes and survived release.

Pacific Rockfish

West Coast rockfish are another deep-water species that present a similar release problem. I spoke with Farron Wallace, a fisheries biologist with the Washington Department of Marine Fisheries, who expressed surprise that I would even choose to cover the release of rockfish, since apparently very few sport fishermen in the Northwest practice it. Wallace told me that any rockfish taken from below 60 feet generally don't seem to be able to overcome the buoyancy of expanded gas. "Above that depth," he said,

"they're usually pretty lively and don't seem to have a problem getting back down."

When asked about the practice of gas deflation, Wallace said he wasn't aware of any studies being done, but directed me to the Seattle Aquarium and its Senior Biologist Pat McMahon. McMahon told me that his staff has experimented with deflation techniques using hypodermic needles (14 gauge) and says it does work with rockfish. He says that rockfish caught below 100 feet are unable to make it back down on their own, but seem to have no problem after deflation. (Unfortunately, I was unable to uncover any data concerning survival after release.) McMahon says that with rockfish, the needle should be inserted about two scales below the fish's lateral line behind the pectoral fin. The needle should also be angled toward the head as it's inserted into the musculature. Again, as with grouper and snapper, deflation should only be practiced if the fish is unable to descend on its own.

Some West Coast bottom fishermen have expressed concern over releasing lingcod. Fortunately, ling have no swim bladder and do not have a problem returning to any depth.

So there you have it, our rather exhaustive treatise on how to release fish. Unfortunately, space did not allow us to cover every game fish, but the general principles of safe release can be applied to most every species. We hope the article has been instructive, that it has convinced you that released fish survive, and that it will get you to release more of your fish. Of course, not every released fish will survive, but you can increase the number that do.

■

Saltwater Fly Fishing With Lefty Kreh

by Gary Diamond

When anglers talk of fly fishing experts, especially in saltwater, they usually refer to Lefty Kreh, a man who for more than four decades, has been considered the world's leading authority. Lefty has fished in all 50 states, throughout Central America, South America, Europe, Iceland, Australia, New Guinea, New Zealand and a number of small islands in both the South Pacific and Caribbean. He's the author of more than a dozen fly fishing books, several videos, holds a staff position on six major outdoor magazines and served on the boards of national fly fishing organizations, where he received numerous awards.

Kreh can do things with a fly rod that most folks only dream about. His fly casting techniques have been taught to avid fly fishermen throughout the world and his fishing success is unmatched. At one time, Kreh held nearly a dozen saltwater fly fishing records, many of which were on species found right in our own back yard. Lefty is one of the few fishermen fortunate enough to land a white marlin, blue marlin, sailfish, bluefin tuna, yellowfin tuna and a host of other big game species on a fly rod.

Before racing to the nearest tackle shop and purchasing a fly rod, Kreh said, "It's important to know that for most saltwater fly fishing, especially in the mid-Atlantic and New England states, you only need two fly rods. First, a size #8 for smaller species such as weakfish, white perch, yellow perch,

Fly fishing expert Lefty Kreh with an albacore. Lefty can do things with a fly rod that most folks only dream about. (GARY DIAMOND)

flounder and false albacore. When the wind is high, or you want to chase larger fish, you'll need a size #10. Modern 10 weight rods made by top manufacturers, such as Sage, Loomis, Orvis and others, can usually handle 10 or 11 weight lines equally as well and they'll whip any striped bass you'll ever catch."

Heavier Rods

Kreh added "There's a tendency for striped bass fishermen, especially those in the Northeast, to use heavier fly tackle than necessary. Some fishermen use size 12 or 13 weight rods, but the problem is, most people can't cast a heavy rod for long periods of time." Because striped bass fishing usually requires casting large, wind-resistant flies, often for extended periods of time, lighter weight rods are preferred. However, when the winds are howling from an easterly direction, heavier rods and lines are often a necessary evil.

Two-Handed Rods

Kreh said this problem was recently solved when a lightweight, graphite version of a 200-year-old salmon fishing rod was introduced by a few manufacturers. "You can now buy a 14-foot, two-handed fly rod that only weighs 9 ounces." said Kreh. "There are a number of advantages to using a two-handed fly rod but until recently, very few people in the Northeast knew they existed. They're really great for striper fishing in the surf."

"When you're fishing from the beach, there are a number of advantages to fishing with a two handed rod. First, a person can cast 25 to 30 feet farther with a 12 to 14 foot rod than they can with a 9 footer. The reason is quite simple. The increased length of the rod makes the tip move a greater distance at a higher velocity, thereby increasing your casting range. This is really helpful when you're trying to catch big blues or stripers in the surf. If you make longer casts, you'll cover more water, which means you'll usually catch more fish."

Kreh says another distinct advantage of using the long, two-handed fly rod is it's ability to keep the line above the waves, preventing the surf from dragging and curling your line. Additionally, Kreh added, "The longer rod makes it easier to pick your line up and make a back-cast. If you're near the end of your retrieve and you're fighting the wave action, it's difficult to lift your line from the water, get it airborne and make a cast. With the longer 12 or 14 foot rod, this problem is minimized."

Kreh says a lot of fly fishermen have a false impression of the casting techniques used with a two-handed rod. In reality, the basic casting procedure is nearly identical to double hauling. Merely hold the rod's foregrip with your casting hand, grasping the line between your index finger and thumb. Grip the rod butt with your other hand and with a short, quick motion, shove it forward as you pick the line from the water for your back-cast. When the line's straight behind you, pull the butt toward your elbow to initiate your power cast. It's that easy.

Kreh says the average person can easily pick 60 feet of line off the water using this technique. The ensuing forward or power cast often travels well over 100 feet. Kreh says special fly lines designed for two-handed rods are now available from Scientific Anglers and Courtland. These lines have designations such as Extra-Long Belly Taper and Special Rocket Taper for two handed rods.

Tippet

"Most fishermen don't really understand the function of a leader, especially when it comes to saltwater fly fishing." said Lefty. "A leader plays several roles, the most important, an invisible connection between the line and fly. However, there are additional, but very important considerations. First, the tippet, which is the smallest part of the leader, has to match the fly. If you were to use a heavy length of monofilament for a tippet and a relatively small fly, it would kill the fly's action, which reduces the number of fish you'll catch. Therefore, tippet is not only an integral part of this invisible connection, but it's weight determines the fly's action."

Leader Length

"If you're fishing for striped bass in a clear New England river or a coastal Long Island back cove that's flat calm, you'll need a longer leader than if you were fishing offshore or in the surf," said Kreh. "The reason behind the extended length is to place the fly line's impact on the water well away from the fly. In calm, clear water, a leader measuring 10 to 12 feet works well."

"Unfortunately, God never lets us fly fish in salt water without first making the weather windy. When the winds are high, the water will be rough and under these conditions substantially shorter leaders are equally as effective," Kreh said. "If you're fishing the surf and conditions are relatively calm, a 9-foot leader is acceptable. When the water's surface is dead calm, you'll do best with a 12- to 13-foot leader. If the surface is choppy, 7 to 8 feet is fine, especially when you're using sinking line."

Kreh added, "If you're using sinking lines, leaders should never be longer than seven to eight feet. The problem is the fly line sinks, but the monofilament leader tends to float. If I want my fly deep, I prefer a maximum leader length of just three to four feet with most types of sinking fly line."

Topwater Versus Sinking Flies

"When you're fishing in water less than 15 feet deep, most of the food consumed by predator fish is consumed on or near the bottom," said Kreh. "Obviously, if you're fishing on the open ocean, pelagic species will feed up and down the water column, but most of the time, they'll feed 10 to 20 feet beneath the surface."

"The major problem you'll encounter when saltwater fly fishing is casting a sufficient distance to get the fly deep, where the fish are feeding." Kreh says most of the time, sinking and fast sinking lines produce far more strikes than floating lines. Because of this, Kreh prefers shooting heads, specially constructed lines that frequently outperform standard weight forward designs because of their decreased wind resistance and improved casting ability.

Kreh says if you encounter situations where floating lines and popping bugs can be productive, such as a school of breaking bluefish or stripers actively feeding on the surface, be sure to attach the popper with a loop knot. This allows the bug to splash erratically as it's being retrieved, giving it the appearance of an injured baitfish. Kreh says the loop knot also aids in lifting the fly from the water's surface before casting.

Line Backing

"I use 30 pound Dacron line for backing. The reason is, 30-pound Dacron resists abrasion much better than 20-pound. Although some anglers use 20-pound Dacron backing because they can put more line on their spool, in most instances, the added length isn't necessary. I've been fishing hard with a fly rod since 1949 and with the exception of some ocean species such as sailfish, tuna and huge tarpon, I have never had a fish run off 200 yards of backing. In fact, any fish that lives within two or three miles of the coast, with the exception of tarpon, will never take 200 yards of backing, plus an additional 30 yards of fly line from your reel. The only advantage to having a lot of backing is it increases the spool's diameter which allows you to recover line at a greater rate. With 200 yards of 30-pound Dacron backing, you can land just about any fish that swims within two miles of shore."

Kreh says never, under any circumstances, use monofilament backing. When under stress, monofilament line stretches, decreases it's diameter and buries itself into the bed of line remaining on the spool. The compressed line eventually becomes weakened and catches within the line's folds, causing it to break when a big fish makes a hard run. Not only do you lose the fish, but in addition, you could lose your $35 fly line.

Kreh says the most important aspect of backing is making sure it's installed properly on the spool. "Most people put backing on a reel by allowing the line to run between their thumb and forefinger while winding it on. Ironically, a lot of novice saltwater fly anglers lose big fish because of this. If the backing isn't extremely tight, it packs down in the folds of the line and snags when the fish takes off on a long run. You should use cotton or leather work gloves, hold the line as tight as possible and make sure it's put on evenly."

Night Fishing

"Some of the most productive fly fishing in the Northeast, especially for big stripers, takes place at night, a time when fish often migrate into the surf to feed. The problem with night fishing is there's no way of telling how much line you have retrieved. If too much line is retrieved, it's impossible to make another cast until you've worked sufficient line out with several false casts. Wouldn't it be nice if you knew exactly how much line was out, then make a single false cast and place the fly right where you want it? It's easy to do during the day when you can see the line, but at night, it's nearly impossible."

Kreh, known by his peers as a creative genius, developed a Braille-type method of marking his fly line so he knows exactly how much line is out while fishing in total darkness. "All you have to do make a few casts during the day and at the point where you normally pick up the line to make another cast, mark it with a pen. Then, using a short length of 10-pound test monofilament line, tie a tight nail knot over the mark. The monofilament will compress the fly line enough so you won't

have to coat the area with Goop or Rubber Cement and to make it pass through the rod guides. At night, when you're striping line in, you'll feel that tiny nail knot as it touches your fingers and know it's time to make another cast." Kreh says the same technique is great for anglers casting Slime Line, a clear fly line that's nearly invisible.

Stripping Baskets

"Most saltwater fly fishermen quickly discover the value of a stripping basket when they're fishing the surf. Good baskets are commercially available, but for $5 you can make one from a plastic dishpan or Tupperware container. All you do is cut a couple of slots in one side and pass a belt through the slots so the pan can be attached to your waist. Then turn the pan over and with a small diameter, heated nail, punch a couple dozen holes through the bottom. Then cut some 2-inch strands of 100 pound monofilament leader, heat one end with a match until a ball is formed and place a piece of mono in each hole. Then, using epoxy or hot melt glue, put a dab at the base of each strand of mono to hold it in place. Now the inside of the striping basket has a bunch of tiny monofilament fingers projecting upward and preventing your line from tangling as you walk. Without a stripping basket, you'll spend a lot of time untangling line from your feet."

Casting Accuracy Makes a Difference

"More often than not, casting accuracy determines your saltwater fly fishing success," Kreh said. "In many instances, especially when you're fishing offshore, you're casting a swirl or trying to place your fly as close as possible to a weedline. If you can't see the line, how can you determine where it's going to hit?" This is one of the reasons Kreh prefers using fluorescent colored fly lines, colors that sharply contrast with both the sky and water.

"If you're fishing properly, you're not throwing fly line directly over the fish. In most instances, you're casting to a spot some distance away from them, to a point where the fly will be intercepted as it's being retrieved. Another big advantage of fluorescent line is after you've hooked a big fish, if the captain has to chase it with the boat, he's not as likely to run over a bright line he can readily see." Kreh added.

Fly Selection

When it comes to which flies to use for a specific species of fish, it's tough to beat the Lefty's Deceiver, a large streamer made from a combination of bucktail hair and long, slender hackle feathers. Although several variations of Lefty's famous fly have been adapted to various fishing situations, the basic pattern he created nearly three decades ago is still effective on a variety of big game, saltwater species.

"One of the advantages of fishing with a deceiver, a fly I designed for catching stripers, is you can make it very large but still maintain a good profile that's easy to cast. Lets face it, big fish tend to take big flies. The Deceiver's a good fly, but more recently, the Clouser Deep Minnow has become one of the best flies you can use in the Northeast. In fact, during the past three years, I've caught 63 different species of fish in fresh and salt water with this particular pattern. It's the single best underwater fly that has been developed in the past 25 years."

"If you're fishing for striped bass, one of the best flies you can use is a chartreuse and white Clouser Deep Minnow measuring about five inches long. During the past two years, especially in the Northeast, this has been a red-hot striped bass fly. That's because sand eels are one of the favorite foods of striped bass and a sparsely dressed Clouser minnow, tied in the same colors as the eel, is one of the best imitations I've ever seen. It's a good idea to tie a bunch of them with different sized lead eyes so you can cover a variety of depths," Kreh added.

"When you're fishing for false albacore and bonito, a very small Clouser minnow, one measuring about two inches long with fairly small lead eyes, has been responsible for some of the best albacore action from North Carolina to New England. During the fall, both species travel close to shore and if you have a good selection of deceivers, Clouser minnows and a few big popping bugs, that's all the flies you'll need to catch all the fish you can handle. Sure, there are lots of other flies that work in saltwater, but if you have these three, you probably won't need the others.

Lefty's Tips for Catching Big Fish

Cobia: "There's a couple secrets to catching big cobia with a fly rod. First of all, cobia will hit a large popping bug faster than any other fly. A 3/0 popper with a face the size of a quarter is just about right for cobia—they rarely take a small fly.

"Teasing cobia is probably the best way to catch them. You can do this by catching a small baitfish, hook it to a heavy boat rod and drag it around near a buoy. Cobia are like sharks in that they're readily attracted to sounds made by a struggling baitfish. If there's a cobia in the area, it won't be long until it appears right under the baitfish. Lift the baitfish from the water and cast your popping bug in the same spot. Unless the fish is spooked by the boat, it will hit the popper like a freight train."

Striped Bass: "Most fly fishing for striped bass in Maryland and Virginia is done in the shallows from a small boat. The fishing usually takes place in Chesapeake Bay tributaries such as the Choptank and Potomac, where big schools are often found during late summer and fall. The best action is usually during the late afternoon and early evening when baitfish frequently congregate on the surface," he said.

"If you see stripers actively feeding—birds diving, fish breaking—toss a big deceiver or popping bug in their general direction and you're going to catch lots of fish. This is fast fishing and the fish don't always cooperate by staying on top for long periods of time. It's a good idea to have a fly rod rigged and ready to cast at all times.

"A trick I use is to take a five-gallon plastic bucket, put it near the transom and then make the longest cast you possibly can, strip the line into the bucket and hook the fly on the rod handle. When you find a school of fish, unhook the fly, make a false cast and the line will shoot out of the five gallon bucket without getting tangled. If it's windy or you're chasing moving schools of fish at high speeds, put a little water in the bucket. It will keep both your fly line and the bucket from blowing out of the boat.

"From New Jersey north to New England, several striped bass fishing options are available to fly rod fishermen. One of the most exciting is catching them from the surf, which is better in the fall than any other time of year. When you hook a big striper in just three or four feet of water, it goes completely berserk.

"There are lots of small boat fishing opportunities for big stripers also, especially in places like Barnegat Bay where big fish can be found in grass beds and near rock piles. These are great places that are often only accessible to 14- to 16-foot aluminum skiffs powered with small outboards.

"One of the best things about fishing from a small boat is you can go way up into a river system or work the edge of a flats or fish drop-offs of small coves. Striped bass love to lay on a drop-off, whether it's in Chesapeake Bay, Barnegat Bay or Penobscot River, if you can locate a drop-off, you can catch stripers close to the bottom. In New England, there are lots of quiet bays formed where river mouths drop back off the coast. It's in these little sloughs, creeks and coves where big stripers feed on baitfish and crabs all

summer long. On calm, overcast days, striper fishing in these locations can be fantastic."

Kreh added: "Jetties are always a good place to fish for striped bass and most of the time, you don't need a boat in order to catch fish. Stripers school near jetties in spring, summer and fall, but here's a trick that will make fly fishing from a jetty easier. Buy an eight foot by eight foot piece of half inch mesh netting, tie a six- to eight-ounce sinker to each corner and lay it over the rocks. Now you can drop your fly line on the netting and it won't get snagged in the boulders. Some people use tarps, but when the wind get under a tarp, it's gone—wind doesn't effect the netting."

Lefty says it's extremely important to read the water by looking for structure that impedes tidal flow and forms turbulent, backwater eddies. "It's the tide that carries the baitfish and they'll congregate on the downtide side of jetties, rock piles, sand bars and other forms of shallow structure, places where they don't have to expend lots of energy to survive. That's why big stripers are usually found in the same locations."

Bluefish: "Bluefish are tough to catch, mainly because they're constantly on the move, trying to find something to eat. Bluefish are essentially eating machines, but unless you're lucky enough to stumble across a migrating school of blues hitting everything that moves, they're difficult to catch. The best way I know to catch bluefish, especially on a fly rod is in a chum slick. It's a lot easier to attract fish to you, than it is for you to find them in the open ocean."

Kreh's technique for catching big blues is unique. His secret to success is to use sinking line, a relatively short leader and a short length of coffee-colored, stainless tippet. "Sometimes I'll tie on a fly that imitates the baitfish attracted to the chum, but my most effective fly looks like a fresh chunk of ground menhaden. The fly is just a 1/0 hook wrapped with enough lead wire to make it sink with the chum. The hook is then wrapped with dark brown and red maribou to make it look like a large piece of chum drifting in the slick. Let the fly drift freely for 30 to 40 feet, flowing with the chum line. If you don't get a strike, retrieve the line and drop the fly at the beginning of the slick. It's just like nymph fishing for freshwater trout. The fish hit on a slack line and it takes fast reflexes to set the hook before it discovers something's wrong with the bait."

Billfish: Lefty is among a handful of individuals who can brag of catching both blue and white marlin on a fly rod. "The hardest billfish to catch is a white marlin. They're a fast-swimming fish that feeds while it's moving extremely fast. The only time it hits a slow bait is after it has been stunned or injured during the chase. That's why they're impossible to catch from a drifting boat."

Kreh says most marlin, blue and white are taken by first luring the fish with a large teaser trolled at high speeds. When a marlin attacks the teaser, the mate drags lure within fly casting range while the boat's still in motion. A large streamer, often measuring 10 to 12 inches, is then dropped behind the teaser. "If your equipment is perfectly matched, your drag's smooth as silk and the hook is razor sharp, you might get lucky enough to sink the

hook beyond the barb. The fish will jump and you'll likely spend the next several hours chasing a marlin all over the ocean," added Kreh.

Tuna: "The easiest tuna to catch on a fly rod is yellowfin and bonito. The bonito are often found close to shore and accessible to small boat anglers. At certain times, especially during late summer and early fall, you'll find them breaking a few miles offshore. Toss a big streamer several feet in front of the fish, strip your line as fast as possible and when they hit, hang on. Bonito are a lot of fun on any kind of light tackle, but they're fantastic on a fly rod," he said.

"The few yellowfin tuna I've taken on a fly were mid-sized, 25 to 50 pounders. Like most saltwater fish with deeply forked tails, they're extremely powerful, but because they don't jump, tuna also have lots of stamina, making them tougher to land than a similar sized marlin." Kreh says when yellowfins are feeding on the surface, they'll slam a big streamer, but after fighting and landing that first fish, few anglers are willing to battle another.

Dolphin: "Dolphin are easy to find and one of the most exciting species you'll encounter while fly fishing in salt water. The secret to success is finding the right kind of bluewater structure. If you're lucky enough to locate an offshore weed line, there's an even chance you'll find lots of dolphin hiding

in it's shadow. You'll also find them lurking in the shade of lobster pots, fish pots, under offshore buoys and beneath floating debris. If you can't locate floating structure, you can make your own by merely placing sheets of newspaper on the water at intervals of 50 to 100 feet. Two or three sheets sandwiched together will float for six or seven hours, but they'll eventually disintegrate, therefore they're not causing pollution. Mark the coordinates on your loran and return to the site within an hour or two. When conditions are right, you'll find a hefty dolphin under every other sheet.

"The easiest way to catch dolphin with a fly rod is to cast from a drifting boat. Simply toss a big streamer close to the weed line or newspaper sheets, let it sink a few feet and retrieve it at a rapid rate. If there's a dolphin under the structure, your fly doesn't have a prayer of making it back to the boat. Most of these fish are only 12- to 20-pounders, but once in a while, a 40- to 50-pounder shows up. If it hits your fly, dig your heels in for a long and exciting battle."

Lefty says fly fishing is an exciting and often new way for many anglers to catch many species of fish that were once reserved only to those fishing with heavy tackle. "It's the ultimate challenge for all saltwater fishermen."

Bottom Bouncing

by Mark Sosin and George Poveromo

Searching for fish along the floors of oceans, bays and sounds ranks as the most popular form of saltwater fishing, and for good reason. Bottom fishing usually offers plenty of action, which can range from rigging gear and baiting hooks to judging when to set up on a pernicious fish that's been

nibbling away at an offering. In contrast to trolling or other specialized forms of fishing, there's always something to keep an angler's mind occupied, and the odds are greater for finding more consistent fishing. Furthermore, most benthic fish provide good to excellent tablefare.

Locating Structure

The concept behind successful bottom fishing is based on an angler's ability to uncover structure that is likely to hold fish. Structure can be defined as wrecks, reefs, rockpiles, depressions in the bottom's contour, weed growth, bridges and assorted rubble, pilings and even channel edges. Anything that offers sanctuary is likely to be an ecosystem that harbors both bait and gamefish. As algae and micro organisms begin to flourish on or near such points, smaller fish move in to feed and seek shelter and, in turn, attract larger fish. Depending on the size and location of the structure, a complete community is often maintained, with the larger benthic fish establishing their own niches within the boundaries. If such territorial fish are removed from the system, there will be others that'll quickly replace them.

Expert anglers realize how critical structure is to success. It's not unusual for them to run long and hard before settling down to fish, with the excessive travel time often rewarded with quality catches. Probably the most valuable aid when it comes to bottom fishing is a dependable chart recorder. Used by all professional captains and an ever-increasing number of recreational anglers, a recorder offers the advantages of illustrating an entire water column. It shows whether a bottom's composition is hard (rocky) or soft (muddy), the exact zone in which the fish are holding and, to some degree, it differentiates between bait and gamefish.

When ferreting out productive structures in an unfamiliar region, anglers should first study a navigational chart. By doing this homework, which includes chatting with local baitshop personnel, one can pencil in, and then locate, several proven areas. The chart recorder helps to pinpoint the exact spot by monitoring the bottom's contour. Furthermore, anglers often run to such spots with their recorders on. They may burn excessive amounts of paper in the process but there's always the possibility of uncovering fish and new structures along the way.

Loran has greatly simplified the ability to find and return to a hot area. In addition, the coordinates of the more popular points are often public knowledge, reducing the amount of effort and headaches associated with

Joey, left, and Nick Andelora with four keeper fluke (summer flounder) caught by bottom bouncing squid and spearing bait in the channels of New Jersey's Barnegat Bay. Fluking is an ideal way to introduce any youngster to fishing. (VIN T. SPARANO)

trying to locate them by other means. A professional captain will always study a chart recorder for structure, placing the loran coordinates of promising areas into the unit's memory. Over the years, these captains have logged hundreds of spots in the pages of their loran books. By taking the time to record their findings, they have literally created a fishing circuit. A captain now has the option of lining up several prominent spots within striking distance of each other. If one point fails to produce fish, he'll simply plug in another set of coordinates and continue on his way. It may take a few years to master, but recreational anglers can build their own collection of numbers, as well as determine what spots are best during the course of the year.

Different Strokes for Different Folks

By developing a basic understanding of the most popular fish frequenting a region, you should have an advantage that will reflect in your catch. Focus on the seasons, the types of structure that appeal to them, the best baits, and

coordinating your terminal gear with the size and species of the fish.

For example, blackfish is a very popular Northeastern groundfish that takes up residence around scattered rocks in sounds and shallow offshore waters, becoming more abundant between spring and fall. These scrappy warriors, often less than four pounds, lurk around structure for protection and to feed on various types of mussels and clams. Anglers fishing Long Island Sound off Rowayton, Connecticut, particularly around Green's Ledge, Budd Reef and The Cows off Shippan Point (just north of the Stamford breakwater), benefit from abundant rockpiles that maintain healthy populations of these tasty fish.

Black seabass are similar to blackfish except that they prefer slightly greater depths and are more prominent offshore of the Carolina and Virginia coastlines. From the Carolinas southward through the Gulf of Mexico, groupers and snappers take over as the most valuable bottom fish.

Wreck Dwellers

Artificial reefs and shipwrecks have improved local fisheries by replacing portions of the bottom that have been damaged, and by adding structure to otherwise barren areas. Most wrecks and artificial reefs are situated offshore, although an increasing amount of attention is being given to developing inshore programs. Species visiting or taking up residence around these points run the gamut from amberjack, barracuda, cobia (ling), snapper, and grouper from the Gulf of Mexico to the Carolinas. Cod, pollack and hake take over in the cooler waters off the New England coast.

Seasons will determine the arrival of migratory species. Peaks can range from the winter in the extreme southern portion of Florida to the spring and early summer off the Southeast and Gulf of Mexico states to mid-summer and early fall off the Northeast. Because of the vast ecosystems supported by these wrecks, pelagic species sometimes linger around the ones situated near deep water. Dolphin, kingfish and mackerel may visit sights in the Gulf of Mexico and Southeastern states, and every now and again there might be a smattering of sailfish and tarpon off some of the South Florida wrecks.

Deep Dwellers

The ultra deep species that reside on the bottom near and beyond the Continental Shelf make up a small recreational fishery due to the vast depths and currents that must be encountered to get a bait down to them. Tilefish are probably the most popular and abundant species, followed by hake and cusk in the Northeast. Since it's sometimes necessary to make a set depth nearing 2,000 feet, especially for the latter two species, electric reels are used to lower and haul up the heavily weighted rigs. You will occasionally find recreational anglers fishing for tilefish in waters around 400 feet deep with electric reels or downriggers that have enough cable to reach them.

Inshore Fish

Inshore species are located in a manner similar to their offshore counterparts, but their structure will consist of scattered debris, channel edges, depressions, oyster bars, etc. The prestigious striped bass is a prime example of an inshore species that frequents shelves and rocky points. It is especially fond of structure at the mounts of rivers or canals that dump fresh and brackish waters into bays and sounds. Compared to blackfish, which can sometimes be found around offshore rocks, striped bass rarely travel seaward.

Gulf coast and southeastern bay anglers know that the popular sheepshead can be found around hard bottom. Alabama's Mobile Bay is just one productive system that yields great numbers of these fish. The remains of the old Dauphin Island bridge and the surrounding oyster beds attract some

real heavyweights that may break five or six pounds. The tasty fish feed mainly on crustaceans that abound around such structure.

Species such as flounder or fluke (summer founder) are fond of structure, too. However, in comparison to hard bottom, these fish enjoy muddy bottoms that are adjacent to shallow flats, as well as various holes, depressions or channels. Their flat configuration and coloration permit them to blend into the ocean floor. This camouflage offers both protection and the ability to attack unsuspecting baitfish such as blood and sand worms, mussels, killifish and sand eels. The fluke grows considerably larger than the winter flounder, with doormats weighing more than ten pounds. It'll frequent sections of inlets and shoals where moderate to swift currents abound.

The Fun Fish Species

If the most sought-after species take a breather, there are always the "fun fish" that will do their best to turn an otherwise unproductive day into a memorable outing. Some of these lesser-known fish aren't recommended for quality tablefare, but practically all of them will put up a determined scrap with anglers who are willing to scale their tackle accordingly. Day savers can include pinfish, which are caught over grassy flats, white perch, grunts, sea robins, and blowfish. All species are prominent inshore and over some offshore structures and are usually under two pounds. Their willingness to consume a variety of small cut baits make them the perfect challenge for youngsters who are just beginning to experience the thrill of salt water angling.

Getting to the Fish

Although some inshore fish, such as flounder, striped bass, porgies and blackfish, can be taken by anglers from bridges, piers or in the surf, increased fishing pressure has limited the better catches to boatowners. After locating

a potential area, an angler must select the baits and use them in conjunction with the proper rigs to get them down to the fish. Always obtain the freshest bait possible. Bottom fish, particularly grouper and snapper, rely heavily on their sense of smell and it often takes the scent of a fresh bait to convince a finicky member to eat. While you may take your fair share of fish on frozen bait, there's no denying that a fresh bait will be the decisive factor in producing fish on slow days.

An experienced bait fisherman always takes into consideration what's happening around him. That is, he's monitoring the water conditions to find out what the fish are feeding on and using the bait that's the most abundant within an area. By "matching the hatch," an angler can increase his chances of catching fish. There are many species that go on a selective feeding pattern, consuming those baits that they have rounded up or which thrive in a system. Striped bass is just one species that tends to specialize at times. Veteran anglers know they'll score more consistently using the predominant bait.

Understand that fish frequenting grass flats or soft bottoms are often pursuing shrimp, crabs or bloodworms and those over rockpiles are ferreting out crabs, mussels and a variety of baitfish. Try tempting the fish with their natural food first, switching strategies only after there's a lull in the activity. Furthermore, it often requires alternating baits when fish become wise to a certain offering. For example, grouper fished over the rockpiles in the Gulf of Mexico are noted for turning off to a specific type of bait that's repeatedly lowered into their domain. That's why successful anglers begin by using only one type of offering, such as Spanish sardines, and switching to another, usually squid, mullet or live pinfish, when the fish cease feeding. By doing so, they can effectively take advantage of a concentration of fish.

Neatness counts in trimming baits. There's more to presenting natural baits than cutting a chunk from a fish and lowering it to the bottom. Consider the current and how much more enticing a strip of squid or mullet will be as it flutters in front of a fish's lair. Baits can be trimmed to create a swimming action, and even to conceal a hook, such as a ballyhoo plug. A streamlined bait will cut accurately through a swift tide, appealing more to fish than a bulky one that resists the flow. Above all, pack several different types of baits on each outing. You'll not only have a greater chance of supplying the fish with what they want, but have an adequate back-up supply that can even be used for chum.

Terminal Gear

Successful bottom fishing requires a precise balance of terminal gear tailored to the desired species. Many fishermen make the mistake of employing gear that is too heavy for their quarry. Such overkill results in fewer strikes, affects a bait or lure's action, and reduces the sensitivity to feel a fish pick up an offering. Whenever applicable, use the lightest monofilament leaders that can handle a species and the least amount of lead that will hold an offering at the bottom. Depending upon the structure and the size of the fish, you may even consider scaling down to light tackle, such as 10- or 12-pound test line. The smaller diameter of a light line allows it to sink quicker than a heavier one and increases its sensitivity. Also, the lighter the monofilament leader, the less hardware a fish is likely to notice.

There will be certain situations that will prohibit the use of light gear. When fishing near wrecks or abrupt structures for large fish such as grouper or snapper, it's often necessary to employ heavy gear to horse the fish away from a potential cutoff. However, by utilizing a monofilament leader that tests slightly above the actual fishing line, you can still benefit by keeping visibility minimal. If an angler is fishing a wreck for grouper averaging 15 or 20 pounds and uses 30-pound test line, his leader's breaking strength should be 40 or 50 pounds. If he uses a 20-pound test outfit, he should reduce his leaders to around 30- or 40-pound test. Grouper don't possess dentures that are detrimental to fishing lines and it's often beneficial to use light to moderate strength leaders for them. Even with toothy fish such as mackerel or kingfish, you'll draw more strikes by using predominantly monofilament leaders. To reduce the risk of a cut-off and still maintain low visibility, tie a three or four inch wire trace leader to the monofilament with an Albright Special knot.

Sinkers come in a variety of sizes and shapes to cover most bottom applications. Among the standard selections that attach directly to the fishing line are the split shots (a small lead that is crimped on a fishing line) and the rubbercore sinker (which is attached by running the fishing line through its groove with a rubber cap or stop at each end to hold it in place). The egg sinker is the common choice of bottom fishermen. If the lead is small enough, it can ride just above the eye of a hook. Otherwise, most applications will find it resting on a swivel or the knot joining the fishing line and leader.

The pyramid sinker is often used in swift currents. In contrast to the weight styles mentioned above, the pyramid actually anchors itself in the bottom, leaving the bait to ride freely just above it. Like the egg sinker, the pyramid can be rigged as slider by running the fishing line through its eye. It also can be used as a base for specialty rigs where two or more hooks are featured.

The type of terminal arrangement an angler chooses will depend on the species and his sporting virtues. For example a rig for striped bass can consist of an egg sinker just above a three or four foot stretch of 60-pound test monofilament leader and a 6/0 or 7/0 live bait hook. The bait can be a live menhaden, or the head section of one. Rigs for blackfish, grouper and seabass can be as simple as a 2/0 hook, a foot or so of 30- or 40-pound-test monofilament leader, and an adequate amount of lead to maintain a proper depth. A more complex dropper rig would incorporate a pyramid sinker at its base and about three or four feet of 60-pound-test monofilament leader equally divided by a pair of three-way swivels, each featuring about a two foot dropper line with a hook.

There are anglers who are fond of a spreader rig, particularly with flounder. Such an instrument is constructed with a three way swivel dividing 20 to 24 inches of stiff wire. The fishing line is tied to the swivel's top eye with a few inches of monofilament and a bank or pyramid sinker attached to the bottom. A dropper hook is then secured to each end of the wire bar.

Regardless of the rigs, hook sizes should be geared to the species of fish. A large hook shows more hardware and requires a serious effort to drive it home, especially with species blessed with bony jaws. Take the time to hone each hook before placing it into action, inspecting it for sharpness throughout the day.

Deep Jigging

Deep jigging involves the art of coaxing a fish to strike an artificial. It's a popular form of fishing that is often associated with light tackle. The advantage of deep jigging is that you work not only the ocean bottom, but the entire water column. Grouper anglers in South Florida, the Bahamas, and the Keys continually see action from pelagic species such as kingfish, mackerel, barracuda and even a sailfish over the deep, offshore reefs. In addition, the boat usually drifts along a reef, allowing an angler to cover more ground and increase his chances of finding fish.

Deep jigs come in a variety of sizes and shapes. The two most prominent designs include the lima bean and arrow heads. The lima bean style features compressed sides that give it a fluttering action when worked through the water. The arrow tends to track straight and accurately. The latter design also penetrates a water column quicker because it exposes less surface area. Jigging spoons are more prominent in northern waters. Like the lead heads, they, too, come in various weights and two main designs that give them an inherent action. The diamond jig slices through the water quickly, while those featuring flat sides maintain a swimming like motion.

To maximize a jig's action and potential, use the lightest weight possible to reach bottom. Depending upon the species, opt for the lightest monofilament leader that can accomplish the job. If you have to use wire to prevent a cut-off, try a trace of about for or five inches. Pay particular attention to the knot, making sure there's an adequate loop for the jig to swing on. Ditto with wire. Never snug a knot against a lead's eye ring, for it will only hinder its performance.

A productive drift pattern is one that covers the shallow and deep sections of a reef. Depending upon the wind and tide, begin your drift at one extreme, repositioning yourself only after you clear the opposite end. By covering various depths and working closely with a chart recorder, you'll be able to discover the most productive zones to concentrate on. For benthic species, a jig should be allowed to reach bottom before being retrieved back to the surface with a hopping motion. It often pays to let the jig sink back to the bottom a second time after initially retrieving it about 20 feet. A solid strike will get an angler's attention in a hurry. Fish often strike a jig on its descent, reducing an angler's ability to "feel" the fish. It there's the slightest interference with a jig destined for the bottom, engage the reel's drag, take up the slack line, and strike if there's any resistance.

Often frowned upon by purists, sweetening a jig with a natural bait is almost a surefire way of luring bottom dwellers into feeding. Sweeteners can include strips of cut bait trimmed so

that they flutter attractively with the jig's motion, or whole baits that are impaled on a hook. Tipped jigs can be retrieved in a fashion listed above or left on the bottom until a fish consumes it. A second hook can even be added to guard against short strikes. Trailing hooks feature open eyes that can be closed with pliers after they've been attached to the lead hook. The lead hook is inserted under the bait's lower jaw and out the upper membrane with the barb of the second hook positioned inside the mid section.

Party Boats

Party or drift boats provide access to bottom fish and are an inexpensive alternative to chartering a private craft. They offer a great day on the water with friends when you don't feel like going through the motions of preparing your own craft. Prices on these boats vary, but you can expect to pay an average of $12 to $25 dollars per person for a half- or full-day ticket respectively. The fishing strategies will also vary with what's running at the time. If migratory species are in, expect the drift and tackle to be geared towards to them. Although you can still drop a bait to the bottom, the odds are that the boat won't be positioned over prime ground fish spots.

Check with a party boat captain in advance to learn what's running, his strategy for the week, prices, and the type of gear he has available. Chances are reservations aren't required and, unless you prefer your own gear, tackle is usually available at a nominal rental fee. Ditto terminal gear. Also, find out what baits he'll have on board, packing your own if you believe a different offering may stack the deck in your favor. Party boats make their money on the number of fishermen they host. Therefore, heavy tackle (30- and 40-pound-test conventional gear), is the norm. If you plan on bringing light tackle, it may be best to consult the captain in advance. If the "rail" is lean, he may let you follow through with your quest.

Otherwise, a disaster is almost sure to occur if a fish hooked on light tackle skirts its way across and tangles the lines of about 40 other paying customers.

Productive positions or hot seats aboard a party boat are those that happen to be near the fish when they're passing through, or right above an edge, shelf, wreck or structure. Many anglers swear by the stern, although their preference may be based on the fact that they're not sandwiched between other anglers, and that their baits can be drifted or worked in the relatively uncrowded waters off that section. If you desire a stern slot, make certain you arrive at the dock well ahead of time to secure it. And by all means, make sure you board the craft at least 15 minutes before departure. Party boat captains adhere precisely to their designated schedule to maximize actual fishing time.

The backbone of any drift boat is the mate. This hard-working lad must cater to the needs of the ship's party. He's in charge of rigging tackle, baiting hooks, untangling lines, keeping anglers happy, cleaning fish for anglers, and keeping the boat and its gear in ship shape and Bristol fashion. He's only too happy to explain the most productive techniques for the designated species, simply looking for a little consideration in the form of a tip back at the dock.

Party boat techniques are as simple as using a strip of bait or a whole fish on a hook and sending it down with the aid of a weight. The idea is to keep the bait just above the bottom which is usually accomplished by taking a few turns on a reel after it reaches its destination. Periodically, drop the bait back down to the bottom to compensate for any line planing due to current. After several minutes, it becomes necessary to reel up, check the bait, and re-drop it to keep an advantageous angle with the bottom. Deep jigging techniques also will produce, although it can become very difficult to entice a fish to strike an artificial when there's plenty of natural bait to be had. Some drift boat captains will go so far as to deploy a live bait or two in hopes of capturing a shark, billfish or other trophy fish for mounting purposes. If you desire to fish a live bait, make arrangements with the captain at least a day or so in advance.

Some drift boats even offer weekend bottom fishing expeditions to remote regions at very attractive rates, especially those sailing from South Florida and the Keys. Drift boats operate half- and full-day trips, as well as some night outings.

Fighting Strategies

Bottom fish can be pursued with almost any type of gear. The smaller members frequenting grass beds, oyster bars, bridges, etc., are enjoyable to wrestle on lines less than 10-pound test. The bigger gladiators are a different story. Depending on an angler's skill, he may attempt to challenge some of these critters on bait-casting gear spooled with lines testing between 12- and 15 pounds. However, when large fish abound over potentially dangerous structures, it often requires stiff rods and a minimum of 20 pound test line to have a chance at them.

The strategy with bottom fish, even with the smaller species on ultra light gear, is to go toe-to-toe with them immediately after setting the hook. By placing as much strain on your tackle as you can and still keeping within the line's breaking strength, you'll have a better chance of disorienting the fish enough o move it away from any structure. Any delays will give the fish a fighting chance, and usually enough time to react and charge into its lair. If a fish holes up, try throwing slack in the line for a few minutes, then engaging the reel's drag and "horsing" the fish after the line becomes taut. There are no guarantees, but sometimes this trick is worthy of a try. The most critical stage of the battle usually ends about ten or 15 feet above the bottom. It's a game of reflexes and judgment that becomes mastered after a few seasons in the field. ■

Fishing by the Birds

by Al Ristori

The modern angler has a multitude of fishing aids arrayed before him when he goes to sea, and they can greatly increase his chances of making a good catch. Yet, all too often, these same fishermen fail to use the powers of observation that were the only stock in trade of their predecessors. Though few fishermen are also birders, they're well-advised to become more acquainted with our feathered friends as they'll often lead us to fish which we'd otherwise be unaware of.

The most important aspect of successful saltwater fishing is being at the right place at the right time. The water volume we cover is huge, and every clue must be considered in order to narrow down the search. No matter how high the tower of the boat, your visibility is of little consequence when compared with that of any bird—and you can bet that their sight is a lot better besides. Best of all, their services in leading us to fish are completely free.

Whether you're fishing for stripers and blues, or marlin and tuna, the assistance provided by seabirds can make or break your effort on many occasions. The trick is to learn what birds will prove helpful for various species in your area and how to interpret their behavior.

Among the most reliable fish indicators in tropical and semi-tropical seas is the frigate, also known as man-o-war. This bird, which can have a wing spread of up to eight feet, is unable to dive for fish. However, there is no

Frigates take advantage of a shrimp trawler's riggers as they wait for trash to fall into the Gulf of Mexico off Key West. (AL RISTORI)

better fish spotter in the world. The frigate hovers far up in the sky and will track a single billfish until it pushes a bait fish to the surface, where it can be plucked off by the swooping bird. If there are no other signs to work with, I'll always steer toward any frigate spotted.

Frigates put me into some of the most exciting striped marlin fishing I've seen off Salinas, Ecuador, years ago as the birds targeted marlin balling bait fish. More recently, those birds led to action with marlin off the coast of La Guaira, Venezuela, as they dove on schools of bait driven so far up on the surface that the frigates could fly in one after another and easily pick off a fish on each pass. On another day off La Guaira, large dolphin were scattered over a wide area offshore of the bank, but our skipper was able to race to each pair as they chased bait to the surface by watching the actions of the frigates. That timing was critical, as the balao were blasted immediately and after the fish were boated it was time to race to another swooping frigate for a sure hook-up.

Feeding isn't usually easy for frigates, and they are notorious pirates—stealing fish from lesser birds. That propensity has to be accounted for as the birds may end up well away from the predator fish you're seeking in the course of a fight for an already captured bait.

Frigates aren't usually much of a problem for fishermen, but that's not the case at Christmas Island. That mid-Pacific bonefishing hot spot has its own species of frigate (*Fregata andrewsi*), which is extremely aggressive. They would dive on plugs trolled along the surface of the lagoon, and while casting plugs I'd have to watch out on my backcast as frigates would swoop down to grab the plug from the tip of the rod. After the cast was made, it became a question of whether a giant trevally would hit before a frigate nabbed the popper.

Frigates aren't the only birds that can be a hindrance to anglers at times. Boobies can be a real pain when

trolling bait in the tropics, as they don't give up easily. There were many occasions in the Galapagos Islands when we had to stop trolling balao because blue-footed boobies wouldn't stay off them. After first picking up a balao and having it pulled away, they'd typically fly off far ahead of the boat as if they were leaving—but would then make a big circle and sneak back in for the same bait. However, boobies don't seem to be as aggressive on plugs as the frigates which often feed with them in the same areas. Boobies are found in most tropical seas and are related to the gannets. They also can plunge below the surface to pick off fish, but make shallower, more angled dives than gannets.

The most fascinating and wide-spread sea bird is the tiny storm petrel. Actually there are 22 species of this smallest web-footed sea bird that is better known to sailors as Mother Carey's chickens. According to David Saunders in his *Sea Birds* (Grosset & Dunlap, N.Y., 1973), petrels were probably named after St. Peter, because they seem to walk on the surface while feeding. Saunders suspects that the popular name may have evolved from the words *Mater Cara*, which is an appellation of the Blessed Virgin Mary.

Wilson's petrel is the most common species of storm petrel, and may well be the most numerous bird in the world. Shark fishermen of the northeast see these constantly flying birds picking at the tiniest scraps in their shark chum slicks, but few realize that the 6-inch petrels migrate north all the way from the Antarctic. Though they have no meaning while in chum slicks, petrels have earned their nickname of "tuna birds" by leading fishermen to everything from schools of smaller tunas up to a single feeding giant. Never overlook a concentration of petrels while trolling!

Sharkers have no problem with storm petrels, but they're occasionally plagued with shearwaters. Those long-winged, slender sea birds are great

divers and can pick off baits at considerable depths. Most of the time you'll just see one or two fly by and check out any chunks which may be in the slick. However, there are times when flocks will sit around the boat and defy you to get a bait in the water. Unlike gannets and pelicans, shearwaters have no need to dive out of the air in order to get below the surface. They can sit on the water and spot a bait well below before swimming down to it like a winged fish.

Shearwaters are excellent tuna indicators when diving on actively-feeding fish, and even when sitting in the water in flocks. It's been my experience that shearwaters rarely rest for long, and a flock on the water indicates very recent action in the area.

Pelicans were once considered threatened, but it would be hard to prove that point in Florida where those big-billed birds hang around boats to grab baits and try to push fishermen aside at cleaning tables in order to swallow anything not protected. I've seen them in the summer as far north as Sandy Hook, N.J., and they've become a permanent winter resident at Hatteras, N.C., even when water temperatures drop into the forties.

Pelicans aren't a very reliable guide to predators in shallow waters because they have the ability to dive on bait fish, sticking their heads underwater in order to scoop up the prey without the aid of predator fish chasing them to the surface. In both the Atlantic and Pacific I've often spotted masses of diving pelicans near shore only to find they were happily feeding in skinny water. Under such circumstances, it's likely the crashing of those awkward-looking birds as they hit the water would probably scare off predators in any case.

On the other hand, pelicans diving in deeper waters are always worth a look for a variety of coastal and oceanic game fish. Off Cabo San Lucas, at the tip of Mexico's Baja California, pelicans dive on baits chased up by striped marlin and the entire fleet will start a high speed chase toward even a single diving pelican.

Sea gulls are the sea bird most familiar to shorebound fishermen, and they can be very effective fish spotters. Like the frigate, gulls can't dive and must look for easy pickings. In the case of the gull, those pickings can be literally anything and they've earned the nickname "flying rats." Yet, gulls are pretty reliable indicators of feeding fish, since they have to wait for dead and dying bait fish pushed up by predators.

Sea gulls are particularly important to striped bass and bluefish anglers in the Northeast. Even a novice fisherman would realize that gulls are probably over feeding fish, but those sitting on the water also may provide a valuable clue that something has recently gone on or is about to happen.

A valuable example of that occurred during a November striper run in Raritan Bay. As the birds got active after sun-up, they clued us into the portion of the open bay where bass would briefly chase bunkers. However, after the action was over, Tony Arcabascio of Staten Island noted that the sitting birds were also a good indication—and almost every time we dropped a live bunker near even a few sitting gulls we raised at least one bass from seemingly dead water.

On the negative side, gulls can be a big problem for anglers attempting to cast lures at breaking fish. Not only do they often try to grab surface plugs, but the cast line may get tangled in their wings. As with all sea birds which get tangled in lines or hooked, it's important to avoid being bitten by sharp beaks. The trick is to drop a cloth over the bird's eyes. Without sight, they usually remain quite calm and you'll be able to get everything cleared so the bird can fly away unharmed.

It was on Cape Cod that I learned how sea gulls can help in navigation. At the time I was running a Mako 19 and fishing for stripers in the fall off Monomoy Island at Chatham. Rather than running the dangerous inlet, I would return on the calm back side of

Monomoy. However, fog was a regular problem, and combined with darkness it was difficult to follow the winding channel through the flats. Yet, I found it was possible to do so in practically zero visibility by stopping to listen for and smell the sea gulls standing on the exposed flats I had to avoid.

Terns are close relatives of the gulls, but these slender birds with long wings and forked tails are much more active. They are very good fish indicators, but can fool you when bait is close to the surface since they're agile enough to plunge partly beneath the surface in order to nab sand eels, rainfish, etc. without any help from predators. Though terns have webbed feet, they prefer to stand on shore or floating objects rather than resting on the water. When terns are in the area, they'll find bluefish long before the gulls arrive, so keep an eye on them.

Since terns can feed on tiny objects, they're often attracted to weed lines. Anything different in the ocean is always worth checking out, as weed lines often indicate contrasting currents and temperature variations. However, terns may be actively picking away in weed lines when there are no predators about. By observing them closely, you'll soon be able to tell at a glance when terns are picking on undisturbed bait fish or working over baits being pushed to the surface—at which time they fly and dip much more erratically.

An illustration of that occurred after the perfect combination of a northeaster followed by a cool, clearing northwester during a recent October when I joined Capt. Frank Rose on his *Miss Diane* from Point Pleasant as Stu Wilk and other marine biologists from the Sandy Hook Marine Lab sought out specimens of fall bluefish for analysis of possible contaminants. There was plenty of bait being marked on Rose's fishfinder in the Shrewsbury Rocks area, but we were surprised to find no bluefish where they should have been thick—a preview of what turned out to be the first fall without a real bluefish migration in decades.

By noon there was considerable tern action on that bait, but it didn't look frantic enough. Purple clouds of bait could be spotted just under the surface and the terns would dive on them every time the school moved just a bit higher and within reach. Sea gulls were sitting on the water, which normally wouldn't be the case if bluefish were feeding.

Though sea birds know enough to stay clear of the sharp-toothed, ravenous blues, which may hit anything in the course of wild feeding, they're probably unaware of their real enemies. Goosefish (angler, monkfish) gained their name by making meals of sitting birds, and tiger sharks seem to be fond of sea gulls. In the course of releasing a 600-pounder from my boat off Montauk I watched it spit up hundreds of gull feathers while I was holding it on the leader for photos—and Captain Bob Rocchetta saw a tiger eat a sea gull off the surface the next day.

Gannets are the cold water, high-diving relatives of the tropical boobies. Measuring up to three feet in length, the North Atlantic gannet circles 100 feet above the water before diving headlong with folded wings to nail the prey well below the surface. Those spectacular dives are punctuated with three-foot splashes that look like bombs being dropped into the water from a distance. Gannets can handle large prey, and should prosper now that the herring population is rebuilding after being decimated by foreign trawlers in the 1960s and 1970s. These birds become abundant in the fall, and can clue anglers into migrating schools of striped bass from great distances.

During the late 1960s, I used to run across to Nantucket with the late Captain Bud Henderson, and we'd spot gannets from a mile or more away. Gulls and gannets made it look like a garbage dump at sea as they fed on herring and squid driven to the surface by acres of stripers. There are no longer such vast schools of bass, and these days there's usually a lot more bait than predators, but gannets will still find those sub-surface bait concentrations that may well have bass below them.

Off the New Jersey coast, we usually start seeing gannets in November. There's no greater assurance that bait is available, though most of the time they're feeding without help from the striped bass we seek. As with the terns, there's a more erratic pattern to the gannet's movements when they're actually on feeding fish—and sea gulls tend to join them quickly when easy pickings are available.

The height of the dive is another indication with gannets as well as with many other birds as to how high the bait and predators are. When birds are flying high they're broadening their range of vision as well as the depth they can see below the surface—a good indication that bait fish are deep. On the other hand, birds fly lower and dives are shallower when bait is close to the surface and, hopefully, being pushed to the surface by the fish we seek.

Though I have a reputation to protect and even in my most desperate hours of fishlessness have never slipped

Bird	Fish Indicated	Behavior
Frigate	Oceanic predators	Check out area they circle over
Pelican	Oceanic predators	Race to diving birds
Gannet	Striped bass	Diving from great heights
Shearwater	Tuna	Troll by even sitting flocks
Petrel	Tuna	Flock to tuna on surface
Sea Gull	All predators	Raucous and erratic

NOTE: Sea birds may react differently in various areas, depending on the bait and predators involved. This table only reflects personal observations of bird behavior in many areas around the world where I've fished. In every case, the angler must decipher the behavior of sea birds in his area—which could be quite different.

to such depths, I must note that the unwary can also be fooled by birds with just a bit of help from certain fishermen who carry bread, oatmeal, or a few dead baits that can be spread upon the waters to create a feeding flurry—drawing boats to an otherwise dead area while they slip off to the real hot spot.

The foregoing only briefly touches on the many sea birds that are far better fishermen than any human being, and whose skills can be utilized by anglers to make themselves look a lot smarter. Keep your eyes peeled whenever you're at sea or on the beach, and there'll be many occasions when you'll be thanking sea birds for saving the day. ∎

A Guide to Offshore Fish-Fighting Teamwork

by George Poveromo

The fight exceeded the three-hour mark before the swordfish began to tire. The weary angler, strapped in the fighting chair with an 80-pound-class outfit, kept at it throughout that still, starlit June evening. He was sure this fish was going to be his. It was 2:30 A.M., but reports of the exciting battle kept the anglers in the 17-boat fleet glued to their radios. As the fish neared the radio went silent.

Then it happened. Instead of a joyous victory shout over the VHF, a depressed voice declared that the fish was gone. I later learned the story. According to the angler's father, when

the swordfish surfaced behind the boat, the captain left the helm to help wire and gaff the fish. But the fish wasn't entirely beaten. With the boat stationary, it was able to swim underneath the transom and cut the line on the lower unit. Had someone remained at the wheel, things might have turned out differently.

Big sportfishing boats, especially those on the tournament circuit, generally have experienced crews who know their roles intimately. But what about the guys in the midsized boats? Do they stand a chance of landing a big fish with a small crew?

Absolutely! All you need is a game plan.

Beating a trophy fish requires quality tackle, an experienced angler, and a sharp boat handler. I've seen and heard of many big fish that were successfully played to the boat, only to have a miscue end the fight on the prop, lower unit, or hull. In fact, it's all too common an occurrence, primarily because the crew isn't aware of the importance of keeping a skilled helmsman at the wheel.

Helmsman is Team Captain

The helmsman's responsibility is to lead the fish to the wireman, giving him a

Fighting a big fish takes teamwork between the anglers and captain, a fact especially true on small boats. (GEORGE POVEROMO)

good, clean angle to work with, while being ready to counter any last-second surges by speeding up, backing down, or spinning around.

Several factors determine when and how the helmsman should assist his crew. Aboard my boat, for instance, I generally have friends who have fished with me for many years. We all know the drill, and any one of us could take over the wheel if necessary.

When trolling, I won't alter the boat's speed and direction on a hook-up. In my opinion, this helps set the hook by getting the stretch out of the monofilament, while leaving the remaining baits working for a possible second hook-up.

Once He's Hooked

Once the hook is firmly set, I shift to neutral. If it's a small to medium fish hooked on heavy tackle (30- or 50-pound test), we'll immediately remove only the lines that might interfere with the fight. For example, if the fish eats the port outrigger bait and swims away from the bait spread, the long center rigger and the port flat line are quickly removed from the water. I like to keep

at least one bait out throughout the fight, which might pick up another fish. In the above case, this would be the starboard outrigger bait and/or the starboard flat line.

If the fish charges the boat, throwing slack in the line, I'll throttle forward, steering the boat to keep the fish off the port stern quarter. Should the fish take off in the opposite direction, I'll remain in neutral and let the angler play the fish, unless he's losing too much line. Once the fish settles down, I'll either stay in neutral, except to adjust the boat to keep the fight off the port stern quarter, or slowly back down a few feet at a time to help the angler regain line (at this point the extra line is reeled in so it won't be run over). I never back down faster than the angler can reel to keep a tight line.

Big-Fish Tactics

If a big fish is hooked, such as a marlin, a big wahoo, or a big tuna, the helmsman's ability becomes critical. He must react immediately—not after most of the spool has been emptied. Our plan, since we're fishing out of an outboard-

powered center console, requires the helmsman to shift into neutral once the hook has been firmly set, then pivot the boat around to chase the fish. While the angler moves to the bow, all remaining lines are quickly reeled in and the outfits stored away. An uncluttered cockpit and gunwales are a must!

If fighting the fish from the bow is a problem, the angler can remain in the cockpit and quarter the fish off the bow during the chase. This is a more practical approach in rough seas or aboard an outboard-powered cuddy or cabin boat. Or, if you have an inboard-powered boat that has the speed and agility, you can simply back down quickly.

One important note: Once the fish is under control and settles into the depths, the angler can move back to the cockpit for the remainder of the fight. By keeping the fish off the stern, the helmsman can lead it to the wireman more effectively, and can quickly counter any last-second runs (a helmsman trying to lead in a fish from the bow always runs the risk of losing control at boatside).

Communicate!

Communication between the helmsman and the angler is crucial throughout the battle. During the chase, the helmsman must gauge his speed: He mustn't charge ahead too quickly, so that the angler can't keep pressure on the fish, or pursue too slowly, so that line can't be gained efficiently. It's a fine balance, and the angler has to let the helmsman know how he's doing. Also, if the fish stops or abruptly alters course, the angler must alert the helmsman immediately.

I become concerned when the spool is nearly half empty, and prefer to start chasing the fish before it gets that far. Some people wait until a reel is at least half spooled before giving pursuit, but I believe this subjects the line to a substantially greater drag pressure, and increases the chance of its getting nicked or cut by a piece of flotsam. I also feel that you begin to lose control of the fish.

When the Fish Goes Deep

When a big fish sounds, such as a tuna, a marlin, or a big dolphin, it can drive even an experienced crew nuts. Once again, the helmsman becomes invaluable. It's up to him to talk with the angler and be aware of what the fish is doing. To keep the line away from the engines on an outboard-powered boat, he must keep the fish off to the side of the stern. On an inboard boat, he must keep the fish either off to the side or well off the transom, where the angler can pump and wind without the line rubbing against the gunwale. The helmsman must also know when to throttle away, establish a more vertical angle, or hold above a stubborn fish, should the angler decide to pivot pump from the chair.

Equally important is knowing how to compensate for a fish that has sounded and managed to cross underneath the boat. In this case, the boat should be spun forward and around the line's entry into the water (if the angler is in the stern), or backed down so the bow spins away from the line's entry into the water. If a fish crosses underneath the boat and begins jumping or running at the surface (where the prop might cut the line on such a maneuver), the angler should dip his rod tip in the water and move to the bow while the helmsman backs down and away from the line's entry into the water.

Planing Him Up

Sometimes the battle becomes deadlocked. It happens with marlin and tuna, and especially big dolphin on light tackle. Here, the helmsman can help by "planing" the fish towards the surface. This is done by slowly throttling forward as the angler backs off the drag a little. After about 100 feet, shift back into neutral. Slowly back down half the distance, letting the angler re-adjust the drag and

gain line. Then motor forward another 100 feet and repeat the process. You'll soon know if the fish has been planed up towards the surface or if its rhythm has been broken. If not, continue the planing process.

One trick that helps the helmsman determine how much line is being gained is to lay a half-inch-long strip of colored string or mono onto the spool as the angler attempts to pump up the fish. As the fishing line is reeled onto the spool, it buries the marker. As long as the marker isn't fully exposed, you're making headway. Add a second marker if another stand-off is reached. Aside from letting the helmsman know the effectiveness of his moves, the marker is a great psychological boost for a tired angler.

Boatside Manners

Arguably, fish are more likely to be lost on the strike and next to the boat than at any other time during the fight. The latter situation is more critical because of the boat (which can become an obstacle) and the person(s) who must handle the fish. There's not much a helmsman can do about a bad gaff shot or a poor wiring job, but he can help the crew by leading the fish directly to them. During the final stages of battle, the helmsman should put the boat in gear and lead the fish in off a stern quarter. Keep the fish coming at a steady angle and swimming forward by inching ahead, occasionally shifting into neutral and letting the angler take up line.

When the leader comes up, shift into neutral and let a crew member take control and lead the fish alongside the boat. Don't relax yet; he may have to turn the leader loose, forcing you to react to the fish's actions. Once the fish is completely under control, that's the time to leave the helm and do the gaffing or releasing honors—if you're short-handed.

Throughout all this, the angler should back off the drag slightly, so the tension won't hinder the crew's efforts,

and be ready in case the fish makes a sudden surge. He should *never* put down the rod or get out of the chair.

The above describes the handling techniques we use on my boat, and they can be applied to most forms of offshore fishing, from trolling to live-baiting. As mentioned, my friends all know what to do when a fish strikes, and that's a big advantage. If you haven't formulated a similar game plan on your boat, do so.

When a big fish decides to eat, there's no time for assigning duties on the spot. If you're at the helm, the ball's in your court, and your performance might be the deciding factor in whether or not your angler comes home a winner. ■

Boaters don't have a clean record when it comes to accidents afloat. Do you know why? It has little to do with the prerequisites of fishing and hunting, but much to do with neglecting to control the boat and guard personal safety aboard. A sportsman who has not schooled himself in basic boating safety and safe habits will forget about it when the action gets lively. Here's your chance to start right.

Safe Boating

IMPORTANT EQUIPMENT

BASIC TOOL KIT

Every boat must be equipped to get home on its own. The exact selection of tools, spare parts, and supplies necessary must be suited to your boat and motor and to problems you are most likely to encounter.

Ordinary pliers	Vise-grip pliers
Diagonal-cutting pliers	Long-nose electrician's pliers
Screwdrivers	
Combination open-end and box wrenches in sizes ⅜ to ¾ inch	Spark-plug wrench to fit
	Sharp knife

SPARE PARTS

Spark plugs of correct specifications
Distributor cap, rotor, condenser, point set
Fuel pump and filter
Oil filter
Water-pump impeller
V-belts to match each size used
Spare fuel lines, cocks, and fittings
Gaskets and hoses
Bailing-pump diaphragm
Fuses and bulbs to double for each used

ALL-PURPOSE KIT

50-ft. chalk line	Insulated wire
Molly screws and pot menders for small cracks and holes	Cotter pins
	Packing
Nails, screws, bolts and nuts, washers	Elastic plastic bandage material
Hose clamps	Small blocks of wood that can be carved
Electrical tape	Machine oil

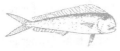

OUTBOARD MOTOR TROUBLESHOOTING CHECKLIST

Check gas supply and tank pressure; squeeze bulb several times.

Check to be sure propeller is not wrapped in weeds, line, or net. If line is wrapped around prop, try slow reverse to loosen it; then cut off pieces until you can pull the rest free.

Look for loose ignition wire at battery terminals.

Remove ignition wire from any spark plug; crank the motor; spark should jump from wire end to engine head; if no spark, check back to ignition switch.

If you have a hot spark, look into fuel feed; pull gas feed line off from side of outboard; blow through line until you hear bubbles in tank.

Clean the carburetor bowl and fuel filter.

Did you remember to add oil to gas tank in right proportion?

SAFE BOATING PROCEDURES

First, it is important to know your boat. Get familiar with its equipment and discover its limitations. If it's a livery rental, check it over completely before you push off.

Make a habit of checking off safety equipment aboard. First, locate the safety items required by law. Then compare your optional equipment with the Coast Guard's list of recommended equipment in the same section.

Count the life preservers, and make sure that each passenger has one that will keep him afloat in the water.

Check the fuel supply, the condition of the tank and feed line. Make sure the spark is strong and regular. Take along at least 1½ times as much fuel as you estimate you will need. If you run into heavy waves, your boat will take more fuel to go the same distance.

Carry a map you can read—a proper chart if the water is a large one—and a compass that is reliable near machinery.

Put tackle, guns, decoys, nets and other gear where they are secure and won't clutter walkways and footing. There is a bonus for the sportsman who keeps everything in place on board: He always knows where to find it when the action gets hot.

Do not overload your boat. Make sure you have safely adequate freeboard before casting off. Look ahead

to water conditions and weather changes you might encounter.

Keep an alert lookout. If you have a boat over 20 feet, name your mate and agree he'll keep lookout any time you can't. You have more to watch for than other boats and shallow water. Watch for obstructions such as big rocks and floating logs.

Swimmers are hard to see in the water. Running through swimmers or a swimming area is the most sensitive violation a boat can make. If in doubt, give beaches and rafts a wide swing.

Your wake is potent. You can swamp small craft such as a canoe or rowboat, damage shorelines and shore property, disturb sleepers, and ruin fish and wildlife sport for hours by running fast through small passages and shallows.

STORM WARNING SIGNALS

SMALL CRAFT

DAYTIME: Red Pennant.

NIGHTTIME: Red Light over White Light.

Indicates: Forecast winds as high as 33 knots and sea conditions considered dangerous to small-craft operations.

GALE

DAYTIME: Two Red Pennants.

NIGHTTIME: White Light over Red Light.

Indicates: Forecast winds in the range 34-47 knots.

STORM

DAYTIME: Square Red Flag with Black Square Centered.

NIGHTTIME: Two Red Lights.

Indicates: Forecast winds 48 knots and above no matter how high the wind speed. If the winds are associated with a tropical cyclone (hurricane), storm warnings indicate forecast winds of 48-63 knots.

HURRICANE

DAYTIME: Two Square Red Flags with Black Squares Centered.

NIGHTTIME: White Light between Two Red Lights.

Indicates: Forecast winds of 64 knots and above, displayed only in connection with a hurricane.

Storm warning signals.

Learn the Rules of the Road and obey them at all times. Copies are available free from the Coast Guard. Most collisions are caused by those "onetime" violations.

Make sure at least one other person aboard knows how to operate the boat and motor in case you are disabled or fall overboard.

Know a plan of action you will take in emergencies—man overboard, a bad leak, motor won't run, collision, bad storm, or troublesome passenger.

Storm signals and danger signs are often informal. Learn to read the weather, and keep alert to what passing boats are trying to tell you.

Wear your life preserver—or at least make sure children and nonswimmers wear theirs. In any case, don't sit on life preservers.

In a capsizing, remember that you are safer if you stay with the boat, where you can be seen. It will help you stay afloat until help arrives.

Under U.S. Coast Guard legislation, it is illegal for anyone to build, sell, or use a craft that does not conform to safety regulations. Check with your dealer, and check with yourself to make sure your boat measures up.

LOADING YOUR BOAT

There are several things to remember when loading a boat: distribute the load evenly; keep the load low; don't overload; don't stand up in a small boat; and consult the "U.S. Coast Guard Maximum Capacities" label. On boats with no capacity label, use the following formula to determine the maximum number of persons your boat can safely carry in calm weather:

The length of your vessel is measured in a straight line from the foremost part of the vessel to the aftermost part of the vessel, parallel to the centerline, exclusive of sheer. Bowsprits, bumpkins, rudders, outboard motors, brackets and similar fittings are not included in the measurement.

Wind Speed/ Sea Height Relationships

Winds	Sea Conditions
0–3 knots	Sea like a mirror
4–6 knots	Ripples, less than 1 foot
7–10 knots	Smooth wavelets, 1–2 feet
11–16 knots	Small waves, 2–4 feet
17–21 knots	Moderate waves, many whitecaps, 4–8 feet
22–27 knots	Large waves, spray, 8–13 feet
28–33 knots	Heaped seas, foam from breaking waves, 13–20 feet
34–40 knots	High waves, foam blown in well-marked streaks, 13–20 feet
41–47 knots	Seas rolls, spray may reduce visibility, 13–20 feet
48–55 knots	Very high waves, white seas, overhanging crests, 20–30 feet
56–63 knots	Exceptionally high waves, 30–45 feet
Over 63 knots	Air filled with foam, sea completely white, over 45 feet

BOAT CAPACITY CALCULATION

Average 150 lbs. per person

$$People = \frac{L \times W}{15}$$

FLOAT PLAN

File a float plan. Tell someone where you are going and when you plan to return. Tell them what your boat looks like and other information that will make identifying it easier should the need arise. Make copies of the following Float Plan and leave it with a reliable person who can be depended upon to notify the Coast Guard, or other rescue organization, should you not return as scheduled. Do not, however, file float plans with the Coast Guard.

1. NAME OF PERSON REPORTING AND TELEPHONE NUMBER.

2. DESCRIPTION OF BOAT. TYPE _____ COLOR_____

   TRIM _____ REGISTRATION NO. _____

   LENGTH _____ NAME _____ MAKE _____

   OTHER INFO. _____

3. PERSONS ABOARD _____

NAME	AGE	ADDRESS & TELE. NO.
_____	____	_____
_____	____	_____
_____	____	_____

4. ENGINE TYPE _____ H.P. _____

   NO. OF ENGINES _____ FUEL CAPACITY _____

5. SURVIVAL EQUIPMENT: (CHECK AS APPROPRIATE)

   PFDs _____ FLARES _____ MIRROR _____

   SMOKE SIGNALS _____ FLASHLIGHT _____ FOOD _____

   PADDLES _____ WATER _____ OTHERS _____

   ANCHOR _____ RAFT OR DINGHY _____ EPIRB _____

6. RADIO YES/NO TYPE _____ FREQS. _____

7. TRIP EXPECTATIONS: LEAVE AT _____ (TIME)

   FROM _____ GOING TO _____

   EXPECT TO RETURN BY _____ (TIME) AND IN

   NO EVENT LATER THAN _____

8. ANY OTHER PERTINENT INFO. _____

9. AUTOMOBILE LICENSE _____ TYPE _____

   TRAILER LICENSE _____ _____ COLOR AND MAKE OF

   AUTO _____

   WHERE PARKED _____

10. IF NOT RETURNED BY _____ (TIME) CALL THE

    COAST GUARD, OR _____ (LOCAL AUTHORITY)

    TELEPHONE NUMBERS _____

    _____

    _____

Taking Your Small Boat Offshore

by Capt. John N. Raguso

Like the Siren's call to the ancient Greek mariners, the lure of the sea is strong. But the sea is also a fickle mistress who is unforgiving to those foolish anglers who would take her "sometimes" benign nature for granted, ignoring the fury that she can often vent without warning to the unsuspecting. With the single-minded specter of crossing paths with a large billfish, high-flying mako, or schools of powerful tuna, many anglers often go further than either their skills or boat's capabilities should take them in pursuit of their sport, which creates a potentially perilous situation.

I've been driving small 19- to 24-foot outboard-powered fishing boats offshore in search of big game sportfishing opportunities since the mid-70s. While I may not take as many calculated risks in downsized craft as some, I have been known to "press the envelope" of sanity on more than one occasion. As recently as this past season, my 24-foot Grady-White Explorer has been as distant as 84.99 nautical miles from the closest Long Island inlet, working the mouth of the fabled Hudson Canyon for tuna and billfish.

And why would anyone in their right mind want to do this in a relatively tiny, peanut-sized craft? Well, for starters, not everyone can afford those 40- and 50-foot gold-plated, super sportfishing platforms that ply the exotic waters of this planet. Plus, some of the smaller boats, with their deep-vee hulls, beefy laminate schedules, foam flotation and outboard power, are actually safer in some respects than their bigger sisters, who if given the right set of circumstances, will sink unceremoniously like the proverbial rock.

Small 22- to 25-foot outboard boats have the advantage over many of their larger, more cumbersome sister craft in numerous ways. They require less horsepower to achieve cruising speeds, typically use less fuel per mile traveled and are a lot easier on the pocketbook. But when you're 50 miles from the nearest inlet when a hostile squall line comes your way, being on that efficient, affordable and economical little fishing boat might be the last place you'd ever want to be! Well, no one ever said that going offshore in a small boat was going to be easy, but it can be eminently do-able. Let's take a closer look on how to improve your odds out there in the big blue.

A Deep-Vee with Twin Power and Plenty of Fuel

Venturing 40 to 50 miles and more offshore demands that your boat can handle the constant stress and pounding of the often-merciless sea conditions that prevail this far off the beach. Modified vee hulls just won't cut it out here, as a tight 3- to 5-foot sea will certainly loosen a few fillings and desensitize numerous brain cells in the process. And a stiff 20-knot crosswind on your beam will make a walkaround or cuddy cabin boat seem like an open center console with no canvas, unless your mini-hull can knock the wind and spray back down and away from the cockpit.

Some of the older classics, like the 23-foot SeaCraft, 24-North Coast and 25-foot Blackfin hulls are still found where big fish roam, but a new generation of bluewater chariots like the new Grady-White SeaV2 hulls, and the latest 1995 vintage running bottoms from Pursuit, Boston Whaler, Regulator, Wahoo, Contender, Ocean Master and Fountain all have what it takes to get you out there and back. A deep-vee design, with 50-degrees or more of entry angle, a raised forward "Carolina" sheer with plenty of flare, offering wide, reversed chines and tapering back to at least 20-degrees of aft deadrise is the minimum hull you should consider for this specialized duty. An 8.5 to 9.5-foot beam is nice, since it usually offers a bit more stability and cockpit space to fight the catch-of-the-day.

Anyone who ventures offshore with only one engine is either truly mad or is just waiting to become a statistic. Even though small boats should always take long distance trips in pairs or threes, don't always count on your friends being there to help you when tragedy strikes. You must always be able to control your own destiny, and this starts by going with twin outboard power on the transom. The optimum bluewater set-up is either twin V-4s or V-6s, depending on your hull's horsepower requirements and efficiency. Remember, the concept of twin outboards is truly maximized when you set up your rig to plane home on one powerplant, with the other tilted up and out of the way.

If your platform cannot perform this simple but essential task, your initial capital investment, and subsequent higher fuel and maintenance bills, will be a continuation of this less-than-desirable situation. Work closely with both the manufacturer of your hull, as well as your local dealer, to set your boat up with the appropriate combination of engines and props that will achieve this critical objective. Laboring home at 8 mph at displacement speeds, while gulping gas at your most inefficient consumption rate, might put you too close to the bottom end of your precious fuel supply.

A viable alternative to the downside of this first scenario is to rig your offshore sportfishing vessel with a single

297

V-6, ensuring a "get-home" strategy with a 20- to 30-h.p. outboard kicker. These larger mid-sized outboards typically have the push necessary to move your hull along at the typical 6.5- to 8-mph displacement speeds you're likely to experience in average offshore sea conditions.

Just remember to install the largest blade diameter, lowest-pitch prop you can find for this auxiliary outboard, which will enable your mill to operate in its designed rpm range and provide maximum performance. If you go this route, be sure to get a heavy duty bracket (like the 40-h.p. version offered by the Garelick Co.) and run the engine at the marina every few weeks to ensure that the little kicker will start right up when you really need it the most. I've run seven different offshore rigs set up this way (versus a trio of twin-outboard platforms), and the lower investment cost, fuel economy over the life of the vessel, and lower overall maintenance costs were right for my situation. I had to come back on auxiliary power from 53 miles offshore once, but I made it back in slightly under 8.5 hours, powered along by a Mercury 25 kicker.

One of the most important considerations for your offshore chariot, the one factor that will truly enable you to roam far and wide in search of your dream catch, is your fuel capacity. Based on my experience rigging 11 offshore fishing machines in the 21- to 24-foot class, if you run a single primary V-6 outboard, you should have at least a 150- to 160-gallon fuel capacity onboard. This will allow you roughly 9 hours of cruising at a consumption rate of roughly 12 gallons-per-hour (108 gallons), plus a generous 6 hours of trolling time at 5 gph (30 gallons), for a total of 138 gallons of fuel used. With about 140 gallons of usable fuel on the 150 gallon fuel cell, you're pushing the envelope a bit too much, and will probably have to sacrifice a little fishing range or trolling time to leave a safety margin, just in case you hit rough weather.

Looking at a typical twin V-6 rig,

assuming 150s or 175s as your power choice, you should opt for an onboard fuel capacity of somewhere between 180 to 200 gallons. At 16 gph for the twin V-6s, figure you'll require the same 9 hours of cruising range (144 gallons). Add 6 hours of trolling time at approximately 7 gph (42 gallons), and you can see that the 186-gallon total would once again necessitate either shortening your trip or your trolling time, or maybe a little of both, especially when you factor-in usable fuel and a 10% buffer for inclement weather.

Safety Gear and Electronics

An "EPIRB" emergency radio beacon can also be a big lifesaver when the going gets rough. There are two types of these Emergency Position Indicating Radio Beacons on the market. Most bluewater anglers are probably familiar with the Class B EPIRBs, which simultaneously transmit emergency signals on two distress frequencies, 121.5 and 243.0 mHz, for recognition by other vessels, aircraft and satellites.

The cost for these Class B units will typically be in the $200 to $300 range, and they are an excellent investment for those who frequent the bluewater.

Looking at the next step up in capability, many offshore aficionados have been opting for the more costly, but more effective, combination 406.0 and 121.5 mHz EPIRBs. These more advanced units comply fully with all USCG requirements, with the major difference in capability being the addition of the 406.0 mHz frequency, which transmits both a positive ID of your vessel and your location to within a fairly narrow-focused 3-mile radius. If you do experience some trouble, the likelihood of the rescue team knowing you're out there and then finding you right away is greatly enhanced. Once help has entered the 3-mile zone of your original 406.0 mHz signal, the 121.5 mHz beam allows rescuers to easily home in on your pulsing distress frequency, if a visual recognition hasn't already been established.

As far as other electronics are concerned, I share the same philosophy as one of the most ancient mariners, Noah, when he was outfitting his fabled ark for the original 40 days and nights journey—take two of everything! I still prefer the accuracy of loran-C over GPS for my primary navigation functions, especially when wreck fishing 40 or 50 miles offshore. The theoretical 10- to 15-meter repeatable accuracy of GPS is neat, but with the Department of Defense playing with the "selective availability" switch with increasing regularity, the signal from the orbiting navigation satellites is scrambled to provide a usable accuracy of ± 100 meters. Compare this figure to loran's ± 50- to 75-foot repeatability, and the old reliable loran-C workhorse navigation system gets my vote, especially when trying to find a 15-foot patch of rocky bottom in 200 feet of water. Since I've been taking more and more charters to the edge of the continental shelf, I typically employ a handheld GPS unit as a backup, just in case my primary Loran-C takes an unannounced vacation. For depth sounders, I usually run two units, one a LCD graph and the other a small 6" color CRT, with each sounder offering both narrow and wide-beam transducers, and operating on different frequencies to prevent "cross-talk." Looking at my VHFs, my primary radio is hooked-up to the best cell-wave antenna I can afford, plus I carry a spare handheld VHF, with a BNC-to-PL259 antenna adapter, so the smaller VHF can use its big brother's main antenna for increased range. I also pack a portable emergency replacement antenna that can be hoisted up on the center rigger, just in case the 8-foot cell wave runs into harm's way.

Yet another invaluable tool for the offshore angler is a FloScan fuel flow gauge. I make excellent use of mine, and it is one of the main reason's I can confidently venture 85 miles offshore (in favorable weather conditions) and know to within a few gallons, how much fuel I have consumed from my Grady 24's 150-gallon onboard fuel cell.

Type I life jackets are an absolute

must, as they will most likely keep the wearer in a face-up position when floating in the open ocean waters, even if unconscious. For cold-water fishing in the early spring and late fall, I've even gone to the extent of purchasing thermal float coats and bib trousers, which will keep you alive for a few hours when swimming in 50-degree waters. According to research conducted by the Mustang Manufacturing Company, one of the leading makers of offshore survival gear, the projected survival time of the average person swimming in 45- to 50-degree water is less than an hour. There are two basic survival problems that result from cold-water immersion, even when you are wearing a lifejacket or other PFD. The first is the initial shock of cold water on your skin, which can cause you to gasp or take sharp and rapid breaths. If your head is under water when this occurs, you may drown. The second problem, hypothermia, is more subtle, but equally as terminal in its effect. Most people can safely lose 5.5 degrees Fahrenheit of body temperature, but as your body cools to below 93 degrees Fahrenheit, you start to lose your mental and physical functions.

Unconsciousness will likely occur when your body temperature drops below 86 degrees Fahrenheit. Wearing flotation clothing that provides insulation from cold-water immersion can greatly enhance your odds for survival.

I've also installed a portable strobe light to each of my five Type I PFDs that I keep aboard my *MarCeeJay*. These strobes feature a super bright 80-pulse-per-minute flash that will last up to 24 hours of continuous use from a standard 9-volt alkaline battery, with a visibility of over 3 miles. Hey, for roughly $28 bucks each, you can't go wrong, especially on a dark, moonless night!

Rough Weather Ahead

After entertaining my charters with the thrill of five canyon adventures without incident this past season, the last excursion turned out to be a real "adventure." NOAA was calling for 20- to 25-knot offshore winds for the afternoon of our last trip and the accompanying 6-foot seas. However, the weather pattern prior to this dire forecast had seen light and variable winds with a 1-foot sea. Against the advice of some fellow charter skippers, as dawn broke the eastern horizon, we headed southeast for the 70-mile trek to the edge. The ride out was absolutely glorious—we averaged 25.5 knots and made the run in less than 3 hours. And the fish didn't disappoint us either. We tomahawked over two dozen 5- to 10-pound dolphin casting live killies under a few productive lobster pots and trolled-up a pair of cooperative 40-pound yellowfins, losing a few others to fight for another day. Come 2:30 P.M., the seas were still only 2 to 3 feet, but the wind was starting to "freshen" just a bit. My sixth sense said it was time to leave, while we still had the chance to make a good run of speed, but then we came upon the opportunity of a lifetime.

We had heard numerous Jersey and Long Island boats talking on the VHF about their experiences with large blue marlin, spooling 50-pound outfits and rasping through 300-pound leaders, and three of our dolphin had fresh slash marks on their sides from aggressive billfish. Suddenly, thirty yards to starboard, the caudal fin of the largest billfish I had ever seen anywhere broke the surface, looking like the periscope of a German U-Boat that used to prowl these same waters 50 years ago. As we approached, we could clearly see the unmistakable shape and colors of a huge blue marlin, as it gently surfed down the building southwest swells. As we brought the boat alongside to within spitting distance of the billfish, it appeared that this 13-footer was in a trance, probably up on the surface to get some sun while it digested a big meal, and didn't even recognize our presence. At that point, my young son Marc decided to take some action and made a sharp starboard turn, dragging the tuna clones and psychobeads directly over the big blue's head.

Well, that sure woke it up! It lit up like a neon sign, dove down into the deep and resurfaced some 50 yards away. We played a game of leapfrog with this fish for over 20 minutes without any luck before I decided to pull the plug. It would have spooled my 30- and 50-pound outfits anyway. Only 15 miles into our return trip, all hell broke loose, and NOAA's weather predictions came through in spades. We slugged it out for the better part of 55 miles in hissing, breaking 6-foot seas, but they were fortunately at my stern quarter, providing some added push back to port. Although we took a few waves over the hardtop when we reached shallower water, we made it back without incident and were lucky to do so!

My best advice when venturing offshore in small boats is to be cautious. Remember, no fish is worth your life—and be sure to know the capabilities of your boat in case rough weather hits. Carry the best PFDs you can afford—as a charter skipper, I'm required to carry Type I vests aboard for every passenger—and be sure to put them on *before* you're stuck in a compromising position, not after it's too late! If the seas are too big to handle running a straight course home, employ a modified zig-zag route, like the way a sailboat might tack down a course, and take the waves on a 30- to 45-degree angle on your bow. To save the wear and tear on vessel and crew, you might also consider slowing down your speed to bare planing attitude, which might be somewhere between 12 and 15 knots, depending on your hull and power configuration.

If the seas are too rough for a return trip back to port, bring your bow into the waves at roughly a 15- to 25-degree angle and use only enough throttle to keep bare steerage while you ride out the worst of the storm—old salts call this "heaving to." Never turn your engine off, if you can help it, as you'll turn sideways to the surfing seas and increase your chances of "broaching." A sea anchor run off the bow can provide a big assist in helping to keep your nose into the slop, especially if you lose power. If given the option, head to deeper water during a storm, where the waves will have a tendency to be a bit less steep and farther apart. Make sure your vessel has a reliable high-capacity bilge pump of at least 1500 gph or more. My 24-footer has two of these aboard, and I check their operation at least once every few weeks. If you have to make a turn in rough seas, try to count the rhythm and duration of the waves and look for a flat spot, particularly after a big sea has passed, to make your move and do it quickly.

In Conclusion

Heading offshore in a 22- to 25-foot outboard boat and enjoying our coastal fishery on a budget is something that just about anyone can do, if done within reasonable parameters. You need a good hull, with a proven rough-water running bottom, super solid construction and a long range fuel capacity. Carrying extra fuel in portable containers is just asking for trouble. You also need the right electronics and safety equipment, plus the knowledge and ability to bring vessel and crew back safely to port, even when the weather turns against you. Hey, it's a real "rush" to catch the big ones 60 miles off the beach from a miniature platform, but no fish that's ever swam the oceans is worth the lives of you and your crew. Enjoy your sport, but be safe out there!

Why Boats Sink

by Vin Sparano

The mere thought of a boat sinking out from under its skipper and his passengers will send chills down the back of the toughest boater. Will he calmly handle the situation or will he go to pieces and panic? Why did it happen? What did he do wrong?

According to Boat/U.S., boaters should worry more about sinking at the dock than out on the water. Statistics show that three out of four recreational boat sinkings happen right at the dock. I thought that was a surprising statistic until a few weeks ago when I climbed into a 14-foot aluminum boat to bail out a foot or so of rain water. It simply did not occur to me that my weight, plus the weight of the water concentrated in the stern, plus the weight of the Yamaha outboard motor, would push the transom below the surface and water would gush into the boat. It took only a second to realize my mistake and I quickly shifted my weight to bring the transom out of the water. It would have been embarassing to sink my boat right there at the dock, but it can and does happen to a lot of boaters every year. Fortunately, most dockside sinkings can be prevented.

First, never depend completely on an automatic float switch to turn on your bilge pump when water gets into your hull. Bilge pumps and switches, because of their location, get dirty and will sometimes jam in the off position and not turn on your pump at all or get stuck in the on positon and kill your battery. Both cases are bad news and could sink an unattended boat.

Check your bilge pump and switches before every trip. In fact, I replace my automatic float switch every other year. These switches are inexpensive and easy to wire to a bilge pump.

Learn how to tie your boat correctly at the dock, especially in tidal water. If your boat swings or drifts too freely at the dock, it could get stuck under the dock and get pushed under the water when the tide rises.

Make it a point of learning every through-hull underwater fitting on your boat. Draw the locations of the fittings on a piece of paper and check them every time the boat is out of the water. Look inside the hull. Do all the fitting have seacocks? Do they all work? Do you close them when you leave the boat unattended? Do you keep them well-lubricated? It's this kind of maintenance and attention that will keep your boat afloat.

Remember that your boat can take on water from above the waterline as well as from below. Check all deck fittings, fastenings and hatches. Not all boat manufacturers use a good sealant on fastenings and some of them leak. Hose down your cabin and decks, then look for leaks inside and in the hull. If you see a leak, fix it. You can sink from rain water just as easily as from a leak below the surface.

I have found that water from washings at the dock can sometimes get trapped in the hull. To get this water out, try this trick: When your bow lifts up, just before you get on plane, manually switch on your bilge. If you have to, keep the bow high until all the bilge water rushes to the pump and gets pumped out.

Continually check all hoses and clamps. Clamps are cheap. If they look rusty, replace them. In fact, you should keep an assortment of different size clamps in your tool box. Pay special attention to hoses that have sharp bends. If any look stressed or kinked, replace them. Replacing a hose when your boat in on a trailer is easy. It's a panic problem, however, if it happens five miles from shore. It's also a good idea to double clamp all hoses.

If you're shopping for a boat, look for designs with self-bailing cockpits. This means the deck is above the waterline. Any water coming into the boat will drain out the transom and not stay in the boat or hull. This is a comforting thought in a heavy sea. Most of

the tough breed of small fishing boats built for offshore fishing have this feature. Many small, less-expensive ski boats, however, do not have self-bailing cockpits.

Make sure your transom drains, transom wells and scuppers are clean and not clogged with dirt. Water must be allowed to drain out. The best time to check these drains and flush them out is when you're washing your boat with a hose and good water pressure.

Maintenance of through-hull fit-

tings, seacocks, hoses, bilge pumps and switches is easy. Make a checklist and do it often. This is especially important if you leave your boat unattended for long periods of time.

If you leave your boat in the water, you should also get a mooring cover that protects your boat from bow to stern. This kind of full cover will give you peace of mind the next time it storms and your boat is 50 miles away at a marina where your boat may not get any attention. ■

Why Boats Blow Up

by Vin Sparano

A day on the water can be an exhilarating experience. But, when things go wrong with your boat, it can also be a frightening experience. The thought of a fire or explosion on a boat is even more terrifying. If you're far from land, there is no safe place to run.

Fires and explosions can only come from faulty fuel systems or human error. Fortunately, both are avoidable if you take certain precautions.

First, let's start with the deck. Is your gas cap clearly labeled GASOLINE? As farfetched as it sounds, there are cases on record where a clueless gas attendant has pumped gasoline into a rod holder or into a water tank.

All boats must have an overside drain or tank vent for your fuel tank. Make sure that excess fuel or fumes at the gas dock will not find their way into your boat or bilge. Make sure your vent has a mesh screen in place, which could keep fumes from igniting in the fuel line.

If your fill hose is worn or frayed, replace it. But make certain you buy the right hose. It should be stamped "USCG TYPE A2," which is fire resistant. Your filler cap should also be grounded

with an electrical wire from the fill opening to the tank, so that any static electricity from the dock hose will flow to the ground without causing a spark.

It's critical that you run your blower to clear your bilge of gas fumes before starting your engine. Check the blower hose and make sure it's not crushed or broken or twisted. After you've run your blower, sniff the bilge with your nose, which is probably the best fuel detector of them all. If you have any doubts, don't start your engine. This is especially true at the fuel dock, where most explosions and fires occur.

If you're buying a new or used boat, check the fuel tanks. Any tank over seven gallons should have a label with the manufacturer's name, date of manufacture, capacity, and material. It should also state: THIS TANK HAS BEEN TESTED UNDER 33 CFR 183.580. If you can't find this label, avoid the boat or have the tank replaced.

Even if you have all the right fittings and parts, you can still get into trouble if you are careless. According to BOAT/U.S., explosions are most likely to occur at the fuel dock, when a leak

in the fill or vent system may not be discovered until the tank is topped off.

When you refuel, take certain precautions. First, close all hatches and turn off the battery switch and stove. Fill the tank yourself, if you can, and never fill it to the very top. If you do, and the gas expands, you could get spillage in your boat and bilge. After refueling, run the blower for a full five minutes or longer, then sniff the bilge with your nose before starting the engine.

If you use outboard-motor tanks, take them out of the boat and do your refueling on the dock. This is the safest procedure. Unfortunately, most inboard and stern-drive boats don't have this option.

Let's suppose, for example, that you don't notice a fuel leak until it is too late and you're out on the water with a bilge full of gas. Do you know what to do?

Here's the best and only procedure. Do not start the engine or use any electrical equipment other than your VHF radio and this should be only after you turn off all other electrical circuits. Next, turn off your battery switch and have all your passengers put on lifejackets and stay on deck. Finally, call the Coast Guard and describe your problem and situation. They will instruct you on the next step.

If you find gas has leaked into your boat at the dock, order all guests off the boat. Turn off the battery switch and shore power. Notify the marina manager and call the fire department.

Don't wreck your day or endanger your guests because you don't know how to handle a gas emergency. Most of these precautions are simple common sense. ■

Man Overboard!

by Vin Sparano

Most fishermen will have their boats in the water before warm summer temperatures arrive. They will push the season and launch for trout, flounder and other species that will start biting in early spring. One truth that is hard to accept is the fact that most fishermen are not dedicated boatmen. Fishermen are usually interested more in fishing than boating... and this means a potential danger to themselves and their passengers.

One distinct danger is falling overboard into cold water. Even if you are a good swimmer, the effects of cold water may be more than your body can handle. Cold water, according to BOAT/U.S., can rob your body of heat very quickly. When your body temperature drops, hypothermia becomes a very real threat to life.

Don't be misled into believing that water has to be 35 degrees to be dangerous to someone falling overboard. Cold water is anything under 70 degrees. When water temperature drops to as low as 35, survival is usually based on the physical condition of the victim.

Panic and shock are the first and most dangerous hazards to a fisherman falling overboard. Cold water can shock the body and sometimes induce cardiac arrest. Remember how your breath was taken away when you dived into the pool? The same reaction happens when you fall head first into cold water. Your first gasp for air will fill your lungs with water. You may also

become disoriented for a minute or two before you realize what is happening to you.

If at all possible, get back into your boat as quickly as possible. Your life may depend on it. Unless you have a big boat, this may not be as difficult as it sounds. The majority of fatal boating accidents involve small boats with outboard motors. Most small boats, even if capsized, can be righted and re-entered.

Small boats are legally bound to have enough flotation to support all occupants. If you can, right the boat, climb back into it and bail out the water. If you can't right the boat, climb onto the hull and hang on. It's critical that you get out of the cold water.

If the boat slips away and you can't reach it, there are certain precautions to take in the water until help arrives. Unless there is no chance for a rescue, do not try swimming. It will drain body heat and, if you're like most people, you will not be able to swim very far in cold water.

Your best bet is to remain still and get into a protective position to conserve heat and wait for a rescue. This means protecting your body's major heat loss areas, such as your head, neck, armpits, chest and groin. If there is more than one person in the water, huddle together to preserve body heat.

Treatment of cold-water victims varies. First signs of hypothermia are intense shivering, loss of coordination, mental confusion, blue skin, weak

pulse, irregular heart beat and enlarged pupils. If the victim is cold and only shivering, dry clothes and blankets may be all that is necessary.

If the victim is semi-conscious, move him to a warm place and into dry clothes. Make him lie flat with his head slightly lower than the rest of his body, which will make more blood flow to the brain. You can also warm the victim with warm towels to the head, neck, chest and groin.

Of course, it's always easier to avoid problems by taking a few simple precautions. First, wear a lifejacket at all times when out on the water during cool weather. Whenever possible wear several layers of wool for insulation. Wool, even when wet, will retain body heat.

If you suddenly find yourself in the water, make sure your lifejacket is snug. Keep clothing buttoned up. The water trapped in your clothes will be warmed by your body heat and keep you warm. ■

Stormy Weather for Captains

by Vin Sparano

I've just read about a terrible boating tragedy that could have been avoided. Eight men in a 28-foot pleasure craft got caught in 20-foot seas and 70-m.p.h. winds 30 miles off the New Jersey coast. In a miraculous Coast Guard rescue, seven men were saved, but one man was never found.

The wife of a survivor told reporters, "I don't understand why the captain took the boat out. The captain didn't want to go. He said it was too windy."

I'll venture a guess why the captain took the boat out. It was probably a long-planned fishing trip, no one wanted to be disappointed and the weather didn't look bad at the dock.

I live and fish in New Jersey. I remember that day and I also remember a weather forecast that would have kept me at the dock. I don't care how many friends showed up to go fishing. I would have treated them to breakfast at a local diner and sent them home. They would be disappointed, but alive. The open water is no place to prove that you have more guts than brains.

Never forget that if you own and run a boat, you are also the captain, and totally responsible for the safety of your passengers. If someone gets hurt on your boat, you have to take the blame.

I get scared when I see a boat pass me with young children sitting on the bow with their feet hanging over the side. One bumpy wake and a child could be easily killed by the prop. I get angry when I see a boater pulling a water skier in a channel with heavy boat traffic.

I also wonder what is going through the minds of small-boat operators who disappear in ground swells as they head offshore when a small-craft advisory flag is flying in plain view. I also say a prayer when I see a family overload a rental boat and head for a day of fishing with two inches of freeboard.

High winds and rough water can turn a pleasant day into a life-threatening nightmare. The best way to stay out of trouble is to learn how to read the warnings, wind and water. And it's equally important to know when to cancel a trip and stay home. This advice is even more important to hunters and fishermen who tend to use smaller boats and go out in marginal weather.

Rule No. 1: Check the weather. The National Weather Service issues marine forecasts every six hours with details of winds, seas, weather and visibility. If you have a VHF radio, check the weather frequently on Channels WX-1, WX-2 or WX-3. Marine forecasts on these channels are broadcast continuously. Heavy static on your AM radio may also indicate nearby storms.

The National Weather Service also posts visible warnings at prominent locations along shore, including Coast Guard stations, lighthouses, yacht clubs and marinas. Although the Weather Service has, unfortunately, discontinued the official system of displaying these warnings, you can still find them at some shore installations. Learn where these warnings are displayed in your area and check them before leaving the dock. Here are the warnings and what they mean:

SMALL CRAFT ADVISORY—Daytime warning signal is a single red pennant. Nighttime signal is a red light over a white light. A Small Craft Advisory means winds as high as 33 knots and sea conditions dangerous to small craft. Small craft generally means boats under 25-feet, but I have seen winds that would keep a 40-footer at the dock. You must use your judgment.

GALE—Daytime signal is two red pennants. Nighttime display is a white light over a red light. Gale means winds in the 34 to 47-knot range.

STORM—Daytime signal is a single square red flag with a black square in its center. Nighttime signal is two red lights, displayed vertically. Storm means winds 48 to 63 knots

HURRICANE—Daytime signal is two red flags with black centered squares. Nighttime warning is a white light displayed vertically between two red lights. Hurricane winds are 64 knots and higher.

One of the problems with weather forecasts is that they are not always right. Sometimes you may have to make judgment calls on your own. Learn to read simple weather signs. Watch for dark threatening clouds which nearly always indicate a thunderstorm or squall. Any steady increase in wind or sea is another sign of bad weather.

If you're on the water, don't wait too long to make a decision. Calm winds and water can turn into a gusty electrical storm in as little as 30 minutes.

You can determine the distance of an approaching thunderstorm, in miles, by counting the seconds between the lightning flash and the thunder and dividing by five. For example, if it takes 10 seconds to hear the thunder, the storm is about two miles away.

If you've taken all precautions and you still get caught in a storm, pinpoint your location or write down your loran numbers on a chart before heavy rain reduces your visibility. Watch for other boats, secure hatches, lower antennas and outriggers, stow all loose gear and, most important, make sure everyone is wearing a lifejacket.

Once the storm hits, try to take the first and heaviest gusts of wind on the bow of the boat. Approach waves at a 45-degree angle to keep the propeller underwater and reduce pounding. If there is lightning, unplug the radio and electrical equipment. Stay away from metal objects and order your passengers to stay low. If you don't lose power, you should be able to ride out almost any storm. ■

How Not to Get Seasick

by Vin Sparano

I haven't been seasick in the last 15 years or so. The night before a trip, I stay away from alcohol and get a good night's sleep. The following morning, I sip a cup of black coffee before I get on the boat. If I still feel good by 10 A.M., I'll start to eat... but never before. Will this simple formula work for you? To be quite honest, I don't know.

Finding a cure for seasickness is often a matter of trial and error. Everyone has a different approach. Some fishermen are convinced that a full stomach before a fishing trip is the best way to avoid seasickness and that may work for some people. It doesn't work for me. I can, however, tell you what doesn't work for everyone. Stay out late, overindulge, get on a boat tired and hung over and I can guarantee that you will get sick in even a small chop.

In simplest terms, seasickness is the inability of your body to adjust to motion. Your body has a built-in gyroscope to keep you on even keel, much the way a gyroscope keeps a rocket upright as it travels in space. This system works on solid ground, but on a rocking boat or a bumpy airplane, the mechanism sometimes fails and you get seasick.

This means, of course, that when you start feeling seasick, you should try to reduce movement as soon as possible. If you are on a boat, sit in the center and at the stern, where movement will be minimized. It also helps to keep your eye on a stationary object, such as a bridge or tower on the shoreline. You are trying to send a message to your brain that you are not really rocking and have no reason to be seasick. It sometimes works.

Fight the urge to go into a cabin. There is nothing stationary in a cabin, you have no fixed object and you will likely get sicker. In fact, if you get seasick and head for the cabin, you will proba-bly be there for the rest of the day.

Over the years I've heard of dozens of concoctions to cure seasick-ness. Some may be effective for some people, but most wacky formulas don't work. A doctor once suggested cold stewed tomatoes and saltines, a formula that originated aboard an oil tanker. I suggested it to a friend and he still got sick. It could, however, work for you.

Fortunately, modern medicine has made great strides in helping people cope with an illness that will make you feel like dying. These seasick drugs fall into two categories: antihistamines and scopolamine. These drugs are designed to inhibit the flow of nerve impulses from the vestibular system to the brain. Which drug will work for you? You may have to try them all until you find the one that works best for you.

Antivert and Bonine are non-pre-scription antihistamines that you take every 24 hours. They will make you drowsy. Marezine is another antihista-mine, but it is taken every four to six hours.

Dramamine is the old standby. If the weather forecast calls for rough seas, I will take a Dramamine tablet with my cup of black coffee one hour before I get on a boat. It works for me. A antihistamine that is taken every four hours, Dramamine is a non-prescrip-tion drug and it will make you drowsy. On my last trip to a pharmacy, how-ever, I did see a Dramamine formula that the company claims will not make you drowsy.

Phenergan and Mepergan are pre-scription antihistamines that will effec-tively prevent and treat seasickness, but ask your doctor about side effects. In some people, they can cause consider-able drowsiness.

Transderm Scop is a comparatively new and perhaps the most effective drug in fighting and preventing seasick-ness. It's an patch on the skin behind the ear that slowly releases scopo-lamine into your system for days. The side effects can sometimes be severe, however, and should be discussed with your doctor.

There's a lot you can do to protect yourself from getting seasick. First, accept the fact that everyone will even-tually get seasick. When someone brags that he never gets seasick, don't believe him. His time at the rail has not yet arrived! There is also no reason to be apologetic or embarrassed about getting seasick.

Finally, never poke fun at someone who is seasick, especially a youngster. You may get paid back on your next trip! ■

Get Ready for Hurricanes

by Vin Sparano

Don't wait for a 12-hour warning to start preparing your boat for a hurricane. Do it now! You may need more time than you think to work out a plan of action that will secure and protect your boat in a storm. Now is the time to think about extra lines and special storm gear.

Even the best plan of action, however, cannot guarantee that your boat will survive a hurricane. In 1992 Hurricane Andrew, for example, proved so violent that boats and people were helpless in its path. Fortunately, not all hurricanes are killers and there are some precautions you can take to keep storm damage to a minimum.

Most boaters believe their real threat of damage comes from wind and waves. This isn't so. Most boat damage comes from storm surge, which means high water. In fact, storm surge accounts for nine out of 10 hurricane-related deaths.

The safest place for your boat is out of the water. If you have a trailer, load your boat on it and take it home. If the boat and trailer fit in your garage, park it there and leave your car outside. Your boat is lighter than your car and can get blown off your trailer in hurricane winds. If you must leave your boat and trailer outside, put it where it will get the best protection from the wind, trees and electrical lines. Let some air out of the trailer tires, block the wheels and make sure the boat is strapped securely to the trailer.

You have two options when you leave your boat on a trailer. First, if it's a heavy boat, take out the drain plug to allow rain water to drain quickly out of the hull. If your boat is light, however, and you are concerned that it may blow off the trailer, leave the drain plug in and fill the hull with water from a garden hose to add more weight. Don't put in too much water or you will damage the hull. Remember that rain will add more water and weight.

Don't trust storage racks, even if your marina says it's a safe place. There may be other lighter boats that could be blown off their cradle and into your boat. Tell your marina to take your boat out of the rack and block it securely in a safe area. Your marina may balk at this, but be insistent.

If you are forced to leave your boat in the water, make sure it is tied securely, which means double lines. Most boats require five lines: two bow lines, two stern lines and one spring line. If a hurricane is approaching, you will need 10 lines. It's also wise to go up one size larger than your normal dock lines. Line your boat with as many rubber fenders as you can find to protect the craft boat from the dock. Always give your lines chafe protection where they will come in contact with the boat or cleats. Neoprene hose is best, but canvas wrapped in place with duct tape will do in a pinch.

If your slip is a small one, look around for a bigger one that's empty and ask your marina if you can use it. The more distance you put between your boat and the pilings and bulkhead, the safer it will be.

Mooring or anchoring in a protected harbor that is not crowded is a safe way to ride out a hurricane, but only if the mooring is a permanent installation and you back it up with two additional storm anchors.

When you leave your boat, take all loose gear and electronics with you and use duct tape to seal all hatches, windows, vents and doors. When you feel your boat is ready for a hurricane, the next step is an important one: Go Home! When hurricane-force winds hit your boat at 100 miles per hour, there will be nothing you can do.

You can now track a hurricane by phone, which may give you enough warning to secure your boat. When a hurricane is headed your way, you can get official hurricane advisories issued by the National Oceanic and Atmospheric Administration (NOAA). A phone call to Boat/U.S. Weather Watch will connect you to the NOAA Hurricane Center in Miami, Florida. Just dial 1-900-933-BOAT. The cost is 98 cents per minute, a small price for a hurricane warning. ■

SIGNALING THE FUTURE

While there's a great deal going on in the world of marine electronics, it's nothing compared to what's about to happen in the near future. To determine the direction of technology, we interviewed numerous manufacturers and put together a summary—their "sense-of-the-industry."

As late as 1995, industry surveys showed there was still consumer hesitancy to switch over from loran to GPS. But GPS and loran manufacturers agree that the market for the satellite-based system is still just barely tapped. Only 10 percent of all boatowners currently own a GPS unit.

Look for better interfacing abilities from "multi-talkers." That's where your instruments can talk in both directions rather than information traveling in one direction only. You'll find this makes your navigation display far easier to use. Also expect to see displays themselves getting larger, night lighting improving, and more disparate instruments hooked together.

GPS

Trimble NT 200

Trimble has introduced its NT family of navigation instruments—the NT 100 GPS, the NT 200 Chart Plotter and the NT 200D, a chart plotter with a built-in differential receiver. The Trimble plotters are Navionics-based cartography units with an interesting twist. They have bi-directional NMEA ports, meaning they can talk to and receive input from other electronics. A small "Smart Card" is used to store data. You can store, LAT/LON, Course over ground, Speed, Time, Position, heading, and cross-track error updates every five seconds and not run out of memory for two days. **Trimble Navigation, 645 North Mary Ave., Sunnyvale, CA 94086, (408) 481-8000.**

Northstar 941X GPS

The 941X is completely waterproof, with a built-in, dual-channel differential beacon receiver, descriptive waypoint names (Nantucket Harbor), heat-resistant LCD display that will never turn black, 24-hour graphic tide display for over 3,000 locations, graphic steering director with waypoint markers, and a feature called Nav Log that is an interactive database telling you how you are progressing on your trip. Northstar provides many useful functions that no one else has. **Northstar, 30 Sudbury Rd., Acton, MA 01720, (508) 897-6600.**

Electronics

by Dean Travis Clarke

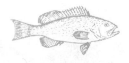

Micrologic Mariner Plus GPS

This is an LCD GPS unit that you can virtually use without reading the manual. There are loads of prompt messages. You can save 500 waypoints by number or name, automatically record your position, speed, day, date, and time periodically in your data log, and read your position in converted TDs. There's even a readout of how accurate your position fix is in meters or feet. The Mariner Plus can be connected to the Micrologic ML-9100 Differential receiver for DGPS accuracy. **Micrologic, 9174 Deering Ave., Chatsworth, CA 91311, (818) 998-1216.**

Magellan Meridan XL

Nervous about changing over from loran to GPS? Magellan's Meridian XL will help you over the hurdle. This tiny handheld GPS will automatically readout your position in converted TDs. In addition, this tiny handheld provides a track plotter, five different navigation screens, 200-waypoint memory, detachable antenna, and differential GPS capability. Magellan is also introducing a very small fixed-mount GPS, the Nav 1200, and a new C-Map-based electronic chart plotter, The Chartmate. **Magellan, 960 Overland Ct., San Dimas, CA 91773, (909) 394-5000.**

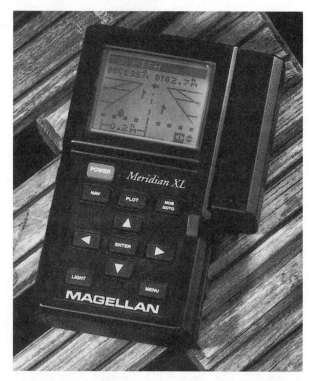

Magellan's Meridian XL has a wide-screen and features easy-to-read displays, large keys and user-friendly operation, making it ideal for the boater looking for a handheld GPS receiver.

VHF

We've all heard about Digital Selective Calling and agree it will be an excellent technology. The problem at the moment is there are only two Coast Guard DSC stations operating and there's no timeline for total system function. Budget constraints are hurting the program. But the turn-of-the-century should see a final mandate in effect.

Long-term, the most significant change in marine radio communications is going to be the low-earth orbit cellular telephone system: when the whole earth is connected via cellular phone with no "out-of-coverage area" even in the middle of the ocean; when instead of using just an EPIRB and hoping someone is listening, you'll suddenly have two-way communications. It probably won't affect VHF substantially since VHF is free and cellular has no provision for vessel-to-vessel traffic. But you can bet it will hammer the Single Sideband business. And it isn't that far off, either. A company called OrbComm already has the earth stations, the assigned frequency space, the satellites ready to launch, the launch dates—it's just around the corner.

ICOM IC-M10 Handheld VHF

How annoying is it to have a supposedly fully charged handheld VHF whose NiCad batteries die when you use it for a half-hour or so? Battery memory is the real stumbling block with handhelds. ICOM now has an innovative unit, the IC-M10, that has all the features of most fixed-mount VHFs. But this handy unit uses alkaline batteries. Never worry about charging again. Also new this year are ICOM's M-15 waterproof handheld—a truly waterproof radio, and the IC-M58 DSC VHF, with emergency calling. Simply press a single button and a continuous, pre-programmed distress call goes out containing your boat's identification, the time, and your vessel's position. And if you want total privacy in your radio transmissions, you can get the optional voice scrambler. **ICOM America, 2380-116th Ave., Bellevue, WA 98004, (206) 454-8155.**

Shakespeare NAV-COM 6000 VHF RADIO

Shakespeare's SE-6000 integrates a Digital Selective Calling VHF radio, with GPS, loran, and electronic compass sensors, displays all the information on a large, highly-visible screen, and can even direct your autopilot. The microphone has buttons to change display readouts. When another radio calls you, the 6000 will act as a receptionist, storing the call information until you are ready to call them back. **Shakespeare, PO Box 733, Newberry, SC 29108, (800) 800-9008.**

Standard Horizon Eclipse VHF

No company has a richer history making radios than Standard. Their new Horizon Eclipse is the smallest fixed-mount VHF in the world! And the Eclipse is loaded with useful features like mike-mounted channel switching, automatic weather alert interruption, instant access to both channel 9 and channel 16, several scanning modes, and an LCD display that comprises almost 25 percent of the face so those of us with eyesight that isn't what it once was can see the channel with ease. Also, unlike other companies' warranty promises, Standard will cover water damage. Chances are good that you won't have any. **Standard Communications, PO Box 92151, Los Angeles, CA 90009-2151, (310) 532-5300.**

LORAN

There's still question about what will ultimately happen to loran. Many European and third-world nationals are distrustful of the U.S. Deptartment of Defense having total control of all GPS satellites. Foreign government representatives question what would happen if we suddenly decided to shut the system down for any reason. Their shipping, aircraft and land-based users would all be stuck.

Throughout the rest of the world, loran is still on the upswing. There are new chains developing and it appears the system is here to stay for the foreseeable future outside the U.S.

However, the U.S. government has no budget to operate two navigation systems. What may happen is some agency other than the Coast Guard, or perhaps even a private enterprise may take over loran's operation. But according to Magellan's Vern Bennet, a former loran station operating chief in southeast Asia, "The Coast Guard will never, ever, turn over control of loran to *anyone!*"

Some people feel loran just isn't taken as seriously as it once was. The association of government officials, academicians, engineers, and international users that promotes loran, called the Wild Goose Association, has changed its name. It is now the International Loran Association.

Si-Tex XJ-9 Loran

This new loran has the *real* answer for those making a switch from loran to GPS. It can interface with the Si-Tex GPS-10 and you can then scroll between real loran and GPS—no conversion algorithms from Lat/Lon to TDs. However, as a straight loran receiver, the XJ-9 has a four-line display, all the normal navigation information, memory for 20 "instant positions" for your daily fishing hotspots as well as 89 waypoints 10 reversible routes and single-button Man Overboard calculations

and readout. Si-Tex, PO Box 6700, Clearwater, FL 34618, (813) 576-5734.

ELECTRONIC CHART SYSTEMS

As Navionics' Dr. Guiseppe Carnevali said, and to a fault, everyone agreed: "The dramatic evolution that we will witness in the next several years can be summarized in one word: 'Awareness.'"

You simply can't imagine how much simpler, safer, and more comfortable using an electronic chart plotter is compared to a straight alpha-numeric readout as in GPS or loran. The human mind likes processing graphic images better than digital data. The world is becoming increasingly aware of electronic charting—not just in boats—but in automobiles, hiking, surveying, interstate commerce, aviation, agriculture and other uses you couldn't even imagine. And every new system introduced has more features and handles information better than the last. Look for "vending machines" that will sell updated charts you can download to your cartridge. Also, every chart you need can be had on one or two CD-ROM disks.

What does ECS really do for you? It relaxes you. It is so easy you can let your mind dwell on fishing rather than navigating. Just a glance at the ECS display will tell you everything you could ever want to know about your location and where you're going.

MarineTek SeaMax Chart GPS/Dual-Frequency Sounder

Heading in the right direction of all your onboard electronics information available from one display, Marinetek's SeaMax Chart System combines a color fish finder, a Navionics-based chart plotter, and a Trimble-engineered GPS engine. Colors are very bright, the resolution is excellent, and SeaMax has an automatic transducer that constantly tunes both transducer frequencies at the same time for optimum signal. Another great feature is the ability to recall a particular track and re-sail that track with cross-track error display. You'll be absolutely certain you're hitting the exact spot where you hooked that last fish. **Marinetek, 2300E Zanker Rd., San Jose, Ca 95131, (408) 526-9288.**

Maptech Pilot

Resolution Mapping introduces their newest electronic charting systems, the Maptech Pilot and Professional. Both display full-color versions of the real charts you're used to. However, the Pilot has half the features of the Professional. But don't scoff. The Pilot has everything the average navigator will ever use and costs less. The Maptech difference is you can use this system on any personal computer with a CD-ROM drive, rather than needing a special expensive instrument dedicated only to navigation. Otherwise, this system does virtually everything the other electronic chart plotters do. The flexibility you have in planning trips at home is amazing. **Maptech, 35 Hartwell Ave., Lexington, MA 02173, (617) 860-0430.**

Cetrek ChartPilot 775

The new Cetrek ChartPilot 775 is a combination autopilot and chart plotter, and is one of the easiest systems to use. It contains the best "onscreen" instructions, a display that covers most of the front of the case for super visibility, and interface ability second to none. Use the trackball to lay out your course line, press the button and the autopilot steers you there. **Cetrek, 640 North Lewis Rd., Limerick, PA 19468, (610) 495-7011.**

KVH Quadro Chart Plotter

KVH, maker of some of the world's best electronic compasses, has broadened its navigation product line with the Quadro LCD GPS Chart Plotter. This compact, splashproof display uses Navionics' seamless cartography, has an automatic zoom, loads of memory and built-in world chart. But the most innovative part is the Quadro's ability to connect with KVH's instrument system. With this feature, your chart plotter can also figure in depth, boat and wind speed, and will even drive your autopilot. KVH has come one step closer to a total navigation suite in one instrument. **KVH Industries, 110 Enterprise Center, Middletown, RI 02842, (401) 847-3327.**

Datamarine Chartlink LCD & CRT

Datamarine's new electronic chart systems are available with a VGA display in either a LCD or CRT forms. Datamarine can interface with most other manufac-

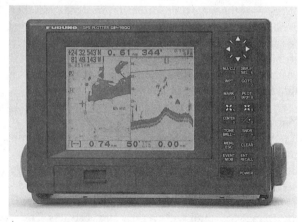

The Furuno GP-1800 is a combination LCD and GPS Plotter. It will track up to eight satellites and uses Furuno chart cards. The GP-1800 will also select and display the most appropriate chart.

turer's equipment, not just Datamarine's. However, it does offer interface ability with all their performance instruments including depth, water temperature, and speed through the water as well as over ground—a good way to determine drift speeds. Waypoint and route storage is substantial internally—but infinite on storage cartridges. Both units offer the option of a built-in GPS or the ability to plug into your existing GPS engine. **Datamarine International, 53 Portside Dr., Pocasset, MA 02559-1900, (508) 563-7151.**

Raytheon Chart Plotters

These C-Map-based chart plotters are available in numerous configurations. The 600XX and RT units can be interfaced with radar for a "real world" electronic view. The 610EST interfaces with a color fish finder and the 610T boasts a huge 14-inch color monitor. Additionally, all can be hooked up to SeaTalk instruments, allowing them to provide depth, speed, wind direction and speed, velocity made good, course made good, speed over ground, distance log, and true wind direction. They also come with a Man Overboard feature that, at the touch of a button, locks the position into memory, sounds an alarm, and gives constant readout of distance and bearing to the position. **Raytheon, 676 Island Pond Rd., Manchester, NH 03109-5420, (603) 647-7530.**

VIDEO DEPTH SOUNDERS

One of the greatest demands from the users of fish finders is visibility—they're just too danged hard to read—from a distance, from any angle other than straight on, in sunlight, or at night.

Other things you can look forward to that will improve sounders is new software and interfacing with GPS and other navigation instruments. For example, have you ever gotten frustrated because your sounder scrolls at pretty much the same speed no matter how fast you're going? Why can't it stop when I stop? Expect to see real time scrolling that will show the bottom passing under your boat at the same speed at which you are traveling. Also, there will be a better perspective. Where is the boat? Which way are the fish traveling? How far back are those marks? All common questions. New software will address these difficulties, offering information so excellent, you'll wonder how you ever managed before.

Furuno FCV-667 Color Video Sounder

Furuno has several new products: Chart Plotters, LCD sounders, combination chart plotters/sounders/GPS units, and autopilots, to name but a few. But one very interesting product for offshore fishermen is the FCV-667 color sounder. It's very compact, having only a six-inch screen. But while the display is small, the capabilities are large. Dual-frequency operation (50/200 kHz) from a single transducer, A-scope, eight color levels, auto-mode, and numerous zoom adjustments. An ideal unit for anglers with little instrument space. Also new from Furuno are their GP-1800, a full-featured chart plotter, and their FAP-300 autopilot. **Furuno, PO Box 2343, South San Francisco, CA 94083, (415) 873-9393.**

Apelco Fishfinder
Apelco's new 460 pumps out 800 watts of power for bottom readings at 600 feet while the 530 puts out an impressive 2,400 watts for reaching the bottom through 900 feet of saltwater. Both units offer Bottom Lock for reading the bottom and a selected distance above. The White Line feature distinguishes bottom fish from the actual bottom, and Bottom Coverage allows the anglerto see where the fish actually are relative to the boat and just how much of the bottom is represented on the screen. **Apelco, 676 Island Pond Rd., Manchester, NH 03109-5420, (603) 647-7530.**

Interphase Probe, Sea Scout, and Echoscan
These new depth sounders from Interphase are specialists indeed. The Probe scans from just below the water's surface ahead to directly below to show you what you are approaching. It also shows you exactly how far ahead the structure is. The Sea Scout tracks the bottom directly below the boat and scans a 90-degree arc from one side of your bow to the other like a searchlight, to detect bait and schools of fish. The EchoScan 8 scans from side-to-side beneath the boat to see structure and fish on either side you might otherwise miss. **Interphase Technologies, 1201 Shaffer Rd., Santa Cruz, CA 95060, (408) 427-4444.**

Humminbird Wide Vision
Wide Vision solves the problems offshore fishermen have with most depth sounders. It reaches bottom at 1,000 feet. It has exceptionally clear display resolution, it allows a very quick glance to determine the exact depth a fish is marked at. It has a screen you can actually see while wearing polarized sunglasses. It gives a constant water temperature and speed readout and is waterproof. In fact, the unit is so good, it took Humminbird a half year to catch up with the demand. Also available this year is Humminbird's new DC5-S handheld VHF. It's not just waterproof. It's submersible. With a full 25-watt output and exceptional saltwater corrosion resistance, this radio is the ideal radio for small boats and an indispensable backup on larger offshore vessels. **Humminbird, 3 Humminbird Lane, Eufala, AL 36027, (205) 687-6613.**

Lowrance X-70A 3D
This 3,000-watt unit has the potential to reach 1,000 feet down to show you fish, bottom composition, and structure. Lowrance has incorporated all the performance

The Humminbird Wide 3D Vision is a three-dimensional sonar that also offers a two-dimensional mode that can be viewed simultaneously. This unit will read bottoms down to 1,000 feet.

and versatility of their 2D picture in their 3D display. The 3D signal will lock onto the bottom rather than being fooled by baitfish or thermoclines. In fact, the X-70A 3D has 2D-mode with all its benefits, allowing the 3D to provide greater information about contour and perspective—the best of both worlds. And no one has better visibility in direct sunlight than Lowrance with their super-twist display. **Lowrance, 12000 E. Skelly Dr., Tulsa, OK 74128-2486, (918) 437-6881.**

MISCELLANEOUS

Simrad Robertson AP3000 Autopilot
This is a Robertson autopilot specially designed for boats less than 40 feet long. Robertson's proprietary "Autotune" feature monitors rudder movement and vessel response for instant and accurate course adjustment. Good for mechanical or hydraulic systems, the AP3000 also offers selectable night vision backlighting in red, green or white. If you want the real story on Simrad Robertson autopilots, ask almost any professional charter boat captain. He probably has one. **Simrad, 19210 33rd Ave. West, Lynnwood, WA 98036, (206) 778-8821.**

Roffer's Ocean Fishing Forecasts Go Online
Roffers, one of the top satellite image-based fishing spot forecasters has gone on-line with an electronic bulletin board. Those of you who modem your way through on-line services and the Internet will appreciate a peek at the numerous menu items such as fishing articles, offshore analyses, expert's forums, satellite imagery, shareware and free filesource, an electronic mailbox and frequent weather update announcements. **Roffers, 2871 SW 69th Ct., Miami, FL 33155-2829, (800) 677-7633.**

Alden Satfind 406 Survival EPIRB

Small, rugged and ideal for smaller offshore fishing boats. Controls are easy to use even in stressful situations. It can be mounted in any position, is water-activated as well as manually. Each unit is coded to broadcast information identifying you, your boat, its size, emergency contacts, and now, with a built-in GPS receiver, constant position readouts. It also broadcasts on 121.5 MHz so aircraft and shipping can home in on your beacon. **Alden Electronics, 40 Washington St., Westborough, MA 01581-0500, (508) 366-8851.**

FloScan 9000 Fuel Computer

Some of the most crucial information to have when you're running offshore is how much fuel you have and how fast are you using it. FloScan's new fuel-management system provides real-time information on miles per gallon, gallons per hour, and total gallons used. Combined with integral RPM input, you can easily build your own performance curves—or simply set your throttles for the most efficient fuel consumption. And unlike the performance charts you see in magazines, these figures are on your boat with all your gear, tackle, ice and anglers aboard. **FloScan, 3016 NE Blakely St., Seattle, WA 98105, (800) 522-3610.**

ACR Mini-B2 EPIRB

Touted as the smallest floating Class B EPIRB, ACR's Mini-B2 broadcasts simultaneously on 121.5 MHz (civilian) and 243.0 MHz (military) Search and Rescue homing frequencies. Operating battery life is 48 hours and the long-life lithium batteries have a replacement life of six years. The Mini-B2 measures an incredible 6″ × 2.6″ × 1.6″ so will fit on even the smallest offshore center console — the type of boat that should really have an EPIRB aboard. **ACR Electronics, 5757 Ravenswood Rd., Ft. Lauderdale, FL 33312, (305) 981-3333.**

Shakespear Art-1 Antenna Tester

Shakespeare has an invaluable antenna tester for a price everyone can afford and simple enough for a child to use. Simply plug this meter between your radio and antenna. It will give you a constant readout of output, the antenna's efficiency (Standing Wave Ratio-SWR) and whether your radio's signal will be transmitted properly. A switch lets you pick between forward or reflective power and a calibrator knob allows you to adjust your SWR for the optimum signal. This should be standard equipment with every radio. **Shakespeare, PO Box 733, Newberry, SC 29108, (800) 800-9008**

Autohelm LCD Radar

Autohelm presents its new ST50, a waterproof, liquid crystal display radar with 16-mile range. In addition to the normal information a radar provides, the ST-50 offers navigation data on waypoints, tide and wind, Electronic Bearing Line (EBL) and Variable Range Marker (VRM), both "big ship" anti-collision features that are extremely helpful. The ST-50 also interfaces with Raytheon's 600XX system, making it a C-Map-based chart plotter. **Autohelm, 676 Island Pond Rd., Manchester, NH 03109-5420, (603) 647-7530.**

ITT Night Mariner Monocular

Night Vision just became affordable. ITT Night Vision has a monocular that sells for about half what the large binocular unit does. And though it's certainly personal preference (meaning loads of people disagree with me), I find it easier to run a boat while looking through the monocular than the binocular. For those who want magnification in addition to their night sight, ITT introduces their 150 DX kit; a 3-way lens offering 3X, 2X and .42 wide angle magnification. Also available now are other lenses to further boost magnification. **ITT Night Vision, 7635 Plantation Rd., Roanoke, VA 24019, (800) 448-8678.**

FIELD CARE AND DRESSING OF FISH

If you sit down at the dinner table and bite into a poor-tasting fillet from a fish you caught, there's a good chance that the second-rate taste is your own fault. In all probability, the fish was not handled properly from the moment it came out of the water. Fish spoil rapidly unless they are kept alive or quickly killed and put on ice.

Here are the necessary steps involved in getting a fresh-caught fish from the water to the table, so that it will retain its original flavor.

First, the decision to keep a fish dead or alive depends on conditions. For example, if you have no ice in your boat, you'll want to keep all fish alive until it's time to head home. Under no circumstances should you toss fish into the bottom of the boat, let them lie there in the sun, then gather them up at the end of the day. If you try that stunt, the fillets will reach your table with the consistency of mush and a flavor to match. Instead, put your fish on a stringer as quickly as possible and put them back into the water, where they can begin to recover from the shock of being caught. (This is something you will want to avoid in shark-filled waters; in that case, make sure you bring a large cooler and lots of ice.)

Use the safety-pin type stringer and run the wire up through the thin almost-transparent membrane just behind the fish's lower lip. This will enable the fish to swim freely, and the fish will recover from this minor injury should you decide to release it at the end of the day.

Do not shove the stringer under the gill cover and out of the mouth. This damages gills and kills fish fast. Also avoid cord stringers, where all fish are bunched in a clump at the end of the cord. Use the safety-pin stringer. It does its job well.

If you're rowing or trolling slowly, you can probably keep the stringer in the water. If you have a big boat and motor, however, it's a good idea to take the stringer into the boat for those fast runs to other hotspots. If the run is fairly long, wet down the fish occasionally. But don't tow a fish in the water at high speed—you'll drown it.

If a fish has been deeply hooked and appears to be dying slowly, however, it's best to kill the fish immediately, gut it, and keep it on ice.

Killing a fish quickly is simple. Holding the fish upright, impale it between the eyes with the point of your knife or rap it on the head with a heavy stick. The important factor is killing it quickly, since the more slowly it dies the more rapidly the flesh will deteriorate.

13

From Hook to Table: Field Care and Nutrition

If you're surf fishing, bury your catch in the damp sand to keep it cool and out of the sun. Just remember to mark the spot. (VIN T. SPARANO)

If you're a surf fisherman, you can bury your catch in the damp sand. Just remember to mark the spot. A burlap sack occasionally doused in the surf also makes a practical fish bag. The important factor is to keep the fish cool and out of the sun.

Regardless of the various ways to keep fish cool, they should first be cleaned properly. With a bit of practice and a sharp knife, the job can be done in less than a minute.

Take a sharp knife, and insert it in the anal opening on the underside of the fish. Slit the skin forward from there to the point of the V-shaped area where the forward part of the belly is attached to the gills. Put your finger into the gills and around that V-shaped area, and pull sharply to the rear. You will thus remove the gills and all or most of the entrails. Then, with the fish upside down, put your thumb into the body cavity at the anal opening, and press the thumbnail up against the backbone. Keeping the nail tight against the bone, run your thumb forward to the head, thereby removing the dark blood from the sac along the backbone.

That completes the cleaning process—unless you want to remove the fins. This is easily done with a knife but is even easier with a small pair of wire clippers or scissors.

One more tip. More good fish meat is probably ruined during the drive home than during any other point in the trip from the water to the plate. Take the time to ice the fish properly for the drive home. Here's how:

Don't pack the fish in direct contact with the ice. The ice is sure to melt, and the fish, lying in the water, might well deteriorate, becoming soft and mushy. It's far better to put the fish in plastic bags, seal the bags so that they are watertight, and then pack the bags in the ice. The fish will stay cool—and dry—until you get home.

When you get the fish home, scale or skin them. For saltwater fish, prepare a heavy brine solution, and brush them thoroughly (a pastry-type brush works well) with the brine until they are clean.

Separate the fish into lots, each of which will make a meal for yourself or your family, and wrap each lot in good freezer paper, sealing tightly to prevent freezer burn. Freeze the fish as quickly as possible.

Some fishermen prefer not to field-dress their fish, but to fillet and skin them. This method, which appears difficult but is actually quite simple, has a number of advantages. First, gutting the fish is not necessary since entrails are left intact and never touched with a knife. Second, messy scaling is also an eliminated step because the fillet is skinned and the skin discarded, scales and all. Finally, and perhaps most important, the fillets are bone free.

Filleting is also a good idea for fishermen on extended trips. Head, entrails, fins, and skin are left behind and only clean and meaty fillets are brought home.

FISH COOKING TIPS

How Much To Cook
The following is an estimate of how much to cook per person, depending on appetite and course of meal served:

Whole or round fish—¾ pound
Dressed or cleaned fish—½ pound
Fillets or steaks—4 to 6 ounces
Crab meat, scallops and peeled shrimp—¼ pound
Unpeeled shrimp or whole squid—½ pound
Crab or lobster, live—1 to 2 pounds
Oysters or clams, shucked—¼ pint
Oysters or clams, in the shell—6 pieces

How Long to Cook?
The 10-Minute Rule: The main point to remember when cooking any seafood is not to cook it too long. Overcooked fish and shellfish becomes tough and dry, and much of the delicate flavor is lost.

FISH: "The 10-Minute Rule" is a good rule of thumb for timing all types of fish cookery, except deep drying and microwaving. Measure the fish at its thickest point. For every inch of thickness, allow 10 minutes cooking time. Double the cooking time for frozen fish that has not been thawed. Observe the changes in the fish as it cooks. Fish is done when it has just turned opaque and it starts to flake when prodded with a fork. Properly cooked fish will be firm yet moist.

Five Basic Cooking Methods
Sautéing: One of the easiest and quickest ways to cook fish, sautéing is ideal for thin fillets, fish steaks, and small whole fish as well as shrimp, scallops, and oysters. Heat a small amount of vegetable oil, butter, or mar-

garine in a heavy skillet. Dip seafood in seasoned flour and shake off excess. Sauté over medium-high heat until browned; turn and brown the second side. Serve immediately.

Baking: Baking requires little attention and works well for almost any fish. Melt a small amount of butter or margarine in a shallow baking pan. Season fish with herbs, salt, and pepper and turn in pan to coat with butter. Bake at 450°F, allowing 10 minutes per inch of thickness.

Broiling/Grilling: Steaks and fillets of firm fish or whole fish may be placed directly on an oiled broiler pan or on the well-oiled grill of an outdoor barbecue. A hinged fish basket is recommended for fragile fish. Cook 4 to 6 inches from the source of heat, turning once and basting frequently to prevent drying. Allow 10 minutes cooking time per inch of thickness.

Poaching: Fish simmered gently in a flavorful poaching liquid can be served either hot or chilled.

Place a whole fish, steaks, or fillets in a boiling liquid to cover. Reduce heat, cover and simmer gently, allowing about 10 minutes per inch of thickness. Remove skin from whole fish while it is warm.

Microwaving: An excellent and quick method for a variety of seafood.

Cut fish into equal portions to facilitate even cooking. Place in shallow microwave-proof dish with thinner parts overlapping in the center to make an even layer. Cover with heavy-duty waxed paper. Allow approximately 3 minutes per pound cooking time at highest setting for boneless fish and 2 to 3 minutes per pound for shellfish. Rotate dish halfway through cooking time. Allow 3 to 5 minutes covered "standing time" to finish cooking.

A Guide to Cooking Fish

Species	Fat or Lean	Broil	Bake	Boil Steam Poach	Fry/ Sauté
Alewife	Fat	.....	Best	Good	
Barracuda	Fat	Good	Best	.....	Fair
Bluefish	Fat	Good	Best	.....	Fair
Bonito	Fat	Good	Best	.....	Fair
Buffalo Fish	Lean	Good	Best	.....	Fair
Bullheads	Lean	.....	Fair	Good	Best
Cod	Lean	Best	Good	Fair	.....
Croaker (Hardhead)	Lean	Good	Fair	.....	Best
Drum (Redfish)	Lean	.....	Best	Good	.....
Eels	Fat	.....	Good	Fair	Best
Flounder	Lean	Good	Fair	.....	Best
Fluke	Lean	Good	Fair	.....	Best
Grouper	Lean	.....	Best	.....	.....
Haddock	Lean	Best	Good	Fair	.....
Hake	Lean	Fair	Best	Good	.....
Halibut	Fat	Best	Good	Fair	.....
Herring, Lake	Lean	Good	Fair	.....	Best
Herring, Sea	Fat	Best	Fair	.....	Good
Hog Snapper (Grunt)	Lean	Good	.....	.....	Best
Jewfish	Lean	.....	Best	.....	.....
Kingfish	Lean	Best	Good	Fair	.....
King Mackerel	Fat	Best	Good	.....	.....
Ling Cod	Lean	Best	Good	Fair	.....

(continued on page 316)

A Guide to Cooking Fish

Species	Fat or Lean	Broil	Bake	Boil Steam Poach	Fry/ Sauté
Mackerel	Fat	Best	Good	Fair	.....
Mango Snapper	Lean	Good	.....	.....	Best
Mullet	Fat	Best	Good	.....	Fair
Pollock	Lean	Fair	Good	Best	.....
Pompano	Fat	Best	Good	.....	Fair
Porgies (Scup)	Fat	Good	Fair	.....	Best
Redfish(ChannelBass)	Lean	Good	Best	.....	.....
Red Snapper	Lean	Good	Best	Good	.....
Rockfish	Lean	.....	Good	Best	.....
Rosefish	Lean	.....	Good	.....	Best
Salmon	Fat	Good	Best	Fair	.....
Sablefish(Black Cod)	Fat	.....	.....	Good	.....
Sardines	Fat	.....	Best	.....	.....
Sea Bass	Fat	Best	Fair	.....	Good
Sea Trout	Fat	Best	Good	.....	Fair
Shad	Fat	Good	Best	.....	Fair
Shark (Grayfish)	Fat	.....	Best	Good	.....
Sheepshead					
(Freshwater)	Lean	.....	Good	Best	.....
(Saltwater)	Lean	Best	Good	.....	Fair
Smelts	Lean	Good	Fair	.....	Best
Snapper	Lean	Good	Best	Fair	.....
Snook	Lean	Good	Best	.....	.....
Sole	Lean	Good	Fair	.....	Best
Spanish Mackerel	Fat	Best	Good	.....	Fair
Spot	Lean	.....	.....	.....	.....
Striped Bass	Fat	.....	Good	Best	.....
Sturgeon	Fat	Good	Best	Fair	.....
Swordfish	Fat	Best	Good	Fair	.....
Tautog (Blackfish)	Lean	Best	Good	.....	Fair
Tuna	Fat	Fair	Best	Good	.....
Weakfish (Sea Trout)	Lean	Best	Good	.....	Fair
Whiting(Silver Hake)	Lean	.....	.....	Best	.....
Whitefish	Fat	Good	Best	.....	Fair
Yellowtail	Fat	Good	Good	Best	.....

Note: All Shellfish are Lean

Index